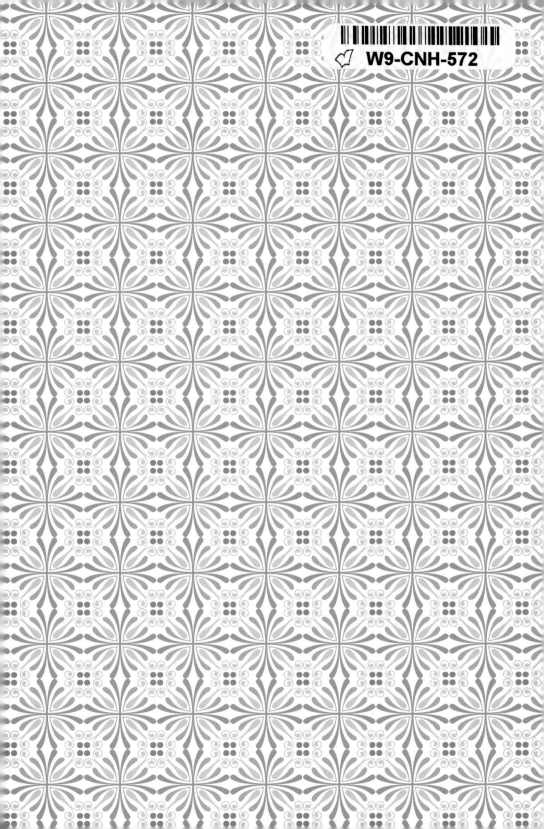

The Book of

Amazing Curiosities

Publications International, Ltd.

Contents

✳ ✳ ✳ ✳

Chapter 1 ✳ **How It All Got Started**   **8**

A Magnetic Curiosity ✦ How It All Began ✦ Survival of a Quote ✦
Pennies and Piggies ✦ Texas Tea ✦ The Toll House Mystery ✦ Inventions
That Stick With You ✦ Clippings ✦ How It All Began, Part II ✦ Bacon and
Hogs ✦ How It All Began, Part III ✦ The Keys to an Invention ✦ Swinging
the Night Away ✦ It Started in Chicago ✦ Who Started Mother's Day? ✦
Popcorn and the Cinema ✦ Going Up ✦ Who Came Up With Chewing
Gum? ✦ In the Red ✦ Grand Old Party Begins in Ripon ✦ You Can Thank
Wisconsin ✦ America Goes to Kindergarten ✦ How It All Began, Part
IV ✦ Chariots of Fire ✦ Labor Day ✦ Bagel Beginnings ✦ On a Roll ✦ The
History of the Birthday Cake ✦ How It All Began, Part V ✦ O Christmas
Tree ✦ The Original Smoke-Filled Room ✦ The Poetry Slam: A Perfect 10
✦ Facial Perfection ✦ You Can Thank Ohio ✦ A Cool Invention ✦ Terrific
Tuxedoes

Chapter 2 ✳ **Nature All Around**   **63**

11 Animals that Use Camouflage ✦ Exposing the Virus ✦ The Upper
Atmosphere ✦ U.S. National Parks: Vacation Highlights ✦ Rooting for
Rudolph ✦ Rodent Fun Facts! ✦ Plants During Biblical Times ✦ Local
Legends ✦ Canny Coyote! ✦ Hurricane 101 ✦ 8 Most Common Blood
Types ✦ Star Words ✦ Top Five Ferocious Prehistoric Creatures ✦ 7
Wonders of the Natural World ✦ The Human Body ✦ Hopping Up the
Wrong Tree ✦ Anatomical Anomalies ✦ The Weird Animals of Texas ✦ Top
Texas Snake Legends ✦ Dino-mite! ✦ Charging Bull ✦ Pet Precipitation
✦ The Ohioan Cockroach to Beat All Cockroaches ✦ Blue Moon? ✦ The
Real-life Dead Zone ✦ When Nature Turns Mean! ✦ The Deadliest Texas
Tornadoes ✦ Collective Nouns ✦ The 1900 Flood: More than Galveston ✦
Howl at the Moon ✦ Treasure Hunting ✦ Do Bed Bugs Really Bite? ✦ Can
the Cold Give You a Cold? ✦ The Dead Sea: It Lives ✦ Poor Pluto

Chapter 3 ✳ **Government and Politics**   **118**

14 of the New Deal's Alphabet Agencies ✦ 17 People in Line for the
Presidency ✦ Heights and Zodiac Signs of 43 Presidents ✦ 30 Countries
and Their Currency ✦ 6 Political Scandals ✦ 9 Political Slips of the Tongue
✦ A Few Facts About the Statue of Liberty ✦ Five Reasons People Think
Nixon Was a Great President ✦ Five Reasons People Think Nixon Was a

Crummy President ✦ You Can't Take Down a Bull Moose ✦ Edward Hyde: Cross-dresser or Double-crossed? ✦ Trashing the White House ✦ Leaders Who Shaped Canadian Destiny ✦ Presidentially Speaking ✦ The USPS: The Check Is in the Mail ✦ All Hail the Emperor ✦ Warren G. Harding ✦ Presidentially Speaking ✦ Fast Facts ✦ Trudeaumania ✦ Kingmaker City ✦ A Long, Strange Line of Governors ✦ Presidential Nicknames ✦ Some Current States and Their Early Names

Chapter 4 ✷ Interesting People and Big Personalities 168

The Castle That Harry Built ✦ Aluminim Siding ✦ Gummo: Marx Brother #5 ✦ Hizzoner! ✦ Tired, Achy Feet? Paging Dr. Scholl ✦ 13 Famous Rhodes Scholars ✦ Josh Gibson ✦ It's Not You, It's Me ✦ 18 Notable People with a Twin ✦ Henry VIII ✦ Goal: Bibles in Every Language ✦ Truth Be Told ✦ The Mighty Pen! ✦ How Marlon Brandon Changed Acting Forever ✦ Who Was Button Gwinnett? ✦ Successful Dropouts! ✦ Annie Get Your Gun: The Story of Annie Oakley ✦ Studs Terkel: Lending an Ear to America ✦ Poet of the Big Shoulders ✦ Keeping It in the Family ✦ Controversial Queen ✦ The King of Ragtime ✦ Stand Tall, the Texas Rangers ✦ Sandy Koufax: Brooklyn's Best ✦ Batter Up! The Babe Ruth Quiz ✦ From Baseball to Bible Thumper ✦ Ghost Hunters Extraordinaire: Ed and Lorraine Warren ✦ 10 Alleged Cases of Feral Children ✦ Who Was Davy Crockett? ✦ Queen of the Nile ✦ Charles Waterton: Britain's Monkey Man ✦ Proust's Weird and Wordy Life ✦ People Who Deserve to Be a Lot More Famous

Chapter 5 ✷ Spooky Events & Strange Coincidences 232

Shakespeare and the 46th Psalm ✦ The Tyler Tragedy ✦ LaLaurie Mansion ✦ The *Poltergeist* Curse ✦ Blue Light Cemetaries ✦ Paramount and the Paranormal ✦ The Curse of Camelot: The Kennedy Family ✦ Curse of the Little Rascals ✦ Unsettling Happenings Aboard UB-65 ✦ World of Wonder ✦ Won't You Come Home, Erie Baby? ✦ Strange Stories from On the Set ✦ Local Legends: the Hodag ✦ Summerwind: Wisconsin's Most Haunted House ✦ Local Legends: Resurrection Mary ✦ Take a Walk on the Other Side ✦ The Phantom Flapper ✦ Near-Death Experiences Are Not All Black or White ✦ Ghosts Live on at the Clovis Sanitarium ✦ Stalked by an Invisible Entity ✦ Local Legends: New York ✦ Do You Pay Half the Rent if Your Roommate Is a Ghost? ✦ Ghost Dogs ✦ Moore Ghosts Gather in Villisca ✦

Chapter 6 ✷ Intriguing Moments in History 291

Zero: To Be or Not to Be ✦ 11 Highlights of 1907 ✦ 9 Bits of Irony ✦ The *Empress of Ireland* ✦ The Times They Are A-Changin' 1913 ✦ Blacklisted! ✦

When Hell Came to Texas ✦ Now That Would Have Been a Great Photo! ✦ In the Year...1919 ✦ Christmas in Space! ✦ Peace in the Midst of War ✦ Bibles for the Masses ✦ The Times They Are A-Changin': 1932 ✦New York News Before the *New York Times* ✦ Debugging ✦ The Other Jackie Robinson ✦ The Times They Are A-Changin': 1942, 1943 ✦ Bay View Tragedy ✦ Showing the Klan the Door ✦ The Great Camel Experiment ✦ An Ominous Chain Reaction ✦ Bringing the World to Chicago ✦ Battle of Harlem Heights ✦ A Call to Action! ✦ Ship of Honor ✦ "Ford to City: 'Drop Dead'" ✦ 17 Bits of Nostalgia from 1957

Chapter 7 ✳ Culture and Traditions   343

Cheers! ✦ Pardon Me? Foreign Slang Terms ✦ Leap Year Luck ✦ Objects of Their Affection ✦ 5 Fabulous Fads from the 1950s ✦ Mistletoe: It's Not Just About Making Out ✦ Sing It Loud! ✦ 7 of the Oldest... ✦ Icarus ✦ Getting Carded ✦ 8 Groovy Fads of the 1960s ✦ Learn to Talk Trucker ✦ Lucky (and Unlucky) Charms ✦ The Lawn Chairs of Winter ✦ Texan Talk ✦ Why Is the Heart Associated with Love? ✦ This Festival Embraces "Unmentionable" History ✦ Don't Sing Too Loudly! ✦ 8 Legends of American Folklore ✦ What Were They Reading? ✦ 8 Awesome Fads of the 1980s ✦ Green River ✦ Military Jargon Gets Mustered Out ✦ Happy Birthday, Dear Valentine? ✦ The Day After Turkey Day ✦ Why Do We Carve Jack o' Lanterns? ✦ Hot Dog! The Warm Glow (and History) of the Advent Wreath ✦ Aren't There Better Ways for Santa to Sneak into a House? ✦ A Thanksgiving Tradition

Chapter 8 ✳ Games and Pastimes   393

The Truth About Monopoly ✦ A Striking Pastime: The Badger Bowling Obsession ✦ Vince Lombardi, Football Hero ✦ Talking Turkey ✦ The Seventh-inning Stretch ✦ From Bingo to Uno: The Origins of Popular Pastimes ✦ Fad Inventions ✦ Bragging Rights ✦ Raising the Stakes ✦ Between a Rock and a Weird Place: The House on the Rock ✦ 11 of the World's Greatest Roller Coasters ✦ Days Gone By: Pinball ✦ The Most Expensive Baseball Card ✦ Curling ✦ Strat-O-Matic Baseball ✦ Institutions of Higher Chicanery ✦ Weird Collections ✦ Most Dangerous Toys ✦ Doin' the Dunk ✦ Before Basketball ✦ All This and Cereal Too? How Did Texas Hold 'Em Gets Its Name? ✦ One Determined Detective ✦ Papa Bear

Chapter 9 ✳ Successes and Fumbles   434

15 Notable People Who Dropped Out of School ✦ Sinking Car ✦ A Mighty Enterprise ✦ 8 Automotive Lemons ✦ Prolific Producers ✦ 11 Design Innovations of Harley Earl ✦ Major Miscues ✦ Dusty Rhodes:

One-Year Wonder ◆ 8 Memorable Ad Campaigns ◆ 9 Famous TV Flops ◆ The Short-Lived 1942 German Invasion of America ◆ Toy Story ◆ Battle for the Sky ◆ Broadway's Biggest Losers ◆ The High-flying Jacob Brodbeck ◆ Up in Flames: The "Fireproof" Crystal Palace ◆ Toxic Times Beach ◆ Millenium Park ◆ Baseball's Darkest Hour ◆ Not Quite Hotcakes: Product Disasters ◆ Blowing a "Razz"-berry ◆ A Ticket to Ride ◆ The *Titanic* of New York ◆ Inventive Women

Chapter 10 ✳ Love and Marriage   492

Proposals: The Preposterous ◆ 22 Romantic Kissing Spots in America ◆ Wedding Announcements ◆ 18 Hopelessly Devoted Couples ◆ Cakes through the Ages ◆ Fast Facts: Wedding Cakes ◆ Weddings the Wiccan Way ◆ A Walk Down the Aisle ◆ Something Old: Saving the Top Tier ◆ Once Wasn't Enough ◆ Italian Wedding Customs ◆ Bachelor Parties and Bridal Showers ◆ The Common and the Covenant ◆ Fast Facts: Weddings ◆ Long Road to Love ◆ On the "Threshold" of Tradition ◆ Marriage by Proxy ◆ The Much-Married Tommy Manville ◆ Meant for Each Other ◆ Flinging Flowers ◆ Bouquet Breakdown ◆ The Continuous Circle of Love ◆ Old Weddings' Tales ◆ Chase Away the Evil Spirits ◆ Jumping the Broom ◆ Japanese Wedding Traditions ◆ A Long-Ago Wedding Remembered ◆ Fast Facts: Wedding Superstitions ◆ Bad Brides ◆ Quiz

Chapter 11 ✳ Screen, Stage, and Song   545

Behind the TV Shows of Our Time ◆ Solo Mission ◆ The Late, Great Buddy Holly ◆ 38 Celebrity Siblings ◆ Roles of a Rebel ◆ Hollywood's Self-Censorship Machine ◆ 19 Popular TV Shows of the 1960s ◆ Acting Up in School ◆ Beatlemania New York Style ◆ Tin Pan Alley ◆ The Best of Broadway ◆ Bragging Rights ◆ Memorable Movie Weddings ◆ Behind the Films of Our Time ◆ Crossing Ed Sullivan ◆ Box Office Disasters ◆ The Secret Side of Elvis ◆ Behind the Music of Our Time ◆ 7 Outrageous Hollywood Publicity Stunts ◆ Frankly Freakish: The Crazed Genius of Frank Zappa ◆ Behind the Films of Our Time ◆ D'oh! I Know That Voice! ◆ The Red Special ◆ Behind the Films of Our Time ◆ Weird Science ◆ Real or Hollywood? ◆ From Chicago to Hollywood ◆ It Wasn't Always a Wonderful Life ◆ From the Playing Field to the Silver Screen ◆ First City of Comedy ◆ Left Behind on the Cutting Room Floor ◆ Steven Spielberg's Tall Tale ◆ How to Get a Star on the Hollywood Walk of Fame ◆ The Making of *King Kong* ◆ The Dummy Did It ◆ Oscar: The Scoop on the Statue ◆ Slasher Films ◆ Films Based on Fact When, In Fact, Those Facts Were Fiction ◆ Actors, Actress, and Directors ◆ For Some, Acting Just Isn't Enough ◆ Sing and Shout ◆ The Wilhelm Scream ◆ Misheard Lyrics

Fumbling Felons, Part I ✦ 8 Outrageous Lawsuits ✦ John Wesley Hardin: The Old West's Deadliest Gun? ✦ The Giant Straw Goat of Gävle ✦ Growing Up Capone ✦ Fumbling Felons, Part II ✦ Odd Ordinances ✦ Bloody Angle: The Most Violent Place in New York? ✦ Sleep with the Fishes ✦ Pirates! ✦ Fumbling Felons, Part III ✦ More Odd Ordinances ✦ Masks Only a Robber Could Love ✦ 9 of the Grisliest Crimes of the 20th Century ✦ Outlandish Laws ✦ Cold and Clammy ✦ Fumbling Felons, Part IV ✦ Criminals Behaving Nicely? ✦ Brazen Armored Car Heists ✦ Even More Odd Ordinances ✦ Bye-Bye Brewskis ✦ That's a Crime, Too ✦ Death from on High ✦ The Sutton-Taylor Fued ✦ Fumbling Felons, Part V ✦ Bluebeard in the Flesh ✦ The Butcher Was a Wienie ✦ The Whitechapel Club ✦ William Desmond Taylor ✦ Who Founded the Mafia? ✦ Fumbling Felons, Part VI ✦ Ohio's Greatest Unsolved Mystery ✦ The Butcher and the Thief ✦ Fumbling Felons, Part VII ✦ Another Set of Odd Ordinances ✦ Berkowitz's Reign of Terror ✦ Murder, Inc. ✦ Mafia Buster! ✦ One Last Set: Odd Ordinances

Explore a World of Weirdness

✳   ✳   ✳   ✳

Welcome to *The Book of Amazing Curiosities*. In this pages, you'll find stories of strange events, fascinating people, and remarkable curiosities. Some of the stories found here concern themselves with world-changing events, while others focus on the trivial and minute, but they're all meant to pique your interest. You'll discover how some traditions started and how they're changed through the ages, read about amazing people who excelled in their field, and wince at stories of disasters or bad decisions.

Some stories will make you laugh, while others might scare you, but all of them will give you a small glimpse into something extraordinary.

Chapter 1

How It All Got Started

Accidental Inventions

A Magnetic Curiosity

It might surprise you to learn that a melted candy bar led to the invention of the microwave.

✳   ✳   ✳   ✳

PERCY SPENCER DIDN'T set out to find a faster way to make popcorn. A self-educated engineer, Spencer had contributed greatly to the Allied efforts in World War II by developing a speedier way of manufacturing *magnetrons*, the crucial element in radar systems used by Allied bombers.

One day in 1945, Spencer was standing near a magnetron at the Raytheon Company in Waltham, Massachusetts, when he noticed that the candy bar in his pocket was melting. Spencer wasn't the first person to notice the phenomenon, but he was the first to wonder what caused it. This was typical of Spencer's insatiable curiosity, which had led him from the Maine farm where he grew up to a career as the world's foremost authority on microwave radiation.

Spencer suspected that the melting was caused by microwaves emitted by the magnetron. To test his theory, he fetched a package of uncooked popcorn and held it near the magnetron. Sure enough, the popcorn heated and popped. Next, he tried cooking an egg—which exploded in the face of a curious coworker who got too close.

Soon after discovering this effect, Spencer patented and built the first microwave oven, the Radarange, a monster of an appliance that stood more than five feet tall, weighed 750 pounds, and cost $5,000—more than $40,000 by today's standards.

How does a microwave oven work? Simply put, microwave radiation causes the molecules in food to move, bumping into each other and causing heat. Objects whose molecules are too far apart (like air) or locked together (like a teacup) do not heat up.

The U.S. Navy gave Spencer the Distinguished Public Service Award for his work on military uses of the magnetron. But Spencer's greatest public service—as far as the rest of us are concerned—was developing the technology that enables us to cook popcorn, or nearly anything else, in a couple of minutes.

How It All Began

Every wondered how some of our everyday inventions and sayings came to be? Read on!

✳   ✳   ✳   ✳

E-mail

E-MAIL WAS DEVELOPED by Ray Tomlinson and sent across the forerunner of the Internet—called ARPANET—in 1971. He chose the [at_sign] symbol to denote an online "address" for the sender. His first message, he has said, was likely "qwertyuiop," familiar to anyone who has ever used a keyboard (it's the top line).

When Tomlinson was asked by people at the time (who clearly had no foresight) why he'd invented something that nobody seemed to want or even have any use for, he responded, "Because it seemed like a neat idea."

"In Cahoots"

When two or more people are up to no good, they're said to be "in cahoots." The phrase may well come from France, where a small cabin was called a cahute. If these cabins were occupied by bandits and robbers planning a heist, the name of the cottages may have become a sort of shorthand to signify what went on inside them.

The Safety Pin

The humble, but modesty-saving, safety pin has its origins in Central Europe, circa 1000 B.C.; this concoction held the pointed end within a curved wire, and while it may have been safer, it was not entirely safe itself. Straight pins, on the other hand, date back 5,000 years and were created from iron and bone by the Sumerians. Archeologists are convinced that the sewing needle is at least 10,000 years old—when fish spines were pierced at the top or the middle to receive a thread.

"Running Amok"

When a crowd of people begins to panic, it's said to "run amok" (or amuck). The phrase comes from the Malay word amok, which means "violent and out of control." It is said that this is what the excited Malaysians yelled when they encountered Europeans for the first time.

The Cold Shoulder

To be "given the cold shoulder" means to be snubbed. In days of yore, it originally referred to a shoulder of meat, often mutton, offered to a traveler. A warm meal was an indication that someone was welcome, whereas cold meat was a warning that, although you'd be fed, the householders weren't particularly enthusiastic about your being there.

Survival of a Quote

"Survival of the fittest," thought to summarize the theory of evolution, is actually a metaphor for natural selection that was not coined by Charles Darwin.

✳ ✳ ✳ ✳

A QUOTE MAY HAVE an original creator, but its evolution occurs independently of the person who said it first. "Survival of the fittest" has a definite creator: 19th-century economist Herbert Spencer. Yet after Spencer coined the phrase in *Principles of Biology* (1864), it took on a life if its own.

Spencer conjured the phrase as a reference to Charles Darwin's theory of natural selection, which Spencer had read about upon the 1859 release of *On the Origin of Species by Means of Natural Selection*. Darwin's theory was strictly biological: Given the preconditions of variation, replication, and heritability, traits favorable to a given environment are preserved over time (natural selection), and thus change occurs (evolution). By means of analogy, Spencer brought this concept into the economic realm to describe how the "fittest" societies evolve over time.

Despite popularizing the same phrase, Darwin and Spencer didn't use it in the same way. By "fittest" Darwin did not mean "best" but rather whatever trait allows an organism to survive and reproduce in a given environment, thereby increasing the frequency of said trait. Spencer, on the other hand, did intend fittest to mean "best," and he applied the idea to social evolution, not biology.

What Darwin meant by natural selection is best summarized by a quote that actually appeared in *On the Origin of Species*, from the first edition ad infinitum: "Any variation, however slight…if it be in any degree profitable to an individual of any species…will tend to the preservation of that individual, and will generally be inherited by its offspring."

Pennies and Piggies

The piggy bank sprang from a play on words.

✳   ✳   ✳   ✳

THE PIGGY BANK is one of America's favorite ways to save. Kids love to hoard their pennies in them, and adults often use them to hold spare change. But the origin of the venerable piggy bank has nothing to do with pigs. It can actually be traced to an English play on words that dates back hundreds of years.

According to historians, the concept of the piggy bank most likely started in England around the mid-1500s. Back then, metal was precious and quite expensive, so the average family used dishes, jars, and cookware made from an inexpensive orange clay called *pygg*, which was probably initially pronounced "pug."

It was common for families to keep extra coins in a pygg jar, which eventually came to be known as the "pygg bank." Centuries later, in the 1700s, the name evolved to "piggy bank." Amused British potters started making clay banks in the shape of pigs, and that's how the piggy bank as we now know it was born.

People quickly became enamored with piggy banks, and their popularity soared throughout England. The earliest piggy banks were ceramic and had to be broken to retrieve the money inside. Later versions came with a hole or other retrieval method so that the banks could be used over and over.

Piggy banks eventually spread outside of England to equal popularity. Adults found them a good way to instill a sense of financial responsibility among children, and versions of the piggy bank can now be found throughout the world.

Texas Tea

The modern American oil industry was born in southeastern Texas on January 10, 1901. That's when the Lucas #1 well on a hill known as Spindletop blew a gusher more than 100 feet in the air. Until then, the nation's leading oil-producing state had been Pennsylvania.

✳   ✳   ✳   ✳

NATIVE AMERICANS HAD known about the oil under the Texas soil for centuries and had used what seeped to the surface as a home remedy for a variety of ailments. Spanish explorers later discovered black tar along the beaches of eastern Texas and used it to waterproof their boots.

In the late 1800s, small amounts of oil were produced in the area around Nacogdoches, a region that eventually became known as Oil Springs. This attracted several oil companies eager to tap the area's natural oil reservoirs. The first major oil-producing field was Corsicana, which, like many other fields, was discovered by accident when locals drilling for water hit oil instead. Many ignored the oil and drilled around it to reach the deeper water wells—after all, you can't drink oil. These early oil wells produced roughly 25 barrels a day, just a fraction of what was being produced in the larger Pennsylvania fields.

A Visionary Pioneer

It would take Patillo Higgins, an amateur geologist who had lost an arm in a teenage encounter with the police, to turn the focus to Spindletop and change everything. Higgins was a forward thinker who believed the coal industry would ultimately be replaced by oil. He was also convinced that large amounts of oil could be found under salt domes—salt domes such as Spindletop.

In 1882, Higgins formed the Gladys City Oil, Gas and Manufacturing Company. Many years of frustration—not to mention derision from local geologists and petroleum industry officials—followed as attempt after attempt to drill proved unsuccessful. The situation finally turned around with the help of John Galey and James Guffey, who had previously left Texas after the Corsicana field failed to produce significant amounts of oil. The men surveyed the area around Beaumont and picked the spot at Spindletop to drill. Exploration began on October 27, 1900. The drill site that produced the famous gusher was the work of Anthony Lucas, a Louisiana mining engineer and oil prospector.

That Spindletop well produced more than 75,000 barrels a day, with peak annual production of 17.5 million barrels in 1902. The boom was on, and an influx of wildcatters descended on the area. With them came related services, supply and manufacturing firms, and refineries. Unfortunately, so did speculators, scam artists, prostitutes, gamblers, and liquor dealers. Such a volatile combination led to gunfights, murders, and mayhem, all of which added to the colorful tales that Texans love to tell about their history.

The Ever-Expanding Industry

Within several years, additional fields were tapped in Sour Lake, Baston, and Humble within the 150-mile radius around Spindletop. Companies were established to develop the burgeoning oil fields, and these evolved into the giants of today's oil industry. Among them were Gulf Oil, Sun Oil, Magnolia Petroleum, the Texas Company, and Humble Oil, which later affiliated itself with Standard Oil of New Jersey to become Esso and then Exxon. The refineries, pipelines, and export facilities that grew along the coastline near Beaumont and Port Arthur became a major industrial region that made millionaires out of the company owners.

Between 1902 and 1910, however, oil fever spread to North Texas. Water-well drillers found oil in Wichita County, and the Electra oil field was created. Subsequent oil fields were found in

Burkburnett, Ranger, Mexia, and eventually in the Panhandle and all across the state. The largest of the discoveries occurred in Rusk County in East Texas when the Daisy Bradford #3 well blew. A free-for-all atmosphere ensued, and derricks started popping up like weeds across the surrounding area. At the time, no regulations for spacing or limits on production existed. Local sheriffs had to institute martial law to control the wildcatters. Bitter rivalries and concern over the exploding industry led to two years of legal battles to institute the regulations that are still used today.

People Swarmed In

The burgeoning industry led to a sudden growth in population in the areas surrounding all these oil fields. This became known as the boomtown phenomenon as hastily erected shacks, tents, and vehicles served as living quarters for the oil-field workers. Businesses in the surrounding rural communities were overrun by workers, and lines were long at eating and banking establishments. Many historians have compared it to the famous California Gold Rush in which whole towns appeared overnight and grew rapidly.

By the time the East Texas field was fully developed, the economy had shifted from an agricultural base to one where the petroleum industry was king. Gradually, the oil industry began to affect ordinary Texans in a trickle-down effect that saw the mechanization of farm work, the replacement of farmland by manufacturing plants, the displacement of the population to the oil fields and manufacturing centers, and the growth of urban areas.

By the Numbers

In the first quarter of 1929, Texas oil operators produced 69,541,834 barrels of so-called black gold. At the end of 1935, there were more than 1,000 operators in the field producing 158,599,275 barrels. With the start of World War II, however, exports to Europe fell by a quarter, and the industry was producing just 60 percent of its potential. The end of the war brought another boom in the oil industry as postwar markets for oil and gas expanded. For the first time in eight years, the Texas Railroad Commission ordered no shutdown days to keep the oil barrels moving.

However, the boom didn't last, and in the 1950s a decrease in domestic demand and the increase of imports once again caused the oil industry to cut back its production. The most notable developments over the next two decades were the improved management of oil production, the expansion of the petrochemical industry, and the discovery of natural gas.

Undercut by Imported Oil

Toward the end of the 1970s, it became evident that the U.S. oil industry was being controlled by decisions made in Washington, D.C., that were related to oil imports from the Middle East and the pivotal changes resulting from the fall of the Shah of Iran's government. Over the next decade, the increased cost of production and exploration, the political environment, and a decline in the price of domestic oil led to failures of oil production, finance, and real estate in Texas.

By the 1990s, the Texas industry started a period of downsizing, and although it continues to produce domestic oil, the percentage of state government revenue contributed by oil money has dropped into the single digits. Today, oil is no longer the driving force behind Texas's economy. However, in the century since Spindletop blew that geyser of Texas Tea into the air, oil has touched the lives of many Texans. The oil industry continues to provide benefits to the citizens of Texas and is still considered a major player in the international oil market.

Ever heard of Notrees, Texas, 79759? It may have the most literal name of any town in the state. When the community, which is 20 miles north of Odessa, got a post office during the first oil boom, it needed to come up with a name quickly. And since there are no trees...

The Toll House Mystery

Warning: This story might make you hungry for cookies.

✳ ✳ ✳ ✳

IN THE 1930S, Ruth Wakefield and her husband operated the Toll House Inn near Whitman, Massachusetts. Wakefield was a dietitian, cookbook author, popular food lecturer, and an excellent cook. One day, she was mixing up a batch of Butter Drop cookies, a popular sugar cookie found in recipe books dating back to the colonial days.

According to oft-repeated legend, the recipe called for baker's chocolate, but Ruth didn't have any, so she used a bar of Nestlé semisweet chocolate instead. But why would a sugar cookie recipe include baker's chocolate? Who knows? In any event, Wakefield broke up the bar and added it to the dough.

Or did she? George Boucher, who was head chef at the Toll House Inn, told a different story. According to Boucher, the chocolate accidentally fell into the mixing bowl from a shelf just above it, knocked off by the vibrations of the electric mixer. Mrs. Wakefield was going to throw out the batter, but Boucher convinced her to try baking it, and the rest is cookie history. (Doubters might wonder why the chocolate would be sitting on a shelf unwrapped, just waiting to fall into the mix.)

The official Nestlé version of the story states that Wakefield expected the chocolate to melt and was surprised when it didn't. But as she was an experienced cook and knew her way around a kitchen, it seems more likely that she was intentionally trying to create a new recipe and added the semisweet chocolate on purpose.

Of this there is no doubt: In 1939, Nestlé invented chocolate chips specifically for the cookies and printed the recipe on the bag. Today, Toll House Cookies are perhaps the most popular cookie in history.

Inventions That Stick with You

Next time you need a Band-Aid, you'll know whom to thank!

✳   ✳   ✳   ✳

On the Cutting Edge

IN 1920, JOSEPHINE Dickson was the young bride of Earle, who worked at Johnson & Johnson in New Jersey, a leading producer of surgical supplies. As the story goes, Earle would arrive home every day to find Josephine cut, burned, or bleeding from some kitchen mishap, so he'd get out the adhesive tape and gauze and bandage up his accident-prone wife.

After a while, it became clear that Josephine needed a way to quickly and easily bandage herself throughout the day, so Earle stuck several pieces of gauze onto individual strips of adhesive tape and covered them with crinoline to keep them secure. He took his idea to work, and the company loved it; in 1920, Johnson & Johnson began making Band-Aids. At first the bandages were quite large—18 inches by 2 inches—and were made by hand. But by 1924 the company had perfected a machine that made the bandages smaller and easier to make. Initially, the public wasn't too interested in Band-Aids. Then Johnson & Johnson launched a PR stunt to give free bandages to Boy Scouts across the country—and soon the sticky strips were a national sensation.

A Clear Winner

Speaking of sticky strips, the ever-useful Scotch tape owes its existence to a lab technician for the Minnesota Mining and Manufacturing Company (3M). Richard Drew had already developed a masking tape in 1925 to help body shops edge a paint job without tearing existing paint off the car. It worked, but it wasn't waterproof. In 1929, a client called asking for a waterproof adhesive to cover the insulation batting in refrigerated railroad cars.

Also new at this time was a waterproof product called cellophane. Drew ordered 100 yards of it to see if his theory was right and adhesive could be applied to cellophane. His theory was correct, but Drew's invention failed to meet the railroad client's needs. Nevertheless, he knew he was on to something. Drew learned that if a primer coat was applied to the back of cellophane, it would coat evenly, and special machinery could keep the cellophane from tearing. On September 8, 1930, the first roll of Scotch Cellophane Tape was given to a customer, who sent back rave reviews.

As for the name, the story is that it comes from feedback that a 3M salesman received from a frustrated auto worker regarding an early version of Drew's masking tape: "Take this tape back to your stingy Scotch bosses and tell them to put more adhesive on it!"

Clippings

Here's something to ponder the next time you put together a chain of paper clips...

❋   ❋   ❋   ❋

Where the Wired Things Are

PRETTY MUCH AS soon as paper-use became widespread (around the 13th century), people started looking for ways to attach more than one piece together. Sure, you could bind pages together in book fashion, but that was unnecessarily formal (and permanent) for things such as letters and reports. For a while, people used ribbons to tie pages together. Then, in 1832, the mechanization of the straight pin popularized the "desk pin"; alas, this too proved problematic: The pins rusted over time, caught on other papers, left unsightly holes, and presented a stabbing hazard.

Around this time, a bendable substance called steel wire hit the market, and creative types began experimenting with new ways to fold it as a paper fastener. Beginning in the 1860s, patent after patent was issued for variations on the "paper clip."

Finally, a solution appeared, and it's the classic model still used today. No one knows who, exactly, first developed the oval "loop within a loop" paper clip, but it was William D. Middlebrook of Waterbury, Connecticut, who revolutionized its production. In 1899, he patented the paper clip-making machine and sold it to manufacturers Cushman and Denison, who named their new paper clip the Gem.

Some say Middlebrook also patented the modern design of the paper clip. Others say the paper clip was designed years before and Middlebrook just mechanized it, while still others claim the paper clip is of British origin.

A Clip on Their Shoulder?

Interestingly, Norway proudly takes credit for the modern shape of the paper clip. They claim countryman Johan Vaaler patented the design in 1899. Despite this discrepancy, Norway's pride continues unabated. A statue has been erected for Vaaler, and during World War II, patriotic Norwegians wore a paper clip on their lapels as a symbol of national unity.

Today, an estimated 20 billion paper clips are sold every year. Though many varieties of paper clips have flooded the market over the years, the most common ones found in office supply rooms and on desks around the world is still the original Gem.

How It All Began, Part II

Every wondered how some of our everyday inventions and sayings came to be? Read on!

✳   ✳   ✳   ✳

Ice Cream

ICE CREAM DATES back to first-century Romans, specifically Emperor Nero, who ordered runners to pass buckets of snow from the northern mountains down the Appian Way to the city, where it was flavored with fruit toppings before being served to hungry Romans.

The Barber's Pole

Although not as prevalent as it once was (but still instantly recognizable), the red-and-white striped pole visible from storefront windows signifies that a barber plies his trade within. There's a gory origin for this symbol. In medieval times, barbers' services included surgery and bloodletting, as well as the trimming of hair and beards. The original poles were brass. A basin at the top was used to store leeches, and one at the bottom was used to hold any blood that flowed. To help blood flow more easily, patients held tightly to a staff, which worked much as a tourniquet does today. The barber pole itself may have originated in that staff, with the stripes acting as a visual representation of bandage strips, both blood-stained and clean.

Eavesdropping

Why is snooping on someone's conversation called "eavesdropping?" At one time, landholders weren't allowed to build right up against a property line—they had to leave room between their space and the neighbors' for the eaves on the house, as well as for water dripping from rainy weather. An "eavesdrip" was only about 24 inches, a small enough space for a curious neighbor to easily hear what went on next door—whether he or she wanted to or not.

Nag

The word nag derives from the Scandinavian nagga, which translates as "to gnaw." During the Middle Ages, many of the houses had thatched roofs. Rats and squirrels would sometimes burrow into these roofs, and late at night, people could hear them as they gnawed and chomped on the straw. In fact, the noise was annoying and would keep people awake. Now, the word serves as a perfect description of constantly being verbally gnawed at by another (the "nagger").

Bacon and Hogs

Well, groundhogs, anyway. Read on to find out about a pork-related saying and a hog-related tradition.

✳ ✳ ✳ ✳

"Bringing Home the Bacon"

THIS EXPRESSION IS now used to denote the person in a marriage or other domestic partnership who earns the larger monetary share of household income, but it once meant exactly what it says. In the 12th century, at the church of Dunmow in Essex County, England, a certain amount of cured and salted bacon was awarded to the couple that could prove (how they proved it is not quite sure) that they had lived in greater bliss than any of their competitors. The earliest record of this contest was 1445, but evidence exists that the custom had already been in effect for at least two centuries. In the 16th century, proof of devotion was determined through questions asked by a jury of unmarried men and women. The curious pork prize continued, albeit in irregular intervals, until the late 19th century.

Groundhog Day

The practice of watching a creature's reaction to its shadow to determine whether there will be six more weeks of winter began with German farmers in the 16th century, although they didn't use a groundhog, but a badger. When German immigrants settled in the area of Punxsutawney, Pennsylvania, 300 years later, they couldn't find any badgers, but there were plenty of local groundhogs to act as stand-ins.

German folklore had it that if the day was sunny and the creature was frightened enough by its shadow to dart back into the ground, there would be six more weeks of cold weather. That meant that the farmers shouldn't plant their crops yet. In more recent times, scientific studies have proven that the groundhog's accuracy in prediction over a 60-year period is only 28 percent.

In other words, for every year the groundhog is correct, there are almost three years in which it is incorrect. And in truth, the only things determining a groundhog's behavior when it emerges from hibernation is how hungry and how sexually aroused it is. If the groundhog is in the mood to mate—and starving, as well—chances are it'll stick around to see if it can get either or both of those cravings satisfied. The weather, at that moment or for the next six weeks, is the least of the groundhog's worries.

How It All Began, Part III

Every wondered how some of our everyday inventions and sayings came to be? Read on!

❋   ❋   ❋   ❋

Banning the Rays

SUNGLASSES HAVE BEEN around a lot longer than you'd think. The Arctic-dwelling Inuit found more functional uses for whalebones than merely as stays in women's corsets. Among these innovations was what may be the first pair of sunglasses: whalebone with narrow slits, designed to reduce snow and ice glare, thus preventing snow blindness.

Inscrutable 14th-century Chinese judges made themselves even more enigmatic by wearing smoked quartz glasses to hide their facial expressions while in the courtroom.

In the 20th century, "shades" became popular. Movie stars wore them. So did pilots, musicians, and gangsters—the latter notably when appearing as witnesses in front of Senate subcommittees.

What's Hot, Corny, and Cool?

Anyone who walks into a ballpark or a 7-Eleven store knows about hot dogs. In fact, the convenience-store chain sells 100 million a year, and the United States has officially declared July National Hot Dog Month.

Since 1938, people have also been treated to corn dogs, a cornmeal-coated wiener on a stick. Then, in 2002, along came a new product. On Red Sox Opening Day in Fenway Park, concessionaires put Cool Dogs on offer.

Cool Dogs look sort of like hot dogs: wiener-shape ice cream in a hot dog bun-shape sponge cake. As for condiments, buyers can choose from whipped cream, hot fudge, cherries, candy—just about anything other than mustard, relish, ketchup, or sauerkraut.

Cool Dogs kept a low profile until 2005 when they turned up at the Super Bowl. Suddenly, the treat was making its mark and began to be available in dairy cases throughout the country.

Mistake Out

Anyone who has ever made a mistake while typing and used Liquid Paper to fix it has Bette Nesmith Graham to thank.

Shortly after World War II, Graham, a Dallas divorcée with a young son to raise, went to secretarial school and found employment as an executive secretary. A perfectionist, Graham loathed the fact that her typed pages often contained errors and thought long and hard on how to fix them.

Graham was an aspiring artist who knew that painters often covered over their mistakes on canvas with more paint, so she mixed some specially tinted tempura in her kitchen and brought it to work. The stuff worked like a charm, covering over her errors as if they'd never been there, and her boss was none the wiser. Graham's colleagues in the secretarial pool soon took notice and asked if they could get some of her special correcting fluid. Graham obliged, placing it in a bottle labeled "Mistake Out."

Graham knew she was on to something and turned Mistake Out, which was later renamed Liquid Paper, into a home business. She worked hard to improve her formula, mixing batch after batch in her electric mixer.

Graham was ultimately fired from her secretarial job, but she took the opportunity to focus exclusively on Liquid Paper, which became a huge success. By 1968, she had moved into her own plant and had 19 employees; six years later, a massive new corporate headquarters and manufacturing facility opened in Dallas. In 1979, she sold the Liquid Paper Company to the Gillette Corporation for $47.5 million. She had little time to enjoy her windfall, however, dying only six months later at the age of 56.

Graham's son, Michael Nesmith, who helped her during the early days of her business, is also quite famous in his own right. He was a founding member of the '60s rock band The Monkees and later had a part in the creation of MTV.

The Keys to an Invention

Mechanical typewriters long ago went the way of the dinosaur, cast aside in favor of various kinds of newfangled word processors. But back in the day, typewriters were the best friend of anyone who had to put words on paper.

✳ ✳ ✳ ✳

EVEN MORE TIME-SAVING than a manual machine was the electric typewriter, which was invented by a finger-weary Texan named James Field Smathers.

Smathers was born in Valley Spring on February 12, 1888. Upon graduating from business school, he taught shorthand and typing for a year then took a job as a typist, accountant, and credit manager with a company in Kansas City, Missouri.

Typing was an integral part of Smathers's job, and he found it both time-consuming and tiresome. An electric typewriter, he reasoned, would do the job much more quickly, so he set to work creating one, and by the fall of 1912, he had developed a working model. Smathers applied for a patent as he perfected his invention, and in 1914, he produced a model that worked with stunning proficiency. In that instant, the lives of secretaries everywhere became much easier.

In 1923, after improving his electric typewriter even further, Smathers was approached by the Northeast Electric Company of Rochester, New York, which offered him a royalty contract for his revolutionary invention. However, it wasn't until 1930, when Electric Typewriters, a subsidiary of Northeast Electric Company, began marketing its Electromatic model that American businesses truly embraced the electric typewriter.

International Business Machines, better known today simply as IBM, purchased Electric Typewriters in 1933 and made it the cornerstone of its new Office Products Division.

Smathers, meanwhile, was awarded the Edward Longstreth Medal by the Franklin Institute in Pennsylvania for "ingenuity in the invention of the electric typewriter." He joined IBM as a consultant in 1938 and remained employed by the company until his retirement in 1953.

Swinging the Night Away

It's country music—like Duke Ellington might have played it. Or jazz, played by a Grand Ole Opry star. Mix them together, throwing in a wailing fiddle, a touch of polka, and a bit of blues and folk. Then give it a pop shine, and it becomes one of America's unique musical art forms—Western Swing.

✳ ✳ ✳ ✳

BORN IN THE heart of Texas and still enjoyed throughout the United States, the dance-oriented country-music sound known as Western Swing came out of the honky-tonks and dance halls favored by hard-working Texans in the 1920s and '30s, places that offered a welcome relief from the oil fields and cattle ranches. The music was upbeat, rhythmic, and infectious, and it got people on their feet.

A Familiar Sound

The biggest name in Western Swing is Bob Wills, the Texan who helped invent the stuff and reigned for decades as its most popular performer. Wills, a native of Turkey in West Texas, took up the fiddle as a child. In search of a career in music, he set off for Fort Worth in the early '30s, where he picked up work playing at parties. With a new friend, singer Milton Brown, he landed a job at radio station KFJZ. The two were hired, along with pianist Alton Stricklin, by the sales manager of the Burrus Mills flour company and dubbed The Light Crust Doughboys, after the company's most famous product.

Forming the Playboys

The Doughboys played a daily radio show, cut a couple of records in 1932 as the Fort Worth Doughboys, and then broke up, leaving three groups in their wake. Wills launched his own band, the Texas Playboys, in Waco, while Brown and his group, the Musical Brownies, continued to rule in Fort Worth. Under new management, The Light Crust Doughboys also continued to flourish. Looking to expand, Wills and his Playboys struck out for fresh territory—Tulsa, Oklahoma, where they became a fixture at a local ballroom named Cain's.

Although personnel shifted several times, the group eventually consisted of Wills, his cousin Johnnie Lee Wills on banjo, fiddler Jesse Ashlock, drummer Smokey Dacus, steel guitar player—a first in country music—Leon McAuliffe, and Wills's old friend, pianist Alton Stricklin. They began to record in 1935, and the rest is history. Milton Brown, who some argue might also have had a claim to the crown of the King of Western Swing, died too young after an auto accident in 1936. The future of Western Swing, then, lay with Wills and the Texas Playboys.

The band drew crowds of 6,000 to their nightly performances at Cain's until 1943. They were broadcast regularly across the country over Tulsa's 50,000-watt powerhouse KVOO radio until late in the 1950s, and they had a slew of hit records over the years, such as "San Antonio Rose," "Take Me Back to Tulsa," "Faded Love," and "Milk Cow Blues."

Widening the Music's Reach

In the '30s and early '40s, Western Swing moved to California with Depression-era migrants. By the 1940s, Western Swing had grown a huge following in California, with stars such as Wills playing venues around the state. Among the literally scores of popular West Coast performers were singer Spade Cooley (who later became notorious for viciously murdering his wife), Hank Thompson and his Brazos Valley Boys, Tex Williams and his Western Caravan, and Dude Martin and his Roundup Boys. The Los Angeles County Barn Dance at the Venice Pier drew 10,000 fans to dances in the early '40s.

Western Swing hasn't remained the popular powerhouse it once was, of course, but its influence can be found in the music of dozens of artists, from bands such as Asleep at the Wheel and the Time Jumpers to Elvis, Willie Nelson, Merle Haggard, Lyle Lovett, and George Strait. It's continuing strong today, with young bands still playing Western Swing to appreciative new audiences from California to Nashville.

It Started in Chicago

A lot of things got their first started in America's Second City.

✳   ✳   ✳   ✳

Car Radios

IN THE 1920S, Paul and Joseph Galvin started a business in Chicago selling devices that allowed home radios to be run on regular electric current rather than on batteries. In 1930, the innovative brothers rolled out a remarkable new invention—a radio that could be mounted in a car, so that motorists could be entertained and informed as they toured the roads of America. Taking advantage of the popularity of their new device, the brothers renamed their company Motorola (a combination of "motor" and "Victrola"), and went on to become one of the largest electronic communications manufacturers in the world.

Italian Beef Sandwich

A Chicago Italian Beef sandwich consists of thinly sliced seasoned beef on a hearty Italian roll, adorned with sautéed peppers—either sweet or hot according to the customer's preference. Now a staple of caterers and fast-food stands around the country, the sandwich was introduced in Chicago during the 1930s. According to Al's Beef and the Scala Packing Company (leading Chicago Italian beef purveyors), the sandwiches became a staple of Depression-era Italian family gatherings because the thinly sliced meat and hearty rolls offered a cheaper way to feed large crowds.

Lemonheads

The Ferrara Pan Candy Company was founded in Chicago in the early 1900s by Italian immigrant Salvatore Ferrara and was originally known for the popular sugar-coated almonds it sold. In 1962, the company introduced Lemonheads, a small, round, sour candy that remains a popular treat today. The candies are made by the "pan" process referred to in the company's name, in which layers of flavoring and coloring are added to a hard candy center as it spins around in a rotating pan. Still owned by the same family today, Ferrara Pan produces more than 500 million Lemonheads a year.

Mail Order

Aaron Montgomery Ward got his start as a Marshall Field clerk. He then worked for a St. Louis dry goods wholesaler as a sales rep assigned to the rural market. In 1872, Ward started his own company using a new distribution method—mail order. His first catalog was just a page long, but by 1876 he was offering 3,000 products. His innovative sales approach opened up a whole new market by making big-city goods available to frontier families. Just before the turn of the century, another

Chicago firm, Sears, Roebuck & Co., entered the mail-order business and soon surpassed Ward's annual sales by allowing patrons to buy on credit. These Chicago-based retail giants pioneered the national distribution model that we know today.

The Skyscraper

As a result of its ambitious plan to rebuild the city in the wake of the Great Fire, Chicago became a leader in urban planning and architecture. In what was likely the most significant architectural feat of the 19th century, William Le Baron Jenney devised an entirely new way to construct large office buildings. His Home Insurance Building, put up in 1885 on the corner of La Salle and Adams, relied on an interior steel frame to bear the load of the building, which allowed the exterior walls to be lighter and the building to be taller. This innovation is still used in the designs of modern skyscrapers. Three of Jenney's skyscrapers still stand: Robert Morris Center (403 S. State St.), the Manhattan (431 S. Dearborn), and the Ludington (1104 S. Wabash), which is now part of Columbia College.

Boy Scouts of America

The Scouting movement was founded in Britain by military figure Lord Robert Baden-Powell. According to Scouting legend, William D. Boyce, a publishing magnate from Chicago, became lost in a dense fog while visiting London. One of Baden-Powell's Scouts helped him find his way and told the American about the British organization. Impressed with the selfless mission of the group, Boyce set up a similar organization after returning to Chicago, and the group grew into the Boy Scouts of America.

McDonald's

In 1940, two brothers opened a barbecue restaurant in San Bernardino, California. Within a few years, they were offering their busy patrons quick service and a pared down menu, including an unusual thin-cut version of French fries. In 1954, restaurant appliance salesman Ray Kroc visited the operation and struck a deal with the brothers to franchise their operation nationwide. Within a year, Kroc had opened the first McDonald's fast-food restaurant in the Chicago area (specifically, in the suburb of Des Plaines), and by 1956 the company had more than 700 stores nationwide. McDonald's is now one of the largest restaurant operations in the world, with outlets in more than 100 countries.

Remote Control

Headquartered in Chicago, the Zenith Corporation offered Americans one of the most well known brands of television sets in the 1950s. The company's popularity skyrocketed, however, when Zenith engineer Robert Adler developed the first practical wireless remote control. The company had previously offered a wired remote, the Lazy Bones, which had a cumbersome 20-foot cable. Adler's Space Command remote, introduced by Zenith in 1956, used ultrasonic sound to send signals to the set without wires.

Modem

In the 1970s, USRobotics was an electronics company operated by five University of Chicago graduates out of a single office on Chicago's North Side. A short while later, the company introduced the world's first commercially available computer modem, setting the foundation for the explosion of the World Wide Web and helping make the Internet a presence in almost every home in the country.

Twinkies

In 1930, Jimmy Dewar was the manager of Chicago's Continental Bakery, which was well known for its Wonder brand bread and Hostess brand cakes. Another popular item the bakery produced was a strawberry-filled shortcake, which could only be made when the berries were in season. Looking for a way to make the snack available year-round, Dewar replaced the strawberries with a banana-cream filling, and the Twinkie was born. During World War II, fruit rationing forced him to switch from the banana filling to the vanilla cream we all know today.

Tinkertoys

Stonemason Charles Pajeau loved watching children at play, and he came up with the idea for a new toy by watching neighborhood kids build models with pencils and empty spools of thread. Working out of his garage in the Chicago suburb of Evanston, he designed a set of colored wooden rods and disks with holes drilled through the center and along the sides. Partnering with businessman Robert Pettit, he introduced his Tinkertoys to local stores in 1915. Before long, the toys were a national sensation.

Cell Phones

In the mid-20th century, AT&T engineers developed a new idea for communications: a network of radio towers that would allow wireless telephone communication through telephones installed in automobiles. AT&T had some success with their car-phone service, but the true revolution in the communications industry came when Martin Cooper's research team at the Chicago-based Motorola company developed a fully portable phone in 1973. Cooper's original phone weighed two pounds and cost nearly $4,000, but consumers were nonetheless anxious to take advantage of the convenience it offered. Within a decade, the Chicago firm had reduced both the size and the cost of the cell phone, leading to a revolution in personal communications.

Who Started Mother's Day?

Celebrations of mothers date back to antiquity, but Mother's Day proper was the brainchild of a West Virginian woman named Anna Jarvis.

❋ ❋ ❋ ❋

RAISED IN GRAFTON, West Virginia, Jarvis was the daughter of a woman who organized events called Mother's Friendship Days, which reunited West Virginia families that had been separated during the Civil War. After her mother died in 1905, Jarvis paid homage to her with an aggressive letter-writing campaign that began in 1907 and urged elected officials and newspaper editors to promote an official holiday to honor all mothers.

Within six years, most states observed Mother's Day. In 1914, President Woodrow Wilson signed a Congressional resolution that designated the second Sunday in May as Mother's Day across the nation. Jarvis had succeeded, but little did she know that, just like Dr. Frankenstein, she had created a monster that would lead to her ruin.

Jarvis suggested that people wear white carnations, her mother's favorite flower, on Mother's Day. But when florists started charging more for carnations, she denounced the practice and chose instead to wear a button to commemorate the day. This was just one of many futile battles that Jarvis waged for the rest of her life against the quick and thorough commercialization of the holiday. Anybody who profited from Mother's Day felt her wrath. She considered Mother's Day cards especially nefarious, opining that giving one was a lazy way to show appreciation for the person who gave you the gift of life.

Jarvis lived off the considerable inheritances that she received after the deaths of her mother and her brother, Claude, who had founded a taxi service in Philadelphia. But while she was wholeheartedly devoting herself to fighting the exploitation of Mother's Day, Jarvis neglected to tend to her own finances. By 1943, she was living in poverty and her health was in serious decline. Friends raised enough money to allow her to live in a sanatorium in West Chester, Pennsylvania, where she died in 1948, childless.

If Jarvis were alive today, she wouldn't be at all pleased with what has happened to Mother's Day. In 2009 the National Retail Federation estimated total Mother's Day spending by consumers to be in the neighborhood of $14.1 billion.

Popcorn and the Cinema

Popcorn could be called the smell of the cinema, but the buttery treat wasn't always favored in movie houses. In fact, theater owners initially resisted the idea of letting the salty stuff inside their doors.

✳   ✳   ✳   ✳

Popcorn Resistance

POPCORN'S ROMANCE WITH the box office started in the 1920s, but in those days, the corn was popping *outside* of theaters, especially in large urban areas. Back then, vendors set up carts outside movie houses and sold the snack to crowds on their way in.

The 1920s was the era of the picture palace, when huge theaters were constructed with elaborate decor designed for comfort, class, and escapism. Greasy popcorn didn't fit with that image. Historians say it wasn't until the Great Depression that theater owners realized that the snack could bring in added profits. That realization was the beginning of the movie industry's most famous partnership.

The Rise and the Pop

By the 1930s, with the rise of the electric popping machine, popcorn in theaters was commonplace. Before that, poppers sent nasty burning smells into the air, but with the olfactory offense eliminated, the path was clear for nonstop popping.

Popcorn was inexpensive to make, which helped it rise in popularity during the Depression. Theater owners could price a bag at an affordable ten cents and still manage to make money from the sales. Popcorn demand skyrocketed as the '30s progressed, and when World War II began, the government's rationing of sugar made popcorn a favored alternative to sweeter snacks.

Popcorn Today

These days, movie theaters rely heavily on snacks to make a profit. The selections have expanded, but popcorn continues to make up a significant part of the equation—and it's one crunch you can count on hearing for years to come.

Going Up

You're standing in an elevator. Against your better judgment, you're tapping your toe to a lush, languid, orchestral version of The Rolling Stones' "Sympathy for the Devil." It sounds more like a duet of Kenny G and Lawrence Welk than the Stones. You'd probably never guess that this gentle, non-offensive, ostensibly soothing music comes to you thanks to a soldier who held a major general's rank in the U.S. Army.

✳   ✳   ✳   ✳

BORN IN 1865, George Owen Squier had only an eighth-grade education when he finagled his way into the United States Military Academy at West Point. He graduated seventh in his class in 1887 and went on to earn a Ph.D. from Johns Hopkins University. Squier had an interest in aviation and was a passenger on one of Orville Wright's earliest flights. In fact, Squier played a major role in convincing the army to start using airplanes.

But his first love was electronics. For much of his career in the military, he served in the signal corps, working to develop and refine communication systems. Squier was an avid inventor who held more than sixty patents, and he created numerous valuable technologies for the army. One of his major achievements came in 1910, when he invented multiplexing, which enabled telephone wires to carry multiple messages at once—he called this technology "wired wireless."

In the early 1920s, as retirement from the military approached, Squier became increasingly interested in the idea of delivering radio signals directly to listeners using wired wireless. He helped found a company called Wired Radio that transmitted programming into homes via electrical wires for about two dollars a month; not surprisingly, people preferred wireless radio because it was free. Wired Radio did, however, have success pitching its services to businesses—the company emphasized research that claimed that music could increase worker productivity. The concept caught on, and eventually, piped-in music could be heard in stores, offices, restaurants, lobbies, waiting rooms, and, yes, elevators.

Not long before Squier died in 1934, he left the world with one last great invention that has reverberated through our culture ever since. He longed for a catchier name than "Wired Radio" for his service, so he combined the word "music" with the name of his favorite innovative company of the day—Kodak—and coined the term "Muzak."

Who Came Up with Chewing Gum?

The legacy of the ancient Greeks included not only democracy, but...chewing gum?

✳   ✳   ✳   ✳

THE ANCIENT GREEKS were the original gum smackers. Thousands of years ago, they were chewing mastic—a rubbery resin from the mastic tree—in order to clean their teeth, freshen their breath, and treat various maladies. It's not clear who exactly came up with the idea, but we know that Hippocrates, the so-called father of medicine, was a big fan—he recommended mastic as a remedy for chronic coughs, upset stomachs, and liver problems.

As for chewing gum as we know it today? Look to the Native Americans, as well as to General Antonio López de Santa Anna (yes, the same Santa Anna who attacked the Alamo). Native American tribes introduced European settlers to a chewing gum that they made from spruce-tree resin. Americans chewed this spruce gum, along with a similar product made from sweetened paraffin wax, through the mid-nineteenth century, but neither was especially popular.

Then Santa Anna brought chicle—a latex product extracted from the sapodilla tree—to the United States in the late 1860s. The Maya of the Yucatán Peninsula had been chewing chicle for ages, probably as a means of staving off thirst during long journeys—chewing the gum helped them produce saliva and, thus, quenched their thirst. But Santa Anna believed that chicle could be used as a rubber substitute in the manufacture of tires. To this end, Santa Anna introduced it to a New York businessman named Thomas Adams.

Adams started importing chicle from the Yucatán, but found that it was unsuitable as a rubber substitute. However, Adams discovered an effective use for his leftover chicle: chewing gum. It became a hit, and before long, Adams had launched flavored gum, the gumball, and the gumball machine. His products were massive successes, though the simultaneous introductions of sidewalk gum, hair gum, and under-the-desk gum weren't quite so popular.

In the Red

Give a youngster a box of crayons, ask for a drawing of a fire engine, and watch those little fingers reach for red. Kids know that red is the right color for a fire truck—it's adults who don't always agree.

* * * *

PRECISELY WHY FIRE engines are red is lost in the smoky recesses of history. Experts from such agencies as the U.S. Fire Administration and the National Fire Protection Association (NFPA) cite theories, but even they admit that no one knows for sure. Most conjecture leads to the nineteenth century, when firefighting in America was an ad hoc pursuit and competition between public, private, and volunteer brigades was fierce. Crews would race each other to a blaze, and the first group on the scene took control. Sometimes it was to secure a claim on any fire insurance money; often it was just for the glory. The rivalry extended to uniforms and equipment: The brighter and more elaborate, the more prestigious. Not only was red the shade most identified with fire, it was the most regal and expensive color with which to paint the firefighting apparatus. Thus was born a tradition.

Another theory holds that red became the accepted color for safety reasons in the early twentieth century, when most automobiles were black and red was thought to stand out best in traffic. Indeed, the visibility of fire trucks to other motorists remains a matter of grave importance. NFPA records show a steady increase in the number of collisions involving fire emergency vehicles going to or from a blaze. In 2006, for instance, there were 16,020 such collisions, resulting in 1,250 injuries and the deaths of nineteen firefighters.

Safety concerns once led to a flirtation with alternatives to fire-engine red. The movement was fueled by research suggesting that hues of yellow or lime are more visible to the human eye, particularly at dusk or nighttime since they are more reflective. Indeed, support for a switch to yellow, lime green, or white from red was strong in the 1970s and 1980s. But subsequent analysis revealed little difference in the number of collisions.

It turns out that color has virtually no effect on how visible a fire truck is to motorists, but lighting and reflective surfaces do. The NFPA never had a requirement for fire truck color, but in 1991 it established new standards that increased the number and size of emergency lights and specified their brightness and location. It also added standards for the size, placement, and color of reflective striping. Though the Federal Aviation Administration stuck with lime-yellow for airport emergency vehicles, municipal fire departments have trended back to the color red. The government's Occupational Safety and Health Administration also favors red in its standards.

Most firefighters couldn't be happier. They say that the public never really associated lime with fire trucks, and anything other than red somehow bucked a proud tradition. Any kid with a crayon in his hand could have told you as much.

Grand Old Party Begins in Ripon

Today, in the little town of Ripon, about 50 miles northwest of Milwaukee, there is a large sign on the front of a one-room schoolhouse that proclaims "Birthplace of the Republican Party." And in a 1954 speech, President Dwight D. Eisenhower credited the party's founding to a meeting that took place 100 years earlier at that very spot. So it must be true, right? Well, yes and no.

✳ ✳ ✳ ✳

Trying Times

IT WAS A time of turmoil in our nation, and there is no doubt that other areas were having anti-Democrat powwows of their own. Jackson, Michigan, and Pittsburgh, Pennsylvania, are two of the other cities that have laid claim to the title of

Republican birthplace. Yet after careful analysis over the years, it appears as though Ripon's party started just a bit earlier than the other events. Even the Republican Party itself credits Ripon as the home of the first informal meeting of the party. The first official meeting of Republicans occurred in Jackson a few months later, and Pittsburgh hosted the first national GOP convention two years after that.

Out with the Old, In with the New

Decades before the Civil War actually broke out, the institution of slavery had become a controversial topic—especially in the northern states. The Missouri Compromise of 1820 had closed the Kansas and Nebraska territories to slavery, but in 1854 Democrat Stephen Douglas introduced a bill that would amend the law and allow settlers to make their own decision regarding slavery in the territory.

So on March 20, 1854, attorney Alvan E. Bovay of Ripon organized a group of people interested in the politics of the day. It is said he went door to door to recruit citizens for his meeting, and he managed to round up 54 of the 100 eligible voters in Ripon. They met at the Little White Schoolhouse, where, at Bovay's urging, these former members of the Whig, Democrat, and Free Soil Parties pledged their allegiance to the antislavery movement and the new Republican Party.

Bovay's friendship with New York publisher Horace Greeley gave the newcomers a boost. In June 1854, Greeley publicly used the term "Republican" for the first time in an editorial against slavery. With Greeley's help, the name—and the values it represented—quickly spread throughout the country.

History Preserved

The Little White Schoolhouse has been moved three times since that famous meeting. In 1908, the Ripon Historical Society, the Ripon Commercial Club, and the Ripon City Council came together to save the schoolhouse. In 1973, the schoolhouse was placed on the National Register of Historic

Places. A year later, the U.S. Department of the Interior declared the site a historic landmark for its role in the formation of the Republican Party.

Today, the Little White Schoolhouse still stands in Ripon and is open to the public as a museum. No matter what your political affiliation may be, a visit to the schoolhouse is an important glimpse into our nation's history.

You Can Thank Wisconsin

Some ways the Badger State made the average American's life even better.

✳   ✳   ✳   ✳

Vitamin D

HARRY STEENBOCK DIDN'T invent vitamin D, but in 1923, the University of Wisconsin-Madison professor figured out that exposing food to ultraviolet radiation increased its vitamin D content. Rather than receive a big payday from the Quaker Oats Company, which wanted the technology to fortify breakfast cereal, Steenbock helped create the first university technology transfer office, the Wisconsin Alumni Research Foundation (WARF). It was a nonprofit organization that ensured university research profits would go toward funding future research. WARF's first action was to sell the license for Steenbock's technology to Quaker Oats and various pharmaceutical companies, netting WARF roughly $8 million by 1945.

The Snowmobile

Joseph Bombardier of Quebec is often considered the father of the modern snowmobile, and rightly so: His endless track vehicle, patented in the United States in 1962, was the first commercially successful model in the nation. However, in 1927, Carl J. Eliason of Sayner received a patent for an oft-forgotten precursor called the snow machine—essentially a toboggan with a seat and a motor. Eliason couldn't find commercial success and ended his endeavor in 1953. Nevertheless, his final K series is credited with influencing companies like Polaris and Arctic Cat.

The Automobile (Kind of...)

Although his name is not usually mentioned along with early automobile pioneers, in 1871, Racine's John Wesley Carhart invented and perfected an oscillating valve for a steam engine, which he used to power a buggy he called the Spark. Though the contraption was deemed too noisy to be practical—local legend says the noise spooked a neighbor's horse, indirectly causing its death and prompting neighbors to demand that Carhart dismantle his invention—it was recognized years later by the American Manufacturers' Association as a forerunner of the automobile.

America Goes to Kindergarten

Kindergarten—which literally means "children's garden" in German—is now considered a normal transition between home and full-time schooling for young children. But initially, America was slow to warm to the idea.

✳   ✳   ✳   ✳

FRIEDRICH FROEBEL FIRST conceived of kindergarten in 1840 as an introduction to art, mathematics, and natural history—a preeducation for children of all classes, as opposed to the custodial religious services that had been created for the offspring of the very poor. But after kindergarten became associated with radical feminist ideals in its German homeland and in Prussia, authorities became upset that women's nurturing skills might be translated into a wider commercial sphere, and kindergarten was soon banned.

You Can't Keep a Good Idea Down

German liberals in exile, however, exported the idea to other countries: Bertha Ronge took it to England, and her sister

Margarethe Meyer Schurz opened the first American (even if it was German-speaking) kindergarten in Wisconsin in 1856. Elizabeth Palmer Peabody created the first English-speaking kindergarten three years later in Boston. But it was Susan Elizabeth Blow who established the first public kindergarten, Des Peres School in St. Louis, Missouri, in 1873. She taught children in the morning and gave seminars to teachers in the afternoon. By 1883, a mere ten years later, every St. Louis public school had a kindergarten, making the city a model for the nation.

The movement really garnered momentum after Commissioner of Education William Harris spoke to Congress on February 12, 1897, in support of public kindergartens: "The advantage to the community in utilizing the age from four to six in training the hand and eye ... in training the mind ... will, I think, ultimately prevail in ... the establishment of this beneficent institution in all the city school systems of our country."

How It All Began, Part IV

Every wondered how some of today's objects and sayings came to be? Read on!

✳   ✳   ✳   ✳

Pirate Jewelry

ONE REASON GIVEN for why pirates wore gold earrings is because no one could be assured of returning from a long, dangerous sea journey back in the bad old days. In case of accident—or an ill-fated sword battle—the hope was that these golden earrings would be taken from the corpse to pay for a decent burial.

"Mad as a Hatter"

The Mad Hatter was popularized in Lewis Carroll's Alice's Adventures in Wonderland, but Carroll did not coin the phrase. Making hats and madness had already been linked.

During the early days of processing felt to use in hatmaking, the toxic substance mercury was used, which resulted in many industry workers developing mental or neurological disturbances. From this unfortunate situation, the phrase "mad as a hatter" came to indicate anyone who had gone insane.

"Crocodile Tears"

When someone is said to be crying "crocodile tears," they are feigning sorrow. This phrase actually does come from crocodiles, specifically a peculiarity in which crocodiles shed tears while eating. This is caused by food pressing against the roof of the animal's mouth, which activates the lachrymal glands that secrete tears. This makes crocodiles appear to be crying without really being sad at all.

Eye of the Beholder

Unless you manufacture them or wear them, it's sort of easy to forget about artificial eyes. The ancient Egyptians even wore them, beginning around the fifth century B.C. Since then, artificial eyes have had a slow but steady evolution.

First came gold and painted enamel eyes, followed by glass, and, finally, acrylic. During the evolution other materials were tried in search of realism: aluminum, sponge, asbestos, rubber, and paraffin, to name a few. Researchers in Toronto have rocketed the science of artificial eyes into the realm of high technology, developing a robotic eye that mimics natural movements by using electrodes implanted in the wearer's head. That takes the development a long way from the Egyptians who simply painted an eye on a piece of cloth, which hung over the eye socket.

The First Alaska Highway

The 1,500-mile Alaska Highway, which runs from Dawson Creek in Canada's Yukon to Fairbanks, Alaska, was not the first Alaskan highway. Sure, it got the name and fame, but it was a highway-come-lately compared to the 1,150-mile Iditarod Trail between Seward and Nome. The Iditarod opened in 1915;

the Alaska Highway in 1942. Granted, the Alaska Highway is open year-round and is paved, while the decidedly more rustic Iditarod Trail is just, well, a trail, navigable only in winter and only by dogsled.

Still, the Iditarod has an international claim to fame. Each winter since 1973, dog mushers from every snowy corner of the world gather to race over the trail in the "Last Great Race on Earth," an annual tribute the history and contributions of the dog sleds, from the gold prospectors who opened Alaska's interior (the dogs would haul the gold), to the dogs that ran serum vaccines to the isolated town of Nome to prevent a diphtheria epidemic in 1925.

So, what exactly is an "Iditarod"? It's a ghost town that was once the midpoint on the trail.

Chariots of Fire

In war and peace, these vehicles served the ancient world well.

✳   ✳   ✳   ✳

ABOUT 3,000 YEARS BEFORE the birth of Jesus Christ, the Mesopotamians invented the ox cart as a means of conveyance. The four-wheeled ox cart was useful for transporting both people and products, but it was slow—certainly too slow to be effective for other uses, such as active warfare. While ox carts could be used to carry weapons from one place to the next, they could not be used in actual battle. Frustration led to invention, and over the centuries, the ancient peoples of the Middle East refined their vehicles until the chariot was born.

Triumph of Human Ingenuity

Before the chariot could be invented, humans had to invent something else: the spoked wheel. Spokes are the rods that radiate from the center of a wheel, allowing for more weight, greater pressure, and faster movement. Archaeologists date the first spoke-wheeled chariots to about 2000 B.C., and within the next 700 years, they were ubiquitous in the ancient world, especially for use in warfare. The solid, wooden wheels that had been both helping and hampering armies were now a thing of the past, and warriors relished the opportunity to use lighter, faster vehicles. But in addition to the invention of the spoked wheel, horses had to be tamed and trained. Once these two things were accomplished, the chariot was inevitable.

In biblical times, chariots were used by the Hebrews, Romans, Greeks, Hittites, and Egyptians. Most chariots were two- or four-wheeled vehicles with a floor to stand on and a waist-high, semicircular guard to protect the lower half of the driver. A driver could lean against this guard while moving or attach himself to it in order to leave his hands free to carry a shield and/or sword. Though most chariots were designed to hold only the driver, others were big enough to accommodate one or two riders as well. The Latin word for chariot is *carrus*, from which we take the name for our modern-day cars. A two-horse chariot was called a *biga*, a three-horse chariot was called a *triga*, and a four-horse chariot was called a *quadriga*.

Battle for the Mediterranean

Once the chariot had been invented, it quickly became a common sight throughout the Middle East and factored into almost every battle until about the 4th century B.C. Some of the greatest charioteers of ancient times were the Hittites. An ancient Anatolian people, the Hittites conquered much of Syria and Mesopotamia with their fierce, chariot-powered army. Indeed, it was the Hittites who fought and won what was probably the largest chariot battle ever: the 1299 B.C. Battle of Kadesh, in which 3,500 to 5,000 chariots (exact number unknown) clashed in a bloody fight for regional dominion. The Egyptians, Assyrians, and Hurrians were put in their place—for a time.

Though the Egyptians lost the Battle of Kadesh, they won many other battles with their brilliantly designed and beautifully ornamented chariots. It was the Egyptians who invented the yolk saddle for their horses, and as the Romans did, they enjoyed making their chariots works of art as well as practical. It was not unusual for wealthy warriors to use fine leather and gold trim on their chariots. But while ancient chariots were often beautiful, they were rarely comfortable due to the lack of suspension. Though military engineers of the time attempted to make a primitive form of springs for chariots, they had little success in this area. Suspension in horse-drawn vehicles would not be perfected until the 19th century. Still, compared to the ox- and ass-drawn vehicles that came before them, chariots seemed positively revolutionary and modern to the peoples of the Bible.

The Word on Chariots

Chariots are mentioned many times in the Bible, especially in the Old Testament. First referred to in Genesis 50:9, they are often used as symbols of power, glory, and dominance. The great Hebrew King Solomon had a huge army that was described in 2 Chronicles 1:14: "Solomon gathered together chariots and horses; he had fourteen hundred chariots and twelve thousand horses, which he stationed in the chariot cities and with the king in Jerusalem."

When the prophet Elijah died and left his mantle to Elisha, "a chariot of fire and horses of fire separated the two of them, and Elijah ascended in a whirlwind into heaven. Elisha kept watching and crying out, 'Father, father! The chariots of Israel and its horsemen!'" (2 Kings 2:11–12). But chariots could also be used in biblical metaphors of a more tender sort; for example, in Song of Solomon 1:9: "I compare you, my love, to a mare among Pharaoh's chariots." Might not sound too "hot" to us today, but back then, it was quite a sexy compliment.

By the time Jesus Christ was around, chariots were no longer used in warfare. Why? Because horses were bred to be bigger and stronger so that warriors could use them alone in battle, without having to attach them to chariots. Chariots were still used in Jesus' time for other reasons, and chariot races were still quite popular, as was shown in the iconic chariot race scene in the 1959 film *Ben-Hur*, starring Charlton Heston. This spectacular action sequence is still considered one of the greatest and most authentic historical scenes ever filmed. Using the largest film set to that time (it took five months to build on 18 acres) and 15,000 extras, it was a grueling five weeks of work for Heston and the other actors, who drove nine chariots that were each pulled by four horses.

Labor Day

Next time you're enjoying time off for Labor Day, relishing cold beer and grilled bratwurst in the backyard, you can thank Peter J. McGuire of New York. Or maybe Matthew Maguire (no relation).

✳ ✳ ✳ ✳

IN THE 1880S, Peter J. McGuire, one of the cofounders of the American Federation of Labor, is said to have developed the idea of a holiday for American workers in homage to those "from whom rude nature have delved and carved all the grandeur we behold." Matthew Maguire, a machinist and secretary of the Central Labor Union, is also credited with that honor.

In any case, the CLU and the Knights of Labor decided to go ahead with the holiday in New York City, and the first Labor Day was observed on September 5, 1882, with a grand parade and festival in Union Square. By 1885, as the labor movement continued to gain ground and organized labor lobbied vigorously in state legislatures, Labor Day was celebrated in cities around the country. The first Monday of September was agreed upon as the official date, roughly halfway between the Fourth of July and Thanksgiving.

Prompted by widespread labor unrest, and perhaps the fact that 1894 was an election year, President Grover Cleveland was eager to appease the labor movement. On June 28, 1894, Congress unanimously named the first Monday in September a legal holiday. That didn't stop labor unrest—the 1894 Pullman strike was still going strong—but it was a step forward.

Today, Labor Day is still marked with speeches and celebrations, though with fewer of the large parades of the past. Many still regard it, as AFL leader Samuel Gompers did in 1898, as "the day for which the toilers in past centuries looked forward, when their rights and their wrongs would be discussed . . . that the workers of our day may not only lay down their tools of labor for a holiday, but upon which they may touch shoulders in marching phalanx and feel the stronger for it."

Bagel Beginnings

Shiny. Chewy. Crusty. A pal to cream cheese and smoked salmon alike. What's not to love about a bagel?

※　※　※　※

POSSIBLY THE ARCHETYPAL New York food—many swear that New York City tap water makes the city's bagels the best in the world—these dense rolls with the hole in the middle have a long and fascinating history. And, as is the case with lots of edible goodies, that history is—wait for it—shrouded in mystery.

The English name is derived from the Yiddish *beygl*, "to bend." Some say it's from the German beugel, a round roll shaped like a stirrup, invented in Vienna in the mid-1600s in honor of the victorious general Jan Sobieski, an avid horse rider. Maria Balinska, author of the definitive *The Bagel: The Surprising History of a Modest Bread*, dates the bagel's beginning earlier, given its mention in the 1610 municipal law of Krakow, Poland. The law, the story goes, provided for a gift of bagels to women in childbirth—perhaps the first acknowledgment of the bagel's status as comfort food.

In any case, the bagel made its way to New York from Eastern Europe in the late 19th and early 20th century. It was so important to the immigrant diet that it spawned the formation of a tightly run International Bagel Bakers Union in 1907.

Until the 1960s, bagels were almost all made by hand. Then, Daniel Thompson invented a machine that could produce hundreds of bagels an hour. Murray Lender successfully used the first of these in a garage in Connecticut for his nascent commercial frozen bagel line. For better or worse, frozen bagels immediately went national. By 1993, Americans averaged one bagel every two weeks, and by 2009 the top ten purveyors of fresh and frozen bagels did better than $650 million in business.

The secret to bagel excellence lies in just the right combination of flour, water, yeast, salt, and malt. Once the dough is made, it rises, and then the bagels are "kettled"—boiled in water—and finally baked. The result, says Balinska, "should be that you feel like a stone has landed in your stomach—in the best possible way, of course."

On a Roll

Ever since the dawn of humanity, people have searched for ways to cleanse themselves after the inevitable, if rather unmentionable, process of elimination. How did today's toilet paper come to be?

✳   ✳   ✳   ✳

ANCIENT ROMANS USED communal sponges (which were then replaced in a bucket of saltwater—*eww*). Over the centuries, different countries and cultures used, literally, whatever came to hand—leaves, hay, fruit skins, or even (ouch) corncobs; the wealthier had rags. Circa A.D. 589, the Chinese were reportedly the first to use something akin to what we now know as toilet paper, and by 1393, the imperial court was going through 720,000 sheets annually, at a massive two by three feet each. The emperor's family itself had its royal rumps massaged by perfumed paper. But it was almost 500 years later before a New Yorker named Joseph Gayetty introduced the first pre-packaged tissue for the masses in 1857.

Marketed as "therapeutic" or "medicated" paper, Gayetty's invention—which sold in packs of 500 for 50 cents—was ahead (no pun intended) of its time in that the "unbleached pearl-colored pure manila hemp paper" also contained aloe vera (an ingredient still employed in some "luxury" toilet tissues), for "the prevention of piles." Gayetty was so proud of his innovation that each loose sheet was watermarked with his name.

Unfortunately, not only was Gayetty's product ultimately not very successful (although it remained available until the 1920s), it soon had competition. Seth Wheeler, of Albany, New York, obtained a patent in 1871 for perforated toilet tissue on a roll (said to have been previously invented by someone from England, whose version flopped). Philadelphia brothers Thomas, Edward, and Clarence Scott adopted the idea of sheets on a roll from an inventor in Great Britain. They began selling it through intermediaries such as drugstores in 1890, privately labeled (they didn't want their name on the actual product) and cut to specifications.

But if it hadn't been for Joseph Gayetty's first attempt at improving the state of the nation's bottoms, we might all still be eagerly awaiting our next mail-order catalog.

The History of the Birthday Cake

This ubiquitous candlelit confection has been a tradition in Western countries for centuries. Read on for the full scoop!

✳ ✳ ✳ ✳

Whose Cake Is This?

THE ORIGIN OF the birthday cake is up for debate. Some scholars place its creation with the ancient Greeks, who made celebratory round honey cakes to offer up to the goddess Artemis; or with the Romans, who would make small savory cakes with honey, cheese, and olive oil. Other folks claim the birthday cake was born in the Middle Ages. At that time in Germany, sweet dough was formed into a petite cake to represent the baby Jesus wrapped in his swaddling clothes. The cake was eaten on Jesus's birthday (or rather, Christmas Day). Later, it became tradition for the cake to be given to children on their own birthdays.

Cake Customs and Custom Cakes

However the trend began, the birthday cake has been claimed by many birthday-celebrating cultures and cake customs have evolved over time. In England starting in the late 1600s, small charms were baked into birthday cakes; each charm foretold the recipient's future: If you bit into a coin, you'd be rich. Got the thimble? Be prepared to die lonely.

For many years, however, only the rich enjoyed birthday cakes. Before the industrial revolution (when cake mixes and home baking became more commonplace), frosted tiers of sugary cake were luxuries afforded only by the wealthy. These days, a birthday cake can be cheaply made at home or purchased at a bakery or grocery store.

Not everyone loves to celebrate their birthday, and plenty of cultures don't celebrate it at all. Jehovah's Witnesses believe the birthday celebration to be a pagan tradition and refuse to celebrate birthdays—no cake for them. And other people do celebrate the anniversary of their birth, but not with cake. In the Netherlands, birthdays are all about fruit tarts served with cream. And in Korea, seaweed soup is the special birthday dish.

How It All Began, Part V

Every wondered how some of today's objects and sayings came to be? Read on!

✳   ✳   ✳   ✳

By the Glass or Gallon

IN MODERN TIMES, when people think gin, they picture complicated, elegant, and expensive cocktails: martinis, Singapore Slings, and gin and tonics. But for about a century after a Dutch doctor invented gin in 1650, it was actually cheaper in Britain than beer. By 1690, Londoners were drinking half a million gallons of gin a year; by 1750, consumption of the drink had risen to 11 million gallons in London alone. The term "Dutch courage" was born because much of the stuff was imported from Holland.

In 1751, however, the British government passed the Tippling Act to reduce gin consumption by reducing its availability. Prohibition in the United States further sullied gin's reputation. "Bathtub gin" was no misnomer—gin is so easy to make that it can be done at home, even in the bathtub, if a person so chooses (and many have).

So much for gin's original application: as a liquor formulated to cure kidney and stomach disorders!

Stick-ups

In 1980, Art Fry and Spencer Silver came up with the Post-it Note. Their invention suddenly made "I'm sorry, I forgot to write it down," the lamest excuse in the Western world. Back in the early '70s, Fry and Silver were employed by office equipment producer 3M. The duo pitched their idea, but the company didn't dig it. Then Fry and Silver began handing out samples to their coworkers. Their colleagues clamored for more; eventually the head honchos at 3M came around. Post-it Notes were launched nationally in 1980 to great success.

Notable Notes:

* Post-its have always been recyclable.

* It would take approximately 506,880,000 Post-it Notes to circle the world (using $2\,{}^{7}/_{8}$-inch square notes).

* The most expensive Post-it Note sold in an auction went for £640—it featured a charcoal drawing by artist R. B. Kitaj.

O Christmas Tree...

Getting ready to deck the halls? Before you trim that tree, spruce up your knowledge of this holiday centerpiece.

* * * *

Origins

ACCORDING TO HORTICULTURAL experts, the use of trees to spruce up a winter holiday dates back thousands of years. The ancient Egyptians celebrated the winter solstice by adorning their homes with date palm leaves, and the Romans enjoyed a seasonal festival called Saturnalia that included decorating one's home with tree branches and lights and exchanging gifts. Sound familiar?

How the Christmas tree came to America is open to debate. Some historians believe it arrived with Hessian troops during the Revolutionary War. Others believe it started when German immigrants settled into Pennsylvania and some of the surrounding states.

The commercial Christmas tree industry as we know it today began in 1851, when an enterprising farmer named Mark Carr had the brilliant idea to take two sleds full of evergreens to New York City. He quickly sold them all, and by 1900, the home Christmas tree had become an established tradition.

The National Christmas Tree

The first National Christmas Tree was a 48-foot balsam fir, erected by the District of Columbia Public Schools on the Ellipse south of the White House in November 1923. About 3,000 spectators gathered that Christmas Eve at 5:00 P.M. to watch President Calvin Coolidge and his wife, Grace, stroll from the White House to the tree. The president then pressed a button to activate the 2,500 electric red, green, and white bulbs on the tree, winning cheers and applause from the cold but excited crowd. Coolidge was especially pleased that the tree came from his home state of Vermont.

The Original Smoke-Filled Room

We all know what the phrase "smoke-filled room" refers to—a place where political bigwigs meet, shielded from the public glare, in order to hammer out the self-serving deals they would prefer to hide from their constituents. This oft-used bit of political shorthand traces its origins to an incident that occurred in a famous Chicago hotel.

❋   ❋   ❋   ❋

WITH ITS REPUTATION for hardball politics, Chicago might seem like a natural place for the term "smoke-filled room" to have originated. But this familiar part of the American political lexicon was not coined to describe any actions of local politicians. Rather, it stems from the 1920 Republican Convention that was held at the Chicago Coliseum (1513 S. Wabash).

The race for the Republican presidential nomination was a particularly hard-fought competition that year, and on Friday, June 11, it became clear that the delegates faced an intractable deadlock. That night, a group of Republican senators arranged a private meeting in suites 408 and 410 at Chicago's Blackstone Hotel (636 S. Michigan). Working late into the night, they finally settled on dark-horse candidate Warren G. Harding as the only viable compromise. The first-term senator was called to the room shortly after 2:00 A.M., accepted the deal offered by the power brokers, and took the nomination shortly thereafter.

An Associated Press journalist reported on the secret meeting in a nationally published article, describing the setting as a "smoke-filled room." Ever since, the phrase has been used to describe any private gathering of political figures where deals are struck, but it is particularly meant to indicate a meeting during which party members choose a candidate to put forth for office.

The Blackstone, a luxury hotel that first opened in 1910, is still in operation today, and guests can stay in the very rooms where the presidential deal was hashed out—though they can no longer smoke there!

The Poetry Slam: A Perfect 10

We know you've scribbled a poem down on a napkin or in your journal with dreams of sharing your brilliant verse with a world that could never understand. The good news, fair poet, is that a Chicago construction worker has invented something called the poetry slam!

✳ ✳ ✳ ✳

IN 1984, A Chicagoan named Marc Smith decided that poetry needed a little livening up. He enjoyed poetry but not poetry readings—they were too stiff and hoity-toity, making them inaccessible to the general public. Smith organized the first poetry slam (named after the grand slam in baseball) at the Green Mill. The rules are simple: The work had to be original, and no props or costumes were allowed.

Smith picked judges from the audience and gave them markers and napkins on which to write their scores from 0 to 10. Smith instructed the rest of the audience to get involved too. If they hated a poet, they were encouraged to boo. If they liked him/her, they should cheer. The winner of the slam received a Twinkie—a worthy prize.

Slam On, Crazy Poet!

Smith's idea caught on. By 1993, the first National Poetry Slam was held in San Francisco; the event continues to be held in a different U.S. city every year and brings more than 80 teams from across the country together for five full days of fierce poetic competition.

Slams have popped up in small towns and big cities across America, as well as in France, Nepal, and the Czech Republic. Marc Smith still hosts the Original Uptown Poetry Slam at the Green Mill every Sunday night. The show's been running for more than 20 years and shows no signs of slowing.

President Barack Obama and First Lady Michelle Obama hosted a poetry slam at the White House in May 2009. James Earl Jones was among the performers.

Facial Perfection

Today, most women—and some men—apply makeup for one simple reason: They want to look good. But how did the practice get started?

✳   ✳   ✳   ✳

THOSE SUBTLE TOUCHES of pigment and shade can make all the difference, hiding flaws in the skin and enhancing the natural appearance of facial features. Call it vanity if you must, but spending quality time in front of a mirror is a daily ritual that millions of Americans can't do without, whether they're preparing for an average day at work, a big event, or a date with that special someone.

It all goes back to the ancient Egyptians, who were the first people to wear makeup. Their motive was the same as ours—just like modern-day supermodels, the well-to-do women of ancient Egypt wanted to look their best and saw the careful application of face-paint as a means to that end.

But they weren't just trying to impress a burly construction foreman who was working on the pyramids or a distinguished assistant to Pharaoh. Their sights were set a little higher—they were trying to impress the gods. Archeological evidence shows that Egyptians were dolling themselves up as early as 4000 B.C., in part because they felt that appearance was directly related to spiritual worth.

So the Egyptians created the first cosmetics. (No word on whether they received makeovers at malls along the Nile.) They applied an eye paint called mesdemet (from the ancient Egyptian word *msdmt*), a mixture of copper and lead ore, around their eyes. Green shades went on the lower eyelids; black and dark gray were applied to the lashes and upper eyelids. Dark colors were said to ward off "evil eyes." To complete the ornate look around the eyes, they added almond shapes of a dark-colored powder—later called kohl—that might have been made of a combination of ingredients such as burnt almonds, oxidized copper, copper ores, lead, ash, and ochre. (Think Johnny Depp as Captain Jack Sparrow or Keith Richards as Keith Richards.) Kohl was believed to have medicinal benefits as well.

Egyptian women put a mixture of red clay or ochre and water or animal fat on their cheeks and lips—the first blush and lipstick—and applied henna to their nails. When it came to removing all of these cosmetics at the end of the day, they used a type of soap that was made from vegetable and animal oils and perfumes.

The connection between beauty and spirituality remained for centuries, until the Romans gained power. The Romans adopted many of the Egyptians' cosmetic formulas, but their primary motive was to improve their appearances for each other and not the gods.

You Can Thank Ohio

These Ohioans invented things that were and are used far beyond the Buckeye state.

✳　✳　✳　✳

Charles Richter

EVER WATCH A news report about an earthquake and hear the reporter say something like "it measured a 5.8"? Thank Charles Richter. In 1935, Richter developed the Richter scale, a mathematical formula that can be used to determine and compare the size of earthquakes.

James Spangler

Menial labor clearly is the mother of invention: In the early 1900s, while working as a janitor in Toledo, James Spangler got an idea. He took an old fan motor, encased it in a soapbox, and attached it to a broom handle. After a couple of tweaks, Spangler successfully created the world's first electric vacuum cleaner, complete with a pillowcase acting as a dust bag.

Henry Timken

A carriage maker by trade, Henry Timken spent many years trying to reduce friction in the axles of his carriages. In 1898, he found his solution when he invented roller bearings. In less than a year, the Timken Roller Bearing Axle Company was created and began shipping bearings across the United States. Today, Timken's invention is used in everything from horseless carriages (that is, cars) to zero-gravity carriages (that is, space shuttles).

Harry Burt

In 1920, Harry Burt, an ice cream shop owner in small-town Ohio, invented the first ice cream confection on a stick. Inserting a wooden stick into the ice cream bar made it "the new, clean, convenient way to eat ice cream." Burt quickly patented his manufacturing process and started promoting the Good Humor bar, in accordance with the popular belief that one's palate affects one's mood. He then sent out a fleet of shiny white trucks, each stocked with a friendly Good Humor Man and all the ice cream bars kids could eat. By 1961, 200 Good Humor ice cream trucks wound their way through suburbia.

When other companies followed suit, Good Humor took them to court, arguing their patent. Burt fought the Popsicle company in a decade-long court battle over the differences between their products, centering on what precise percentage of milk constitutes ice cream, sherbet, and flavored water. Popsicle and Good Humor have settled their differences and are now owned by the same corporation.

A Cool Invention

Anyone who's ever spent August in New York—where the concrete and asphalt keep things steamy even in the wee hours of the—morning, will certainly understand why the city was the natural birthplace of what some say is the world's greatest boon to mankind: cool air on demand.

✳   ✳   ✳   ✳

CHANGING TEMPERATURES AND humidity inside the Sackett-Wilhelms Lithographing Company in 1902 Brooklyn were causing quite a problem. The varying conditions caused the printing plant's paper to expand and contract, and its colored inks became misaligned or out of register. Willis H. Carrier, just 25 years old and a year out of Cornell University with an engineering degree, was called upon to invent a system to stabilize the plant's interior air. His response to this problem—air conditioning—earned him the nickname, "The Father of Cool."

While many attempts had been made around the world to cool interior temperatures—one required using half a million tons of ice every two months—Carrier was the first to carry it off successfully. It wasn't yet called *air conditioning*, however—that term was later used by another inventor for his system that added moisture to the air in textile manufacturing plants.

Carrier's basic ideas revolutionized the fledgling field and still provide the foundation for modern air conditioning. He further refined his idea of how to condition, clean, dehumidify, and cool air, he claimed, on a foggy night while waiting for a train. The inventor patented his "Apparatus for Treating Air" in 1906, and in 1911 he unveiled his Rational Psychrometric Formulae, which is now known as the Magna Carta of the air conditioning industry.

In 1915 Carrier and several others in New York founded the Carrier Engineering Corporation—a company that today employs 45,000 in 172 countries. Among the milestones in Carrier's career were the first residential air conditioner (1914), the first air-conditioned department store (1924), and the air conditioning of such places as Madison Square Garden, Grauman's Chinese Theatre in Los Angeles, the Canadian Houses of Parliament, and the USS *Forrestal*. Carrier died in New York City in October 1950.

Terrific Tuxedos

Every guy looks good in a tuxedo—and we have New Yorker (and wealthy tobacco magnate) Pierre Lorillard IV to thank for it.

✳   ✳   ✳   ✳

THIS FORMAL SUIT has been the epitome of male fashion finery for generations, and yet most people don't realize that it originated in the appropriately named Tuxedo Park region, a haven for the rich and famous located just outside New York City.

In October 1886, the story goes, Lorillard commissioned a new type of formal wear, which he had designed and intended to wear to the Tuxedo Club's Autumn Ball. The outfit, which Lorillard himself named after the tony area in which he lived, was most notable for its tailless black jacket—a dramatic departure from the era's traditional long tailcoat and white tie.

But for reasons unknown, Lorillard did not wear his new design to the ball—instead, his son, Griswold, and a handful of Griswold's buddies, did. It was a bold fashion statement, completely out of character for the times but one that was met with glowing approval by others in attendance. In short, the tuxedo was a hit.

But from where did the elder Lorillard receive his fashion inspiration? Some believe the tuxedo was modeled after a special dinner jacket designed by Henry Poole & Company of London's famed Savile Row, whose high-society clients included the Prince of Wales, later to become King Edward VII. Others believe Lorillard was inspired by the shorter red jackets often worn during fox hunts.

Regardless of its source, the tuxedo quickly found its way into the closet of every man who wanted to look dashing at a formal event, be it a wedding, a high school prom, or a high-society fund-raiser. To wear anything else was to look like a slob.

So the next time you find yourself stuffed into what is also sometimes called a penguin suit, take a moment to thank (or blame) Pierre Lorillard, the New York fashion plate who made it all possible.

Chapter 2

Nature All Around

11 Animals that Use Camouflage

The animal kingdom is a wild, wacky place where animals have to be clever in order to survive. One of the most amazing techniques for survival is animal camouflage. Animals have the ability to mimic plants, ground cover, or even other animals in order to hide or hunt. The following is a list of some animals that are particularly gifted in the art of invisibility.

※　※　※　※

1. Chameleons

Contrary to popular belief, chameleons only change color when in imminent danger. Their everyday skin color, a light khaki, keeps them hidden from enemies during those not-so-dangerous times. Nearly half the world's chameleon species live in Madagascar, but they're also found in Africa, the Middle East, and southern Europe.

2. Leopards

Whether their coats are spotted (useful for hiding in sun-dappled areas in the African outback) or black (perfect for nighttime stalking or lurking in shadows), these elegant and deadly cats are born with fashionable camouflage. Rabbits, young buffalo, and monkeys don't stand a chance when a hidden leopard makes a surprise attack.

3. Polar Bears

Other bears and human poachers are the biggest threats to the majestic polar bear, but by blending into the blindingly white snow of the Arctic with equally white fur coats, some danger can be avoided. Only a polar bear's nose and foot pads are without fur.

4. Turtles

If you're a fish, you better look twice before resting near that big rock . . . it could be an snapping turtle. There are hundreds of species of turtles and tortoises that use camouflage to blindside their prey and hide from large predators like alligators. Sadly, camouflage can't protect turtles from the poacher's fishnet.

5. Arctic Owls

Ah, the Arctic tundra: cold, barren, and totally white. Arctic owls have a coat of snow-white feathers to keep them warm and safe from predators, such as foxes and wolves.

6. Bark Bugs

For most bugs, birds are the bad guys. For bark bugs, which hang out on trees around the world, this is especially true. In order to hide in the middle of nature's birdhouses, bark bugs appear to be part of the tree itself.

7. Ornate Wobbegongs

If you're ever swimming in the shallow waters off Australia or New Guinea, look for the ornate wobbegong—though you probably won't be able to see it! This shark's body flattens out on the seafloor where its spots and blotchy lines resemble rock and coral. Wobbegongs take camouflage a step further with a little "beard" under their chins that looks like seaweed. Prey that swim in front of their mouths are gobbled up without knowing what hit them.

8. Gaboon Vipers

In order to hide from their prey, gaboon vipers—among the most venomous snakes on Earth—make the most of their brownish-gray, mottled scales. These big snakes hide in the layer of dead leaves that carpets the African rain forest floors. They also like to snuggle into forest floor peat and sneak up on unsuspecting prey.

9. Leaf Butterflies
Complete with fake leaf stalk, fake leaf veins, and perfect dead-leaf coloring, leaf butterflies have the whole camouflage thing down pat. Birds pass them by without a second glance since these insects from southeast Asia look more like dead leaves than butterflies.

10. Dragon Lizards
Spiders, snakes, birds, and even other lizards all want a piece of the dragon lizard, so they have some of the most effective camouflage around. Not only do dragon lizards look nearly invisible when hanging out on a tree branch, they keep extraordinarily still, knowing that their predators react to the smallest movements. It doesn't make for an exciting life, but at least they live to tell about it.

11. Flower Mantises
Careful—that flower you're thinking about smelling might have a flower mantis hiding inside. The flower mantis of western Africa uses colorful, pistil-and-stamen-like camouflage to trick smaller insects into smelling the roses, then snap—lunch is served.

Exposing the Virus

Is the common cold caused by a bacteria or a virus? What about the flu? Can viruses ever benefit humanity? Read on to find out the answer to those questions and more...

✳   ✳   ✳   ✳

✳ A virus that infects and destroys bacteria is called a "bacteriophage," ("phage," for short). Phages exist in some preserved foods, including pickles and pastrami.

* The deadliest disease in history was the Influenza Pandemic of 1918, also known as Spanish Flu. In just two years, the strain took more than 50 million victims worldwide—nearly twice as many as were killed in World War I.

* Unlike most flu outbreaks, Spanish Flu did not pose a greater danger to very young children, people in poor health, or the elderly. The virus invaded the body's immune system and caused it to attack its victims' lungs, so it killed more people with strong immune systems than those with weak ones.

* The word vaccination comes from the Latin word vacca, meaning "cow." The first European vaccinations infected people with cowpox, a disease similar to but less severe than smallpox. After the cowpox infection cleared, people were then immune to smallpox as well.

* Antibiotics treat only bacterial infections (e.g., strep throat), but people often take them for viral illnesses, such as common colds or the flu. This misuse contributes to the development of antibiotic-resistant bacteria.

* In the United States in 1989, a new strain of Ebola killed a large number of monkeys in a primate facility in Reston, Virginia. The source of Ebola Reston was infected monkeys imported from the Philippines, and it is the only Ebola strain known to be spread by air.

* Because each virus targets a specific type of cell, certain strains can be used to treat, or even cure, diseases. Scientists are currently using "virotherapy" to genetically engineer a virus that attacks only cancer cells, and the use of virotherapy to treat the human immunodeficiency virus (HIV) is being investigated.

The Upper Atmosphere

Next time you look up to admire a sunset, think about all the layers of atmosphere above us...

✳ ✳ ✳ ✳

Q: What's ozone?

A: It's oxygen. Honest. The oxygen we breathe is O2, a fairly stable chemical compound of two oxygen atoms. Ozone is O3 and is much less stable (breaks up more easily). Passing electricity through breathable oxygen can produce ozone; it has an acrid smell and it hurts to breathe. It is toxic, even lethal in significant concentrations.

Q: Why does it help to have a layer of ozone?

A: As long as it's about 9 to 20 miles up in the stratosphere, where you won't get a lungful of it, ozone filters out the most harmful wavelengths of the sun's ultraviolet (UV) light. If pollutants react with the ozone, there's less of it to stop the incoming UVs, so you have an "ozone hole" where the UV light gets through to cause harm.

Q: Can the ozone layer recover on its own?

A: Under normal circumstances it does, with O3 constantly changing to O2 and back to O3 as UVs hit it. Many of the offending pollutants are now banned, but the residue may stick around and cause trouble for 50 to 100 years. So if we leave it alone, yes, it'll recover in time.

Q: What's in the ionosphere?

A: Not much—it begins about 50 miles up and tops out at roughly 250 miles as the outermost layer of Earth's atmosphere. It varies quite a bit. We bounce radio waves off it so that you can ignore the stifling monotony of your daily commute.

U.S. National Parks: Vacation Highlights

The U.S. National Park Service administers about 400 sites of historic, scientific, cultural, scenic, or other interest. These include national monuments, national parks, national battlefields, national rivers, and national cemeteries. Here are some details.

✳ ✳ ✳ ✳

✳ Delaware is the only state with no national park territory.

✳ Some sites are international rather than national. St. Croix Island International Historic Site, between Maine and New Brunswick (Canada), is situated in Maine but is managed in cooperation with Parks Canada (the two often hold joint events on the site). A similar situation exists with the International Peace Garden (North Dakota) and the Waterton-Glacier International Peace Park (Alberta/Montana).

✳ Although Yellowstone was the first national park (designated on March 1, 1872), it wasn't the first area set aside as a park. That honor is shared by the National Capital Parks, the White House, and the National Mall, all designated on July 16, 1790.

✳ National park status doesn't last forever. A couple dozen sites have been turned over to the states or to other federal departments. For example, the Park Service transferred New Echota Marker National Memorial (a Cherokee heritage memorial) to the state of Georgia in 1950.

✳ In 2006, there were 272,623,980 recreational visits to national parks.

✳ The highest point in a national park is the summit of Denali (aka Mt. McKinley) in Alaska. At 20,320 feet, it's also the highest point on the North American landmass.

* In Alaska's Kobuk Valley National Park, there are approximately 25 square miles of rolling sand dunes, and summer temperatures can hit 100° Fahrenheit.

* The lowest point is Badwater Basin in California's Death Valley National Park, which is 282 feet below sea level. From 1931 to 1934, just over half an inch of rain fell there, and summer temperatures can exceed 130° Fahrenheit.

* Death Valley National Park also has a mountain, Telescope Peak, which tops out at 11,049 feet above sea level. From the top of this mountain to Badwater Basin it's twice the vertical drop of the Grand Canyon.

* The northernmost point in a national park is Inupiat Heritage Center at Barrow, Alaska, while the southernmost point is the National Park of American Samoa, below the equator.

* While a portion of California's Yosemite National Park has all the conveniences of a small city, 95 percent of the park is designated as wilderness.

* The farthest national park from Washington, D.C., is War in the Pacific National Historical Park in Guam. It's far closer to the Philippines than to Hawaii, let alone the continental United States.

* The Grand Canyon has a lesser-known peer: Colorado's Black Canyon of the Gunnison National Park. The dark gneiss walls of the canyon (more than a half mile deep) narrow to a quarter mile wide, presenting a majestic, shadowy abyss.

* The longest arch at Arches National Park in Utah measures 306 feet from base to base. A football field is 300 feet long.

* Oregon's Crater Lake National Park is a corpse—a volcanic corpse, that is. Ancient Mt. Mazama coughed up one last violent eruption during the earliest stages of human

civilization, and then its walls collapsed into the dead volcano's caldera. Precipitation fell and melted to form a shimmering six-mile-wide lake.

✳ Devil's Tower in Wyoming began its history buried—a tall pillar of magma that leaked or burned through the other rock in the area, then cooled underground. Millions of years of erosion laid bare the 1,267-foot tower.

Rooting for Rudolph

All about Rangifer Tardanus, *otherwise known as reindeer.*

✳   ✳   ✳   ✳

✳ The word "reindeer" is in no way related to the word "reins." Rather, the Old Icelandic word *hreinn* (meaning reindeer) is the source of the first syllable, but its original spelling was lost in translation.

✳ Because a reindeer can pull twice its weight for miles over snowcovered terrain, the Saami people of Lapland have used its muscle power for 5,000 years as a primary means of transportation.

✳ Antlers are made of the fastest-growing tissues know to humans, growing up to an inch a day. Antlers appear within weeks of a reindeer's birth. Regardless of age or sex, every reindeer grows a new set of antlers each year. Antlers are actually bone, while horns are made of keratin, a protein similar to a human's fingernails.

✳ The secret's out: Reindeer aren't equipped with built-in GPS. Instead, it's their supernatural sense of smell—so keen that they can detect food up to 3 feet below snow—that helps guide Santa's sleigh.

✳ The furry layer on a reindeer's antlers is called velvet. Each fall, reindeer rub the velvet off their antlers to signal the rutting, or mating, season.

* Blessed with nature's version of an orthopedic shoe, reindeer have wide splayed hooves that distribute their weight evenly. That way, reindeer can walk across snow without sinking, with their hooves working in much the same way as snowshoes.

* If only red-blooded American *homo sapiens* could be as lucky as reindeer. In the antlered set, dominant male reindeer called bulls keep harems of females, or cows, throughout the winter for mating purposes. Calves are born each spring, and most cows have one or two. Interestingly, reindeer twins are more common in Europe than North America.

* Santa's actual reindeer were probably not reindeer at all, but a compilation of traits from several members of the deer family. In some pictures, the reindeer have white tails—not a trait of the Lapland reindeer—as well as the facial structure of an antelope.

* So much for those wild reindeer games—at least in Lapland. It seems that the last of the wild herds were hunted out around 1900. Around the same time, the U.S. government imported 1,300 reindeer from Siberia to Alaska to provide food for Eskimo peoples. Herds grew to a million over the next 30 years but were also decimated by white hunters. In 1972, Alaska wildlife officials set quotas to protect the remaining herds of reindeer.

* Reindeer are generally herbivores, which means they prefer vegetation over other forms of food. In the summer, they eat leaves and herbs. In the winter, they eat lichen and moss. During dry spells when vegetation is sparse, however, they have been known to eat bird eggs and small birds. Well-endowed male reindeer use their imposing antlers like a shovel to break through the upper crust of snow to reach the vegetation underneath.

✳ Contrary to belief, reindeer don't run very fast. In fact, a normal-size deer could outrun a reindeer. And not only can reindeer swim, but their soft, hollow hair is buoyant. Talk about getting special perks from the guy in the red suit . . . Before a poem entitled "The Children's Friend" and then Clement Clarke Moore's "'Twas the Night Before Christmas," Santa had to hoof it from house to house. (Moore apparently drew inspiration from the previous poem.) Moore was the first to outfit Santa with a sleigh and eight, albeit "tiny," reindeer.

✳ Behind every successful male is, well, a female, and in Santa's case, there are nine to be exact. Believe it or not, all of Santa's reindeer—including Rudolph—are probably of the feminine persuasion. According to the Alaska Department of Fish and Game, both male and females in the deer family Cervidae grow antlers, but most male reindeer drop their antlers at the beginning of winter, usually in late November to mid-December. Female reindeer, however, keep their antlers until after they give birth in the spring, meaning they are the only ones to have antlers during the holiday season. So much for the theory of a testosterone-powered sleigh!

✳ If you're ever lost in a snowstorm, make sure you're with a few reindeer. That's because these hooved holiday creatures have fur so insulated that when they lie down on snow, the snow underneath doesn't melt from their body heat. Furthermore, their fur can accommodate vast fluctuations in temperature, from 80 degrees below zero up to 115 degrees above zero.

✳ I say "caribow," you say "caribou." Either way, it's the name reindeer go by in North America. The name is derived from the Micmac Indian language and describes the way the animals dig and root around for food in the snow.

✳ Worldwide, there are 40 species of reindeer in existence today. Santa's reindeer are from Lapland, the place where the northern Scandinavian countries of Finland, Sweden, and Norway meet. In North America, reindeer/ caribou live in Canada and Alaska.

✳ Reindeer aren't always brown. In fact, they come in various colors, including white and dark gray, depending on the time of year. Males can also have light-colored manes, necks, and shoulders.

Rodent Fun Facts!

Because who doesn't want to know more about rodents?

✳   ✳   ✳   ✳

✳ Rodents are some of the most common animals on the planet. In fact, nearly half of all mammal species on earth are rodents.

✳ Mice can get by with almost no water; they get most of the moisture they need from the food they eat.

✳ Rats have been known to chew through wood, glass, cinder-block, and lead.

✳ Mice become sexually mature at six to ten weeks and can breed year-round. Female mice average six to ten litters annually.

✳ If a pair of mice started breeding on January 1, they could theoretically have as many as 31,000 descendants by the end of the year.

✳ The bubonic plague pandemic that killed millions through-out Europe in the mid-1300s was predominantly caused by fleas carried by rats.

✳ The largest rodent in the world is the capybara. Indigenous to South America, it can measure as large as 4 feet in length and 20 inches in height.

* The world's 4,000 known rodent species are divided into three suborders: squirrellike rodents (*Sciuromorpha*), mouselike rodents (*Myomorpha*), *and porcupinelike rodents* (*Hystricomorpha*).

* According to the Centers for Disease Control and Prevention, more than 45,000 Americans are bitten by rats each year.

* Rodents in the United States spread a horrifying array of diseases, including bubonic plague, murine typhus, salmonellosis, trichinosis, and hantavirus.

* Rats are the NBA stars of the rodent world. They can jump three feet straight up and four feet outward from a standing position.

* Approximately 20 percent of fires of unknown origin are believed to be caused by mice and rats chewing through electrical wires.

* Rats can enter a building through a hole just half an inch in diameter.

Plants During Biblical Times

In an agricultural society, plants mean everything—whether as food for humans, animal fodder, construction material, or landscaping.

✳   ✳   ✳   ✳

Farming

PALESTINE IS RELATIVELY near to Mesopotamia, to which many edible grains are native. Barley, one of the most important, tended to be a crop of the poor. Wheat, of course, grew well when the weather cooperated—as it did in Exodus, when a hailstorm trashed the barley but spared the wheat because the latter wasn't up yet. Beans, especially lentils, provided nutritious sustenance.

Biblical agriculture also produced two extremely valuable nonfood crops: papyrus and flax. Papyrus is a grassy plant that can get very tall if it gets enough water; it still grows today in Israel. If you had writing to do—unless you wanted to write on parchment, which is animal hide—you did it on papyrus. If kept dry, papyrus would keep for a very long time—witness the fact that some of the Dead Sea Scrolls are on papyrus. Flax stems produce fibers, which were separated and woven into cloth. Probably every person mentioned in scripture wore flaxen clothing at some point.

Orchardry/Vintery

If properly cared for, some trees live for millennia. A few olive trees still survive from the time of Christ . . . maybe even from the time of the Exodus! To destroy an orchard was the height of scorched-earth scriptural warfare. Olives, of course, have always been a staple of Holy Land orchardry: The oil was delicious and healthy, and the fruit itself added to many meals. Dates, which come from date palm trees, are less prevalent today but were very important for their sweet fruit.

Nut trees, especially almonds, were very important in the Holy Land as a source of food and oil. When Aaron's staff produced almonds overnight in the Tent of the Covenant, the Lord ordered the fruitful staff placed in a special position to warn rebels. Probably those were the bitter almond variety, which can cause cyanide poisoning.

Fig trees not only produced leaves for wrapping (so the old idea about a fig leaf of protection isn't that big a joke) but a tasty fruit still popular today. Without grapes, of course, there wouldn't have been much wine. When Moses sent scouts ahead to the Promised Land, the grapes they brought back signified good things to come. Even the leaves made tasty wrappings, as anyone who enjoys stuffed grape leaves can attest. The emblem of the pomegranate, a fruit containing numerous juicy seed casings, adorned priestly robes and even the Temple of Solomon.

While scripture refers to apples, we have good reason to believe they meant another fruit, quite probably apricots, which (unlike apples) thrive in the Holy Land and otherwise match biblical descriptions.

Gathering

Frankincense is a resin that was harvested from the tree of that name (somewhat like maple syrup is tapped—a frankincense tree can take a lot of punishment); the resin was burned for its rich, pleasant smell. Myrrh, at least the Palestinian version, came from Commiphora trees of various varieties; people also tapped these small trees for the myrrh. Of course, scripture records it as one of the gifts of the wise men at the birth of Jesus and as an embalming agent for him after the Crucifixion—so myrrh would seem special to Christians, as it was part of Christ's birth and death.

Exodus and Leviticus specify hyssop for ritual Israelite cleansing usage. Since it was good to plant between grapevines and attracted many bees, hyssop was a good companion crop—probably many Israelite farms grew a little. For building, the region's cedars remain famous today, just as they were specified for Solomon's Temple with their delightful fragrance and amazing mix of color patterns in lumber. Another important tree was the acacia, used to set up the tabernacle in the wilderness as specified in Exodus.

Local Legends

The myth that albino alligators sightlessly prowl the New York City sewer system has its roots in an alleged decades-old fad.

✳ ✳ ✳ ✳

SOME SAY VACATIONERS brought the infant 'gators home from Florida, while others insist that New York pet shops enjoyed a thriving trade in such babies (the reptiles sometimes sold in stores today are actually caimans, crocodilians from

South America). When these 'gator tots grew too large for apartment dwelling, they were supposedly dispatched by flushing down the toilet—a trip these hardy creatures survived all the way down to the sewers, where, it was claimed, they evolved over the years, adapting to their new environment by becoming blind and losing their pigmentation. The legend grew legs, as it were, when an alleged eyewitness—a retired sewer official who swore he'd seen a colony of the things back in the 1930s—was quoted in a 1959 book entitled *The World Beneath the City.* Thomas Pynchon also wrote of them in his 1963 novel V.

Reports of regular alligators in New York City might be a little bit more believable. In 1932, "swarms" of alligators were reportedly spotted in the Bronx River, and on February 10, 1935, the *New York Times* wrote that several urban teens had pulled a seven-footer from an open manhole while clearing snow—and had beaten the beast to death after it snapped at them. The paper suggested that perhaps the animal had escaped from a ship "from the mysterious Everglades." Even before this—a full century earlier in 1831—a little-known paper called *The Planet* noted a 'gator sighting in the East River.

However, any herpetologist worth his or her scales will tell you that it's impossible for the tropical-thriving 'gator to get through a New York City winter, in polluted waters, no less. One explained that alligators can't digest food when they're cold. Plus, living without sun destroys their ability to utilize calcium, which would result in too soft of a skeletal structure for the creature to survive. As one spokesperson for the city's Department of Environmental Protection, who has been denying the rumors for 30 years, wearily sighed: "Sewers simply are not a prime environment for alligators."

But you're still going to check before you sit down, though—right?

Canny Coyote!

Central Park is home to a variety of birds and animals—though usually not coyotes. But several of the canny canines have striven to move from the surrounding wilds into the big city.

✳   ✳   ✳   ✳

PET DOGS ARE a common sight in New York City, coyotes less so. There's no surprise in that, of course, but in March 2006, a coyote nicknamed Hal loped into the Hallett Nature Sanctuary with the apparent intention of calling the place home. Park workers tried to capture the cagey critter, but Hal proved to be an adept escape artist. He eluded his pursuers by jumping into a lake and then led them on an exciting two-day chase before finally being taken down with a tranquilizer dart near the Wollman Rink ice skating facility.

How Hal managed to make his way into Manhattan had wildlife officials scratching their heads. Coyotes are much more common upstate, so it's a good assumption that that's where he came from, moving unnoticed along the Hudson River and through the Bronx. But how did he get into Manhattan? Did he cross a railway bridge over the Harlem River? Did he swim? No one can say for sure.

New Yorkers became enamored with the gutsy coyote and closely followed his saga in the newspapers and on the local news. Cheers went up when he was captured alive and apparently well, but the story ended on a sad note when Hal died while being tagged and prepared for release into California Hill State Forest in Putnam County, New York. A necropsy revealed that he probably died of internal hemorrhaging from the ingestion of rat poison, complicated by a case of heartworms.

Hal wasn't the first coyote to have a run through Central Park. In 1999, another one was captured there and given to the Flushing Zoo in Queens.

Though coyotes in Central Park inevitably make the front pages, city officials don't consider them a serious threat to people. The animals are shy by nature and tend to avoid humans whenever possible, say wildlife experts.

Hurricane 101

Hurricanes are huge tropical storm systems that can measure up to 600 miles across. Powerful winds (ranging from 75 to more than 200 miles per hour), flooding rains, and huge storm surges can leave utter devastation in their wake.

✳ ✳ ✳ ✳

A Storm by Any Other Name...

HURRICANES ARE ONLY called by that name in the Atlantic Ocean, Gulf of Mexico, and the Eastern Pacific Ocean. In the Western Pacific Ocean, such storms are called *typhoons*. In the Indian Ocean, the Bay of Bengal, and Australia, they are known as *cyclones*.

Hurricanes by the Numbers
1953:

the year the U.S. Weather Bureau started giving hurricanes women's names. Previously, they were named by the phonetic alphabet (Able, Baker, Charlie)

5:

the number of categories in the Saffir-Simpson Hurricane Wind Scale

6 months:

the length of the official "hurricane season" (June 1–November 30). The Eastern Pacific hurricane season extends from May 15 through November 30

8,000:

the estimated number of deaths caused by the category 4 hurricane that ravaged Galveston, Texas, on September 8, 1900

$25 billion:

the estimated amount of damage caused by Hurricane Andrew, which struck Dade County, Florida, in 1992

$75 billion:

the estimated amount of damage caused by Hurricane Katrina, which devastated New Orleans and the Mississippi Gulf Coast in 2005

8 Most Common Blood Types

In love, they say that opposites attract. But when it comes to blood types, opposites can be deadly. Scientists have discovered eight major blood types; some are compatible, but others are not. See which types you're compatible with.

✳   ✳   ✳   ✳

1. O+: 38 percent

O+ blood is needed more often than any other blood type because it's the most common. O+ blood can be given to a person with A+, B+, AB+, or O+ blood. A person with O+ blood can receive blood from O+ or O- donors.

2. A+: 34 percent

A person with A+ blood can receive A+, A-, O+, or O- blood. However, A+ blood can be given only to a person with the A+ or AB+ blood types.

3. B+: 9 percent

B+ blood can be given only to those with either AB+ or B+ blood. This blood type can receive blood from B+, B-, O+, or O- donors.

4. O-: 7 percent

O- is considered the universal donor because it can be given to anyone, regardless of blood type. However, a person with the O- blood type can receive blood only from other O- donors.

5. A-: 6 percent

A- blood can be given to a person with AB-, A-, AB+, or A+. This blood type can only receive blood from O- or A- donors.

6. AB+: 3 percent

AB+ is considered a universal receiver because people with this blood type can receive blood of any type. But AB+ blood can only be given to a person who also has AB+ blood.

7. B-: 2 percent

B- blood can be given to those with B-, AB-, B+, or AB+ blood. A person with B- blood can receive blood from O- or B- blood types.

8. AB-: 1 percent

AB- is the least common blood type. A person with this type can give blood to AB+ or AB- blood types, but must receive blood from O-, A-, B-, and AB- blood types.

Star Words

When discussing astronomy, someone invariably mentions black holes, quasars, supernovas, or white dwarfs, among other references. Though we tend to nod knowingly, in fact, most of us haven't a clue what these terms mean. Help has arrived.

✳ ✳ ✳ ✳

Galaxy: This is a large group of stars rotating around a central nucleus. Ours, the Milky Way, is part of a 20-fold cluster that clings together like a bunch of grapes. In 1920, we learned that the Sun was not the center of our galaxy, as we had previously assumed. Soon after that, powerful telescopes revealed a host of other galaxies, and humankind began to comprehend the immensity of the universe. Just how big is our galaxy? Traveling at the speed of light, it would take 100,000 years to cross it. The Sun, situated toward the outer edge of the galaxy, takes 200 million years to complete its orbit around the galactic center.

Nebula: This is the name given to an interstellar cloud of gas and dust. Nebulas are among the most beautiful objects in the night sky. Within nebulas, new stars are born when the diffuse matter condenses under the force of gravity into contracting regions of gas. These huge balls of gas stabilize when they reach the temperature at which nuclear reactions begin in the core of the cloud, preventing further contraction. Thus, a star is born, often in conjunction with others. Combined, these make up a star cluster.

Red giant: After a star has burned out its hydrogen supplies (which could take billions of years), the core contracts. The outer layer of the star then expands and becomes cooler, giving off a reddish glow. These red giants are up to ten times larger than our Sun. When the Sun has exhausted its hydrogen supplies (in about 5 billion years), it will become a red giant. This relatively short phase in a star's life ends with a celestial fireworks display. The star, burning any remaining helium, ejects its outer layers, forming a planetary nebula that glows because of energy received from its mother star. Eventually, the star contracts to become a faintly shining white dwarf.

White dwarf: This small white star (about the same radius as Earth) is actually the remnant core of a star that has completed fusion (nuclear collision) at its core. It is composed mainly of carbon.

Brown dwarf: A brown dwarf is larger than a planet but not as big as a star. Unlike a true star, it doesn't contain enough mass to convert hydrogen to helium. As a result, these "failed stars" have only a short period during which helium burns before they cool and fade. Brown dwarfs are often too dim to be detected easily.

Super giant: The biggest type of star, it is many times more luminous and several times larger than a red giant. Its diameter is several hundred times that of the Sun, and its luminosity is about a million times stronger. Super giants, however, have a relatively short life span and die out after only a few million years.

Supernova: A supernova is the explosion that ends the life of a star that was originally much more massive than the Sun. Huge amounts of dust and gas are spewed into space by violent shock waves at speeds of more than 6,000 miles per second. The light of the explosion is so bright that it outshines a billion suns, appearing as a sparkling diamond in the sky. The energy liberated in a single supernova explosion corresponds to the total energy that the Sun would radiate in 9 billion years.

Pulsar: A pulsar is what remains of a supernova. The once huge star has now become a fast-spinning globe approximately 20 miles in diameter. A beam of radio waves rotates with the star, like the beam of a lighthouse, appearing as a pulse to an observer (hence, the name pulsar). Pulsars are also called neutron stars because they are principally composed of tightly packed neutrons.

Black hole: Current understanding is that a black hole is simply the result of an exploded supernova. Such an event would cause the force of gravity to continue beyond the pulsar stage, so the star would actually disappear, leaving behind only its gravity and a black hole where it used to be. This hole would act as a super-charged cosmic whirlpool—ready to devour whatever comes too close to it.

Dark matter: This is a term used to describe celestial matter that is invisible but can be detected by the gravitational effect it exerts upon other bodies. Swiss astrophysicist Franz Zwicky first proposed dark matter in 1933, theorizing the existence of unseen mass based on the motions of galaxies. The speed of orbit he observed would have required 400 times more mass than was visible. The solution to this problem of missing mass was the existence of dark matter.

Big Bang: This theory suggests that the universe was formed from a single point in space as the result of a massive explosion some 18 billion years ago. A consequence of this explosion is that the universe continues to expand. Some astronomers suggest that the rate of expansion is slowing and will eventually come to a halt. At that point, gravity will pull the galaxies inward, back to where they began, merging in a mass of matter that will "blow up" in another big bang. Some believe this process will be repeated over and over, so that the universe "oscillates." Each cycle would take about 80 billion years—40 billion to expand, and 40 billion to contract.

Quasars: In the 1960s, strong radio signals were picked up from objects far beyond our local group of galaxies. These objects were called quasars because of their similarity to stars. But astronomers were perplexed by the prodigious energy quasars emitted. The most luminous one is approximately 10,000 times as bright as the Milky Way, and the most distant ones detected are more than 10 billion light-years away. After two decades of intensive study, astronomers have concluded that these distant quasars are very active nuclei of outlying galaxies.

Top Five Ferocious Prehistoric Creatures

Think that Tyrannosaurus rex was the most fearsome creature to roam the earth? Think again. Eons ago, the planet was literally teeming with toothsome, terrifying monsters. Here are five of the most ferocious.

✳ ✳ ✳ ✳

1. *Giganotosaurus*
Averaging 47 feet in length and weighing 8 tons, *Giganotosaurus* would have made T. rex run home to its mama. Luckily, these monstrous behemoths lived millions of years apart. What made *Giganotosaurus* so menacing? Well, its eight-inch-long serrated teeth didn't hurt.

2. *Spinosaurus*
According to paleontologists, *Spinosaurus* is the largest carnivorous dinosaur known to have existed. It measured a whopping

55 feet in length, weighed almost 10 tons, and had long, croco-dilian jaws that sparked terror in anything foolish enough to cross its path. It also sported a sail on its back that was more than six feet tall.

3. Megalodon
Sharks are some of the oldest creatures on the planet, and *Megalodon* was the granddaddy of them all. It measured nearly 60 feet in length—longer than a city bus—and weighed more than 75 tons. To survive, *Megalodon* had to consume an esti-mated 2,500 pounds of food every day. That's a lot of sashimi.

4. Tylosaurus
Equal to Megalodon in ferocity, *Tylosaurus* was one of the most vicious creatures ever to swim the oceans. It measured more than 45 feet in length, and its jaws were lined on each side with two rows of cone-shaped teeth. What did *Tylosaurus* eat? Anything it wanted to, including other *Tylosauruses*.

5. Saber-Tooth Tiger
Known scientifically as *Smilodon*, the saber-tooth tiger was a dominant carnivore during the early days of humans. Though smaller than today's large cats, it was twice as heavy and sported 11-inch-long canine teeth. Luckily, *Smilodon* went extinct about 10,000 years ago.

7 Wonders of the Natural World

Each of the following sites captures the imagination with its natural power and beauty. And they have one thing in common: Nothing made by humans can approach their majestic dignity.

✳   ✳   ✳   ✳

1. Grand Canyon
The Grand Canyon in northwestern Arizona was formed by the erosive power of the weather and the Colorado River and its tributaries as they scoured away billion-year-old rocks. Although known to Native Americans for thousands of years,

the vast gorge was not discovered by the first Spanish explorers until 1540. Grand Canyon National Park was established in 1919, preserving the more than 1.2 million acres of colorful cliffs and waterways that are home to 75 species of mammals, 50 species of reptiles and amphibians, 25 species of fish, and more than 300 species of birds.

The canyon stretches 277 miles, with some sections reaching a mile deep and 18 miles across. More than five million visitors view the canyon annually, often hiking or riding mules down to the canyon floor, while the more adventurous opt for boating or rafting the Colorado River through the canyon.

2. Aurora Borealis (Northern Lights)

The aurora borealis (also called the northern lights) consists of awe-inspiring twirls of light in the sky, caused by "solar wind"—electrically charged particles interacting with Earth's magnetic field. The aurora borealis can be up to 2,000 miles wide, but it fluctuates in size, shape, and color, with green being the most common color close to the horizon while purples and reds appear higher.

Named after Aurora, Roman goddess of dawn, and Boreas, Greek god of the north wind, these ribbons of color are best viewed in northern climates like Alaska, but have been seen as far south as Arizona.

3. Mount Everest

Mount Everest, part of the Himalayan Mountains between Nepal and Tibet, was formed about 60 million years ago due to the shifting of Earth's rocky plates. Named after Sir George Everest, a British surveyor-general of India, Everest is the highest mountain on Earth, looming some 29,035 feet high and growing a few millimeters every year. Climbing Everest isn't easy, due to avalanches, strong winds, and thin air. Nevertheless, in 1953, Edmund Hillary and Sherpa Tenzing Norgay were the first climbers to reach the peak. More than 700 others have done so since.

4. Paricutin

Paricutin provides one of nature's best lessons in how volatile Earth is. Exploding out of a Mexican cornfield in 1943, Paricutin was the first known volcano to have witnesses at its birth. Within a year, the cone had grown to more than 1,100 feet high. The flow eventually spread over 10 square miles, engulfing the nearby towns of Paricutin and San Juan Parangaricutiro. The eruptions ceased in 1952, and the cone now soars 1,345 feet high.

5. Victoria Falls

Victoria Falls, originally called Mosi-oa-Tunya ("smoke that thunders"), was named after Queen Victoria of England in 1855. The raging waters of the Zambezi River pour 19 trillion cubic feet of water per minute into a gorge that is 1.25 miles wide and 328 feet deep, making this the largest curtain of falling water in the world. Located between Zambia and Zimbabwe, Victoria Falls is flanked by national parks and is now one of the world's greatest tourist attractions, with resorts, hiking trails, and observation posts springing up around it. Whitewater rafting at the foot of the falls makes for a thrilling adventure.

6. Great Barrier Reef

The Great Barrier Reef blankets 137,600 square miles and extends a dramatic 1,242 miles along Australia's northeastern coast, making it the largest group of reefs in the world. The reef began forming more than 30 million years ago and is made up of the skeletons of marine polyps. Four hundred species of living polyps can also be found there, along with 1,500 species of fish, as well as crabs, clams, and other sea life. The area is an Australian national park and is visited by around two million tourists a year.

7. Giant Sequoia Trees

Ancient giant sequoia trees are nature's ever-growing wonders. Giant sequoias grow naturally on the western slopes of California's Sierra Nevada Mountains at elevations from 5,000 to 7,000 feet. Some are as tall as a 26-story building, with their trunks spanning up to 100 feet and the bark on the older specimens reaching two to four feet thick. California's Sequoia National Park is home to several noteworthy giants, including the General Sherman, which is the world's largest tree by volume, measuring 274.9 feet high, almost 103 feet around, and comprising 52,508 cubic feet of wood. Giant sequoia trees are estimated to be between 1,800 and 2,700 years old. Depending on the tree and where it is situated, giant sequoias can grow up to two feet in height every year, producing almost 40 cubic feet of additional wood each year.

The Human Body

How well do you know yourself?

✳ ✳ ✳ ✳

The Human Brain

Estimated size of human brain capacity, in terabytes: between 1 and 1,000

Total size of collections in Library of Congress, in terabytes: approximately 50

Average Human Brain Size: 1350 cc

Average Neanderthal Brain Size: 1600 cc

Homo neanderthalensis, better known to modern humans as the Neanderthal, has long existed in the popular imagination as an apelike primitive ancestor of modern man. Yet recent anthropological and genomic studies have indicated that Neanderthals were remarkably similar to modern humans and may, in fact, have coexisted with our ancestors. According to DNA studies, Neanderthals not only had physical and cultural traits similar to their human contemporaries, but they actually had larger brains as well.

The Speed of Humans

Speed at which fingernails grow: .004 millimeter per hour

Speed of a human sneeze: around 100 mph

Speed of hair growth: .16 millimeter per hour

Speed of blood: about 2 miles per hour

Human top foot speed: 28 mph

Hopping Up the Wrong Tree

Planes, trains, automobiles, and Christmas trees? Some North American frogs unintentionally discovered a new form of transportation.

✳   ✳   ✳   ✳

WHEN RELOCATING TO a new home, most people rent a moving van, but when Pacific Chorus frogs want to move, apparently they just hitch a ride on Christmas trees bound for Alaska. In December 2009, the *Anchorage Daily News* reported that some of these critters were showing up in the Anchorage area during the holiday season, having traveled discreetly on trees imported from Oregon. (Who knows, maybe they just wanted to see the Northern Lights or go whale watching!)

Unfortunately for the Pacific Chorus frogs (so-named because of their raspy vocal trills), city officials didn't exactly leap for joy at their arrival. In Alaska, these amphibians are nonnative and have the potential to carry the disease-causing chytrid fungus, which has caused amphibian population declines around the world. Although the frogs didn't appear to be invasive, the Alaska Department of Fish and Game encouraged residents to take precautionary measures by killing the frogs (euthanizing them with a toothache anesthetic, such as Orajel) or putting them in the freezer. Then locals were supposed to bring in the frozen frogs for inspection.

Not a very "hoppy" Christmas for these critters!

This wasn't the first time that Pacific Chorus frogs traveled far from home. In 2007, members of this North American species showed up in Guam—again riding Christmas trees. (Maybe this time they were in search of sandy beaches and mangrove forests!) They also found their way to the Queens Charlotte Islands in British Columbia, where they spread fairly quickly, thus raising the possibility that the Pacific frogs could eventually become established in Alaska, too. But in order to do so, they'll have to steer clear of toothache medication and subfreezing temperatures!

Anatomical Anomalies

Mother Nature isn't always right. Here are a few examples.

✳ ✳ ✳ ✳

But Can It Wag?

MANY PEOPLE DON'T know that every human embryo actually starts life outfitted with a tail, though we usually lose them before birth. The reason why there are only several dozen known cases of people born with "true human tails" is because almost as soon as the embryonic tail develops, its growth is suppressed by *apoptosis*, or programmed cell death. True human tails, when they are retained by newborns, range from one to more than five inches in length—and, yes, they are able to wag!

Breathe Easily—If You Can

Flying is a strenuous activity requiring vast amounts of oxygen and an efficient respiratory system. Birds have a flow-through system of ventilation, which doesn't let freshly oxygenated air mix with the depleted air leaving the body. Mammals, however, mix fresh air with depleted air when they breathe, which is very inefficient. This is unfortunate for bats, since these flying mammals must take to the sky with inferior ventilation systems. Too bad they can't swap lungs with flightless birds such as emus and penguins, who still have the avian flow-through system that is of little use to them on the ground.

Picasso's Dream Fish

The bony flatfish has evolved to lay flat on the seabed. The most sensible way to flatten itself would be back-to-stomach, like a ray, so that both eyes are on top of its head. However, most bony fish are flat sideways, which means lying down flat would leave one of their eyes pointing uselessly at the ground. But where there's a will, there's a way: The flatfish asymmetrically reshapes its skull during adolescence, so that one of its eyes migrates over the top of the head and winds up on the other side! The result is both comical and creepy.

The Weird Animals of Texas

Texas is full of unusual critters. Here are some of its strangest.

❋ ❋ ❋ ❋

❋ The Texas state small mammal is the nine-banded armadillo, an insect-eating relative of sloths and anteaters. Originating in South America, the armadillo migrated to Texas via Mexico in the 19th century. Its fear response is to jump in the air, which is why so many are found dead on Texas highways. Selling armadillos is illegal in Texas because they're the only animal besides humans to carry leprosy.

❋ The horned toad, horny toad, or horned frog is really a horned lizard and the Texas state reptile. The mistaken identities come from the lizard's round body and blunt snout, and the name comes from the scaly spikes on its back, sides, and head. Unrelated to the name, the male also has two sexual organs.

❋ The Houston Toad is an endangered toad species discovered in and around Houston in the late 1940s. Only between a few hundred to a few thousand remain, and they're gone from the city that gave them their name. The largest group of these loud amphibians is in Bastrop State Park.

✳ When people think of Texas, they often think of the long-horn. Longhorn cattle are a hybrid descended primarily from the first cattle brought to the United States by the Spanish and mixed with English cattle. The horns can measure 120 inches tip to tip for steers (which are castrated males) and up to 80 inches for cows and bulls. Longhorns might have been bred out of existence if not for members of the U.S. Forest Service, who saved a herd of breeding stock in 1927.

✳ At five feet in height, the whooping crane is North America's tallest bird and an endangered species. An estimated 340 exist in the wild. The largest group spends the summers in Wood Buffalo National Park in Alberta, Canada, and migrates south in the winter to the Texas Gulf Coast, set-tling primarily near Corpus Christi on the Aransas National Wildlife Refuge and Matagorda Island.

✳ Found only in the Guadalupe and a few other Texas rivers, the Guadalupe bass is the Texas state fish. A black bass and member of the sunfish family, the Guadalupe bass is called the "Texas trout" by fishers because of its fighting ability.

✳ Mexican free-tailed bats live in caves across the western and southern United States, but the largest colony—nearly 20 million bats—hangs out in Bracken Cave, north of San Antonio. Another huge colony of 1.5 million free-tails spends its summers under the Congress Avenue Bridge in Austin, just ten blocks from the state capitol building, mak-ing it the largest urban bat colony in North America. Those numbers helped make the Mexican free-tailed bat the official "flying mammal" of Texas.

✳ The greater roadrunner, a member of the cuckoo family, believe it or not, is a year-round resident of Texas, although it can be found in other southwestern deserts, as well. It can fly if necessary, but it prefers to stay on the ground, where it can reach speeds of more than 15 miles per hour. Although roadrunners try to stay clear of coyotes, they are willing to attack a snake for a nice meal.

✳ At the small end of the Texas critters scale, the Texas leaf-cutter ant is a fungus-farming ant species that likes to dine on more than 200 types of plants. Considered a major pest by Texas farmers, leafcutter colonies can contain as many as 2 million ants, and one colony with high hopes can strip a citrus tree of its leaves in less than a day.

✳ It sounds strange, but many Texans, particularly goat farmers, fear a creature known as the Chupacabra—Spanish for "goat sucker"—because of its reputation for attacking goats and other livestock and then drinking their blood. Unexplained livestock disappearances are often blamed on this creature, which is said to be the size of a small bear with fangs and huge claws, have spines down its hairless leathery back, and be bluish-greenish-gray in color. In 2004, a San Antonio rancher killed a creature many believed to be a Chupacabra, but DNA analysis identified it as a coyote with a mange problem. Even though no credible evidence of such a creature exists, it has built up quite a reputation.

Top Texas Snake Legends

Snakes are a favorite topic when Texas storytellers tell tall tales by the campfire. Here are a few stories that may not be entirely true, but Texans will assure campers that they're darn near factual.

✳   ✳   ✳   ✳

Eternal snakes: The Karankawa people lived along Texas's Gulf coast and believed that some snakes never died. According to their lore, rattlesnakes do not grow old and, unless deliberately killed by a human or animal, will live forever.

The fatal boots: A Texas cowboy wore his new snakeskin boots to court the prettiest girl in town, but he died days later. He left his boots to his best friend, who also died after wearing them with the same young lady. When a third victim died, the coroner found a venomous rattlesnake fang embedded in the lining of the boots.

The 50-rattle rattlesnake: According to legend, settlers along Texas's Colorado River killed a rattlesnake more than ten feet long with 50 rattles on its tail.

The longest rattlesnakes in Texas: In the summer of 1877, a Dallas newspaper reported an 18-foot snake in a rural area northwest of San Antonio; its tail had 37 different rattles.

The fattest rattlesnake: In the mid-1840s, a tiger hunter was touring Texas and sat down to rest on what he thought was a fallen tree. That "tree" turned out to be a rattlesnake about a foot and a half across and 17 feet long.

The second-fattest rattlesnake: Around 1840 near the Nueces River, explorers found a rattlesnake as big around as the thigh of an average man and at least nine feet long.

Flying snakes: Texas's flying snake legends date to before Europeans arrived in North America. In June 2008, a flying snake appeared in video footage from a security camera in Lajitas.

Dino-mite!

Dinosaur Valley State Park provides a trip back in time.

✳ ✳ ✳ ✳

For anyone who loves all things prehistoric—and who doesn't?—a trip to Dinosaur Valley State Park in Somervell County, Texas, should be at the top of the list for gotta-see vacation destinations. Located just northwest of tiny Glen Rose, just past the Creation Evidence Museum,

Dinosaur Valley State Park is the Lone Star State's answer to Jurassic Park, complete with a life-size *Tyrannosaurus rex* and Brontosaurus (*Apatosaurus*). The only difference is that these are fiberglass models rather than real-life, attorney-munching behemoths.

Dinosaurs to Spare

The statues, located at the entrance to the 1,500-acre park, are relics from the Sinclair Oil Company's 1964 New York World's Fair display. In fact, Sinclair Oil had a whole menagerie of leftover dinosaurs, which it offered to the Smithsonian Institution when the World's Fair ended. The Smithsonian didn't want them, however, so the prehistoric beasties found new homes across the country.

Ankylosaurus ended up at the Houston Museum of Natural Science; *Corythosaurus*, in Independence, Kansas; *Stegosaurus*, at the Dinosaur National Monument in Vernal, Utah; *Struthiomimus*, in the Milwaukee Museum—and *T. rex* and Brontosaurus at Dinosaur Valley State Park.

Walk Where Dinos Walked

The faux monsters set the stage for the park's most impressive attraction: approximately 100 actual dinosaur footprints preserved in the bed of the Paluxy River. At 113 million years old, these are some of the best-preserved dinosaur tracks in the world. They have become both a popular tourist attraction and a scientific boon; over the years, the tracks have shed great insight into how dinosaurs walked.

The tracks are visible only when the water is low, so it's a good idea to call ahead to check on current river conditions before a visit. If the tracks aren't easy to spot, however, a replica of them is also available.

Charging Bull

Think you've got what it takes to beat a charging bull? An average bull weighs in the ballpark of 2,000 pounds—more than ten times the weight of a typical man. Unless you're a trained rodeo performer used to sidestepping an angry bull, you probably want to follow these steps if you find one staring you down:

✳ ✳ ✳ ✳

✳ First of all, stay still. Bulls tend to attack when they're angry, so the last thing you want to do is provoke that massive hunk of meat.

✳ You may have run track in high school, but the bull can outrun you. Use your wits to find a nearby place where it won't be able to follow you, such as a building with an open door or a high fence you can quickly climb. If you spot such a place, make a mad dash for it. Otherwise, just stick with staying still.

✳ Assuming escape's not an option, take a deep breath and get ready to play the rodeo clown. Those clowns throw around red cloths for a reason: They work. Pull off your shirt and wave it around to distract the bull. But it doesn't have to be red; bulls respond more to the movement than to the color.

✳ Once the bull starts heading toward the shirt, toss it as far away as you can. The bull should charge toward it, leaving you a window to run like the wind while it's distracted.

✳ In the case of a full-on stampede, don't mess with the distraction part—it's too tough to divert an entire group's attention. Your only options are to get out of their path or to run with them to keep from getting run over. Once those fellas are charging, though, don't stay still, or they will trample right over you—and that's no load of bull.

Pet Precipitation

While the idiom "raining cats and dogs" might conjure images of domestic denizens being heaved from the heavens, the conception of the cliché is more down-to-earth.

✳ ✳ ✳ ✳

WHILE THERE IS considerable speculation as to the exact genesis of the idiom "raining cats and dogs," there is no doubt about one thing: It describes a vicious storm where all kinds of solid materials are spewed and strewn about by the sheer velocity of the downpour. But things get murky from there. Some theorists claim the phrase originated in the Middle Ages. Back then, tenuous, almost transparent thatched roofs covered many domestic dwellings. These anemic canopies consisted of intertwined batches of vented vegetation such as straw, heather, and other porous particles. It was common for dogs and their feline brethren to climb into the comblike confines of these roofs in an effort to keep warm and dry. However, in a downpour, these rickety roofs would often give way, causing pets to plunge down from their lofty lairs, creating the illusion that they were raining from the sky.

Another theory offers a more gruesome justification for the origin of this phrase. In the Middle Ages, it wasn't uncommon to dispose of perished pets by simply dumping them in a street-side gutter or a garbage-strewn alley. Since sewer systems at the time were inadequate at best, a thundering rainstorm would deluge the drains and swamp the alleys, causing the deceased pets to drift down the streets and give the impression that their untimely demise was caused by the harsh rain.

Jonathan Swift, the Anglo-Irish author best known for his tall tale *Gulliver's Travels*, may also be responsible for introducing the lifeless litter to literature. In his satirical poem "A Description of a City Shower," first published in the October 17, 1710, edition of *Tatler Magazine*, Swift writes of "Drown'd

Puppies, stinking Sprats, all drench'd in Mud, Dead Cats and Turnip-Tops come tumbling down the Flood." And it's on that cheerful note, that we take leave of this discussion. Keep those umbrellas handy!

The Ohioan Cockroach to Beat All Cockroaches

In 1999, one of the largest specimens of cockroaches ever found turned up in Ohio. Lucky for contemporary Ohioans, the biggest cockroach from Ohio lived more than 300 million years ago.

✻ ✻ ✻ ✻

CARY EASTERDAY, A geology master's student at The Ohio State University, unearthed the largest known complete fossil of a cockroach in 1999. This massive critter, measuring three and a half inches, lived 300 million years ago, making it more recent than the oldest known (but less complete) cockroach fossil from 350 million years ago. Three and a half inches is pretty colossal for a cockroach—though there are some modern cockroach species in the tropics that are just as large. What makes this Ohio-bred bug special is the amazing perfection of its preservation.

The cockroach fossil that Easterday found, member of a long-extinct species known to scientists as *Arthropleura pustulatus,* was discovered at the 7–11 Mine in northeastern Ohio, which lies right at the intersection of Ohio State Routes 7 and 11. These digging grounds are renowned for yielding perfectly preserved fossils. The cockroach was preserved so well that its mouth, its antennae, the veins in its wings, and even the little splotches that indicate color patterning could be clearly seen. It is generally difficult to find well preserved insect fossils, since insects lack bones or hard shells.

Cockroaches infested the earth 150 million years before dinosaurs showed up, and they are among the most resistant of Earth's species. Cockroaches were so common during the Carboniferous Era (between 359.2 million and 299 million years ago) that paleontologists jokingly renamed this time period the Age of Cockroaches.

Indeed, cockroaches seem to have evolved little during massive time periods—although back in the Carboniferous Era, there were no humans around to pester.

Blue Moon?

Blue moon, You saw me standing alone, Without a dream in my heart, Without a love of my own.

—From the song "Blue Moon"

✳ ✳ ✳ ✳

ACCORDING TO THE many performers who have recorded this Rodgers and Hart classic—including Elvis Presley, Frank Sinatra, and Bob Dylan—there most certainly is such a thing as a blue moon, and it acts as a celestial matchmaker for the lovelorn. Of course, not everyone is as sappy as the aforementioned singers. When most people mention a blue moon, they are referring to an event that is highly unusual. As our lovelorn crooners might say, "I have a date once in a blue moon."

The phrase "blue moon" dates back to 1528. It first appeared in a work by William Barlow, an English bishop, the wonderfully titled *Treatyse of the Buryall of the Masse*. "Yf they saye the mone is belewe," Barlow wrote, "we must beleve that it is true." (Trust us; he's saying something about a blue moon here.) After Barlow's usage, which no doubt confused as many readers as it edified, the term came to represent anything absurd or impossible.

It was only later that "blue moon" connoted something unusual. Most etymologists trace this usage to the wildly popular 1819 edition of the *Maine Farmer's Almanac*, which suggested that when any season experiences four full moons (instead of the usual three), the fourth full moon was to be referred to as the "blue" moon.

As is often the case with these things, somehow the *Maine Farmer's Almanac's* suggestion was misinterpreted—researchers blame the incompetent editors of a 1946 issue of *Sky & Telescope* magazine—to mean a second new full moon in a single month. Consequently, in present-day astronomy, that second new full moon is referred to as a "blue" moon. This frequency, ironically, isn't all that unusual, at least as astronomical events go: once every two and a half years.

As for whether the moon really can appear blue, the answer is yes. After massive forest fires swept through western Canada in 1950, for example, much of eastern North America was treated to a bluish moon in the night sky. However, events such as this occur, well, once in a blue moon.

The Real-Life Dead Zone

The Dead Zone is a popular book by Stephen King that was made into a movie and television series. But it is also a terrifying reality. There are currently hundreds of dead zones in the world's oceans, which threaten marine life, and possibly, humanity as well. Unfortunately, this isn't a fictional horror story.

✳   ✳   ✳   ✳

Death from Life

DEAD ZONES ARE areas of bottom waters in oceans where the oxygen is too depleted to support most life. They first began being noticed in 1910, when four such zones were identified. As of 2008, that number had increased to a staggering 405, and current scientific studies suggest that dead zones may increase by a factor of ten or more by the year 2100. In a worst-case scenario, more than 20 percent of the world's oceans could one day turn into dead zones.

These zones are scattered up and down the eastern and southern coasts of the United States. They are also found in several West Coast river outlets. However, the problem isn't only domestic—dead zones are found throughout the world. In fact, the largest dead zone to date is in the vast expanse of the Baltic Sea—its bottom waters do not contain oxygen year round.

Agricultural fertilizer is the primary cause of dead zones. Fertilizer contains large amounts of nitrogen, which runs off of fields into rivers, and eventually finds its way into the ocean. Algae feed on this nitrogen. The algae die and sink to the bottom of the ocean, where they are eaten by microbes. And these microbes consume oxygen as they feed. So the more algae, the more microbes there are feeding, which robs more oxygen from the water.

Mobile fish and bottom-dwellers can escape this oxygen loss, but others that are not as quick-moving (such as clams) die off in massive numbers. Then the microbes that thrive in oxygen-free environments move in. They form vast bacterial mats, which produce the toxic gas hydrogen sulfide.

Comeback . . . and Disaster

Sometimes a dead zone can recover—just take a look at the Black Sea. Formally a dead zone, it recovered between 1990 and 2000, when fertilizer became extremely costly after the Soviet Union collapsed and took the planned agricultural economies of many central and eastern European countries with it.

Ironically, one of the most cataclysmic events in recent U.S. history—Hurricane Katrina—actually helped the local dead zone problem. The largest zone in the United States is at the mouth of the Mississippi River, measuring approximately 8,500 square miles (an area equivalent to the size of New Jersey).

When Katrina came along, it acted like a giant blender: The storm's awesome power mixed the oxygen-filled surface water with the oxygen-free water on the bottom. Hard on Katrina's heels came Hurricane Rita, which finished the job. This temporarily dissipated the dead zone in that area. But waiting for massive hurricanes to come along and repair dead zones is a poor way to solve the problem. Global warming also throws a wrench into the works. Since warmer water holds less oxygen than cooler water, global warming reduces the ocean's ability to store oxygen at the same time it decreases the amount of oxygen available in deeper water.

Computer simulations by Danish researchers indicate that dead zones caused by global warming will last for thousands of years. "They will be a permanent fixture [of the oceans]," said University of Copenhagen researcher Gary Shaffer.

Searching for a Solution

Scientists are currently scrambling for solutions to dead zones. One idea is to pump air into smaller areas of water and see what happens, much like a pond is aerated to prevent low oxygen. Ultimately, however, it may take massive revolutions in agriculture and human behavior to save the world's oceans from becoming a giant dead zone. And that's a future we don't want to see happen.

When Nature Turns Mean!

Man and nature are supposed to live in harmony, right? But sometimes certain animals don't get the memo. The following tales are incredible stories of man (and woman) versus beast in a remarkable fight for survival.

✳   ✳   ✳   ✳

Bearing Down

ON NOVEMBER 1, 1999, hunter Gene Moe of Anchorage, Alaska, was dressing a freshly killed deer atop a mountain on Raspberry Island when an 8-foot-tall, 700-pound Kodiak bear attacked him. Armed only with a 3 3/4-inch-long hunting knife, Moe went toe-to-toe with the snarling behemoth in a terrifying battle to the death.

Moe first tried to shove his knife down the bear's throat but missed, allowing the bruin to tear away a large flap of flesh on his right arm. Moe repeatedly stabbed the animal in its neck and back each time it attacked, but the bear managed to get in a few more licks of its own, at one point mangling Moe's right leg with a vicious bite and slashing one of his ears. When the bear lunged at him a final time, Moe met the assault with a wild punch to the animal's face, a blow that managed to sever the bear's already damaged vertebra. With that, the beast fell dead at Moe's feet.

But Moe's ordeal wasn't over yet. Bleeding heavily and in excruciating pain, he crawled two miles down the mountain to where the rest of his party was waiting. In the hospital, Moe received more than 500 stitches. But he recovered well enough to go hunting again the following year.

A Game of Cat and Bicyclist

On January 8, 2004, Anne Hjelle of Mission Viejo, California, was riding her mountain bike with her friend, Debi Nicholls, at Whiting Ranch Wilderness Park when she was ambushed and knocked to the ground by a 110-pound mountain lion. When Nicholls arrived on the scene, the big cat had latched on to Hjelle's head with its powerful jaws and was trying to drag her into the brush. Nicholls's first instinct was to throw her bike at the animal, but it barely flinched. She then grabbed Hjelle by the leg, engaging the lion in a life-or-death game of tug-of-war.

Nicholls struggled to keep the lion from dragging Hjelle down into the ravine, but the cat was strong and managed to pull both women about 30 feet into the brush before a group of other cyclists heard Nicholls's screams and rushed over. With Nicholls still clinging desperately to Hjelle's leg, the other cyclists threw rocks at the killer cat until it finally let go and slunk away into the underbrush.

Hjelle's left cheek was almost completely ripped off in the attack, and she suffered numerous other lacerations on her head and face. However, her plastic surgeons did a remarkable job of sewing her back up, and Hjelle was back riding her bike within a few months.

Honeymoon Surprise

In August 2001, Krishna Thompson of Central Islip, Long Island, took his wife, AveMaria, to Freeport, Grand Bahama, to celebrate their wedding anniversary. On their second morning there, a shark attacked Thompson while he was out for an early-morning swim in the ocean.

The shark grabbed Thompson's left leg and started to drag him out to sea. Once in deeper water, the shark submerged, taking Thompson with him. As the light above him grew dimmer, Thompson desperately reached down and tried to pull the shark's jaws apart. He lacerated his hands on its razor-sharp teeth, but finally succeeded in making it release him. Thompson then punched the shark several times, until it turned and swam away.

Thompson swam to shallow water, then hopped to the beach on his uninjured leg and screamed for help. A physician who was jogging nearby tended to Thompson until an ambulance could take him to the hospital. The lacerations on Thompson's left leg were so severe that the limb had to be amputated. Thompson was later fitted with a computerized prosthetic limb. Today, Thompson lectures as a motivational speaker.

The Deadliest Texas Tornadoes

Texas sits at the southern end of a geographic area called Tornado Alley. Each year, during spring and summer months, deadly tornadoes wreak havoc through the countryside. Here are the deadliest tornadoes in modern Texas history.

✳   ✳   ✳   ✳

1. **The Waco Tornado, May 11, 1953:** The day after Mother's Day wasn't a good one as this F5 tornado, about a third of a mile wide, raged through town, killing 114 people and hurting 597 more. About 600 buildings and homes were destroyed, and another 1,000 were damaged.

2. **The Goliad Tornado, May 18, 1902:** This F4 tornado also had a death toll of 114. It demolished hundreds of buildings including a Methodist church where many citizens had taken shelter. A total of 250 people were injured.

3. **The Rocksprings Tornado, April 12, 1927:** This F5 tornado demolished 235 of the town's 247 buildings. Almost one-third of the population was affected by the twister, which resulted in 74 fatalities and 205 injuries.

4. **The Sherman Tornado, May 15, 1896:** This F5 tornado took a path straight through the most populated section of the town of Sherman, killing 73 citizens and injuring 200.

5. **The Glazier-Higgins-Woodward tornadoes, April 9, 1947:** A massive two-mile-wide tornado was part of a family of storms that started in Texas and moved on to Oklahoma and Kansas. In Texas, the monster twister destroyed the town of Glazier, resulting in 17 deaths and 40 injuries, and severely damaged the town of Higgins, which recorded 51 fatalities and 232 injuries.

6. **The Wichita Falls Tornado, April 10, 1979:** This mile-wide F4 tornado took a direct path into Wichita Falls. When

the winds subsided, citizens found 3,000 homes destroyed and significant damage done to public buildings and schools, as well as 42 fatalities, 1,700 injuries, and as many as 20,000 homeless.

Collective Nouns

Here are some ways to describe a group of animals, birds, or general, well, things.

✳ ✳ ✳ ✳

It's a bird! It's a plane! It's a . . .

blessing of unicorns

generation (or nest) of vipers

shrewdness of apes

pod of dolphins

trip (or tribe, herd, drove) of goats

charm of hummingbirds

pride of lions

zeal (or herd) of zebras

flock of camels

company of parrots

herd of llamas

sleuth (or sloth) of bears

leap (or leep) of leopards

phalanx of umbrellas

babble of barbers

husk of jackrabbits

erudition of editors

swarm of eels

quarrel (or host, ubiquity) of sparrows

string of ponies

passel of possum

soufflé of clouds

dray (or scurry) of squirrels

streak of tigers

hover of trout

cast (or business) of ferrets

The 1900 Flood: More than Galveston

Many remember Hurricane Katrina with horror, but the 1900 Galveston hurricane and flood did far more damage.

✳   ✳   ✳   ✳

GALVESTON IS AN island city that basks in the sun about an hour southeast of Houston. Nearby, vacationing families enjoy the Houston Space Center, Moody Gardens, Armand Bayou Nature Center, Kemah Boardwalk, and the Forbidden Gardens. Every three years or so, Galveston can expect a brush with a major storm. Every ten years, it's likely to receive a direct hurricane hit. Usually, the city breezes through those storms with ease. But September 8, 1900, was another story.

Unprepared and Vulnerable

In 1900, tropical storms and hurricanes weren't assigned names. Galveston residents knew that bad weather was coming, but the U.S. Weather Bureau discouraged use of terms such as *hurricane*. In addition, geographers claimed that the slope of the sea bottom protected the city against harsh ocean conditions.

Galveston, the fourth-most-populous city in the state at the time, didn't even have a seawall.

By the time the Category 4 hurricane hit the city, fewer than half its residents had evacuated. In fact, the city was busy with tourists who'd arrived to enjoy the warm gulf waters and watch the eerie, oncoming clouds.

To date, Galveston's 1900 flood, which resulted from that storm, is America's worst natural disaster, killing approximately 8,000 people with a 15-foot storm surge that destroyed roughly half of Galveston's homes and businesses and devastated the surrounding area. The flood has been the subject of books, movies, and songs. In 1904, crowds lined up to see the "Galveston Flood" attraction at New York's Coney Island. Most people don't realize, however, that the storm's damage extended far beyond Galveston.

A Wide Swath

During the 18-hour storm, the winds were so intense that telegraph lines as far away as Abilene—more than 300 miles from Galveston—were leveled. Between the Gulf of Mexico and Abilene, the 1900 storm snapped trees and crushed houses. On J. E. Dick's ranch near Galveston, 2,500 cattle drowned. Throughout East Texas, cities and towns were destroyed. Katy is just one of them.

Today, Katy is an upscale community about 25 miles west of Houston and 60 miles inland from Galveston. Before the Europeans arrived, it was a winter feeding ground for buffalo and a major hunting ground of the Karankawa. By the late 19th century, settlers had built farms and other businesses there. Katy—or "KT"—was named for the MKT (Missouri, Kansas, and Texas) railroad line that terminated in the area.

The 1900 hurricane, however, almost wiped Katy off the map. Only two houses were undamaged when the winds blew through the town's streets and swept homes and businesses from their foundations. Today, those two homes—Featherston House and Wright House—are part of Katy Heritage Park.

Houston was also in the storm's path. Much of the area's economy relied on farms and ranches that were ill prepared for the devastation that was coming. Winds and rising waters destroyed almost every barn in the hurricane's path. Waters up to ten feet deep flooded local pastures. Across East Texas, entire forests were crushed. One news reporter observed "no large timber left standing as far as the eye can see."

From there, it's not clear whether the storm headed due north or if it doubled back. Many believe it retraced its path to the Florida Keys and then continued up the East Coast. By the time it reached New York City, the winds were still raging at 65 mph.

Digging Out

In the aftermath of the storm, the Galveston community dredged sand to raise the city up to 17 feet above sea level. The city also built a 17-foot-tall seawall to protect it from storm surges. Likewise, Houston and the cities around it improved drainage and created reservoirs and flood plains to absorb the water from future storms that were sure to come.

Howl at the Moon

Do dogs really howl at the moon? Why?

❋   ❋   ❋   ❋

A DOG, COMMON WISDOM tells us, is man's best friend. And it's true that dogs are loyal, playful, and protective. But they also smell, shed, pee in the house, and bark at everything in existence: cars, squirrels, other dogs, people—you name it. But perhaps nothing is more perplexing to us than the canine instinct to bark at the moon. Frankly, it seems a little pointless, not to mention irritating for the person who is trying to sleep through it. (Trust us—we know from experience.) So you'll have to forgive us for any glaring errors we make while trying to write this, bleary-eyed, after another sleepless night courtesy of the neighbor's hound.

According to canine experts, the howling of domesticated dogs is related directly to their wolf ancestry. For wolves, howling is an important part of social interaction and protective behavior. Not all howls are equal—a number of different types of howls have been identified, including "lonesome" howls, "confrontational" howls, and "chorus" howls. Each of these serves a different purpose. For example, a "lonesome" howl might be unleashed when a wolf gets separated from its pack and wants to let its buddies know where it is. A "chorus" howl—when multiple wolves howl at the same time—can be used to encourage potential predators to stay away. (Interestingly, wolves are able to modulate their howls, so just a few wolves can make a clamor that sounds like an enormous pack.)

Evolutionary biologists believe that domesticated dogs have retained the howling instinct of their distant wolf cousins. The howling you hear in your neighborhood is a form of communication between doggie neighbors or sometimes a response to noises that they mistake for fellow howlers (which is why dogs often howl in response to a siren).

What does this have to do with Fido barking at the moon? Actually, there is no evidence that dogs howl at the moon. Scientists say that this is a figment of the public's imagination. Dogs may be more active on moonlit nights, experts say, because they can see better, which may lead to increased howling. Or perhaps humans are more active on bright evenings. Either way, biologists are adamant about the fact that neither wolves nor dogs howl at the moon. To which we say: Try sleeping at our house sometime.

Treasure Hunting

How does a dog find its buried treasure weeks or maybe months later? It follows its nose.

✻ ✻ ✻ ✻

EVER WATCHED YOUR dog bury a bone? After covering its treasure with dirt, it'll press its nose into the ground as if it's literally tamping the soil down with its snout. You can always tell when a dog's been digging, because its dirty nose is a dead giveaway.

How does the dog find the bone again? The enzymes that are released by decomposing bones, especially raw ones, give off a distinctive odor. We can't smell it, but a dog certainly can— dogs can smell one thousand to ten thousand times better than humans can. A dog that's looking for its buried bone will sniff around, keeping its nose to the ground until it finds the spot.

Incidentally, this ability to detect decomposing bones is what enables dogs to help law enforcement officials find corpses. Dogs can even be used at archaeological digs to locate ancient burial grounds.

A dog's propensity for burying bones is what zoologists call cache behavior. It's also found among wolves, wild dogs, and foxes. When a kill is too large to be devoured at a single sitting, these animals bury what they can't eat in safe places. Canines are highly territorial. Your dog will never bury its bones in another dog's yard, though it may try to sneak in and dig up its neighbor's cache on the sly. Wild canines also bury food in areas that they have marked as their own, which they defend fiercely. During lean times, they will dig up their hidden food stores— it's sort of like having something set aside for the proverbial rainy day.

Do dogs always retrieve the bones they bury? Not necessarily. Cache behavior is an important survival technique for canines in the wild, but well-fed domestic pets may simply have no need for their buried leftovers. Furthermore, cooked bones don't hold the same allure as raw ones—they disintegrate faster, and their scent is sometimes masked by the odors of the surrounding soil.

Stop, Spot, Stop

If your yard is full of holes, you're probably wondering how you can stop your dog from burying bones. Well, the cache instinct is so powerful that there isn't much you can do to deter it. As any experienced dog owner can tell you, a dog will always bury something. If Fido doesn't have a bone, a favorite toy or even an old shoe will do. Indoor dogs often hide their toys under beds or behind sofa cushions. Some veterinarians recommend giving a dog its own sandbox or a pile of pillows where it can "play" at hiding and seeking. These vets add that encouraging cache behavior can be a great interactive way of getting to know your pet better.

So join the fun. Instead of punishing your dog for doing what comes naturally, roll up your sleeves, grab that tattered old stinky sneaker, and dig in.

Do Bed Bugs Really Bite?

You better believe they do. In fact, it's pretty much the only thing they do.

✳   ✳   ✳   ✳

A BROWNISH-RED, FLAT, AND oval-shaped wingless insect, the common bed bug (*Cimex lectularius* if you're a Latin lover) grows to about a quarter-inch in length and feeds exclusively on the blood of animals. This includes you, sleepyhead.

Bed bugs are nocturnal, hiding in cracks and crevices during the day and emerging at night to feed on a host. They use an elongated beak to puncture the skin and can spend three to ten minutes drawing blood. Often, the victim never feels a thing.

If you awake with itchy, reddish welts on your skin, it's possible that you were the main course at a bed-bug feast. But symptoms vary, and some people don't react to the bites at all. Thankfully, under normal circumstances, bites from bed bugs don't spread disease, just a measure of discomfort.

Bed bugs don't prey exclusively on humans—they can also be found around the nests of birds and bats, for example. But they have demonstrated an enduring affinity for people: Literary references to bed bugs date to the days of Aristotle.

The little suckers were on the run in America in the years following World War II, however. The rise of such household cleaning staples as vacuum cleaners and pesticides helped diminish their forces.

But as pesticides with the broad-spectrum killer DDT were replaced by more specialized products aimed specifically at such pests as roaches and ants, bed bugs regained their foothold. And because they travel well in clothing and luggage, they've been slowly reintroduced to North America, notably in hotels (and not just the cheap ones), homes, and hospitals.

"Don't let the bed bugs bite" isn't just a quaint saying. These pesky predators are back in business.

Can the Cold Give You a Cold?

No, you won't catch a cold by running around in the frigid air while wearing only underwear (not that you would ever do such a thing) or traipsing through town with wet hair. Sorry, Mom—and old wives.

* * * *

WHILE IT'S TRUE that colds are more prevalent during the nippy months from September to April, the cold temperatures are probably not to blame. These just happen to be the months when viruses are typically spread.

One study did conclude that cold temperatures might indeed give you a cold. Researchers at Cardiff Common Cold Centre in Wales asked 180 volunteers to sit with their feet in bowls of ice-cold water for twenty minutes. Over the next five days, 29 percent of the cold-feet volunteers caught a cold, compared to 9 percent of an empty-bowl control group. It's thought that cold temperatures can constrict the blood vessels of the nose, turning off the warm blood supply to white blood cells (the ones that fight infections).

However, most research continues to show that being physically chilled or wet really has nothing to do with catching a cold. We spend more time indoors during the winter, oftentimes exposed to sniffling coworkers who refuse to take sick days. (Are they still hoping to win a gold star for perfect attendance?) Before you know it, January rolls around and you're drowning in a mound of Puffs Plus and begging someone—anyone—to make you a batch of chicken noodle soup.

Who hasn't been there? That's why it's the "common cold." More than two hundred types of viruses can cause it. There are the rhinovirus (the leading cause of the common cold, made famous in Lysol disinfectant TV commercials), the respiratory syncytial virus, and lots, lots more. These nasty bugs lurk on telephones, cutting boards, computer mice, doorknobs, hand towels, and pretty much everywhere hands are meant to go.

So wipe those areas down with disinfecting sprays or wipes and be vigilant about cleansing your hands with antibacterial soap and water or hand sanitizer gel. Dr. Neil Schachter, author of *The Good Doctor's Guide to Colds and Flu*, says that people who wash their hands seven times a day get 40 percent fewer colds than the average person.

You know what else? It really can't hurt to throw on your ski mask and thermal snowsuit when the temperature dips below freezing. At least it will make your mom feel better.

The Dead Sea: It Lives

The Red Sea isn't really red, and the Black Sea isn't really black—so what are the odds that the Dead Sea is really dead?

❋   ❋   ❋   ❋

IF YOU'VE EVER gone for a dip in the Dead Sea, you'll know that there is at least a shred of truth to the name. The Dead Sea's otherworldly qualities make swimmers buoyant—everyone's doing the "dead man's float."

Located between Israel and Jordan, the Dead Sea is, at 1,300 feet below sea level, the lowest surface point on Earth. The very bottom is 2,300 feet below sea level. Water flows into the Dead Sea from the Jordan River, but then it has no place to go, since it's already reached the lowest possible surface point on the planet. The fresh water that flows into the Dead Sea evaporates quickly because of the high temperatures in the desert, and it leaves behind a deposit of minerals.

These minerals have accumulated to make the Dead Sea the pungent stew that it is today. Slightly more than 30 percent of the Dead Sea is comprised of minerals, including sodium chloride, iodine, calcium, potassium, and sulfur. These minerals have been marketed as therapeutic healing products for people with skin conditions; many cosmetic companies have their own line of Dead Sea products.

The Dead Sea is reported to be six times saltier than an ocean, and salt provides buoyancy for swimmers. No form of life could survive in these conditions, right? Not exactly. It's true that every species of fish introduced into this body of water has promptly died, but in 1936, an Israeli scientist found that microscopic pieces of green algae and a few types of bacteria were living in the Dead Sea. So the Dead Sea can't technically be considered dead.

Poor Pluto

It once held the title of the smallest planet. Now it's not considered a planet at all. What happened?

✻　✻　✻　✻

POOR PLUTO. IT was welcomed into the exclusive club of planets in 1930 after being discovered by American astronomer Clyde Tombaugh, but then was unceremoniously booted out on August 24, 2006, by the International Astronomical Union (AIU). Because Pluto's orbit around the sun takes approximately 247.9 Earth years, it didn't even get to celebrate its first anniversary of being a planet.

Pluto didn't change. What did?

Discoveries and Definitions

The word and original definition of "planet" are derived from the Greek *asteres planetai,* which means "wandering stars." Planets are known as wanderers because they appear to move against the relatively fixed background of the stars, which are much more distant. Five planets (Mercury, Venus, Mars, Jupiter, and Saturn) are visible to the naked eye from Earth and were known to people in ancient times.

Three other planets would not have been discovered without modern advancements. Uranus was discovered by William Herschel in 1781, using a telescope; Johanne Galle discovered Neptune in 1846, using sophisticated mathematical predictions; and Pluto was discovered when the astronomer Tombaugh laboriously flipped through photographic plates of regions of the sky captured at different dates that showed the special wandering that denotes a planet.

Continued improvements in telescopes and mathematical modeling, among other advancements, have helped astronomers find all sorts of things in a solar system that previously seemed somewhat vacant. Classifying all of these objects—especially with respect to what is a planet and what's not—has proven to be tricky. On August 24, 2006, the IAU established a cut-and-dried definition of a planet. To be a planet, an object must orbit the sun, have enough mass so that it is nearly round, and dominate the area around its orbit.

A Sudden Demotion

This turn of events was bad news for Pluto because it doesn't meet the third part of the definition—it doesn't dominate its "neighborhood." For one thing, planets are supposed to be much larger than their moons, and Pluto's moon, Charon, is about half its size. Second, a planet is supposed to clear the neighborhood around its orbit—meaning it should, in the words of National Geographic News, "sweep up asteroids, comets, and other debris"—and Pluto isn't particularly effective at doing that.

The IAU didn't completely diss Pluto. It now is classified as a dwarf planet, meaning that it orbits the sun, is round, and isn't a satellite of any other object, despite not clearing its orbit. There are dozens of known dwarf planets, and scientists expect the number to grow rapidly because so many objects fit the criteria. It's a much less elite club.

NASA also has given Pluto its due (though it did so before it was declassified as a planet). On January 19, 2006, NASA launched an unmanned probe called New Horizons that is bound for Pluto. After traveling three billion miles, the probe is expected to enter the Pluto system in the summer of 2015. It carries some of the ashes of Tombaugh, who no doubt would have been horrified to learn that his grand discovery has been reduced to a dwarf.

Chapter 3

Government and Politics

14 of the New Deal's Alphabet Agencies

When Franklin Delano Roosevelt took office in 1933, America was in the darkest depths of the Great Depression. But Roosevelt promised a "New Deal"—an America free from economic deprivation—and he kept his word, launching major legislation in his effort to revitalize the American spirit and its fading dream. Between 1933 and 1939 dozens of federal programs, often referred to as the Alphabet Agencies, were created as part of the New Deal. With FDR's focus on "relief, recovery and reform," the legacy of the New Deal is with us to this day. The following are 14 of the most notable Alphabet Agencies.

✳ ✳ ✳ ✳

1. CCC (Civilian Conservation Corps)

The CCC was created in 1933 and lasted for ten years. Its function was the conservation of resources, which it achieved by hiring more than 2.5 million young men to work on environmental projects such as planting trees, building roads and parks, and fighting soil erosion on federal lands. These men earned $30 per month and contributed to many of the outdoor recreation areas that exist today, including the Blue Ridge Highway. Between 1934 and 1937, this program also funded similar programs for 8,500 women.

2. CWA (Civil Works Administration)

This agency, created in 1933, lasted only one year, but it provided construction jobs for more than four million people who were paid $15 per week to work on schools, roads, and sewers. Some of these jobs were considered frivolous, such as raking leaves. But this program contributed to the morale and self-esteem of millions of displaced people by providing them with steady employment.

3. FDIC (Federal Deposit Insurance Corporation)

During the summer of 1933, the Glass-Steagall Act was passed, setting forth stringent regulations for banks and providing depositors with insurance of up to $5,000 through the newly formed FDIC. The FDIC successfully restored confidence in the nation's banks and encouraged savings because people no longer feared that all their money would be lost in a bank failure.

4. FERA (Federal Emergency Relief Administration)

Established in 1933 by Harry Hopkins, a close advisor to Franklin Roosevelt, this agency was the first of the New Deal's major relief operations. It provided assistance for the unemployed, supporting nearly five million households each month by funding work projects for more than 20 million people. It also provided vaccinations and literacy classes for millions who could not afford them. Both Hopkins and Roosevelt believed in a work ethic based on payment for services and that "earning one's keep" was an important aspect in building the morale and self-esteem of the dole recipients.

5. TVA (Tennessee Valley Authority)

Of all of the reform programs initiated by the Roosevelt administration, the TVA was by far the most ambitious. Created in 1933 for the purpose of developing the Tennessee River watershed, this comprehensive federal agency revitalized the region by building 16 dams to control flooding, generate hydraulic power, and increase agricultural production. This agency also provided jobs, low-cost housing, reforestation, and many other conservation-related services to the region.

6. FCC (Federal Communications Commission)

The Communications Act of 1934 established the FCC as the successor to the Federal Radio Commission. Its function was to merge the administrative responsibilities for regulating broadcasting and wire communications into one centralized agency. Today, this independent, quasi-judicial agency is charged with the regulation of all nonfederal governmental use of radio and television broadcasting and all interstate telecommunications (wire, satellite, and cable), as well as all international communications that originate or terminate in the United States. It is much more powerful today than in the days of its inception, given the incredible growth of the communications industry over the last 70 years.

7. FHA (Federal Housing Administration)

Established in 1934 as part of Roosevelt's recovery campaign, this program focused on stimulating the growth of the building industry. A similar agency, the Home Owners' Loan Corporation (HOLC) was also established. The FHA promised a stable future by providing the funds necessary to construct low-income housing. Today, percentage-wise, more Americans own homes than people in any other country in the world. More than 70 years since its inception, the FHA is the largest insurer of home mortgages in the world.

8. SEC (Securities Exchange Commission)

Established by Congress in 1934 as an independent, nonpartisan regulatory agency, the SEC was created primarily to restore the stability of the stock market after the crash of October 1929 and to prevent corporate abuses relating to the offering and sale of securities. Today, the SEC is responsible for the enforcement and administration of the laws that govern the securities industry. It also serves as a federal watchdog against stock market fraud and insider manipulation on Wall Street and offers publications on investment-related topics for public education.

9. NLRA (National Labor Relations Act)

Also known as the Wagner Act of 1935, this reform legislation created the National Labor Relations Board, whose purpose was to protect the rights of organized labor by legalizing practices such as "closed shops" in which only union members could work and collectively bargain.

10. REA (Rural Electrification Administration)

The purpose of this legislation was to supply electricity to rural communities. Before the onset of the New Deal, only 10 percent of areas outside cities had electricity. Established in 1935, the REA granted low-cost loans to farm cooperatives to bring electric power into their communities. The program was so successful that 98 percent of American farms were equipped with electric power under this initiative.

11. SSA (Social Security Administration)

The original purpose of the SSA, which was established in August 1935 under the Social Security Act, was to administer a national pension fund for retired persons, an unemployment insurance system, and a public assistance program for dependent mothers, children, and the physically disabled. Today, it is the nation's most important and expensive domestic program, covering nearly 49 million Americans and accounting for about 20 percent of the federal budget. However, as the population ages, more and more funds will be needed to keep recipients above the ever-shifting poverty line.

12. WPA (Works Progress Administration)

The WPA, which lasted from 1935 to 1943, was the largest and most comprehensive New Deal agency, affecting every American locality. It employed more than eight million people to build roads and highways, bridges, schools, airports, parks, and other public projects. In total, the WPA built 650,000 miles of roads, 78,000 bridges, 125,000 buildings, and

700 miles of airport runways. Under the arts program, many artists, photographers, writers, and actors became government employees, working on a myriad of public projects ranging from painting murals to writing national park guidebooks.

13. FSA (Farm Security Administration)

This relief organization was originally called the Resettlement Administration Act of 1935. Its purpose was to improve the lot of the poor farmers so poignantly depicted in John Steinbeck's novel The Grapes of Wrath. The FSA established temporary housing for Dust Bowl refugees from Oklahoma and Arkansas who had migrated to California in hopes of finding employment. In total, the FSA loaned more than a billion dollars to farmers and set up many camps for destitute migrant workers.

14. FLSA (Fair Labor Standard Act)

This labor law, enacted in 1938, was the last major piece of New Deal legislation intended to reform the economy, and it is still with us today. This law established the minimum wage, which at the time was twenty-five cents an hour. It also set the standard for the 40-hour work week and banned the use of child labor.

17 People in Line for the Presidency

It's common knowledge that if the president of the United States dies or is removed from office, the vice president takes over. But what happens if the V.P. is unavailable? President Harry Truman signed into law the Presidential Succession Act of 1947, placing the Speaker of the House second in line for the presidency and creating the following order of successors to the White House.

✳ ✳ ✳ ✳

1. Vice President
2. Speaker of the House of Representatives

3. President Pro Tempore of the Senate

4. Secretary of State

5. Secretary of the Treasury

6. Secretary of Defense

7. Attorney General

8. Secretary of the Interior

9. Secretary of Agriculture

10. Secretary of Commerce

11. Secretary of Labor

12. Secretary of Health and Human Services

13. Secretary of Housing and Urban Development

14. Secretary of Transportation

15. Secretary of Energy

16. Secretary of Education

17. Secretary of Veterans Affairs

Heights and Zodiac Signs of 43 Presidents

President	Height	Zodiac Sign
1. George Washington	6' 2"	Pisces
2. John Adams	5' 7"	Scorpio
3. Thomas Jefferson	6' 2"	Aries
4. James Madison	5' 4"	Pisces
5. James Monroe	6' 0"	Taurus
6. John Quincy Adams	5' 7"	Cancer

7.	Andrew Jackson	6' 1"	Pisces
8.	Martin Van Buren	5' 6"	Sagittarius
9.	William Henry Harrison	5' 8"	Aquarius
10.	John Tyler	6' 0"	Aries
11.	James Polk	5' 8"	Scorpio
12.	Zachary Taylor	5' 8"	Sagittarius
13.	Millard Fillmore	5' 9"	Capricorn
14.	Franklin Pierce	5' 10"	Sagittarius
15.	James Buchanan	6' 0"	Taurus
16.	Abraham Lincoln	6' 4"	Aquarius
17.	Andrew Johnson	5' 10"	Capricorn
18.	Ulysses S. Grant	5' 8"	Taurus
19.	Rutherford B. Hayes	5' 8"	Libra
20.	James Garfield	6' 0"	Scorpio
21.	Chester Arthur	6' 2"	Libra
22.	Grover Cleveland	5' 11"	Pisces
23.	Benjamin Harrison	5' 6"	Leo
24.	William McKinley	5' 7"	Aquarius
25.	Theodore Roosevelt	5' 10"	Scorpio
26.	William Howard Taft	6' 0"	Virgo
27.	Woodrow Wilson	5' 11"	Capricorn
28.	Warren Harding	6' 0"	Scorpio
29.	Calvin Coolidge	5' 10"	Cancer
30.	Herbert Hoover	5' 11"	Leo

31.	Franklin Delano Roosevelt	6' 2"	Aquarius
32.	Harry Truman	5' 9"	Taurus
33.	Dwight Eisenhower	5' 10"	Libra
34.	John F. Kennedy	6' 0"	Gemini
35.	Lyndon B. Johnson	6' 3"	Virgo
36.	Richard M. Nixon	5' 11"	Capricorn
37.	Gerald Ford	6' 0"	Cancer
38.	Jimmy Carter	5' 9"	Libra
39.	Ronald Reagan	6' 1"	Aquarius
40.	George H. W. Bush	6' 2"	Gemini
41.	Bill Clinton	6' 2"	Leo
42.	George W. Bush	5' 11"	Cancer
43.	Barack Obama	6' 1"	Leo

30 Countries and Their Currency

1. Algeria   Algerian dinar (DZD)
2. Argentina   Argentine peso (ARS)
3. Brazil   real (BRL)
4. Bulgaria   lev (BGL)
5. Chile   Chilean peso (CLP)
6. China   renminbi (yuan) (CNY)
7. Denmark   Danish krone (DKK)
8. Ecuador   U.S. dollar (USD)
9. Guatemala   quetzal (GTQ), U.S. dollar (USD)

10.	Hungary	forint (HUF)
11.	Indonesia	Indonesian rupiah (IDR)
12.	Iran	Iranian rial (IRR)
13.	Iraq	new Iraqi dinar (NID)
14.	Japan	yen (JPY)
15.	Nigeria	naira (NGN)
16.	Panama	balboa (PAB); U.S. dollar (USD)
17.	Peru	nuevo sol (PEN)
18.	Poland	zloty (PLN)
19.	Romania	new leu (RON)
20.	Russia	Russian ruble (RUR)
21.	Slovakia	Slovak koruna (SKK)
22.	South Africa	rand (ZAR)
23.	South Korea	South Korean won (KRW)
24.	Switzerland	Swiss franc (CHF)
25.	Thailand	baht (THB)
26.	Turkey	Turkish lira (YTL)
27.	Uganda	Ugandan shilling (UGX)
28.	United Kingdom	British pound (GBP)
29.	Venezuela	bolivar (VEB)
30.	Vietnam	dong (VND)

6 Political Scandals

Political scandals in the United States have been around since the birth of the nation and don't show any signs of going away, much to the satisfaction of late-night comedians and talk show hosts. Who needs soap operas when real life in Washington is so scandalous? Check out these infamous political scandals.

✳   ✳   ✳   ✳

1. Teapot Dome Scandal

The Teapot Dome Scandal was the largest of numerous scandals during the presidency of Warren Harding. Teapot Dome is an oil field reserved for emergency use by the U.S. Navy located on public land in Wyoming. Oil companies and politicians claimed the reserves were not necessary and that the oil companies could supply the Navy in the event of shortages. In 1922, Interior Secretary Albert B. Fall accepted $404,000 in illegal gifts from oil company executives in return for leasing the rights to the oil at Teapot Dome to Mammoth Oil without asking for competitive bids. The leases were legal but the gifts were not. Fall's attempts to keep the gifts secret failed, and, on April 14, 1922, The Wall Street Journal exposed the bribes. Fall denied the charges, but an investigation revealed a $100,000 no-interest loan in return for leases that Fall had forgotten to cover up. In 1927, the Supreme Court ruled that the oil leases had been illegally obtained, and the U.S. Navy regained control of Teapot Dome and other reserves. Fall was found guilty of bribery in 1929, fined $100,000, and sentenced to one year in prison. He was the first cabinet member imprisoned for his actions while in office. President Harding was not aware of the scandal at the time of his death in 1923, but it contributed to his administration being considered one of the most corrupt in history.

2. Chappaquiddick

Since being elected to the Senate in 1962, Edward M. "Ted" Kennedy has been known as a liberal who champions causes such as education and health care, but he has had less success in his personal life. On July 18, 1969, Kennedy attended a party on Chappaquiddick Island in Massachusetts. He left the party with 29-year-old Mary Jo Kopechne, who had campaigned for Ted's late brother Robert. Soon after the two left the party, Kennedy's car veered off a bridge and Kopechne drowned. An experienced swimmer, Kennedy said he tried to rescue her but the tide was too strong. He swam to shore, went back to the party, and returned with two other men. Their rescue efforts also failed, but Kennedy waited until the next day to report the accident, calling his lawyer and Kopechne's parents first, claiming the crash had dazed him. There was speculation that he tried to cover up that he was driving under the influence, but nothing was ever proven. Kennedy pleaded guilty to leaving the scene of an accident, received a two-month suspended jail sentence, and lost his driver's license for a year. The scandal may have contributed to his failed presidential bid in 1980, but it didn't hurt his reputation in the Senate. In April 2006, *Time* magazine named him one of "America's 10 Best Senators."

3. Watergate

Watergate is the name of the scandal that caused Richard Nixon to become the only U.S. president to resign from office. On May 27, 1972, concerned that Nixon's bid for reelection was in jeopardy, former CIA agent E. Howard Hunt, Jr., former New York assistant district attorney G. Gordon Liddy, former CIA operative James W. McCord, Jr., and six other men broke into the Democratic headquarters in the Watergate Hotel in Washington, D.C. They wiretapped phones, stole some documents, and photographed others. When they broke in again on June 17 to fix a bug that wasn't working, a suspicious security guard called the Washington police, who arrested McCord and four other burglars.

A cover-up began to destroy incriminating evidence, obstruct investigations, and halt any spread of scandal that might lead to the president. On August 29, Nixon announced that the break-in had been investigated and that no one in the White House was involved. Despite his efforts to hide his involvement, Nixon was done in by his own tape recordings, one of which revealed that he had authorized hush money paid to Hunt. To avoid impeachment, Nixon resigned on August 9, 1974. His successor, President Gerald Ford, granted him a blanket pardon on September 8, 1974, eliminating any possibility that Nixon would be indicted and tried. *Washington Post* reporters Bob Woodward and Carl Bernstein helped expose the scandal using information leaked by someone identified as Deep Throat, a source whose identity was kept hidden until 2005, when it was revealed that Deep Throat was former Nixon administration member William Mark Felt.

4. Wilbur Mills

During the Great Depression, Wilbur Mills served as a county judge in Arkansas and initiated government-funded programs to pay medical and prescription drug bills for the poor. Mills was elected to the House of Representatives in 1939 and served until 1977, with 18 of those years as head of the Ways and Means Committee. In the 1960s, Mills played an integral role in the creation of the Medicare program, and he made an unsuccessful bid for president in the 1972 primary. Unfortunately for Mills, he's best known for one of Washington's juiciest scandals. On October 7, 1974, Mills' car was stopped by police in West Potomac Park near the Jefferson Memorial. Mills was drunk and in the back seat of the car with an Argentine stripper named Fanne Foxe. When the police approached, Foxe fled the car. Mills checked into an alcohol treatment center and was reelected to Congress in November 1974. But just one month later, Mills was seen drunk onstage with Fanne Foxe. Following the incident, Mills was forced to resign as chairman of the Ways and Means Committee and did not run for reelection in 1976. Mills died in 1992, and despite the scandal, several schools and highways in Arkansas are named for him.

5. The Iran-Contra Affair

On July 8, 1985, President Ronald Reagan told the American Bar Association that Iran was part of a "confederation of terrorist states." He failed to mention that members of his administration were secretly planning to sell weapons to Iran to facilitate the release of U.S. hostages held in Lebanon by pro-Iranian terrorist groups. Profits from the arms sales were secretly sent to Nicaragua to aid rebel forces, known as the contras, in their attempt to overthrow the country's democrat-ically-elected government. The incident became known as the Iran-Contra Affair and was the biggest scandal of Reagan's administration. The weapons sale to Iran was authorized by Robert McFarlane, head of the National Security Council (NSC), in violation of U.S. government policies regarding terrorists and military aid to Iran. NSC staff member Oliver North arranged for a portion of the $48 million paid by Iran to be sent to the contras, which violated a 1984 law banning this type of aid. North and his secretary Fawn Hall also shredded critical documents. President Reagan repeatedly denied rumors that the United States had exchanged arms for hostages, but later stated that he'd been misinformed. He created a Special Review Board to investigate. In February 1987, the board found the president not guilty. Others involved were found guilty but either had their sentences overturned on appeal or were later pardoned by George H. W. Bush.

6. The Keating Five

After the banking industry was deregulated in the 1980s, sav-ings and loan banks were allowed to invest deposits in commer-cial real estate, not just residential. Many savings banks began making risky investments, and the Federal Home Loan Bank Board (FHLBB) tried to stop them, against the wishes of the Reagan administration, which was against government interference with business. In 1989, when the Lincoln Savings and Loan Association of Irvine, California, collapsed, its chairman, Charles H. Keating, Jr., accused the FHLBB and its former head Edwin J. Gray of conspiring against him. Gray testified that five senators had asked him to back off on the Lincoln investigation. These senators—Alan Cranston of California, Dennis DeConcini of Arizona, John Glenn of Ohio, Donald Riegle of Michigan, and John McCain of Arizona—became known as the Keating Five after it was revealed that they received a total of $1.3 million in campaign contributions from Keating. While an investigation determined that all five acted improperly, they all claimed this was a standard campaign funding practice. In August 1991, the Senate Ethics Committee recommended censure for Cranston and criticized the other four for "questionable conduct." Cranston had already decided not to run for reelection in 1992. DeConcini and Riegle served out their terms but did not run for reelection in 1994. John Glenn was reelected in 1992 and served until he retired in 1999. John McCain continues his work in the Senate.

9 Political Slips of the Tongue

Presidents and other politicians have a lot to say and not much time to say it; in their haste, the message often gets lost on its way from the brain to the mouth and comes out in funny, embarrassing, and memorable quotes. Here are some favorites.

✳ ✳ ✳ ✳

1. **Ronald Reagan:** As president, Reagan sometimes veered from his carefully written speeches with disastrous results. In 1988, when trying to quote John Adams, who said, "Facts are stubborn things," Reagan slipped and said, "Facts are stupid things." Not known as an environmentalist, Reagan said in 1966, "A tree is a tree. How many more do you have to look at?" His most famous blooper came during a microphone test before a 1984 radio address when he

remarked, "My fellow Americans, I am pleased to tell you I just signed legislation which outlaws Russia forever. The bombing begins in five minutes."

2. **Al Gore:** Al Gore served as vice president under Bill Clinton from 1993 to 2001. During the 1992 campaign, he asked voters skeptical of change to remember that every Communist government in Eastern Europe had fallen within 100 days, followed by, "Now it's our turn here in the United States of America." Gore has often been incorrectly quoted as saying that he invented the Internet, but his actual comment in 1999 was, "During my service in the United States Congress, I took the initiative in creating the Internet."

3. **Richard Nixon:** Richard M. Nixon was the 37th president of the United States, serving from 1969 to 1974. He is the only U.S. president to have resigned from office. Famous for telling reporters, "I am not a crook," Nixon once gave this advice to a political associate, "You don't know how to lie. If you can't lie, you'll never go anywhere." Nixon couldn't cover up Watergate and he couldn't cover up bloopers like that either.

4. **Richard J. Daley:** Mayor Richard J. Daley served as the undisputed leader of Chicago during the turbulent 1960s. The Democratic National Convention was held in Chicago in August 1968, but with the nation divided by the Vietnam War and the assassinations of Martin Luther King, Jr., and Robert F. Kennedy fueling animosity, the city became a battleground for antiwar protests, which Americans witnessed on national television. When confrontations between protesters and police turned violent, Daley's blooper comment reflected the opinion of many people: "The police are not here to create disorder, they're here to preserve disorder."

5. **Texas House Speaker Gib Lewis:** A true slow-talkin' Texan, many of Texas House Speaker Gib Lewis's famous bloopers may have influenced his colleague, future president George W. Bush. While closing a congressional session, Lewis's real feelings about his peers slipped out when he said, "I want to thank each and every one of you for having extinguished yourselves this session." He tried to explain his problems once by saying, "There's a lot of uncertainty that's not clear in my mind." He could have been describing his jumbled reign as Texas speaker when he commented, "This is unparalyzed in the state's history."

6. **Dan Quayle:** Before President George W. Bush took over the title, Dan Quayle was the reigning king of malaprops. Serving one term as vice president from 1989 to 1993, Quayle's slips of the tongue made him an easy but well-deserved target for late-night talk shows. His most famous blunder came in 1992 when, at an elementary school spelling bee in New Jersey, he corrected student William Figueroa's correct spelling of potato as p-o-t-a-t-o-e. Quayle didn't really help the campaign for reelection when, at a stop in California, he said, "This president is going to lead us out of this recovery."

7. **Spiro Agnew:** Spiro Theodore Agnew served as vice president from 1969 to 1973 under President Nixon, before resigning following evidence of tax evasion. This slip expressed his true feelings on this matter, "I apologize for lying to you. I promise I won't deceive you except in matters of this sort." Agnew also didn't endear himself to poor people in 1968 when he commented, "To some extent, if you've seen one city slum, you've seen them all."

8. **George W. Bush:** Reflecting about growing up in Midland, Texas, President George W. Bush said in a 1994 interview, "It was just inebriating what Midland was all about then." Back in those days, Dubya was known to be a heavy

drinker, so misspeaking the word invigorating was a real Freudian slip. During his time in the White House, the junior Bush has had enough malaprops to give a centipede a serious case of foot-in-the-mouth syndrome.

9. **George H. W. Bush:** With Dan Quayle as his vice president, the bloopers of President George H. W. Bush sometimes got overshadowed, but he still managed some zingers. While campaigning in 1988, he described serving as Ronald Reagan's vice president this way, "For seven and a half years I've worked alongside President Reagan. We've had triumphs. Made some mistakes. We've had some sex ... uh ... setbacks." When it comes to presidents 41 and 43, you could say that the slip doesn't fall far from the tongue.

A Few Facts About the Statue of Liberty

✳   ✳   ✳   ✳

✳ The statue's real name is "Liberty Enlightening the World."

✳ Lady Liberty was sculpted by Frédéric Auguste Bartholdi; Alexandre Gustave Eiffel was the structural engineer.

✳ The statue was completed in Paris in June 1884, given to the American people on July 4, 1884, and reassembled and dedicated in the United States on October 28, 1886.

✳ The model for the face of the statue is reputed to be the sculptor's mother, Charlotte Bartholdi.

✳ There are 25 windows and 7 spikes in Lady Liberty's crown. The spikes are said to symbolize the seven seas.

✳ The inscription on the statue's tablet reads: July 4, 1776 (in Roman numerals).

✳ More than four million people visit the Statue of Liberty each year.

* Lady Liberty is 152 feet 2 inches tall from base to torch and 305 feet 1 inch tall from the ground to the tip of her torch.

* The statue's hand is 16 feet 5 inches long, and her index finger is 8 feet long. Her fingernails are 13 inches long by 10 inches wide and weigh approximately 3.5 pounds each.

* Lady Liberty's eyes are each 2 feet 6 inches across, she has a 35-foot waistline, and she weighs about 450,000 pounds (225 tons).

* Lady Liberty's sandals are 25 feet long, making her shoe size 879.

* There are 192 steps from the ground to the top of the pedestal and 354 steps from the pedestal to the crown.

* The Statue of Liberty functioned as an actual lighthouse from 1886 to 1902 and could be seen 24 miles away.

* Until September 11, 2001, the statue was open to the public. Visitors were able to climb the winding staircase inside the statue to the top of her crown for a spectacular view of New York Harbor.

Five Reasons People Think Nixon Was a Great President

Believe it or not, Nixon was once very popular. In his 1972 reelection bid, he carried 49 states and 60.7 percent of the popular vote—one of the widest margins in history. And his greatest hits are nothing to sneeze at either.

* * * *

1. China

In the 1940s, Nixon made his political mark as an anticommunist crusader. So, it surprised many when he became the first U.S. president to go to China—after years of hostility between the nations—in February 1972. Nixon met with Chinese Premier Chou En-lai and Communist Party Chairman Mao Zedong, laying the groundwork for the establishment of full diplomatic relations with China in 1979.

2. Détente

Only three months after his visit to China, Nixon accepted Soviet Premier Leonid Brezhnev's invitation to meet in Russia. During the visit, Nixon and Brezhnev signed the Strategic Arms Limitation Treaty and the Anti-Ballistic Missile Treaty. This ushered in a period of reduced Cold War tensions called *détente*, which lasted until the early 1980s.

3. Ecology

Nixon had a spotty environmental record, but he did establish the Environmental Protection Agency in 1970. He also signed the Marine Mammal Protection Act in 1972, the Endangered Species Act in 1973, the Safe Drinking Water Act in 1974, and enacted amendments to the Clean Air Act in 1970 that set the course for curbing auto emissions.

4. OSHA

In 1970, Nixon established the Occupational Safety and Health Administration, a government agency dedicated to making workers safer.

5. School Desegregation

In 1970, Nixon committed to enforcing the Supreme Court's 1954 ruling against school segregation. His landmark discussions with leaders from seven holdout Southern states led to peaceful integration of the last segregated schools.

Five Reasons People Think Nixon Was a Crummy President

✳   ✳   ✳   ✳

Nixon claims the dubious honor of being the only U.S. president to resign from office. Before his hasty exit, his approval rating plummeted to a dismal 23 percent. Here's why:

1. Watergate

On June 17, 1972, five men were caught breaking into Democratic Party offices at The Watergate complex. They were there to bug phones and photograph private documents to help Nixon win reelection. Damning testimony and Nixon's own recordings of Oval Office conversations implicated the president in a cover-up conspiracy. Nixon resigned before he could be impeached.

2. Vietnam

In his 1968 campaign, Nixon promised to end the war. Yet, during his first term, he expanded U.S. combat operations into neighboring Cambodia, which had long been neutral, and authorized secret bombings there.

3. The Economy

When Nixon took office, unemployment was at 3.3 percent. It rose to 9 percent in 1975, in the aftermath of his presidency. Inflation jumped from 5 percent to 12.1 percent while he was in office. The economy saw an upturn just before the 1972 election, but by the time Nixon left office, the nation was in a recession.

4. The Plumbers

Before Watergate, Nixon assembled a Special Investigation Unit (SIU)—better known as "The Plumbers"—to stop White House leaks. The SIU specialized in illegal capers, including breaking into Daniel Ellsberg's psychiatrist's office to dig up dirt after Ellsberg released classified Vietnam documents.

5. His Big Mouth

Because of the Watergate investigation, Nixon was forced to hand over around 3,700 hours of Oval Office recordings. The recordings released to the public painted Nixon as devious, anti-Semitic, paranoid, and exceptionally foul-mouthed.

You Can't Take Down a Bull Moose

✳   ✳   ✳   ✳

During a 1912 Milwaukee political speech, Teddy Roosevelt took a lickin' (or rather, a bullet) but kept on tickin'.

A Four-Way Race

AMERICAN POLITICS WERE in a state of chaos during the presidential election season of 1912. Ex-President Theodore Roosevelt had broken with the Republicans and established the Progressive Party, which then nominated the "Bull Moose" himself as its candidate. Incumbent President (and Republican) William Howard Taft was running for a second term, Woodrow Wilson waged a high-minded campaign on behalf of the Democrats, and Eugene Debs was running as a Socialist. Roosevelt needed every vote in this contentious four-way race. In particular, he needed to win over Progressives allied with Wisconsin senator Bob LaFollette, who had expected to receive the Progressive party's nomination and was increasingly critical of Roosevelt. To this end, Roosevelt included Milwaukee at the end of an extensive speaking tour.

Milwaukee Turns Deadly

On the evening of October 14, a large crowd gathered to see the Bull Moose leave from his Milwaukee hotel for a speech at the auditorium. Roosevelt stepped into a waiting car where Henry F. Cochems, Chairman of the National Speakers' Bureau of the Progressive party, was seated. As Roosevelt stood waving to the crowd from the open car, John Schrank, a New York City saloonkeeper who had followed Roosevelt across the country, stepped forward and fired a Colt revolver into Roosevelt's chest.

Roosevelt's stenographer leapt upon the shooter. The Bull Moose's knees buckled at first, but he straightened and raised his hat to the crowd. Roosevelt barked to a crowd of people looking to do harm to Schrank, "Don't hurt him; bring him to me here!" Schrank, still struggling for possession of the weapon, was dragged to Roosevelt who studied him while Cochems secured the revolver. Later Roosevelt admitted that he had no curiosity concerning Schrank: "His name might be Czolgosz or anything else as far as I'm concerned," he said referring to the assassin who felled President McKinley in 1901 (giving Vice President Roosevelt the presidency). Later, Schrank said he was convinced by a dream that Roosevelt was responsible for McKinley's death, and that he believed no president should be allowed to serve three terms.

Saved by a Speech (and Some Suspenders)

Though he was bleeding steadily from a hole below his right nipple, Roosevelt refused to be taken to the hospital. He could tell that the bullet, slowed first by his heavy overcoat, then his folded 50-page speech, his metal glasses case, and finally his thick suspenders, had not penetrated his lung. At the auditorium, in front of a crowd of 9,000–12,000 people, Roosevelt's first words were: "Ladies and gentlemen, I don't know whether you fully understand that I have just been shot; but it takes more than that to kill a Bull Moose." Someone yelled, "Fake!" but Roosevelt smiled and opened his vest to reveal his blood-stained shirt. The room went silent.

Roosevelt vs. LaFollette

Instead of collapsing, Roosevelt spoke for 90 minutes. When aides tried to cut short his speech, he quipped: "I am all right and you cannot escape listening to the speech either." When a woman near the stage said, "Mr. Roosevelt, we all wish you would be seated;" the candidate quickly replied: "I thank you, madam, but I don't mind it a bit." LaFollette supporters yelled protests at each mention of their beloved senator's name, but Roosevelt ignored their outbursts.

After speaking, Roosevelt was rushed to the hospital where exploratory surgery revealed that the bullet was inoperable. Roosevelt later admitted that he never believed the wound fatal. "Anyway... if I had to die," he laughed, "I thought I'd rather die with my boots on." During his weeklong hospital recovery, both Wilson and Taft suspended their campaigns.

Still, Schrank got his wish in the end: Although Roosevelt's Milwaukee speech was sensational, it failed to impress the LaFollette Progressives who voted overwhelmingly against Roosevelt, denying him the third term.

Edward Hyde: Cross-dresser or Double-crossed?

Edward Hyde, Viscount Cornbury, Third Earl of Clarendon, was governor of New York and New Jersey from 1701 to 1708, yet his legacy is one that politicians wouldn't want to touch with a ten-foot pole. Aside from doing a generally terrible job, rumors of Hyde's cross-dressing ways landed him a sullied spot in the annals of political history.

✳ ✳ ✳ ✳

Here, Have a Job!

A S THE STORY goes, being of noble English lineage, Edward Hyde was able to buy an officer's commission in the British army. While in that position, he helped overthrow his commander (and uncle), King James II. The king who replaced James was William III, who was quite pleased with Hyde's assistance in getting him the throne, so in 1701, William made Hyde governor of New York as a way of saying thanks. Later,

William's successor (and Hyde's first cousin), Queen Anne, also threw in the governorship of New Jersey for Hyde. Suddenly, a woefully underqualified guy from England was in charge of two of the most prominent colonies in the New World.

Corruption, Colonial Style

When Hyde arrived in New York in 1703 to assume his new post, he didn't make a very good impression with the struggling, toiling colonists. His luxurious house was filled with sumptuous linens, curtains, silverware, furniture, and art. To make matters worse, he soon found it necessary to divert public defense funds toward his new country house on what was then christened "Governor's Island."

It didn't take long for the bribery to start. At first, Hyde reportedly turned down a bribe from a New Jersey proprietor, but it appears he only passed because the bribe wasn't big enough. The man, hoping to get preferential treatment of some kind, then upped the ante. Hyde accepted the bribe the second time around and did the businessman's bidding.

Soon, a group of the governor's favorites controlled tax and rent collections across the area. The bribes were constant, and the governor sank deeper and deeper into corruption. He was described at one point as "a spendthrift, a grafter, a bigoted oppressor and a drunken vain fool."

By 1707, a desperate New Jersey assembly wrote to Queen Anne to ask her to take Hyde back to Britain. One assembly member, Lewis Morris, made a list of Hyde's crimes and added a juicy bit: He claimed the corrupt governor was fond of dressing in women's clothing. That little item of gossip didn't sit well with the queen, and Hyde lost his job. What isn't often mentioned is that Hyde, thrown into disgrace (and into debtor's prison) for some time, actually rallied later in life and held office in England where he became a respected diplomat of the Privy Council.

Right This Way, Mrs. Hyde?

The question remains whether Hyde really was a cross-dresser or just the victim of a rumor drummed up by his enemies to help push him out of office. One story tells of Hyde costumed as Queen Anne in order to show deference and respect—but could that really be true?

According to certain historians, there is no hard evidence that Hyde was fond of wearing dresses. Only four contemporary letters contain any information pertaining to his cross-dressing, and they don't include eyewitness accounts. Experts maintain that if the governor of New York and New Jersey really did don full petticoats and silk taffeta, it would have been plastered across every newspaper in the Western Hemisphere—people in the 18th century loved a scandal as much as people do now.

Still, the rumors persisted for years and stories of his behavior grew—there is even a period portrait of a scruffy man in women's clothing that is said to be Hyde. Yet, art historians say there's no proof that the painting is of anyone other than an unfortunate-looking young woman.

Trashing the White House

When did democracy come to America? Many historians say that winning the American War of Independence introduced democracy to the country. Others, however, may point to an incident that occurred during the inauguration of Andrew Jackson as the true birth of democracy: the trashing of the White House.

✳ ✳ ✳ ✳

Man of the People

As simply put by the government's own Web site, Andrew Jackson "More nearly than any of his predecessors . . . was elected by popular vote; as President he sought to act as the direct representative of the common man."

Jackson was a popular figure and a war hero. In 1824, he was one of four candidates who sought the presidency. He won the most popular votes, but because no candidate won a majority of Electoral votes, the election went into the House of Representatives. There, presidential candidate Henry Clay threw his support to fellow contender John Quincy Adams, supposedly in return for a promise to be named Secretary of State. Adams became president and did indeed name Clay his Secretary of State. This "corrupt bargain" infuriated Jackson and his supporters, who campaigned vigorously against it for four years. In 1828, they were rewarded when Jackson overwhelmed Adams in a rematch to become the seventh President of the United States.

On March 4, 1829, Jackson was inaugurated president. A crowd of 15,000–20,000 people swarmed around the Capitol building and the surrounding streets to see and hear their hero take the oath of office. After he did, the enthusiastic crowd burst through a chain holding them back and mobbed around Jackson, congratulating him. Jackson was barely able to get away, and he was spirited into the building.

King Mob

Jackson exited from the Capitol and mounted a white horse for the trip to the White House, where a public reception had been planned. "As far as the eye could reach," said an onlooker, "the side-walks of the Avenue were covered with people on foot, and the centre with innumerable carriages and persons on horse-back." This massive throng—country boys, dandies, ladies and gentlemen of all races—moved en masse with Jackson to the White House. The Man of the People had won the election, and the people intended to celebrate.

When Jackson arrived at the Executive Mansion, its lower floor was filled with a teeming mass of humanity from all classes and walks of life. "I never saw such a mixture," said a witness. "The reign of KING MOB seemed triumphant."

Melee!

Waiters opened the White House doors to bring barrels of orange punch outside. Bad move. The crowd rushed forward and plowed into the waiters like a flying wedge in football. Waiters, glasses, pails of liquor, and guests collided, sending people and implements flying.

The free-for-all was underway. Men in muddy boots tramped onto satin-covered chairs to get a better look at Jackson. People surged into the building through the doors or leaped in through open ground-floor windows. Expensive china and glasses were broken and the pieces crushed underfoot. The mob flowed throughout the White House, unrestrained and unfettered. One senator called it a "regular Saturnalia."

"Ladies fainted, men were seen with bloody noses," said one stunned participant. "A rabble scrambling, fighting, romping…" Most folks could only escape by jumping back out of the windows.

Everyone wanted a piece of Jackson, the opportunity to shake his hand, touch his sleeve, congratulate him, or shout words of encouragement. Eventually Jackson, who was still in mourning because of the recent death of his wife, became exhausted and was taken away by several aides. The crowd only left the White House when punch tubs were placed on the lawn.

Amidst the confusion, a small girl disappeared. Her parents later found her jumping up and down on a sofa in Jackson's private quarters. "Just think, mama!" she yelled. "This sofa is a millionth part mine!"

Ah, democracy.

Leaders Who Shaped Canadian Destiny

Canadian history would be a subtopic of U.S. history but for key turns of the national steering wheel by determined Canadians. Of course, not all leadership is political (or even lawful). Here are some Canadian leaders—or outside leaders embraced by Canadians—who shaped Canada in interesting ways.

✳   ✳   ✳   ✳

Air Marshal William "Billy" Bishop (1894–1956): When he flunked his first year at the Royal Military College, no one would have predicted a bright future for Cadet Bishop. Leaving the cavalry to join Britain's Royal Flying Corps, he became the second-highest-scoring Allied ace of World War I—and the highest-scoring Commonwealth ace, a fact no Canadian or Briton could ignore.

Major General Sir Isaac Brock (1769–1812): Without "the Hero of Upper Canada," it might be "Ontario, the Hudson Bay State." General Brock gets the primary credit for beating back the U.S. invasion of Upper Canada (today, Ontario) during the War of 1812. He also won his enemies' respect. He died doing his duty, and the British fired 21 guns in salute at his funeral. The nearby U.S. garrison at Fort Niagara, though a wartime enemy, fired a similar salute to General Brock that same day.

The Right Honourable Avril P. D. "Kim" Campbell (1947–): This Vancouver Island native smashed the ice ceiling, becoming Canada's first woman prime minister in 1993. Unfortunately for Campbell, her predecessor, Brian Mulroney, had poisoned the party's well in the public mind; she couldn't manage to shake that legacy. Though few characterize her brief administration as a success, she went where no Canadian woman had gone before.

Samuel de Champlain (c.1567–1635): This Frenchman founded the city of Quebec, and with it the colony of New

France (later Lower Canada, still later the Province de Quebec). He did have one rough spot, siding with the Hurons against the Iroquois (thus authoring 150 years of lousy Franco-Iroquois relations), but de Champlain is still the father of French Canada—arguably, of Canada itself.

Lieutenant General Sir Arthur Currie (1875–1933): Considered by many to be Canada's greatest military man, he became its first general—and a strong advocate for keeping Canadian troops together in the World War I trenches rather than dispersing them around the front. As the commander responsible for the defining Canadian victory at Vimy Ridge in 1917, he ensured that friendly and enemy nations alike wouldn't take Canadian valor lightly.

Lieutenant General Roméo Dallaire (1946–): Dallaire was in command of the United Nations Observer Mission in Rwanda. As the 1994 genocide unfolded, he was the voice in the wilderness: First he tried to alert the United Nations to the magnitude of the problem, then attempted to halt it himself in defiance of orders. His moral courage embodied the best of Canada's national commitment to peacekeeping.

Sir Sandford Fleming (1827–1915): As railways shot across the western United States, this Scottish visionary realized that Canada must either have its own transcontinental railway or start drafting a petition for statehood. He helped with nearly every aspect of the project and was present when the last spike was driven to finish the job in British Columbia (1885). He also devised the 24-zone global time system we use today.

Elijah Harper (1949–): In his view, the painfully negotiated Meech Lake Accord (1990) disregarded First Nations rights. A Cree from Manitoba, Harper rejected it in style—by standing up with an eagle feather in his hand and leading the filibuster that prevented Meech Lake's ratification. This stubborn stand may have annoyed some people, but it got Canada's undivided attention.

Sir Wilfrid Laurier (1841–1919): A Quebecois farmer's son, this gifted lawyer became Canada's first Francophone prime minister, and he helped create the Royal Canadian Navy. His passion for Canadian unity made his position difficult—the French/English divide in Canada predated him by well over a century—but his persuasive ability bridged that canyon as well as any Canadian could.

René Lévesque (1922–1987): While French Canadians have often struggled to preserve their distinct society and its language, Lévesque took it to the next level. He was the first premier of Quebec to mount a credible bid for Quebecois independence. It didn't happen, but the national dialogue continues to this day.

Sir John A. Macdonald (1815–1891): When the British North America Act created the Dominion of Canada on July 1, 1867, Canadians elected a Parliament with Macdonald as the first prime minister. Sir John laid the foundations for the modern Canadian state.

William L. Mackenzie King (1874–1950): Though not always popular in or after his time, this Liberal Party stalwart established Canada's independence in foreign policy. He also invented the Canadian. That's no misprint: Until a resolution introduced by Mackenzie King's government in 1946, Canadians were technically British nationals. Fittingly, Mackenzie King received the first-ever certificate of Canadian citizenship.

Agnes C. Macphail (1890–1954): This rural Ontario schoolteacher and penal reformer—the first woman elected to Federal Parliament—would be reelected four times. As her funeral procession struggled through the snow and wind to her final rest, an old farmer gave a eulogy she might have liked: "She came in on a Grey County storm and she's bloody well going out on one."

Nellie L. McClung (1873–1951): Although this Western activist believed that women were people (as opposed to what, one might wonder), Canada's founding British North America Act wasn't specific on the matter. This made it awkward for Canadian women in politics, because most people prefer to be governed by other people. McClung's petition in 1927 began a process that led to equality (and personhood) under law for Canadian women.

Louis Riel (1844–1885): The cultural hero of Canada's Metis (mixed French and First Peoples culture), Riel was part prophet, part visionary, and part revolutionary. From the Metis perspective, he ended a martyr when authorities strung him up for his role in the failed Northwest Rebellion. His memory is a central rally point for modern Metis pride.

Jeanne Sauvé (1922–1993): In Canada's parliamentary monarchy, the governor-general represents the Crown and exercises its powers (for example, the Royal Assent to a bill of law). Sauvé was doubly important: first female governor-general (1984) and first woman speaker of the House of Commons. This also marked the first time a reigning queen had a governor-general of her own gender.

Joey Smallwood (1900–1991): Newfoundland remained a British Dominion through World War II. Smallwood, a charismatic, forceful "Newfie," was the tugboat pushing his seafaring homeland into Canada (1949). He retired from politics in 1972 as the only premier Newfoundland had ever known. Never mind his somewhat overbearing style; anyone who brings a province into Confederation is by definition an influential Canadian leader.

Superintendent and Major General Sir Samuel Steele (1849–1919): Steele's most enduring contribution to Canada was police work. During the gold rush, the Northwest Mounted Police under Superintendent Steele was the law in Yukon Territory. American gold-seekers pouring through Soapy Smith's private thieving preserve of Skagway (Alaska) were shocked to reach the border and find NWMP constables enforcing law.

Chief and Brigadier General Tecumseh (1768–1813):
Shawnee chief, orator, and general. In his effort to protect and establish free Native American territory, he allied his warriors with General Sir Issac Brock's British and Canadians in the War of 1812 and helped capture Detroit. Though a rebel from the United States' standpoint, Tecumseh is honored by Canadians as a brave, capable ally who gave his life defending Canada from U.S. invasion.

Presidentially Speaking

"About the time we think we can make ends meet, somebody moves the ends."

—HERBERT HOOVER

"A radical is a man with both feet firmly planted in the air."

—FRANKLIN DELANO ROOSEVELT

"Do you realize the responsibility I carry? I'm the only person standing between Richard Nixon and the White House."

—JOHN F. KENNEDY

"If one morning I walked on top of the water across the Potomac River, the headline that afternoon would read: 'President Can't Swim.'"

—LYNDON BAINES JOHNSON

"An atheist is a man who watches a Notre Dame–Southern Methodist University game and doesn't care who wins."

—DWIGHT D. EISENHOWER

"There is no pleasure in having nothing to do; the fun is having lots to do and not doing it."

—ANDREW JACKSON

"If you can't convince them, confuse them."

—HARRY TRUMAN

"When a man is asked to make a speech, the first thing he has to decide is what to say."

—GERALD FORD

"Being president is like running a cemetery: You've got a lot of people under you and nobody's listening."

—William Jefferson Clinton

"No matter how much cats fight, there always seem to be plenty of kittens."

—Abraham Lincoln

"Leadership to me means duty, honor, country. It means character, and it means listening from time to time."

—George W. Bush

"Mankind, when left to themselves, are unfit for their own government."

—George Washington

"Free nations are peaceful nations. Free nations don't attack each other. Free nations don't develop weapons of mass destruction."

—George W. Bush

"The fact that my 15 minutes of fame has extended a little longer than 15 minutes is somewhat surprising to me and completely baffling to my wife."

—Barack Obama

"In my many years I have come to a conclusion that one useless man is a shame, two is a law firm, and three or more is a congress."

—John Adams

"When you reach the end of your rope, tie a knot in it and hang on."

—Thomas Jefferson

"The man who reads nothing at all is better educated than the man who reads nothing but newspapers."

—Thomas Jefferson

"I like the job. That's what I'll miss most . . . I'm not sure anybody ever liked this as much as I've liked it."

—William Jefferson Clinton

"Philosophy is common sense with big words."

—James Madison

"Better to remain silent and be thought a fool than to speak out and remove all doubt."

—ABRAHAM LINCOLN

"A little flattery will support a man through great fatigue."

—JAMES MONROE

"As to the presidency, the two happiest days of my life were those of my entrance upon the office and my surrender of it."

—MARTIN VAN BUREN

"All the measures of the Government are directed to the purpose of making the rich richer and the poor poorer."

—WILLIAM HENRY HARRISON

"I'm a Ford, not a Lincoln."

—GERALD R. FORD

"I am not one who—who flamboyantly believes in throwing a lot of words around."

—GEORGE H. W. BUSH

The USPS: The Check Is in the Mail

What is now known as the United States Postal Service was established in 1775 by the Continental Congress, which also appointed Benjamin Franklin the first postmaster general. It was a job with which Franklin had some experience—he worked as postmaster of Philadelphia under the British Parliamentary Post and later as one of two deputy postmasters of North America. (The other was a less famous guy named William Hunter.)

✳ ✳ ✳ ✳

Through Rain and Sleet . . .

There are 32,741 post offices throughout the United States. Combined, they employ 656,000 career employees and manage 221,000 vehicles—the largest civilian fleet in the world. Here's more:

46 million: the number of address changes processed each year

8.5 million: the number of passport applications accepted in 2008

597,000: the average number of postal service money orders issued daily

300: the number of "employee heroes" recognized by the postal service in 2008 for saving the lives of customers on their routes

For Your Protection

* The Postal Inspection Service is one of the oldest federal law enforcement agencies and was the first to offer federal agent careers to women.

* More than 9,000 suspects were arrested in 2008 for crimes involving the mail or for crimes against the postal service.

* Postal inspectors prevented 800,000 fake checks—worth an estimated $2.7 billion—from entering the United States in 2008.

Mail by the Numbers

203 billion: pieces of mail processed in 2008

667 million: the approximate number of mail pieces processed each day

28 million: pieces of mail processed each hour (on average)

463,000: pieces of mail processed each minute (on average)

36.6 million: the number of stamps printed in 2008

1963: the year the Zoning Improvement Plan (ZIP) Code was launched

Neither snow, nor rain, nor heat, nor gloom of night stays these couriers from the swift completion of their appointed rounds."

—THE MOTTO OF THE U.S. POSTAL SERVICE

All Hail the Emperor!

Meet Mr. Joshua Abraham Norton: businessman, citizen of San Francisco, and the first Emperor of the United States of America.

❊ ❊ ❊ ❊

Humble Beginnings

JOSHUA NORTON, AMERICA'S first and only "Emperor," was born in England in 1819. Soon after his birth, Norton and his family relocated to South Africa. When his father died, Norton found he was the recipient of $40,000 from his father's estate.

With inheritence money in pocket, 30-year-old Norton headed to San Francisco in 1849 where he quickly set about amassing a small fortune in real estate. However, a failed attempt to corner the San Francisco rice market left Norton in financial ruin. After declaring bankruptcy in 1858, Norton left the Bay area for a short time.

He returned a year later, but the stress and strain caused by his economic downfall had taken its toll on Norton, who not only lost his money, but also his marbles. No longer having use for the United States and its government, on September 17, 1859, Norton officially proclaimed himself "Emperor of These United States."

The Reign of Emperor Norton I

As the self-proclaimed emperor, Norton quickly (though impotently) moved to dissolve Congress, ordered the U.S. Army to forcibly stop the meeting of said body, and abolished both the Republican and Democratic parties.

Norton also demanded the construction of a bridge spanning the bay to connect San Francisco and Oakland. He was a man of the people, and so the Emperor spent his days tirelessly inspecting the streets of his hometown until his death on January 8, 1880.

On the occasion of his funeral, more than 20,000 of his subjects, "from capitalists to the pauper, the clergyman to the pickpocket, well-dressed ladies and those whose garb and bearing hinted of the social outcast," took to the streets to show their appreciation for their fallen faux leader.

Warren G. Harding

Few presidents have had a reputation such as that of Warren G. Harding, the publisher-turned-politician who, after a landslide presidential victory, wrought havoc upon the United States for two years before dying while in office.

✳   ✳   ✳   ✳

A BUSINESSMAN, FREEMASON, AND consummate Republican, Warren G. Harding was born not far from Marion, Ohio, in 1865. He remained there for much of his adult life, becoming a prominent member of the business community before entering political life in 1898. He served two terms as a state senator and briefly held the post of lieutenant governor before running an unsuccessful gubernatorial campaign. After introducing fellow Ohioan and then–nominee for the presidency William Howard Taft at the 1912 Republican National Convention, Harding, who was by all accounts a captivating but hollow orator, quickly rose to political stardom.

He was elected to the U.S. Senate two years later and by 1920 was campaigning for the White House. Harding became the Republican candidate for president only as the result of a deadlock between the other candidates, but he nevertheless defeated James M. Cox, the Democratic governor of Harding's native Ohio, in a landslide victory with a little more than 60 percent of the popular vote.

The Ohio Gang

Harding's presidency is not usually revered for its policy, which sought to overturn major legislation from the Wilson administration, deregulate large businesses, and limit American involvement in international affairs. Most historians agree that Harding's policies contributed greatly to the economic collapse at the end of the 1920s. Still, Harding performed the ceremonial functions that officially brought World War I to a close, supported both the railroads and domestic agriculture, and created the federal budget. Though he died in the middle of his first term, many of his policy goals were carried out by his successors: Calvin Coolidge, his vice president, and Herbert Hoover, his secretary of commerce.

However destructive they may have been, Harding's failed policies have been largely overshadowed by the magnitude of his administration's corruption, which included fraud, bribery, embezzlement, and drug and alcohol trafficking. The most serious offense was the Teapot Dome scandal, when Secretary of the Interior Albert B. Hall illegally leased government land (the Teapot Dome oil field in Wyoming) to oil companies in exchange for bribes and under-the-table private loans. Hall and other members of the administration—known as the Ohio Gang, though none actually hailed from the Buckeye State— were forced to resign amidst a sea of public outrage; Hall went to prison, and his colleague Jess Smith committed suicide.

And That's Not All

Though the Teapot Dome affair went on under Harding's watch, many historians question whether he was even aware of the corruption in his cabinet. The only offense attributed directly to Harding is his rumored alcoholism. Despite his unwavering support for Prohibition, Harding was, by all accounts, a drunkard, regularly consuming contraband liquor in the White House even when it was against federal law to do so. For good measure, he was also accused of fathering a child out of wedlock with a fawning admirer from Marion named Nan Britton. Britton made the accusations public when she published a lurid account of their supposed relationship, *The President's Daughter*, in 1927.

Harding died of a heart attack in 1923 after less than two and a half years in office. He is regularly ranked among the worst presidents in U.S. history, both for the rampant corruption in his administration and his support of policies that discouraged regulation and indirectly led to the Great Depression. Perhaps that's why no Ohioan has been elected president since.

Presidentially Speaking

"If this is coffee, please bring me some tea; but if this is tea, please bring me some coffee."

—ABRAHAM LINCOLN

"I can think of nothing more boring for the American people than to have to sit in their living rooms for a whole half hour looking at my face on their television screens."

—DWIGHT D. EISENHOWER

"You know nothing for sure . . . except the fact that you know nothing for sure."

—JOHN F. KENNEDY

"It's a damn poor mind that can only think of one way to spell a word."

—ANDREW JOHNSON

"I only know two tunes. One of them is 'Yankee Doodle,' and the other isn't."

—ULYSSES S. GRANT

"Man cannot live by bread alone; he must have peanut butter."

—JAMES GARFIELD

"Sensible and responsible women do not want to vote. The relative positions to be assumed by man and woman in the working out of our civilization were assigned long ago by a higher intelligence than ours."

—GROVER CLEVELAND

"Always be sincere, even if you don't mean it."

—HARRY TRUMAN

"I am only an average man but, by George, I work harder at it than the average man."

—THEODORE ROOSEVELT

Blessed are the young for they shall inherit the national debt."

—HERBERT HOOVER

"Things may come to those who wait, but only the things left by those who hustle."

—ABRAHAM LINCOLN

"Never kick a fresh turd on a hot day."

—HARRY TRUMAN

"Any man who wants to be president is either an egomaniac or crazy."

—DWIGHT D. EISENHOWER

"My brother Bob doesn't want to be in government—he promised Dad he'd go straight."

—JOHN F. KENNEDY

"We've uncovered some embarrassing ancestors in the not-too-distant past. Some horse thieves and some people killed on Saturday nights. One of my relatives, unfortunately, was even in the newspaper business."

—JIMMY CARTER

"I do not like broccoli. And I haven't liked it since I was a little kid and my mother made me eat it. And I'm president of the United States and I'm not going to eat any more broccoli."

—GEORGE H. W. BUSH

"You can put wings on a pig, but you don't make it an eagle."

—WILLIAM JEFFERSON CLINTON

"It's clearly a budget. It's got a lot of numbers in it."

—GEORGE W. BUSH

"The fact that a man is a newspaper reporter is evidence of some flaw of character."

—LYNDON B. JOHNSON

Fast Facts

✳ Calvin Coolidge liked having his head rubbed with Vaseline at breakfast.

✳ In 1930, Herbert Hoover predicted unemployment would be eliminated within 60 days.

✳ Almost as many Americans fought *for* the British during the American Revolution as fought *against* the British.

✳ In 1828, Philadelphia tried to sell the Liberty Bell for scrap.

✳ Despite popular belief, Confederate President Jefferson Davis was not wearing women's clothing when he was captured at the end of the Civil War.

✳ The first Emancipation Proclamation was not issued by Abraham Lincoln, but by British Royal Governor Lord Dunmore of Virginia in 1775.

✳ In early 1865, the Confederacy told England and France that it was willing to emancipate its slaves in return for recognition as an independent country.

✳ In 1659, the leaders of the Massachusetts Bay colony passed a law against celebrating Christmas.

✳ The Pilgrims first landed at Provincetown, Massachusetts—not Plymouth.

✳ When he died, George Washington had but a single real tooth left in his mouth.

Trudeaumania

Canadians called him PET, but this prime minister could bite.

✳   ✳   ✳   ✳

The Man for All Seasons

PIERRE ELLIOT TRUDEAU, Canada's prime minister during the 1970s, was no rock star, but rock stars might well envy his ability to enthrall a crowd. Prior to his election, the usually reserved country was awash in "Trudeaumania." So much so that his swooning electorate familiarly knew Trudeau by his initials, PET.

A Renaissance man, Trudeau was as quick to quote Plato as paddle a canoe down the Amazon or shepherd legislation through a lupine Parliament. While he had the dashing charisma of former American president John F. Kennedy, he wasn't so easily tied down: Throughout his first campaign for leadership he was an eligible bachelor. When he married in 1971, it was to a 22-year-old beauty he'd met in Tahiti. He was 51.

Trudeau's background included University of Montreal Law School, the Sorbonne, the London School of Economics, and Harvard, all while he used his downtime to wander around the world. He savored life, and let Canadians know it. The nation ate it up, even relishing Trudeau's occasional outbursts of temper. On one occasion, an annoyed Trudeau gave the finger to the entire Opposition party in Parliament. In 1969, he chastised a boy throwing grain at him while he was giving a speech in Saskatchewan: "If you don't stop that, I'll kick you right in the ass."

The End of an Era

Trudeau often showed his fun side, notably during the most solemn of ceremonies. When he did a pirouette behind the back of the Queen of England while she was signing Canada's new Constitution, all but Canada's staunchest royalists and rabid Anglophobes were delighted. PET was their guy, and he served for three terms, formally retiring in June 1984. When his term ended, he opted to whisk himself over the hill in his Mercedes sports car rather than ride in the official black limo.

Kingmaker City

Presidents past and present have tipped their hats to Chicago.

✳   ✳   ✳   ✳

LONG BEFORE HYDE Park resident Barack Obama became the nation's 44th president, Chicago was an important stop on the road for any candidate. Other political hotspots (Alaska, anyone?) may take the limelight, but few places have played a bigger role in electing the nation's chief executives in the past 150 years than Chicago.

A Gracious Host City (for the Most Part)

Chicago has hosted more presidential nominating conventions (14 for Republican, 11 Democrat) than any other American city, and many of these conventions went well beyond the scope of merely nominating a candidate. In 1896, Democratic candidate William Jennings Bryan gave his famously fiery "Cross of Gold" speech in Chicago, whipping the crowd into a frenzy, and in 1968, the nation watched anxiously as protestors and police clashed outside of that year's Democratic convention.

Much of the city's historical attractiveness for political conventions comes from its central location, but right from the start, the city also simply had more space than other locations. The 1860 Republican convention was held in a temporary structure called the Wigwam, a great place for a powwow of 12,000 participants. In 1880, Republicans met in the Interstate Industrial Exposition Building, a huge, barnlike structure on Michigan Avenue at Monroe Street. The Chicago Coliseum at 63rd Street and Stony Island Avenue, was home to the 1896 Democatic convention, and between 1952 and 1968, the 9,000-seat International Amphitheater at 43rd Street and Halsted held no fewer than five conventions.

A Cherished Right

Beyond these gatherings, Chicago is best known for its ability to get out the vote. The expression "Vote early and vote often" is variously attributed to Al Capone, Richard J. Daley, and William Hale "Big Bill" Thompson. Historically, Chicago's citizenry prepared to vote (whether only once or several times a day) by marching in a torchlight parade each Election Eve. No parade was more significant than that of 1960, when Mayor Richard J. Daley accompanied John F. Kennedy and hundreds of thousands of marchers to the Chicago Stadium, where Kennedy spoke to a massive rally. Kennedy's narrow victory over Richard Nixon is often credited to the ability of Mayor Daley to turn out the vote: Kennedy won Cook County by a staggering and somewhat suspicious 450,000 votes.

The Lowest Lows and the Highest Highs

No Chicago political event is as notorious as the 1968 Democratic convention. Fueled by opposition to the Vietnam War, protesters clashed with police in battles beamed around the world by television. So divisive were the events of 1968 that Chicago didn't host another convention until Bill Clinton accepted his reelection bid in the newly constructed United Center in 1996. In between, however, Chicago continued to be a fertile hunting ground for votes.

One of the most memorable moments from the 1968 convention was when Abraham Ribicoff of Connecticut took to the podium to endorse George McGovern of South Dakota. In his speech, Ribicoff was critical of the tactics the Chicago police were using to handle protestors outside the convention. Ribicoff's words enraged Mayor Daley, who was sitting in the front row. Daley's response was not caught by microphones, but television viewers had no problem reading his lips.

A Long, Strange Line of Governors

Not every Texas chief executive deserves to be on a list of oddball governors, but more than a few of them should feel right at home. Here are a couple of early examples.

✳   ✳   ✳   ✳

MAYBE IT'S BECAUSE of Texas's long-standing independent streak, or maybe there's something in the water, but for hundreds of years there has been a parade of eclectic (to put it kindly) characters at the helm of the Lone Star State. In fact, Texas has had a love-hate relationship with independence and impeachment right from the start.

Setting the Standard

The first American governor of Texas was Henry Smith. Texas was technically part of Mexico at the time, but Texans never were much for technicalities. In 1834, Mexican officials appointed Smith chief of the department of the Brazos, but neither that appointment nor the fact that he'd been deeded his land by the Mexican government quelled his thirst for Texas independence.

Within a year, Smith was heading up the War Party, which set the creation of the independence movement into motion. By the end of 1835, he was named governor of the provisional breakaway government, but perhaps the "War Party" moniker was too literal—he wasn't able to survive political wars with his rivals. No sooner had he attempted to dissolve the provisional government's council than council members fought back by impeaching him.

But, setting a tradition that would be repeated some four decades later, Smith refused to leave office. Texans eventually got rid of him the next year when a new constitutional congress came and created a "do over" for the new Republic of Texas.

A Convoluted Personal Life

Smith's first wife, Harriet Gillette, died in 1820 when they lived in Missouri, seven years before Smith emigrated to Texas. He didn't have to look far for wife number two: In 1822, he married Harriet's sister Elizabeth. But Elizabeth died of cholera in Texas in 1833. Fortunately, Elizabeth had a twin sister, Sarah, who became Smith's third wife. Breaking the curse of the Smith wives, Sarah outlived Henry, who died in 1851 in a mining camp during the California gold rush.

Smith may have had his problems, but he also had a sense of propriety as far as legal documents were concerned. Legend has it that he created what would become the official seal of Texas. As head of the provisional government of Texas in December 1835, he had to seal his first official document, which appointed John Forbes, Sam Houston, and John Cameron as commissioners to negotiate with American Indians in the area. Having nothing official in place for the newly minted state, Smith—still according to legend—took a brass button off his coat, dipped it in some sealing wax, and stamped in the impression of a five-pointed star. It was the beginning of Texas's most common nickname: the Lone Star State.

Leaving Office Is Hard to Do

Giving up the position of governor was definitely not easy for the 14th governor of Texas, either. Edmund Jackson Davis was a Union general in the Civil War and a Radical Republican during Reconstruction. His approach to governing was marked by everything from imprisoning political opponents to suppression and intimidation of newspapers. Davis wasn't a popular guy after all this, and he lost reelection in 1873 to Richard Coke by a margin of two to one. Taking a page from Henry Smith, Davis refused to leave the ground floor of the Capitol, locking himself in his office and asking President Ulysses S. Grant to send troops to his aid (Grant refused). Eventually Davis left of his own accord—locking the office door behind him, so Coke's supporters still had to use an ax to break in.

If You Liked Me, Wait Till You Meet My Wife

Impeachment should spell the end for most political careers, but Jim Ferguson found a way not only to survive but to thrive after being impeached. Given that Ferguson was run out of Austin in 1917 during his second term with accusations of misappropriation of funds and embezzlement, not to mention that it was illegal for a successfully impeached governor to ever run for office again, there was no way that he would regain the governorship. Well, it may have been impossible for *him*, but it wasn't illegal for his *wife* to run.

With Jim's guidance in 1924, the genteel, highly educated Miriam Ferguson was rebranded "Ma" on the campaign trail. Her new image was carefully crafted with pictures of chicken coops and a bonnet someone borrowed along the way. Inexplicably, Ma won, and she and her husband returned to Austin triumphant.

The second woman governor in the United States, Ma Ferguson had her husband's desk placed right next to hers in the governor's mansion and would reportedly ink over documents Jim had written in pencil. A number of significant laws were passed during her administration, such as one attacking the Klu Klux Klan by banning the wearing of masks in public. She also prohibited smoking and drinking in the governor's mansion—a policy that was quietly overturned the minute she was gone. Ma Ferguson ran again and won in 1932, giving the Fergusons a total of three and a half terms in office.

Football and Politics Don't Mix

Texas's well-known passion for football actually led to the demise of one governor. Nowadays, Governor Rick Perry, who took office after the previous governor, George W. Bush, was elected to the presidency, is the longest-serving governor in Texas history. But before him, William P. Clements held that distinction. He served two nonconsecutive terms, from 1979 to 1983 and again from 1987 to 1991. Clements's tenure was particularly surprising because of his garish taste in sports coats—plaid in a number of colors (it was the '70s, after all). But he is perhaps most notorious for his involvement in a pay-for-play scandal at his alma mater, SMU.

Needing to clean up its image after a series of NCAA football recruiting violations, SMU brought Clements in to head its board of governors. Although the football program was sanctioned and promised to clean up its act, nefarious goings-on continued behind the scenes. During the 1970s, the school had begun paying cash to athletes to attend and play football at SMU, a direct violation of NCAA rules. Clements and other university officials believed they'd made a commitment to these players and continued to pay them.

Two months into his second term as governor, Clements held a press conference to come clean. The NCAA, needless to say, came down even harder on SMU, imposing a "death penalty" and shutting its football program down completely for 1987; SMU officials decided themselves to extend that condition through the 1988 season. This was too much for even the most rabid college football fan. Although he had almost his entire second term in front of him, Clements may have decided then and there that he could not run for reelection.

The Man the Voters Turned Away

In the category of "also-rans" stands Stanley Edward Adams, who ran for office in 1990. He actually listed his occupation as "alleged white collar racketeer," winning a tongue-in-cheek "truth in advertising" award from the *Washington Post*.

Adams was infamous for his involvement with one of the larger Texas savings and loan failures in 1988 and was implicated in everything from shady real estate deals to money laundering for arms dealers. He had applied for permission to open up a branch office of Lamar Savings and Loan Association on the moon, with the stated purpose of serving the needs of individuals there and on other celestial bodies.

Presidential Nicknames

Here are the origins of some of the more interesting presidential nicknames throughout the years.

Sam: President Hiram Ulysses Grant earned this nickname at West Point. He enrolled as Ulysses Hiram Grant (a move some say was an attempt to avoid having the initials HUG embroidered on his clothing). Somehow, the name was entered as Ulysses S. Grant instead. Grant's classmates were the first to call him "Sam" based on his newly acquired middle initial.

The Phrasemaker: President Woodrow Wilson was known as an acclaimed historian who seldom used speechwriters.

Washington of the West: President William Henry Harrison was a general, like George Washington, and was remembered for his victories at the Battle of Tippecanoe and the Battle of the Thames.

Young Hickory: President Andrew Jackson was "Old Hickory," so his protégé President James Knox Polk became Young Hickory.

The Abolitionist: President John Quincy Adams routinely brought up the issue of slavery and earned the nickname after returning to Congress following his presidency.

The Negro President: President Thomas Jefferson earned this nickname following his victory in the 1800 election, which he won because of the Three-Fifths Compromise.

The American Cincinnatus: Known as the Father of His Country, George Washington was often compared to that famous Roman, who also became a private citizen instead of a king.

Ten-cent Jimmy: President James Buchanan earned this nickname because of a campaign claim that 10 cents was enough for a man to live on.

Some Current States and Their Early Names

❋ Delaware—Lower Counties on Delaware

❋ Connecticut—Connecticut Colony

❋ Rhode Island—Colony of Rhode Island and Providence Plantations

❋ Vermont—Province of New York and New Hampshire Grants

❋ Kentucky—Virginia (Kentucky County)

❋ Tennessee—Province of North Carolina, Southwest Territory

❋ Ohio—Northwest Territory

❋ Maine—Massachusetts

❋ Texas—Republic of Texas

❋ California—California Republic

❋ Oregon—Oregon Territory

❋ Hawaii—Kingdom of Hawaii, Republic of Hawaii

Chapter 4

Interesting People and Big Personalities

The Castle that Harry Built

All Harry Andrews wanted was some land and a castle to call his own—so he built it by hand.

✳   ✳   ✳   ✳

A S A YOUNG man born in 1890 and raised on the streets of New York City, the last thing on the mind of young Harry Andrews was castles. But a strange thing happened when Harry enlisted as a medic in World War I and was sent overseas: He fell in love with European castles. That love was so serious that when he came back stateside, he built one of his very own. In 1929, Andrews took up residence on a small tract of land in Loveland, Ohio, right alongside the Little Miami River, and began building his castle.

In the beginning, Andrews only worked on the castle as a sort of hobby. He was quite busy with his job at the local newspaper and volunteering to teach Sunday school. Still, Andrews felt that his castle, when finished, could serve as a place for young boys to come and scout. Andrews named this group of boys the Knights of the Golden Trail. It was for these boys that Andrews started spending more and more time working on the castle. In 1955, Andrews turned 65 and retired from his jobs and began working on the castle full time.

How the Castle Was Built

Most amazing of all was how Andrews chose to construct his castle. Every morning, he took two empty five-gallon pails and walked down to the Little Miami River. There, he filled the pails with rocks and carried them back up the hill. These were the rocks Andrews used to make his castle. It has been estimated that Andrews made that round-trip to the river and back more than 50,000 times. No wonder Andrews named his castle Chateau Laroche (French for "rock castle").

Andrews accepted certain items as donations. Obviously, rocks were among those items. Wandering through the halls of Chateau Laroche, one will find stones carved with the names of cities from around the world, all donated by friends of the castle. Another interesting item Andrews accepted as a donation was old-style cardboard milk containers. He would take the empty containers, cut the tops off, and then fill them with concrete. When they were hardened, he peeled pack the cardboard, and voilà—instant bricks! Andrews himself kept track of all 32,000 of the empty milk containers.

The Castle Today

In April 1981, Andrews was up on the roof of the castle burning garbage (although some say he was cooking). Either way, his pants somehow caught on fire, burning him severely. A little more than two weeks later, Andrews passed away.

Even though Andrews had worked on his castle for more than 50 years, it was still incomplete at the time of his death. But what he left behind stands a stunning three stories tall with more than 15 rooms, including bedrooms, a great hall, an armory, a grand banquet hall, a dungeon, and even an "ax-proof" wooden door. So while Andrews may be gone, the love of his life, Chateau Laroche, is still standing tall. It remains open for tours, some of which are conducted by the Knights of the Golden Trail themselves.

Aluminum Siding

Back in the day when the greening of America meant dabbing the decks with emerald-colored paint, and long before recycling was routine, Houston householder John Milkovisch decided to put the empty beer cans that constantly clogged his closets and garnished his garage to good use.

✳ ✳ ✳ ✳

MOST PEOPLE WITH an excess of beer cans cluttering their house would take the consumed containers to the nearest salvage storehouse. Not Houston's John Milkovisch, though. Instead, he crushed the canisters and paneled his palace with the aluminum.

Rethinking and Reusing

Milkovisch, an upholsterer for the Southern Pacific Railroad, initially began his unique home makeover project in 1968. Tired of mowing the lawn, he re-worked the grounds around his suburban residence by replacing the grass with concrete inlaid with designs made of marbles, rocks, and metal. A cold libation or two not only helped temper his thirst, it also provided the budding artist with the raw materials needed to accomplish his next assignment: covering the outer walls of his residence with flattened, empty beer cans.

Over the next 20 years, Milkovisch cut, crushed, compacted, and compressed more than 50,000 beer cans and mortared them to the outside of his home until he had completely covered it from ceiling to cellar with aluminum empties. Do beer cans provide effective insulation? Apparently not. But with the walls finished, Milkovisch started using lids and pull-tabs to make curtains and fences for shade, and even windchimes. Milkovisch's energy bills dropped.

One might wonder how the woman of the house felt about all this, but Mary Milkovisch remained living there for more than a dozen years after her husband passed away, until her own death in 2001. In 2008, the Beer Can House became a legitimate tourist attraction, opening its doors to the public for tours and visits.

Gummo: Marx Brother #5

Everyone has heard of the Marx Brothers. Many can name three; buffs can name four. If you know all five, you're a true Marxist!

✳ ✳ ✳ ✳

MILTON "GUMMO" MARX was born October 23, 1892, in Manhattan to Sam and Minnie Marx, Jewish immigrants from France and Germany. The couple eventually raised five sons (from eldest to youngest): Leonard ("Chico"), Adolph ("Harpo"), Julius ("Groucho"), Milton ("Gummo"), and Herbert ("Zeppo").

Milton began doing vaudeville around 1905 as the dummy in his uncle's ventriloquism act. The brothers were all naturals at the performing arts, especially music. Milton had a fine singing voice and vocalized with Julius onstage beginning in 1907. The brothers seem to have coined their nicknames in 1914. Why "Gummo"? The obvious problem with asking Marx brothers to explain nicknames is that any explanation could be a joke. Potential reasons, in order of plausibility:

✳ Gummo liked to sneak up on people backstage, like a gumshoe (detective).

✳ He wore gum (rubber) boots to avoid wet feet as a boy because he was susceptible to illness.

✳ He would never stick to the stage (Gummo's usual wisecrack).

He Did It His Way

The United States entered World War I in 1917. Gummo was the only Marx brother the Army wanted. Onstage, Zeppo stepped in while Private Gummo defended his nation. Gummo finished military service in 1919 and tried to start a dressmaking business. It failed, but Gummo landed on his feet as a theatrical agent and manager for his brothers and for numerous others. He developed such an honest reputation that his clients rarely wanted or needed a contract; Gummo's word was golden.

After a long and prosperous career, Gummo died in 1977.

Hizzoner!

New York City has had its share of colorful mayors over the years. Many worked hard to make the Big Apple a better place to live, while others spent their careers embroiled in controversy.

✳ ✳ ✳ ✳

THE GOVERNOR MAY reign over the state of New York, but it's the mayor—or "hizzoner," as the tabloids usually refer to him—who controls New York City.

The municipality's first mayor was Thomas Willett, who was appointed to the post in 1665 by Governor Richard Nicolls. For more than a century and a half, the position of mayor would remain an appointment that came with limited authority. Today, however, the mayor heads the executive branch of the city government and oversees an annual budget of $50 billion—the largest municipal budget in the country. Here are some of the most memorable characters to hold the job of mayor:

Robert Van Wyck (1898–1901). A graduate of Columbia University Law School and former chief judge of the city court, Van Wyck was a product of the Tammany Hall machine. His race against political reformer Seth Low was a bloody battle that Van Wyck managed to win despite refusing to give a single public speech. A man of few words, Van Wyck's acceptance speech consisted of just two sentences.

Van Wyck's single term as mayor was rife with political scandal, including allegations that he was part of a scam to artificially inflate the price of milk. An investigation by the state legislature concluded that he was a "dictator" who remained under the influence of Tammany Hall bosses. Following the inauguration of his successor, it was reported that Van Wyck left City Hall via a back entrance and walked unrecognized into the crowd outside.

George Binton McClellan (1904–09). The son of renowned Civil War general George McClellan, George Binton McClellan was a bit of a political prodigy, winning a congressional seat at age 27 and becoming president of the New York City Board of Aldermen at 30. Although he ran and won on the Tammany Hall ticket, McClellan quickly proved that he wasn't beholden to his political bosses. He won his second term as mayor by defeating newspaper mogul William Randolph Hearst but spent the remainder of his tenure suffering almost daily attacks from Hearst's muckraking newspapers. Much to the chagrin of his political patrons, McClellan also spent much of his second term attempting to dismantle the Tammany Hall machine.

William Jay Gaynor (1910–13). Gaynor holds the distinction of being the only New York City mayor to have an attempt made on his life: Early in his first year, he was shot in the throat by a disgruntled city employee. Gaynor survived the shooting, but the bullet could not be removed; he died three years later from residual effects of the attack.

James "Jimmy" Walker (1926–32). One of the city's more flamboyant mayors, Walker was an accomplished actor and musician as well as a state politician. (Among his most famous works was the ballad "Will You Love Me in December as You Do in May?") Another product of the Tammany Hall machine, Walker paid off his political benefactors with cushy jobs and lucrative city contracts. Citizens of New York City were willing to overlook this until the Depression revealed just how neglected many city services had become. In 1932, accused of accepting bribes from business leaders with ties to the city, Walker was called before the governor. He resigned as mayor in the middle of the hearings and moved to Europe with his mistress.

Fiorello La Guardia (1934–45). Considered by most historians to be one of the most effective mayors in the city's history, La Guardia worked extremely hard to better the lives of his constituents. He strived to eliminate the corruption that infested city government, strengthened the city's infrastructure, and quickly gained renown for putting the city before political gain. He often used the radio to reach out to the citizens of New York, and in 1945 turned to that device to read the Sunday funnies during a newspaper delivery strike, an act that endeared him to many.

John Lindsay (1966–73). Lindsay served during one of the most turbulent times in modern American history and hoped to make city government more accessible to the poor and disenfranchised through efforts such as the Urban Action Taskforce and Neighborhood City Halls. However, things didn't start smoothly for Lindsay—on his first day in office, a transit strike threatened to bring the city to its knees. It was just the first of many such emergencies Lindsay would face. While still mayor, Lindsay mounted a short-lived bid for the 1972 Democratic presidential nomination. Two decades later, his finances a wreck, he accepted honorary city posts from Mayor Rudy Giuliani, in order to have health insurance and a pension.

Abraham Beame (1974–77). New York's first Jewish mayor, Beame came into office with the city on the verge of bankruptcy, a situation that forced him to make drastic cuts to the city's budget and eliminate numerous jobs. However, in 1976, Beame managed to land annual federal loans that helped keep the city financially solvent.

Edward Koch (1978–89). Koch inherited the financial difficulties that had plagued Beame but was able to restore the city's credit and put it on better financial footing. A gregarious man with a strong personality, he became famous for greeting his constituents with the amusingly self-serving question, "How'm I doing?" Koch hoped to be NYC's first four-term mayor, but corruption scandals and revelations of his harsh dealings with other officials stopped him at three.

Rudolph Giuliani (1994–2001). A former U.S. Attorney, Giuliani became mayor with a pledge to help the failing city get back on its feet and improve the lives of all New Yorkers. He established a zero tolerance policy against crime and was influential in transforming some of the sleazier sections of the city into places where citizens and tourists felt safe. Terrorist attacks against the World Trade Center on September 11, 2001, propelled Giuliani into the national spotlight. Even though his tenure was ending, he quickly stepped up to reassure New Yorkers and help lead them through those trying times. A 2008 run at the GOP presidential nomination went nowhere, despite Giuliani's mention of 9/11 at every opportunity during his campaign.

Tired, Achy Feet? Paging Dr. Scholl ...

This "arch" Chicagoan never practiced medicine, but he brought pain relief to millions.

✳   ✳   ✳   ✳

YOU MIGHT SAY that foot care was in William Mathias Scholl's blood. Born in 1882 on a farm in Indiana, Scholl had a chance encounter with his grandfather's shoemaking kit that led him to cobble together a career centered around foot care.

At age 18, Scholl set off for Chicago and soon landed on his feet, getting a job at Ruppert's, a downtown shoe store. Many of his customers complained that their dogs were barking; Scholl quickly realized that something was afoot, and bad shoe design was the culprit. Scholl enrolled in night classes at a medical school. He never wanted to practice medicine in the traditional sense, and he never did. Instead, he marched to his own drummer, inventing and patenting various foot-care devices, the first of which was an arch support called the Foot-Eazer that he developed when he was just 22 years old.

Scholl may have been a born cobbler, but he was also a born salesman. Rather than hiring salespeople, Scholl hit the ground running by personally making the rounds of Chicago shoe stores, dressed in a white doctor's coat. He would often hold a skeletal model of the foot against his products to give store owners a visual demonstration of exactly how the products would support feet.

Dr. Scholl was a pioneer who realized that an ill-fitting shoe affected the wearer's spinal alignment. This understanding led to the invention of his famous sandals, along with cushion insoles and bunion pads. By the mid-1950s, such "corny" Scholl-written slogans as "When your feet hurt, you hurt all over" were ubiquitous. When he died in 1968, the Dr. Scholl brand was worth $77 million. Today, his legacy lives on at Chicago's Dr. William M. Scholl College of Podiatric Medicine.

13 Famous Rhodes Scholars

When British businessman Cecil Rhodes died in 1902, his fortune was used to establish the Rhodes scholarship, which brings outstanding students from around the world to study at the University of Oxford in England, generally for two years. Students from any academic discipline are selected on the basis of intellectual distinction, as well as the promise of future leadership and service to the world. Around 90 scholarships are given annually, and some of the most famous scholars are listed below.

✳   ✳   ✳   ✳

1. **Edwin Hubble:** Famous astronomer Edwin Hubble received his scholarship in 1910. Having studied science

and mathematics at the University of Chicago, he used his time at Oxford to study law. Hubble then returned to the States to continue his work in astronomy, most notably discovering the existence of galaxies beyond the Milky Way.

2. **Dean Rusk:** Dean Rusk, who used his 1931 Rhodes scholarship to study history and political science, served as U.S. Secretary of State from 1961 to 1969 under presidents John F. Kennedy and Lyndon B. Johnson.

3. **Lord Howard Florey:** Australian pharmacologist Lord Howard Florey was awarded his scholarship in 1921 and studied medicine at Oxford. In 1945, he was awarded the Nobel Prize in Medicine along with Alexander Fleming and Ernst Chain for their work in discovering penicillin.

4. **James William Fulbright:** James William Fulbright, who used his 1926 Rhodes scholarship to study law, was elected to the House of Representatives in 1943, then served in the Senate from 1945 to 1974. Soon after, he established the Fulbright Program to provide grants for students and professionals to study, teach, and conduct research abroad. To date, more than 250,000 individuals have received Fulbright grants.

5. **Bill Bradley:** William Warren Bradley already had an Olympic gold medal for basketball when he began his study of politics, philosophy, and economics at Oxford in 1965. He went on to have a Hall of Fame career in basketball before entering the Senate in 1978 and running as a presidential candidate in the 2000 primary.

6. **Bill Clinton:** Former President Bill Clinton received his Rhodes scholarship in 1968. While at Oxford, he studied law and also played an active part in student life, particularly in protests against the Vietnam War. Fellow Rhodes scholar David E. Kendall later became Clinton's personal lawyer.

7. **Strobe Talbott:** Strobe Talbott, who also won his scholarship in 1968 and spent his time at Oxford translating Nikita Khrushchev's memoirs into English, was another of Clinton's Oxford friends. He went on to be Deputy Secretary of State from 1994 to 2001. Talbott was also president of the Brookings Institution—a Washington, D.C.-based political research facility that helped negotiate an end to the war in Yugoslavia in 1999.

8. **George Stephanopoulos:** George Stephanopoulos used his 1984 Rhodes scholarship to earn a master's degree in theology. During the 1992 presidential campaign, Stephanopoulos served as Bill Clinton's senior political adviser, then as communications director during Clinton's presidency.

9. **Kris Kristofferson:** Well-known musician and actor Kris Kristofferson received his Rhodes scholarship in 1958. He studied English literature, and it was while he was at Oxford that he began his performing career. Since then, his hit records have won him several Grammys.

10. **Terrence Malik:** Best known as director of *The Thin Red Line* and *Badlands*, Terrence Malik won a Rhodes scholarship in 1966. He studied philosophy but had a disagreement with his adviser over his thesis (the concept of the world in the writings of Kierkegaard, Heidegger, and Wittgenstein) and left Oxford without finishing his doctorate.

11. **Naomi Wolf:** American author and feminist social critic Naomi Wolf used her time at Oxford from 1985 to 1987 to begin the research that eventually became the international best seller *The Beauty Myth*, which condemns the exploitation of women by the fashion and beauty industries.

12. **Cory A. Booker:** Cory A. Booker began his studies at Oxford in 1992, gaining an honors degree in modern his-

tory. He is now a Democratic politician and went on to become mayor of racially diverse Newark, New Jersey, the largest city in the state. In 2013, he became a U.S. Senator.

13. **Randal Pinkett:** Randal Pinkett, who earned a masters degree in computer science as a 1994 Rhodes scholar, gained celebrity status when he was hired by Donald Trump after winning season four of The Apprentice.

Josh Gibson

This catcher may have been the greatest power hitter of all time.

✳ ✳ ✳ ✳

Born: December 21, 1911; Buena Vista, GA

MLB Career: None. Kept out of the majors by the color line. Played in Negro Leagues 1930–1946.

Hall of Fame Resume: Some say he hit more than 800 home runs in his career, as many as 75 in one season.

Inside Pitch: Although Gibson was hardly talkative, he did have one famous quote: "A homer a day will boost my pay."

The statistics are sketchy, the stories only hearsay from people who have little documentation to prove their points. The Negro Leagues operated under constraints that made keeping close track of player performance an impossible task, but those who watched these banished stars usually agreed on one thing: No one hit a baseball further and with greater frequency than catcher Josh Gibson.

Growing up in Pittsburgh, Gibson began playing semipro ball as a teenager and, as legend has it, was watching the Negro League Homestead Grays in action when he was pulled from the stands and put behind the plate after the Grays catcher hurt his finger. A star on the Grays within a year, the stocky, 6'2" right-handed batter moved on to the Pittsburgh Crawfords in 1934. There, he played alongside fellow future Hall of Famers Judy Johnson, Oscar Charleston, and James "Cool Papa" Bell in Black Ball's version of "Murderer's Row." On occasion Gibson also formed half of the most intimidating battery in Negro League history along with pitching Hall of Fame legend Satchel Paige.

Fun-loving and popular among his teammates, Gibson—known as "the black Babe Ruth"—drew high praise from players black and white for his abilities. Roy Campanella said Josh was "the greatest ballplayer I ever saw." Walter Johnson claimed he "catches so easy, he might as well be in a rocking chair." Jimmy Powers of the *New York Daily News* wrote in 1939, "I am positive that if Josh Gibson were white, he would be a major-league star," an argument Gibson supported by blasting three homers off Hall of Fame pitcher Dizzy Dean in two exhibition matchups.

One set of partial Negro League statistics credits Gibson with 146 home runs and a .362 average in 501 games spread over 16 seasons (in Negro League games alone). In reality, he may have slugged as many as 84 homers annually playing in more than 200 contests a year in winter (in the Puerto Rican League), spring, and summer. Sometimes the Crawfords or Homestead Grays (to which Gibson returned for his last five seasons) secured big-league ballparks for their games, and stories abound of Gibson belting homers to the deepest points of Comiskey Park and Yankee Stadium.

Pirates owner William Benswanger and Senators boss Clark Griffith both claimed an interest in bringing Josh to the majors, but the man with a reported 850 to 900 home runs was still blasting them for the Grays when Jackie Robinson signed with Brooklyn in 1945. Gibson might still have made the big leagues, but struggles with alcohol and illness shrouded his final years. He died of a brain hemorrhage at age 35 in January 1947, three months before Robinson's debut with the Dodgers.

It's Not You, It's Me

Fraternal twins come from two different eggs that have fertilized separately but implant in the womb together. Identical twins started out as the same fertilized egg, but that egg splits and each develops into two separate babies. With that in mind, here are a few famous twins of both kinds.

✳ ✳ ✳ ✳

✳ Perhaps the most famous twins in history are Romulus and Remus. According to mythology, these identical boys were the victims of political jealousy and rage and were ordered to be killed, along with their mother. Abandoned rather than murdered outright, they were raised by wolves until a kind-hearted shepherd brought them into his home.

✳ The lovelorn and those in despair had two different advice columnists from which to choose: Ann Landers (real name, Eppie Friedman Lederer) began dispensing advice when she took over for a deceased columnist, using the same pen name, in 1955. A few months later, her identical twin sister (Pauline Friedman Phillips) created advice rival Abigail Van Buren (Dear Abby).

✳ While Chang and Eng Bunker were certainly not the first conjoined (therefore, identical) twins, they were arguably the most famous. Born in 1811 in Siam, they spent many years traveling as a sideshow exhibit with P. T. Barnum's circus. In their later years, they became gentlemen farmers, married, moved to North Carolina, and raised separate families. Other famous conjoined twins were vaudevillians Daisy and Violet Hilton and former slaves Millie-Christine, usually referred to by one hyphenated name.

✳ If your household members are divided in their NFL loyalties, imagine the Barber house. Identical twins Ronde and Tiki Barber played for different NFL teams.

* White House watchers had lots to watch when fraternal twins Jenna and Barbara Bush lived on Pennsylvania Avenue.

* Other famous twins: Actresses Mary-Kate and Ashley Olsen (they're fraternal twins, believe it or not); country singers Jim and Jon Hager; and Ross and Norris McWhirter, creators of *Guinness World Records*.

18 Notable People with a Twin

1. Kofi Annan — twin sister, Efua
2. Isabella Rossellini — twin sister, Isotta
3. Kiefer Sutherland — twin sister, Rachel
4. Scarlett Johansson — twin brother, Hunter
5. Alanis Morissette — twin brother, Wade
6. Mario Andretti — twin brother, Aldo
7. Vin Diesel — twin brother, Paul
8. Ashton Kutcher — twin brother, Michael
9. Billy Dee Williams — twin sister, Loretta
10. José Canseco — twin brother, Ozzie
11. Aaron Carter — twin sister, Angel
12. John Elway — twin sister, Jana
13. Jerry Falwell — twin brother, Gene
14. Deidre Hall — twin sister, Andrea
15. Pier Angeli — twin sister, Marisa Pavan
16. Montgomery Clift — twin sister, Roberta
17. Maurice Gibb — twin brother, Robin
18. Jim Thorpe — twin brother, Charlie

Henry VIII

Just the facts about one of England's most famous kings...

❋   ❋   ❋   ❋

❋ Henry was the third child and second son of Henry VII and Elizabeth of York. Two brothers and two sisters predeceased their father, while Henry and two sisters survived. When his older brother, Arthur, died at the age of 15, Henry became heir to the throne. Henry wasn't the only sibling to hold a throne. His sister Margaret became the queen of Scotland, and his sister Mary was briefly the queen of France.

❋ Henry was crowned king just before he turned 18, and he died at age 55, one of England's most beloved, and feared, monarchs.

❋ One of Henry's first acts as king was to execute his father's two most successful (and therefore hated) tax collectors, Edmund Dudley and Sir Richard Empson.

❋ Henry was at least six-foot-three, one of the tallest kings in English history. His suits of armor, some of which are still on display in the Tower of London, give a good idea of his formidable size.

❋ Although famous for having had six wives, Henry was married to his first, Catherine of Aragon, for more than 20 years.

❋ Queen Catherine was the widow of Henry's brother, Arthur (they were married only six months). This caused considerable speculation over whether her marriage to Henry was ever legal.

❋ Henry's great passion for his second wife, Anne Boleyn, led to the Protestant Reformation in England. The Pope refused to dissolve Henry's marriage to his first wife, so Henry split from the Catholic Church, declared himself head of the Church of England, and ordered his own annulment.

* Jane Seymour was said to have been Henry's favorite wife, as she was the only one to give birth to a son, Edward. Henry was buried with Jane, and she is featured in all of the dynastic portraits.

* Legend has it that when Jane Seymour was in labor with Prince Edward, she was having such difficulty that the doctors asked the king which they should save—his wife or his child. Although he loved her, the callous king is said to have replied, "Save the child, by all means, for other wives may be easily found."

* King Henry had ten children by his first three wives, but only three—Mary, Elizabeth, and Edward—survived infancy. All three eventually ruled England, but none had children of their own.

* One of Henry's favorite sports was tennis. The athletic king popularized the game in England, and in 1529 he built a tennis court on the grounds of his Hampton Court palace. It was rebuilt in 1625 and is now the oldest tennis court in existence.

* Though his break with Rome fueled the Protestant Reformation, Henry considered Protestants to be heretics. His reforms were more legal than religious—the religion was still basically Catholic, but the king took the role of the Pope. The real disagreement between Catholicism and Protestantism was fueled by Henry's children—Mary was a strict Catholic, and Edward and Elizabeth strongly supported Protestantism.

* Henry was the first king to authorize an English translation of the Bible.

* For all his claims of chivalry and honor, Henry seemed to have no problem making up charges in order to arrest and execute people he considered an irritation or a threat.

* Henry spent the equivalent of approximately 2 million pounds on clothing each year.

* After his brother Arthur's death, Henry's childhood became stifling. He was kept under strict supervision and forbidden any activities that could possibly jeopardize his safety. Henry's friends had to get his father's permission before they were allowed to visit.

* Henry was well known as a talented musician who frequently composed his own music. Contrary to popular lore, however, he did not write "Greensleeves."

Goal: Bibles in Every Language

While the Christian missionary William Cameron Townsend was working with the Cakchiquel Indians in Guatemala in the 1930s, a local man asked: "If your God is so great, why doesn't he speak my language?" Flummoxed, Townsend thought deeply about the problem and soon established the Wycliffe Translators, an organization devoted to translating the Bible into every language in the world.

* * * *

CONVINCED THAT EVERY person should be able to read God's Word in his or her own language, William Cameron Townsend established a linguistics school for Bible translators in 1934 and named it for John Wycliffe, the 14th-century reformer who was the first to translate the Bible into English. Once students completed training, Townsend sent them into the field to develop alphabets for languages that had none so they could translate scripture into that language.

One of the first to go into the field was Kenneth Pike. In 1935, Pike traveled to Mexico, where he committed himself to learning Mixtec, an Indian dialect, with the help of an old Mixtec man. Pike's efforts were almost foiled from the start when he discovered that the words for "one" and "nine" differed only in pitch and sounded exactly alike to his ears. At a loss to master the tone problem, Pike sought help from former linguistics professor Edward Sapir, who explained his own system for analyzing the tones of Navajo. Using Sapir's technique, Pike cracked the Mixtec system, but it took him ten years. Today, computers are often used to chart and organize sounds and find symbols to represent them. If Sapir had only had a computer, how much easier his work would have been! His Mixtec New Testament was published in 1951. It was the first of hundreds of Wycliffe translations.

Forming Two Corporations

Wycliffe Bible Translators was incorporated in 1942, as was its affiliate, the Summer Institute of Linguistics, which operates as a secular society in order to gain admission into countries that prohibit missionary activity. Wycliffe translators work hard to identify cultures that have no written language, develop writing systems for them, and translate scripture into those languages. Sometimes requests for help come from the people themselves, but more often, people are identified through surveys. Young people trained by Wycliffe drive and hike through remote areas of the world for days or weeks at a time, combating foul weather, loathsome leeches, and bombarding insects. On their travels they interview dozens of people to determine which groups need scripture in their own language. The groups that are chosen are later visited by translators who first develop writing systems, then ultimately publish the Bible in the language of the people.

Numbers Are Staggering

Since incorporating in 1942, Wycliffe Bible Translators and the Summer Institute of Linguistics have been involved in translating 24 complete Bibles and 735 New Testaments, potentially reaching some 107 million people. Yet this is only the tip of the iceberg. About 6,900 languages are spoken by the 6.9 billion people on earth. At the start of 2010, only 459 of these languages had decent versions of the full Bible and only 1,213 had adequate New Testaments, though scripture portions appeared in another 836 languages.

Wycliffe forges on and continues to be a leader in producing scripture in obscure languages. Though other organizations, most notably the United Bible Societies, have produced Bibles in many languages, Wycliffe has an impressive track record. At the start of 2010, Wycliffe translators were involved in rendering scripture into 1,363 languages, which are spoken by about 939 million people. This constitutes some 68 percent of the 1,990 active Bible-translating programs in the world. But there's still a long way to go.

Future Plans

In 1999, Wycliffe International initiated a campaign called Vision 2025, determining that by the year 2025 they will have translation projects started—though not necessarily completed—in every language that needs one. It's an ambitious program. Current estimates suggest that about 353 million people, speaking 2,252 languages, may have a need for a Bible translation. The Wycliffe translators will need all the stamina they can muster—and lots of help from on high.

Truth Be Told

Freed slave Sojourner Truth was a vocal advocate of social justice and an inspiring religious orator.

✳   ✳   ✳   ✳

SOJOURNER TRUTH WAS unique among 19th-century preachers—she was a former slave who fought for women's rights and other social causes, and she steadfastly refused to back down in the face of adversity. Her life was rife with abuse and heartache, but she always found comfort in the Bible.

Truth was born into slavery as Isabella Baumfree in 1797, in a Dutch enclave in upstate New York. She was sold around age 9 for $100 (which also included a flock of sheep) and endured physical abuse at the hands of her new master because she spoke limited English, her first language being Dutch. It was during this period that Truth first sought solace in religion, praying loudly whenever she was frightened or hurt.

Finding Freedom

Truth was sold several more times in the ensuing years. She married another slave in 1817 and bore four children. Freedom seemed at hand when the State of New York enacted legislation that called for the end of slavery within the state on July 4, 1827. Her owner promised to set her free a year early, but he reneged at the last minute. Angry and bitter at being lied to, Truth worked until she felt she had paid off her debt then walked away. She arrived at the home of Isaac and Maria Van Wagenen, who agreed to buy her services for the rest of the year for $20. The Van Wagenens treated Truth well and insisted she call them by their given names.

It was while working for the Van Wagenens that Truth experienced a religious epiphany that inspired her to become a preacher. She began attending a local Methodist church, and in 1829, she left to travel in the company of a white female evangelical teacher. Truth began preaching at regional churches and developed a reputation as an inspiring speaker. She later joined a religious reformer named Elijah Pierson, who became her mentor until his death in 1834.

Truth moved to New York City, where she decided to become a traveling minister. She changed her name from Isabella Baumfree to Sojourner Truth and set out on the road, relying on the kindness of strangers to make her way. In 1844, Truth joined a Massachusetts commune known as the Northampton Association of Education and Industry, which had been founded by a group of abolitionists who espoused women's rights and religious tolerance. She left when the collective disbanded in 1846.

Literary Success

Truth began dictating her autobiography, *The Narrative of Sojourner Truth: A Northern Slave*, shortly after, and renowned abolitionist William Lloyd Garrison privately published the book in 1850. The memoir was a success and brought Truth both a needed income and promotion as a public speaker.

Soon, Truth found herself in great demand, speaking about women's rights and the evils of slavery, often turning to her own experiences as illustration. In 1854, she gave one of her most famous lectures, titled "Ain't I A Woman?" at the Ohio Woman's Rights Convention in Akron.

Through everything, religion was Truth's personal mainstay. She was very active during the Civil War, enlisting black troops for the Union and helping runaway slaves. In 1864, she worked at a government refugee camp for freed slaves on an island off the coast of Virginia, and she even met President Abraham Lincoln. Following the war, she continued her efforts to help newly freed slaves through the Freedman's Relief Association.

Truth pursued her work on behalf of freed blacks until her death on November 26, 1883, from complications related to leg ulcers. She was buried next to her grandson, Sammy Banks, in Oak Hill Cemetery in Battle Creek, Michigan.

A Lasting Legacy

Sojourner Truth's legacy of spiritual pursuit and social activism resulted in numerous honors in the decades following her death. Among them were a memorial stone in the Stone History Tower in downtown Battle Creek; a portion of Michigan state highway M-66 designated the Sojourner Truth Memorial Highway; induction into the national Women's Hall of Fame in Seneca Falls, New York; and a commemorative postage stamp.

The Mighty Pen!

Thomas Nast was one of the most important editorial cartoonists of his day—and an unrelenting foe of political corruption.

✳   ✳   ✳   ✳

WHEN HE PICKED up his pen, he drew beautifully. He invented Santa Claus as we know him today, created the Republican elephant and the Democratic donkey, and used his skilled pen to fan the fires of patriotism during the Civil War. But it was his efforts to draw attention to New York City's corrupt political system for which cartoonist Thomas Nast is best known today.

Nast was born in Landau, Germany, in 1840 and emigrated to New York City with his mother and sister at the age of six. (His father followed three years later.) A natural talent, Nast studied art, and at age 15 he was hired as a reportorial artist for *Frank Leslie's Illustrated Newspaper*. He later went to work for the *New York Illustrated News*, which sent him to Europe to cover, among other things, Giuseppe Garibaldi's military campaign in Sicily.

A National Audience

In 1862, Nast accepted a full-time position with the prestigious *Harper's Weekly*, for whom he had previously freelanced. The magazine sent him to the battlefields of the Civil War, where his artistic talent shone. An avowed Union supporter, Nast unabashedly used his pen to criticize, with dramatic flair, the Confederate war effort and rouse support for the North.

His gig with *Harper's Weekly* made Nast nationally famous, and after the war he was solicited to illustrate books. Nast enjoyed such work and accepted numerous illustration jobs while he continued to work for *Harper's Weekly*. It is estimated that over the course of his career, Nast provided drawings for more than 100 volumes.

Tweed in the Crosshairs

In 1868, Nast turned his pen against William Magear "Boss" Tweed, the corrupt leader of New York City's Tammany Hall political machine. Tweed used his influence to put almost all of city government and much of the state legislature in his pocket. Tweed was the worst kind of political crook, and Nast was unrelenting in his artistic attacks against Tweed's administration. The cartoonist's campaign in *Harper's Weekly* and the *New York Times* lasted nearly three years.

Tweed and his cronies quickly felt the effects of Nast's drawings, which depicted the politician and his followers as sleazy scum with their hands in the public till. Legend has it that Tweed became so incensed over Nast's illustrations that he told his underlings, "Stop them damn pictures. I don't care what the papers write about. My constituents can't read. But, damn it, they can see the pictures."

At one point, intermediaries for Tweed visited Nast and offered him a $100,000 "gift" to study art in Europe. Naturally, Nast realized he was being bribed, so he played along, upping the payoff amount until it reached $500,000—which Nast then declined.

The End for Tweed

Nast's cartoons helped bring an end to Tweed's culture of corruption. In 1871, Tweed was kicked out of office by angry voters and eventually jailed. However, he managed to escape in 1876 and tried to flee to Spain. In an ironic twist, he was recognized and arrested by a customs official who could not speak English but who recognized Tweed from Nast's dead-on caricatures!

In the years that followed, Nast's relationship with *Harper's Weekly* began to sour. Nast left the magazine in 1886. He freelanced for various magazines until 1892, when he established his own, *Nast's Weekly*. Unfortunately, the publication lasted only six months.

Nast had difficulty finding substantial illustration work in the years that followed, and in 1902 he accepted an appointment from President Theodore Roosevelt as consul general to Ecuador. Nast contracted yellow fever while abroad and died on December 7, 1902.

To this day, Thomas Nast is revered as one of the most influential political cartoonists who ever lived, demonstrating every time he put ink on paper that the pen really is mightier than the sword.

How Marlon Brando Changed Acting Forever

Marlon Brando revolutionized stage and screen technique by leading the influx of a new wave of actors after World War II. His role as Stanley Kowalski in Tennessee Williams's Broadway smash A Streetcar Named Desire *led to the Hollywood version, both directed by Elia Kazan, which catapulted Brando to mainstream stardom.*

✳   ✳   ✳   ✳

THE NEW YORK theater scene in the 1940s was rich ground for acting coaches. Lee Strasberg, Stella Adler, and Stanford Meisner were all disciples of Constantin Stanislavski. The Stanislavski System was a kind of "grammar" for actors. By breaking down a task or interaction into objectives and obstacles, an actor could better get "in the moment" of a scene. In New York, Strasberg and others adapted the Stanislavski System to focus more on the actor personally identifying with the character and using techniques to understand psychological motives. Students led the charge for a new kind of acting: The Method. In this new guard were Paul Newman, Marilyn Monroe, James Dean, and Marlon Brando.

Brando followed his older sisters to New York in 1943. He studied with Stella Adler and traveled to Massachusetts to do an in-person audition for Tennessee Williams for his new play, *A Streetcar Named Desire*. *Streetcar*, which would go on to win the Pulitzer Prize, tells the story of Blanche DuBois, an alcoholic Southern belle who moves in with her sister, Stella Kowalski, and Stella's abusive working-class husband, Stanley. Stanley and Blanche clash physically and emotionally, which leads to assault and Blanche's nervous breakdown.

Stanley

Brando wandered around the stage during rehearsals. He didn't know his lines. The ones he did remember he muttered softly. Director Elia Kazan encouraged his antics. Brando spent hours touching and examining every object on the set. By handling the objects, he used their familiarity to get himself into the emotional tenor of a scene. Repetition often brought staleness to performances, but Adler, Kazan, and Brando believed that spontaneity could reinvigorate a scene. Brando would ad lib and improvise to inject new life into the play. He didn't just act; he reacted.

His behavior frustrated costar Jessica Tandy, who came from the classical tradition: Hit your mark, know your lines, and say them. At one point Tandy shouted, "Speak up! I can't hear a bloody word you're saying." Costar Kim Hunter was more forgiving: "Some nights he made terrible choices, but they were always *real*."

The play opened in three cities (New Haven, Boston, and Philadelphia) before hitting Broadway on December 3, 1947. Brando (as Stanley Kowalski), Tandy (as Blanche), Hunter (as Stella Kowalski), and Karl Malden (as Mitch) received standing ovations and 12 curtain calls. "In those days people stood only for the national anthem," said producer Irene Selznick.

The reviews were gushing. Brando's mumbling and habitation of the set during the weeks of rehearsal caged a sexuality and violence that, when released, fired the first shot of the "great revolution in American acting." The Actors Studio was founded just prior to the play's opening, and Method actors soon flooded Broadway and Hollywood, having been electrified by Brando's performance.

Imitators

Talents as bright as Montgomery Clift, Paul Newman, and James Dean were inspired by what Brando had achieved. But there was an inevitable downside to Brando's influence. Among many lesser actors, precise diction gave way to imitations of Brando's mumbling. T-shirts replaced neat attire. Some young actors struck poses or attitudes instead of truly acting their parts. "Lots of the actors were just slobs," said Alice Hermes, Brando's diction coach at Erwin Piscator's Dramatic Workshop. "Brando mumbled only when appropriate."

Who Was Button Gwinnett?

His invasion of Florida was a disaster and he may have plagiarized his most lasting composition, but Button Gwinnett still managed to get his signature on the Declaration of Independence.

✳   ✳   ✳   ✳

From England to Georgia to Pennsylvania

IN 1762, BUTTON Gwinnett emigrated from England to the colonies, where he dabbled in trade before borrowing a large sum to establish a plantation. He served as a representative to the colony's House of Commons until 1773. After losing his land and slaves, Gwinnett allied himself with the burgeoning revolutionary cause, but his English birth made him politically unpopular, so Gwinnett's rival, Lachlan McIntosh, was given the honor of leading Georgia's Continental battalion. Denied the laurels of military leadership, Gwinnett went to Philadelphia as one of the state's representatives to the Continental Congress. It was in this role that he signed the Declaration of Independence in 1776.

Elected to the Georgia legislature, Gwinnett used a pamphlet given to him by John Adams as the basis for the new state's constitution. When the governor died in early 1777, Gwinnett was appointed to the post. At a time when the struggling nation could ill afford intrigue, he worked to undermine his old rival General McIntosh by spreading dissent among his officers, devising a questionable plan for invading Florida, and then appointing one of McIntosh's subordinates to lead the ill-fated expedition. After a mere two months in office, Gwinnett lost the governorship.

Lachlan's Loose Tongue

Like Gwinnett, McIntosh was a boastful man who delighted in the embarrassment of his rivals. In the days following Gwinnett's defeat, McIntosh publicly derided the ex-governor. Finally, Gwinnett challenged him to a duel. On May 16, 1777, the two Georgians stood 12 paces apart and discharged pistols. Both men were wounded; McIntosh survived, but Gwinnett succumbed to gangrene. He died days later at age 42.

Successful Dropouts!

Parents commonly tell their children, "You'll never become successful without a college education!" Sound advice to be sure, but it's not always true.

✳   ✳   ✳   ✳

1. **S. Daniel Abraham** Made billions by founding Slim-Fast. Never attended college.

2. **Christina Aguilera** One of the most successful pop singers in the world. Dropped out of high school.

3. **Paul Allen** Made billions as one of the cofounders of Microsoft. Dropped out of Washington State.

4. **Bill Bartman** Made billions as a successful businessman. Dropped out of high school.

5. **Richard Branson** Billionaire founder of Virgin Music and Virgin Atlantic Airways. Dropped out of high school.

6. **Andrew Carnegie** One of America's first multibillionaires. Dropped out of elementary school.

7. **Jack Kent Cooke** Billionaire owner of the Washington Redskins. Dropped out of high school.

8. **Ron Popeil** Multimillionaire inventor and television pitchman. Dropped out of college.

9. **Kjell Inge Rokke** Billionaire Norwegian businessman. Dropped out of high school.

10. **J. K. Rowling** Billionaire author of the *Harry Potter* series and one of the richest women in Great Britain. Never attended college.

11. **Frederick Henry Royce** Made millions as the cofounder of Rolls-Royce. Dropped out of elementary school.

12. **Vidal Sassoon** Made millions as the founder of Vidal Sassoon hairstyling salons and hair care products. Dropped out of high school.

Annie Get Your Gun: The Story of Annie Oakley

Despite being neglected as a child and suffering an accident later in life, Oakley rose to personal triumph and inspired young girls all over the country.

✳ ✳ ✳ ✳

ANNIE OAKLEY BECAME a star in Buffalo Bill Cody's "Wild West" show in the late 19th century as a female sharpshooter. Her lasting image as a self-reliant, hearty, and highly skilled shooter represented the best values of the Old West just as that era was fading. Oakley was not born in the West, nor had she been part of its settlement—but she embodied ideals that were important to Americans.

A Quick Study

Born Phoebe Ann Mosey in 1860 in the remote farmland of Darke County, Oakley endured a horrible childhood. Her father died after a protracted illness, leaving her mother with eight mouths to feed. To help, little Phoebe took her father's rifle into the woods and taught herself how to shoot, bringing home game for the family to eat. Despite her daughter's growing skills with the gun, her mother could not provide for the family, and eight-year-old Phoebe was sent to live at the Darke County Infirmary—put simply, the poorhouse. She would be in and out of this establishment, between living with abusive farming families, running back home, and eventually returning to her family after her twice-widowed mother's third marriage.

Phoebe became a professional hunter to help with the household expenses, killing game birds to sell to local hotels. Within a few years, she had paid off the mortgage on her mother's farm. Phoebe's mother then sent her to Cincinnati to live with an older sister and attend school, but the young girl preferred the shooting galleries where she could hone her skills.

When Phoebe was 15, she was asked to participate in a public sharpshooting match with a man named Frank Butler. To the crowd's delight, the tiny teenager bested the tall, broad-shouldered Butler. Despite the defeat, Butler began to correspond with the little girl with the big gun while he toured the vaudeville circuit. The two were married the following year. From Butler, Phoebe learned about show business. By 1882, she had changed her name to Annie Oakley and joined him onstage.

More Than Just Sharpshooting

When it became obvious that Oakley was the act's main attraction, Butler became her manager. Around 1884, they approached Buffalo Bill Cody about a position with his traveling western show. After an impressive audition, she joined the extravaganza. The legendary Sioux leader Sitting Bull, who was also part of Cody's show, called her "Little Sure Shot" and legally adopted her. Cody merely called her "Missie."

Oakley's act was more than just shooting at a target: She could shoot glass balls while galloping around the arena on a horse; with a gun in each hand, she could hit two targets at once; and she could shoot upside down and backward while looking in a mirror. Annie stayed with Buffalo Bill Cody's Wild West Show for 17 years, longer than any other performer. After a train accident left her with a slight paralysis in 1901, she quit the show but continued performing as a shooter for 20 more years.

Rather than resting on her laurels, Oakley used her celebrity to help young women become self-reliant. She taught young girls to shoot (a skill still mostly associated with men at that time), and never forgetting her own turbulent childhood, she used her wealth to support and educate 18 orphan girls. Oakley died on November 3, 1926. Never separated from Annie in life, Butler joined her in death 18 days later.

Studs Terkel: Lending an Ear to America

This Chicago oral historian never tired of his work.

✳   ✳   ✳   ✳

FEW CHICAGO PERSONALITIES so captured the energy and pulse of the city as Studs Terkel. In his long career, the writer, actor, and broadcaster focused his attention on the lives of ordinary citizens. Tape recorder in hand, he initiated conversations with all sorts of people—from farm workers and folksingers to switchboard operators and valets—and ultimately popularized the oral history form.

Louis Terkel was born in the Bronx in 1912. He later took the name "Studs" after the protagonist of novelist James T. Farrell's

Studs Lonigan trilogy. In 1923, the Terkel family moved to Chicago, where his parents managed hotels, including a rooming house on Grand Avenue and Wells Street, aptly named the Wells-Grand. Here, and at Bughouse Square—a legendary gathering place for speakers, "soapboxers," and poets—the energetic and ever-curious Terkel absorbed the stories of working-class Chicagoans.

After studying law at the University of Chicago, marrying social worker Ida Goldberg, and completing a year of civil service in Washington, D.C., Terkel returned to Chicago and honed his communication skills. Along with other now-famous writers (including the Chicago-based Nelson Algren, Richard Wright, and Saul Bellow), he participated in the WPA Writers' Project, a Depression-era initiative to keep writers busy and well funded. Terkel worked in the radio division, which led him to gigs on radio soap operas, news shows, and eventually to the stage.

In 1945, he disc jockeyed his own WENR program called *The Wax Museum*, playing a mishmash of jazz, gospel, folk, country, and opera. He then went on to star in an unscripted TV drama called *Studs' Place*, in which he played himself as the owner of a local barbecue joint. NBC axed the show in 1952 (under pressure from the House Committee on Un-American Activities) due to Terkel's left-leaning politics.

Though his television contract was canceled, this action did little to silence Terkel. In fact, he began to make a career out of conversation—asking people questions and encouraging them to voice their opinions and experiences. His most successful radio project was *The Studs Terkel Program*, which broadcast daily from 1952 to 1997 on Chicago's fine arts station, WFMT. On the show, Terkel spoke with a wide variety of guests— labor organizers, performing artists, architects, historians— Chicagoans and non-Chicagoans alike. In 1980, his journalistic work earned him the prestigious Peabody Award.

In 1956, he published his first book, *Giants of Jazz*, followed by many important volumes of oral history. *Division Street: America* (1967) featured interviews with people who had lived in and around the Windy City. "I was on the prowl for a cross section of urban thought, using no one method or technique," Terkel said of this work. "I was aware it would take me to suburbs, upper, lower, and middle income, as well as to the inner city itself and its outlying sections. It finally came down to individuals, no matter where they lived."

He followed this best seller with *Hard Times: An Oral History of the Great Depression* (1970) and *Working: People Talk About What They Do All Day and How They Feel About What They Do* (1974). In 1985, he won the Pulitzer Prize for *The Good War*, which collected citizens' memories and perspectives of World War II. In 2001, he published his last book of oral history, *Will the Circle Be Unbroken? Reflections on Death, Rebirth, and Hunger for a Faith*.

In Terkel's later years, he maintained a jam-packed schedule of writing, interviewing, and community appearances. He published the memoirs *Touch and Go* (2007) and *P.S.: Further Thoughts From a Lifetime of Listening* (2008). In archiving the hopes and daily lives of Americans, he never lost a close connection to Chicago, the city he called "America's dream, writ large. And flamboyantly." The lifelong listener passed away on October 31, 2008, at age 96.

Poet of the Big Shoulders

Who knew a scrappy high school dropout from Galesburg, Illinois, would one day give the City of the Big Shoulders its most fitting nickname?

✳   ✳   ✳   ✳

CARL SANDBURG'S ABILITY to capture the feel of Chicago in the industrial age through his lyrical-yet-gritty poetry secured him a place in the hearts of the working people and in the annals of literary history. Sandburg's vision of the city shaped it for generations to come.

Portrait of Sandburg as a Young Man

The house where Carl Sandburg's remains now rest is the same house in which he was born. The son of Swedish immigrants, Sandburg was the second of seven kids. After finishing eighth grade, Carl went on to various odd jobs, from shining shoes to delivering milk. Ten years later, Sandburg decided to see the world. He got around as best he could, hitchhiking and riding the rails. Later, when he began to write, these hobo days would provide plenty of inspiration.

Influences and Experiences

When the Spanish-American War broke out in 1898, Sandburg—who was still working odd jobs—joined the Sixth Illinois Volunteers. During his service, Sandburg wrote dispatches for the *Galesburg Evening Mail*. When the fighting was over, Sandburg returned to Illinois and entered college (he never received his high school diploma, but his status as a war veteran earned him admission and free tuition at Lombard College in Galesburg). Once in school, he found that he enjoyed writing and reading—poetry, especially—and soon joined a group that called themselves the Poor Writer's Club. The club was made up of socialist thinkers, and Sandburg was heavily influenced by conversations with these peers.

Never one for the conventional path, Sandburg took only the courses that interested him and quit college before he graduated. He began working on his first poetry collection and took odd jobs to support himself. Over the next few years, several volumes of Sandburg's poetry would be published by a small press owned by one of his professors.

Poetry for the People

The poetry that Carl Sandburg wrote was different from much American poetry that had come before it. While Sandburg's poems were rich with imagery and offered exquisitely crafted words and phrases, there was a realism to his work that readers found refreshing and inspiring. This was because much of the writer's poetry turned a reporter's eye on what was happening in America at the turn of the 20th century. Sandburg was used to approaching writing from a journalist's perspective: He had written dispatches during the Spanish-American War and World War I, and he wrote for the *Chicago Daily News* for a number of years.

The country was booming during the early part of the 20th century; Rockefeller, Carnegie, and other tycoons were funneling massive wealth into various industries that created jobs in steel mills, slaughterhouses, and agriculture. But the boom caused problems too. Great numbers of people swarmed into the rapidly growing cities, and soon there were far more people than jobs.

Poverty and illness raged through these communities, and Sandburg, along with other socialist thinkers, grew disgusted with a country that would allow a few to get rich while the masses suffered.

In "Chicago," his most famous poem, he personifies the city, elevating the plight of workers into an almost heroic quest:

Hog Butcher for the World,
Tool Maker, Stacker of Wheat,
Player with Railroads and the Nation's Freight Handler;
Stormy, husky, brawling,
City of the Big Shoulders

Such descriptive language made Sandburg instantly popular; both his *Chicago Poems* in 1916 and *Cornhuskers* in 1918 were big hits with a public who loved his conversational style and everyman themes.

And He Could Sing Too!

Sandburg's longtime love of folk songs led him to publish *The American Songbag* in 1927. It included more than 300 songs (picked up during his hobo days) and played a big part in legitimizing folk music in America. Sandburg performed some of these tunes when he was invited to appear publicly, and he continued to play the guitar and sing throughout the '50s and '60s.

Happily, Sandburg enjoyed success throughout his long life—no long-suffering starving artist stuff here. Sandburg is primarily known for his poetry, and he won his first Pulitzer in 1919, for *Cornhuskers*, a collection of his poems. The second installment of his biography of Lincoln earned him another Pulitzer, and he won the prize a third time, in 1950, for *The Complete Poems of Carl Sandburg*.

Further proving that he was seriously in touch with the pulse of the times, Sandburg won a Grammy in 1959. The Best Spoken Word award was given for his audio recording of a work about Lincoln backed by the New York Philharmonic.

Sandburg died in 1967, having published dozens of books of poetry, songs, children's stories, biographies, and his own autobiography, all of which reflected his tough-but-lovable, strong-willed midwestern identity. He will long be remembered not just as a quintessential American writer, but as a quintessential Chicagoan too.

Carl Sandburg was once asked if there was a word he didn't like. He replied that he never liked the word *exclusive* because it carries the implication that you are shutting people out of your mind and heart.

As a young boy, Sandburg preferred to be called "Charlie" because he thought it sounded more American. He reverted to "Carl" around 1910, with encouragement from his wife.

Keeping It in the Family

How many famous people can one family produce? Let's count 'em down.

✳ ✳ ✳ ✳

The Baldwins

THIS SLICK-HAIRED BAND of brothers includes eldest brother Alec (of *30 Rock* and paparazzi-hating fame), Daniel (of rehab fame), William (Mr. Chynna Phillips), and Stephen (minister and D-list celebrity).

The Barrymores

The "Royal Family" of acting includes Maurice Barrymore, Lionel Barrymore, Ethel Barrymore, John Barrymore, and Drew Barrymore. (Numerous spouses and ex-spouses also dabbled in stage and screen work.)

The Fondas

Henry Fonda (not to mention first wife, Margaret Sullavan), his kids Jane and Peter, and grandchildren Bridget Fonda and Troy Garity. 'Nuff said.

The Hemingways

Talent and tragedy followed the Hemingway family, so it seems. Author Ernest Hemingway committed suicide in 1961 after a lifetime of depression. A similar fate awaited his granddaughter, model and actress Margaux Hemingway. Fortunately, granddaughter Mariel Hemingway, an actress and author, has fared better.

The Marx Brothers

An early stage mom, Minnie Marx made sure that all of her boys got a chance in vaudeville. So it came to be that brothers Chico, Harpo, Groucho, Gummo, and Zeppo—the Marx Brothers—carved a niche in history. Gummo ultimately found that he enjoyed life outside the limelight and left the act to become a talent agent. (See page 171.)

Controversial Queen

In establishing the identity of the Egyptian queen Nefertiti, scholars find themselves up to their necks in conflicting info.

✳   ✳   ✳   ✳

L IKE CLEOPATRA, NEFERTITI is one of the most famous queens of ancient Egypt. She's also often referred to as "The Most Beautiful Woman in the World," largely due to the 1912 discovery of a painted limestone bust of Nefertiti depicting her stunning features: smooth skin, full lips, and a graceful swanlike neck—quite the looker! Now housed in Berlin's Altes Museum, the likeness has become a widely recognized symbol of ancient Egypt and one of the most important artistic works of the pre-modern world. But the bust, like almost everything about the famous queen, is steeped in controversy.

Conflicting Accounts

It wasn't until the bust surfaced in the early 20th century that scholars began sorting out information about Nefertiti's life. Her name means "the beautiful one is come," and some think she was a foreign princess, not of Egyptian blood. Others believe she was born into Egyptian royalty, and that she was the niece or daughter of a high government official named Ay, who later became pharaoh. Basically, no one knows her origins for sure.

When the beautiful one was age 15, she married Amenhotep IV,who later became king of Egypt. Nefertiti was thus promoted to queen. No one really knows when this happened— other than it was in the 18th Dynasty—but it's safe to say that it was a really long time ago (as in, the 1340s B.C.). Nefertiti appears in many reliefs of the period, often accompanying her husband in ceremonies—a testament to her political power.

An indisputable fact about both Nefertiti and Amenhotep IVis that they were responsible for bringing monotheism to ancient

Egypt. Rather than worship the vast pantheon of Egyptian gods—including the supreme god, Amen-Ra—the couple devoted themselves to exclusively worshipping the sun god Aten. In fact, as a sign of this commitment, Amenhotep IV changed his named to Akhenaten. Similarly, Nefertiti changed her name to Neferneferuaten-Nefertiti, meaning, "The Aten is radiant of radiance [because] the beautiful one is come." (But we're guessing everyone just called her "Nef.") Again, it's unclear as to why the powerful couple decided to turn from polytheism. Maybe there were political reasons. Or perhaps the two simply liked the idea of one universal god.

Disappearance/Death?

In studying Egyptian history, scholars discovered that around 14 years into Akhenaten's reign, Nefertiti seems to disappear. There are no more images of her, no historical records. Perhaps there was a conflict in the royal family, and she was banished from the kingdom. Maybe she died in the plague that killed half of Egypt. A more interesting speculation is that she disguised herself as a man, changed her name to Smenkhkare, and went on to rule Egypt alongside her husband. But—all together now—*no one knows for sure!*

During a June 2003 expedition in Egypt's Valley of the Kings, an English archeologist named Joann Fletcher unearthed a mummy that she suspected to be Nefertiti. But despite the fact that the mummy probably is a member of the royal family from the 18th Dynasty, it was not proven to be female. Many Egyptologists think there is not sufficient evidence to prove that Fletcher's mummy is Nefertiti. So, that theory was something of a bust.

In 2009, Swiss art historian Henri Sierlin published a book suggesting that the bust is a copy. He claimed that the sculpture was made by an artist named Gerard Marks on the request of Ludwig Borchardt, the German archeologist responsible for discovering the bust in 1912.

Despite the mysteries surrounding Nefertiti, there's no question that she was revered in her time. At the temples of Karnak are inscribed the words: "Heiress, Great of Favours, Possessed of Charm, Exuding Happiness . . . Great King's Wife, Whom He Loves, Lady of Two Lands, Nefertiti."

The King of Ragtime

Scott Joplin was the most famous ragtime composer of all time. He became known as the King for compositions including "The Entertainer" written in 1902, although he may have gained his greatest fame and renown more than 50 years after his death as composer of the music in The Sting.

❊ ❊ ❊ ❊

DESPITE HIS ENDURING musical legacy, the details of much of Scott Joplin's early life remain imprecise. His birth date is often recorded as November 24, 1868, although it seems likely that it may have been as much as a year before that. He was born near Linden, Texas, where Jiles Joplin, his father and a former slave, worked as a laborer. It appears as though Mr. Joplin boasted at least a rudimentary knowledge of music that he delighted in passing on to his son.

By the time that he was seven years old, Scott Joplin was already an experienced banjo player, and when his family moved to the Texas/Arkansas border town of Texarkana, he was introduced to the instrument that would make him famous. His mother, Florence, did domestic work for a neighboring attorney, who allowed young Scott to experiment on his piano.

The Father of Ragtime

The elder Joplin saved enough money to buy his son a used piano, and Scott's talent quickly blossomed. At age 11, Joplin began taking free lessons from Julius Weiss, a German-born piano teacher who helped shape Joplin's musical influences, including European opera. As a teen, Joplin formed a vocal quartet and performed in the dance halls of Texarkana before venturing out as a pianist on the saloon and honky-tonk circuit that stretched from Texas all the way to Louisiana, Missouri, Illinois, and Kentucky.

In St. Louis, Joplin encountered a style of music that featured abbreviated melody lines called "ragged time," or "ragtime" for short. Joplin adopted the principles of ragtime into longer musical forms including a ballet—*The Ragtime Dance*, written in 1899—and two operas—*The Guest of Honor* in 1903 and *Treemonisha* in 1910. While the orchestration scores for both operas were sadly lost during the copyright process, a piano-vocal score for Treemonisha was later published. It was, however, Joplin's shorter compositions that earned him the title "The King of Ragtime."

From the Maple Leaf to New York

One of his first compositions to be published, "Maple Leaf Rag" in 1899, went on to sell more than one million copies of sheet music. The piece was named after one of the music clubs Joplin enjoyed playing in Sedalia, Missouri, the Maple Leaf Club. Joplin occasionally returned to Texarkana to perform, but by 1907 he was living in New York City. It was here that he wrote his instructional manual, *The School of Ragtime*. In 1916, Joplin's health deteriorated in part due to syphilis, which he'd contracted a few years before. His playing became inconsistent, and he was eventually forced to enter the Manhattan State Hospital, where he died on April 1, 1917. Joplin was married and divorced twice. His only child, a daughter, died in infancy.

Legacy

It wasn't until years after his death that Scott Joplin achieved the full recognition his work deserved. In 1971, the New York Public Library published his collected works, but his music found a whole new audience with the release of the popular 1973 Paul Newman and Robert Redford movie, *The Sting*.

Joplin's work, adapted by Marvin Hamlisch, was featured heavily in the film's score, which won an Academy Award. "The Entertainer," released as a single from the movie, became a bona fide top ten hit.

Joplin himself was posthumously awarded a Pulitzer Prize in 1976 for *Treemonisha*, which has been recognized as the first grand opera by an African American composer. Today, a large mural on Texarkana's Main Street depicts the life and accomplishments of one of the town's most famous sons.

Stand Tall, the Texas Rangers

Among the most revered of Texas's iconic institutions must be the Texas Rangers, whose rich history and daring frontier exploits have thrilled generations.

✳   ✳   ✳   ✳

THE OLDEST LAW enforcement agency in North America, the Texas Rangers has been compared with the FBI, Scotland Yard, and the Royal Canadian Mounted Police. The group's heritage began with the earliest settlements in Texas, and it became a significant part of the story of the Old West and its mythology.

Getting Off the Ground

In Mexican Tejas, the Comanche and Tonkawa raided Texian settlements on a regular basis. Stephen F. Austin, responsible for founding and developing many of these settlements from America, realized he needed a militia of some kind to ward off Native American raids, capture criminals, and patrol against intruders. He set up two such companies, which today are considered the ancestors of the modern Texas Rangers.

In 1835, in what is often considered the official founding of the Rangers, the Texas council of representatives created a Corps of Rangers and set pay at $1.25 per day. These enforcers of the law had to provide their own mounts, weapons, and equipment.

As they were often outnumbered during battles, many carried multiple pistols, knives, and rifles. The most popular weapons were Spanish pistols, Tennessee and Kentucky rifles, and Bowie knives. Later, Sam Colt built his reputation on the fact that the Texas Rangers were the first to use the Colt revolver.

Like the state of Texas itself, the Texas Rangers had multicultural roots. Company rosters show that Anglos, Hispanics, and American Indians served in the ranks. In addition, a number of immigrants were also present; Ireland, Germany, Scotland, and England each contributed native sons to the Rangers.

As the cause for independence from Mexico heated up, the Rangers played a key role in protecting civilians fleeing Santa Anna's army, harassing Mexican troops, and providing intelligence to the Texas army. And it was the Rangers who responded to Colonel William Travis's last minute plea to defend the Alamo. Even so, the Rangers did not participate in actual combat as often as they may have preferred.

Texas president Sam Houston sought good relations with Native Americans, so a fighting force to be used against them was not high on his list of priorities. Texas's second president, Mirabeau B. Lamar, however, felt differently and strengthened the Rangers and their responsibilities when he got into office. He wanted them to clear the frontier of Native Americans who were in the way of Texas settlement and expansion, and the Texas Rangers rose to that call very effectively. The Cherokee War of 1839 expelled most Cherokee from Northeast Texas, and the Battle of Plum Creek moved the Comanchee farther west out of central Texas. When Houston regained the presidency in 1841, he recognized the Rangers as an effective frontier protection agency and threw his support to them.

Making Their Name

In the Mexican-American War that followed closely after Texas annexation, the Texas Rangers distinguished themselves as ferocious fighters. They supported the U.S. Army under

Generals Zachary Taylor and Winfield Scott, working as scouts and extremely effective warriors. This brought them a worldwide reputation as *Los Diablos Tejanos*, the Texas Devils.

For a time after the war, however, it looked as though the Rangers might have had their best days behind them. Once Texas became a U.S. state, the protection of its frontier was a federal issue, and there was no obvious place for the Rangers. Although it wasn't dissolved, the agency saw its purpose wither away and its best officers leave for greener pastures. There was a slight revival under Captain John S. "Rip" Ford in which the Rangers attacked and killed Comanche leader Iron Jacket, but the coming Civil War gave those interested in fighting another focus. Many Rangers and former Rangers served with the Confederacy, but there was no official connection. Reconstruction, likewise, offered little opportunity for the Texas Rangers, as their former frontier duties were handled by the Union Army.

Back in the Battle

That all changed, however, when the Democrats took back the governor's mansion in 1874. The state legislature passed a bill that year formally creating the Texas Rangers (thus making that name official). The Reconstruction government hadn't been entirely successful in maintaining order, so the Rangers had their work cut out for them. Two branches were created by the legislation: the Special Force, focusing on law enforcement, and the Frontier Battalion, protecting the western frontier and borders. The Special Force did what was necessary to get the job done. In one particular infamous incident, Rangers took the bodies of dead cattle rustlers and stacked them in the Brownsville town square as a show of force.

The Frontier Battalion, focusing on gunfighters in addition to Native Americans, had its share of high-profile captures, as well. Not bound by the borders of the state, Ranger John Armstrong captured one of Texas's deadliest outlaws, John

Wesley Hardin—reputed to have killed more than 30 people—on a train in Pensacola, Florida. In the course of the capture, Hardin was knocked out, and one of his three companions was killed; the remaining two surrendered. Another famous train and bank robber, Sam Bass, was killed by four Rangers in an 1878 shoot-out at Round Rock.

By the 1890s, Texas Rangers were upholding the law in mining towns and tracking down train robbers. They were once even called upon to prevent an illegal prizefight. Records show that in one year, the Rangers scouted nearly 174,000 miles, made 676 arrests, returned 2,856 head of livestock, assisted civil authorities 162 times, and guarded jails on 13 occasions.

Into Tomorrow

The role of the Texas Rangers has continued to evolve. Today, they are part of the Texas Department of Safety, and a Ranger is far more likely to have a laptop computer than a horse. Even so, they continue to investigate cattle thefts as well as other major felony crimes. And the stories of their heyday during the early days of Texas live on to support the mythos of the officers who stand tall.

Sandy Koufax: Brooklyn's Best

Sandy was a Jewish son of Brooklyn who became a Dodger. How bittersweet that he didn't show Hall of Fame form until he was playing in Los Angeles!

✳ ✳ ✳ ✳

BORN SANFORD BRAUN in Brooklyn on December 30, 1935, Sandy changed his last name at age nine when his mother remarried. The family moved from Borough Park to Long Island but returned to Brooklyn during Sandy's later teens.

Sandy excelled in basketball at Lafayette High. He walked onto the University of Cincinnati's hoop squad, earning a partial scholarship. Sandy also tried out for baseball and proved a terror on the mound—not always in a good way. A blazing lefthander, he struck out 51 players in 32 innings, which means shock and awe . . . but he walked 30, which means he was wilder than a bag of bobcats.

Artless Dodger

Sandy left Cincy after his freshman year and accepted an offer from the Brooklyn Dodgers that included bonus money. In an unfortunate twist, the bonus probably shortened his career. Why? Well, at the time, baseball rules required "bonus babies" to spend two years on a major league roster—no minor league—and that could stunt their development. Sandy Koufax never got the gradual grooming one would see today in the minor leagues.

Instead, Sandy Koufax went home to Brooklyn and made his big league debut on June 24, 1955. A wild, inconsistent spot starter and reliever, he won nine games and lost ten in the borough. Had he retired rather than gone to Los Angeles, only dedicated Dodger nuts would remember him today. On the bright side, Sandy did get a 1955 World Series championship ring—without throwing a pitch.

On to L.A.

As every loyal Brooklynite knows, in 1957 Walter O'Malley "stole" the Dodgers and lured the Giants away to California with him, leaving the city a National League-free (and Sandy Koufax-free) zone. Once on the West Coast, Sandy gradually improved, working into the starting rotation. However, through 1960, only once did he lead the league in a pitching category: In 1958 he sailed a league-high 17 wild pitches. After the '60 season, he seriously considered quitting baseball.

But as every baseball fan knows, Sandy didn't ditch baseball. From 1961 to '66, he became a nightmare for National League hitters, winning 129 games and losing just 47. He led the league in strikeouts four times, wins and shutouts three times, and earned run average five times. He won four World Series games, three Cy Young Awards, and copious other performance awards. He threw four no-hitters, one of which was the rarest of the rare: a perfect game. Koufax accomplished most of this while in pain from worsening arthritis, using an abused left arm that had come to the major leagues far too early.

But the pain aside, Sandy's dominance while in California was one of the weirdest and most complete career turnarounds in the history of sports, making Koufax a lock for the Hall of Fame. What changed between Brooklyn and L.A.?

It started with advice during 1961 spring training from catcher (and fellow Jewish New Yorker) Norm Sherry, who counseled Koufax to work on being subtle rather than overpowering. Sandy improved his curveball, stopped trying to blow the fastball past everyone, and concentrated on motion, timing, and control. In simple terms, Koufax became a pitcher rather than a thrower.

Shalom

After one last sparkling season in 1966 (27–9, 1.73 ERA), Sandy Koufax retired at age 30. It was that or risk losing the use of his left arm, so bad was the arthritis. He was inducted into the Hall of Fame at 36, an age when most stars are just starting to fade. He then began to rove the country, offering guidance to young big league players and prospects, a lifetime student of the physics of pitching. He's one of the most admired figures in sports.

Koufax did get one opportunity for a comeback. In 2007, when a baseball league finally started in Israel, the septuagenarian Koufax was the final player drafted. Sandy declined to suit up again, but it's no stretch to suppose that the opportunity warmed his soul.

Batter Up! The Babe Ruth Quiz

How much do you know about the Sultan of Swat? Try to answer these 17 hard-hitting questions!

1. On what day was Babe Ruth born?

   February 6

2. What was Babe Ruth's real name?

   George Herman Ruth Jr.

3. Who was the only one of Babe's siblings to live past infancy?

   A sister named Mamie

4. From what minor league team did the Boston Red Sox purchase Ruth?

   The Baltimore Orioles

5. Which major league team had first crack at buying Ruth before the Red Sox?

   The Philadelphia Athletics

6. How old was Ruth when he was purchased by his first major league team, the Red Sox?

   19 years old

7. Who was the Red Sox owner who bought Ruth?

   Joseph J. Lannin

8. What was the maiden name of Helen, Ruth's first wife?

   Woodford

9. Who was Ruth's first manager with Boston?

   Bill Carrigan

10. How many home runs did Ruth hit in the major leagues between 1914 and 1916?

Seven

11. What instrument was Ruth often photographed holding in 1920 during the St. Mary's Industrial School Band's tour to raise money?

The tuba

12. How many games did it take Ruth and the New York Yankees to win their first World Series in 1923?

Six

13. Ruth was suspended by Yankee Manager Miller Huggins in 1925. How much was he fined?

$5,000

14. What did Ruth keep under his baseball cap to keep him cool?

A cabbage leaf, which he'd swap out every few innings

15. Ruth had names for his bats. What was the name for the bat he used to hit his 60th home run in 1927?

Beautiful Bella

16. Who succeeded Huggins as Yankee manager in 1929 after he passed away?

Art Fletcher

17. Off of what pitcher did Ruth hit his famous "called shot" home run in the 1932 World Series?

Charlie Root

From Baseball to Bible Thumper

Billy Sunday was a good baseball player—and an exceptional evangelist who preached to millions.

✳ ✳ ✳ ✳

PREACHERS OFTEN COME from unusual backgrounds, but it's safe to say that Billy Sunday is the only one to play professional baseball before taking up the Lord's calling.

Born on November 19, 1862, near Ames, Iowa, Sunday's early life was less than ideal. His father died weeks after he was born, and his stepfather died prematurely as well. As a result, his impoverished mother had no choice but to send Sunday and his older brother to the Soldiers' Orphans Home in Glenwood, Iowa, when Sunday was around 10 years old. There, Sunday received a good education and developed the prowess that would serve him well as a professional athlete.

From Player to Preacher

Sunday experienced a religious conversion in 1886, and he began speaking at churches and YMCAs throughout the Chicago area. In 1891, he turned down a $3,000 baseball contract to accept an $83-per-month position with the Chicago YMCA, where he honed his preaching skills. Two years later, Sunday became the full-time assistant to renowned evangelist J. Wilbur Chapman, who gave Sunday a crash course in public speaking.

Sunday eventually struck out on his own. A savvy promoter, he used his reputation as a baseball player to help publicize his revival meetings, which drew huge crowds.

It is believed that Sunday preached to more than one million people over the course of his career—all without the aid of a microphone. He made a small fortune as a result, but he donated large amounts to various charities. Billy Sunday died in 1935, following a mild heart attack.

Ghost Hunters Extraordinaire: Ed and Lorraine Warren

There are paranormal investigators and demonologists and then there are psychic research soul mates. This describes Ed and Lorraine Warren, who are considered to be among the pioneers in the field of paranormal research. Ghosts and demons were their bread and butter for more than 50 years until Ed joined the spirit world in 2006.

✳   ✳   ✳   ✳

Home Sweet Haunted Home

ED WARREN—WHO WAS born in Bridgeport, Connecticut, in 1926—lived in a haunted house from age 5 until age 12. His father—a police officer—took a commonsense approach: He explained away the mysterious sights and sounds. But even at a young age, Ed knew better. He heard rapping and pounding on the walls and footsteps roaming the hallways; he also saw ghosts. Although he was frightened, Ed was also fascinated by the phenomena going on around him, and he yearned to know more.

In 1945, Ed married Lorraine, his high-school sweetheart; they were both 18. In the early years of their marriage, Ed worked as an artist, painting landscapes, seascapes, and haunted houses; he sold his works for $3 or $4 each. But of course, you need to *find* haunted houses in order to paint them.

Coming of Age

Although Ed was exposed to spirits as a child, his specialty was demonology—the study of demons and fallen angels. Unlike her husband, Lorraine didn't immediately recognize that she had an affinity for the paranormal, but that soon changed. The pair was on a drive with another couple when they spotted a house near Henniker, New Hampshire, that was rumored to be haunted. Lorraine rang the doorbell and persuaded the caretaker to let them inside. There, Lorraine got more than she bargained for: her first out-of-body experience, during which she hovered near the ceiling.

This was not her imagination or an exaggeration. Since then, Lorraine has refined her abilities, and her skills have been documented by experts. She is what is known as a light-trance medium, meaning that she is able to communicate with spirits; she's also a clairvoyant, meaning that she senses phenomena that are beyond normal perception; in other words, she has a sixth sense. Lorraine can also see the auras—or energies—that surround the living.

A Match Made in Heaven

Simply put, Ed and Lorraine were the perfect couple—perfect for each other, at any rate. Together they investigated more than 4,000 cases, and they were the top psychic research team in the United States for more than 30 years. They lectured at colleges across the country and were interviewed on radio and television shows in the United States, Great Britain, Australia, and Japan. The Warrens were among the few paranormal investigators who were allowed into the "Amityville Horror" house, where they were permitted to take photos—something that only a handful of people were allowed to do.

Over the years, the Warrens' interest in the supernatural only increased; in fact, they founded the New England Society for Psychic Research (NESPR) in 1952. They also opened the Warren Occult Museum in Monroe, Connecticut, which houses numerous items that are allegedly cursed or haunted, including a mirror that was used to conjure spirits.

The Warrens built their reputations through hard work and many years of investigating and documenting the paranormal. Keep in mind that when they began, the field was very small. There were no TV shows featuring ghost hunters, and technology was relatively arcane. The couple investigated with only their experiences and senses.

The Warrens' investigations have been detailed in ten books, two of which (*The Haunted* and *The Devil in Connecticut*) were made into TV movies. Every day, Lorraine receives as many as a dozen calls from people seeking help with paranormal activity. And it all began because Ed needed to find a few haunted houses to inspire his painting career. Looks like the spirits found *them*.

10 Alleged Cases of Feral Children

According to legend, Rome was founded by twin brothers Romulus and Remus, who had been nursed by a wolf. Since then, there have been hundreds of stories about children being raised by animals. Many of these reports are hoaxes. In other cases, the children are not literally feral but are the victims of abusive parents. But there are some surprising incidents that could give the phrase "a walk on the wild side" a whole new meaning.

✳   ✳   ✳   ✳

1. In 2007, a boy approximately ten years old was reported to be living among wolves in the Kaluga Region of Central Russia. He was captured and sent to an orphanage in Moscow, but he managed to escape and is still thought to be living in the wild.

2. Traian Caldarar of Brasov, Romania, became lost and lived among stray dogs between the ages of four and seven. In 2002, he was discovered and returned to his mother. He eventually relearned human language and became a normal boy again.

3. In 2004, social workers found seven-year-old Andrei Tolstyk living in an abandoned house in Bespalovskoya, Siberia, with only a dog for company. They believe he had survived there for almost seven years after his alcoholic parents deserted him when he was an infant. He was placed in an orphanage but reportedly never learned to speak.

4. One of Russia's most famous "wild boys" not only lived with dogs, he actually became leader of his pack. In 1998, six-year-old Ivan Mishukov was finally separated from his beloved pack of stray dogs and placed in a Moscow orphanage. Because he had only been living among the dogs for two years, he was able to relearn language fairly rapidly.

5. Abandoned by her parents at the age of three, Oxana Malaya of the Ukrainian village of Novaya Blagoveschenka spent five years among wild dogs. Rescued at the age of eight in 1991, she eventually acquired language skills and was featured in a 2004 Discovery Channel documentary on feral children.

6. In 2000, ten-year-old Alex Rivas was found among a pack of 15 wild dogs on the outskirts of Talcahuano, Chile. Social workers believe he had been living with the pack for about two years and may have even suckled milk from one of the female dogs. At the childcare center, he could communicate in basic Spanish. He also liked to draw pictures of his favorite subject—dogs.

7. Not all feral children live among canines. Several have been discovered in the company of nonhuman primates. A seven-year-old girl known only by the name Baby Hospital was discovered living among wild chimpanzees in Sierra Leone in 1984. She reportedly never learned how to speak, though she did cry—a trait unusual in feral children.

8. Saturday Mifune of Kwazulu-Natal, South Africa, lived with a tribe of wild chimpanzees for at least a year. Found in 1987 at the age of five, he was placed in an orphanage. Even after living among humans for a decade, he still behaved in a chimplike fashion, leaping from furniture and clapping his hands to his head when disturbed. He died in 2005 of unreported causes.

9. Two-year-old Bello of Nigeria lived with a band of chimpanzees for a year after his parents abandoned him. In 1996, villagers discovered him and placed him in an orphanage. Reports indicate that he never learned how to speak.

10. John Ssabunnya lived with a colony of African Green Monkeys after his parents died in the Ugandan civil war. He was found in 1991, at the age of six, and placed in an orphanage. At 14, he joined the Pearl of Africa Children's Choir, a group dedicated to raising funds for Africa's orphans.

Who Was Davy Crockett?

Just who exactly was Davy Crockett? Was he a rough-and-tumble pioneer, a man whose fearless exploits helped tame the wilderness? Or was he an ambitious and self-promoting politician, made famous by a well-orchestrated public relations campaign and a little help from Hollywood?

✳   ✳   ✳   ✳

A Man from Tennessee

SOME ASPECTS OF David "Davy" Crockett's life are not in dispute, though much of it is. We know that he was born on August 17, 1786, in eastern Tennessee. His first wife was Mary "Polly" Finley, who died in 1815. He soon remarried, taking the widow Elizabeth Patton to be his bride.

Crockett was an excellent hunter. Often his rifle enabled him to provide food for his wife and five children. But he wasn't entirely an outdoorsman: He was elected to the Tennessee legislature in 1821, then the United States House of Representatives in 1827. For the next decade he was in and out of Congress, and when he found himself in a hard-fought battle for the Congressional seat in 1835, he threatened that if he lost the election he would tell his constituents "to go to hell" and move to Texas. He lost the vote and kept his word, departing to Texas, where he met his end at the Alamo on March 6, 1836.

Two Men the Same—Two Men Different

Crockett is always lumped together with Daniel Boone as one of the two premier American frontiersmen, blazing trails through untamed wilderness. Without question, Boone was the real deal. He explored Kentucky when it was populated almost primarily by Native Americans, built the Wilderness Road to provide greater access to the region, led settlers into Kentucky when it was just a howling wilderness, and narrowly escaped death numerous times.

Crockett's life followed a different path. Bitten by the political bug upon his first foray into elected office, he progressed from justice of the peace to U.S. Congressman in a remarkably short time, particularly because political campaigns then—as now— cost money, and Crockett's low-budget campaigns would have embarrassed a shoestring.

Crockett was a natural for politics. Independent-minded and loyal to his backwoods constituents, he was also gregarious, quick-witted, and personable. Once, a flock of guinea hens showed up at an outside political debate and squawked so loudly that his opponent was completely unnerved. Crockett, however, joked that the birds had actually been chanting "Crockett, Crockett, Crockett," which is why the other candidate was spooked. He won the debate and the election.

Contrast that with the stoic and reclusive Boone, who probably would have preferred to swim the entire length of the Mississippi River rather than hobnob and glad-hand. As one story has it, Boone once welcomed a visitor to his cabin and in conversation asked where the man lived. When informed that his guest resided about 70 miles from Boone's home, Boone turned to his wife and said, "Old woman, we must move, they are crowding us."

A Lion with a Touch of Airth-Quake

Crockett enjoyed his reputation as a humble backwoodsman in sophisticated Washington, D.C. This reputation was spread even further by the wildly popular 1831 play *The Lion of the West*. The main character, obviously based on Crockett, is a Congressman from Kentucky named Nimrod Wildfire, who boasts that he's "half horse, half alligator, a touch of the airth-quake, with a sprinkling of the steamboat." Beginning in 1835, with the publication of the so-called *Crockett Almanacs*, he was portrayed in an even more sensational light—as biographer Mark Derr calls him, a "comic Hercules."

Thanks to Walt Disney in the mid-1950s, Crockett became one of the first media sensations of the modern age. By the time Disney was finished with his legend, people everywhere were singing about Tennessee mountaintops and wearing coonskin caps (which Crockett never wore). From then on, Crockett's image as an authentic American hero was set.

A Little of This, a Little of That

So who was Davy Crockett? Like all of us, he's hard to pin down—a combination of different factors that make a characterization difficult. Part frontiersman and part politician mixed with a keen wit, unabashed honesty, and a friendly nature, Davy Crockett in the end was 100 percent uniquely American.

Queen of the Nile

You've got to hand it to Cleopatra: The girl's got some serious staying power. One of the few figures from ancient history to still have a place in the modern cultural landscape, Cleopatra's story continues to fascinate.

✳   ✳   ✳   ✳

✳ Interestingly, one of Egypt's most famous rulers wasn't Egyptian at all—Cleopatra's family was Macedonian Greek in origin.

* Born 69 B.C., Cleopatra (actually, she was Cleopatra VII) was the daughter of Ptolemy XII Auletes, the Macedonian king of Egypt. Cleopatra had several brothers and sisters, most notably her brother Ptolemy XIII. When her dad was dying, he bequeathed the throne to Cleopatra, then age 17 or 18, and Ptolemy XIII, age 12.

* It cannot be denied that Cleopatra was an exceptional young woman. She was extremely intelligent in the ways of business and politics and seriously ambitious to boot. She didn't take being ruler lightly and quickly went to work making sure everyone knew just who was in charge.

* Cleo decided early on to win a few points with the locals. Though her family had ruled Egypt for 300 years, they kept the Greek aristocracy firmly in place by speaking and acting Greek. Cleopatra was the first in her family to learn to speak Egyptian. She observed many of the Egyptian religious customs, too, making the Goddess Isis her patron deity.

* Cleopatra could speak nine languages.

* Her brother and his supporters kicked Cleo out of Egypt in 48 B.C., but then they lost Alexandria to Julius Caesar. According to lore, in order to gain access to the palace, the exiled queen had herself rolled into a large Persian rug to be given to Caesar as a gift. When the rug was delivered, she rolled out onto the floor. Caesar was smitten.

* In 47 B.C., Cleopatra had a son with Caesar named Caesarion. With Marc Antony she had fraternal twins named Alexander Helios and Cleopatra Selene, and later, she had another son, Ptolemy Philadelphos.

* After Caesar's death, Marc Antony entered the picture. The two met in 41 B.C. and they made political magic together, among other things. Antony married Cleopatra four years later.

* She lived a pretty lush lifestyle. Cleopatra was said to bathe daily in milk and had dozens of servants attending to her at every hour of the day.

* When things went downhill for Antony and Cleo, they went down fast. In 31 B.C., Antony and his troops defended Egypt against Roman attacks. It wasn't going so well. The following year, Antony mistakenly heard that his beloved was dead, and reportedly he killed himself in response. When Cleo heard what her husband had done, she killed herself.

* Cleo died as a result of poison. The exact story isn't verifiable, however: Some accounts say Cleopatra knowingly allowed an asp (or two) to bite her. Another version claims she poisoned herself the old-fashioned way—straight poison, no snakes needed.

* Cleopatra was the last of the Ptolemy dynasty and the last pharaoh in Egypt. Rome took over after her death on August 30.

* Most modern stories about Cleopatra cast her as a stunning beauty. Some of the world's most beautiful women (i.e. Theda Bara, Elizabeth Taylor) portrayed Cleopatra in well-known movie versions of her story. But was she really all that? It's hard to say, especially since ideals of beauty change over time. But consider that more than 2,000 years later, we're still mad about the girl.

Charles Waterton: Britain's Monkey Man

Charles Waterton once referred to himself as "the most commonplace of men." He couldn't have been more off the mark. With monkeylike agility and a rude habit of biting friends in the leg, Squire Waterton was not your ordinary British nobleman.

✳ ✳ ✳ ✳

Get Down From There!

CHARLES WATERTON, BORN in 1782 in Wakefield, Yorkshire, had an interesting motto: "He falls not from the bridge who walks with prudence." It was a maxim he fulfilled. In 1817, the Englishman shocked Rome when he scaled a statue of an angel mounted upon the Castel Sant'Angelo, and then assumed the one-legged stance of a stork atop the angel's head. While in the city, he also climbed to the top of St. Peter's Basilica and left a glove behind on the building's lightning rod. Pope Pius VII asked him to remove it, for fear that the rod would no longer work. (Waterton complied.)

A naturalist, Waterton was also obsessed with the thought of flying, and after much study of bird wings, constructed his own flying contraption and dragged it to the top of an outhouse for a test. Friends could barely restrain him from jumping.

The Frankenstein of Taxidermy

Waterton was also passionate about all forms of wildlife, and he began the world's first nature preserve on his family's estate. He traveled to South America to study and collect birds and became famous for catching an alligator by riding it bareback and wrestling it to shore. He invented his own form of "hollow" taxidermy, using mercuric chloride to harden animal skins. In one formal portrait, Waterton is shown with his hair closely shorn in an unfashionable crew cut, with a taxidermied bird on his finger and the head of a cat resting on a book.

But he took his art a step further by sewing parts from different animals together to create weird, Frankenstein-like conglomerations. Waterton's most famous invented creature was called "the Nondescript," rearranging the rear end of a howler monkey to make it resemble a weird monkey/man hybrid. He enjoyed making up stories about its origins, often claiming that it was a new species he'd found on his travels. He was also known to insist it was the head of a British customs agent against whom Waterton held a long-time grudge.

A devout Catholic, Waterton sometimes used his odd creations to make religious statements. He put together an owl and a bittern, for instance, and dubbed it a "Noctifer," explaining to people that it symbolized a new Dark Age brought to England by the Protestants.

Mad Dogs and Englishmen

Waterton's personal life was also, well, *interesting*. He was married at age 47 to a friend's 17-year-old daughter. After his beloved wife died of a fever after childbirth, he refused to sleep in a bed. Instead, he snoozed on wooden planks with an oaken block under his head. Waterton also allegedly kept a tree sloth in his room as a pet. His good friend Dr. Richard Hobson learned to avoid the entrance hall table when invited to Waterton's Yorkshire home, as the squire was often waiting underneath, ready to leap out and bite the good doctor on the leg.

Hobson also witnessed Waterton scratching himself behind the ear with his foot when the squire was well into his 70s. Another time, Hobson saw him hop on one leg across the edge of a rock that leaned over a great chasm. Unfortunately, Waterton's motto failed him in 1865 when he took a bad tumble on his estate. He died a few days later at age 82. His vast collection of artifacts and preserved animal oddities can still be seen at the Wakefield Museum in Yorkshire, England.

Proust's Weird and Wordy Life

Some people just don't know when to stop. French writer Marcel Proust spent the last 13 years of his life penning a novel that topped out at more than one million words.

✳ ✳ ✳ ✳

MARCEL PROUST (PRONOUNCED "Proost") was born to well-to-do parents in France in 1871. A known eccentric, at one point he helped bankroll a house of male prostitution. He wore a fur coat year-round, was a bisexual bachelor, and traveled in the highest circles of Parisian society. Proust became a keen observer of the ways of the wealthy, and he scribbled notes on the white cuffs of his dress shirts while at parties.

After the death of his mother in 1905, Proust dramatically changed his lifestyle. His busy nightlife was abandoned, and he lined his apartment with cork to keep out noise. He wrote all night, propped on his bed with a pile of pens, so that he would have a fresh pen handy should it drop. Once one hit the floor, Proust considered it too germ-laden to reuse.

Proust had already published many short essays and stories when he started his final work in 1908. The title, *À la recherche du temps perdu*, has translated as both *In Search of Lost Time* and *Remembrance of Things Past*. Based on the social intrigue Proust had observed in upper-class Parisian parlors and nightclubs, the book ultimately filled seven volumes. The final installments of the book appeared after the Proust's death in 1922. His massive masterpiece is now considered one of the world's major literary achievements.

From Proust's Pen

✳ "If a little dreaming is dangerous, the cure for it is not to dream less but to dream more, to dream all the time."

✳ "Like many intellectuals, he was incapable of saying a simple thing in a simple way."

People Who Deserve to Be a Lot More Famous

Sadly, inheriting a fortune can make you a superstar while saving countless lives may not. These folks deserved better.

✳   ✳   ✳   ✳

✳ **Philo T. Farnsworth** You can hardly blame him for reality shows, but you should credit this self-taught Utah inventor with the first fully electronic television system.

✳ **Stanislav Petrov** On September, 26, 1983, Soviet Lieutenant Colonel Petrov likely saved 100 million Americans when he recognized an apparent U.S. missile attack as a satellite error and stopped an all-out counterstrike.

✳ **The Funk Brothers** The house band at Motown Records played on more number one singles than The Beatles, The Rolling Stones, The Beach Boys, and Elvis combined.

✳ **Sam Philips** Speaking of Elvis, we have producer Philips to thank for launching his career. He also recorded early records for Johnny Cash, Roy Orbison, and Jerry Lee Lewis.

✳ **Norman Borlaug** This Nobel Peace Prize winner developed high-yield varieties of grain crops that averted mass famine in developing nations, saving hundreds of millions of lives.

✳ **Joseph Rochefort** In World War II, Rochefort cracked the Japanese Navy's JN25 code and intercepted plans for an assault on Midway Atoll. Because of this, the Allies won a crucial victory that shortened the war, saving countless lives.

✳ **Alan Turing** Speaking of codebreakers, Turing deserves credit for cracking the infamous Nazi Enigma code, which saved many lives as well. He also came up with the concept of modern computer hardware and software.

* **Edith Wilson** After President Woodrow Wilson suffered a stroke in 1919, First Lady Edith took over many duties, effectively functioning as co-president.

* **George Mason** In 1776, the "Forgotten Founding Father" wrote the Virginia Declaration of Rights, which inspired parts of the Declaration of Independence. Mason also helped draft the Constitution but ultimately opposed it because it lacked a Bill of Rights and made compromises to defend slavery.

* **Shigeru Miyamoto** Dubbed "the Walt Disney of the digital generation," he's the designer behind Nintendo's *Mario*, *Legend of Zelda, Donkey Kong, and Metroid* games, among many others.

* **Roy Sullivan** Between 1942 and 1977, park ranger Sullivan survived seven direct lightning strikes—certainly worthy of fame.

* **Stan Musial** Between 1942 and 1963, the St. Louis pitcher racked up 3,630 hits, played in 24 All-Star games, led the league in doubles eight times, and had 6,134 total bases—more than anybody but Hank Aaron.

* **Leif Eriksson** The Norse explorer was the first European on record to set foot in North America, beating Columbus by 500 years.

* **Steve Ditko** Stan Lee often gets sole credit for creating Spider-Man, but the reclusive Ditko was the artist who actually came up with the outfit and web shooters, among other details.

Chapter 5

Spooky Events and Strange Coincidences

Shakespeare and the 46th Psalm

It was April 1610, the 46th birthday of William Shakespeare, already England's most acclaimed actor-playwright. He had already written and produced Romeo and Juliet, Hamlet, A Midsummer Night's Dream, and dozens of other masterpieces.

⁂　⁂　⁂　⁂

MEANWHILE, KING JAMES I had decided to authorize a new English translation of the Bible, gathering an impressive crew of scholars and wordsmiths to do so. They had been working on the project since 1607. It would be published in 1611.

Surely these translators were familiar with Shakespeare's work. As literary men themselves, they probably admired his ability to turn a phrase. The story goes(and there's no proof of this) that for Shakespeare's 46th birthday some of the translators decide to slip an homage into the text of Psalm 46. It begins:

*God is our refuge and strength, a very present help in trouble. Therefore will not we fear, though the earth be removed, and though the mountains be carried into the midst of the sea; Though the waters thereof roar and be troubled, though the mountains **shake** with the swelling thereof.*

The 46th word is *shake*.

And here are the last three verses:

*He maketh wars to cease unto the end of the earth; he breaketh the bow, and cutteth the **spear** in sunder; he burneth the chariot in the fire. Be still, and know that I am God: I will be exalted among the heathen, I will be exalted in the earth. The lord of hosts is with us; the God of Jacob is our refuge.*

The 46th word from the end is *spear*. Count 'em up yourself. Shake ... spear.

Coincidence? Maybe. Or perhaps a really cool birthday gift.

The Tyler Tragedy

John Tyler was sometimes called the "accidental" president since he only became America's Chief Executive because of the death of President William Henry Harrison. But once in office, Tyler was almost the victim of another accident that would have removed him from the presidency—and this world.

✻ ✻ ✻ ✻

Technical Marvel

ON FEBRUARY 28, 1844, U.S. President Tyler and a few hundred government officials, dignitaries, and invited guests—including Dolley Madison, widow of President James Madison—had gathered on board the warship USS *Princeton*. The ship was scheduled to take a leisurely journey up the Potomac River.

The *Princeton* was the pride of the U.S. Navy. It was one of the most technologically advanced ships in the world, a steam-powered frigate propelled by a screw propeller instead of a paddle wheel. Its engines were silent and smokeless, using high-grade anthracite coal for fuel. It carried many heavy-duty cannons and two massive guns named "Peacemaker" and "Oregon." The Peacemaker was the largest gun ever forged from wrought iron.

It was able to fire a 212-pound projectile more than three miles, obliterating any target of metal and wood. Nothing could stand in its way.

Fateful Request

In the early afternoon of February 28, the Navy put the ship through its paces for the important people in attendance, including demonstrations of the Peacemaker's awesome firepower.

Later in the day, someone noticed that they were sailing past Mount Vernon. They asked for a final firing of the Peacemaker in honor of George Washington. *Princeton* Captain Robert Stockton refused, saying "No more guns tonight." However, Secretary of the Navy Thomas Gilmer, who was on board, overruled Stockton and asked that the gun be fired.

Everyone who had been down below partying raced up to the deck to see the impressive gun at work again. Meanwhile, Tyler, who had been below deck about to offer a toast, lingered there a moment longer to hear a song sung by his son-in-law William Waller. It was a decision that saved his life.

Carnage

The crowd watched from the deck as the Peacemaker's ease of movement was demonstrated. Senator Thomas Hart Benton moved to the right to get a better view and opened his mouth to try to protect his ears from the roar of the gun. He saw the gun's hammer pull back, heard a tap, and then saw a flash. A moment later he was lying on the deck, unconscious.

The Peacemaker had exploded with terrifying force, sending jagged pieces of iron hurtling into the assembled crowd. When Benton woke up he saw "two seamen, blood oozing from their ears and nostrils, rising and reeling."

Captain Stockton, with his hat blown off and his face blackened by powder, was "staring fixedly upon the shattered gun." "My God!" Stockton screamed. "Would that I were dead, too."

The deck was like a scene out of a slaughterhouse. Blood and body parts were strewn everywhere. Among the dead were David Gardiner, father of the woman Tyler was wooing, with his arms and legs blown off; Navy Secretary Gilmer, with a gaping head wound; Secretary of State Abel Upshur, his stomach torn open; retired diplomat Virgil Maxey; two seaman, a commodore, and Tyler's black slave, Henry. Others wandered around, dazed and bleeding.

Divine Retribution?

The explosion was seen by many anti-slavery advocates as divine retribution, for the deaths of Gilmer and Upshur eliminated two of the strongest advocates for annexing pro-slavery Texas into the Union.

The tragedy was unprecedented in American government at the time, but it was not Tyler's last brush with death. Several days later, returning from the burial services, Tyler's carriage horses inexplicably bolted, sending his coach careening at breakneck speed through the streets of Washington. Just when all seemed lost, an African American man stepped out and stopped the horses, saving the president's life.

LaLaurie Mansion

There is no city in the American South as haunted as New Orleans, which is not surprising given its dark history of death, murder, war, slavery, and on occasion, downright depravity. New Orleans is a city that stands as a prime example of the deeds of the past creating the hauntings of today.

✳   ✳   ✳   ✳

THERE ARE SCORES of ghost stories in the city, but there is no story as famous as that of the LaLaurie Mansion. It has long been considered the French Quarter's most haunted house, and in many early writings of the city, its infamy was so great that it was simply referred to as "the haunted house."

The origins of the ghostly tales centering on 1140 Royal Street began around 1832, when Dr. Louis LaLaurie and his wife, Delphine, moved into the mansion. It was regarded as one of the finest houses in the city and one that befit their social status—the family was noted for its grand affairs and respected for its wealth and prominence.

Madame LaLaurie was considered one of the most intelligent, beautiful, and influential women in the city. She was known for her grand dinner parties that showed off her fine china and imported rugs and fabrics. One of the things that nearly all of her guests recalled about her was her extraordinary kindness.

A Darker Side

This was the side of Madame LaLaurie that her friends and admirers saw. But beneath the delicate and refined exterior was a cruel, cold-blooded, and possibly insane woman—a side that some were forced to see on a regular basis.

The finery of the LaLaurie house was attended to by dozens of slaves. Many guests to the mansion remembered the finely dressed servants, who made sure that guests wanted for nothing. Other slaves, sometimes glimpsed in passing, were not so elegant. In fact, they were surprisingly thin and hollow-chested. Rumors began to swirl that Madame LaLaurie abused these slaves. It was said that she kept her cook chained to the kitchen's fireplace and that many other slaves were subjected to treatment that went far beyond mere cruelty.

Mr. Montreuil, a neighbor on Royal Street, was one of the first to become suspicious that something was not quite right with the slaves in the LaLaurie house. Parlor maids were replaced with no explanation, and stable hands suddenly disappeared, never to be seen again. Montreuil made a report to the authorities, but little, if anything, was done.

One day, another neighbor heard a scream and saw Madame LaLaurie chasing a young servant girl across the courtyard with a whip. The neighbor watched as the girl was pursued from floor to floor until she and Madame LaLaurie at last appeared on the rooftop. The child ran down the steeply pitched roof and vanished. Moments later, the neighbor heard a horrible thud as the child's small body struck the flagstones below. Stunned, the neighbor watched the house that night and told authorities that she witnessed the girl being buried in a shallow grave.

When the authorities investigated the neighbor's claims, the LaLaurie slaves were impounded and sold at auction. Unfortunately, Madame LaLaurie coaxed some relatives into secretly buying them back for her. The entire incident had been a terrible accident, she said. Some believed her, but many others didn't, and the LaLaurie social standing began to slowly decline. Soon, everyone would know the truth.

Unspeakable Horrors

In April 1834, a huge fire broke out in the kitchen of the LaLaurie Mansion. The story goes that the fire was set by the cook, who couldn't handle any more torture at the hands of Madame LaLaurie. As the fire swept through the house and smoke filled the rooms, the streets outside began filling with people. Soon the volunteer fire department was on hand carrying buckets of water, and bystanders began crowding into the house, trying to offer assistance.

Throughout the chaos, Madame LaLaurie remained calm. She directed the volunteers to carry out expensive paintings and smaller pieces of furniture. She was intent on saving the house but would not allow panic to overcome her.

Montreuil, the neighbor who had been suspicious of Madame LaLaurie, came to assist during the fire. He asked if the slaves were in danger from the blaze and was told by Madame LaLaurie not to interfere in her family business. Montreuil appealed to a local official who was also present. They began searching for the rest of the servants and were joined by several firefighters. They tried to enter the attic but the door was locked, so firefighters broke it down.

What they saw in the attic was unlike anything they could have imagined. They found slaves chained to the walls. Cruel experiments had been carried out where people had their mouths sewn shut, eyes poked out, limbs removed, and skulls opened while the slaves were still alive. The men were overwhelmed by the terrifying sight, as well as the stench of death and decaying flesh permeating the confined chamber.

Although the chamber contained a number of dead bodies, many of the slaves were still alive. Some were unconscious and some cried in pain, begging to be killed and put out of their misery. The men fled the scene in disgust, and once the fire was extinguished, bystanders helped the surviving slaves out of the attic and provided them with food and water. It is uncertain just how many slaves were found in Madame LaLaurie's torture chamber. Only a few were strong enough to leave the chamber of horrors under their own power.

As the mutilated slaves were carried out of the house, a crowd gathered outside. Nothing happened for hours, but word of the atrocities began to spread. Madame LaLaurie was responsible for the atrocities in the house, and the people wanted vengeance. Threats were shouted as the crowd grew restless. Suddenly, the gates to the mansion opened and a carriage clattered onto the street. The coach sped past, carrying its passengers out of sight. Madame LaLaurie had escaped, fleeing to a ship that took her far away from New Orleans.

The seething mob on Royal Street was enraged. They decided to take their anger out on the mansion the LaLauries had left behind. They broke furniture, shattered windows, and looted the fine china, expensive glassware, and imported foods before the authorities arrived and restored order. The house was eventually closed and sealed, and it sat on Royal Street, completely empty for years. Or so it seemed at the time.

The Haunted House on Royal Street

Recently discovered letters signed by Madame LaLaurie show that she escaped to France where her dark past was unknown. No legal action was ever taken against her, and she was never seen in New Orleans, or her mansion, again. The same cannot be said for her victims....

Tales of ghosts at 1140 Royal Street began soon after the LaLauries fled. As the mansion began to fall into disrepair, neighbors and passersby claimed to hear cries of terror from the deserted property. They saw apparitions of slaves peering out from the windows and walking in the overgrown gardens.

The house was eventually sold, but the first owner kept it for only three months. He heard groaning sounds and cries in the darkness and soon abandoned the place. He attempted to operate it as a boarding house, but renters usually only stayed for a few days and then moved out. Finally, he gave up, and the house was abandoned again.

The LaLaurie house switched owners several times until the late 1890s, when it was converted into a boarding house for recent immigrants.

A number of strange events occurred during that time. One story told of a tenant being attacked by a naked man in chains, who quickly vanished. There were stories of children being chased by a spectral woman with a whip; screams and weeping sounds from the attic; and on one occasion, a mother was frightened to see a woman in a formal gown gazing into the crib where her infant slept. Even cheap rent was not enough to convince tenants to stay for longer than a week or two, and soon the house was empty once again.

The Haunted Saloon

Over the years, the house served as a saloon, a furniture store, and a refuge for poor and homeless men. In 1969, the mansion was converted into 20 apartments before a new owner, a retired

New Orleans doctor, purchased it. The house was restored to its original condition and turned into condominiums. Apparently, tenants are a little easier to keep today than they were a century ago.

That owner did not observe any supernatural occurrences in the house, but past tenants have told of doors that opened and closed by themselves, water faucets that inexplicably turned on, toilets that flushed under their own power, and other small irritations. Others told of a lingering scream that was sometimes heard in the courtyard at night.

Madame LaLaurie's Secret Graveyard

During a remodeling of the house that took place some years ago, workers discovered an unmarked graveyard under the floorboards of the house. The skeletal remains had been placed there haphazardly and with no sense of organization or ceremony. When officials investigated, they found the remains to be from the early to mid-1800s. Some believe that Madame LaLaurie may have buried these bodies in secret, solving the mystery of why some of the slaves simply disappeared.

But how many of her slaves did she kill? And how many of them have never found peace?

The *Poltergeist* Curse

Considering its paranormal story line and the number of tragic and untimely deaths it's been associated with, it's not surprising that rumors of a curse have become attached to the movie Poltergeist (1982).

✳   ✳   ✳   ✳

COWRITTEN AND COPRODUCED by Steven Spielberg, *Poltergeist* was one of the most successful movies of the 1980s, earning three Academy Award nominations. However, not everyone associated with the movie was able to bask in its success or enjoy their fame.

Only a few months after the movie's release, Dominique Dunne, who played the older sister, died under brutal circumstances. The 22-year-old actress's ex-boyfriend choked her to death in her Los Angeles home.

In 1986, the first sequel, appropriately titled *Poltergeist II*, hit movie theaters. By that time, veteran actor Julian Beck, who played Kane, had already died of stomach cancer. It was hardly unexpected, though, as the 60-year-old actor had been battling the disease for 18 months, including during the movie's production. A second member of the *Poltergeist II* cast passed away in 1987. Will Sampson, best known for his role as the Native American patient in *One Flew Over the Cuckoo's Nest* (1975), died in a Houston hospital six weeks after undergoing a heart-lung transplant. He was only 53.

Then, in 1988, the rumor of a curse really took off following the tragic death of 12-year-old Heather O'Rourke, who starred in all three movies. O'Rourke played Carol Anne, the little girl who first encountered the poltergeist and made "They're heeeere!" the catchphrase of 1982. A few months before the release of *Poltergeist III*, she suffered septic shock from a bowel obstruction and died on the operating table at Children's Hospital in San Diego.

While a number of deaths have occurred among the cast of the three *Poltergeist* movies, the idea that there is a curse on the franchise is about as believable as a young girl disappearing inside a television set. The truth is that four actors who appeared in one or more of the movies have since died, but only two were untimely and unexpected deaths. Most of the cast members, including Craig T. Nelson and JoBeth Williams who headlined the original 1982 release and the first sequel, are still alive and well. As stories of curses go, this one just isn't all that convincing.

Blue Light Cemeteries

Under the full moon, some cemeteries in Texas are known for eerie, flashing blue lights and ghostly figures hovering over certain graves.

✳ ✳ ✳ ✳

Texas's many intriguing mysteries include "blue light" cemeteries. Many people believe that these blue lights and figures are ghosts, angels, or even demons. Others blame the phenomena on swamp gas or foxfire, a luminescent fungus that glows in the dark. The more likely explanation is simpler... and perhaps more mystical.

Geologists explain that normal flashes occur when the mineral labradorite is exposed to bright, natural light. Although they can happen at any time, these flashes become especially obvious at night. The effect is so unique, it's called *labradorescence*.

No Need to Be Alarmed

Labradorite is a blue-green stone that's found in Finland, Nova Scotia, Newfoundland, and Labrador. The mineral has been used for gravestones, especially in Louisiana and Texas. Unfortunately, natural cracks and refractions within the mineral cause it to crumble, especially after years in the hot sun.

Thus, in cemeteries throughout Texas, pieces of crumbled labradorite glisten beneath the moon. Hidden in the grass, those shards reflect moonlight and spark ghost stories.

Or Is There?

According to folklore, labradorite can connect the living to the spirit world. Some psychics use labradorite to communicate with "the other side." Perhaps labradorite gravestones connect the worlds, too.

One of Texas's most famous blue light cemeteries is just west of Houston near Patterson Road. For more than 20 years, curiosity seekers have ignored poison ivy, spiders, snakes, and barbed wire to explore Hillendahl-Eggling Cemetery. It's been called "Blue Light Cemetery" since the 1940s when the surrounding German community moved to make room for a Houston reservoir. Other Texas "blue light" cemetery locations include Andice, Cason, and Spring.

Paramount and the Paranormal

The studios of Paramount Pictures in Hollywood opened their doors in 1926. Since then, they've hosted everyone from early stars such as Rudolph Valentino and Clara Bow to modern mainstays such as Tom Cruise and Harrison Ford. Paramount has been home to some of the greatest performers in Hollywood history—and a few have even stuck around after death.

✳   ✳   ✳   ✳

Location, Location, Location

WHEN YOU CONSIDER the location of Paramount's studios, it's not surprising that they're said to be haunted. After all, the back of the lot shares a border with the famous Hollywood Forever Cemetery. And just as not everyone interred at Hollywood Forever is famous, some of the ghostly residents of Paramount are relatively anonymous. One, a nondescript elderly woman, has been spotted roaming the halls of the Ball Building late at night. Certain that she's lost, several guards have tried to help her, but she always disappears before they can.

A ghost that seems to be afraid of the dark likes to wander around the second floor of the Chevalier Building. Guards say that the floor's lights mysteriously turn on at night after everyone has left the building; but when they investigate, nobody is there. Then there's the woman whose strong, flowery perfume can be smelled on the second floor of the Hart Building. She most often makes her presence known to men by throwing objects from desks onto the floor.

Next-Door Neighbors

Hollywood Forever Cemetery is a prominent neighbor of the studios, and guards working at the Lemon Grove Gate—the entrance closest to the graveyard—tell several spooky stories. One playful yet anonymous spirit seems to revel in getting the Paramount guards to chase it to the gate; then, just as the guards close in, it walks through the wall and into Hollywood Forever Cemetery.

One of Paramount's best-known visitors from next door was also one of its most famous stars. Rudolph Valentino was a heartthrob of the silent era whose most famous role was as the title character in *The Sheik* (1921). In 1926, when he died unexpectedly at age 31, fans the world over were devastated. A riot broke out at his funeral, and rumors persist that a few women took their own lives rather than live in a world without him. For decades, Paramount guards have reported seeing the original "Latin Lover" hanging out by the soundstages. Others say that he comes in through the Lemon Grove Gate entrance, leaving his tomb to visit the film studio that made him famous.

She's Heeeeere

One of the youngest ghosts that haunts Paramount made her mark, ironically enough, in a movie about a haunted house. Heather O'Rourke began her film career with a role in *Poltergeist* (1982), and she quickly became a star. Soon after, she was on Stage 19 at Paramount shooting episodes of *Happy Days*. Sadly, in 1988, she died during surgery at age 12. Her friends and costars remembered fondly that she enjoyed running around the catwalks of Stage 19 between takes, filling the air with sweet laughter. In the 1990s, Stage 19 became home to a new sitcom called *Wings*, and the cast and crew of that show reportedly heard a child laughing and playing on those same catwalks. However, no child actors were cast as regulars on *Wings*, and the people who worked on the show were convinced that it was Heather. Paramount is clearly a place where people are dying to get in, and the dead never want to leave.

The Curse of Camelot: The Kennedy Family

The Kennedys were as close as America got to royalty. Educated, attractive, and about as well-placed in society and politics as possible, the Kennedy family put the "A" in "A-list." But all the beauty, brains, and big bucks in the world can't keep a family safe from natural disaster, calamity, and death—and the Kennedys have endured so much of all three that some wonder if there's a curse on the whole crew.

✳   ✳   ✳   ✳

Incriminating Evidence

OKAY, SO MAYBE if this family had stayed away from the White House and off of airplanes, things would have worked out differently. But for a family so heavily involved in world politics and jet-setting affairs, that has never really been an option. As a result, the Kennedys have seen a rather high number of family tragedies in the sky and on the political road:

President John F. Kennedy's brother Joseph Jr. and sister Kathleen both died in separate plane crashes in 1944 and 1948, respectively.

Another one of JFK's sisters, Rosemary, was institutionalized in a mental ward after a failed lobotomy when she was 23.

America's 35th president, John F. Kennedy, was assassinated in 1963 at age 46.

JFK's brother Robert was assassinated in 1968.

JFK's youngest brother, Senator Ted Kennedy, survived a plane crash in 1964. In 1969, he was driving a car that went off a bridge and caused the death of Mary Jo Kopechne.

In 1984, Robert's son David died of a drug overdose. Another son, Michael, died in a skiing accident in 1997.

In 1999, John F. Kennedy Jr., his wife, and his sister-in-law died when the small plane he was piloting crashed into the Atlantic Ocean.

In addition, JFK's wife, Jackie, suffered a miscarriage and had a stillborn baby during their marriage. When Jackie remarried, her stepson Alex Onassis died in a plane crash and stepdaughter, Christina, died in Argentina of a drug overdose. Several other Kennedy relatives have also died in plane crashes or were involved in deadly car accidents.

Is It a Curse or Bad Luck?

Unlike many rumored curses, there's no ancient origin of the Kennedy curse—no angry king, no agitated 16th-century wizard, no funky tribal hex. No, the Kennedy family's alleged curse seems to have been born out of a general dismay at all the awful things that seem to happen to them. People think one family couldn't possibly fall victim to that many tragedies; thus, they must be cursed!

It's more likely that the general public is more aware of these tragedies because the Kennedy family for generations has lived life in the public eye. Your Aunt Myrtle might've passed away from a strange Amazonian jungle disease on the same day your dog died, but no one's claiming your family is cursed. The Kennedys have lived under scrutiny for decades, which makes the public and media more apt to draw conclusions based on non-corollary information.

In addition, the Kennedy family is big—bigger than most (JFK was one of nine children, and Robert had 11 kids), which increases the likelihood of accidents. The more people there are, the more chance there is that someone's going to die in a remarkable way.

Furthermore, when your entire family spends a lot of time in private jets on international missions, in fast sports cars, and with high-rolling people who tend to live dangerously, the chances are much higher that some of you might perish in plane crashes, auto accidents, and drug overdoses.

Only time will tell if the next generation of the Kennedy clan will fare any better, or if the "curse" will prove to be more than just a popular myth.

Curse of the Little Rascals

Beginning in 1922, the mostly kid cast of the Our Gang *comedies, more commonly referred to as The Little Rascals, filmed a staggering221 episodes over the course of several decades. After the series ended, many of the cast members met strange or untimely deaths.*

✳　✳　✳　✳

Alfalfa

AFTER LEAVING THE Little Rascals gang, Carl "Alfalfa" Switzer was never able to find steady acting work, but he did seem to find a lot of trouble. In late 1958, Switzer was shot and wounded while getting into his car, by an unknown assailant. On January 21, 1959, 32-year-old Switzer was shot and killed during an argument with another man over a $50 debt. The shooter was acquitted when it was ruled he acted in self-defense.

Chubby

His unnatural girth may have brought lots of belly laughs, but off-camera, Norman "Chubby" Chaney's weight was the cause of some concern. When he first joined the series in 1929, Chaney was an 11-year-old who wasn't quite 4 feet tall and weighed more than 110 pounds. In 1935, in bad health and with his weight at around 300 pounds, Chaney underwent an operation to correct a glandular problem. After the operation, Chaney quickly lost more than 135 pounds, but his health continued to deteriorate. Chaney passed away on May 29, 1936, at age 18.

Froggy

Forever known for his bizarre, croaking voice, Billy "Froggy" Laughlin will also be remembered as the youngest Rascal to die. On August 31, 1948, the 16 year old was riding a scooter in La Puente, California, when a bus or truck struck him. He died instantly.

Mickey

Mickey Daniels had the unique opportunity of having been a child on the series and then returning as an adult, playing a truant officer and even providing the laugh of the gang's donkey, Algebra. After the series ended, however, Daniels sank into alcohol-induced obscurity. On August 20, 1970, Daniels's body was discovered in a San Diego hotel room. The official cause of death was complications from cirrhosis of the liver.

Jay

Freckly Jay R. Smith replaced Mickey in 1925. Although he lived to age 87, far longer than many of the other Rascals, Smith still suffered one of the most violent deaths. After he was reported missing from his Las Vegas home in October 2002, a massive search was launched. Several days later, Smith's body, riddled with stab wounds, was found dumped in the desert. An investigation found that Smith had been murdered by a homeless man that he had recently tried to befriend and help.

Scotty

Scott "Scotty" Beckett was one of the most-loved members of the Little Rascals. After leaving the series, Beckett enjoyed a successful acting career that was suddenly cut short by a series of run-ins with the police, including a shootout. On May 8, 1968, Beckett checked himself into a Hollywood nursing home, needing medical attention for what appeared to be wounds from a fistfight. Two days later, the 38 year old was found dead in his bed. Despite the fact that a suicide note and a bottle of pills were said to have been found on his nightstand, the coroner claimed he was unable to determine the cause of death.

Wheezer

Born March 29, 1925, Robert "Wheezer" Hutchins was only two years old when he appeared in his first *Our Gang* episode. Over the next six years, Hutchins would star in nearly 60 shorts. After graduating high school, Hutchins joined the Army Air Corps during World War II (though he didn't see overseas combat). After the war, Hutchins decided to become an air cadet. On May 17, 1945, Hutchins was killed when his plane collided with another aircraft during training exercises at Merced Army Air Corps Field in California. He was only 20 years old.

Unsettling Happenings Aboard UB-65

You've probably heard of ghost ships or ghosts that inhabit ships, but how about a submarine that takes such spooky folklore beneath the waves? German sub UB-65 was one such vessel. From ghostly sightings to freakish tragedies that led many to fear for life and limb, the tale of the "Iron Coffin" is an ominous part of military history.

✳ ✳ ✳ ✳

Das Boot

DURING WORLD WAR I, the German U-boat was feared above all other war machines. It could sink other vessels from great distances without being detected. But the U-boat had its drawbacks. For example, unlike conventional vessels that floated on the water's surface, U-boats were virtually doomed if underwater explosives were detonated near them while they were submerged. But submariners—who are a uniquely brave lot—generally accept such perils as part of their job. This makes the fantastic tale of German submarine *UB-65* all the more interesting.

Commissioned in 1917, *UB-65* seemed cursed from the start. From mysterious mishaps and tragic accidents to ethereal events terrifying enough to scare even the bravest sailors, the events associated with the "Iron Coffin" suggest that it was one wicked vessel.

Devil's Playground

Most warships manage to celebrate their launches before any casualties occur onboard. Not so with *UB-65*. While still under construction at a shipyard in Hamburg, Germany, a structural girder broke free of its chain and fell directly on top of a workman. Pinned by its crushing weight for a full hour, the man shrieked in pain. When the girder was finally lifted off of him, the man died.

Later, just prior to the submarine's launch, another tragedy occurred. This time, a chloride gas leak claimed three lives in the vessel's engine room when dry-cell battery tests went awry. Were such tragedies simply unfortunate coincidences, or was *UB-65* showing distinct signs of being cursed? No one could say with certainty, but many sailors leaned toward the latter.

Chilling Sea Trials

After launching on June 26, 1917, *UB-65* moved into her sea-trial phase. Designed to debug the vessel before it commenced active duty, *UB-65's* "shakedown" tests would prove deadly. Macabre events began when *UB-65* surfaced to perform a hatch inspection. Clearly underestimating the ferocity of a storm that was raging outside in the turbulent North Atlantic, the seaman performing the inspection was swept overboard to his death. This event took a heavy toll on the crew's morale, but sadly, even more misfortune was yet to come.

During a test dive, a ballast tank ruptured and seawater began to fill the engine room; noxious vapors that greatly sickened all on board were produced as a result. It took 12 long hours before events were finally brought under control. This time, the seamen had survived and had seemingly beaten the curse, but just barely. The next event would turn the tables once again and grant the Grim Reaper his much-pursued bounty.

Kaboom!

If there were any doubts about *UB-65* being cursed, they were quickly erased by an incident that took place when the vessel was being fitted with armaments for its first patrol. As crew members loaded torpedoes into firing tubes, one of the warheads inexplicably detonated. The blast claimed the life of the second officer, injured many others, and sent shudders through the submarine. Afterward, crew members were given several days off to bury their fallen comrade. It was a somber period and a much-needed time for healing. Unfortunately, ethereal forces were about to wreak further havoc on the submarine and rattle the men's nerves like never before.

Second Life for the Second Officer

After the crew reboarded for *UB-65*'s first mission, a scream was heard coming from the gangplank. It came from an officer who had witnessed something that his mind couldn't quite grasp. Later, when pressed about the incident, the officer swore to the captain that his recently buried comrade had boarded the sub directly in front of him. Soon after, another crewman reported seeing the dead sailor as well. Believing that his crew was suffering from hysteria, the captain pushed on with the mission. But the situation only got worse when the engine room staff reported seeing the deceased officer's apparition standing where he had perished. Hoping to stave off panic, the captain ordered all talk of ghosts to cease.

Everything went well until January 1918—the pivotal month when the captain himself became a believer. The turnabout took place while *UB-65* was cruising on the surface. A frightened lookout bolted below deck claiming that he'd seen the second officer's ghost topside. Hoping to put an end to spirit-related nonsense, the captain grabbed the lookout and led him back up the ladder. When they reached the deck, the captain's smugness morphed into terror. There, just inches before him, stood the ghost of the dead second officer.

Exorcism

With numerous documented sightings on their hands, the German Navy knew that it had a problem. The sub was temporarily decommissioned, and a Lutheran minister was brought on board to perform an exorcism. Afterward, a new crew was assembled and the vessel was put back into service, but it didn't take long for the fright-fest to start all over again. In May 1918, at least three ghost sightings were reported. One sailor was so frightened to see the second officer's spirit that he jumped overboard and drowned.

That was the last death aboard *UB-65* until mid-July 1918, when the sub mysteriously disappeared while patrolling in the North Atlantic. Conjecture abounds over what exactly happened aboard *UB-65*: Accidental causes or explosive depth charges head up the list of probable culprits for the vessel's demise. In 2004, an underwater expedition located *UB-65* in the vicinity of Padstow, England, but researchers still couldn't produce a conclusive reason for why the sub was lost.

What is known for sure is that this cursed "Iron Coffin" took 37 souls down with her. The Grim Reaper, determined as always, had received his ill-gotten spoils.

World of Wonder!

The laws of nature appear unenforceable at Mystery Hill, a popular tourist attraction in Marblehead, Ohio.

✳   ✳   ✳   ✳

MYSTERY HILL IS located near a limestone quarry that, for years, shipped rock throughout the Great Lakes. However, the small area of the quarry upon which Mystery Hill is located was never excavated and remained untouched. The plot was sold, and in 1953 a house was built there. Today, that's where visitors can marvel at what appears to be nature run amok. Water flows uphill, balls refuse to roll downhill, and chairs easily balance on two legs. Visitors comfortably lean at an almost 45-degree angle without falling over.

The Forest Inside the Hill

Mystery Hill is part of a larger attraction that also includes Prehistoric Forest, a trip back in time to when dinosaurs still ruled. Sure, they're brightly painted plastic dinosaurs, but they're life-size and still pretty impressive—especially when they roar.

Visitors to Prehistoric Forest enter through a volcano and walk under a thundering waterfall where a huge serpent lies in wait. The ten-acre park is a tranquil natural forest that harkens back to Ohio's earliest days. Dinosaurs and other prehistoric creatures lurk among the trees, ready to give guests a fright, and there's also a dig site where youngsters can search for plastic dinosaur bones. Further exploration will reveal such ancient mysteries as Water Wars and miniature golf. There are other bizarre, gravity-defying locations found in Lake Wales, Florida, and Santa Cruz, California, among others. But at Mystery Hill, as it is with much of the unexplained phenomena in Ohio, the mystery and wonder of the natural world can't overcome an Ohioan's entrepreneurial spirit.

Won't You Come Home, Erie Baby?

Lake Erie is the site of old lighthouses, numerous shipwrecks, and even its own lake monster. But a local taxidermist began a fiery debate on the nature of life itself when he discovered a carcass of dubious origin washed up on the lake's shore.

✳ ✳ ✳ ✳

IN 1992, CLEVELAND taxidermist Larry "Pete" Peterson was walking along the Lake Erie beach when he saw a strange carcass washed up on the shore. Having a professional interest in such things, he took it home, mounted it, and set off a firestorm of arguments about the origin of life itself.

Fun with Carcasses

When Peterson found the carcass, it was already a little decayed, and its head was deformed where seagulls had pecked at it. The fishhook in its mouth suggested it had at some point been caught and broken the line. Although Peterson couldn't identify the species, he decided to have a little fun with the carcass and turn it into a display for taxidermy shows. He created flippers for it out of loose flaps of skin, notched its back fin to make it look more like a dragon, and mounted it in a sea serpent's traditional S-shape. At the trade show, Peterson's trophy made a splash, delighting onlookers with its spooky resemblance to a sea monster. Peterson gave the mounted fish a position of honor on display in his shop when he returned home.

In 1998, creationist Kent Hovind visited Peterson's shop and was struck by the specimen. He believed it looked like a young plesiosaur, a type of marine reptile that lived at the same time as the dinosaurs. He took a picture of the display, which he posted on his Web site, and began writing and lecturing about it, using it to advance his theories of a young Earth.

Rally Around Baby Erie

Shortly thereafter, a creationist from Texas named Carl Baugh heard about the display and traveled to Cleveland to see it for himself. He purchased it from Peterson and took it back to display in his Creation Evidence Museum near Glen Rose, Texas, where he renamed it "Baby Erie." According to Baugh, after Baby Erie moved to Texas, museum staff ran several tests including X-rays and CAT scans on the specimen to try to determine its origin. Due to taxidermic tampering, however, they were unable to make any definitive judgments. In recent years, Baugh has admitted that it is unlikely to be a plesiosaur, and that he had taken the sample to a number of academic marine biologists who declared it to be an unidentified eel and a possible missing link to prehistoric marine creatures (and therefore still proof of Baugh's young Earth theories).

Hovind and Baugh's theories caught the imagination of creationists all over the world, many of whom in turn began promoting, teaching, and writing about the "Erie baby" in their pulpits and on Web sites. Most of the Web sites disappeared, however, when the trophy was identified as a modified carcass of a burbot—a long, codlike fish. Despite that revelation, the sad, mutilated carcass of a strange-looking fish remained on display in Texas, proof either of a taxidermist's skill or that cohabitation of man and dinosaurs—as depicted in *The Flintstones*—is not entirely fictional.

Strange Stories from On the Set

Hang around a movie buff long enough and you're sure to hear about strange things that happened on the set while famous movies were being filmed. These are the kind of stories that leave you wondering, "Could that really be true?" Well, curious reader, read on and you might be surprised at what you learn!

❋ ❋ ❋ ❋

Indiana Jones and the Scene-Stopping Stomach Virus

BELIEVE IT OR NOT, one of the most famous scenes in *Raiders of the Lost Ark* (1981)—when Indy decides to simply shoot a sword-wielding enemy rather than fight him—was not originally in the script. Rather, the scene was improvised by Harrison Ford himself. Why? Well, the script called for Indy and the swordsman to engage in a massive fight that would have required several shots and hours of shooting. But Ford, who had come down with a rather nasty case of dysentery, was weak and in pain, making it too difficult for him to do the extensive swordplay that the script called for. So he asked director Steven Spielberg, "Can't I just shoot the guy?" Fortunately for moviegoers, his wish was granted.

Bob Geldof Hits *The Wall*

In a scene from the cult classic *Pink Floyd: The Wall* (1982), actor and musician Bob Geldof, playing the role of Pink, is called upon to trash his hotel room. As cameras rolled, Geldof started breaking everything in sight. But when he pulled down the venetian blinds, he inadvertently cut his left hand. Undeterred, Geldof simply wrapped some cloth around his bloody hand and allowed cameras to keep rolling. The entire scene was later edited down, but scenes showing Geldof cutting his hand, as well as the bloody cloth on his hand, were left in.

Willy Wonka's Somersault

The famous scene in the original *Willy Wonka & the Chocolate Factory* (1971), in which Mr. Wonka greets the lucky winners with a somersault, wasn't in the original script. When first offered the role, actor Gene Wilder said he would do it under one condition: He wanted to do a somersault after faking a limp when he was first introduced. Wilder believed that the act would show audiences that Willy Wonka was capable of all sorts of surprises and that anything could happen. The director agreed, and the now-famous scene was added.

James Dean Takes Method Acting One Step Further

He only made three movies before his life was tragically cut short, but James Dean was known for giving all he had in every scene. Case in point, in *Rebel Without a Cause* (1955), during the scene in which Dean's character, Jim Stark, angrily pounds on a desk in a police station, Dean got so into character that, according to costar Jim Backus, he broke two bones in his hand. The scene was left in the finished film, so when viewers see Dean writhing in pain with tears in his eyes, those emotions are the real deal.

Martin Sheen's Rampage

The scene that opened Francis Ford Coppola's *Apocalypse Now* (1979) didn't look like much on paper. It simply called for actor Martin Sheen to mime a bit of drunken despair in a hotel room, over which his voiceover would eventually be added. But Sheen, a method-style actor, decided that he wanted to explore the dark side of the character from the inside out, so prior to shooting he got intoxicated and then worked himself up into an intense emotional state. Once cameras started rolling, Sheen launched into the unscripted, improvised breakdown of his character, which included accidentally smashing his right fist through a real glass mirror. Despite pleas from the frightened crew, Coppola, who remains an advocate of the method and character improvisations, ordered them to keep filming. The final product was edited down and used in the finished film and has since become one of the legendary performances from the Film School Generation of actors.

Spider's Fake Gunshot Wounds

While filming the scene in *GoodFellas* (1990) in which Michael Imperioli's character, Spider, is shot to death while carrying a drink to Joe Pesci's character, Tommy, Imperioli cut his hand on a glass and had to be taken to the hospital. Seeing the fake gunshot wounds all over Imperioli, emergency room attendees immediately began preparing to operate. When they were told the wounds were fake, they were so outraged that they ordered Imperioli back into the waiting room, where he sat for three hours before being seen.

Local Legends: the Hodag

If you're ever in Wisconsin's northern forests, especially if you happen to be near Rhinelander, be sure to beware the fearsome Hodag. But what exactly is a Hodag?

❋ ❋ ❋ ❋

THE HODAG IS an unusual creature that was discovered in 1893. It is savage and ferocious. It walks on four legs, is anywhere from seven to eight feet long, weighs roughly 265 pounds, and has two horns on its head and a row of spines down its back and tail. It appears to be somewhat like a dinosaur, yet it's covered with short, dark fur. Fortunately, the Hodag is exceedingly rare. It was thought to be a lumberjack's tall tale, something like Paul Bunyan, until one was captured by a man named Gene Shepard.

Or at least, that's what Shepard said. The story of the Hodag is also very much his story, too.

Gene Shepard was born in 1854, in Hortonia. He grew up in south central Wisconsin and eventually settled near Rhinelander, where he worked as a timber cruiser—a surveyor and estimator for the logging industry. He was so successful that he eventually was able to live a rather independent lifestyle, but his real genius took an unusual form: He loved to play practical jokes.

This was the age of the humbug. Audiences enjoyed the miraculous, even when they knew they were being fooled. For example, in 1869, a famous and popular New York attraction was the Cardiff Giant, which was a huge "petrified man" supposedly discovered underground by well diggers. When P. T. Barnum, of circus fame, was unable to purchase the stone giant for his own exhibit, he had another one carved and put it on display as the original.

Shepard's bizarre temperament led him to occasionally pretend to be a hobo. He entertained business associates by serving them roast beef and afterward "revealing" that it had actually been dog meat. He doused ordinary moss with cheap perfume and sold samples of it as a naturally scented rarity. In short, he was the ultimate hoaxer.

The Lore of the Lumberjacks

Lumberjacks already spoke of the Hodag and also told stories of other strange beasts, such as the Gumberoo, the Whirling Whimpus, and the Side Hill Gouger. But in 1893, Shepard claimed to have actual proof of the Hodag's existence.

According to Shepard, he and a party of hunters had cornered a specimen of the beast and, after a fierce battle, finally destroyed it with dynamite. The charred remains were exhibited in town for all to see—if they paid first.

Three years later, a Hodag was finally captured alive, after being drugged in its den with chloroform. Shepard and his crew dragged it back to Rhinelander and exhibited it in a pit. The moment of capture was documented in a photograph, which became a popular postcard—the first of countless Rhinelander Hodag souvenirs.

The Hodag was subsequently shown inside dim tents at fairs in Antigo, Wausau, and even at the Wisconsin State Fair, amazing all (for the cost of a dime) with its slow, mechanical movements and guttural growls. Supposedly, the Smithsonian Institution even inquired about the creature. Shepard finally removed the specimen to a hut on his Rhinelander property, where it was accidentally destroyed in a fire.

Legacy of the Beast

Shepard passed away in 1923, but the Hodag lives on, as the City of Rhinelander's official mascot. The beast serves as the city's goodwill ambassador, and the high school's teams call themselves the Hodags. An annual Hodag Country Festival is held. The beast's image is featured on local advertising and even police cars, and several Hodag statues are on display in the area.

Was it all a hoax? Shepard is said to have admitted as much, but it is a fact that the legendary Hodag of the lumberjacks looks quite a bit like another supposedly mythical creature, the "water panther" of the Ojibwa (Chippewa). It's shown in Native American pictographs throughout the Great Lakes area. Images portray a long and low creature just like the Hodag, with two horns and a row of spines down its back. Perhaps Shepard used that legend as his inspiration...

Summerwind: Wisconsin's Most Haunted House

On the shores of West Bay Lake, in northeastern Wisconsin, are the ruins of a once-grand mansion known as Summerwind. The house is long gone, but the memories remain—as do several ghostly legends.

✳ ✳ ✳ ✳

A Frightening Beginning

SUMMERWIND WAS BUILT by Robert P. Lamont in 1916 as a summer home. It provided a quiet place for Lamont to escape the pressures of life in Washington, D.C., where he worked in politics, later serving as the secretary of commerce under President Herbert Hoover.

But life was not always sublime at Summerwind. Those who claim ghost stories of the house were "created" later on forget the tale of Lamont's spirit encounter. According to legend, Lamont fired a pistol at a ghost inside the house, and bullet holes remained in the basement door for years as evidence of this encounter. After Lamont's death in 1948, the house was sold several times, and nothing out of the ordinary occurred for years.

Insanity and Spirits

Arnold and Ginger Hinshaw and their six children moved into Summerwind in the early 1970s. They stayed for only six months, but it was an eventful time. As soon as they moved in, the Hinshaws saw strange things in the house. Vague shapes and shadows moved down the hallways. Voices mumbled in dark, empty rooms but stopped when the rooms were entered. More alarming was the apparition of a woman who was often seen floating past the French doors off of the dining room.

The family wondered if they were imagining things, but events convinced them otherwise. Appliances, a hot-water heater, and a water pump mysteriously broke down and then started working again before a repairperson was called. Windows and doors opened on their own. One particular window raised and lowered itself at all hours. Out of desperation, Arnold drove a heavy nail through the window casing, and it finally stayed closed.

One morning, Arnold walked out to his car to leave for work when the vehicle suddenly burst into flames. No one was near it. Of course, it's unknown whether the source of the fire was supernatural in origin or not, but no cause was ever found.

Despite the strange events, the Hinshaws wanted to make the best of their house, so they hired workers to make renovations. Crews would often skip work, claiming illness. Some told Ginger they avoided Summerwind because of its haunted reputation. The Hinshaws eventually gave up and tried to do the work themselves.

One day, while painting a bedroom closet, Arnold pulled out a shoe drawer from the back of the closet and noticed a large, dark space behind it. He wedged himself into the narrow opening and looked around with a flashlight. Suddenly, he jumped back, scrambling away from the opening—there was a body in the wall!

Thinking that it was an animal, Arnold tried to get a better look, but he couldn't fit into the space. So he asked his daughter Mary to take a better look. She crawled into the space with a flashlight and screamed—it was a human corpse! Hinshaw claimed they found a skull with strands of dark hair still attached and several long bones.

For whatever reason, the Hinshaws never contacted the authorities. They decided to leave the body where it was, not thinking that the hidden remains might be the cause of supernatural activity in the house. Things then took a turn for the worse at Summerwind.

Arnold began staying up late, madly playing an organ the Hinshaws had purchased when they moved in. His playing became a frenzied mix of notes that seemed to make no sense and grew louder as the night wore on. Arnold claimed voices in his head demanded he play. He would often stay up until dawn, frightening his family so badly that they huddled together in a bedroom, cowering in fear.

Soon after, Arnold apparently suffered a nervous breakdown, and Ginger attempted suicide around the same time. Were the strange stories of Summerwind merely the result of two disturbed minds? But what about the children who also reported ghostly encounters?

Return to Summerwind

The Hinshaws eventually divorced after Arnold was sent away for treatment. Ginger later remarried and settled into a new, peaceful life but was shocked a few years later when her father, Raymond Bober, announced he was going to buy Summerwind. Bober planned to turn the mansion into a restaurant and an inn.

Ginger was horrified at her father's plan and begged him not to buy the property. His mind was made up—he knew the house was haunted and claimed that he knew the identity of its ghost. Bober said the ghost was Jonathan Carver, an 18th-century explorer who was searching for a deed that was given to him by the Sioux nation—allegedly giving him rights to the northern two-thirds of Wisconsin. Carver believed the deed was in a box, sealed into the foundation. Bober claimed that Carver had asked for his help in finding it.

The story goes that shortly after Bober bought the house, he, his son Karl, Ginger, and her new husband, George Olsen, spent a day exploring the house. After Ginger told them about the bones, they opened the hidden chamber to search for the remains, but they were gone. Where had the corpse gone? Had it ever been there at all?

History Lost

Bober's plans did not go smoothly. Workers refused to stay on the job, complaining of tools disappearing and feeling as though they were being watched. The project went over budget and was eventually abandoned. However, Bober did not give up on finding Jonathan Carver's deed. He spent many days searching, chipping away at the foundation. To this day, the mysterious deed has never been found.

The house was abandoned in the early 1980s and fell deeper into ruin. In 1986, investors reportedly purchased the house, hoping to revive Bober's idea of a restaurant, but Summerwind was struck by lightning two years later and it burned to the ground. Today, only the foundation, the stone chimneys, and perhaps the ghosts remain.

Local Legends: Resurrection Mary

Most big cities have ghost stories, and Chicago is no different. But beyond the tales of haunted houses and spirit-infested graveyards, one Chicago legend stands out. It's the story of a beautiful phantom that nearly everyone in the Windy City has heard of. Her name is "Resurrection Mary," and she is Chicago's most famous ghost.

✳   ✳   ✳   ✳

THE STORY OF Resurrection Mary begins in the mid-1930s and centers around the Oh Henry Ballroom (known later as Willowbrook Ballroom), located in the southwestern suburbs on Archer Avenue. Several young men began relating similar stories of meeting a girl at a dance, spending the evening with her, and then offering her a ride home at closing time. Her vague directions always led to the gates of Resurrection Cemetery—where the girl would inexplicably vanish!

A short time later, numerous drivers began reporting a ghostly young woman on the road near the gates of Resurrection

Cemetery. Some drivers claimed that she was looking for a ride, but others reported that she attempted to jump onto the running boards of their automobiles as they drove past. Some drivers even claimed to have accidentally run over the girl outside the cemetery, but when they went to her aid, her body was gone. Others said that their automobiles actually passed through the young woman before she disappeared through the cemetery gates.

Police and local newspapers began hearing similar stories from frazzled drivers who had encountered the mysterious young woman. These firsthand accounts created the legend of Resurrection Mary.

One Last Dance

One of the prime candidates for Mary's real-life identity was a young Polish girl named Mary Bregovy. Mary loved to dance, especially at the Oh Henry Ballroom, and was killed one night in March 1934 after spending the evening at the ballroom and then downtown at some of the late-night clubs. She was killed along Wacker Drive in Chicago when the car she was riding in crashed into an elevated train support. Her parents buried her in Resurrection Cemetery, and a short time later, a caretaker spotted her ghost walking through the graveyard. Stranger still, passing motorists on Archer Avenue soon began telling stories of her apparition trying to hitch rides as they passed by the cemetery's front gates. For this reason, many believe that the ghost stories of Mary Bregovy may have given birth to the legend of Resurrection Mary. Many believe she is continually returning to her eternal resting place after one last dance.

Will the Real Resurrection Mary Please Stand Up?

However, there may be more than one Resurrection Mary haunting Archer Avenue. Descriptions of the phantom have varied. Mary Bregovy had bobbed, light-brown hair, but some reports describe Resurrection Mary as having long blonde hair. Who could this ghost be?

It's possible that this may be a young woman named Mary Miskowski, who was killed along Archer Avenue in October 1930. According to sources, she also loved to dance at the Oh Henry Ballroom and at some of the local nightspots. Many people who knew her believed that she might be the ghostly hitchhiker.

We may never know Resurrection Mary's true identity. But there's no denying that sightings of her have been backed up with credible eyewitness accounts. Witnesses have given specific places, dates, and times of their encounters with Mary— encounters that remain unexplained. Besides that, Mary is one of the few ghosts to ever leave physical evidence behind!

She Left Her Mark on the Cemetery Gates

On August 10, 1976, around 10:30 P.M., a man driving past Resurrection Cemetery noticed a young girl wearing a white dress standing inside the cemetery gates. She was holding on to the bars of the gate, looking out toward the road. Thinking that she was locked in the cemetery, the man stopped at a nearby police station and alerted an officer to the young woman's predicament. An officer responded to the call, but when he arrived at the cemetery, the girl was gone. He called out with his loudspeaker and looked for her with his spotlight, but nobody was there. However, when he walked up to the gates for a closer inspection, he saw something very unusual. It looked as though someone had gripped the oxidized bronze bars with such intensity that handprints were seared into the metal. The bars were blackened and burned at precisely the spot where a small woman's hands would have been.

When word got out about the handprints, people from all over came to see them. Cemetery officials denied that anything supernatural had occurred, and claiming that the marks were created when a truck accidentally backed into the gates and a worker tried to heat them up and bend them back. It was a convenient explanation, but most people still had their suspicions.

Cemetery officials were disturbed by this new publicity. In an attempt to dispel the crowds of curiosity seekers, they tried to remove the marks with a blowtorch. This made them even more noticeable, so they cut out the bars, with plans to straighten or replace them. Removing the bars only made things worse, as people wondered what the cemetery had to hide. Local officials were so embarrassed that the bars were put back into place, straightened, and then left alone so that the burned areas would oxidize and eventually match the other bars. However, the blackened areas of the bars did not oxidize, and the twisted handprints remained obvious until the late 1990s, when the bars were finally removed. At great expense, Resurrection Cemetery replaced the entire front gates, and the notorious bars were gone for good.

A Broken Spirit Lingers

Sightings of Resurrection Mary aren't as frequent as in years past, but they do continue. Even though a good portion of the encounters can be explained by the fact that Mary has become such a part of Chicago lore that nearly everyone has heard of her, some of the sightings may be authentic. Whether you believe in her or not, Mary is still seen walking along Archer Avenue, people still pick her up during the cold winter months, and she continues to be the Windy City's most famous ghost.

Take a Walk on the Other Side

At England's Falstaff's Experience, ghosts—and the ghostly possession of visitors—are routine occurrences.

❋ ❋ ❋ ❋

BY DAY, THE Falstaff's Experience in England's Stratford-upon-Avon is an amusing historical and ghost-themed attraction. Costumed mannequins, coffins dripping fake blood, and a re-creation of a "plague cottage" are among the displays that provide chills and thrills to visitors. At night, however, the atmosphere can turn sinister. In total darkness, dozens of spirits freely roam both floors of the building and appear on the staircases between them. Only ghost hunters with nerves of steel should join one of the "midnight vigils" at the Falstaff's Experience.

A Beastly Barn

The land under the Falstaff's Experience is believed to have been a Saxon cemetery in the sixth century. As Christianity became popular in Britain, early burial grounds such as this were typically dismissed as pagan and built over. By the 12th century, the site included a home and a barn used for trading sheep and wool (hence it's name: Sheep Street). However, that wool became infamous in the 14th century when it carried fleas infested with bubonic plague to the area. Thousands of people died; their homes became known as plague cottages.

Later, the barn and house belonged to one of King Henry VIII's archers, William Shrieve. Even today, many people refer to the site as "Shrieve's House," particularly because his ghost has been seen there.

During the English Civil War in the 17th century, the barn was used as a hospital, and some people think the spirits of many wounded soldiers have never left the building. The soldiers died slow, bloody, and feverish deaths in an era when painkillers barely existed. When the TV show *Most Haunted Live* filmed at the Falstaff's Experience in 2004, medium Derek Acorah was possessed by a soldier whose arm was being amputated. From Acorah's slurred speech and drunken singing, it seems that the soldier's only anesthetic was liquor. Today the barn is known as one of the most haunted places in Britain.

Midnight Vigils

During the midnight vigils at the Falstaff's Experience, visitors explore several ground-floor rooms of the old barn before they're led up the stairs. People often report feeling a sense of dread as they climb these steps—some even leave the tour before reachingthe upper floor. Many visitors describe the feeling of invisible hands grabbing them around the ankles; others have seen bloody soldiers who prevent them from continuing. Other people talk about a sense of imminent danger or even death. For those who make it up the stairs, even more haunting experiences await.

Visitors have been known to see streetlights shining through an open window several feet above the haunted staircase. This seems normal enough, until the tour guide turns on the building's interior lights to reveal that there is no window and nothing to explain the lights. Some believe the image is from an earlier time when a window was there; others feel it may be a portal to another, ghostly dimension. Women are especially vulnerable near the staircase, where they may encounter the malicious spirit of John Davies.

Sharpened Senses

In the Middle Ages, John Davies traveled the countryside sharpening knives and axes. The weapons came in handy, for Davies is known as one of England's earliest serial killers. Several of his victims, usually women, were killed on Sheep Street, where he often conducted business.

When Davies's ghost appears at the Falstaff's Experience, it's been said that he's an average-looking man wearing a white shirt and brown breeches. Of particular note are the bloody knife he appears to be carrying and the stench of his breath. His ghost has been known to frighten women by breathing on them—usually on the cheek or neck—in the upper floor of the barn.

Playful Lucy

As visitors move past the staircase and onto the upper level, they'll come to Lucy's room. Little Lucy is a mischievous ghost-child whose mother was accused of witchcraft in the 1700s. The young girl was questioned, tortured, and killed, but she never betrayed her mother.

Today, Lucy allegedly pats visitors' hair, tugs at jewelry, and moves small items around her room. People have taken off their necklaces and held them out, only to find ghostly hands pulling at the jewelry. It's as if she never gets tired of playing. Lucy's innocence is in sharp contrast to other areas of the Falstaff's Experience.

Ghostly Slideshow

Visitors courageous enough to stand directly beneath the upstairs smoke alarm may see something startling. In the eerie green light from the alarm, a visitor's appearance is often transformed to resemble a ghost. A few seconds later another ghost manifests, and so on. People have seen as many as half a dozen different apparitions of varying ages, genders, and hairstyles. Some wear jewelry, and even their clothing may be visible. Those who volunteer are not permanently possessed. Apparently, the ghosts are simply using the person as a backdrop to project their images—think of it as Possession Lite. Mostly, volunteers have described a sense of imbalance, saying the experience is not scary, just very strange.

Don't Look Back

History has shown that after leaving one room in the Falstaff's Experience, it's best not to go back into it. Visitors who have returned to an earlier room have described feeling disoriented. Some ghost hunters have seen a hooded figure when they returned to Lucy's room. Others felt as if the furniture was floating around them or they were sinking into another dimension. Videos taken by visitors have shown unexplained figures moving in front of the camera. It's as if the ghosts are willing to let people pass through their home, but they want them to keep moving. The one exception is Davies, the knife sharpener. He often follows guests from room to room until they finally leave.

No matter the experience, it's pretty safe to say that the Falstaff's Experience is one of the few places in the world where you can safely get a sense of what it's like on "the other side."

The Phantom Flapper

Nearly every Broadway theater seems to have a resident ghost. For example, the ghost of Samuel "Roxy" Rothafel, the man who opened Radio City Music Hall in 1932, is said to make an appearance at the world-famous venue on the opening night of every new production. But few, if any, Broadway palaces seem to be as notably haunted as the New Amsterdam Theatre—a glamorous Art Nouveau structure located on 42nd Street.

For many years, the New Amsterdam Theatre, which was built in 1903, served as the home of the Ziegfeld Follies—an elaborate, highly successful series of theatrical productions and variety shows. The theater was hit hard during the Great Depression, and by the late 1930s, it was turned into a movie house. By the end of the 20th century, the once-lavish venue was crumbling along with many other buildings nearby. But since then, the New Amsterdam has been restored to its original grandeur, and it features at least one ghostly reminder of its past.

※　※　※　※

The Original Flapper

BORN IN 1894 into a working-class family, Olive Thomas was married at age 16. In 1914, she won a beauty contest for the "most beautiful girl in New York." This landed her a job as a model, which, in turn, got her portrait featured on the cover of the *Saturday Evening Post*.

After appearing in a bit part in the *Ziegfeld Follies*, Olive was given a juicy role in *Ziegfeld Midnight Frolic*, a racier production that was held after hours at the New Amsterdam's rooftop garden. During her performance, Olive was expected to sing songs with a strict sense of decorum while dressed only in balloons that male patrons could (and did) pop with their cigars. The rooftop stage also featured a glass catwalk that extended over the audience, upon which the girls would "fish for millionaires." It is said that some wore bloomers and some did not.

After putting in her time as a showgirl, Olive made the move to silent films. She appeared in more than a dozen features and shorts, but it was her starring role in *The Flapper* (1920) that would define her career and her generation.

But all the while, Olive kept a secret from the public: In 1915, she had divorced her first husband, and a year later, she married Jack Pickford, whose sister Mary was the most famous actress in the world at the time. Mary Pickford was "America's Sweetheart," and her family didn't approve of Jack marrying a girl like Olive, who had a reputation for scandal.

A Fallen Star

The stress of dealing with Jack's disapproving relatives and the couple's busy careers (which kept them apart for long periods at a time) put great stress on their union. In 1920, they finally found time to take a vacation to Paris, but their trip would end in tragedy. While in the dark bathroom in her hotel room, Olive accidentally drank a large quantity of the poison bichloride of mercury, thinking that it was a different medication (the blue bottle's label was written in French). She died in a hospital three days later amid rumors that she had been murdered or had committed suicide after a wild night of partying. In reality, her death was simply a tragic accident.

Gone but Not Forgotten

Most ghosts tend to haunt the places where they died. But almost immediately after Olive's death, baffled stagehands at the New Amsterdam Theatre reported seeing her apparition backstage. Nearly everywitness claimed that the spectral Olive was carrying a blue bottle.

Over the years, the theater fell into disuse and disrepair, and sightings of Olive's ghost tapered off. But in the 1990s, the Walt Disney Company leased the theater and began a massive restoration project. Early in the process, Dana Amendoula— whom Disney left in charge of the theater—was awakened in the middle of the night by a frantic phone call from a security guard. The guard said that he'd been making his rounds when he encountered a young woman wearing a green dress and a beaded, flapper-style headdress; she was walking across the stage carrying a blue bottle. When he shouted to get her attention, she simply floated off the stage and walked through a wall.

Sightings of Olive continued throughout the theater's four-year renovation. She appeared almost exclusively to men, and, once or twice, she was even heard to say "Hiya, fella!" in a flirty voice.

Her presence in the theater became so well known that, to this day, employees have a habit of saying "Good morning, Olive" when they arrive for work and "Good night, Olive" when they leave. Olive seems to be a friendly spirit, but she has been known to cause disturbances when new shows are performed and on nights when veterans of the original *Ziegfeld Follies* were present. (The theater used to stage *Follies* reunions, but the last surviving cast member, Doris Eaton Travis, died in 2010 at age 106.) Rattling scenery and inexplicable lighting issues are common during these times.

In 2005, Amendoula told *Playbill* (the magazine of the Broadway world) that Olive had also been seen floating around in an empty upstairs room—the room that was once the rooftop garden and the home of the *Ziegfeld Midnight Frolic*. She may have died nearly a century ago, but it appears that Olive Thomas may still be at the New Amsterdam Theatre "fishing for millionaires."

At the Belasco Theatre on 44th Street in New York City, there's at least one person who's no longer in the program but still shows up for every curtain call: the ghost of former owner David Belasco, who built the neo-Georgian playhouse in 1907. Once one of the most important men on Broadway, Belasco was so passionate about the theater that he has continued to attend opening night performances since his death in 1931. Sometimes, his spirit is accompanied by that of a woman known simply as "the Blue Lady."

Near-Death Experiences Are Not All Black or White

Nothing about a near-death experience (NDE) is black or white—except, of course, for the light at the end of the tunnel. No matter what you believe about the afterlife (or lack thereof), one thing is certain: We're all going to die someday. Some deaths are premature, however, and when this is the case, the person gets sent back to earth with a memory to last a lifetime.

✳   ✳   ✳   ✳

IN 2009, AFTER enduring 30 years of back pain due to arthritis, Marcia Bergman decided that she'd had enough. Although there were plenty of doctors near her home in suburban Indianapolis, Marcia followed a friend's recommendation to see a doctor in Kentucky. That's where her unusual and eerie journey began.

A Change of Plans

Marcia's doctor scheduled her for back surgery, but when she underwent routine X-rays prior to the procedure, a small spot was discovered on her lung. The back surgery was immediately put on hold and the growth was biopsied; unfortunately, it was found to be cancer. Suddenly, instead of preparing for back surgery, Marcia was facing an operation to remove a malignant tumor from her lung.

The tumor was small and the surgery went well, and the doctors were confident that they'd removed all of the cancer. The near-death experience happened later, when Marcia was almost ready to go home. In fact, the nurse had just removed the central line from Marcia's jugular vein. To make the blood clot at this site, the nurse was supposed to hold his thumb over the vein for five minutes. But he was apparently distracted by *The Oprah Winfrey Show*, which was on the television set in Marcia's room. Marcia started to feel a little funny and she suspected that the process was taking too long. It was. Essentially, the nurse kept his finger on Marcia's jugular vein for too long, and his carelessness stopped the blood flow to her brain, causing her to die right there in the chair.

View from Above

The next thing that Marcia remembered was floating above her body. She heard the nurse call her name and she watched herself fall over.

Unlike some people who see a white light, Marcia said that she went from seeing herself in the hospital room to seeing nothing but black all around her. The next thing she knew, she was waking up in the intensive care unit—three days later.

Seeing the Light

"Looking back, I really think this all happened for a reason," Marcia said. "The doctor I saw later in Indiana doesn't take presurgical X-rays, so they never would have found the cancer." Two years later, Marcia was still cancer-free, and her back had also been repaired, allowing her to enjoy her favorite hobby: working in her flower garden.

Marcia said that her NDE may not have been as complete as some; after all, she didn't see a white light or reunite with dead relatives. But she said that the experience has made her more spiritual. "When I thought about this sort of thing, I always hoped I'd be a white-lighter," she laughed, "but I'm just happy to be here. I think each step I took led me to this place."

Part of the Plan

And if Marcia thinks about God and her life a little more now…well, that's only natural. After her NDE, she was sitting in front of her makeup mirror one day when she may have received another message from above.

"I was deep in thought, thinking of God and of my father, who died when I was four," she recalled. "All of a sudden, the mirror's lights dimmed, went off, and then came back on, from low to medium and then back to high. The lights in the room never changed."

Marcia doesn't know what the message was supposed to be, but she said that she's not afraid of dying. And until that time, she said, "I guess I'm just not done planting flowers."

Ghosts Live On at the Clovis Sanitarium

Picture this scene at the emergency call center in Clovis, California: "Hello. 911. What's your emergency?" Dead silence. "Hello? Is anyone there?" More silence. So the dispatcher checks to see where the call is coming from and finds that it's 2604 Clovis Avenue: the former home of the Clovis Sanitarium—a building that has no electricity and no working phone. It's probably not a life-or-death situation, since whatever is making the call is already dead.

❋　❋　❋　❋

ODDLY, THIS TYPE of phone call is not uncommon in Clovis—a city of 95,000 that is located just northeast of Fresno. Nicknamed "the Gateway to the Sierras," Clovis was the home of Anthony Andriotti, who built a magnificent mansion for his family in 1922. Unfortunately, he miscalculated the cost of the building's upkeep, and he went bankrupt, turned to alcohol and opium, and died in 1929 at age 36.

The estate sat empty until it was reopened in 1935 as the Hazelwood Sanitarium for tuberculosis patients. In 1942, it became the Clovis Avenue Sanitarium, which was dedicated to serving the area's physically and mentally ill.

A Place to Die

Families whose loved ones suffered from dementia or schizophrenia brought these unfortunate souls to the Clovis Sanitarium to die. It is said that at one point, the death rate at the facility reached an average of one person per day. Still, the building soon became overcrowded, with ten beds to a room and one nurse overseeing two or more rooms. Former employees told sad tales of patients who were abused and neglected.

When patients died, their bodies were stored in the relatively cool basement until they could be removed. Locals started talking about strange happenings at the sanitarium, and rumors began to suggest that the place was haunted. But it wasn't all idle gossip: It seems that there *were* some pretty strange things going on at 2604 Clovis Avenue.

A Call for Help

In 1992, the Clovis Sanitarium closed; that's when the mysterious phone calls began. Sometimes neighbors or passersby would call the police regarding trespassers or vandals. But then there were the other calls—the ones that came directly from the vacant building that had no working phone line.

Unfazed by these odd stories, Todd Wolfe bought the property in 1997 with hopes of creating a haunted-house-type Halloween attraction. Initially a skeptic, Wolfe was surprised when his employees complained about spirits interfering with their work. They saw apparitions and reported being touched and grabbed by unseen hands. It wasn't until he had his own encounter in "Mary's Room"—where he actually saw a shadowy apparition—that Wolfe began to believe. Today, Mary's Room is furnished with only original furniture because it seems that "Mary" gets quite upset when changes are made. And a disturbed Mary leads to increased paranormal activity, including phantom breathing, shoving by an invisible force, and objects that move seemingly on their own.

Many paranormal groups have visited the Clovis Sanitarium, and all agree that it is indeed haunted. They've heard shuffling footsteps and strange voices, and many have reported feelings of being watched.

Energetic Spirits

When the *Ghost Adventures* team visited the Clovis Sanitarium in a 2010 episode, they were greeted by a laughing spirit and a spike in electromagnetic energy (in a building with no electricity). Later, in the basement, the crew used a state-of-the-art ultraviolet camera to record a mysterious purple form; the shape even appeared to sit on a couch for a while. The team also captured some amazing EVPs (electronic voice phenomena), including one that told the group to "Get out."

Investigator Zak Bagans observed that the ghosts of Clovis Sanitarium are an unusual bunch. The original owners were a family with young children who lived a lavish lifestyle, full of happiness and laughter. But combine those feelings with those of the mentally ill who were neglected and abused after being brought there to die, and the mix becomes volatile. As Bagans concluded, "That contrasting energy has to do something weird to the atmosphere."

Stalked by an Invisible Entity

In November 1988, when Jackie Hernandez moved into a small bungalow on 11th Street in San Pedro, California, she was looking to make a fresh start. But her hopefulness quickly turned into what she described as the "nightmare of all nightmares."

✳   ✳   ✳   ✳

FROM THE TIME that Jackie moved in to her new place, she felt a presence in the house. At first, it made her feel safe—as if someone was looking out for her. But Jackie soon realized that the presence was less than friendly. Shortly after their arrival, Jackie and her young children heard a high-pitched screeching noise throughout the house. Then, in February 1989, Jackie's unseen houseguests manifested in the form of two separate apparitions: One was an old man that Jackie's friend also witnessed while she was babysitting in the home; the other was a disembodied head that Jackie saw in the attic.

Call in the Cavalry

In August 1989, Jackie asked a group of paranormal researchers to investigate the phenomena; parapsychologist Dr. Barry Taff, cameraman Barry Conrad, and photographer Jeff Wheatcraft had no idea how the case would impact their lives. On August 8, during their first visit to the Hernandez home, the group noted a foul odor in the house, heard noises in the attic, and captured glowing orbs of light in photographs. Skeptical of Jackie's claim of seeing a phantom head in the attic, Wheatcraft took several photos in the darkened space. But he left the room in terror after an unseen force yanked the camera from his hands. When he summoned the courage to go back into the attic (this time with a flashlight), he found the body of the camera on one side of the room and the lens on the other, inside a box.

Later that same evening, while Wheatcraft and Conrad were in the attic, Wheatcraft was violently pushed by an invisible hand. After they returned to the main level of the house, loud banging noises were heard coming from the attic, as if someone (or something) was stomping above them.

When the researchers returned to the house later that month, they observed a liquid oozing from the walls and dripping from the cabinets. Samples that were analyzed at a lab determined that the substance was blood plasma from a human male. Why it would be oozing from the walls was anyone's guess.

Get Out and Don't Look Back

The phenomena that Jackie and the investigators experienced on the night of September 4, 1989, shook them to their very cores. During the day, the poltergeist ramped up its attention-seeking behavior. After watching objects fly through the air and hearing mysterious moaning and breathing noises, Jackie called the researchers for help.

Wheatcraft and Conrad's friend Gary Boehm were inspecting the pitch-black attic and were just about to leave when

Wheatcraft screamed. Boehm took a photo hoping that the flash would illuminate the room so he could see Wheatcraft and help him. Boehm's photo captured the spirit's latest attack on Wheatcraft, who was hanging from the rafters with a clothesline wrapped around his neck; the cord was tied with a seaman's knot. Boehm was able to rescue Wheatcraft, who was understandably shaken by his encounter with the evil entity that seemed to have a personal vendetta against him.

After observing several other paranormal phenomena that night, Jackie and the researchers left the San Pedro house, never to return.

You Can Run but You Can't Hide

Frightened for the safety of her young children, Jackie moved her family nearly 200 miles away to Weldon, California. But it didn't take long for the poltergeist to find her. The haunting started with unusual scratching noises that came from a backyard shed; then, a black, shapeless form was spotted in the hallway of the home. As had been the case in San Pedro, others witnessed the phenomena as well: While moving an old television set out of the storage shed, Jackie's neighbors saw the ghostly image of an old man on the screen.

In April 1990, when the researchers heard that the paranormal activity had followed Jackie to her new home, they drove to Weldon to continue their work on the case. Besides, Wheatcraft had a personal interest in the matter: He wanted to know why the entity was focusing its physical attacks on him.

Hoping to provoke the spirit, Jackie, her friend, and the researchers decided to use a Ouija board. During the session, the table that they used shook violently, candles flickered, and the temperature in the room dropped dramatically. But the group may have received the answers it was seeking: Through the Ouija board, the spirit told them that he was a sailor who had been murdered in 1930 when his killer drowned him in San Pedro Bay. He also said that his killer had lived in Jackie's former home in San Pedro. When Wheatcraft asked the spirit why he was being targeted, the entity said that Wheatcraft resembled his killer. It then picked up Wheatcraft and threw him against the wall. He was naturally frightened, but he was not injured.

After that, Conrad searched old newspaper records to see if the information that they'd received from the spirit could be verified; it was. In 1930, sailor Herman Hendrickson was found drowned in San Pedro Bay. Although he'd also suffered a fractured skull, his death was ruled accidental. Perhaps Hendrickson's spirit was trying to make it known that his death was not accidental but that he was murdered.

Spirit Stalker

In June 1990, Jackie moved back to San Pedro and rented an apartment on Seventh Street. This time, she had a priest bless the place before she moved in. Nevertheless, the glowing orbs of light returned.

Later that year, Conrad's home was also infested with poltergeist activity, which he witnessed along with Boehm and Wheatcraft. Objects were mysteriously moved to new locations, burners on the gas stove turned on by themselves, scissors flew across the kitchen, a broom was left standing on top of the stove, and scissors were found underneath pillows in the bedroom. Also, Wheatcraft was again pushed by the invisible force, which left red scratch marks on his back.

The phenomena greatly diminished after that, although subsequent residents of the house on 11th Street in San Pedro also claimed to witness poltergeist activity; since then, it is said that no one has lived in the house for more than six months.

Although Jackie was terribly frightened by the mysterious activity at the time, she later said that she was grateful to have had a firsthand encounter with the Other Side, which not many people get to experience. Although some folks might welcome a visit from a ghost, few would want it to be as distressing as what Jackie went through.

Local Legends: New York

The 1960s sparked some of the wildest urban legends ever to come out of the Big Apple. Two, in particular, continue to make the rounds and are still believed by many: that the crime rate plummeted nationwide the night The Beatles appeared on The Ed Sullivan Show *in 1964, and that the city's birthrate skyrocketed nine months after the Great Blackout of 1965.*

✳   ✳   ✳   ✳

The Beatles Sweep America: It's true that The Beatles were already wildly popular when they made their first trip to the United States in 1964 and that their February 9 appearance on *The Ed Sullivan Show* drew 73 million viewers, the largest audience the show had ever seen. But the claim that the crime rate dropped during their appearance, first made by an editor at the *Washington Post* and later picked up by others, is more fancy than fact. In truth, the comment wasn't even a compliment but a put-down of the band's fans, which were perceived by many at the time to consist primarily of lazy, criminally inclined teenagers. Only in the repeated retelling was the statement transformed into a positive reflection of The Beatles' general popularity. Regardless, an examination of police records for that evening from New York—or any town—will show that crime did, indeed, continue apace.

Getting Busy During the Blackout: And the "skyrocketing" birthrate that supposedly followed the Great Blackout of November 9, 1965? Also unfounded, say researchers. The 12-hour blackout, which affected more than 30 million people throughout eight American states and Ontario, Canada, was huge news at the time. And it's certainly likely that a lot of couples, lacking electricity and thus in need of something to pass the time, jumped into bed for an amorous romp. However, despite reports by the *New York Times* and other outlets, a review of hospital birth records nine months after the blackout show no statistically significant spike in births, compared to the same period in the previous five years, anywhere in the affected area.

Do You Pay Half the Rent if Your Roommate Is a Ghost?

Upon first glance, the 1856 Gothic Revival town house at 14 W. Tenth Street in New York City looks like any other apartment building on a quiet street in Greenwich Village. Shaded by trees, the red brick structure blends in with the expensive brownstones and other town houses that line the block. But its quaint facade masks the sinister activities that took place inside.

* * * *

A PLAQUE ON THE building explains that famed author Mark Twain resided there in 1901. However, it does not note that Twain may not have left, as his ghost reportedly haunts the stairwell—and he's not alone. Over the years, 22 people have died in the building—many in horrific ways—and all are said to haunt the place.

One of the first grisly occurrences at the so-called "House of Death" was a murder/suicide that took place in the early 1900s. In the 1930s, a young girl was tortured and starved to death by her immigrant parents. Among the many abuses they heaped upon her, she was forced to walk around the apartment while tied to a chair. Not surprisingly, she died due to mistreatment and neglect.

Then, on November 1, 1987, criminal defense attorney Joel Steinberg beat and terrorized his partner Hedda Nussbaum and their adopted children, Lisa and Mitchell. Authorities found Mitchell tied to his playpen with a rope. Six-year-old Lisa was discovered unconscious with a fractured skull; Joel had beaten her during a crack-induced rage and left her on the bathroom floor for hours. Like the young girl in the building five decades earlier, Lisa died at the hands of her abuser.

The ghosts of 14 W. Tenth Street have many reasons for hanging around; rent control and the high cost of living elsewhere in the city, unfortunately, aren't among them. The hallways and stairwell abound with sightings of the immigrant girl, Mark Twain, Lisa, and many other spirits that don't want to leave their former residence. The ghosts don't seem to bother anyone, but potential renters and visitors should beware.

Ghost Dogs

Cynophobia is the fear of dogs. But the canines discussed here are ghostly dogs that have stuck around after passing away. The following is a list of places where, if you're not careful, you might find yourself staring down a phantom hound.

❋ ❋ ❋ ❋

Colebrook Furnace

IT IS A horrifying tale that dog lovers everywhere hope is merely a legend: A Pennsylvania man who was furious at his pack of hunting dogs ordered his servants to throw all 40 of the hounds into the roaring flames of Colebrook Furnace, a massive structure that was used to melt iron ore. As the story goes, shortly after the heinous deed, ghostly howls and cries began emanating from the furnace. Even after the structure was dismantled in the 1850s, the sounds could still be heard. In addition, a pack of phantom dogs has been seen running through the woods nearby. Those reports continue today, although with a minor twist: Some believe that the strange cries belong to the ghost of the guilty man, who is forced to spend eternity in torment due to his inhumane actions.

Woodland Cemetery

There's something to be said for the unconditional love that's shared between a boy and his dog. A prime example of this is the story of five-year-old Johnny Morehouse and his scruffy pooch. In the mid-1800s, Johnny could often be seen playing by the Miami & Erie Canal near Dayton, Ohio, with his faithful dog beside him. One morning in 1860, Johnny slipped and fell into the icy water. Seeing his master struggling, the dog jumped into the water and tried to save him. Even though the dog aided several men who pulled Johnny from the water, it was too late for the little boy.

Legend has it that after Johnny was laid to rest at Woodland Cemetery in Dayton, his faithful dog refused to leave the grave site; instead, he kept watch over his young master. When the dog passed away in 1861, a monument was erected at Johnny's grave; it depicts the boy sleeping while his dog stands watch over him. Many believe that, even in death, Johnny's dog is still watching over him. Some say that the statue often comes to life and if you place your hand under the dog's nostrils, you can feel it breathing; others have reported seeing the ghosts of Johnny and his dog running together through the cemetery.

Peddler's Rock

If you ever find yourself in the historic town of Port Tobacco, Maryland, ask the locals to show you the way to Peddler's Rock, where you just might catch a glimpse of a spectral blue dog. Although the animal is not technically blue in color, it is said to be the spirit of a blue mastiff. A long-standing legend states that a man and his dog were brutally murdered at Peddler's Rock in the 18th century; the culprits were never caught and brought to justice.

Today, it is said that the ghost of the blue mastiff paces back and forth across the top of Peddler's Rock. Occasionally, its loud, bone-chilling howls are also heard cutting through the night air.

Borley Rectory

Often dubbed the "Most Haunted House in England," the Borley Rectory was built in the 1860s and quickly gained a reputation for being home to all sorts of ghosts. In the late 1930s, famous ghost hunter Harry Price rented the building and began an investigation that lasted many months. During that time, Price and his team encountered ghostly nuns, a headless specter, and flying bricks. Of course, no haunted house would be complete without a ghost dog, and Borley did not disappoint in that regard. On more than one occasion, Price and his team heard the eerie sound of a hound howling from somewhere inside the building; however, no dog was ever found. Several investigators also described seeing a large spectral canine walking slowly across the rectory grounds.

Bonaventure Cemetery

Bonaventure Cemetery is the largest city cemetery in Savannah, Georgia. But the graveyard's real claim to fame is that it was featured in John Berendt's best-selling novel *Midnight in the Garden of Good and Evil* and the 1997 movie that was based on the book. It's also a place where ghost dogs are said to prowl.

For many years, a pack of phantom dogs has been known to chase people out of the cemetery, especially if they are trespassing late at night. If the idea of being pursued by a pack of spectral canines isn't spooky enough, consider that no one has ever actually seen the dogs—not even those who have been chased by them; rather, only their barking and snarling is heard as they draw near. Those of you who'd rather not risk being run down by the phantom dogs should just roll down your windows as you drive by and listen closely—you just might hear the baying of the hounds.

Sunnybank

Albert Payson Terhune may be best remembered as an author who wrote books about dogs, but his devotion to canines went much deeper than that. In 1912, Terhune decided to take up full-time residence at Sunnybank, his family's summer home in Wayne, New Jersey; it was there that he began breeding and raising rough collies. Eventually, Terhune became so successful at breeding that he opened Sunnybank Kennels. Some of the dogs from these kennels later made their way into Terhune's books—including Rex.

Rex was different from most of the other dogs at the kennels: He was not a purebred, but rather a collie/bull terrier mix. Also, Rex had a large, unique scar on his head. Rex loved Terhune, and the feeling was more than mutual. It was often said that if you wanted to know where Terhune was, all you had to do was find Rex and Terhune wouldn't be far away. That was true even after Rex's death: Shortly after the dog's passing, friends reported seeing his ghost following Terhune around the property and even lying at his feet. Those who were unaware that Rex had died even mistook the apparition for the real dog. Incidentally, Terhune himself never claimed to see Rex's ghost.

After Terhune passed away in 1942, the kennels and the surrounding property fell into disrepair and were eventually sold. Much of the original estate is now maintained as a park that is open to the public. While Rex is rumored to be buried there, his grave site was never marked. Still, many locals claim to see Rex's ghost wandering through the park at night.

Moore Ghosts Gather in Villisca

Villisca was once a bustling town in southwestern Iowa. In the early 1900s, it was home to more than 2,500 citizens, a busy train station, and dozens of businesses. But on June 10, 1912, a local family was brutally murdered in their home. The crime was never solved, and the town has since dwindled in size to about half as many residents. You might say that Villisca has become a ghost town...literally.

❋　❋　❋　❋

How It All Began—and Ended

THE HOME OF Josiah Moore and his wife, Sarah, was much like many other houses of its time. Built in 1868, it was a well-kept two-story white house on a quiet street in the heartland of America. After attending a Children's Day event on the night of June 9, 1912, the Moores and their four children, as well as Lena and Ina Stillinger—two young neighbor girls who were sleeping over—returned to the house and went to bed.

The next morning, Mary Peckham, the Moores' next-door neighbor, went outside to hang her laundry and was struck by the silence that greeted her from the Moore house; after all, a family of six was rarely quiet. Peckham called Josiah's brother Ross, who then came over to check things out.

Bungled Bungalow

Ross unlocked the door and entered the parlor; the home was covered in a blanket of eerie silence. But when he opened the door to one of the bedrooms, he was confronted with a horrific sight: the bloody bodies of the Stillinger girls lying in a bed.

Peckham called the police, who arrived to find the lifeless bodies of Josiah, Sarah, Herman, Katherine, Boyd, and Paul Moore, as well as the Stillinger girls—they had all been brutally murdered with an ax, which had been wiped off and left by the door of the downstairs bedroom.

That the crime was never solved is no real surprise due to the mayhem that ensued. As word of the carnage spread, friends and hundreds of curious onlookers raced to the house, where police soon lost control of the contaminated crime scene. With all of this chaos and none of today's technology, police were unable to solve the case—a fact that haunted them for the rest of their lives.

The Suspects

Among the leading suspects was Frank F. Jones, a local businessman who was angry with Josiah for leaving his company and poaching one of its best clients. People who believe in this theory suggest that Jones hired hit man William Mansfield to do the dirty work. Although police were suspicious of the pair, they did not find enough evidence to prosecute either of them. Another school of thought suggests that a drifter committed the murders. Two men fit the bill: Andy Sawyer, a vagrant who traveled with an ax, and Henry Moore, who was later convicted of killing his mother and grandmother with an ax and was a suspect in several other ax murders. But no evidence connected either to the Villisca murders.

Traveling preacher George Kelly was another prime suspect. A rather odd character, Kelly had been present at the Children's Day event at the Moores' church. He left town the morning that the bodies were discovered and reportedly told fellow train passengers that he'd had a vision that told him to "Slay and slay utterly." When he was arrested for another crime in 1914, he admitted to the Moore murders but later withdrew his confession. Nevertheless, Kelly was tried twice for the Moore murders: One trial ended in a hung jury, and he was acquitted in the other.

If You Renovate It, They Will Come

After the murders, the Moore house changed hands several times because, really, who wants to live in a house where eight people were killed? By 1994, the house was dilapidated and in danger of being torn down; that's when a realtor presented Darwin and Martha Linn with a proposal. The couple operated the Olson-Linn Museum in Villisca, and the realtor hoped that they'd be interested in purchasing the house to preserve another piece of the town's history; they were.

The Linns secured state funding to restore the house. Using old photographs, they remodeled and redecorated it with items from the early 1900s. They removed the electricity, water, and working bathrooms and restored the building to its 1912 condition. It was placed on the National Register of Historic Places in 1998.

After the renovation was complete, the Linns began giving tours of the house. On these tours, visitors get a glimpse of

Villisca in the early 1900s and learn the details of the grisly murders. Other topics of discussion include possible suspects and how the crime and the eventual trial of Reverend Kelly affected the small town.

They're Baaaaack

With the house looking almost exactly as it had in 1912, it seems that the spirits of the Moore family were drawn back to it. Visitors have reported seeing apparitions and hearing voices whisper in their ears. Closet doors open and close by themselves, and balls mysteriously roll across the floor.

Darwin Linn said that he always felt a pull toward this house, and he'd heard stories about the spirits that linger there. But when the renovations went smoothly, he dismissed the idea ... until he saw the youngsters who came through the house on tours: He saw them interacting with other children—children who weren't there. "That makes the hair stand up on the back of my head," he said. That's when he became convinced that the Moore family is still around.

Many ghost hunters and paranormal investigators have toured the house and found evidence of spirits there. Orbs have been captured in photos and mysterious voices have been recorded on audio devices. But some of the most interesting documentation was collected by Maritza Skandunas, who related her harrowing firsthand account on the TV show *My Ghost Story*.

1912 Again

Skandunas, the founder of San Diego Ghost Hunters, decided that if most people take tours of the Moore house, she'd like to go one step further and spend the night there. Darwin Linn said that he was a little surprised by the request, but he was open to the idea; he didn't even charge her for the lodging. So Skandunas and a couple of ghost-hunting friends settled in at the dark and primitive house. "It felt like you went back a hundred years," she said. "You could almost relive what they felt and the screaming that must have been going on, and no one heard it." Skandunas said that she felt that pure "evil was [permeating] out of the walls."

As Skandunas and her friends walked through the house absorbing the energy, they were able to imagine what took place in each room. Soon, they noticed a black shadow following them; they believe that it was the spirit of the murderer. Skandunas said that it gave off "a very hateful energy."

In the master bedroom, Skandunas felt something touch her arm; that sensation was validated when she took a picture of the room's mirror and saw the image of Sarah Moore staring back at her in the photo.

In one of the children's rooms, the investigators discovered the spirits of youngsters who were hoping to interact with the living. When they asked Herman, the eldest, to open the closet door, the door opened, even though no one was near it. When Skandunas's friend suggested reading one of the children's books aloud, the ghostly excitement was palpable. But shortly thereafter, the black shadow appeared and the reader began to feel nauseated. The killer obviously didn't want any happiness in the house, but when the group left the room, an audio recorder captured the voice of a child saying, "Don't go."

When the investigators asked the kids if they knew who committed the murders, they said no, but added clearly that it was two people. It seems that the Moores may have stuck around to offer clues about that terrible night.

Evil Energy

Even a seasoned ghost hunter like Skandunas was shaken by the night's revelations. "I had goose bumps," she said. "I would never go into that house alone."

According to historical records, the town was named "Villisca" after a Native American word meaning "pleasant view." But others claim that the town was originally called "Wallisca," which means "evil spirit." Now that sounds about right.

Chapter 6

Intriguing Moments in History

Zero: To Be or Not to Be

You might think that zero is an insignificant little number worth nothing. But you'd be wrong. When did humans first use the concept of zero?

✳   ✳   ✳   ✳

THE ORIGIN OF the number "zero" was not as neat as the subtraction of one minus one. In fact, there was no symbol for zero for centuries. Before a symbol was used for zero, most archeologists believe various cultures used an empty space to stand in zero's stead.

It is thought that the Babylonians were the first to use a place-holder for zero in their numbering system in 350 B.C. But it was not a zero; instead, they used other symbols, such as a double hash-mark (also called a *wedge*), as a placeholder. Why the need for a placeholder—or a number that holds a place? Merchants and tax collectors in particular needed such a tool. After all, their numbers became larger as trade developed and more taxes were levied. The placeholder became extremely necessary; for example, the number 5,000 implies that the three places to the right of the 5 are "empty" and only the thousands column contains any value.

The first crude symbol for zero as a placeholder may have been invented around 32 B.C. by Mesoamericans in Central America—most notably in a calendar called the Long Count Calendar. No one really agrees if it was the Olmecs or the Mayans who first used a shell-like symbol for zero. Either way, the idea of using a symbol for zero remained a secret for centuries, as isolation hindered the Mesoamericans, never allowing their concept of zero to be spread around the world.

More than 100 years later, another symbol for zero was invented either in Indochina or India. In this case, the culture was not averse to spreading their number system—including the concept of zero—around the world in trade and commerce. And by around A.D. 130, Greek mathematician and astronomer Ptolemy, influenced mainly by the Babylonians, used a symbol representing zero along with the alphabetic Greek numerals—not just to hold a place, but as a number.

But because zero technically means nothing, few people accepted the concept of "nothing" between numbers. Not every culture ignored the idea, though; Hindu mathematicians often wrote their math in verse, using words similar to "nothing," such as *sunya* ("void") and *akasa* ("space"). Finally, around A.D. 650, zero became an important number in Indian mathematics, though the symbol varied greatly from what we think of as our modern zero. The familiar Hindu-Arabic symbol for zero—essentially an open oval standing on one end—would take several more centuries to become accepted.

Why all the excitement after zero was "invented"? It turns out that all the wonderful, exotic properties of zero made it a necessity to the development of science and technology over time—in everything from architecture and engineering to our checkbooks. The properties are many: You cannot divide by zero (or in other words, divide something by nothing); zero only in the numerator (top number) of a fraction will always be equal to zero; it's considered an even number. Probably its most endearing quality is that when zero is added or subtracted from any number, the result is that number. Add nothing, subtract nothing, and you get the original number—a handy device to have when it comes to counting on anything.

11 Highlights of 1907

In 1907, Americans had a life expectancy of just 45.6 years for men and 49.9 for women. Even worse, this was the year that typhoid, an abdominal disease spread through water and food supplies, ravaged the nation. But alas! Public health officials discovered that 47 people stricken with the disease were all from families that employed a cook named Mary. With "Typhoid Mary" safely quarantined, these were the highlights of that year.

✳ ✳ ✳ ✳

1. **The Creation of Mother's Day:** After her mother died, Anna Jarvis started a letter-writing campaign in support of the celebration of mothers everywhere. A minister in Grafton, West Virginia, obliged and dedicated the second Sunday in May specifically to the late Mrs. Jarvis. Ironically, the woman who is credited with creating what we now know as Mother's Day never became a mother herself.

2. **The Invention of the Paper Towel:** The paper towel was created by a crafty teacher in Philadelphia who found a way to keep her students from perpetuating a cold epidemic. Instead of sharing the same cloth towel, she put her scissors to use and cut some paper into individual squares. The Scott Paper Company, which was already making toilet paper, got wind of the story. As luck would have it, the company had an entire railroad car full of paper that was rolled too thick to be used in the bathroom. Arthur Scott came up with a way to copy the teacher's design on a bigger scale. It didn't take long before he was selling them as a product called the Sani-Towel.

3. **The Beginnings of UPS:** Seattle entrepreneur James E. Casey was only 19 in 1907 when he borrowed $100 to create a delivery service he called the American Messenger Company. He and his friends ran errands and delivered packages and trays of food. Most deliveries were done on foot, with longer trips made via bicycle. A Model T Ford was added six years later and the name was changed to Merchants Parcel Delivery. By 1919, the company had expanded beyond Seattle and was renamed United Parcel Service.

4. **The First Electric Washing Machine:** By 1907, U.S. power companies were growing in technology and scale. As a result, life became a little easier for housewives, especially when the Thor washing machine was introduced by Hurley Machine Company of Chicago. To go with the Thor, a company in Düsseldorf, Germany, came up with the first household detergent in the same year. It was called Persil.

5. **Swimming Without a Skirt is a Police Matter:** When Australian long-distance swimmer Annette Kellerman decided to swim at Boston's Revere Beach in a one-piece bathing suit—without a skirt—she was arrested. The charge? Indecent exposure, of course! The 22-year-old wasn't the only one under scrutiny. Even infants were required to wear complete bathing costumes in the land of the free until a quarter of a century later.

6. **The "Monobosom" and Other Fashionable Styles:** Ladies of the early 20th century certainly didn't show much skin. However, they were very creative in enhancing their fully clothed silhouettes. The hourglass figure was highly coveted, but if you weren't a full-bodied woman by nature, you simply had to work harder. Corset strings were pulled so tightly that the hips were forced back and the chest thrust forward creating a "monobosom." But things loosened up a tad after dark. To show off their fine

jewelry, women of 1907 wore low sweetheart necklines often accented with feathered boas.

7. **And Now for the Tresses:** In 1907, America was at war against tuberculosis, which killed hundreds of people from the 1880s to the 1950s. To complement their pale complexions, survivors opted for masses of ringlets, thanks to the invention of the waving iron in the 1870s. Hair coloring was frowned upon, but the brave went for it anyway, using herbs, rust, and other concoctions. To promote hair growth, petroleum jelly, castor oil, and gallic acid were also part of the beauty arsenal.

8. **No One Wanted Their MTV:** A lucky few enjoyed phonographs in 1907, but the most common way to hear a new song was by piano. People would trade, borrow, and collect the sheet music to their favorite songs. A popular choice was George M. Cohan's "You're a Grand Old Rag" from his hit Broadway musical *George Washington, Jr.* The song quickly spread beyond New York City and became a staple in piano benches across the country. Eventually, Cohan changed the title to "You're a Grand Old Flag," and the song remains a national treasure.

9. **A Movie for a Nickel:** Way before the TV network and even before the Ryan and Tatum O'Neal film, the word nickelodeon meant a small neighborhood theater where people would gather to see a movie. The cost? A nickel, of course! These theaters held about 200 chairs and featured live piano music before each show. Movies were comedic sketches, animal acts, or vaudeville acts that lasted around 15 minutes each.

10. **An Economic Boom:** Industrial capitalism was on the rise in 1907 and with it came lots of jobs. New businesses created a need for more clerical help and a new "white collar" mentality was born. More and more workers received a salary instead of an hourly wage. Retail jobs also flourished.

11. **The Chicago Cubs Win the World Series!:** The World Series was only four years old in 1907. What's more, Ty Cobb was merely 20. But youth was on the side of the Chicago Cubs as they won the World Series, beating Cobb and his Detroit Tigers four games to none. The Series wasn't without its share of drama—the first game was called because of darkness.

9 Bits of Irony

Throughout history, people have made bold proclamations that were not only incorrect but many times contradicted their own actions. Here are a few examples.

⁂ ⁂ ⁂ ⁂

1. **The Beatles:** On January 1, 1962, Paul McCartney, John Lennon, George Harrison, and Pete Best auditioned at Decca Records, performing 15 songs in just under an hour. The songs included Lennon-McCartney originals and covers of other songs, but their performance was mediocre. In fact, producer Mike Smith flatly rejected them saying, "We don't like their sound. Groups of guitars are on their way out." The Beatles went on to sign with producer George Martin at EMI Records and proved Smith extraordinarily wrong.

2. **Take Me Out to the Ball Game:** Next to the national anthem, the song most associated with the game of baseball is "Take Me Out to the Ball Game," an early-20th-century song usually played during the seventh-inning stretch. Ironically, it was written by two men who had never attended a baseball game. Jack Norworth wrote the words in 1908, after seeing a sign that said, "Baseball Today—Polo Grounds." Albert Von Tilzer added the music. The song gained popularity in vaudeville acts, and now it's played at nearly every baseball game in the country.

3. **James Dean:** In 1955, actor James Dean advised teens about the dangers of speeding and drag racing in a two-minute televised public service announcement. Dean talked about how he used to "fly around quite a bit" on the highways, but then he took up track racing, and after that he became "extra cautious" on the highways. He also warned, "The life you save may be mine." On September 30, 1955, Dean was pulled over for speeding in his Porsche 550 Spyder on his way to a race in Palm Springs, California. Later that afternoon, an oncoming vehicle crossed into Dean's lane and the two cars collided almost head-on. Dean was pronounced dead at the hospital.

4. **Clark Gable:** William Clark Gable was a high school dropout with big ears who eventually became known as the "King of Hollywood." In 1924, Gable's friendship with Lionel Barrymore helped him land a screen test at MGM. Producer Irving Thalberg thought Gable's screen test was awful and referred to his ears as "bat-like." In spite of that, he was signed to a contract and went on to make a number of hit movies for the studio. When MGM head Louis B. Mayer decided that Gable was getting difficult to work with, he loaned the actor to the Columbia studio. Ironically, Gable won an Academy Award for his 1934 performance in the Columbia film *It Happened One Night.*

5. **Tom Seaver:** In 1966, baseball pitcher Tom Seaver signed with the New York Mets and was assigned to a minor league team in Jacksonville, Florida. After seeing Seaver pitch, Chicago Cubs scout Gordon Goldsberry said, "He won't make it." On the contrary—when Seaver was called up by the Mets in 1967, he had 18 complete games with 16 wins, including two shutouts. Seaver was named the National League Rookie of the Year and went on to a 20-year career with 311 wins, 3,640 strikeouts, and a 2.86 ERA. Nicknamed "Tom Terrific," Seaver was elected to the Baseball Hall of Fame in 1992.

6. **Ludwig van Beethoven:** German composer Ludwig van Beethoven is generally regarded as one of the greatest composers in history and was a dominant figure in the transitional period between the Classical and Romantic eras in Western music. Around age 28, Beethoven developed a severe case of tinnitus and began to lose his hearing. His hearing loss did not affect his ability to compose music, but it made concerts increasingly difficult. According to one story, at the premiere of his Ninth Symphony, he had to be turned around to see the applause of the audience because he could not hear it. In 1811, after a failed attempt to play his own Piano Concerto No. 5, Emperor, he never performed in public again.

7. **Gus Grissom:** Virgil "Gus" Grissom was America's second astronaut in space aboard the capsule Liberty Bell 7. After landing in the Atlantic, a hatch on the capsule opened prematurely, and Grissom nearly drowned before being rescued by helicopter. To prevent this from happening again, Grissom recommended to NASA designers that the hatch on the three-man Apollo capsule be made more difficult to open. Ironically, while testing the Apollo capsule before its first flight, Grissom was killed in a fire along with fellow astronauts Ed White and Roger B. Chaffee when the new hatch proved too difficult to open.

8. **Television:** Darryl F. Zanuck was an actor, writer, producer, and director who helped develop the Hollywood studio system in the 1920s. He also cofounded Twentieth Century Pictures in 1933. In 1946, television was in its infancy, but the movie industry was worried. When asked his thoughts, Zanuck said, "Television won't be able to hold on to any market it captures after the first six months. People will soon get tired of staring at a plywood box every night." Of course, television thrived, but it did not bring an end to movies.

9. **Charles Justice:** In 1900, Charles Justice was serving time at the Ohio State Penitentiary in Columbus. While performing cleaning duties in the death chamber, he thought of a way to improve the restraints on the electric chair. Justice suggested that metal clamps replace the leather straps, allowing the inmate to be secured more firmly and minimizing the problem of burnt flesh. These changes were made, and Justice was later paroled from prison. In an ironic twist of fate, after his release, he was convicted of murder and sentenced to death. On November 9, 1911, justice was served and the inmate found out firsthand how well those metal clamps worked on the same electric chair he had improved.

The *Empress of Ireland*

In the wee hours of May 29, 1914, the Canadian steamship Empress of Ireland *sank in the St. Lawrence River after a collision with the Norwegian collier* Storstad. *What happened?*

✳ ✳ ✳ ✳

THE TWO SHIPS had crossed paths just east of Rimouski, Quebec, on a narrow stretch of the river. Of the nearly 1,500 people aboard the *Empress*, more than 1,000 died. After the tragedy, questions would come with rapid-fire succession. Why did the liner sink just 15 minutes after the collision? Why were so few of its lifeboats launched? How could the *Storstad* emerge from such a violent collision virtually unscathed?

History would list fog as the principal cause for the disaster, but it wasn't the only culprit. In an ironic twist, *Empress's* Captain Henry Kendall made a bad situation worse when he ordered an evasive turn to starboard. Instead of striking the *Storstad* a glancing blow as he had hoped, reports suggest that the *Storstad's* bow pierced the "liner's steel ribs as smoothly as an assassin's knife." With the super-hardy *Storstad* (specifically fortified to break through ice) doing the piercing, there was little doubt which ship would come out on top. With a sudden list to starboard that prevented the launch of most of her lifeboats, the *Empress* gave up the ghost. The last living survivor was Grace Martyn, who passed away in 1995. She was eight years old at the time of the sinking.

Today the *Empress of Ireland* rests approximately 130 feet below the surface of the St. Lawrence River. Despite its relatively shallow depth, extremely cold temperatures and severe tidal currents make reaching the craft a dicey proposition. But even with such hazards acting as a natural shield, unscrupulous divers have found their way to the wreck. Since the 1980s, underwater marauders have caused much damage at the site, including the removal of skeletal remains.

The Times They Are A-Changin': 1913

* After ten years of construction, Grand Central Terminal opens in New York City on February 2. It is the largest train station in the world, with 44 platforms and 67 tracks.

* The "Armory Show" introduces Post-impressionism and Cubism to shocked American art lovers. The show moves from New York to Chicago, where students of the Art Institute burn Henri Matisse in effigy.

* Mohandas Gandhi is arrested in South Africa for leading 2,500 Indian citizens in protest against discriminatory laws, his first experiment with the techniques of nonviolent noncooperation that he later uses to fight for Indian independence from Great Britain.

* The first-ever crossword puzzle appears in the *New York World*.

* Henry Ford opens the first assembly line, reducing the time needed to build a car from 12.5 hours to 1.5 hours.

* On March 3, thousands of suffragettes demanding women be given the right to vote march down Pennsylvania Avenue in Washington, D.C. Crowds of jeering men greet the marchers with insults, obscenities, and finally, physical violence. The Washington police refuse to protect the marchers. Finally, a cavalry troop is called to control the crowd.

* In May, the First Balkan War ends with the division of the Ottoman Empire's European possessions between Bulgaria, Serbia, Greece, and Montenegro. A month later, Bulgaria begins the Second Balkan War, setting the stage for the assassination of Archduke Ferdinand by a Serbian nationalist the following year and the start of World War I.

Blacklisted!

During the Red Scare, hundreds of film and television careers were destroyed by a vindictive hunt for Communists in Hollywood.

* * * *

IN SEPTEMBER 1947, Dalton Trumbo was at the height of his career as a screenwriter. He was highly acclaimed, well paid, and still basking in the accolades he received for his work on two patriotic war films: *A Guy Named Joe* (1943) and *Thirty Seconds Over Tokyo* (1944). That month, an FBI agent delivered Trumbo a subpoena from the House Un-American Activities Committee (HUAC), a special investigative committee of the U.S. House of Representatives. Trumbo, along with 42 other film industry professionals—actors, directors, producers, and writers—were named as key witnesses in HUAC's probe into Communist subversion in Hollywood. The good times were about to end for Dalton Trumbo.

The Hunt for Reds in October

HUAC was created in 1937 to "investigate disloyal or subversive activities in America," such as the Ku Klux Klan and organizations sympathetic to Nazi Germany. HUAC also worked diligently to ferret out American Communist Party (ACP) members and supporters in the U.S. government and media. HUAC cooled its heels during World War II, when the Soviet Union was an ally, but ramped up its pursuits with the postwar onset of the Second Red Scare, which later gave rise to a similar but totally unrelated Red-baiting phenomenon: Joseph McCarthy and the notorious Senate Committee hearings of the 1950s. But in 1947, HUAC had turned its attention to Hollywood.

Citing Soviet-sympathetic war films such as *Mission to Moscow* (1943) and *Song of Russia* (1944), HUAC announced formal hearings to determine if Hollywood filmmakers were undermining U.S. security and freedom by covertly planting Communist propaganda in American films. Those subpoenaed by HUAC were expected to provide details of Communist activity in Hollywood and, more importantly, name names.

On October 20, 1947, the hearings opened with testimony from several "friendly" witnesses. One of them was Walt Disney, who readily fingered several individuals as Communists, claiming that they incited labor unrest in Hollywood. Ronald Reagan, then-president of the Screen Actors Guild, also testified and claimed that Communist intrigue was rampant in Tinseltown.

The Hollywood Ten

Disney and Reagan were followed by ten individuals (including Trumbo, Samuel Ornitz, and John Howard Lawson—screenwriters who were also members of the Writers Guild of America, which Lawson founded) who refused to cooperate with an investigation that they considered a modern-day witch hunt. These "unfriendly" witnesses condemned the hearings as unconstitutional and invoked their Fifth Amendment rights when asked about their involvement with Communist organizations. For their defiance, the Hollywood Ten, as they were dubbed, were cited for contempt of Congress on November

24. They were also fired by their respective studios and the Motion Picture Producers and Distributors of America barred them from working in Hollywood until they were acquitted or purged of contempt and declared under oath that they were not Communists.

The ten remained unrepentant, and in early 1948, they were convicted of contempt. In 1950, after failed appeals, they began serving six-month to one-year prison sentences. Trumbo and his cohorts also became charter members of the now-notorious Hollywood blacklist.

The List that Ate Hollywood

During the next several years, the blacklist grew into a monster that devoured Hollywood careers—a monster that was willingly fed by numerous anticommunist organizations. In 1949, the American Legion presented Hollywood execs with a list of 300 film industry members that they suspected of Communist affiliation. Fearing Legion-organized film boycotts, the studios adopted it as their de facto blacklist. In 1950, a pamphlet known as *Red Channels* pegged 151 TV and radio professionals as Communist sympathizers. Those named were blacklisted from their respective industries to avoid boycotts of products sponsored by the shows.

From 1951 to 1952, HUAC launched more hearings in which witnesses sold out others to save their own careers. Among them was director Edward Dmytryk, a guilt-ridden member of the Hollywood Ten, who betrayed 26 colleagues in exchange for an early jail release and the resumption of his career.

HUAC reports produced another blacklist of 212 Hollywood professionals who soon lost their jobs. Most were writers who were relatively unknown outside Hollywood. But several prominent actors, producers, and directors landed on the list, including Charlie Chaplin, Lee Grant, Zero Mostel, Orson Bean, and Larry Parks. Many on the list also had earlier screen credits omitted.

Unable to earn a living, dozens of blacklisted professionals left Hollywood (and even America) to continue their careers elsewhere. Approximately 90 percent of those blacklisted never worked in Hollywood again.

Breaking the Blacklist

Open resistance to the blacklist began to emerge in 1956, when TV and radio personality John Henry Faulk sued the group Aware Inc. after its erroneous labeling of him as a Communist supporter kept him from getting a job at a radio station. Faulk's court victory in 1962 put an end to the blacklist altogether. Soon afterward, several television productions began hiring and crediting blacklisted artists. Even before then, there were signs that the blacklist was losing strength. In 1960, director Otto Preminger named Dalton Trumbo as the screenwriter for his upcoming film *Exodus*. That same year, Universal Pictures announced that Trumbo would be similarly credited on *Spartacus*, having been hired two years before by the film's executive producer and star, Kirk Douglas. Dalton Trumbo's 13-year nightmare was coming to an end.

Few knew it then, but Trumbo had already trumped the blacklist. During the 1950s, some blacklisted artists, including Trumbo, worked under different names. Trumbo wrote *Roman Holiday* (1953) under the alias Ian McLellan Hunter. He also penned *The Brave One* (1956) using the name Robert Rich as his "front." Both efforts earned Oscars for Best Writing, which meant golden redemption for Dalton Trumbo.

When Hell Came to Texas

The Texas City explosion was one of the worst industrial accidents in history.

✳   ✳   ✳   ✳

TEXAS HAS SEEN its share of devastation over the years, most of it caused by massive hurricanes or killer tornadoes.

But on April 16, 1947, the residents of Texas City experienced a disaster unlike any they had seen before, a bizarre shipboard explosion that killed hundreds and set the Galveston County port town ablaze.

Instant Devastation

That morning, just before 8 A.M., longshoremen were loading ammonium nitrate fertilizer into Hold 4 of the French Liberty ship SS *Grandcamp* when smoke suddenly started billowing from the ship's belly. After a series of failed attempts to get the fire under control, including the use of pressurized steam that succeeded only in blowing off the hatch covers, the Texas City Fire Department was called.

The town's entire contingent of 28 firefighters was struggling to douse the blaze when, at 9:12 A.M., the *Grandcamp* suddenly exploded with a fiery blast that was felt 100 miles away in Port Arthur. The devastation was horrifying: The entire dock was destroyed, along with the nearby Monsanto Chemical Company, grain warehouses, and several oil and chemical storage tanks. In addition, more than 1,000 residences were damaged or destroyed. Adding to the chaos, flaming debris rained down over the area, igniting a series of smaller explosions and fires, while columns of thick, oily smoke blackened the sky.

The explosion killed all 28 firefighters and annihilated the town's firefighting capability. Also killed were numerous ships' crews and scores of curious bystanders drawn by the fire earlier that morning. The explosion's shockwave was so intense that it knocked down buildings and caused deadly metal shrapnel to rain over the community. A wave of water estimated to be 15 feet tall swept inland, grounding a 150-foot steel barge. The receding water then carried debris and many of the dead and injured back out to sea.

Unprepared for the Aftermath

Because Texas City was relatively small, it had no municipal hospital and only three clinics, which were immediately overwhelmed by the large number of burned and injured. But within hours, hundreds of doctors and nurses began arriving from nearby cities and military bases, working together to establish temporary hospitals and morgues.

Unfortunately, Texas City's problems weren't over just yet. The *Grandcamp* explosion had also damaged the SS *High Flyer*, which was in dock for repairs and, like the *Grandcamp*, was loaded with thousands of tons of ammonium nitrate fertilizer. These chemicals ignited, as well, but it was several hours before rescue workers realized the danger. Tug boats were dispatched from Galveston to tow the *High Flyer* away from the dock, but they were unable to maneuver the ship, and as the flames grew higher and higher, the tugs pulled back. Not much later, the *High Flyer* also exploded, causing more damage to the waterfront area and starting fresh fires among the port's petroleum storage tanks. Luckily, casualties were minimal because the area had already been evacuated.

Among the Worst Ever

The explosion of the SS *Grandcamp* remains one of the worst industrial accidents in U.S. history. It's unknown exactly how many died during the event, given the force of the explosion and the intensity of the resulting fires. However, a monument lists 576 persons killed, with 398 positively identified and 178 listed as missing. Many of the dead were never recovered. In addition, an estimated 3,500 people were injured—nearly a quarter of the town's population. Property loss was believed to be around $100 million, in addition to the loss of nearly 1.5 million barrels of petroleum. A third of Texas City's homes were condemned, leaving nearly 2,000 residents homeless.

But while Texas City was down, it was not out. Residents and businesses immediately turned to the task of rebuilding, invigorated by insurance money and aid donations from individuals and corporations.

Now That Would Have Been a Great Photo!

If only we had a camera—and a time machine—to capture these historic events. Unfortunately, each took place prior to the development of modern photography in the 1820s.

✳ ✳ ✳ ✳

1. **The Big Bang** No need for flash photography at the Big Bang...though the images may have been overexposed.

2. **Dinosaurs** Doesn't matter if they're from the Triassic, Jurassic, or Cretaceous period, they would've looked awesome!

3. **Neanderthals** Their ability to make fire and advanced tools would have made a great "how-to" book filled with step-by-step instructions and illustrations.

4. **Egyptian Pyramids** Another great "how-to" book!

5. **Birth of Christ** Whatever your religious beliefs, you have to admit that this would have been the ultimate baby album.

6. **Destruction of Pompeii** Spectacular color photography would have emerged from that fateful day in A.D. 79—provided the photographer didn't get too close to Mount Vesuvius.

7. **Charlemagne Is Crowned** It's not every day that someone becomes Holy Roman Emperor.

8. **Magna Carta Is Signed** And history is made.

9. **Mona Lisa Is Painted** Maybe it's a good thing there was no photography in 1503; Leonardo da Vinci would have gotten off too easy.

10. **Christopher Columbus "Discovers" the New World** Send a couple of snapshots back to Queen Isabella and let her know you're okay.

11. **Henry VIII of England** Acting as official royal wedding photographer to King Henry VIII would surely have kept any shutterbug busy.

12. **The Pilgrims' First Thanksgiving** Pilgrims and Indians—what's not to love?

13. **Declaration of Independence** Benjamin Franklin could have called in some favors from his days as a newspaper editor to get a photographer into the 1776 signing.

14. **War of 1812** We could use a couple of photos of the rockets' red glare and the bombs bursting in air to accompany the lyrics to "The Star-Spangled Banner."

15. **George Washington's** First Presidential Inauguration Hail to the chief!

In the Year...1919

* Jerome David (J. D.) Salinger meets the world on January 1. His 1951 book, *The Catcher in the Rye*, would come to hold the simultaneous distinctions of being the most banned book in the United States and the second most taught in public schools.

* It is a big year for commercial air travel, with the advent of U.S. air passenger service and delivery of the first U.S. international airmail, transported from Seattle to Victoria, British Columbia, by pilot William Boeing.

* The Volstead Act passed by Congress enacts Prohibition in the United States.

* Congress declares the Grand Canyon a national park.

* Curly Lambeau founds the Green Bay Packers.

* The American Communist party is established.

* Henry Ford steps down as head of the Ford Motor Company, passing the job to his son Edsel.

* Carl Sandburg wins the Pulitzer Prize for his collection of poetry titled *Cornhuskers*.

* Eight members of the Chicago White Sox, along with the second baseman for the St. Louis Browns, are kicked out of Major League Baseball for "throwing," or intentionally losing, games in the World Series. The term "Black Sox" is often associated with the scandal that darkened the reputation of Chicago's South Side team, but the term's origins are clouded in mystery. Some say it refers to a jab at the legendarily cheap team owner Charles Comiskey, who wouldn't cough up the change to launder the team's uniforms.

* W.E.B. DuBois organizes the first Pan-African Congress in Paris.

* More than 3,000 Chinese student protesters march on Tiananmen in support of a democratic revolution in China.

Christmas in Space!

For a few shining minutes, the crew of Apollo 8 *offered Christmas cheer to a tumultuous world.*

✳ ✳ ✳ ✳

THE YEAR 1968 WAS rough for the United States and the world. The war in Vietnam was ramping up, and civil unrest was rife on college campuses. But one bright spot that year was a televised Christmas address from the crew of *Apollo 8*.

Apollo 8's mission—to orbit the moon and return safely—was vital to the American space program, but it barely registered on the public consciousness at the time.

That changed on December 24 when Commander Frank Borman, Command Module Pilot Jim Lovell, and Lunar Module Pilot William Anders greeted the world with a holiday message from lunar orbit.

Vast Loneliness of Space

During the presentation, the astronauts showed pictures of the earth and the moon as seen from their space capsule. "The vast loneliness is awe-inspiring," said Lovell, "and it makes you realize just what you have back there on earth."

Anders took the mic: "For all the people on earth, the crew of *Apollo 8* has a message we would like to send you." The astronauts then took turns reading the first ten verses of the book of Genesis.

Though *Apollo 8* didn't garner nearly as much attention as *Apollo 11*, which landed the first men on the moon, the Christmas message from its crew was viewed by an estimated one billion people around the world, making it the most widely watched television broadcast at the time. There was, however, a bit of controversy: Atheist activist Madalyn Murray O'Hair sued NASA because of the overtly religious broadcast. The case was eventually dismissed by the Supreme Court because of lack of jurisdiction.

Interestingly, *Apollo 8* was not the only mission to have a religious component. During *Apollo 11*, Edwin "Buzz" Aldrin quietly received communion on the lunar surface shortly after he and Neil Armstrong made their historic landing.

Peace in the Midst of War

Troops on both sides of the Western Front forgot to kill one another for one day.

✳   ✳   ✳   ✳

STRETCHING THROUGH BELGIUM and Northeastern France, the Western Front of 1914 was a place of misery, death, and despair. On one side were the armies of the German Empire and Austria-Hungary and on the other were troops from the United Kingdom. Though they came from different cultures, practiced different methods of Christianity, and felt a fervent hatred for the cause of their respective enemies, all the men on both sides of the Front had one thing in common: the grinding, constant squalor of life in the trenches.

Not Really Diggin' the Trenches

Few experiences are as harsh and filthy as trench warfare. This form of fighting came about because advances in firepower were not met with satisfactory mobility solutions. Both sides in World War I had plenty of weapons, but both sides also had trouble figuring out how to effectively haul these weapons from one location to the next. This resulted in troops literally "digging in" along the Western Front and living in the same trenches for months, even years, on end. Living in these trenches was not only physically unpleasant, but mentally excruciating. On Christmas Eve 1914, both the British and German troops along the front were cold, depressed, and homesick. The Germans began setting candles on the edges of their trenches, then singing Christmas carols. Soon they heard the British troops—who in some areas were a mere 30 yards away—answering with their own carols. Holiday greetings were shouted across no-man's land, and then the soldiers came out of their trenches and actually exchanged gifts of tobacco and liquor. Through Christmas Day, the guns were silent, as both sides honored a common tradition.

Bibles for the Masses

The Gutenberg Bible was the first to be printed using movable type, a process that ultimately made the books available to all.

✳ ✳ ✳ ✳

I F IT WEREN'T for Johannes Gutenberg, the book you're holding in your hands right now would not be possible. The German printer developed the first functioning printing press to use movable type, a process that eventually made books inexpensive enough for everyone to own.

Though the Bible wasn't Gutenberg's first project using his new press, it's the one for which he would became most famous. Prior to the development of the movable-type press, most mass-produced books were created using engraved wood blocks, which were coated with ink and pressed against a piece of paper. This was fine for printing pictures on a page, but it was unsuitable for books comprised primarily of text. As a result, books such as the Bible had to be meticulously handwritten, a process that could take years to complete.

Man of Mystery

Little is known about Gutenberg's early life or how he came to actually invent the movable-type press. Once he had created a prototype, he experimented by printing single sheets and small books, such as a simple textbook of Latin grammar.

Gutenberg began work on the Bible in 1450, using quality paper imported from Italy. Each page contains a unique watermark, which is visible when held up to the light. Gutenberg also printed some copies on a higher-grade material called vellum, which was made from scraped calfskin. The ink he used was oil-based and deep black in color due to its high metal composition.

Some historians speculate that Gutenberg had more than one movable-type press in his shop due to the high number of

Bible pages he had to print. But even with movable type, it was a time-consuming process. A typesetter had to carefully place the individual pieces of type for each line of text within a frame, which was then placed on the bed of the press and inked using balls stuffed with horsehair. A sheet of paper was then lightly moistened and placed over the frame, which was then pressed to create the printed page.

Not Available at Barnes & Noble

The exact number of Bibles produced by Gutenberg is unknown, though it is believed to be around 180; there were 145 on paper and 35 on the more expensive vellum. The books were nearly finished by October 1454 and made available for sale by March 1455. Though movable type made publication easier than hand transcription, Gutenberg's Bibles were almost certainly beyond the wallets of even the period's wealthiest individuals and likely were purchased primarily by churches and monasteries.

Though printed via press, each copy of the Gutenberg Bible was unique. The Bible was sold in folded sheets and bound and decorated according to the instructions of the owner. As a result, each copy contained a number of distinctive features, such as the addition of red paint to capital letters and paragraph marks, painted decorations, and individual marks of ownership.

Though his new printing press changed the world, Johannes Gutenberg did not become rich as a result. In fact, he was forced to turn over some of his printing equipment to a wealthy benefactor who sued him for the return of a sizable loan. The benefactor, Johann Fust, then went into partnership with Gutenberg's assistant, Peter Schoffer, and started his own successful printing business.

A Revolutionary Invention

Nonetheless, Gutenberg's movable-type press revolutionized book publishing by making it possible to produce a large number of copies of any document in a relatively short period of time. The process quickly spread throughout Germany, then into Italy, France, and the rest of Europe. The first book to be printed in English on a Gutenberg press was *Recuyell of the Historyes of Troye* by Raoul Lefevre, published by William Caxton in 1473–74.

Only a handful of Gutenberg Bibles are known to still exist, including 48 complete copies on paper and 11 on vellum. If you'd like to see one, a fine copy can be found at the Harry Ransom Center, located at the University of Texas at Austin. Make sure you bring your German-to-English dictionary.

The Times They Are A-Changin': 1932

* Ten years after a woman was appointed to the U.S. Senate (and served for one day), Hattie W. Caraway becomes the first woman to be elected to the office.

* Radio City Music Hall opens in New York City. Over the next 75 years, 300 million visitors will attend shows at this spectacular "palace for the people."

* The Dow Jones Industrial Average bottoms out at 41.22, the lowest level of the Great Depression.

* Aviator Charles Lindbergh makes headlines when his son, Charles Lindbergh III, is kidnapped. The boy is found dead 11 days later in Hopewell, New Jersey, about four and a half miles from the Lindbergh home.

* Residents of Archie, Missouri, are surprised when an 11.2-pound chondrite type meteorite crashes into their community, breaking into at least seven pieces.

* Comedian Jack Benny launches his first radio show, *The Jack Benny Program*. The wildly successful show airs until 1955.

* Amelia Earhart makes history twice this year. She is the first female pilot to make a non-stop solo flight across the Atlantic Ocean, flying from Newfoundland to Ireland. Three months later, she becomes the first woman to fly non-stop across the United States from Los Angeles to Newark.

* The Federal Bureau of Investigation (FBI) opens its first Crime Lab in Washington, D.C., with a single employee, agent Charles Appel.

* President Franklin Delano Roosevelt defeats opponent Herbert Hoover in a landslide victory. It will be the first of his four historic terms.

New York News Before
The New York Times

In the once-budding metropolis of New York City, no newspaper was unbiased enough to cross the myriad political and ethnic lines that were drawn everywhere. And then came The New York Times, *which published only the news that was fit to print.*

*   *   *   *

"Extra! Extra!"—Not Everyone Wanted to Read All About It

IN ORDER TO understand the founding of *The New York Times*, one has to envision New York City in 1851, the year the newspaper was founded. The population stood at half a million, and new people came every day. The city's rapid development created gaping power vacuums, and corrupt groups vied for control and influence.

There were many types of printed news sources. Some were frivolous and suited to popular culture; others were highbrow and political. Unlike today, newspapers made little attempt to appear "objective." They explicitly linked with political parties, and sensationalist editorials lampooned some groups while revering others. The two founders of *The New York Times*, Henry Jarvis Raymond and George Jones, met in the office of New York's most popular newspaper in the 1840s: *The New York Tribune*. Jones was working in business management, whereas Raymond was an editorial assistant. *The New York Tribune* was masterminded by Horace Greeley, who imbued his paper with politics; Greeley was a Whig (the forerunner of the Republican Party) with socialist leanings, and one needn't read between the lines too much to figure the rest out.

The Herald was another popular paper of the time; it was the first to focus on hard news coverage of the urban underbelly: stories of crime, drugs, and prostitution were common, which was not appreciated by those who held to the Victorian ideals of the time. On the opposite end of the spectrum, pretentious newspapers with smaller circulations, intended for an elite readership, were still preferred among the upper classes. No single paper transcended these complex class lines.

One Paper for a Mass Readership

What journalism needed was a new approach that would appeal to academics and laypeople alike: a paper that focused on news without sensationalizing sex and violence; a paper that was political but nonpartisan; a paper that was intelligent, yet accessible to the growing literacy of the lower and middle classes. Raymond and Jones were aware of this need, and for years they tossed around the idea of starting a paper together.

The moment finally came in 1851. Jones was a businessman at heart, so he'd moved to Albany to redeem bank notes—a profitable venture in the days before standardized bank practices. In 1851, legislation was in the works that would regulate bank note redemption. One day, Jones and Raymond were walking along the Hudson, and Raymond mentioned that in the previous year, *The Herald* had brought in a profit of $60,000. By the end of that fateful stroll, Jones and Raymond made an agreement: If the bank note legislation passed, the two would start a paper together. The bill passed. With the help of additional investments from mutual friend E. B. Wesley, the paper was officially established in September as *The New-York Daily Times* (the name was changed in 1857).

The founders committed to objectivity and temperance in opinion; the paper was to be "the best and the cheapest daily family newspaper in the United States," and it was "not established for the advancement of any party, sect, or person." The first issue was published on September 18, 1851, with the prophetic pronouncement that "we publish today the first issue of *The New-York Daily Times*, and we intend to issue it every morning (Sundays excepted) for an indefinite number of years to come."

Debugging

Was the original computer bug literally a bug?

✳   ✳   ✳   ✳

THE MARK II Aiken Relay Calculator was built at Harvard University for the U.S. Navy just after World War II. The Mark II wasn't a calculator like we know them today—it was a primitive computer, one of those comically giant, room-filling monstrosities that featured endless wires, switches, and relays. Today you see the Mark II in history books, with serious-looking technicians in lab coats posed in front of it.

One September day in 1947, the Mark II wasn't working properly. Computer operators investigated and found the problem on Panel F: A dead moth was gumming up relay number 70. The moth was removed and taped to the operator's log. The following words were written on the log beneath the moth: "First actual case of bug being found."

The Mark II moth has since gained some fame and is now enshrined at the National Museum of American History in Washington, D.C. It sometimes is referred to as the inspiration for the term "bug," and some people believe that it was the cause of the first-ever computer bug. Both claims are nonsense, of course.

The fact that the operators recognized the joke—that an actual bug was the "bug" in their computer system—suggests that the term already existed. And indeed it did. The term had been used to describe glitches in mechanics and electronics for many years. The *Oxford English Dictionary* traces its use back to 1889, in a published account of Thomas Edison working on "a bug" in his phonograph.

And it certainly wasn't the first time someone had a problem with a computer. You think your PC gives you headaches? There's a reason why none of those technicians in lab coats were smiling.

The Other Jackie Robinson

Jackie Robinson's story has been well documented and celebrated. Larry Doby's story is not as well known, but that doesn't make it any less remarkable or his actions less courageous.

✳   ✳   ✳   ✳

ON APRIL 15, 1947, Jackie Robinson trotted out onto Ebbets Field for the National League's Brooklyn Dodgers, smashing the color barrier that barred African Americans from major-league baseball.

On July 5, 1947, Larry Doby walked from the dugout of Comiskey Stadium in Chicago to pinch-hit for the Cleveland Indians, blazing the trail for African Americans in the American League.

Because Doby followed Robinson, some have deemed Doby's achievement less significant, and his story less compelling. "Jackie's number is hung in every ballpark in the country," former Cleveland player Ellis Burks said in 2003, in reference to Major League Baseball retiring Robinson's number 42. "But Larry Doby never did get enough recognition for what he did."

That shouldn't be the case, because Doby's accomplishment was every bit as important as Robinson's—and certainly as arduous. "It was eleven weeks between the time Jackie Robinson and I came into the majors," Doby said about the experience. "Eleven weeks. Whatever happened to him happened to me."

Unwelcome and All Alone

Whereas several Brooklyn Dodger players circulated a petition during spring training in 1947 refusing to play on the same field as Robinson, some of Doby's Cleveland teammates refused to shake his hand when he was first introduced in the Indian clubhouse—a moment he would recall as one of the most embarrassing of his life.

In his first game with the Indians, initially, none of the players volunteered to do warm-up tosses with him until player Joe Gordon stepped up. "You don't know what a terrible feeling that was," Doby later said. Like Robinson, Doby heard the racial slurs and verbal attacks from the fans and other players. Like Robinson, he was not allowed to stay in the same hotels or eat in the same restaurants as the rest of his teammates. Like Robinson, he had to brave his ordeal alone, having no black peer to take solace with on the field or on the road.

But, also like Robinson, Doby persevered by maintaining a stoic dignity and excelling on the diamond. "I couldn't react to [prejudice] from a physical standpoint," he once explained. "My reaction was to hit the ball as far as I could." And hit it he did: He was a seven-time All-Star and won the American League home run crown in 1952 and 1954. He cemented his place in Cleveland sports history by helping lead the Indians to their last World Series title (so far) in 1948, batting .318 in the six-game series and belting the game-winning homer in Game 4. He was ranked with Joe DiMaggio and Duke Snider as one of the best center fielders of his era.

A Tougher Journey into History

Some have suggested that it was actually Doby, not Robinson, who had the tougher go of things. Dodgers president Branch Rickey brought Robinson along slowly, allowing him to play 18 months in the minors before debuting in Brooklyn. Rickey protected Robinson, carefully planning and guiding the whole process so that Robinson could survive it. Robinson had the time to prepare himself for what lay ahead.

Contrast that to Doby, who made his major league debut *one day* after being signed from the Negro League Newark Eagles by Indians owner Bill Veeck. Doby's protection: two black Chicago police detectives who sat on the bench with him during only his first game to shield him from abusive fans.

Doby, however, never saw it that way. "I look at myself as more fortunate than Jack. If I'd gone through hell in the minors, then I'd have to go through it again in the majors. Once was enough."

Larry Doby reached another landmark in 1962, when he became the second African American to sign with Japan's Nippon Professional Baseball League.

The Times They Are A-Changin': 1942

* Here comes the sun! Daylight Saving Time is reintroduced in the United States.

* President Franklin D. Roosevelt invokes Executive Order 9066, which calls for the internment of more than 120,000 Japanese Americans to "relocation centers" until the end of World War II.

* Physicist Enrico Fermi successfully produces a controlled nuclear reaction at the University of Chicago. The experiment is part of the Manhattan Project, the U.S. government's top-secret effort to create a nuclear bomb.

* A mine explosion in Honkeiko Colliery, Manchuria, kills 1,549 miners.

* On June 12, Anne Frank receives a diary for her 13th birthday. A month later, her family is forced into hiding in an attic above her father's Amsterdam warehouse office.

* Glenn Miller and his orchestra have 11 Top Ten hits in 1942; they play together for the last time in September before Miller enters the U.S. Army.

* Pan American Airlines becomes the first commercial airline to offer a flight that goes around the world.

* In WWII news, the United States' first aircraft carrier, the USS *Langley*, is sunk by Japanese warplanes.

* Barbra Streisand, Jimi Hendrix, and Harrison Ford are born.

* The average cost of new house is $3,770. The average annual income is $1,880.

* The Battle of Midway begins when the Imperial Japanese Navy attacks Midway Island upon the orders of Japanese Admiral Chuichi Nagumo.

* Albert Camus writes his existential classic, *L'Etranger (The Stranger)*.

* Movies are a popular release; top films this year include *Casablanca, Road to Morocco, and Bambi.*

The Times They Are A-Changin': 1943

* Wartime rationing continues in the United States.

* On October 30, the one and only time Bugs Bunny is outwitted is released in the Merrie Melodies animated short, "Falling Hare."

* In January, Franklin Roosevelt and Winston Churchill plan an Allied war strategy at the Casablanca Conference. They agree that the ultimate goal is "unconditional surrender" by Germany and Japan.

* Rodgers and Hammerstein's *Oklahoma!* opens on Broadway. The first musical to treat music, dance, and story as an integrated unit, *Oklahoma!* runs for an unprecedented 2,000 performances and transforms American musical theater.

* From April 19 to May 16, inhabitants of the Warsaw Ghetto revolt against the occupying German troops. Although the Jewish resistance is poorly armed and malnourished, it takes the German garrison more than a month to subdue, and finally massacre, the ghetto's 56,000 residents.

* The Supreme Court rules that U.S. children do not have to salute the flag in school if it is against their religion.

* The Pentagon is built in Arlington, Virginia. It is the largest office building in the world.

* W. E. B. DuBois becomes the first African American member of the National Institute of Letters.

* On September 21, Congress adopts a "one-world" resolution drafted by J. William Fulbright, the freshman representative from Arkansas. The Fulbright Resolution is the first step toward U.S. participation in what would become the United Nations.

* Dr. George Nicholas Papanicolaou publishes his study on the use of the vaginal smear test (now known as the Pap smear) to diagnose cervical cancer, then the leading cause of death among American women.

Bay View Tragedy

"Eight hours for work, Eight hours for rest,
Eight hours for what we will."

Those were the words emblazoned across a banner carried during a parade of some 3,000 Milwaukee industrial workers on Sunday, May 2, 1886. They demanded that their workdays be reduced to eight hours. Just a few days later, organized labor's "Eight Hours" campaign would shut down the city's bustling factories and culminate in a bloody showdown near the shores of Lake Michigan.

✳   ✳   ✳   ✳

All Work and No Play

ALTHOUGH MILWAUKEE LABORERS had staged several strikes before and after the Civil War, they preferred to use the ballot box to elect politicians sympathetic to their cause. By the late 1880s, however, the entire country was buzzing about labor's demand for an eight-hour workday, and Milwaukee workers were eager to join the fight. Conditions were ripe for reform. The city's industrial laborers typically toiled for ten hours a day, six days a week, earning little more than a dollar per day. In machine shops and mills, workers endured dangerous conditions that threatened their lives and their health.

About half of the city's blue-collar workers were members of the Knights of Labor, led by German immigrant Robert Schilling. As a union organizer and editor of the *Volksblatt*, a daily labor newspaper, Schilling was a prominent voice arguing locally for the adoption of the eight-hour day. A more strident voice was that of the Central Labor Union's Paul Grottkau, a Socialist and editor of another German-language labor newspaper, *Arbeiter Zeitung*.

When the unions called for a May 1, 1886, deadline for adoption of the eight-hour day in Milwaukee, the city's industrial workers were ready to drop their tools and strike until their employers agreed to the demand. Julius Perry, a machinist who joined the Knights of Labor in 1884, recalled the mood of the workers at the time in a 1930 interview with the *Milwaukee Leader* newspaper's Jessie Stephen.

"The eight-hour day strike of 1886 was a time of great excitement," Perry said, "not only in Milwaukee, but all over the country."

The Big Day

When Saturday, May 1, dawned, about 7,000 people were either on strike or locked out of Milwaukee businesses. They included tailors, bakers, carpenters, joiners, cabinetmakers, slaughterhouse hands, clothing cutters, broom-makers, mill hands, laborers, and brewers. In the following days, about 16,000 blue-collar workers would be idled.

Grottkau's Central Labor Union organized a parade on Sunday morning, May 2, to bang the drum for the cause. About 2,500 laborers, six buses full of tailors, and a series of marching bands paraded through the streets of Milwaukee. About 20,000 spectators were urged to join the march, which ended with a picnic at the Milwaukee Garden beer garden.

The festive atmosphere took a serious turn on Monday, May 3, when about 14,000 workers either walked off their jobs or were locked out by their employers. Eight of the nine Milwaukee breweries were all but deserted. Strikes broke out across the city, and laborers marched on businesses that were still open, urging those workers to join the protest.

Milwaukee Mayor Emil Wallber and law enforcement officials were becoming increasingly anxious as Governor Jeremiah "Uncle Jerry" Rusk arrived in Milwaukee and called out the militia. On Tuesday, May 4, a crowd of about 3,000 men marched on the only factory still open, the North Chicago Rolling Mill in Bay View, calling for workers inside the plant to come out and join them. When the Kosciusko Guards militia detachment arrived to repel the crowd, the soldiers were met with a shower of sticks, stones, and insults. The militia fired warning shots into the air, and the crowd dispersed.

Frightening Turn of Events

Meanwhile, a crowd of strikers in Chicago was gathering in Haymarket Square to demonstrate against the shootings of several protesters the day before. At the end of the rally, a bomb was hurled into a group of police officers, killing eight. The news of this event escalated an already hair-trigger situation in Milwaukee.

About 1,000 strikers regrouped at St. Stanislaus church on Milwaukee's south side on Wednesday morning, May 5. With a banner demanding an eight-hour workday waving before them, the crowd began to march toward the Bay View rolling mill. Major George P. Trauemer, in command of the militia, ordered the strikers to halt, but the workers pressed ahead. This time, the soldiers' volleys would be aimed squarely at the strikers. Trauemer had orders from the governor to fire directly at them.

Perry, the Knights of Labor machinist, remembered the next terrifying moments: "I was in the front rank of the parade carrying the American flag as we started our march. Just before we got to the mills, I handed the flag to the man next to me to carry for a while and it was only a few minutes later that he was shot down right next to me."

When the shots rang out, the strikers scattered in chaos, leaving the dead and dying behind. Some say five strikers died, while others insist nine people lay dead. The historical records are unclear. Among the victims were two uninvolved bystanders—a 12-year-old boy and a retiree who was watching the confrontation from his backyard.

Rusk became a hero, hailed as the man who saved Milwaukee from anarchists. But on the first Sunday in May, the city's labor leaders commemorate the "Bay View Tragedy" as they gather near a historical marker on a bluff overlooking Lake Michigan. There, on the site of the old rolling mill, they raise a banner in support of the eight-hour workday.

Showing the Klan the Door

Riding a wave of resentment against African Americans, Jews, Catholics, and immigrants, the Ku Klux Klan enjoyed a startling surge of popularity in the early 1920s. Championing "100 percent Americanism," the Klan reached out to white Protestant men who felt threatened by the hedonism of the Jazz Age and the encroachment of diversity in big cities.

✳ ✳ ✳ ✳

NOWHERE WAS THE clash of cultures more pronounced than in Chicago, home to 110,000 African Americans, 125,000 Jews, 1,000,000 Catholics, and 800,000 immigrants. By late 1922 the Klan claimed 100,000 members in the city and another 100,000 in the suburbs. A unifying force was a weekly local newspaper called *Dawn* that featured Klan-related news and advertising, such as a coffee company that promoted its "Kuality Koffee and Kourtesy."

As the Klan began to influence local politics, the African American community and its newspaper, the *Chicago Defender*, decried the organization. The city council reacted, officially condemning the Klan and passing a largely worthless ordinance outlawing masks. But as a legal entity that remained largely nonviolent in Chicago, the KKK thrived.

A Force from the South

The city's most organized anti-Klan forces rallied behind an unlikely figure—Grady K. Rutledge. Born in Alabama, Rutledge was a reporter who claimed to be a direct descendant of Edward Rutledge, the youngest signer of the Declaration of Independence. Grady Rutledge had recently moved to Chicago to start a publicity firm that raised money for several large charities. He hired Ben Hecht, a popular Chicago journalist, and together they raised millions of dollars.

In 1922 Rutledge joined with various community leaders to form an anti-Klan association called the American Unity League (AUL). The league launched a newspaper called *Tolerance* and also published booklets with such catchy titles as "Is Your Neighbor a Kluxer?" Using a network of spies, *Tolerance* obtained and printed lists of Klansmen's names; they figured that, since the Klan reveled in secrecy, the best way to attack them would be through exposure. The approach was novel and effective; circulation reached 150,000 by year's end.

A Wrigley-Size Whoops

One AUL operative claimed that chewing gum magnate William Wrigley Jr. was a Klansman. Rutledge was skeptical and resisted printing the story, but other AUL leaders overruled him. Wrigley was implicated in the December 31, 1922, issue of *Tolerance*, based on what was later proved to be fraudulent evidence. *Tolerance* was soon crushed under the weight of lawsuits filed by Wrigley and others. In a bizarre twist, Rutledge joined the Klan and wrote a series of articles for *Dawn* exposing the AUL's shady tactics.

Dawn lasted about a year longer than *Tolerance*. Its last issue appeared in February 1924. By 1925 interest in the Klan had dissipated as quickly as it had erupted. Exposure had ruined many Klan-friendly businessmen, and internal squabbling weakened the organization.

Hecht became a renowned literary figure and prolific Hollywood screenwriter, winning an Oscar for *Underworld* and working on many films, including *Wuthering Heights* and *Gone with the Wind*. In his autobiography, Hecht portrayed Rutledge as witty but temperamental, a heavy drinker, and a fraud who skimmed the funds he raised for charity. Perhaps Rutledge's conscience caught up with him. In September 1926 he was found dead in his Park Ridge home, an apparent suicide at age 35.

The American Unity League's stated goal was "the creation of better feeling between the several racial and religious groups making up America."

The Great Camel Experiment

One of the most interesting military experiments prior to the Civil War involved 77 camels and a native of Syria called Hi Jolly. Who came up with the idea of camel caravans in Texas?

❊ ❊ ❊ ❊

IN 1836, MAJOR George Crosman recommended to Congress that the U.S. Army consider using camels, arguing that they require less water and forage than mules and horses. He also passed that suggestion to Major Henry Wayne, who, in the late 1840s, began to investigate the feasibility of using camels as pack animals.

Wayne proposed that camels would move faster than mules, carry more supplies, and naturally adapt to the Southwest, which mimicked the geographic areas he called "Camel Land." He submitted a formal proposal to the War Department recommending the importation of camels to test the feasibility of a camel cavalry. The cause was also supported by Army Lieutenant Edward Beale, who had surveyed Death Valley and agreed that camels were hardy animals that could assist the Army in developing the Texas territory and surrounding Southwest.

A Growing Consensus

Jefferson Davis, U.S. Secretary of War in the 1850s, had listened closely to Wayne and Beale and set out to do his own research. Being an avid historian, he knew that the French had used camels during the Napoleonic campaign in Egypt. Davis had previously served in the Mexican War and was keenly aware of the challenges of a desert climate. With Davis's backing, Congress appropriated $30,000 to purchase camels and hire camel drivers.

So with visions of camel caravans winding their way across Texas, Major Wayne and Lieutenant David Porter were sent to the eastern Mediterranean on a Navy supply ship to purchase camels. Wayne, an experienced horse trader, haggled with the natives and chose a team of 33 camels. The savvy businessman paid $250 per beast and gained two more through the birth of two colts during the voyage.

The Triumphal Arrival

On the excursion's return to Texas, locals watched as the camels were unloaded at Powder Point, near Indianola. Displaying typical camel stubbornness and aggravated by the long period of confinement onboard ship, the animals snorted, reared, broke halters, and kicked handlers. Many onlookers thought a circus had come to town. And indeed the circuslike atmosphere continued as the beasts were herded towards Houston with their drivers wearing colorful red coats and blue pants and the jingle of bells on the camels' harnesses echoing through the countryside.

In February 1857, a second cargo of 41 camels landed on the Texas coast. Eventually, a permanent camel camp was established near San Antonio. Camp Verde became the proving ground for the Texas Camel Experiment.

Hadji Ali, a Syrian camel wrangler, was hired to teach the soldiers how to handle the camels and pack and load supplies on a camel's back. The Texans had trouble pronouncing his foreign name, so they gave him the nickname Hi Jolly.

Into the Desert

The first caravan, led by Beale and Jolly, left Texas in June 1857 and made its way to California. The camels carried 600 to 800 pounds each and traveled an average of 25 to 30 miles a day. The caravan made it to California and back successfully. However, the grand plans for the camel experiment were cast aside as the Civil War loomed. Although the next secretary of war petitioned Congress for 1,000 additional camels, the affiliation of the project with Jefferson Davis, who would become president of the Confederacy, soured the enthusiasm.

The camels that were already available were eventually seized by the Confederates, who quickly lost interest in them. Many wandered away from the forts, and some were taken by Mexicans across the border. For many years after, there were camel sightings across Texas and the Southwest, with the last official sighting in 1901. Unsubstantiated sightings, however, lasted into the 1940s.

An Ominous Chain Reaction

Few events have changed the course of history as greatly as the movement of a few simple particles at the University of Chicago one sobering December afternoon in 1942.

✳ ✳ ✳ ✳

A S THE UNITED States braced itself for a second year of war both in Europe and in the Pacific, the world's top scientists set off a mesmerizing chain reaction that proved possible the development of nuclear technology. Its consequences were also, however, devastating and final, capable of obliterating civilization with the press of a button. The atomic bomb was born at 3: 25 P.M. on December 2, 1942.

The Split Heard 'Round the World

By the close of the 1930s, the Axis powers were said to have begun developing a weapon that would harness atomic energy in order to cause vast, devastating damage. Urged by a letter from physicists Albert Einstein and Leó Szilárd, U.S. President Franklin Roosevelt created a committee of scientists to research the feasibility of such a project, the first in a series of official measures taken by the American government to develop the bomb. After Allied scientists working in England discovered Uranium's fissile properties (or, more specifically, the fact that the isotope Uranium-235 had the ability to split), the project was given the full resources of the military. Physicists and engineers were recruited from throughout the world to work on what became known as the Manhattan Project.

Numerous labs and thousands of personnel throughout the country worked overtime to understand, first, how to enact nuclear fission and, second, how to safely harness its energy. Under the auspices of the now-defunct Office of Scientific Research and Development, the Manhattan Project constituted the most complex integration of science and military technology in modern history.

The Chicago Metallurgical Laboratory, the ultra-secret midwestern arm of the project, was overseen largely by Leslie Groves, a meat-and-potatoes brigadier general, while Enrico Fermi, an Italian academic and Nobel Laureate—and namesake of Fermilab, which still conducts nuclear research outside Chicago—worked with a team of physicists to create the conditions necessary for nuclear fission and the subsequent chain reaction.

A Most Imposing Pile

Using the work of such theorists as Szilárd, who had discovered the process of nuclear chain reaction, and the expertise of his engineering team, Fermi constructed a block—a "pile"—of Uranium and other materials called Chicago Pile 1. This was the famous reactor, and it stood almost 26 feet high. From the pile, a rod coated in the element Cadmium would be withdrawn, causing neutrons to collide with and split the Uranium isotopes, and by doing so, cause more collisions. Slowed by the non-Uranium materials and quickly shut off by reinserting the Cadmium rod, the reactor showed the potential for larger reactions in an uncontrolled setting.

Though his famous reactor was meant to be constructed outside of the city, at the Argonne National Laboratory in nearby DuPage County, a labor strike forced Fermi to find another space. Since named a historic landmark by the federal government, the room Fermi chose was a squash court beneath some rusty bleachers at the University of Chicago's long-abandoned Stagg Field. While scores of fellow scientists, officials, and dignitaries looked on, Fermi's team completed a successful self-sustaining nuclear reaction—the world's first. Just three years later, detonated in a split second, the same type of reaction would annihilate a city.

Sources say that the mood that day was both exhilarating and terrifying; after the war, Fermi and Szilárd expressed ambivalence about the consequences of their work, which held immense promise for energy production but could also result in such destruction and utter despair.

Bringing the World to Chicago

The 1893 World's Columbian Exposition, also known as the Chicago World's Fair, was the largest event of its kind ever held. The Fair was so expansive—more than 200 individual buildings spread over 633 acres, with exhibits from 36 foreign nations and 46 U.S. states and territories—that organizers estimated a visitor would have to walk for three weeks and cover more than 150 miles to see every exhibit.

✳   ✳   ✳   ✳

THE FAIR OPENED on May 1, 1893, and proved to be a huge success, with more than 27.5 million admissions over its six-month run. People happily paid 50 cents each (25 cents for children) to see a world of things they'd never seen before. Among the more unusual attractions were:

✳ A "palace of corn" built in the Pompeian style of architecture, as part of the Iowa exhibition.

* The first Ferris wheel, constructed by George Ferris at a cost of $250,000. Each of its 36 cars held 60 passengers. Cost: 50 cents per ride (this was in addition to the entrance fee).

* The Streets of Cairo, a detailed representation of the Egyptian capital manned by real Egyptians who came over specifically for the Fair. The most popular attraction: camel rides.

* Buffalo Bill Cody's Wild West Show. Cody gave 318 shows over six months and pocketed nearly $1 million.

* A British cannon surrendered at Yorktown during the Revolutionary War.

* A mammoth skeleton (part of the Smithsonian exhibit).

* A life-size silver statue of Christopher Columbus. The Fair celebrated the 400th anniversary of Columbus's voyage to the New World.

* The largest telescope in the world (at the time) and a print of the first photograph of the moon.

Battle of Harlem Heights

If you stroll the campus of New York's Columbia University on the city's Upper West Side, the quiet walks and elegant buildings create a sense of tranquility and peace—but it hasn't always been that way.

＊　＊　＊　＊

NOTHING ABOUT THE area near Columbia suggests that it was once the site of a bloody battle, unless you happen to look for, or stumble upon, a bronze marker set in a grassy triangle on Riverside Drive at 121st Street. The modest plaque commemorates the September 16, 1776, Revolutionary War Battle of Harlem Heights, a fierce skirmish between green Continental Army troops under George Washington and a seasoned British Army led by General William Howe. An unplanned, unanticipated fight, the American victory there encouraged the ragtag Continental troops to believe that they could, just maybe, win a war with the greatest military power on earth.

A Surprise for Both Sides

While Washington expected to encounter British troops when they crossed from Queens to the north end of Manhattan Island, General Howe pulled a fast one. His troops, supported by a bombardment from five British frigates with some 86 cannons, landed far south, at Kips' Bay. The largely inexperienced American troops—hungry, underequipped, and, in many cases sick—retreated in a panic. General Washington was furious. Regrouping at Harlem Heights, Washington sent a party of Connecticut Rangers out to determine how far north the British had marched.

The party met with fire at today's West 106th Street, and in retreat the troops were taunted by a bugle call from the enemy that traditionally signaled the end of a foxhunt and the going to ground of the fox. Stung, Washington immediately sent a larger force to engage the British. After a bloody, daylong encounter, the British were sent flying—the first time, it's said, that Continental troops saw the backs of Redcoats and Hessians. Though the victory was short-lived—the Continental Army was soon pushed north—the Battle of Harlem Heights was a critical turning point in American morale.

A Call to Action!

The Stonewall Rebellion wasn't the first salvo in the fight for gay rights—but it did help bring the issue to the public's attention.

✳   ✳   ✳   ✳

IN THE EARLY hours of June 28, 1969, members of the NYPD raided the Stonewall Inn, a popular gay hangout on

Christopher Street. Such police raids were fairly common—transvestism was out and out illegal in New York—but this time things went differently. Rather than meekly disappearing into the night, as had happened so often in the past, the angry crowd fought back.

This confrontation has come to be known as the Stonewall Rebellion. While it certainly wasn't the first push toward the public recognition of gay rights, it remains a defining moment in that ongoing movement.

Enough Is Enough

The Stonewall Inn was a Mafia-owned bar where gay men met to mingle and have a good time. Police frequently targeted the Stonewall and other gay establishments, arresting transvestites and harassing other patrons.

What sparked the rebellion on June 28 remains a mystery. Some cultural historians speculate that patrons were still upset over the recent death of gay icon Judy Garland. Others say the crowd had simply had enough and decided to push back. Regardless, police found themselves confronted by an angry mob that refused to be cowed. Rocks, bottles, and even an uprooted parking meter pelted the cops. Several patrons were beaten and arrested.

But the unrest didn't end that night. The Stonewall Rebellion struck a nerve, and the rights of gay men and women became as important (and as legitimate) as those of other minorities. More protests occurred in the days that followed, making public a cause that had always been kept quietly in the closet.

Men and women who had previously kept their sexual identities closely guarded secrets "came out" to family, friends, and the world, consequences be damned. Gay pride was suddenly on the cultural radar.

Ship of Honor

As a tribute to those who perished on 9/11, the USS New York *contains more than seven tons of steel from the World Trade Center.*

✳ ✳ ✳ ✳

Y̲OU COULD CALL it history that now lives on the sea: The USS *New York*, an amphibious transport dock ship, was commissioned on November 7, 2009, more than eight years after terrorist attacks that destroyed New York City's World Trade Center.

There's an important connection between the two events. The *New York's* bow was constructed using seven and a half tons of steel salvaged from the skyscrapers' wreckage. Five days before it was officially commissioned, the *New York* paused across from the World Trade Center site, dipped its flag, and delivered a 21-gun salute before an assembled crowd that included members of the Fire Department of New York, the New York Police Department, Port Authority Police, and family members of those who perished in the 2001 attack.

Strong as Steel

In the months following the tragic events of 9/11, New York Governor George Pataki wrote the Department of the Navy to request that it revive the name USS *New York* in honor of those who died, and that steel from the Twin Towers be incorporated into the construction of the ship. "The significance of where the WTC steel is located on the 684-foot-long ship symbolizes the strength and resiliency of the citizens of New York as it sails forward around the world," observed Navy Commander Quentin King.

The *New York* isn't alone in honoring the victims of 9/11; two other amphibious assault ships were constructed using steel salvaged from terrorist attack sites. The bow of the

USS *Arlington*, named for the Virginia county in which the Pentagon is located, was cast using metal from the Pentagon building's structural girders, and the bow of the USS *Somerset* contains steel from a crane used to excavate United Airlines Flight 93, a hijacked plane forced to crash by brave and quick-thinking passengers before it could reach its intended target in Washington, D.C.

"Ford to City: 'Drop Dead'"

Two words may have killed a U.S. president's reelection chances—but did he really say them?

✳   ✳   ✳   ✳

WHEN A REQUEST for help is met with a nasty refusal, it's hard to take, especially if it's from a good friend or a close relative. However, when that dose of tough love is doled out by the president of the United States, it can be an even more bitter pill to swallow.

In 1975, New York City was broke. Following years of fiscal mismanagement, a downturn in the national economy pushed the Big Apple to the brink of disaster. While its lawyers filed a bankruptcy petition in the State Supreme Court, Mayor Abraham Beame was forced to beg the White House for a bailout. On October 29, in a speech before the National Press Club, President Gerald R. Ford likened the city's profligate spending to "an insidious disease" and asserted that he was "prepared to veto any bill that has as its purpose a federal bailout of New York City to prevent a default."

Hooked on Heroin?

Meanwhile, Ford's press secretary, Ron Nessen, compared the city to "a wayward daughter hooked on heroin. You don't give her $100 a day to support her habit." None of this sat well with Mayor Beame, who accused the President of "writing off New York City in one speech." The next day, a banner headline on the front page of New York's *Daily News* announced: "FORD TO CITY: 'DROP DEAD.'"

Those two words, although never uttered by the President, did capture the essence of his remarks—at least, as perceived by many New Yorkers. Yet, even the President did an about-face just two months later, signing legislation for federal loans. But the damage had been done, and Ford later acknowledged that the *Daily News* interpretation of his thoughts probably cost him the 1976 election, when Jimmy Carter narrowly carried New York State. Galvanized by the President's speech, a defiant New York City never did drop dead.

17 Bits of Nostalgia from 1957

Life in America in 1957 was much simpler. Everybody loved Lucy and Father always knew best. Make yourself a root beer float, sit on the davenport, and take a look at life in 1957.

✳   ✳   ✳   ✳

1. **You know what they say about the size of a man's fin.:** General Motors and Ford were duking it out with their "Olds vs. Edsel" wars. Ford's Edsel included such forward-thinking features as lights that reminded drivers that it was time to service the engine. Chevrolet opted to put their money into advertising. This is the year that had Dinah Shore singing "See the USA in your Chevrolet" on radio and TV spots. Whatever people chose to drive, the average cost of a car was only $2,749. Brace yourself—gasoline was only 24 cents a gallon!

2. **"Welcome to Babyville.":** After World War II, people were settling down and getting back to the business of creating the American dream. Record numbers of babies were born between 1946 and 1964, and, even today, this generation is referred to as the "Baby Boomers." By 1957, everybody on the fast track was moving out to the suburbs.

Doctors, lawyers, teachers, and cops created a mass exodus to the land of lawn mowers and charcoal grills. With all the new babies being born, it's no wonder that suburbia became known as "Babyville."

3. **All eyes toward the sky.:** In July 1957, American John Glenn set a new transcontinental speed record. The navy test pilot flew a supersonic jet from California to New York in just 3 hours, 23 minutes, and 8.4 seconds.

4. **What's with all the hips?:** Music lovers had plenty of choices in the year when rock 'n' roll took over the charts. Songs like Sam Cooke's, "You Send Me" and Jimmie Rodgers's "Honeycomb" were popular, but the true sensation of the year was Elvis Presley. He rocked teens across the country with hits like "All Shook Up" and "Jailhouse Rock." You could buy a 45-rpm record (that's the little one) for 79 cents or an album (the big one) for about three bucks. The only problem was that a hi-fi record player cost $79.95.

5. **And the Oscar goes to . . . :** *The Bridge on the River Kwai*, for Best Picture. Alec Guinness also won the Oscar for Best Actor for his role in the movie. Joanne Woodward claimed her statue for Best Actress in *The Three Faces of Eve*. Other favorites were *An Affair to Remember*, *12 Angry Men*, and that kid who swivels his hips in a movie called *Jailhouse Rock*. With the average price of a movie ticket at just 50 cents, you could afford to see them all!

6. **The Braves win the World Series!:** They weren't from Atlanta, however. In 1957, they were the Milwaukee Braves (just four years earlier they were the Boston Braves). In the 1957 World Series, the Braves, led by Hank Aaron, beat Mickey Mantle and the New York Yankees, but it wasn't easy; it took all seven games.

7. **Does this price include the white picket fence?:** The American dream was a whole lot cheaper in 1957. You could buy your very own house for about $12,200. A custom built, split-level cost a little more—around $19,000. For those who weren't quite ready to buy, rent was only about $90 a month!

8. **It's all relative.:** Those house prices look pretty good, but what was the average household income in 1957? On average, people made around $4,500 a year. If you sold cars, you made $7,000 to $10,000 a year. A secretary made about $3,900 a year. So, could you afford to own?

9. **It was a small world, after all.:** In 1957, the Census Bureau reported that there were 171,984,130 people in the United States, and 2,889,768,830 in the entire world. Today, there are 6.6 billion people in the world, including more than 300 million Americans.

10. **Rabbit ears were popping up all over the place.:** In 1957, there were 47,200,000 TV sets in America; the RCA Victor model cost $78. What was everybody watching? Top shows included *Gunsmoke, The Danny Thomas Show, I Love Lucy,* and *The Ed Sullivan Show.*

11. **What's a Sputnik?:** Before astronauts, space missions flew without a crew. The first of these, Sputnik, came from the Soviet Union. Sputnik technically wasn't a satellite, it was a 184-pound basketball-size bundle of radio transmitters that took only 98 minutes to orbit Earth. When it was launched on October 4, 1957, during the height of the Cold War, the United States was caught completely by surprise and the "Space Race" was on!

12. **This black and white had nothing to do with TV.:** In the interest of school desegregation, President Eisenhower sent army troops to keep the peace at Central High School in Little Rock, Arkansas, so that nine black students could

attend the formerly all-white school. These kids are forever stamped in history as the Little Rock Nine.

13. **Who's Dick Clark?:** People started bopping in the middle of the family room in 1957 when ABC began airing *American Bandstand*, hosted by Dick Clark. Teens danced to the hits of the day and each week a different band performed. After each song, Clark would interview the teens and have them rate the song for its "danceability." The first nationwide audience poll ranked Patti Page as American Bandstand's favorite female vocalist of the year. The show went off the air in 1989.

14. **Teen idols were "dreamy.":** Teenage girls had plenty of swooning to do thanks to the many teen idols of the late 1950s. Ricky Nelson rocked and rolled on his family's hit TV show, *Ozzie and Harriet*, and people tuned in every week just to see if he'd sing. And Pat Boone cut such a wholesome image in his white patent leather shoes that even parents couldn't object. In 1957, he topped the charts with "Love Letters in the Sand."

15. **"Fashion Forward" had nothing to do with Paris.:** In 1957, American women had houses to clean, children to rear, and parties to plan. With cardigans, pearls, knee-length skirts, and heels, a lady always looked good. Teenage girls opted for bobby socks, saddle shoes, and poodle skirts. Females young and old even wore pants from time to time, especially pedal pushers or Capri pants. For guys, a leather jacket or a letterman sweater was a must.

16. **Lennon and McCartney meet for the first time.:** In 1957, a chance meeting at a church in Liverpool would forever change the face of rock music. On July 6, The Quarrymen, a skiffle group led by singer and guitarist John Lennon, performed a gig at the Woolton Parish Church. Among those in attendance was a young musician named Paul McCartney. The two future Beatles were introduced

by a mutual friend, and McCartney helped Lennon set up for the gig. Lennon was so impressed with McCartney's musical abilities that he invited him to join the group. The Quarrymen eventually became The Beatles, and the rest is music history.

17. **Baseball moves to California.:** Due to aging stadiums and slumping ticket sales, the archrival Brooklyn Dodgers and New York Giants moved west following the 1957 season. The Dodgers played one final game at Ebbets Field on September 24, 1957, before moving to Los Angeles. The stadium remained without a team until it was torn down in 1960. The Giants played one last game at the Polo Grounds on September 29, 1957, before heading to San Francisco. The stadium was vacant until the Mets moved in for the 1962 and 1963 seasons. It was demolished in 1964.

Chapter 7

Culture and Traditions

Cheers!

Raising glasses to one another is a custom that occurs in dozens of countries around the world. Here are some of the many ways to toast.

※   ※   ※   ※

Cheers—English, North America

Ivjeli—Croatian

Fisehatak—Arabic

Prost—German

Salud—used in many Latin countries, including Spain, Mexico, and Argentina

Na zdorov´ya—Bulgarian

Gan bei—Mandarin

Pura vida—Costa Rican

Kippis—Finnish

À votre santé—French

Sláinte—Irish (Gaelic)

Yamas—Grecian

Okole maluna—Hawaiian

L´Chaim—Hebrew

Egészségedre—Hungarian

Pro—Indonesian

Kampai—Japanese

Chukbae—Korean

Saha wa´afiab—Moroccan

Skål—Norwegian

Sanda bashi—Pakistani

Na zdrowie—Polish

A sia saide—Portugese

Noroc—Romanian

Chtob vse bylizdorovy—Russian

Seiradewa—Sri Lankan

Afya—Swahili

Choc-tee—Thai

Pardon Me? Foreign Slang Terms

English borrows freely from nearly every language it comes into contact with. However, there are still many concepts and situations for which Anglophones still lack le mot juste. *Here are some suggested foreign words to add to the English dictionary.*

✳ ✳ ✳ ✳

Backpfeifengesicht (German): a face that's just begging for someone to slap it—a familiar concept to anyone fond of daytime TV.

Bakku-shan (Japanese): a girl who looks pretty from the back but not the front. This loanword would in fact be a loanword regifted, since it's already a combination of the English word "back" with the German word *schoen*, meaning "beautiful."

Kummerspeck (German): literally this means "grief bacon": excess weight gained from overeating during emotionally trying times.

Ølfrygt (Viking Danish): the fear of a lack of beer. Often sets in during trips away from one's hometown, with its familiar watering holes.

Drachenfutter (German): literally "dragon fodder": a makeup gift bought in advance. Traditionally used to denote offerings made by a man to his wife when he knows he's guilty of something.

Bol (Mayan): For the Mayans of South Mexico and Honduras, the word *bol* pulls double duty, meaning both "in-laws" as well as "stupidity."

Uitwaaien (Dutch): walking in windy weather for the sheer fun of it.

Karelu (Tulu, south of India): the mark left on the skin by wearing anything tight.

Blechlawine (German): literally "sheet metal avalanche": the endless lineup of cars stuck in a traffic jam on the highway.

Leap Year Luck

Why do we have Leap Years? What can you to celebrate the day?

* * * *

Ladies' Leap

EVERY FOUR YEARS, the standard calendar year is punctuated with a "Leap Day." In the standard year of 365 days, the earth completes a revolution around the sun in 365 days and 6 hours. Due to the extra six hours, every four years we accumulate an extra day—and that's how we get a Leap Day.

In a custom that dates back to 1288, women can propose to men during any leap year. As the story goes, it allegedly started when Scotland's Queen Margaret legislated that women ask for their fella's hand during a leap year. However, if the man felt that he wasn't ready and rejected the proposal, he was bound to provide a kiss, one pound currency, and a pair of dress gloves.

Objects of Their Affection

Amulets and talismans allowed ancient peoples to feel they had some control over their lives.

* * * *

EVERYDAY LIFE IN biblical times could be a frightening experience. Fear and superstition were widespread, and many people felt they had no control over their own lives and the world around them. They did not understand the viruses and genetic conditions that caused plagues and ill health. They did not understand the mental problems that caused some people to behave as though they had "demons" inside them. They did not fully understand the weather that affected their crops and livestock or the construction of the solar system that controlled the weather. All this ignorance led people to find comfort and security in objects that they imbued with power; these objects are called amulets and talismans.

Good Luck with That

The word "amulet" comes from the Latin *amuletum*, meaning "an object that protects a person from trouble." In other words, a good luck charm. The earliest recorded use of the word that historians have been able to find is in *Naturalis Historia*, an encyclopedia published by Pliny the Elder in about A.D. 78. Pliny and other learned people of the Roman Empire sought to banish the ignorance that led people to use security objects, but they didn't have much luck. Various peoples—Jews, Christians, and Muslims—had been using amulets for centuries, and old habits die hard. Educators could lecture and scold, but where would they be when the next swarm of locusts showed up? Blessed objects were believed to bring protection and healing, and those who put their trust in them did not want to give them up.

Talismans are closely related to amulets, in that they are objects that are considered to be protective. But talismans usually have a more religious or sacred aspect to them. Perhaps the most obvious talisman is the *tallis*, the fringed and tasseled shawl that Jewish men wear over their shoulders while praying. It is just a coincidence that the word "tallis" sounds so much like "talisman." They are not related, since "talisman" is Greek, not Hebrew, in origin. The Jews have other talismans, such as the mezuzah, a small case filled with scripture that is placed on one's doorpost, and the kimiyah, a similar case that is worn on the body. While many modern Reformed and Conservative Jews no longer use such talismans, most Orthodox cling to these sacred objects. For them, talismans are not a sign of ignorance but of faith in God and his Law. Because of the biblical prohibition against idols, Jewish amulets and talismans involve text and names rather than images of God or man.

Controversy That Rages On

While some Jews use amulets and talismans and some Jews do not, there is not much arguing over it amongst them. Most tend to have a "live and let live" attitude about it. Not so in

Christianity. From the very earliest days of the Christian church, the issue of sacred objects, or *sacramentals*, has been a contentious one. Catholics (and some Anglicans) continue to use such sacramentals as crucifixes, rosaries, and holy water, but even many Catholics look askance when their co-religionists seem to be worshipping the dead body parts of saints or seeing images of the Virgin in windowpanes and tree bark.

During the Reformation, which swept across Europe approximately 500 years ago, men like Martin Luther and John Calvin raged against amulets and talismans as a vile form of idolatry. Luther despised the Jews, and felt that it was they who were originally responsible for luring Christians to their security objects. Both Luther and Calvin continually preached the doctrine of *sola scriptura*, the belief that the words of the Bible were all any person needed to lead a holy life.

Centuries after the Reformation, the argument rages on. Some Catholics take their amulets and talismans very seriously, and some Catholics wear things such as St. Christopher medals. Some Protestants wear crosses around their necks, while more reformed Protestants see even a simple cross as a form of idolatry. Whether powerful, harmless, or wicked, these objects don't seem to be going anywhere.

5 Fabulous Fads from the 1950s

If you were around in the 1950s, you probably remember the Korean War and McCarthyism. But that's not the fun stuff to visit on Memory Lane. It's much more fun to remember the fads, the crazes, and the pop culture sensations that emerged in an age when moms still made dinner every night and a car with fins could get you a date. The following is a list of some of the most decade-defining fads and trends of the 1950s. Don't get too excited, though—nice boys and girls never do.

✳   ✳   ✳   ✳

1. **Poodle Skirts:** Undoubtedly, the poodle skirt was one of the most iconic fashion trends of the 1950s. The long, swingy, often pastel-hued skirts had a motif appliquéd below the knee. Some common images were musical notes, flowers, and, of course, poodles. Dancing to the new rock 'n' roll music was popular, but it required dancers to wear clothes that allowed them to move. Since women rarely wore pants at the time, A-line poodle skirts were a nice alternative.

2. **Sock Hops:** Those 1950s teens were so thoughtful! Informal high school dances were named "sock hops" because students would remove their shoes so as to not scuff the floor while they danced. And they really liked to dance! Elvis made his famous appearance on *The Ed Sullivan Show* in 1956, and youngsters across the country were moving to the beat of the neat, new sound of rock 'n' roll. The always chaperoned sock hops were hugely popular—where else could you show off your hand-jive, bop, stroll, or box step?

3. **3-D Movies:** Just as the proliferation of downloadable music sent the record industry scrambling at the turn of this century, the advent of television spooked movie executives. Would anyone go to the movies when they could be entertained at home? In an attempt to offer something unique, studios like Warner Brothers released movies in "3-D." This meant that the movies were projected simultaneously from two different angles in two different colors, red and blue or green, and viewed with special glasses. The colored filters in the funky, paper-framed glasses separated the two different images so each image only entered one eye, creating a three-dimensional effect. Early 1950s titles included Bwana Devil and House of Wax. In 1953, there were more than 5,000 theaters in the United States equipped to show 3-D movies.

4. The Conical Bra: Though it was invented in 1943, the cantilevered brassiere really came into the spotlight in the 1950s. Jane Russell sported one of the bras in The Outlaw, and her lifted and separated bosom caused quite a sensation. The new silhouette was invented by none other than director, eccentric, and ladies' man Howard Hughes, who directed Russell in the movie. The look became popular and heavy-duty brassieres stuck around—at least until women started burning them a decade later.

5. Beatniks: Every generation has a rebellion and the "beats" emerged from the 1950s underground. These writers, artists, and musicians were pushing cultural expectations and embracing taboo subject matter. Writers Jack Kerouac and Allen Ginsberg were admired by this group of largely New York City-based artists. Today, the beatnik has been reduced to an image of a guy with a goatee wearing sunglasses and a beret and beating bongo drums. That's not exactly what the beats had in mind, but many were intrigued by their acts of "spontaneous creativity" that blended words and music, and they continue to influence poetry and music today.

Mistletoe: It's Not Just About Making Out

Ah, mistletoe. The little plant—hung on doorways across the land—conjures up quaint images of stolen kisses and blushing cheeks. The age-old tradition of kissing is what people think of when they consider the small green plant with white berries, but there's much more to mistletoe than just a peck on the cheek.

✻ ✻ ✻ ✻

Kissing Under the . . . Parasite?

WHAT YOU MIGHT think is a pretty little berry producing plant is actually a bloodthirsty— okay, plant-thirsty—

parasite. Mistletoes are hemiparasitic flowering plants, or angiosperms, that obtain their nutrition by living off other plants. There are only a few of these class of plant in the plant world, so to that extent, mistletoe is special straight out of the gate. In case you've never seen actual mistletoe, the plant sports smallish, dark to light green leaves and small, hard white berries. Mistletoe usually grows on oak or silver birch trees, as well as many varieties of shrubs. Mistletoe plants are found almost everywhere and actually first grew in the tropics. The hardy parasite traveled easily, however, and was soon found flourishing all over the West, where its lore was born.

Mythic Mistletoe (Say That Three Times Fast!)

The ancient Greeks saw mistletoe as special, too, and incorporated it into their mythology from the start. Remember Aeneas' "Golden Bough"? Aeneas planned a trip through hell, and on his way he had to pass through a dark and creepy forest. Two doves led him to a mistletoe plant, and Aeneas took a branch with him. The mistletoe lit his way, and when he got to the river Styx, all he did was show his plant to the ferryman and he and his men were immediately transported to the netherworld. Not bad for a twig and some berries! There is also a Norse legend that tells of the goddess Frigga and her son, Balder. Frigga petitioned the gods to keep her beloved child safe from fire, earth, air, and water. Thinking she had her bases covered, she relaxed. Then Loki, evil god that he was, made a poison-tipped arrow from mistletoe, since it grew in neither the earth nor the sea, but from the branches of other plants. He struck Balder down, and it was said that Frigga's tears turned into the white berries on the mistletoe plant.

The Celts Start the Trend

One of the earliest known examples of the importance of mistletoe, however, comes to us via the Druids, revered priests in the Celtic religious order. The Druids were big fans of trees, believing them to possess mystical properties. In fact, the word *Druid* means "oakknower." Since mistletoe grows on oak trees, the Druids thought it had major significance, especially since oaks shed leaves in winter but the mistletoe (being, unbeknownst to them, a parasite) remained vibrant. There was also a summer ritual that involved slaughtering animals—and a few humans—that was begun by clipping mistletoe plants off the boughs of an oak tree. The word "mistletoe" meant "all-healing" in the ancient language of the Druids, which gives you a good idea of how important the little leafy green was.

Mistletoe: An Idea That Stuck

In ancient Europe (think several hundred years B.C.), trees were seen as life-giving sources and were used in medicines, rituals, and all types of ceremonies and holy goings-on. Once Christmas came into play, some of these leftover tree traditions held on, including the Christmas tree, the yule log, and yes, the mistletoe. As the Middle Ages rolled into town, mistletoe hung on in people's minds as having special powers. Folks cut bunches to hang above their doors—not to inspire kissing but to ward off demons and bad spirits. Other uses included fire prevention (Sweden) and a cure for nightmares (Austria), as well as a poison antidote and an aphrodisiac. The idea that mistletoe could cure all ills was a widely held belief, and many tried it out in potions and other medicines in hopes that they could make barren animals conceive or epileptics cease to have seizures. In the third century A.D., mistletoe was incorporated into the traditions of Christianity as the faith became more and more widespread. This is where the origins of mistletoe as kissing cue may have begun. With all the powers mistletoe was believed to have, many thought it could help with fertility and conception. Therefore, kissing under a bough of the berries was sure to help bring a child into the world. And remember Frigga, the Scandanavian goddess? Well, she was eventually able to bring her son Balder back to life. In her joy, the happy mother kissed everyone who passed beneath the now berryfilled tree that had caused her so much sorrow. Some believe that this is the reason we kiss under the mistletoe today.

Before You Head Off to a Holiday Party...

Mistletoe continues to be a typical holiday tradition, though it's more common to see plastic mistletoe plants than the real thing these days. The next time you find yourself in a house or office with mistletoe hanging, you should know that there's actually a bit of etiquette involved. Traditionally, a man is supposed to kiss a woman under the branches—sorry gals, but that's the way it's supposed to go. Once a guy kisses a gal, he is to remove one of the berries from the plant. Once all the berries have been plucked, the plant should be removed and replaced with a fresh one, since all its "powers" have been used up. If a couple kisses under the mistletoe, not only do they get that nice, just-kissed feeling, they'll also have good luck in the coming year and a long and happy marriage in general, according to legend. Conversely, the couple that's too cool to smooch under the doorway is in for bad luck. If you're a single woman lingering under the mistletoe and you don't get any takers, tradition says you'll be single for another year. If you do get kissed, you'll be lucky in love. And if you don't want to deal with the whole kissing aspect of the tradition, you could always resort to fire. Burning a mistletoe plant is thought to foretell a woman's future in marriage. A mistletoe plant that burns slowly and steadily prophesies a healthy marriage, while spotty, smoky flames warn of a bad marriage or an ill-suited mate. Pucker up!

Sing It Loud!

Gospel music in its varied forms has inspired millions of Christians since the genre's birth in the 1800s.

✳   ✳   ✳   ✳

MUSIC HAS LONG played an essential role in organized religion, and its place in Christianity is strong. Hymns, for example, have been an important part of most church services for generations, but a unique variation known as gospel music brought the Lord's message to a wider audience.

Gospel music dates back to the Negro spirituals of the 1800s, which evolved from the hymns learned when slaves were often required by their owners to attend Christian church services. Later in the century, revival and camp meeting songs became popular, and it was from these musical declarations of praise and worship, sung with unreserved gusto, that contemporary gospel music was born.

In the Beginning

The word "gospel" in music is believed to have first been coined in the 1870s. At that time, the musical form was really starting to take shape, thanks to a number of especially talented pioneers such as Charles A. Tindley, George F. Root, P. P. Bliss, and Ira Sankey.

In the 1930s, composer/performer Thomas A. Dorsey, whose songs include such classics as "There Will Be Peace in the Valley" and "If you See My Savior," took gospel music to a whole new level. Originally a bluesman, Dorsey worked with some of the nation's all-time great blues singers, including Bessie Smith and Ma Rainey. Later, he turned to writing religious music that was heavily influenced in composition by the jazz and blues so popular in that era. At first, many conservative churchgoers didn't care for Dorsey's new gospel style, but it eventually caught on and today is considered a cornerstone of the genre.

Thanks in large part to Dorsey's fearless approach, other composers found themselves unrestricted and eager to push gospel in new and exciting directions. As a musical form, it evolved and stretched but never lost its spiritual heart and soul. Helping it along was the ever-growing popularity of radio, the only source of entertainment for many Americans.

National Respectability

By the 1950s, gospel had become established as a thriving musical force. So popular was gospel that singer Mahalia Jackson—one of the most celebrated gospel singers of her generation—produced several best-selling albums for Columbia Records and even performed on *The Ed Sullivan Show* and other national stages.

Today, gospel music remains as popular as ever. At first a predominantly African American musical form, it has become quite integrated. Numerous radio stations nationwide feature nothing but gospel, and many fans are excitedly rediscovering the genre's earliest stars. Meanwhile, gospel music continues to go in unique and varied directions as musicians and composers declare their love of God through their work.

Different Styles of Gospel

Modern students of gospel music like to divide the genre into various subcategories. Among them:

* Urban contemporary gospel, sometimes known as "black gospel."

* Christian country music, also known as country gospel, is characterized by a distinct country influence. In the 1990s, Christian country was so popular that many secular country musicians released gospel albums, including Larry Gatlin and Barbara Mandrell.

* Southern gospel, which typically describes how God helps people overcome daily problems and difficult times. It's a popular cross-over style of music.

* Bluegrass gospel, which has its roots in traditional rural mountain music. If it ain't got a banjo and a whole lot of praisin', it ain't bluegrass gospel.

* Gospel blues, a hybrid of blues music with religious lyrics.

Gospel music has many different roots and influences, but one thing is certain—it's distinctly American music. It remains very popular inside church and out, and it never seems to go out of style.

7 of the Oldest...

Western culture has become so age-obsessed that people in their thirties are trying to recapture that youthful glow. Well, outta the way, kiddies! There's something to be said for withstanding the tests of time, so this list pays homage to the old!

✳   ✳   ✳   ✳

1. **Oldest Tavern in America:** Established in 1795, Boston's Bell in Hand Tavern is the longest continuously running tavern in America. Founded by town crier Jimmy Wilson, the Bell in Hand still serves frosty mugs and food to an often full house. Famous customers have included Paul Revere and President McKinley.

2. **Oldest City:** In 2001, archaeologists found signs of an ancient city in the Gulf of Cambay in western India. In the 5.6-mile stretch of submerged city, carbon dating found evidence dating back to 7500 B.C., about 4,500 years older than what were believed to be the first cities, located in the Sumer Valley of Mesopotamia.

3. **Oldest Company:** Headquartered in Osaka, Japan, Kongo Gumi Co., Ltd., has been continuously operating for more than 1,400 years. Their business? Construction. Since A.dD 578, when the company built the still standing Shitennoji Temple, Kongo Gumi has had a hand in building Osaka Castle (16th century) and other famous Japanese buildings and temples. In 2006, the company had financial trouble and liquidated its assets, but it still maintains its identity and continues to function in Japan as a wholly owned subsidiary of the Takamatsu Corporation.

4. **Oldest Professional Chorus Line:** When the Tivoli Lovelies of Melbourne, Australia, entered Guinness World Records in 2004, the ten dancers had a combined age of 746 years and some change.

5. **Oldest Nut Collection:** In 2003, scientists at the University of Bonn uncovered a burrow containing 1,800 fossilized nuts. They were digging in a mine near Garzweiler, Germany, and came across the nuts, probably winter food supplies stashed away by a large hamster or squirrel more than 17 million years ago.

6. **Oldest Person to View Earth from Space:** John Glenn was a U.S. pilot during World War II and, in 1967, became a national hero as the first American and third person to orbit Earth when he rode in the Friendship 7, a NASA space capsule that successfully circled the globe three times. In 1998, Glenn went back into the great beyond at age 77, making him the oldest person to travel into space. The reason? To test the effects of space travel on the elderly, of course.

7. **Oldest Person:** Some come close, but so far, no one's been older than Jeanne Louise Calment, who died at age 122 in Arles, France in 1997. Calment was born in February 1875, a year before Alexander Graham Bell invented the telephone. She met Vincent Van Gogh at age 13 and was famous for her wit until her death, famously saying, "I've only ever had one wrinkle and I'm sitting on it."

Icarus

It's an ancient story, but the figure of Icarus still resonates today.

✳   ✳   ✳   ✳

IN GREEK MYTHOLOGY, a man named Daedalus built a labyrinth for King Minos. Despite this generous act, Daedalus fell out of favor with the king and was shut up in a tower with his son, Icarus. (The lesson here: be careful of coming to the attention of kings.)

Daedalus decided he and his boy should escape. Using feathers collected from birds that flew through their tower, Daedalus and Icarus created huge wings for themselves and attached them to their backs with wax. Before they leaped out of the window to fly to freedom, Daedalus cautioned his son to stay close to him. "If you get too close to the water, the wax will stiffen up. If you get too close to the sun, it will melt."

After father and son launched into flight, an exhilarated Icarus cried, "This is great!" and decided to fly higher. The wax melted and Icarus plunged into the sea, perhaps providing the genesis of the parental phrase, "Didn't I tell you . . . ?"

Modern musicians (from Joni Mitchell to Kansas to Third Eye Blind) have embraced Icarus imagery in their music. In U2's "Even Better than the Real Thing," Bono sings, "We're free to fly the crimson sky/the sun won't melt our wings tonight."

The story of Icarus is a myth, but people throughout history have tried to improve on Icarus's plan of flight:

✳ In 1020, English monk Oliver of Malmesbury jumped off a tall tower with cloth wings fashioned after those of Icarus. He didn't fly and actually broke most of his bones.

✳ Leonardo da Vinci is actually credited with giving the world the first plans for human flight. In the 1480s, he began a serious study of the subject, amassing more than 100 draw-ings that represented the relationship between birds and mechanical flight.

✳ A French locksmith named Besnier created a glider contrap-tion in 1678 that used rods and blades controlled by his hands and feet. Besnier's claims to have flown successfully are unsubstantiated.

Getting Carded

Back when you were a kid, Grandma used to send you a birthday card with a Washington inside. You were happy to get the dollar, but you probably didn't give much thought to the card itself. Let's change that, shall we?

✳   ✳   ✳   ✳

THE VERY FIRST greeting cards were believed to have been sent by the Chinese and early Egyptians thousands of years ago. The Germans made woodcut cards in the 1400s, and at least one English paper Valentine survives from that century.

By the mid-1800s, greeting cards were enormously popular in Europe, inexpensive to create and send, and an important keepsake for the recipient.

The notable exception to that paper happiness was the Penny Dreadful Valentine card, which cost one cent. As the name implies, these cards were nasty: The pictures and verse were insulting, and the cards were generally delivered to someone the sender disliked. Penny Dreadfuls (also known as Vinegar Valentines) were (un)popular starting in the 1850s.

Though Louis Prang is usually said to have started the greeting card industry in the United States in 1856, Esther Howland was hand-making Valentines in Massachusetts four years earlier. Prang, however, developed a lithographic method of card-making that made his products more vivid and brought them into demand.

Only a few years before Prang started his business, the first Christmas cards had appeared in London. By the late 1800s, both Brits and Americans were exchanging Yuletide greetings among friends. Back then, Christmas cards were elaborate, unusually shaped, and featured artwork by popular artists of the times.

In the early part of the 20th century, many American greeting card companies formed to meet the demand of the public. Patriotic and war-themed greetings were trendy during World War II, and greeting cards with humor made their entry in the 1950s. By the 1980s, greeting card manufacturers were mass-producing cards for every imaginable holiday, as well as for no holiday at all!

8 Groovy Fads of the 1960s

With so many straight-laced teens in the 1950s, it was only natural that there would be a backlash. Welcome to the 1960s! Free love, flower power, hippies, psychedelic drugs, and political mayhem—these were the trends of a decade that saw upheaval of social mores and cultural behaviors. As The Beatles rocked and Bob Dylan rolled, the world saw changes in the political climate (Vietnam War protests, the sexual revolution, civil rights), the fashion world ("It's called a 'mini-skirt,' Mom"), and even in the realm of food (the mighty processed cheese slice). Read on to learn about some of the most iconic fads of the decade that just wanted everyone to get along.

✳   ✳   ✳   ✳

1. **Hippies:** U.S. troops were sent to Vietnam in 1954 and, by the 1960s, thousands of soldiers had died fighting a war that was growing more and more unpopular by the day. The cry "Make Love, Not War" was a mantra among the hippies—the antiestablishment, counterculture of America. Hippies were easily spotted: both men and women grew their hair long, wore ethnic-inspired clothes accessorized with puka shells, dabbled in Eastern religions, used words like groovy, and referred to "the Man" when talking about the flawed government. They were known to experiment with mind-altering drugs (marijuana, mushrooms, LSD) and hang out in places such as Greenwich Village in New York City and the Haight-Ashbury section of San

Francisco. The hippie movement sparked music, art, and cultural dialogue that continues well into the 21st century.

2. **Go-go Boots and Minidresses:** The postwar baby boom had produced 70 million teenagers by the time the 1960s came along. All of those hormones dictated some changes in the world of fashion. Long gone was the poodle skirt. Skirts in the '60s got shorter—much, much shorter. Skirts and minidresses often came up four to five inches above the knee in the United States and an eye-popping seven to eight inches above the knee in the UK. While skirts got shorter, boots got taller. The most popular boot was the go-go boot, which was often white patent leather and went almost to the knee. Singer Nancy Sinatra and TV's *The Avengers* helped popularize the look.

3. **Fallout Shelters:** With the Cold War in full force, the Cuban Missile Crisis exposed, and the constant threat of nuclear attack, many people in the early 1960s decided that building a fallout shelter wasn't such a paranoid notion. Kits began at around $100 (flashlight, shortwave radio, can opener), but a family could spend thousands on special basements equipped with board games, gas masks, and escape hatches.

4. **Surfing:** What better place than a sunny beach to spread peace, goodwill, and free love? Polynesians had been surfing for centuries, but when lightweight surfboards became affordable in the late 1950s, everyone could grab a board and hang ten. By the early 1960s, the fad had really caught a wave, and movies like Beach Party and Beach Blanket Bingo helped popularize surfing and beach culture.

5. **Peace Symbol:** Thanks to British graphic designer Gerald Holtom, no hippie had to go without a peace symbol talisman. Holtom, who was hired to create an image for the Campaign for Nuclear Disarmament, claimed his inspiration for the symbol came from the shape of the letters N

and D in the semaphore alphabet. The icon was adopted by the hippies and remains as popular today as it was when protests and antiwar marches were daily events.

6. **The Twist:** This dance craze of the early 1960s came as the result of Chubby Checker's number one song of the same name. The Twist was the first modern dance style that did not require a partner, and couples did not have to touch each other while dancing. Checker said, "It's like putting out a cigarette with both feet, [or] coming out of a shower and wiping your bottom with a towel to the beat of the music." It seemed like everyone was jumping on the bandwagon with a Twist record. Checker also recorded "Let's Twist Again," and Joey Dee and The Starliters reached number one with "The Peppermint Twist," while Sam Cooke was "Twistin' the Night Away."

7. **Tie-Dye:** The ancient fabric dyeing method of shibori began in Japan centuries ago, but it became a fashion trend symbolic of the 1960s. By wrapping fabric around sticks or gathering and securing it with rubber bands, then submerging it in a bucket of dye, a funky, almost hallucinogenic pattern emerges when the sticks or rubber bands are removed. This homemade method became popular with hippies, providing living color to the ethnic look that so many embraced during the era of free love and liberation. Tie-dyed clothing is still pretty much the standard uniform for peaceniks today.

8. **Lava Lamp:** Invented by Edward Craven Walker, this novelty lighting instrument featured a glass bottle full of wax and oil with a coil in the metal base. When the lamp was turned on, the coil would heat up and globs of wax would bubble around in the oil, producing a "lava" effect. Some claimed the lava lamp was meant to simulate the hallucinogenic visuals from the drugs that were becoming so popular.

Learn to Talk Trucker

Learn these trucker terms, and you'll become the king (or queen) of the road!

✳ ✳ ✳ ✳

Bear: term for a cop; also "smokey" or "smokey bear" —Full-grown bear: state trooper —Bear in the air: cop in a helicopter

Motion lotion: fuel

Bumper sticker: car following too close behind

Cash register: toll booth

Chicken coop: weigh station

Double nickel: 55 mph speed limit

Flip-flop: U-turn; also refers to the return trip ("Catch ya on the flip-flop")

Gator: tire tread lying in the road

Good neighbor: also known as "bubba," a friendly term between drivers. This has replaced "good buddy," which is now considered an insult and used only sarcastically.

Granny lane: the right, or slow, lane

Hammer lane: the left, or passing, lane; to "hammer down" means to drive fast

Gumball machine: lights on top of a police car

Takin' pictures: police using a radar gun to catch speeders (gear jammers). These cops are also called "Kojak with a Kodak."

Ten-four/Forty-two: two ways of expressing agreement. Ten-four means "I heard what you said." Forty-two means "right on" (another driver says, "I love me some Waffle House," and you say, "Forty-two").

Lucky (and Unlucky) Charms

Ever wonder why casinos are often named "Horseshoe" and black cats frequent Halloween? Toss some salt over your shoulder, grab a four-leaf clover, and find out more about the history of these popular symbols of luck and lucklessness.

✳ ✳ ✳ ✳

Lucky Charms

Horseshoe: Not only is the horseshoe forged from iron—which the ancient Egyptians believed was the sacred metal of the sky—but it's also in the shape of the crescent moon, another sacred sign. The horseshoe's reputation as a symbol of good luck could also come from its two-pronged, animal-horn shape, which some ancient peoples thought repelled the evil eye. Though many cultures believe tacking a horseshoe over a doorway brings good fortune, there's disagreement if the prongs should point up, to keep luck from running out, or down, so luck endlessly diffuses.

Four-leaf clover: Four-leaf clovers have been considered lucky for so long, no one quite knows when it began. Doubtlessly it has something to do with their rarity, but the oldest accounts suggest that Eve (before her eviction from the Garden of Eden) picked a four-leaf clover, which served as a reminder of paradise.

Knocking on wood: This custom likely comes from the Christian practice of touching wood on happy occasions to show gratitude to Jesus Christ, who died on a wooden cross. Other experts say the tradition is pagan in origin, stemming from the ancient Druids, who believed deities lived in trees. Knocking (respectfully) on trees also ensured good fortune.

Rabbit's foot: Legend has it that if you rub a lucky rabbit's foot, the characteristics of the animal will rub off on you. It was believed that rabbits were born with their eyes open, so they could recognize (and flee!) the devil from their earliest moments. Others thought the bunny's famous fertility brought prosperity.

Bad Omens

Black cat: This icon of evil dates back to the Middle Ages, when black cats were believed to be the companion of witches. A book called *Beware the Cat* (1584) warned that black cats are witches in disguise—and don't bother killing a cat, because witches can inhabit them up to nine times (a belief that dates back to the Egyptian cat-headed goddess, Bast, who was said to have nine lives). Interestingly, in England, it's the white cat that's considered bad luck and the black cat that's good.

Walking under a ladder: The underside of a ladder is a resting spot for spirits. Don't buy that? Try this: In cultures where the triangle is sacred, the natural triangle formed by a ladder leaning against a wall is considered a holy space to be revered and thus avoided. The ladder also recalls early gallows, when victims climbed a ladder to be hanged to death.

Spilling salt: The lucklessness of spilling salt likely comes from the vital role it played in ancient cultures, which valued the seasoning as much as gold; in fact, Greek and Roman soldiers received part of their pay in salt. Others say the stigma of spilled salt comes from the belief that Judas knocked over the saltshaker at the Last Supper (as depicted in the Leonardo da Vinci painting). In any case, the tradition of throwing spilled salt over the left shoulder comes from the ancient belief that evil spirits are perched there, waiting to attack. Salt thrown over the shoulder—and presumably into their eyes—acted as a kind of pepper spray, putting them out of commission.

Breaking a mirror: Ancient Greeks considered mirrors the gods' porthole into the future: If a mirror broke, it meant the future held ugly things the gods didn't want to show. The penalty of "seven years bad luck" dates back to the ancient Roman belief that a person's health changed every seven years. Since mirrors reflected a person's appearance and health, to break one was to shatter your health for the next seven years.

The Lawn Chairs of Winter

While driving in a brutal Chicago winter can be difficult, the real challenge most Chicagoans face is parking on streets piled high with snow. The unwritten rule of the city is that if you shovel out a parking space, you're entitled to save it, and woe unto the driver who dares to violate your claim—or rather, woe unto his car.

* * * *

THE MEAN STREETS of Chicago get just a little meaner during the city's notoriously harsh winters, as residents vie for precious parking spots amid the mounds of frozen snow. The city has an unwritten rule, often referred to as the "dibs" system, under which anyone who shovels out a parking space in front of their house can reserve it with milk crates, sawhorses, weight benches, or—most commonly—lawn chairs. Of course nothing prevents another driver from removing the placeholder and taking the spot—nothing, that is, except the retribution that's almost certain to come from the spot's "owner."

Many drivers have reported having their side mirrors broken or their tires deflated when they've taken "someone else's" spot. Truly dedicated vengeance seekers have gone so far as to get out their shovels, bury the offending vehicle in a mound of snow, and then pour buckets of water over it, leaving it encased in an icy tomb until the weather makes its way back up above freezing—this being Chicago in winter, that can take a while.

Saving spots is a violation of the city ordinance that prevents obstruction of the public way; many residents oppose the practice, but Chicago officials seem inclined to sympathize with the shovelers. When Alderman Tom Allen was asked why city leaders don't clamp down on the parking space squatters, he responded, saying residents "might string us up." Even former Mayor Daley publicly came out in defense of the system: "If someone spends all that time digging their car out, do not drive in that spot. This is Chicago—fair warning."

Texan Talk...

Here are a few colorful phrases from Texas.

✳ ✳ ✳ ✳

✳ If he were any faster, he'd catch up to yesterday.

✳ That girl's faster'n a Texas blue norther tearin' through the Panhandle.

✳ She's as mean as a bobcat in a burlap sack.

✳ His mouth was a-goin' like a cotton gin in pickin' time.

✳ I'm as happy as a pig in a peach orchard.

✳ It's hotter than a black Cadillac in July.

✳ I'm hungry enough to eat a bear with the hair still on it.

✳ Anytime you pass by my house, I would appreciate it.

✳ They call her "blister" because she shows up when the work is done.

✳ He don't know big wood from kindlin'.

✳ You're as mad as a rooster in an empty hen house.

✳ She's as nervous as a long-tailed cat in a room full of rocking chairs.

✳ She's got lines in her face from trying to straighten out the wrinkles in her life.

✳ He's mean enough to steal his mama's Christmas money.

✳ She was so poor she had a tumbleweed for a pet.

✳ I'm mad enough to eat rattlesnakes.

✳ He's not afraid of hard work, 'cause I've seen him lay down and go to sleep right next to it.

Why Is the Heart Associated with Love?

Who doesn't eagerly await Valentine's Day? It's a day to celebrate your true love in the name of Saint Valentine, the patron saint of lovers. That Valentine became a saint by being beaten, stoned, and beheaded is rarely considered.

* * * *

UNLESS YOU'RE IN a really bad relationship, Valentine's Day is not about beheadings, but about hearts: heart-shaped flower arrangements, heart-shaped cards, heart-shaped balloons, heart-shaped boxes of chocolates, and heart-shaped candies that taste like chalk. Hearts. Hearts everywhere. There's no escaping the hearts.

Since the time of the ancient Greeks, people have associated the heart organ with love. Aristotle posited that affections were housed in the human heart. But how did the heart shape become so ubiquitous, not only on Valentine's Day but in relation to anything associated with love? Think about it for a moment—does the [heart] symbol really look anything like a human heart? Not unless you have some serious cardiac issues. In fact, the heart shape now associated with love may not have had anything to do with hearts in the first place.

There are a couple of explanations for the origin of the symbol. The first has its roots in the ancient city of Cyrene, a Greek colony located in what is now Libya. Archeologists unearthed silver coins used in Cyrene that were stamped with the shape of the seed of a now-extinct plant, silphium.

The plant was important to ancient Cyrenians—silphium was used as a contraceptive. Interestingly, the seed's depiction is almost identical to the contemporary [heart] shape associated with love. This theory holds that the use of the plant, coupled with the prevalence of its image on circulating money, led to a natural marriage of the heart shape with romantic love (or, at least, with passion).

This is an intriguing explanation, but like many stories of origin, it may not be entirely accurate. More likely, the development of the heart symbol is a slower, less racy tale. In fact, the heart symbol may have its roots in ivy-leaf motifs found in ancient art. Pottery and frescoes unearthed from ancient Minos, Crete, and Afghanistan all show prominent use of the heart-shaped ivy leaf. This motif was borrowed by later artists, including religious painters and sculptors, who incorporated the heart shape into depictions of Jesus and Mary as symbols of pure, unconditional love.

Once the Sacred Heart devotion of Catholicism co-opted the symbol in the Middle Ages, it became more popularly associated with love. Shortly afterward, the heart became a standard suit on playing cards, and soon the symbol was integrated into depictions of courtly love.

When the first Valentine's Day was celebrated in the late fifth century, it was only natural to associate the heart symbol with the lovers' day. Now the symbol is linked with love, relegating future generations to an onslaught of heart-shaped kitsch.

This Festival Embraces "Unmentionable" History

Piqua, Ohio, sought a festival theme that would honor its past. Instead of honoring a local food or town founder, however, Piqua's answer was as close as, well, the underwear drawer.

✳   ✳   ✳   ✳

PIQUA HAS THE dubious distinction of once having its major industry be the manufacture of unmentionables. The community's textile mills thrived, thanks in part to Piqua's convenient location along the Miami-Erie Canal. In fact, from the

1880s through the 1980s, as many as 15 different companies made underwear, long johns, and other knit undergarments.

The Fabric of the Town

While earning the title "Underwear Capital of America" carries a certain honor, it also had some social consequence. During the late 1800s, the flourishing industry drove a wedge between residents who felt women should remain unemployed home-makers and those who supported a more liberated viewpoint. However, as women entered the workforce en masse, the cash flow that dual incomes brought on effectually ended the debate on women in the workplace.

The underwear business also changed the social fabric of Piqua, as women launched social clubs with like-minded female coworkers. The industry so permeated residents' lifestyles that future generations began to prepare for textile careers through high school classes.

In 1988, townspeople launched the Great Outdoor Underwear Festival as a way to celebrate Piqua's "unmentionable" history. The annual fall festival included events such as the Long John Parade, the Undy 500, the Boxer Ball, and the Drop-Seat Trot. Celebrities such as Pat Boone and Loni Anderson even donated their underwear for festival fund-raisers. Although the Great Outdoor Underwear Festival ceased in 1998, Piqua still beck-ons tourists with an impressive 23-block section of town that is listed on the National Register of Historic Places.

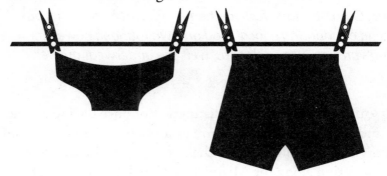

Don't Sing Too Loudly!

Many people believe that "Happy Birthday to You"—the most frequently sung song in the English language—is a traditional folk melody that rests comfortably in the public domain. In fact, the song is protected by strict copyright laws.

✳ ✳ ✳ ✳

THAT FOUR-LINE DITTY is as synonymous with birthday celebrations as a cake full of candles. According to the *Guinness Book of World Records*, the most popular song in the English language is "Happy Birthday to You." What is less well known, however, is that it is not a simple tune in the public domain, free for the singing by anyone who chooses. It's actually protected by a stringent copyright. You are legally safe to sing the song at home, but doing so in public is technically a breach of copyright, unless you have obtained a license from the copyright holder or the American Society of Composers, Authors, and Publishers.

The popular seven-note melody was penned in 1893 by two sisters, Mildred J. Hill and Patty Smith Hill, as a song titled "Good Morning to All." It remains unclear who revised the words, but a third Hill sister, Jessica, secured copyright to the song in 1935. This copyright should have expired in 1991, but through a number of revisions to copyright law, it has been extended until at least 2030 and now lies in the hands of AOL Time Warner. The company earns more than $2 million a year from the song, primarily for its use in movies and TV shows. Because licensing the rights to the song is a costly endeavor, low-budget movies have to cut around birthday scenes, and many popular chain restaurants insist that their employees sing alternate songs to celebrate their customers' birthdays. Unless you license the rights, singing the song in public could result in something decidedly unhappy.

8 Legends of American Folklore

The grit and determination of the American pioneers was truly impressive. Those who crossed the country to settle the West, slogged through the muggy South, and fished the seas and wild rivers all had to face formidable obstacles including famine, predators, and what must have been extended periods of sheer boredom. Without television and movies, entertainment in late 18th- and early 19th-century America was limited to campfire stories and tales told around the fireplace. You can't blame storytellers for embellishing here and there to raise interest levels and inspire tired and weary listeners. The following folk legends helped pioneers cope with uncertainty during hard times and inspired the ambition needed to explore the American frontier.

1. **Paul Bunyan:** If it weren't for Paul Bunyan, America just wouldn't be as interesting geographically. French-Canadian lumber camp legends about Bunyan, which were later adapted by Americans, claimed that he was delivered to Earth by five giant storks, since he was already dozens of feet tall as a baby. Wherever he went as he got older, he created major landmarks. His footprints created Minnesota's 10,000 lakes; his shovel created the Grand Canyon as it dragged behind him; his use of rocks to extinguish a campfire created Mount Hood. Bunyan was accompanied by his blue ox, Babe, who was almost as big as he was. Statues of Bunyan and Babe have been erected all across the country as a testament to America's love of a tall tale.

2. **John Henry:** Unlike a lot of the tall tales from America's formative years, the story of John Henry is somewhat based in fact. There probably really was a John Henry who was born a slave in the South in the mid-1800s. Legend has it that he was around six feet tall and weighed more than 200 pounds. In those days, that was big enough to guaran-

tee you'd be given exceptionally tough work—like building railroads or tunnels. If Henry did exist, he likely worked on the Big Bend Tunnel that went through the mountains of West Virginia. From there, the legend has thousands of variations. Some say Henry challenged the tunnel-making machinery to a duel to see who could drive stakes and blast rock faster. Most stories claim that he won, but that he died from exhaustion after the contest. Some say he won and went on swingin' his hammer from coast to coast.

3. **Sally Ann Thunder Ann Whirlwind Crockett:** Women in tall tales were few and far between, but there are some who made it into folklore as hard as nails, larger-than-life folks. Sally Ann Thunder is one that emerges, however infrequently, as the wife of Davy Crockett. In reality, Crockett married several times and none of the record books have him married to anyone with Thunder in her name. But stories do exist of a gun-totin', fast-talking lady who helped get Davy out of sticky situations and wouldn't miss a trick. She reportedly wore a real beehive as a hat and enjoyed wrestling alligators in her spare time.

4. **Johnny Appleseed:** If you dig too deep into the origins of American folk heroes, you might be disappointed—the man known as Johnny Appleseed wasn't a magical scatterer of apple seeds from sea to shining sea, he was just a regular guy named John Chapman who worked as a nurseryman in the late 1700s. While that's not as exciting as the legend, Chapman's real life was interesting enough—he owned land from Ohio to Indiana, worked as a Christian missionary, and helped make peace between Native Americans and white settlers.

5. **Mike Fink:** Tales of Mike Fink originated in the 19th century and were based on a real man born near Pittsburgh around 1780. The real Fink sailed keelboats on the Ohio and Mississippi rivers and fought against various tribes of

Native Americans. Fink was noted as being an exceptional marksman, though he was reportedly a rather hard-drinking and hard-living character. By many accounts it was Fink who started spreading tall tales about himself, which may explain his low standing among more noble legends like Paul Bunyan and John Henry. Still, tales of Fink being "half-man, half-alligator" and being totally impervious to pain keep him in the canon.

6. Pecos Bill: Pecos Bill, one of the most popular American tall tales, was lost while crossing the Pecos River with his parents. He was found by a pack of coyotes and lived among them until he met a cowboy and realized his true calling. No one was better at ranching than Pecos Bill because he had an uncanny ability to convince animals to work for him. Bill married a nice girl named Slue Foot Sue and lived a long life of ranching, herding, and singing by the campfire.

7. Geronimo: Geronimo, an Apache leader from the Arizona area, was captured and forced onto a reservation by the U.S. Army in 1876. The persecuted Apache leader fled to Mexico, but after that, things get murky and exaggerated. The story goes that Geronimo's wrath toward the white man was such that he killed thousands over the years, using magical powers and ESP to seek them out. It's said that it took many thousands of soldiers and scouts to track the warrior down. By the time Geronimo finally surrendered in 1886, his group consisted of only 16 warriors, 12 women, and 6 children. Geronimo and his people were shipped to Florida, then relocated to Alabama and Oklahoma where they were placed in prisons and reservations. Geronimo died a prisoner of war in 1909.

8. Old Stormalong: Though stories about Stormalong vary, most place him in Cape Cod as a big baby—a baby more than 18 feet tall! Stormalong, a gifted sailor, joined the crew

of a ship. When the ship had an encounter with a kraken—
a beast from Norse mythology—Stormalong fought back
but didn't kill the sea giant. Eventually, he wound up back
on the high seas in search of the kraken that had escaped
him. The ship he used was said to have slammed into the
coast of Panama, forming the Panama Canal. According to
legend, the same boat supposedly got stuck in the English
Channel, requiring the crew to slick it up with soap in
order to get it out. The soap and the scraping action turned
the White Cliffs of Dover white.

What Were They Reading?

Uncle Tom's Cabin *is probably the most famous best seller from
the Civil War era. Here's a list of some of the other popular reading
of the time.*

✳   ✳   ✳   ✳

Ten Nights in a Bar Room and What I Saw There
Timothy Shay Arthur

Considered the *Uncle Tom's Cabin* of the temperance movement, this novel set out to convince people of the evils of liquor.
The story is told from the point of view of Simon Slade, an
ambitious tavern owner who relates the sad and disturbing
effects alcohol has on his patrons. Arthur believed that alcohol
and drunkenness were the first steps on a slippery slope that
could ultimately lead to degeneracy, gambling, and murder.

The Sword and the Distaff
William Gilmore Simms

This book was the most successful of about two dozen so-
called "anti-Tom novels." Written to counterpoint *Uncle Tom's
Cabin*, these books portrayed loving relationships between
slaves and their masters and tried to put a happy face on slavery.
Set during the Revolutionary War, the novel centers around
Captain Porgy, a benevolent master whose obedient slave (also
named Tom) helps him in his patriotic duties.

The Planter's Northern Bride
Caroline Lee Hentz

Another "anti-Tom novel," this book tried to win over Northerners with a protagonist from their own backyard. The novel focuses on a Northern abolitionist's daughter who marries a Southern plantation owner and quickly learns the "truth" about slavery. While Hentz pushes the notion of a familial relationship between the slave and the slave owner, she also introduces the specter of slave rebellions, bringing in several evil, homicidal characters in an effort to show that blacks could not be trusted to mind their own affairs.

Beulah
Augusta J. Evans

This Alabama author portrays the coming of age of the unusually independent Beulah Benton in a huge bestseller shortly before the war. The orphaned Beulah survives a troubled childhood determined never to marry or accept the traditional woman's role. Beulah and author Evans give in by the end of the book, however, when Beulah finds true love and settles down.

"Paul Revere's Ride"
Henry Wadsworth Longfellow

Narrative poetry was a popular form that readers would memorize and recite for others. First published in *The Atlantic Monthly* in January 1861, the poem told the exciting story of Paul Revere, who warned Massachusetts colonists that the British army was coming at the start of the American Revolution. Revere had been a minor historical figure before this time, but this transformed him into a national legend and a symbol of Northern patriotism at a time when a new call to arms was needed.

"Barbara Frietchie"
John Greenleaf Whittier

This was another narrative poem that first saw life in *The Atlantic Monthly*. It ostensibly told the tale of an elderly woman in Frederick, Maryland, who refused to be cowed by Stonewall Jackson and his invading troops. When they took down the Union flag flying at her home, she replaced it. When they fired upon it, she called out to them. "'Shoot, if you must, this old gray head, / But spare your country's flag,' she said." In response, Jackson ordered his troops to let the flag continue flying. There really was a Barbara Frietchie (whose name was sometimes spelled Fritchie or Frietschie), but although poet Whittier claimed to be relaying what he had been told, the story itself is apocryphal.

8 Awesome Fads of the 1980s

In the 1980s, the hair was big, the clothes were big (nice shoulder pads), the music was big, and the political climate was grandiose, too (Reaganomics, Star Wars). With the introduction of the cellular phone and cable television, this decade triggered much of the tech boom that would really get cooking in subsequent decades. With the ever-increasing range and scope of the media, music- and electronics-based fads got bigger and faster in the '80s. Here are a few fads that took the country by storm and helped define the generation that just wanted its MTV.

✳ ✳ ✳ ✳

1. **"Valspeak":** Did you, like, realize that in the '80s, like, everyone totally got pulled into this thing called Valspeak? Seriously! The old way of talking with, like, specificity and declarative statements was, like, super lame-o! Like, whatever! So, like, the San Fernando Valley in California was, like, the place where it started. But soon it was a nation-wide, like, trend. Can you even stand it? And it's totally still, like, a thing? You know, like, a totally awesome way of speaking. And, like, you thought Valley Girls were a passing fad. Whatever!

2. **The Walkman:** Though the technology looks ancient to us today, we wouldn't have the beloved iPod if it wasn't for the

Walkman. In 1979, Sony introduced their first portable music player in Japan. By 1980, America had jumped on the bandwagon, and there were dozens of portable cassette players on the market. They were heavy, didn't deliver great sound quality, and initially cost upwards of $150, but it didn't matter—they were delivering tunes to the masses, one tape at a time.

3. **Atari:** The name of the gaming system that started them all loosely translates from Japanese to mean "prepare to be attacked." Thus, it's fitting that the first video games were simple UFO shooting games or games such as Frogger, which required players to move a frog across a busy road without getting squished. Atari, Inc., was formed in 1972, and five years later one of the most successful gaming consoles of all time—the Atari 2600—was released. Millions of consumers bought the devices and spent hours (and days) glued to the TV set, playing Q*Bert, Pac-Man, and Space Invaders. The Atari company consolidated a few years ago but still has a hand in shaping today's much more advanced gaming world.

4. **Break Dancing:** When DJ Kool Herc took the dance break sections off vinyl records and remixed them into one another to create a longer, funkier song, break dancing was born. These extended breaks gave NYC street dancers all the time in the world to showcase their gravity-defying moves, including the pop and lock, the windmill, the freeze, the moonwalk, the worm, and the closing "suicide." As the media attention grew for this competitive, visually exhilarating dance style, so did its popularity.

5. **Parachute Pants:** If you're thinking about break dancing, you'd be wise to consider your outfit—not only do you need to look "fresh" and "fly," you need to be able to slide, slip, and spin on a dance floor and regular pants just won't do. Baggy in the thigh and narrow at the ankle, parachute

pants increased mobility for dancers who needed flexible clothing. The pants were often made of synthetic materials (you can backspin way better in a poly-blend than you can in cotton) and usually came in bright colors. As break dancing became cooler, the clothes of these street dancers became the "in" fashion trend and even kids in the suburbs were donning parachute pants.

6. **Swatch Watches:** In 1983, the Swatch Group, Ltd., of Switzerland had an idea. They thought that watches could be less of a financial investment for the stuffy and time-conscious and more of a disposable, funky accessory. Their idea was a big hit. Swatch watches came in hundreds of different colors and styles, and some were even scented! Many people chose to wear several styles at once, loading up two, three, even six Swatches on their wrists at the same time.

7. **Hair Bands:** The heavy-metal music of the 1980s was typified by a heavy, guitar-and-drums-centered sound with highly amplified distortion, fairly raunchy lyrics (for the time), and plenty of dramatic builds. The heavy-metal lifestyle was typified by beer, girls, leather, and really big hair. As the music got louder and bolder from groups like Warrant, Mötley Crüe, and Poison, the hair got bigger and fluffier—and we're not just talking about the girls. These "hair bands" were so named because of the impossible-to-ignore hair swung around by the men onstage.

8. **Preppies:** While some kids were break-dancing, and others were coiffing their hair sky-high with hair spray, preppies were busy wearing chinos and loafers, talking about sailboat races, and working with their financial advisors. Preppie was a word used to describe the clean-cut teens, twenty- and thirtysomethings of the '80s who could usually be spotted wearing pink and playing tennis. With the release of the tongue-in-cheek *Official Preppy Handbook* in 1980, it was easy to spot a preppie—or a preppie wannabe—anywhere.

Green River

There are many secrets in an old city like Chicago, but one that fascinates the public every spring is exactly how 40 pounds of orange powder dyes the Chicago River a startling shade of green.

❋　❋　❋　❋

IN 1961, ONE widely spread story goes, a plumber walked into the Chicago Plumber's Union office with bright green stains on his overalls. He'd been checking pipes for leaks, trying to determine sources of pollution in the river. His supervisor, Stephen Bailey, was a boyhood friend of Mayor Richard J. Daley and brought the idea of a new St. Patrick's Day tradition to the Mayor's Office. In 1962, the city started dyeing the river to add to their already exuberant St. Patrick's Day parades.

Other than the men in the boats on the river, the only thing that's changed over the years is the actual dye itself. In 1962, the team used an oil-based dye that was so potent it kept the river green for nearly a week. Organizers then substituted a vegetable dye, and officials say it's harmless to the river's ecology (a claim that leaves many environmentalists skeptical).

The exact dye recipe is a closely guarded secret. The public knows that it's delivered to the river as an orange powder that is slung into the water by the scoopful. Once there, it clumps and then awaits "stirring" by the propellers of a single small boat piloted by a favored crew of plumbers. The resulting emerald green hue is so startling, many think there just *has* to be something harmful in it. But organizers swear that—while they won't give out the secret formula—the dye only adds harmless fun in a city strong with Irish spirit.

Miltary Jargon Gets Mustered Out

These interesting military phrases have seeped into civilian life so successfully that many people don't realize they started out as soldier slang.

✳   ✳   ✳   ✳

Blockbuster

Today the word refers to a wildly successful movie, but during World War II it was a nickname used by the Royal Air Force for large bombs that could "bust" an entire city block. "Blockbuster" retired from the military in the 1950s when advertisers started using it as a synonym for *gigantic*.

Bought the Farm/Gone for a Burton

Because they face death daily, most soldiers try to avoid talking about it. During World War I, U.S. soldiers often said that someone missing or killed had "bought the farm"—which is what what many families did with their loved one's death benefits. Heavy-hearted British soldiers in World War II would raise a glass—in this case a British beer called Burton—to a departed brother, saying he'd "gone for a Burton."

Push the Envelope

If you're tired of your boss urging you to "push the envelope," blame World War II test pilots. They listed a plane's abilities—speed, engine power, maneuverability—on its flight envelope and then did their best to get the plane to outperform its predetermined limits.

Bite the Bullet

During the Civil War, the "anesthetic" often used on wounded soldiers was a bullet or block of wood on which to bite down. The patient, with no alternative, was forced to endure the procedure and excruciating pain so he could get on with the process of healing.

Show Your True Colors/With Flying Colors

Military regiments would end a victorious battle "with flying colors," or with their flag ("colors") held high. To "show your true colors," which has come to mean revealing your intentions, derives from early warships that would temporarily fly another nation's flag to deceive an enemy into feeling safe.

Over the Top

Nobody wanted to go over the top during World War I—that is, to charge over the parapets toward the enemy, a maneuver that resulted in high casualties. Soldiers who went over the top were considered incredibly—even excessively—brave.

Boondocks

In the early 1900s, U.S. troops in the Philippines fought guerillas hiding in the remote *bandok*—Tagalog (the primary language of the Philippines) for *mountains*. Soldiers translated the word as boondocks.

Grapevine

Civil War soldiers likened telegraph wires to grapevines, the latter having a gnarled appearance. News that arrived by "grapevine telegraph" (or simply "grapevine") was eventually considered to be "twisted" or dubious.

Happy Birthday, Dear Valentine?

Why do we celebrate St. Valentine's birthday? We don't. Instead, we commemorate his martyrdom.

✳ ✳ ✳ ✳

Who was St. Valentine? The Catholic Church says there were actually three St. Valentines, and all were martyrs. So which one does Valentine's Day honor? The most likely candidate was a Roman priest during the reign of Claudius II, emperor of Rome from A.D. 268 to 270. Desperate for men to fight his wars, Claudius forbade soldiers to marry. According to the legend, young lovers came to Valentine to be married, and performing these unauthorized marriages led to his imprisonment. While awaiting his execution, he fell in love with his jailer's daughter. Shortly before his death on February 14, he wrote her a letter and signed it "From Your Valentine."

The problem is that there's no proof that any of this actually happened. Valentine's name is not on the earliest list of Roman martyrs, and there's no evidence that he was put to death on February 14. In fact, in 1969, the Catholic Church removed Valentine's Day from the list of official holy days.

How did Valentine become associated with a celebration of love? It may be that February 14 was chosen by the early Church to replace a Roman fertility festival called Lupercalia, which fell on the same date. Another explanation is that the sentimentality of Valentine's Day can be traced to the Middle Ages, an era fixated on romantic love. It was popularly believed that birds chose their mates on February 14, a legend Geoffrey Chaucer referenced in his poem "Parliament of Foules": "For this was on St. Valentine's Day, when every fowl cometh there to chooses his mate."

The Day After Turkey Day

Where did the term Black Friday come from?

✳   ✳   ✳   ✳

FOR MOST SANE, rational humans, the day after Thanksgiving is best spent in the comfort and quiet of home. They know that venturing out can quickly turn into a nightmare. The stores open at 4: 00 AM, but even this isn't early enough for the mindless consumers who camp out overnight in frigid weather to get a first crack at discounts on the gifts du jour. Escalators are jammed, grown adults shove each other out of the way to get to the toy section, and parking lots resemble a bumper car rink at the county fair.

This orgy of consumerism is popularly termed Black Friday, and anybody unfortunate enough to have to travel—or God forbid, run errands—on the day after Thanksgiving can appreciate the appropriateness of such a sobriquet. Nothing can more aptly describe the mood of somebody caught in post-Thanksgiving traffic.

Where the term "Black Friday" originated is the subject of a couple of theories. The one most commonly given in filler newspaper articles is that this is the busiest shopping day of the year and pushes retail stores into profitability—or, in accounting terms, into the black. It's a pithy explanation, but there's no real evidence to support it. According to the International Council of Shopping Centers, the day after Thanksgiving isn't the busiest shopping day of the year; that honor is usually reserved for one of the days right before Christmas.

The true origin of Black Friday is rooted in a deeper tradition than post-holiday sales. The concept of terming days of the week as "black" dates back to at least the Fisk-Gould scandal of 1869, when on September 24—known as Black Friday—plunging gold prices left many investors ruined. The same type of color coding was used again during the 1929 stock market crash, when not one, not two, but three days were black—Black Thursday, Black Monday, and Black Tuesday—and history books are filled with photos of Wall Street investors cramming the streets during this economic disaster. It's possible that this imagery led to the current usage of Black Friday.

According to dialect historians, the day after Thanksgiving was called Black Friday in the mid-1960s by Philadelphia policemen who dreaded the vast, slavering crowds that they were sure to encounter. Black Friday took on an even darker connotation on the day after Thanksgiving in 2008. Shoppers at a Wal-Mart in Valley Stream, New York, were so impatient to get to the bargains that they broke down the doors and shoved their way into the store, trampling an employee to death.

Why Do We Carve Jack-o'-Lanterns?

Who doesn't fondly remember the Halloweens of yore? You'd choose a big orange pumpkin from a local farm, cut off the top to scoop out the mushy insides, and spend an entire evening painstakingly carving out the features. Then finally, with tired eyes, aching fingers, and a sense of pride, you'd place your glowing work of art on the front porch ... where it would last about 18.4 minutes before some kid would smash it into smithereens.

✳   ✳   ✳   ✳

THOUGH THE PRACTICE seems somewhat futile in our pumpkin-smashing present, the tradition of carving jack-o'-lanterns dates back centuries. There is no definitive explanation for how present-day jack-o'-lanterns came into being, but we do know that ancient Celts—as well as other sects of the era—believed that flames would ward off evil spirits.

In the Celtic tradition, the harvest season ended on November 1. This date, according to Celtic legend, also signified a dangerous event: a time when the boundary between the living and dead blurred. For one day, potentially harmful spirits could wreak havoc on the living. To keep these spirits at bay, ancient people built large bonfires as part of their end-of-harvest festivals—festivals that live on today as Halloween celebrations.

But why do we carve jack-o'-lanterns? In the absence of documented evidence, most people cite an Irish folktale called "Stingy Jack." In a small Irish village, the legend goes, lived a deceitful, lying, drunken fellow named Jack. He was also a cheap bastard, so he was known to the locals as Stingy Jack. One evening, Stingy Jack, out on a drunken spree, ran into the devil, who informed Jack that due to his derelict behavior, he was going to hell. The devil asked Jack to kindly prepare his soul to be taken. Jack suggested a drink beforehand. The devil—apparently a truly Irish evil spirit—agreed.

When the bill came, the devil and Stingy Jack looked at each other awkwardly. Stingy Jack reminded the devil of his nickname and said that he had a reputation to uphold. The devil informed Jack that Lucifer, Lord of Hell, didn't buy people drinks. The barkeeper said he didn't care who they were—no one drank for free.

They were at a stalemate, but then Jack had an idea: What if the devil transformed himself into a silver coin with which Jack would pay their bill? The devil, who had perhaps had a few too many drinks, inexplicably thought this to be a brilliant idea. Upon transformation, though, Jack promptly put the numismatic devil into his pocket, along with a silver crucifix to prevent the devil from reverting to form. It was only after he extracted a promise from the devil to not take his soul that Jack released the captive demon.

Much later, when Stingy Jack died, he was denied entrance to heaven. The devil also refused him entrance at the gates of hell, citing the promise he had made long before. He did, however, offer Jack a perpetually glowing piece of coal. Stingy Jack was doomed to wander the countryside for eternity, with nothing but his glowing coal from hell to light the way.

To ward off the spirit of Stingy Jack—also known as "Jack of the Lantern"—people in ancient Ireland, Scotland, and England began to carve scary faces into hollowed-out turnips and potatoes. When the first British settlers came to North America, legend suggests that they continued the tradition, using the native North American pumpkin. It was, after all, larger, simpler to carve, and easier to smash into smithereens.

Hot Dog!

A lot of big corporations have company cars, but Madison's Oscar Mayer has taken that to the extreme with the Oscar Mayer Weinermobile, a 27-foot-long hot dog on wheels.

* * * *

THE FIRST WEINERMOBILE (a mere 13 feet long) was created in 1936 by Oscar Mayer's nephew Karl, as a way to promote the company's products at grocery stores throughout the Midwest. It caught on, and Oscar Mayer's staff steered the sausage around the country. There are currently seven in use—each assigned to a different part of the country.

In 1969, a prototype was actually designed and built by Oscar Mayer mechanics right at the Madison headquarters. The same design was used, this time by Plastic Products in Milwaukee, to create another Weinermobile in 1975. The newest addition to the Weinermobile family is more of a smoky link. It's a smaller replica of its big brother—just 15 feet long, on top of a Mini Cooper chassis.

A Recipe for Success

Today the full-sized Weinermobiles weigh as much as 150,000 hot dogs. They put 1,000 miles on their buns per week and clock about 50,000 miles a year. The interior sports a hot dog-shape instrument panel, catsup-and-mustard-colored seats, and a removable bun roof.

So who drives such a thing? Well, the hot doggers, of course—recent college graduates who attend Hot Dog High at the Oscar Mayer plant in Madison. They bulk up their knowledge of the company's history and products and hit the road for a year. The competition for hot doggers is tough, and hundreds apply each year. Essentially a public relations job, the new hot doggers are ambassadors for the company—and all of them relish their jobs.

The Warm Glow (and History) of the Advent Wreath

Don't mistake this Christmastime object as just another decoration—it's got plenty of symbolism and history behind it.

✳ ✳ ✳ ✳

N OT ALL WREATHS are hung on doors at Christmas. The Advent wreath is placed on a table or other flat surface and holds lit candles in its greenery. Advent is the beginning of the church year for most churches in the Western tradition.

Way Back When

The origin of the Advent wreath is probably best traced to the Scandinavians, who would light candles around a wheel and pray that the god of light would turn the wheel of the earth back toward the sun. (Wintertime in Scandinavia is pretty rough.) The Christians picked up the practice around the Middle Ages, but for them, Christ was the bringer of light, so they adapted the practice accordingly, switching out the wheel for a wreath. By about 1600, both Lutherans and Catholics had formal Advent wreath practices.

The Wreath Part

The actual wreath itself is chock full of meaning. Not only does it symbolize the crown of thorns that Christ wore at his crucifixion, its never-ending, no-beginning-no-end nature of a circle reminds followers that God's love is infinite. Traditional Advent wreaths are made from fresh evergreen, and the various elements have symbolism, too: Laurel signifies victory over persecution and suffering, pine and holly represent immortality, and cedar signifies strength.

The Candle Part(s)

But what's an Advent wreath without its candles? The four lit candles in an Advent wreath are what make it special for Christmas. The candles represent a thousand years each, summing up the 4,000 years that passed from Adam and Eve to Christ's birth. For those wanting to honor the "old school" Advent wreath, only colored candles will do: three purple and one pink or rose colored. The atypical Christmas colors are there for a reason. The purple candles, lit the first, second, and fourth weeks of Advent, represent prayer, penance, and the charitable work and good deeds people do during the time leading up to Christmas. The pink or rose-colored candle is lit on the third week, called Gaudete Sunday (that's the midpoint of Advent). The priest who lights it wears matching rose vestments at Mass, and the rose candle symbolizes rejoicing.

Aren't There Better Ways for Santa to Sneak into a House?

Except for a few sour souls, everyone loves Santa Claus. How could you not? He spends his days in an enchanted world of elves and toys, he has an awesome flying sleigh, and he has the godlike ability to watch all the world's children at the same time. Yet for somebody who is supposed to be such a magical, all-knowing being, it appears that Santa Claus possibly isn't very bright. Case in point: this chimney business.

❋   ❋   ❋   ❋

COME ON, CLAUS. Do you really need to shimmy down a filthy chimney to deliver your presents? And with that ridiculous diet of cookies and milk, how much longer will you fit down it?

In Santa's defense, there's a lot of tradition behind his chimney act. Even though the image of the red velvet-clad Santa known to most Americans is a fairly recent development, the figure of Father Christmas is rooted in traditions dating back centuries. And though most people know that the Christian figure of Santa Claus is loosely based on St. Nicholas from the fourth century—St. Nick is one of Santa's nicknames, after all—most of Santa's behavior and magical powers are actually drawn from pagan sources.

Indeed, historians claim that not only Santa Claus, but also much of the holiday of Christmas itself is rooted in pagan tradition. Back in pre-Christian Europe, Germanic people celebrated the winter solstice at the end of December with a holiday known as Yule. Christmas, which later supplanted the pagan winter solstice festivals during the Christianization of Germanic people, maintained many of the pagan traditions. One was the belief that at yuletime, the god Odin would ride a magical eight-legged horse through the sky. Children left food for the horse, which would be replaced by gifts from Odin, a custom that lives on today in the form of cookie bribery for Kris Kringle and his flying reindeer.

As for sliding down the chimney, folklorists point to another Germanic god: Hertha, the goddess of the home. In ancient pagan days, families gathered around the hearth during the winter solstice. A fire was made of evergreens, and the smoke beckoned Hertha, who entered the home through the chimney to grant winter solstice wishes.

It wasn't until 1822, when literature professor Clement Clarke Moore penned "'Twas the Night Before Christmas," that Santa sliding down the chimney became a permanent fixture in popular Christmas tradition. Moore's poem became even more influential 40 years later, when legendary cartoonist Thomas Nast illustrated it for *Harper's* magazine. In Nast's depiction, Santa was transformed from the skinny, somewhat creepy-looking figure of earlier traditions into a jolly, well-bearded soul. Despite Santa's physical transformation, other traits from his early incarnations linger, including the bewildering habit of crawling down chimneys.

But just because something is a habit doesn't make it excusable. The figure of Santa has morphed over the centuries, and there's no reason why he can't break the chimney routine in the future.

A Thanksgiving Tradition

The Macy's Thanksgiving Day Parade has become the official kick-off for the Christmas season. Here's how it all came together. For more than 85 years, Macy's in New York City has entertained America with one of the largest, most impressive holiday parades in the world. In fact, the event has become so popular that hundreds of thousands of eager spectators rise before dawn to ensure that they'll get a glimpse of the parade's famous character balloons, lavish floats, and big-name entertainment.

✳ ✳ ✳ ✳

Welcome to America

To THINK IT all started primarily as a way for the store's immigrant employees to celebrate the American holiday of Thanksgiving. The first parade, held in 1924, was called the Macy's Christmas Parade. It wound from 145th Street in Harlem to the Macy's store on 34th Street, and it featured colorful floats, marching bands, and live animals on loan from the Central Park Zoo. That year, and every year since except one, the parade concluded with the arrival of Santa Claus.

The procession was renamed the Macy's Thanksgiving Day Parade in 1927, and it quickly grew in both popularity and scope. Today, it takes nearly three hours to complete.

Also in 1927, live animals were replaced with the oversized character balloons that have become one of the parade's most popular attractions. Produced by the Goodyear Tire and Rubber Company in Akron, Ohio, the first balloons included Felix the Cat, a dragon, an elephant, and a toy soldier. The balloons were filled with air, but the following year they were filled with helium and released into the air at the conclusion of the parade. Starting in 1929, a special tag was sewn into each balloon, and whoever found it received a prize from the store. In 1931, aviator Clarence Chamberlain caught the pig balloon in midair so he could claim the $25 reward. As a result, the practice of releasing the balloons was discontinued in 1933. By the 1930s, the Macy's Thanksgiving Day Parade had achieved national acclaim, and nearly a million spectators lined the streets to enjoy the show, which was broadcast locally via radio. In 1933, the parade was filmed by newsreel crews for the first time and shown in theaters across the country.

Full of Hot Air

Mickey Mouse joined the parade as a helium-filled balloon in 1934, and he was followed by dozens of other popular characters in the years that followed. Today, character balloons range from Spider-Man to the Pillsbury Doughboy.

The Macy's Thanksgiving Day Parade was halted during World War II. The nation wasn't in much of a celebratory mood, but more importantly, the war effort needed the rubber and helium that went into the manufacture of the parade's trademark balloons. The celebration resumed in 1945, and two years later the parade achieved unique cultural status when it was featured prominently in the movie *Miracle on 34th Street*, which contained footage filmed during the 1946 parade.

Because it is an outdoor event, the parade has experienced its share of mishaps, including escaped and deflated balloons and even a snowstorm. To avoid potential problems, the balloons, which are inflated the day before the parade, are now carried closer to the ground for greater control during windy conditions.

The Big Guy

Of course, celebrities are another important aspect of the Macy's Thanksgiving Day Parade. A veritable who's who of entertainment has taken part over the years. At the end of the day (or end of the parade!), however, it's Santa Claus the crowds come to see, and for good reason. The arrival of the jolly old elf means the arrival of the Christmas season itself. And few things are more exciting to the child in all of us.

Chapter 8

Games and Pastimes

Toys & Games

The Truth About Monopoly

When the nation was in the depths of the Great Depression, people needed a distraction. If they couldn't corner the stock market in the real world, why not become property moguls on the game board?

※　※　※　※

MONOPOLY IS AS American as apple pie or Norman Rockwell. Yet the story of how the most commercially successful board game came to be is a rather sordid tale. Apparently, the game's manufacturer, "creator" Charles Darrow, was not its true inventor at all. Darrow actually passed off Elizabeth Magie Phillips's concept as his own.

On January 5, 1904, Phillips, a.k.a. Lizzie J. Magie, received a patent for The Landlord's Game. It was based on economist Henry George's belief that landowners should be charged a single federal tax to extend equality to renters, from whom landlords were, in George's opinion, disproportionately profiting. Magie created an educational game, demonstrating how a single tax would control land speculation.

Except for the fact that properties were rented rather than purchased, The Landlord's Game was suspiciously identical to

Parker Brothers' Monopoly, which premiered almost 30 years later. Through the years, The Landlord's Game was passed through communities, evolving along the way. It eventually picked up the name Monopoly, despite Magie's intention that the game be a teaching tool against the very idea of monopolies. The Atlantic City–inspired properties were also incorporated. This chain of events led to Charles Darrow, who learned the game at a hotel in Pennsylvania.

Enthralled, Darrow produced his own copies of the game and subsequently patented and sold "his" idea to Parker Brothers. The company conveniently forgot its refusal to buy the same game (under its old name) from Magie years earlier and promptly covered those tracks. It slyly bought out Magie's patent for a paltry $500, paid off at least three other "inventors" who had versions circulating, and cranked up its propaganda machine. It worked: Monopoly has since sold in excess of 250 million copies.

A Striking Pastime: The Badger Bowling Obsession

Almost everyone has done it—or at least you've thought about it. Maybe they've even daydreamed about doing it with a coworker, or even a complete stranger. Rest assured, there's no shame in pursuing this fantasy in Wisconsin, where everyone is welcome to go bowling!

✳ ✳ ✳ ✳

Bowling is the sport of the common man and woman and is as much a part of the Wisconsin cultural landscape as beer, cheese, and bratwurst. But this is no new obsession.

Over the millennia there have been many games similar to bowling. The ancient Egyptians played something very much like it; Moses' pharaoh may well have had a gilded bowling shirt. In colonial times, the little men played ninepin while lulling Rip Van Winkle into a two-decade sleep. That game was played on an alley consisting of a single plank. The modern game grew directly from that humble pursuit, thanks to the ingenuity of German immigrants.

"It was part of their religious culture. They used to have it at church festivals centuries ago," says Milwaukee bowling historian Doug Schmidt, author of *They Came to Bowl.*

As Germans started landing in New York in the 1800s, they quickly set up bowling clubs. Eventually, these immigrants started making their way to the Midwest, and bowling followed them. Tavern owners, among others, began installing bowling lanes for their customers.

Originally, it was a game of ninepin set up in a diamond formation. Gambling was a popular feature, and as a result the game was outlawed. The immigrants added another pin, changed the formation to a triangle, and satisfied the courts that it was a different game. Modern bowling was born—almost.

Go Play Outside!

As strange as it may sound today, bowling was originally outdoor fun, played in the sun. In the 1850s, "the only bowlers were Germans and the only alleys were crude ones at the picnic groves and other German resorts," wrote historian Andrew Rohm in 1904. In Milwaukee, in the late 1800s, brewers Frederick Pabst and Frederick Miller each opened their own private pleasure parks and pavilions. There, the German biergarten tradition incorporated their favorite game. Gradually, for year-round enjoyment, bowling moved inside.

Almost every small Wisconsin town once had a bowling alley, or at least a couple of lanes inside a lodge hall. Sometimes, as with Fountain City on Wisconsin's western edge, there was even an alley inside city hall. In Madison, the university's Memorial Union had a basement alley. Today, it's still a strong sport on campus. In 2009, the University of Wisconsin-

Madison men's bowling team won its fourth consecutive Wisconsin Collegiate Bowling Conference championship. And Milwaukee could be called the capital of bowling—it's home to the United States Bowling Congress.

Wisconsin is also home to such legendary bowlers such as Connie Schwoegler, who, in 1948, invented the "fingertip grip." In 1930, Wisconsinite Jennie Hoverson became the first woman to bowl a perfect game in the history of league bowling. Her recognition came much later, however.

Something for Everyone

For much of its American history, bowling was a northern pastime. Besides sexism, nationally there was worse bowling bigotry. African Americans were not allowed into sanctioned league bowling until 1951, four years after Jackie Robinson broke the color barrier in baseball. While that fact shames league bowling of the era, in the 1940s, African Americans were already enjoying the game in Milwaukee. They had come to the area in search of factory jobs and found themselves near taverns with bowling alleys. They assimilated into the game, and many African Americans enjoyed the sport and became well-known bowlers. As Wisconsin grew, social networks formed around the game—people who worked together bowled together.

Today, bowling's best features remain as satisfying as ever: The cost is low, the rules are simple, and the bowling alley provides all of the equipment. Then there's the satisfying, almost-musical crash of the maplewood pins. And what other sport has ten second chances? There's also the camaraderie, or, in other words, waiting.

"The big advantage is that it's a team sport that promotes social interaction," says Schmidt. With other games, such as football or baseball, "you're either out on the field or on the sidelines, where in bowling you're sitting around connecting with each other while you're waiting for your turn."

Keep the Good Times Rolling

In Wisconsin, as in the rest of the north, bowling tends to peak over the winter months, as people seek indoor recreation. In warmer parts of the country it's enjoyed equally all year. Even so, bowling is not as popular as it once was.

There are more activities than ever for young people and, as in baseball, experts argue that changes to the game and equipment have artificially inflated scores compared to years past. However, there are some signs of a comeback for bowling. Thanks to the cult movie *The Big Lebowski*, for many people bowling is hip. Also, there are trendy clubs, like one in north shore Milwaukee, where the elite meet to enjoy the menu of exotic martinis—and to bowl.

Young people are attracted to new multi-activity entertainment centers that offer video games and food in addition bowling. More and more high schools are also taking it up as an organized sport and even awarding varsity letters for it. The advantage, for young and old, is that you don't have to be the biggest and strongest to make the team.

"Bowlers come in all shapes and sizes. I think it is something that has no limitations on who it attracts," Schmidt says.

Vince Lombardi, Football Hero

A lot of little boys want to grow up to be football stars. It's not really clear whether young Vince Lombardi felt that way, but what we do know is this: Lombardi grew up to make football stars, and his success with the Green Bay Packers is legendary.

❋　❋　❋　❋

A Coach Is Born

BORN IN BROOKLYN, New York, in 1913, Lombardi studied for the priesthood for two years before he transferred to St. Francis Preparatory High School. He transferred his energy into sports and soon became a fullback on the football team.

Lombardi then enrolled at Fordham University. He played one year on the freshman team before his coach took notice and moved him to the varsity squad, where as a guard he became part of an offensive line known as "The Seven Blocks of Granite."

After graduation, Lombardi turned to coaching. His first steps down that path were modest—but exhausting. He coached football, basketball, and baseball at Cecilia High School in Englewood, New Jersey, while also teaching Latin, algebra, physics, and chemistry. He did all of this for $1,700 a year.

When his alma mater came calling in 1947, Lombardi answered. And just like when he was a student, he spent a year with the Fordham freshman team before moving on to the varsity squad. After that, he got a job working with the defensive line at West Point Academy, which he did for five years before heading to the pros. In 1954, Lombardi took an assistant coaching job with the New York Giants, and his defensive strategy helped turn the team into champions within a few years.

The Beginning of a Golden Era

Then, in 1958, Lombardi took the position of head coach with the Green Bay Packers. In the season before Lombardi arrived, Green Bay had won just a single game. One can only imagine the skeptical looks from players and personnel at the first team meeting when he told them that if they followed his rules, they could be a championship team. Yet, no one was doubtful when those words came true.

Lombardi was a force to be reckoned with. His confidence and enthusiasm won him both the coaching job in '59 and the general manger position. He wasted no time, winning Coach of the Year honors and leading the Packers to a 7–5 season in his first year. The next year, the Packers reached the NFL championship game but lost to the Eagles. But in 1961, Lombardi's Packers beat the Giants for the NFL championship—the seventh for Green Bay and the first for Lombardi.

In his nine years with the Packers, Lombardi amassed numerous wins, records, and honors, including historic victories at Super Bowls I and II. He was named NFL Man of the Decade, won six division titles, and five NFL titles with the Packers. And he'll always be remembered for coaching the Packers to a win in the famous Ice Bowl of 1967 against the Dallas Cowboys in sub-zero weather.

The Lombardi Sweep

Lombardi's drive to win was as strong as his work ethic, and he excelled at motivating his players. His offense employed methodical, no-frills plays, but these tactics worked so well that other teams soon adopted them. Lombardi retired from coaching after the 1967 season but remained with the Packers as general manager for the 1968 season. In 1969, he returned to coach the Washington Redskins to their first winning season in 14 years.

Sadly, this would be his last football season, as he was diagnosed with intestinal cancer. He died on September 3, 1970, and more than 3,500 came to pay their respects at his funeral. Jim Taylor, one of Lombardi's players, put it best when he said, "All he wants from you is perfection."

Talking Turkey

In bowling, why are three strikes in a row called a Turkey?

✳   ✳   ✳   ✳

WE LOVE BOWLING—AND why not? We love the mustaches, the tinted glasses, the fingerless gloves. We love that air-vent thingy on the ball rack, and we love the swirling balls that are inscribed with names like Lefty and Dale. We love the satin shirts and the multicolored shoes (okay, maybe not the shoes so much). But what we love most are the terms. The Dutch 200, the Brooklyn strike, the Cincinnati, the Jersey, the Greek Church, and especially the Turkey.

We have no idea what any of these terms mean, but we love them all the same.

Believe it or not, bowling wasn't always the sexy, hip sport played by highly trained athletes that it is today. Some historians trace bowling's roots back to 3200 BC, while others place its origin in Europe in the third century AD. Regardless, some form of bowling has been popular for centuries.

For much of this history, however, bowling didn't have a particularly sterling reputation. Quite the opposite: Legend has it that King Edward III banned bowling after his good-for-nothing soldiers kept skipping archery practice to roll. And well into the nineteenth century, American towns were outlawing bowling, largely because of the gambling that went along with it.

Despite these attempts at suppression—or perhaps because of them—bowling increased in popularity. In 1895, the American Bowling Congress (which is now known as the United States Bowling Congress) was formed, and local and regional bowling clubs began proliferating. It was around this time that the term "Turkey," which signifies three strikes in a row, arrived on the scene.

In an attempt to cash in on the burgeoning popularity of the newly sanctioned sport, as well as draw customers, many bowling alley proprietors offered a free live turkey to bowlers who successfully rolled three strikes in a row during Thanksgiving or Christmas week. Sadly, turkeys are no longer awarded at bowling alleys, although the tradition of shouting "Turkey" when somebody manages three strikes in a row continues.

So the next time you cry "fowl" at the bowling alley, you can take pride in knowing that you're continuing a time-honored tradition. Now if we could just figure out who decided two-toned bowling shoes were a good idea, we'd really be on to something.

The Seventh-inning Stretch

In a time-honored tradition, baseball fans rise from their seats between the top and bottom of the seventh inning to sing a hearty rendition of "Take Me Out to the Ball Game." Was this custom really started as a nod of respect to President William Howard Taft?

✳ ✳ ✳ ✳

RATHER THAN BEING remembered for his one-term residency in the White House and for being the only man to serve as both president and chief justice of the Supreme Court, Taft is probably best known as the fattest man ever to serve as commander in chief.

Indeed, Taft's girth was impressive, and it sometimes restricted his movements, especially when he attended Washington Senators baseball games (a pursuit that was his preferred method of relaxation). After sitting through a few innings of action, Taft would extract himself from the compressed confines of his chair, stand, stretch, and waddle off to the men's room. The denizens sitting near him would also rise, showing a measure of respect for their honored guest. This presidential pause for the cause was rumored to have occurred in the seventh-inning break.

However, there's no proof that the president was responsible for instituting or influencing the tradition. Taft attended many ball games, but he rarely stayed as late as the seventh inning. It's been said he had more pressing matters on his home plate—running the country, for instance.

From Bingo to Uno: The Origins of Popular Pastimes

Life isn't all fun and games. But we sure wish it could be! Here's a look at the origins of some popular games.

✳ ✳ ✳ ✳

Bingo

Bingo started sometime around 1929 as "Beano." A smart entrepreneur named Edwin Lowe spotted a crowd playing Beano at a fair and ran with the idea. As the story goes, he was hosting a Beano game at his house, and a woman playing the game got her tang all tongueled up. Upon winning, she couldn't blurt "Beano" correctly, and instead said "B-b-ingo!" Lowe jumped on it and started marketing the game as Bingo.

Stratego

The first boxed Stratego set in the United States came out in 1961, but the game's origin is much older than that. An ancient Chinese game called Jungle or Animal Chess very much resembles Stratego. A Frenchwoman patented its modern incarnation as *L'attaque* in 1910.

Scrabble

Would you believe that Scrabble was invented by a guy whose parents named him "Alfred Mosher Butts"? (Arrest them for that!) Al first invented a similar game called Lexiko in 1931, revising it into the equivalent of Scrabble in 1938. The name change came ten years later.

Go

This classic territorial-capture board game originated in China some 4,000 years ago. Legend has it that an emperor invented it to sharpen his dumb son's thinking. Played with black and white stones on a grid, Go has a following in Asia similar to that of chess in the West.

Twister

The Milton Bradley Company released this unique game in 1966, and it was the first one in history to use the human body as an actual playing piece. Worldwide, approximately 65 million people have entwined in a game of Twister.

Playing Cards

Playing cards have been a tradition in China for millennia, but their present markings date back to 14th-century France. The four suits represent the major classes of society at that time. Hearts are taken from the shield, translating to nobility and the church; the spear-tip shape of spades stands in for the military; clubs are clover, meant to represent rural peasantry; and diamonds are similar to the tiles then associated with retail shops and were therefore intended to signify the middle class.

Uno

Is Uno ancient? Only if 1969 seems ancient to you, since that's when a barber from Ohio invented the popular all-ages card game. Creator Merle Robbins sold Uno to a game company in 1972 for $50,000 plus royalties.

Fad Inventions

If we could figure out the next hottest trend, we'd all be millionaires, right? Here are some seemingly crazy ideas that turned out to be both lasting and lucrative.

✳   ✳   ✳   ✳

Hacky Sack

Mike Marshall created this version of the footbag in 1972 to help his friend John Stalberger rehabilitate an injured leg. After they marketed it, the Hacky Sack rehabilitated their bank accounts as well. In Oregon in 2006, Tricia George and Paul Vorvick set a doubles record of 1,415 footbag kicks in ten minutes.

Pet Rock

Its genesis makes sense when you consider the occupation of its inventor. In the mid-1970s, advertising executive Gary Dahl packaged ordinary beach stones in an attractive box and sold them with instructions for their care and training. They cost a penny to manufacture and sold for $3.95, and though the fad lasted less than a year, it made Dahl millions.

Super Soaker

The giant water gun was invented in 1988 by aerospace engineer Lonnie Johnson. An intriguing feature was the incorporation of air pressure, which enabled more water to be sprayed at greater distances. Some of today's pump-action models can "shoot" water accurately as far as 50 feet.

Yo-Yo

The first historical mention of the yo-yo dates to Greece in 500 B.C., but it was a man named Pedro Flores who brought the yo-yo to the United States from the Philippines in 1928. American entrepreneur Donald Duncan soon bought the rights from Flores. Sales of the toy peaked in 1962, when more than 45 million units were sold.

Bragging Rights

"Faster, higher, stronger" may be the motto for the modern Olympic Games, but it's also an apt description for the athletes who stretched the boundaries of human endurance and initiated the Ironman competition.

✳ ✳ ✳ ✳

THE OLD CLICHÉ "anything you can do, I can do better," along with a spirited discussion over the true meaning of "better," ultimately led to the creation of the Ironman Triathlon.

During the awards ceremony for the 1977 Oahu Perimeter Relay, a running race for five-person teams held in Hawaii, the winning participants, among them both runners and swimmers, became engrossed in a debate over which athletes were more fit.

As both sides tossed biting barbs, rousing rhetoric, and snide snippets back and forth, a third party entered the fray. Navy Commander John Collins, who was listening to the spirited spat, mentioned that a recent article in *Sports Illustrated* magazine claimed that bike racers, especially Tour de France winner Eddy Merckx, had the highest recorded "oxygen uptake" of any athlete ever measured, insinuating that cyclists were more fit than anyone. Collins and his wife, Judy, suggested the only way to truly bring the argument to a rightful conclusion was to arrange an extreme endurance competition, combining a swim of considerable length, a bike race of taxing duration, and a marathon foot race. The first Ironman Triathlon was held on February 18, 1978, in Honolulu, Hawaii. Participants were invited to "Swim 2.4 miles! Bike 112 miles! Run 26.2 miles! Brag for the rest of your life." This rousing slogan has since become the registered trademark of the event.

But the Ironman competition was not the first triathlon event. The first competition to combine swimming (500-yard race), bike racing (5-mile course), and running (2.8 miles) was held on September 25, 1974, in San Diego, California.

Raising the Stakes

We're willing to bet you're interested in learning how a lowly token came to supplant both money and sanity.

✳   ✳   ✳   ✳

YOU HAVE TO hand it to the inventor of the poker chip. Here's an item that spends like money, bets like money, has people lusting after it like money, yet it doesn't quite *feel* like money. Ask any gambler—they'll tell you that poker chips, or gaming chips as they're now called, seem like Monopoly money when compared to the real thing. This is especially true when you're down on your luck because the mystical quality of the chip makes the reality of losing hard-earned dollars a little fuzzy. What evil genius devised such a thing? The fact is, nobody seems to know for sure. History records evidence of substitute money being used as betting chips as far back as the 18th century, but the modern chip that we've come to love or loathe (depending upon individual luck) didn't make an appearance until the early 20th century.

Although such crude chips (generally made from ivory, bones, or clay) represented a breakthrough in gaming convenience, they also invited attempts at forgery. Industrious types would simply manufacture similar-looking bits at home and smuggle them into gaming parlors. Today, gaming chips are constructed of composite materials and feature such high-tech extras as microchips within the chip to foil would-be forgers. Thanks to mass production, casino-quality chips are now available to home gamblers as well

Between a Rock and a Weird Place: The House on the Rock

If you've ever said to yourself, "Gee, I wish there was a big house full of fake antiques, a giant plaster squid, the world's largest carousel, and a fully automated pipe organ 'played' by mannequins," then do we have the place for you! You can thank Alex Jordan Jr., a man who decided to build a house and fill it with everything listed above and a whole lot more. But is the House on the Rock an obsessive collection? A weird museum? A potentially haunted house? The answer? Yes.

✳   ✳   ✳   ✳

I'll Show That Frank Lloyd Wright!

THE HOUSE ON the Rock is a tourist attraction near Spring Green, Wisconsin. It's not a house per se, and although part of it is located on an outcropping of rock, the grounds of this odd attraction comprise buildings and structures that rest on 240 acres of farmland. So begins an attempt to describe a place that defies description.

The tale begins with Alex Jordan Sr., an aspiring architect and fan of the legendary Frank Lloyd Wright. The story goes that sometime around 1920, the elder Jordan had designed a women's dormitory for the University of Wisconsin. He took the plans to Wright's well-known property, Taliesin, to show them to his hero and perhaps land a job. Wright, who was not known for his warmth or diplomacy, snapped, "I wouldn't hire you to design a cheese case for me, or a chicken coop." Jordan was none too pleased with this assessment and vowed to get back at the big shot who had spurned him, though the "revenge" would actually be taken by his son, Alex Jordan Jr., years later.

In 1953, the younger Jordan spotted an odd piece of land outside of Spring Green called Deer Shelter Rock. A virtual chimney of rock, it stood 450 feet tall and offered a 70 by 200-foot expanse at the top. Jordan saw it as the perfect place to build a house that would ultimately gain as much attention as any Frank Lloyd Wright house. He began building immediately with funding from his dad.

The original section of the House on the Rock was completed in 1959, and it garnered plenty of attention. The house featured nine rooms with low-slung ceilings, fireplaces, and indoor waterfalls. The rooms spill into each other, and the whole place is incredibly dark. The decor has an Asian feel, but because Jordan favored accumulation over typical Asian minimalism, the effect is unique. Carpeting runs throughout the house, even on the walls in some places.

Let's Go Crazy!

Why the expansion? By 1962, curious people were paying 50 cents a head for a tour of the strange house built on the rock. Jordan Jr. figured that to bring in more people, they'd have to offer more, so five rooms were added.

Jordan supposedly hated to travel, but that didn't stop him from amassing a huge collection of antiques and artifacts over the years. Let the tourist beware: Some of the pieces on display at the House on the Rock are the real deal, such as certain toys and furniture, but others are fake, like the "Tiffany" lamps. With the help of friend and craftsman Don Martin, Jordan built whatever his heart desired and let the public think what they would.

Dim room by dim room, the collection reveals itself. The Oriental Art Room contains pieces similar to those found in the house's original section. The Blue Room and the Red Room contain fully mechanized organs, some with mannequins that "play" instruments in time to the music. There are doll rooms packed with dolls, dolls, and more dolls. The Model Circus Room, the Organ Room, and the Wildlife Room are all aptly named to describe their contents. A visitor can expect to find everything from taxidermic animals to carriages to grotesque masks hanging near old machine parts.

If it sounds weird, you're following along. The House on the Rock tour is said to take four hours and could take even longer if you actually attempted to look at everything. No visit would be complete without a peek at the largest indoor carousel in the world, which, at 80 feet in diameter, features 20,000 lights and 269 creatures (none of which are horses). The carousel revolves in a cavernous room to demonic merry-go-round music. No touching allowed.

There are no placards on items at the House on the Rock, no tour guides to explain origins or histories. The whole rambling structure seems to sort of live and breathe on its own. In defense of the curators (which included Jordan Jr. until his death in 1989), what could you really say about a three-level blimp hangar, dominated by a 200-foot-long sea monster battling a giant squid? Or all those topless angel mannequins that hang from the ceiling in the Carousel Room? Or the Cannon

Room, featuring the world's largest cannon—an object so large the room had to be built around it?

See for Yourself

When Jordan Jr. passed away at age 75, it's believed that he left most of his fortune to his girlfriend of 45 years. Details of his life are murky, and the house he built (which he never lived in) was as mysterious as he was.

The House on the Rock reportedly gets around a half million visitors every year, making it the most popular tourist attraction in Wisconsin and much of the Midwest.

11 of the World's Greatest Roller Coasters

On Coney Island—a spit of Brooklyn beachfront—the first American roller coasters were created in the late 1880s. One of the pioneer coasters, the Flip-Flap Railway, had the unfortunate problem of snapping riders' necks due to the extreme g-forces experienced when accelerating through its circular loop. Engineering innovations and steel construction have made coasters safer, and now the sky's the limit. Here are some of today's biggest thrillers.

❋   ❋   ❋   ❋

1. **The Matterhorn Bobsleds:** While not necessarily the tallest, fastest, or scariest ride in the world, the Matterhorn deserves a nod as the grandfather of modern coasters. Still thrilling riders at Disneyland, this ride was the world's first major steel coaster when it opened in 1959. Inspired by the Matterhorn, a 14,692-foot mountain in the Swiss Alps, the structure is made up of two linking steel roller coasters with loops and corkscrews. Top speed is 18 miles per hour.

2. **Kingda Ka:** Kingda Ka, at Six Flags Great Adventure in Jackson, New Jersey, is the ultimate ride on several fronts.

As of 2007, it was the tallest and fastest roller coaster on the planet. Reaching 128 miles per hour in 3.5 seconds, the train rockets straight up to the 456-foot apex. Crossing over the pinnacle, the train plummets straight down into a vertical, hair-raising descent through a spiral twist at speeds of more than 100 miles per hour. Riders then face a 129-foot tall hill that bounces them out of their seats for a few scary seconds.

3. **Apollo's Chariot:** Opened in 1999, Apollo's Chariot is an award-winning steel coaster at Busch Gardens in Williamsburg, Virginia. Holding the world record for a gulping 825 feet of drops on a coaster, Apollo's Chariot starts with a 170-foot lift hill, then hits a maximum speed of 73 miles per hour. At the peak, riders drop down a few teasing feet before the cars swoop down 210 feet to graze a water-filled gully at a 65 degree angle. Riders then soar up a second hill and back down a 131-foot drop. Then, the coaster screams through a short tunnel and then takes off up a third incline, before screeching around a curved 144-foot plunge. Riders slow down with a series of bunny bumps before the train returns safely to the station.

4. **Steel Dragon 2000:** Steel Dragon 2000, located at Nagashima Spa Land Amusement Park in Japan, represents "The Year of the Dragon." As of 2006, it had the longest track of any coaster in the world, hurtling its riders along at speeds up to 95 miles per hour for 8,133.17 feet. With a peak at 318.25 feet, it is also the world's tallest coaster to use a chain lift: Two chains are utilized, one for the bottom half and one for the top half because a single chain would be too long and heavy. For earthquake protection, more steel was used in this $50 million machine than in any other coaster in the world.

5. **Dodonpa:** When it first opened in 2001 at Fuji-Q Highland in Japan, Dodonpa was the world's fastest steel

coaster, but by 2006, it had slipped to third place. However, it retains the title for the fastest acceleration in the world, reaching a top speed of 106.8 miles per hour in a mere 1.8 seconds! At speeds like that, ride time is only 55 seconds, but that seems like an eternity when rushing down 170 feet at a 90-degree angle.

6. **Son of Beast:** Son of Beast, built in 2000 at Paramount's Kings Island in Cincinnati, Ohio, is touted as the world's tallest and fastest wooden coaster, with a 218-foot apex and speeds up to 78 miles per hour. At the time of its construction, Son of Beast was also the world's only looping wooden roller coaster, although in 2007, the loop was removed. Son of Beast's daddy, The Beast, was constructed at King's Island in 1979 and holds the title as the longest wooden roller coaster, at 7,400 feet.

7. **Rock 'n' Roller Coaster:** Located at Disney parks in Florida and France, the Rock 'n' Roller Coaster is an indoor experience, called a "dark ride." Accelerating to 57 miles per hour in 2.8 seconds, windblown hair is guaranteed. But the highlight of this coaster is that rides are accompanied by music by Aerosmith, including songs such as "Back in the Saddle," "Sweet Emotion," and "Love in an Elevator."

8. **Dueling Dragons:** Located at Islands of Adventure in Orlando, Florida, Dueling Dragons is the world's first high-speed, dueling inverted roller coaster; inverted means that the cars travel under the track rather than on top of it. Dueling Dragons is actually two roller coasters, one representing fire and the other ice. Each has several throat-gulping inversions, including corkscrews, vertical loops, and a cobra roll. Top speed is 55 miles per hour with a maximum height of 125 feet. Riders on each track zoom within inches of each other in three near-miss experiences that elicit plenty of screaming.

9. **Magnum XL-200:** Opened in 1989 at Cedar Point in Sandusky, Ohio, Magnum XL-200 is a steel roller coaster that was the first constructed circuit roller coaster to break the 200-foot barrier, with its 205-foot peak and 194.67-foot drop. The view of Lake Erie from the pinnacle is breathtaking, with plenty of opportunity to see the countryside along the nearly mile-long track. That is, if passengers can keep their eyes open while speeding along at 72 miles per hour. Expert riders prefer the third row of seats in the first car because of numerous, intense airtime moments.

10. **Superman—Ultimate Flight:** If you've ever wanted to fly like a superhero, this is the ride for you! Located at Six Flags theme parks in Illinois, New Jersey, and Georgia, this ride's specially-designed cars tilt passengers facedown into a flying position, so that they're suspended horizontally from the track above. Riders get a bird's-eye view at the top of a 109-foot hill, before sailing through the air at 60 miles per hour in a series of loops, spirals, turns, and rolls. And with the first-of-its-kind pretzel-shaped loop, this truly is a unique thrill ride.

11. **The Raptor:** The Raptor is a steel inverted coaster at Cedar Point, America's roller coaster capital, in Sandusky, Ohio. When it opened in 1994, this sweet ride was the largest of its type ever built. Passengers soar up 137 feet before gliding down 119 feet. Reaching a maximum speed of 57 miles per hour, there are six inversions, including a cobra roll and two corkscrews that are great for shaking up the digestive system. Rides last an enjoyable 2 minutes, 16 seconds—an adventure enjoyed by nearly two million thrill seekers every year.

Days Gone By: Pinball

Once considered an untoward distraction, pinball survived early disapproval and even banishment to become the popular predecessor to today's video games.

✳ ✳ ✳ ✳

Prohibition

PINBALL WAS INVENTED in the 1930s, inspired by the 19th-century game bagatelle, which involved a billiards cue and a playing field full of holes. Some early pinball arcades "awarded" players for high scores, and in the mid-1930s, machines were introduced that provided direct monetary payouts. These games quickly earned pinball the reputation as a fun diversion—and a gambling device. Thus, starting in the 1940s, New York City Mayor Fiorello LaGuardia declared pinball parlors akin to casinos ("magnets for the wrong element"), ushering in an era of pinball prohibition. Chicago, Los Angeles, and other major American cities followed suit with their own pinball bans. New York's pinball embargo lasted until 1976, and city officials destroyed 11,000 machines before it was lifted. The turning point: Writer and pinball wizard Roger Sharpe called his shots during a demonstration in front of the New York City Council, proving that pinball was indeed a game of skill. The council members voted 6–0 to legalize pinball in the Big Apple.

Rise and Fall

Despite the fact that pinball was banned in the three largest U.S. cities, it became a favorite pastime among adolescents and teens in the 1950s. This changed in 1973 with the advent of the video game, but pinball enjoyed the first of several revivals later in the 1970s, thanks to its association with such rock-and-roll luminaries as The Who, Elton John, and Kiss. The last pinball renaissance peaked with Bally's The Addams Family game, introduced in 1991 to tie in with the release of the movie. The Addams Family became the best-selling pinball game of all time, with 22,000 machines sold. In the 1990s, the bottom dropped out of the pinball market, and as of 2007, there was only one American manufacturer, Stern Pinball.

Origin of the Flippers

Gottlieb's Humpty Dumpty, designed by Harry Mabs in 1947, was the first pinball game to feature flippers (three on each side) that allowed the player to use hand-eye coordination to influence gravity and chance. Many pre-flipper games were essentially dressed-up gambling contraptions, and players could just tilt the machines to rack up points. Humpty Dumpty and the thousands of flipper games that followed were true contests of skill. In 1948, pinball designer Steven Kordek repositioned the flippers (just two) at the bottom of the playfield, and the adjustment became the industry standard.

The Most Expensive Baseball Card

A 100-year-old baseball card turns grown men into little kids.

✳   ✳   ✳   ✳

Honus wagner was either the most noble of all early 20th-century baseball players—a man who cringed at the thought of his likeness being used to hawk a tobacco product—or a guy who was ticked that he wasn't getting a big enough share of the profits.

Regardless of the reason, the "Flying Dutchman" pitched a fit when the American Tobacco Company, a cigarette manufacturer, released its T206 series of tobacco cards in 1909. Approximately 50 cards picturing Wagner in uniform with the Pittsburgh Pirates are estimated to have made it to cigarette packs back in the day before being yanked. Only a tiny percentage of those 50 made it to the late 20th-century marketplace.

Flash-forward a hundred years, and that T206 card, the "Holy Grail" among baseball card collectors, is considered the most valuable card of all time. One such exemplar has been owned by hockey Hall of Famer Wayne Gretzky, who—along with a business partner—purchased the T206 card for $451,000 in 1991. Gretzky later sold it in 1995 for $500,000 to Wal-Mart, which used it as part of a store promotion. The winner—a Florida postal worker—was thrilled…until she had to sell it to cover the taxes on her good fortune.

And so Wagner's travels continued as the card was auctioned for $640,000 and again on the online auction site eBay for almost twice that: $1.27 million. Oh, but the news just keeps getting better, as an anonymous collector with gobs of money shelled out $2.35 million for this cardboard classic in 2007. Looking to make a quick buck, that same collector turned around and sold it six months later…for a record $2.8 million.

Somewhere, a 110-year-old man is kicking himself for sticking his Honus Wagner card in the spokes of his bicycle.

Curling

For some people, curling is an Olympic sport; for others it's a fun social activity. Here's some information on a sport that's akin to shuffleboard or bowling on ice.

✳   ✳   ✳   ✳

History

CURLING BEGAN IN Scotland in the 1500s, played with river-worn stones. In the next century, enterprising curlers began to fit the stones with handles. With Canada's heavy Scottish influence and northerly climate, curling was a perfect fit. The Royal Montreal Curling Club began in 1807, and in 1927, Canada held its first national curling championship.

Today, curling has millions of enthusiasts around the world. Canadian curlers routinely beat international competition, a source of brimming national pride.

How to Curl

The standard curling rink measures 146 feet by 15 feet. At each end are 12-foot-wide concentric rings called houses, the center of which is the button. There are four curlers on a team. Each throws two rocks (shoves them, rather; you don't really want to go airborne with a 44-pound granite rock) in an effort to get as close to the button as possible. When all eight players have thrown two rocks each, it concludes the end (analogous to a baseball inning). A game consists of eight or ten ends.

Curling Strategy

You try to knock the other team's rocks out of the house, and thus out of scoring position, while getting yours to hang around close to the button. After all throws, the team with the rock nearest the button scores a point for each of its rocks that's nearer the button than the opponent's nearest rock (and inside the house).

Proper Ice-keeping

The players with the brooms aren't trying to keep the ice clear of crud. The team skip (captain) determines strategy and advises the players using the brooms in the fine art of sweeping. Skips can guide the stone with surprising precision by skillfully sweeping in front of it with their brooms, but they can't touch (burn) that rock or any others in the process.

"Good curling!" "Thanks, you too."

Curling is a game that values good sportsmanship. Curlers even call themselves for burns. When a team is so far behind it cannot win, it is considered proper sportsmanship to concede by removing gloves and shaking hands.

Curling Jargon

Bonspiel: a curling tournament

Curler: curling player

Draw: shot thrown to score

Hack: foot brace curlers push off from, like track sprinters

Hammer: last rock of the end (advantageous)

Hog line: blue line in roughly the same place as a hockey blue line. One must let go of the rock before crossing the near hog line—and the rock must cross the far hog line—or it's hogged (removed from play).

Pebble: water drops sprayed on the ice at the beginning of the game, making the rock move over the ice surface and "curl"

Takeout: shot meant to knock a rock out of play

Up! Whoa! Off! Hurry! Hard!: examples of orders the skip might call to the sweepers

Weight: how hard one slides the rock

Strat-O-Matic Baseball

It's been around since 1961, a tabletop baseball game that includes a detailed stats card for every real-life player. Today, people still spend obsessive amounts of time replaying vintage games, recording statistics, and communicating on message boards.

❋ ❋ ❋ ❋

ON A GIVEN day each February, dozens of men converge on Glen Head in Long Island, New York. Many come from the Tri-State area, but some may come from Alberta or Texas or Michigan. They stand bundled up in line before a cinder-block building, talking baseball, sharing coffee from thermoses, brimming with excitement. A few camped out the night before, like Deadheads hoping to score concert tickets.

But these guys aren't on Long Island for a concert or to purchase the latest technological gadget. Instead, they're here to pick up the new-season cards for a tabletop baseball game.

No, really. Shortly after "Opening Day," thousands more fans across the continent watch for the UPS or mail delivery like eager children. These are stockbrokers, accountants, store managers, janitors—the gamut of life. Most started playing this game as boys.

The Game in Brief

In Strat (as most enthusiasts call it), each Major League Baseball player has a batting or pitching card. Half the time (at random) the result of an at-bat comes from the hitter's card, and half the time from the pitcher's. The result is great statistical clarity, with players rated for fielding range, pitching endurance, clutch hitting, bunting, leading off base, and so on. People take Strat's fielding ratings so seriously that big league ballplayers phone owner Hal Richman to complain about the ratings on their own Strat cards. Fans even heckle players at games: "You're a 5, Jones!" (In Strat, 5 is the worst fielding range rating; players not only get the reference, they resent it.) Strat-O-Matic Game Co., Inc., also makes football, basketball, and hockey games, but baseball remains the core product.

Deep Hal

Strat is the brainchild and life achievement of entrepreneur Hal Richman. Born in 1936 to a domineering insurance salesman from the Lower East Side, the cerebral, introverted Hal had a difficult childhood in Kew Gardens. Whether he was bullied for being Jewish, or just for shyness, young Hal retreated into baseball—simulated baseball. At 11, the gifted young mathematician began finding flaws in spinner-based baseball games. Over the next 15 years, he evolved what would become Strat-O-Matic Baseball.

With only selected players and/or teams, the game's first release was a sales flop. Only when Richman began to include all teams and all significant players did Strat start to sell. John F. Kennedy was president when Hal made that decision—and Hal is still in business.

Very Old School

Strat doesn't even take baseball's word for its own statistics—it compiles them from old box scores. Strat still calls its computer version "CD-ROM Baseball." The company has been in the same building since 1975, slow to change anything. Sometimes lack of change is good, though; gamers have long respected Strat for its scrupulously honest reputation. Hal Richman personally reads and acts upon his mail, ensuring that customers receive fair value.

Well he should, because Strat is boy-howdy expensive, especially for a text-based game. But it's not just average Joes playing. Many big league ballplayers grew up playing Strat, and some still do. Mets great Keith Hernandez has played it since childhood. Spike Lee still loves the game. Trip Hawkins, founder of Strat semicompetitor Electronic Arts, is still rolling the dice. (The baseball game from EA has graphics, costs less, and includes the current season, not last season. Strat junkies remain indifferent to EA.)

Strat Today

It hasn't been easy for Strat, of course. The rights to use player names, the imbroglios created by baseball strikes, an aging customer base, and graphics-based games pose big challenges. But like the single-minded Jewish kid from Queens who borrowed money from a grumpy dad to start his company, Strat-O-Matic is a survivor.

Institutions of Higher Chicanery!

When it comes to clever pranks, some colleges and universities get an A1!

✳   ✳   ✳   ✳

PRACTICAL JOKES AREN'T part of the curriculum at most colleges and universities, but that hasn't stopped generations of students from perpetrating some very clever pranks.

Here are seven of the most impressive:

1. Football rivalries have sparked some genuinely notable pranks over the years. During the 1961 Rose Bowl game between the Washington Huskies and the Minnesota Golden Gophers, for example, students from Caltech cleverly switched the colored placards that were distributed to spectators sitting on the Washington Huskies' side of the field. As a result, instead of hailing the Huskies when held up on cue during halftime, the placards spelled out "CALTECH." The prank was viewed by millions on television and is still considered one of the most impressive (and elaborate) college stunts ever.

2. In 1933, the staff of the Harvard *Lampoon* took it upon themselves to steal the Massachusetts Sacred Cod, a five-foot-long carving that traditionally hangs over one entrance to the Massachusetts State House. When no one was looking, the students simply cut down the fish, hid it in a flower box, and casually strolled away. A few days later, after a lot of hubbub, two *Lampoon* staffers, wearing disguises, returned the cod to the Harvard chief of police.

3. The United States isn't alone in its love of a good college prank. In 1958, students at Cambridge University successfully placed an Austin Seven automobile atop the roof of the Senate House. The students needed just one night to place the car, but it took civil planners a week to figure out how to get it down. Amazingly, the pranksters were never caught, though they did finally reveal themselves during a reunion dinner in 2008.

4. The more difficult a prank, the better, as evidenced by a 1988 endeavor in which students at Rice University successfully turned the one-ton statue of William Marsh Rice so that it faced the university library instead of having its back to it. The stunt was an amazing feat of engineering that went unappreciated by school officials, who

forced Patrick Dyson—one of the students involved in the prank—to pay to have the statue returned to its original position. However, Dyson didn't have to pay a penny out of his own pocket; his fellow students raised the money for Rice's turnaround by selling commemorative T-shirts.

5. More recent college pranks often take advantage of new technologies. In 2006, students at UC Berkeley pulled a fast one on USC basketball star Gabe Pruitt by enticing him with an attractive girl named Victoria via Facebook. Victoria didn't really exist, but Pruitt didn't know that until a game in which UC students started chanting "Victoria! Victoria! Victoria!" and Pruitt's cell phone number, which he had divulged to his nonexistent paramour. The chanting continued throughout the game and truly rattled Pruitt, who shot just 3 for 13 that day.

6. In 1993, three Ohio State University students sent out a fake news release promoting a program to donate guns and ammunition to the homeless, backed by a nonexistent organization called Arm the Homeless Coalition (ATHC). Many news organizations, agencies, and prominent individuals fell for the prank and expressed their outrage by condemning the ATHC. The students finally confessed to the hoax, saying they were just trying to draw attention to the issues of guns and violence, the homeless, and media manipulation in society, but others soon took up the "cause" with similar pranks around the country.

7. Not all college pranks go as planned. In 1958, students at UCLA plotted a devious caper against archrival USC that involved dumping hundreds of pounds of manure from a rented helicopter on to USC's fabled Tommy Trojan statue. Unfortunately for the pranksters, the pull of the helicopter's rotors sucked the manure back into their faces and dropped very little on their intended target.

Weird Collections

Some people collect baseball cards. Others collect belly button lint. Yes, you read that correctly—belly button lint. Now that's a collection that brings a whole new meaning to the phrase "one person's trash is another person's treasure"!

✳ ✳ ✳ ✳

IN 1984, GRAHAM Barker's navel gazing led to an interesting hobby. You can see the results online at his Incredible World of Navel Fluff, where samples of his personal lint are neatly displayed in labeled jars. But maybe you'd prefer to visit the Museum of Burnt Food? Or take a gander at Becky Martz's array of banana stickers (she has more than 7,000, though not all are online)? Or view New Zealand artist Maurice Bennett's Toast Portraits of Famous People?

Some collections that might be classified as "weird" actually have a serious purpose. Dr. Bindeshwar Pathak created the Sulabh Museum of Toilets in New Delhi, India, to educate people about the need for sanitation. The Trash Museum in Harford, Connecticut, will surely boost your commitment to recycling. And after visiting the Museum of Hoaxes in San Diego you're not likely to be hooked by tales of fur-bearing trout or swallow any stories about Italian spaghetti trees. Here's something to keep in mind if you ever drop by the Icelandic Phallological Museum: Most of the 245 embalmed penises on display are from real Icelandic animals, but curator Sigurur Hjartarson has mixed in a few from "elves" and "trolls" just to keep natural historians on their toes.

A passion for collecting goes way back in human history. The Egyptian pharaohs of the Ptolemaic dynasty (332–30 B.C.) collected enough papyrus scrolls to establish the world's first library. A few centuries later, around A.D. 10, Roman Emperor Augustus scoured his empire for unusual objects, including the bones of sea monsters (which we now recognize as whales).

Collecting really took off during the Renaissance, however, when wealthy merchants used *Wunderkammers*, known in English as Wonder Cabinets, to display their collections of antiques and oddities. Today, thanks to the wonders of the Internet, almost anyone can have a Wonder Cabinet in cyberspace. In addition to those mentioned above, here are a few of our top picks when it comes to the weirdest of the weird:

* Jef Beck's collection of vintage Ken dolls, among them the rare "Business Ken" and "Coca Cola" Ken, which was produced as a promotional gimmick along with "Coca Cola" Barbie.

* Chocolate freak Martin Mihál's collection of 38,579 chocolate bar wrappers, including 8,700 from his native Germany.

* A must-see for office mavens is the Acme Staple Company's collection of antique staplers. The Early Office Museum has a collection of staples to fit those machines.

* The Air Sickness Bag Virtual Museum displays more than 2,000 barf bags from around the world. Curator Steven J. Silberberg insists he's never been out of North America. Perhaps the instructions on Virgin Australia airline's "Fully Sick" bag are one good reason why.

* It's natural to move from the barf bag museum to the gallery of moist towelettes. Michael Lewis's Web site, Modern Moist Towelette Collecting, even gives awards in categories such as "Humor," "Most Original Use for a Towelette," and "Strangest Place to Find a Towelette."

* Hygiene does seem to fuel many collectors' obsessions. Carol Vaughn of England has more than 5,000 bars of soap and Dr. Val Kolpakov of Saginaw, Michigan, displays 1,407 different brands of toothpaste at his Toothpaste World online. In Malaysia, they brush with DawnMist, in Russia with Splat, and in the United States with something called Warheads, in three flavors, no less.

* Finally, if you want to know the future of collecting, consult the Museum of Talking Boards, a collection devoted to the art and history of Ouija boards. Or try the Weird Fortune Cookie Collection. Still no answer? Shake a Magic 8-Ball. According to antique dealer Deanna Dahlsad, there are plenty of these little "spheres of influence" floating around out there just waiting for someone to collect them. Which gives us an idea...

Most Dangerous Toys

"You'll shoot your eye out, kid!" Anyone who has seen A Christmas Story *is familiar with this line from the movie, which follows (more or less) the story of a kid who wants a BB gun for Christmas. The familiar refrain from adult after adult: "You'll shoot your eye out, kid!" Yes, some toys are clearly dangerous. But it might surprise you to learn which toys are the most dangerous.*

✳   ✳   ✳   ✳

You'll Want to Stay Away from These...

OVER THE YEARS, numerous toys have been recalled because they posed a danger to users. Here are a few of the most hazardous:

1. **Gilbert U-238 Atomic Energy Lab** This one dates back to the 1950s, but it's a doozy. For $50, kids received three *radioactive* (yep, that's right—radioactive) compounds, a Geiger-Mueller radiation counter, and a Wilson Cloud Chamber. Perfect for the mad scientist in every family!

2. **Lawn Darts** Perhaps the most dangerous game ever created, steel-tipped lawn darts were responsible for an estimated 6,700 injuries and 4 deaths before they were finally taken off store shelves in the 1980s.

3. **Easy-Bake Oven** An oven door that trapped little fingers and a painfully hot lightbulb led to this toy being recalled in 2007.

4. **Clackers** Two acrylic spheres connected by a cord, Clackers were popular among kids in the 1970s. Unfortunately, the spheres had a nasty habit of smacking users in the face or unexpectedly shattering on impact.

5. **Aqua Dots** These Chinese-made craft sets featured tiny beads that could be sprayed with water to create a sculpture. On the downside, the dots metabolized into the date-rape drug gamma hydroxybutyrate (GHB) when swallowed. Good thing little kids don't put stuff in their mouths—oh, wait a minute...

6. **Snacktime Cabbage Patch Dolls** Designed to teach kids how to feed their younger siblings, the dolls' mechanized jaws munched on anything placed inside them—including children's hands.

7. **Creepy Crawler Thingmaker** The idea was simple: Pour plastic goop into a mold then cook at 310 degrees. The result? For many, a trip to the ER.

Toys by the Numbers

18: the number of toy-related deaths among children younger than age 15 reported nationally in 2007 (Most common causes of death: riding toys, including nonmotorized scooters, and small toy balls.)

232,900: the estimated number of toy-related injuries, among all ages, treated in U.S. hospital emergency departments in 2007

34: percentage of toy-related injuries involving children younger than five years of age

This Little Piggy Went Kaboom!

Japanese parents, like most, encourage their children to save money. But they're not on board with a quirky piggy bank introduced by TOMY toys in 2007. If the money-hungry porker isn't fed with coins on a regular basis, it explodes, showering those around it with loose change.

Doin' the Dunk

The slam dunk is one of the moves in basketball that never fails to elicit gasps and groans. Here's how it all began.

✳ ✳ ✳ ✳

WHETHER IT'S CALLED a dip, slam, jam, punch, stuff, flush, or dunk, the act of rising above the basketball rim with a single agile, athletic leap and propelling the ball down the barrel has become something of an art. But the dunk itself wasn't exactly invented; rather, it evolved as players grew in height and athletic ability.

George Mikan, a pioneer in pro basketball, who played for the Chicago American Gears and the Minneapolis Lakers through the 1940s and '50s, was probably the first man to use the dunk as an offensive weapon. Mikan would plant himself under the basket and use his 6'10 frame to his advantage. Back then, there was no rim hangs or wham-slam jams. Instead, Mikan would gently guide the globe, dropping the disc through the hoop. Purists pleaded for the NBA to ditch the dunk, but the league declined. However, college basketball officials weren't so reticent. In 1967, they introduced legislation forbidding the flush that became known as the Lew Alcindor Rule. Alcindor, the 7'2 star of the UCLA Bruins, went on to NBA fame as Kareem Abul-Jabbar. The rule was dropped in 1976.

The dunk as an art form was perfected by Julius "Dr. J" Erving, who used flamboyant moves and powerful slams to become the NBA's most electrifying entertainer in the 1970s. Gus Johnson (Baltimore Bullets, Phoenix Suns) and Darryl "Chocolate Thunder" Dawkins (Philadelphia 76ers, New Jersey Nets), added new panache to the plunge by ripping the rim from the backboard and shattering the glass. Dawkins memorably named one move "The Chocolate-Thunder-Flying, Robinzine-Crying, Teeth-Shaking, Glass-Breaking, Rump-Roasting, Bun-Toasting, Wham-Bam, Glass-Breaker-I-Am-Jam."

And new breakthroughs in dunking continue. Candace Parker became the first female to flush, dipping the ball in a NCAA tournament game, while in 2002, her 65 teammate on the Los Angeles Sparks, Lisa Leslie, became the first woman in the WNBA to do the dunk.

Before Basketball

Meet James Naismith, the man behind basketball.

✳   ✳   ✳   ✳

The Man Behind the Ball

BORN IN 1861, James Naismith was raised in the small Canadian village of Bennie's Corners, Ontario. Naismith grew up both morally and physically fit, performing heavy chores, walking five miles across frozen fields to school, and playing with his friends near the village blacksmith shop.

Later, at McGill University in Montreal, Naismith earned degrees in philosophy and Hebrew while playing hard-hitting sports such as rugby and lacrosse. Despite the prevailing Victorian opinion that sports were violent and vice-ridden, James was convinced that sports could be used to instill good values. He attended International Young Men's Christian Association Training School in Springfield, Massachusetts, where he worked toward his divinity degree while teaching physical education.

Playing Naismithball

In 1891, the school's superintendent challenged Naismith to develop an indoor sport that would keep the boys busy during the cold winter months and that would be "fair for all players, and free of rough play."

Naismith carefully planned this new sport. Games with larger balls were less violent, he noted, so he chose to use a soccer ball. Abuse between players occurred more frequently when the ball was near the goal. Naismith's new game would have goals placed above the player's heads. He also noticed that injuries occurred most often between players in motion. The players in his game would stop as soon as they had possession of the ball.

To solve the problem of how to get the ball into the goal, Naismith showed his students how to throw using a lobbing motion he and his friends developed while playing a game called "Duck on a Rock" in Bennie's Corners.

Armed with their "Duck on a Rock" skills, Naismith's students played the first game of basketball in December 1891, using wooden peach baskets nailed to the walls of the gym. School members called for the game to be named "Naismithball" after its inventor, but he stuck to his guns and the game became known as "Basket Ball."

All This and Cereal Too?

It's rare to find toys in cereal boxes today, but there was a time when no self-respecting kid would buy a breakfast cereal that didn't boast its own rubber spider or Fred Flintstone magnet hiding beneath all those corn flakes and marshmallow hearts.

❋　❋　❋　❋

Cardboard Records The cardboard record may be one of the most unusual cereal box toys of them all. You had to cut the record from the back of your favorite cereal box, which meant that you'd have to wait until you finished the cereal inside—if you were patient enough. You could then play these records on a real record player!

In 1954, General Mills offered some of the earliest cardboard records when the company released a series of 78-rpm children's songs that kids had to cut from the backs of Wheaties boxes. Some of the songs included in the series were "Take Me Out to the Ball Game" and "On Top of Old Smokey."

Other favorites include a cardboard record packaged on Alpha Bits with several songs from the Jackson 5, including "I'll Be There" and "Never Can Say Goodbye," and a Monkees record on Honeycomb cereal that included the songs "Pleasant Valley Sunday" and "I'm a Believer."

Vintage Space Adventure In the 1940s, Cheerios offered kids the chance to send away for a Moon Rocket Kit. They only had to mail in a Cheerios box top and a label from a can of V8 vegetable juice. That's right: They wanted kids to drink tomato juice.

The Moon Kit itself came with plastic astronauts, a rocket, and a poster of the moon that boasted different targets. Kids were supposed to shoot the astronauts at the highest-scoring targets.

How Did Texas Hold 'Em Get Its Name?

Tune in to any televised poker tournament, and the game most likely being played is Texas Hold 'Em, a "community" card game where players use any combination of the five face-up "community" cards and their own two "hole" cards to make a poker hand. But where did Texas Hold 'Em come from and get its popularity?

✳   ✳   ✳   ✳

SOME HISTORIANS WAGER that poker originated in China around A.D. 900

when the Chinese developed many gambling games. Others bet it evolved from a German game called *Pochspiel* or the Persian card game *ganjifa*. The Spanish game *primero* is another possibility. Many historians, however, put their money on the idea that it started in France as *poque*. The French brought *poque* to the United States in the 1700s, where it evolved into the many variations played today.

The Lone Star Variation

The Texas State Legislature officially recognizes Robstown as the birthplace of Texas Hold 'Em, which was probably first played there in the late 1890s or early 1900s. As it spread to big cities such as Dallas in the 1920s, the game became popular with cowboys and miners as saloon entertainment. It was sometimes called Devil's River or Styx, which may explain why the final card in Texas Hold 'Em is traditionally called "the river."

The most popular explanation for Hold 'Em is that it was once called "Hold Me Darling" then shortened to "Hold Me" and finally dyslexically changed to "Hold 'Em." "Texas" was added in 1967 when Texas gamblers Crandell Addington, Doyle Brunson, and Amarillo Slim began playing it in Las Vegas.

In 1970, Benny and Jack Binion staged the World Series of Poker at their Horseshoe Casino in Las Vegas and made no-limit Texas Hold 'Em the main event the following year. With the televising of the World Series, it being featured in the movies *Rounders* and *Casino Royale*, and the advent of online gambling, Texas Hold 'Em has become the most popular poker game in the world.

One Determined Detective

Graphic novels have come into their own over the years, receiving accolades for great storylines and artistic merit. They all owe a debt of gratitude to one of the biggest names in the business—Chester Gould, creator of the Dick Tracy universe.

✳   ✳   ✳   ✳

FROM A YOUNG age, Chester Gould dreamed of creating a comic strip for the *Chicago Tribune*. Gould finished his studies at Northwestern and the Art Institute, got a little room on North La Salle Street, and set about getting his foot in the door at the paper.

It took Gould almost 10 years, but the *Tribune* finally liked one of his ideas. The strip that got him the job was a detective story, filled with fast-paced action and colorful characters. Gould named the strip after its protagonist: Dick Tracy.

The strip first appeared on October 4, 1931, in the *Detroit Mirror*, a paper owned by the *Tribune*. The *New York Daily News* soon began running it as well, and finally the *Tribune* ran it too. Before long, the strip, which readers had begun to follow religiously and loved for its gritty subject matter, had become so popular that it appeared on the front page of many papers.

For 46 straight years, Gould created the *Dick Tracy* world. His characters were borderline outrageous (i.e., "The Mole," "Flattop," and "Breathless Mahoney") and his use of fantastic gadgets kept readers' imaginations firing (i.e., the classic "2-Way Wrist Radio"). The character of Tracy went through changes over the years; Gould experienced periods of great success, but times of backlash too (for instance, readership dropped during the "space period," when Gould catapulted Tracy and company into space adventures).

Gould stopped drawing the strip in 1977, but the cult of *Dick Tracy* lives on. There have been various television adaptations of the comic strip, countless comic books, cartoon versions, and several films, as well, so it's still easy to get your fill of the crime fighter with the banana yellow hat and trench coat.

Papa Bear

George S. Halas was one of Chicago's most enduring sports legends and a towering figure in the National Football League. Player, coach, owner, executive, recruiter—he did it all, on his own terms, and better than just about anybody else.

✳   ✳   ✳   ✳

BORN IN CHICAGO in 1895 to an immigrant family, Halas attended the University of Illinois, where he studied engineering and excelled at several sports. After a short stint in the Navy and an even shorter one on the roster of the New York Yankees, he returned to his hometown and resigned himself to a career of building bridges.

In 1920, A. E. Staley, the owner of a large starch manufacturer in Decatur, recruited Halas to coach and manage the company's football team. Halas jumped at the chance. He led the Decatur Staleys to a 13–1 season, and then, at a meeting of other teams in Canton, Ohio, became one of the founders of the American Football Association, which soon changed its name to today's National Football League.

Everyone Else Will Have to Step Aside

Faced with financial difficulties, Staley encouraged Halas to move the Staleys to Chicago, where the large population would offer greater support. Chicago already had two professional teams, the Cardinals and the Tigers, but Halas muscled his way into town anyway and changed the team's name to the Bears.

These early years were difficult for the sport, which had a reputation as being a lowbrow, thuggish game. Even the best-known teams were hard-pressed to draw more than a few thousand spectators to a game. In 1925, Halas helped change all that by making one of the most brilliant promotional moves of his career. He recruited college running sensation Harold "Red" Grange during his senior year at the University of Illinois, then took the Bears on a barnstorming tour across the country, playing 17 games in only a few weeks. The contests in New York City and Los Angeles drew in excess of 70,000 fans, unheard of numbers for football in those days. Thanks in part to Halas's stunt, the sport was well on its way to becoming a staple of American entertainment.

Uncompromising Brilliance

While Halas is remembered for his key role in founding professional football, he is revered in the sports world for the amazing record he compiled over his career. During the Bears' first 25 years, Coach Halas took the league championship six times and endured only one losing season. Three different times he turned the coaching reins over to others, then took them back after a restless year or two on the sidelines. He completed a total of 40 seasons as head coach, earning a league-leading 324 wins by the time he hung up his clipboard and whistle for good at age 73.

Halas was also well-known for his temper and bare-knuckle demeanor. Some say that in the early years, when he didn't like the way the referees had called a game, he would pay them by tossing their salary on the ground at their feet—one dollar at a time.

Tough, uncompromising, and talented, he was the perfect personality for this working-class city and its notoriously bruising football crew. In a testament to how well loved he had been by Chicagoans, after his death in 1983, the Bears modified their uniforms by adding the initials GSH to the left sleeve.

✳ Halas successfully lobbied to have Bears games broadcast on the radio. He was also the first coach to institute the practice of studying films of opponents' previous games.

Chapter 9

Successes and Fumbles

15 Notable People Who Dropped Out of School

Everyone knows how important it is to stay in school, get a good education, and graduate with a diploma. But it may be hard to stay focused after reading about the success of these famous dropouts. Hard work, drive, natural talent, and sheer luck helped them overcome their lack of education, but many still returned to school later in life.

✳   ✳   ✳   ✳

1. Thomas Edison

Thomas Edison is probably the most famous and productive inventor of all time, with more than 1,000 patents in his name, including the electric lightbulb, phonograph, and motion picture camera. He became a self-made multimillionaire and won a Congressional Gold Medal. Edison got a late start in his schooling following an illness, and, as a result, his mind often wandered, prompting one of his teachers to call him "addled." He dropped out after only three months of formal education. Luckily, his mother had been a schoolteacher in Canada and home-schooled young Edison.

2. Benjamin Franklin

Benjamin Franklin wore many hats: politician, diplomat, author, printer, publisher, scientist, inventor, founding father, and both coauthor and cosigner of the Declaration of Independence. One thing he was not was a high school graduate. Franklin was the fifteenth child and youngest son in a family of 20. He spent two years at the Boston Latin School before dropping out at age ten and going to work for his father, and then his brother, as a printer.

3. Bill Gates
Bill Gates is a cofounder of the software giant Microsoft and has been ranked the richest person in the world for a number of years. Gates dropped out of Harvard in his junior year after reading an article about the Altair microcomputer in *Popular Electronics* magazine. He and his friend Paul Allen formed Micro Soft (later changed to Microsoft) to write software for the Altair.

4. Albert Einstein
Although he was named *Time* magazine's "Man of the Century," Albert Einstein was not an "Einstein" in school. The Nobel Prize-winning physicist, famous for his theory of relativity and contributions to quantum theory and statistical mechanics, dropped out of high school at age 15. Deciding to continue his education a year later, Einstein took the entrance exam to the prestigious Swiss Federal Institute of Technology, but failed. He returned to high school, got his diploma, and then passed the university's entrance exam on his second attempt.

5. John D. Rockefeller
Two months before his high school graduation, history's first recorded billionaire, John D. Rockefeller, Sr., dropped out to take business courses at Folsom Mercantile College. He founded the Standard Oil Company in 1870, made his billions before the company was broken up by the government for being a monopoly, and spent his last 40 years giving away his riches, primarily to causes related to health and education. Ironically, this high school dropout helped millions get a good education.

6. Walt Disney

In 1918, while still in high school, future Oscar-winning film producer and theme park pioneer Walt Disney began taking night courses at the Academy of Fine Arts in Chicago. Disney dropped out of high school at age 16 to join the army, but because he was too young to enlist, he joined the Red Cross with a forged birth certificate instead. Disney was sent to France where he drove an ambulance that was covered from top to bottom with cartoons that eventually became his film characters. After becoming the multimillionaire founder of The Walt Disney Company and winning the Presidential Medal of Freedom, Disney received an honorary high school diploma at age 58.

7. Richard Branson

Britain's Sir Richard Branson is a self-made billionaire businessman. He founded Virgin Atlantic Airways, Virgin Records, Virgin Mobile, and most recently, a space tourism company to provide suborbital trips into space for anyone who can afford them. Suffering from dyslexia, Branson was a poor student, so he quit school at age 16 and moved to London, where he began his first successful entrepreneurial activity, publishing Student magazine.

8. George Burns

George Burns, born Nathan Birnbaum, was a successful vaudeville, TV, and movie comedian for nearly nine decades. After his father's death, Burns left school in the fourth grade to go to work shining shoes, running errands, and selling newspapers. While employed at a local candy shop, Burns and his young coworkers decided to go into show business as the Peewee Quartet.

After the group broke up, Burns continued to work with a partner, usually a girl, and was the funny one in the group until he met Gracie Allen in 1923. Burns and Allen got married, but didn't become stars until George flipped the act and made Gracie the funny one. They continued to work together in vaudeville, radio, television, and movies until Gracie retired in 1958. Burns continued performing almost until the day he died in 1996.

9. Colonel Sanders

Colonel Harland Sanders overcame his lack of education to become the biggest drumstick in the fried chicken business. His father died when he was six years old, and since his mother worked, he was forced to cook for his family. After dropping out of elementary school, Sanders worked many jobs, including firefighter, steamboat driver, and insurance salesman. He later earned a law degree from a correspondence school. Sanders' cooking and business experience helped him make millions as the founder of Kentucky Fried Chicken (now KFC).

10. Charles Dickens

Charles Dickens, author of numerous classics including *Oliver Twist*, *A Tale of Two Cities*, and *A Christmas Carol*, attended elementary school until his life took a twist of its own when his father was imprisoned for debt. At age 12, he left school and began working ten-hour days in a boot-blacking factory. Dickens later worked as a law clerk and a court stenographer. At age 22, he became a journalist, reporting parliamentary debate and covering election campaigns for a newspaper. His first collection of stories, *Sketches by Boz* (Boz was his nickname), were published in 1836 and led to his first novel, *The Pickwick Papers*.

11. Elton John

Born Reginald Kenneth Dwight, Rock and Roll Hall of Fame member Sir Elton John has sold more than 250 million records and has more than 50 Top 40 hits, making him one of the most successful musicians of all time. At age 11, Elton entered London's Royal Academy of Music on a piano scholarship. Bored with classical compositions, Elton preferred rock 'n' roll and after five years he quit school to become a weekend pianist at a local pub. At 17, he formed a band called Bluesology, and, by the mid-1960s, they were touring with soul and R&B musicians such as The Isley Brothers and Patti LaBelle and The Bluebelles.

The album *Elton John* was released in the spring of 1970 and, after the first single "Your Song" made the U.S. Top Ten, Elton was on his way to superstardom.

12. Ray Kroc
Ray Kroc didn't found McDonald's, but he turned it into the world's largest fast-food chain after purchasing the original location from Dick and Mac McDonald. Kroc amassed a $500 million fortune during his lifetime, and in 2000 was included in *Time* magazine's list of the 100 most influential builders and titans of industry in the 20th century. During World War I, Kroc dropped out of high school at age 15 and lied about his age to become a Red Cross ambulance driver, but the war ended before he was sent overseas.

13. Harry Houdini
The name Houdini is synonymous with magic. Before becoming a world-renowned magician and escape artist named Harry Houdini, Ehrich Weiss dropped out of school at age 12, working several jobs, including locksmith's apprentice. At 17, he teamed up with fellow magic enthusiast Jack Hayman to form the Houdini Brothers, named after Jean Eugène Robert Houdin, the most famous magician of the era. By age 24, Houdini had come up with the Challenge Act, offering to escape from any pair of handcuffs produced by the audience. The Challenge Act was the turning point for Houdini. With its success came the development of the spectacular escapes that would make him a legend.

14. Ringo Starr
Richard Starkey is better known as Ringo Starr, the drummer of The Beatles. Born in Liverpool in 1940, Ringo suffered two serious illnesses at age six. First, his appendix ruptured, leaving him in a coma for ten weeks. After six months in recovery, he fell out of the hospital bed, necessitating an additional six-month hospital stay. After spending a total of three years in a hospital, he was considerably behind in school. He dropped out after his last visit to the hospital at age 15, barely able to read or write. While

working at an engineering firm, 17-year-old Starkey joined
a band and taught himself to play the drums. His stepfather
bought him his first real drum set, and Ringo sat in with a variety
of bands, eventually joining Rory Storm and The Hurricanes.
He changed his name to Ringo Starr, joined The Beatles in 1962,
and is now one of the best-known drummers in history.

15. Princess Diana

The late Diana Spencer, Princess of Wales, attended West Heath
Girls' School where she was regarded as an academically below-
average student, having failed all of her O-level examinations
(exams given to 16-year-old students in the UK to determine
their education level). At age 16, she left West Heath and briefly
attended a finishing school in Switzerland before dropping out
from there as well. Diana was a talented amateur singer and
reportedly longed to be a ballerina. Diana went to work as a
part-time assistant at the Young England Kindergarten, a day
care center and nursery school. Contrary to claims, she was not a
kindergarten teacher since she had no educational qualifications
to teach, and Young England was not a kindergarten, despite
its name. In 1981, at age 19, Diana became engaged to Prince
Charles and her working days were over.

Sinking Car

*Thousands of drivers accidentally steer themselves into lakes or
rivers every year. Most cars take only a few minutes to submerge.
Would you know how to get out alive? If you know how to handle
the situation, the disaster doesn't have to turn deadly.*

✳ Stay calm and unbuckle

The first rule of thumb is never panic. Remain calm, unfasten
your seatbelt, and get ready to exit the vehicle.

✳ Roll down the window

Don't wait: Roll down your driver-side window as quickly
as you can. Even electric windows will open if you try soon

enough. If it doesn't work, you'll have to smash the glass. A heavy object is your best bet, but you can try to kick out the window with your feet, too. (Take an easy precaution and leave a screwdriver or hammer inside your glove box, just in case.) Aim for the bottom or corner edge of the window. Whatever you do, don't try to open the door—there's too much pressure from the water outside.

* Work your way out

Take a deep breath and force yourself out through the open space. Then start swimming upward.

* If the window won't open

If you can't get the window open or broken, your only option is to wait until your car has almost been overtaken with water. Climb into the back seat, as it'll be the last to fill up. Unlock the door right away so you don't forget. Then, once the water is as high as your neck, push the door open—once the water is inside the car, there should be enough pressure for the door to give without much trouble. As soon as it opens, swim as fast as you can out of the vehicle and toward the surface.

A Mighty Enterprise

The USS Enterprise *had a humble wartime start, but went on to launch the Doolittle raid on Tokyo, serve as flagship in the pivotal battle of Midway, set a record for continuous combat, survive multiple kamikaze attacks—and emerge as the most decorated ship of the war.*

* * * *

ODD FOR A great fighting ship, the USS *Enterprise* was financed in part by a public-welfare program. In summer 1933, at the worst of the Great Depression, President Roosevelt signed New Deal legislation that authorized $40 million for the construction of two new carriers. As part of this program for defense and jobs, the keels of *Enterprise* and sister ship the USS *Yorktown* were laid the following year at Newport News, Virginia. In 1936, the *Enterprise* was christened as the seventh U.S. ship to bear that name. Her skipper, Captain Charles Pownall, started a lasting precedent of keeping the ship in the highest readiness.

A Near Miss at Pearl

On December 7, 1941, the *Enterprise* was supposed to be in Pearl Harbor. For weeks the more than 800-foot-long aircraft carrier had been ferrying planes and pilots to Guam and Wake Island as part of a buildup to counter possible Japanese aggression. Stalled by rough weather, the *Enterprise's* return was delayed. That fateful morning, she was still about 150 miles west of Pearl Harbor. Her radio operators listened in horror as *Enterprise* flyer Manuel Gonzales tried to land at Fort Island's naval air station. "Please don't shoot! . . . This is an American plane!" he screamed. Then he was heard telling air crewman Leo Kozelek to bail out. Both died. The 19,800-ton ship spent the next two days searching futilely for the retreating Imperial fleet in the waters southwest of Hawaii. When the *Enterprise* slipped into Pearl Harbor at sunset on December 8, surviving sailors called out, "Where in hell were you?" and "Get the hell out of here or they'll nail you too!" Under the wavering light of still-smoldering ships, the crew frantically took on fuel and, by dawn, returned to the protection of the open ocean.

1942

With the war's start, the *Enterprise* began a remarkable 20-month run of critical objectives. In April 1942 it served as Vice Admiral William "Bull" Halsey's command ship on a daring mission. Accompanied by the carrier USS *Hornet*, *Enterprise* steamed with-in 700 miles of Japan. The *Hornet* launched Lieutenant Colonel James Doolittle's 16 medium B-25Bs for their surprise raids on Tokyo, Osaka, Kobe, Nagoya, and Yokohama.

On June 4–6, the *Enterprise, Hornet,* and *Yorktown* were the carriers in the Pacific war's turning point, the Battle of Midway. During it, the "Big E" served as flagship for fleet commander Vice Admiral Raymond Spruance. The carrier's air group commander, Wade McClusky, according to Admiral Chester Nimitz, "decided the fate of our carrier task force and our forces at Midway." While scouting for the Japanese, McClusky later explained, a "stroke of luck met our eyes. Both enemy carriers had their decks full of planes which had just returned from the attack on Midway." Caught by surprise, the Japanese carriers *Kaga* and *Akagi* were sunk, along with flattops *Hiryu* and *Sorya*, shortening Japanese Fleet Admiral Isoroku Yamamoto's post-Pearl Harbor dream of "a year to run wild."

In October, the *Enterprise* and *Hornet,* with the support of one battleship and six cruisers, went against Japan's four carriers, eight cruisers, and four battleships in the Battle of Santa Cruz. The U.S. forces killed 400 enemy aircrew members and lost 44 of their own crew. In November, during the Naval Battle of Guadalcanal, the *Enterprise* was instrumental in thwarting the Japanese effort to reinforce Imperial forces on Guadalcanal, leading to the Marines' successful defense of that vital island. From October 26 through December, as its five fellow carriers had been sunk or damaged, the *Enterprise* was the only U.S. carrier operating in the Pacific. Its hangar boasted a sign, "Enterprise vs. Japan."

The ship's Yorktown-class design was key to its considerable success. Capable of 32.5 knots and more maneuverable than its predecessors the USS *Saratoga* and *Lexington,* the *Enterprise* could dodge enemy attacks. If a torpedo or bomb did strike, its hundreds of watertight compartments limited the damage.

1943

In the midst of other missions, the "Galloping Ghost" was accorded the first Presidential Unit Citation given an aircraft carrier in May 1943. In July, the ship returned to the States, berthing at the Bremerton, Washington, navy yard. The weary crew took 30-day shore leaves while the *Enterprise* underwent major repair and retrofitting.

"Engineers, welders, steamfitters, metalworkers, and mechanists of Bremerton Navy Yard swarmed over the ship," according to the USS *Enterprise* CV-6 Association, installing 90 new and replacement radar-controlled 20- and 40-mm Bofors antiaircraft guns, a protective torpedo "blister" around most of the hull, and a wider, longer flight deck.

1944

The revamped *Enterprise* left the States on November 19, not to return for 560 days. In January 1944, the Big E's aircraft bombed the Marshall Islands. In February, while raiding Truk, Japan's major base in the mid-Pacific, the *Enterprise* set a new mark for the quantity of bombs delivered in one day.

In June during the invasion of the Marianas Islands, it assailed Japan's carriers in the Battle of the Philippine Sea, ending the Imperial fleet's ability to use carrier planes effectively. *Enterprise* narrowly avoided serious harm during the battle when a torpedo exploded in its churning wake.

After wide-ranging raids on Japanese bases in the Philippines and Formosa (now Taiwan), in December it was back to drydock at Pearl Harbor. There the ship was transformed into a night carrier. Deck lighting was installed, maintenance crews were carefully retrained, and radars were placed on the larger planes. It became the first flattop to conduct 24/7 warfare, including regular night missions. But those missions were "sheer terror," recalled crewman Joe Hranek. "I was never sure where we were until [a returning pilot] cut the engine and the deck lights suddenly appeared."

1945

In 1945, even as the war seemed won, *Enterprise* underwent its most dangerous missions. The carriers *Saratoga* and USS

Independence joined its Night Air Group 90. The *Enterprise* attacked Japanese aerodromes, ports, and radar stations in Indochina and South China and, on February 16–17, Tokyo. Two days later it supported the Marines' invasion of Iwo Jima. There, the Big E spent 174 straight hours in combat, setting the record for continuous air-sea combat. After a storm forced a respite, the ship conducted operations for seven more consecutive days.

The carrier's run of luck began to dry up in March during raids on air bases in the Japanese home islands of Shikoku and Kyushu, part of the run-up to the invasion of Okinawa. On March 20, while under attack by Japanese bombers, two 5-inch shells from an escort ship missed the planes—and hit the *Enterprise*, igniting 40- and 20-mm shells, killing seven.

After ten days of repairs, the carrier steamed to Okinawa, where in April two kamikaze planes missed it by yards but exploded close enough to wrench its hull, wounding 18. After three weeks of repairs, it again bombed Kyushu.

During the war, 1 of every 14 kamikazes hit their targets. On May 14, one finally penetrated the wall of lead thrown up by the escorts, the fighters on combat air patrol, and the carrier's own radar-controlled guns. The plane crashed into the deck next to the forward elevator and threw the 30,000-pound lift 133 yards into the air. Twelve were killed, 72 wounded.

The "Galloping Ghost" kept fighting until May 16, then sailed across the Pacific to Bremerton for its last overhaul. The war ended while it was in dry-dock.

The *Enterprise*, stated Secretary of the Navy James Forrestal, was "the one ship that most nearly symbolizes the history of the U.S. Navy in World War II."

8 Automotive Lemons

Automakers aim for excellence with every new car they introduce, but sometimes things don't pan out as planned. The following is a sampling of automobiles that were branded "lemons."

❈   ❈   ❈   ❈

1. **1958–1960 Edsel:** Perhaps the most famous automotive flop, the Edsel wasn't a truly bad car. From an engineering standpoint, it was in step with most other brands of the late 1950s. Unfortunately, its wide-at-the-top, narrow-at-the-bottom vertical grille resembled a collar used to harness draft horses, giving it a controversial look. It also had the misfortune of hitting the market in September 1957 as an economic recession was brewing, slowing down sales of medium-priced cars. Then, too, promotion for the Edsel made it sound as if the car would revolutionize the industry when, mechanically, it really wasn't much different from other Fords and Mercurys. Ford stopped producing Edsels in November 1959.

2. **1962 Plymouth and Dodge:** About 15 years before "downsizing" became the rage in Detroit, Chrysler tried it on its two lowest-priced makes. Unfortunately, this was still the era of "bigger is better." Chrysler exec William Newberg erroneously believed Chevrolet was going smaller for 1962 and ordered chief stylist Virgil Exner to trim the size of the '62 Plymouths and Dodges under development. However, scaling them down from the bigger cars they were intended to be ruined their proportions, and Exner was fired when the cars flopped.

3. **1975–1980 AMC Pacer:** Had this disco-era compact come with the smooth, lightweight, GM-built rotary engine that was planned, perhaps the Pacer hatchback's styling would have seemed appropriately adventurous. But with a conventional powertrain, the Pacer was just plain odd. "America's

first wide small car" ran a six-cylinder engine—and briefly a V8—after GM canceled its rotary program when the engine wouldn't meet emissions and fuel-mileage targets. It was roomy inside, but with its rounded body, large windows, hatchback, and no discernible trunk, the Pacer resembled a "fishbowl on wheels," making it the butt of many jokes.

4. **1981–1982 DeLorean DMC-12:** When flamboyant John Z. DeLorean left General Motors in 1973, he did so intending to start a company to build an "ethical" sports car. He wound up with a movie prop and a world of financial trouble. The car was famous for its stainless-steel body and gull-wing doors—hinged at the top rather than the sides, resembling a gull in flight when open. Moviegoers remember it from *Back to the Future*. But poor quality control and tepid performance from its Renault-supplied V6 engine quickly tarnished its sexy image.

5. **1986–1991 Yugo GV:** The Yugo originated from a plant that had been making Fiat-based cars since 1954. The GV, which reached America in mid-1985, was billed as the cheapest car on the market with a starting price of $3,990, compared to $5,340 for a Chevrolet Chevette, the lowest starting price for a domestic car. Soon owners figured out the reasons why: little power, shoddy quality and reliability, and scary crashworthiness. The little hatchback was later joined by a convertible, but bankruptcy in the United States and civil strife back home in a disintegrating Yugoslavia ended things.

6. **1996–1998 Suzuki X-90:** This little two-seater tried to make a sports car out of the Suzuki Sidekick. But the X-90 would have looked more at home in a circus, disgorging a steady stream of clowns. The compact SUV had a petite 86.6-inch wheelbase and a 95-horsepower four-cylinder engine. Noisy at highway speeds, the X-90 also had

a bouncy ride, minimal cargo space, and tiny radio buttons that were nearly impossible to use in the dark.

7. 1996–2003 General Motors EV1: After talk of alternatives to the petroleum internal-combustion engine started gaining momentum in the 1980s, General Motors plugged in to the pursuit of electric technology. The EV1 was the result, and it was leased through certain Saturn dealers. However, it was a two-seat economy car with a luxury-car price, and it had limited range before it needed to be charged. (Range was severely limited in colder climates, which made the EV1 even more impractical in those areas.) Some lessees wanted to buy their EV1s, but GM, wary of future liability concerns, wouldn't sell.

8. 2001–2005 Pontiac Aztek: This was Pontiac's first stab at a "crossover" vehicle, a mix of car and sport-utility vehicle that was a new market segment at the beginning of the 21st century. Derived from Pontiac's Montana minivan platform, the Aztek suffered from incoherent, angular styling that was roundly criticized. From the rear, it looked tall, narrow, and ungainly. Off-road capability was limited in all-wheel-drive models, and interior materials and finish left something to be desired.

Prolific Producers

These "movers and shakers" are responsible for more than their fair share of the world's greatest accomplishments.

✳　✳　✳　✳

✳ If fruitful production can be traced to its very roots, **Mrs. Feodor Vassilyev** has no equal. Between 1725 and 1765, the peasant from Shuya, Russia, gave birth to a whopping 69 children. Her pregnancies included 16 sets of twins, 7 sets of triplets, and 4 sets of quadruplets—but interestingly, no single births.

✳ If asked which country hosts the largest diamond mine, many will guess South Africa. They will, in fact, be wrong. With an average annual production (since 1994) of more than 35 million carats, Australia's **Argyle Diamond Mine** is the world's largest single producer of diamonds.

✳ World War I ace **Baron von Richthofen** (the infamous Red Baron) has nothing at all on World War II super-ace **Erich Hartmann.** The German pilot, dubbed the "Black Devil" by his enemies, is credited with 352 "kills," making him the all-time "ace of aces."

✳ Unlike the textbook definition of a prolific inventor, **Johannes Gutenberg's** gift to the world was singular, but it kept giving and giving and giving, much like a philanthropic Energizer Bunny. Fact is you wouldn't be reading this right now had Gutenberg not first invented a practical means with which to duplicate print. That breakthrough came in 1440 with the metal "movable type" printing press, a device that made the laborious handwritten manuscript obsolete and consequently made modern book publishing possible. For his amazing invention that begat immeasurable off-spring, Gutenberg is credited with bringing the Middle Ages into the Renaissance.

✳ With more than 300 inventions to his credit, **George Westinghouse** (best known for his Westinghouse brand of home appliances) helped take our world from a quaint, low-tech environment into an anything-is-possible wonder-land brimming with modernity. Breakthroughs such as the air brake and rotary steam engine owe their existence to the visionary from Central Bridge, New York, and alternating current (AC) underscores Westinghouse's genius each and every time a light switch is flicked on. "If someday they say of me that in my work I have contributed something to the welfare and happiness of my fellow men, I shall be satisfied," exclaimed the prolific inventor when asked of his legacy.

11 Design Innovations of Harley Earl

Harley Earl, generally considered the father of American automotive design, was born in Los Angeles, California, in 1893. In the late 1920s, Earl's design talent caught the eye of General Motors Chairman Alfred Sloan, who offered him a position directing the styling of all GM car lines.

Earl accepted, moved to Detroit, and soon wielded unprecedented control over GM's new product development. During Earl's 31-year career with the company, General Motors reigned supreme as an industry leader. Under his direction, designers and stylists pioneered countless innovations, such as the following, which propelled the company to the forefront of automotive design.

❋　❋　❋　❋

1. **The Auto-Styling Studio:** Prior to Earl's arrival in Detroit, cars were designed almost entirely by engineers who often showed little talent for attractive, cohesive forms. The Art and Colour Section (which Earl later renamed Styling) changed all that. GM's new division revolutionized the auto industry, and rival manufacturers soon developed styling studios of their own. A car's appearance became just as important as its mechanicals in Detroit's new product development process.

2. **The Wraparound Windshield:** The groundbreaking 1951 LeSabre concept car boasted an innovative new windshield design in which the glass curved sharply at the ends to meet the windshield pillars. This gave a futuristic look and a panoramic view. The design soon saw production on the 1953 Cadillac Eldorado and the 1953 Oldsmobile Fiesta and quickly became *de rigueur* on most American cars in the 1950s.

3. Model-Line Hierarchy: One of GM Chairman Alfred Sloan's great innovations was a model-line hierarchy of increasing price and status. The idea was that General Motors would have an appropriate product for consumers at each level of the automotive marketplace, and consumers would aspire to the next rung up the GM product ladder. Harley Earl's work dovetailed perfectly with this strategy, as he designed a natural progression of increasing style and prestige into Chevrolets, Pontiacs, Oldsmobiles, Buicks, and Cadillacs.

4. The Dream Car: Earl popularized the idea of the "dream car" or concept car, a one-off, non-production vehicle built for auto-show display. Earl's dazzling, futuristic dream cars forecast tomorrow's styling innovations and whet the car-hungry public's appetite for the "next big thing" in automotive design. Public reaction to the new designs was also used to gauge the popularity of future production models. Earl's 1938 Buick "Y-Job" was the first full-fledged dream car.

5. Clay Modeling: Even before he arrived at General Motors, Earl was a pioneer in the concept of taking a design from a two-dimensional drawing to a three-dimensional form by producing clay models of his creations. The use of clay as a modeling tool greatly simplified and sped up the design process by allowing designers to visualize shapes and forms that were difficult and time-consuming to create in steel.

6. Dagmars: Among the 1951 LeSabre dream car's many design innovations were large, bullet-shaped bumper guards. These protrusions, which were nicknamed "Dagmars" after a buxom TV personality of the day, became standard styling flourishes on 1950s Cadillacs.

7. The Chevrolet Corvette: Harley Earl put more than 45,000 miles on the LeSabre show car, using it as his personal car and driving it to automotive events. In September

1951, Earl took the LeSabre to a sports car race at Watkins Glen, New York. Seeing the passion these enthusiasts had for their cars, most of which were imported, Earl decided America needed an affordable sports car of its own. The Corvette debuted at the New York Motorama in January 1953, and the rest is history.

8. **Integrated Body Design:** When Harley Earl first started out in automotive design, cars were a hodgepodge of disparate parts. Earl visualized a car as a cohesive whole and designed individual components so they would harmonize with the overall design of the car.

9. **Tailfins:** Earl was infatuated with aircraft design motifs and loved incorporating them into automotive designs. In particular, the twin-boom tail of the Lockheed P-38 Lightning caught his eye. The 1948 Cadillac was the first production car to receive these ornamental appendages, which sparked a trend that culminated in the skyrocketing fins of the 1959 Cadillac. Tailfins became more subdued each year and had mostly disappeared by the mid-1960s.

10. **Copious Chrome:** Chrome trim was a simple way to add visual pizzazz to cars, and Harley Earl was a master at effectively using this automotive bling. However, he eventually took the "more is better" approach, and by 1958, GM designers had gone overboard, piling on the brightwork until cars looked like gaudy, chrome-encrusted chariots. Detroit began toning down the chrome soon after.

11. **Rear-Mounted Television Cameras:** Earl loved automotive gadgetry. In place of rearview mirrors, the 1956 Buick Centurion show car boasted a functional TV camera that transmitted the rear view to a small screen on the dashboard. Rearview cameras that supplement rearview mirrors began showing up on SUVs and large luxury cars in the early 2000s. Earl was definitely ahead of his time.

Major Miscues

What's that they say about life? Oh yeah, that it's not fair. Well, baseball legacies aren't always fair either. Consider Fred Merkle, Mickey Owen, and Bill Buckner, for example. All were above-average players, at times All-Star caliber performers, who were assets to pennant-contending teams. Sadly, this was not to be their legacy in the game. A bonehead play, a passed ball, a missed grounder. Big blunders in baseball are hard to forget.

* * * *

Merkle's Boner

September 1908. With the pennant on the line in a crucial late-season game against the Chicago Cubs, Al Bridwell of the New York Giants swatted an apparent game-winning two-out RBI single in the bottom of the ninth. Rookie Fred Merkle was the runner at first. When Moose McCormick scooted home from third to score, according to major-league rules all Merkle had to do was advance to second base and touch the bag in order for the run to officially count. When young Merkle failed to do so and instead started to run toward the clubhouse in center field, Cubs second baseman Johnny Evers frantically called for the ball to force him out. The Giants' coach, Joe McGinnity, wrestled the ball away from him, even going so far as to throw it into the stands, but Evers retrieved it and touched second base.

Oddly, this wasn't the first time this had happened. It wasn't even the first time Evers had been involved in such a play. Just two weeks prior, umpire Hank O'Day had turned down a similar appeal by Evers, in part because O'Day had already left the field and hadn't seen the second baseman touch the bag. Furthermore, umpires of the day rarely enforced the rule that stipulates each runner must advance to the next base on a game-winning play with two outs. This time, O'Day came up with a different decision, though he did not announce it right away. Well after thousands of fans had poured onto the field and most of the players had made their way back to the club-house, he called Merkle out, negating the run. Either on the field or later that night—it's not clear which—O'Day declared the game a tie.

Amid a sea of confusion, and with countless fans scattered over the field, O'Day and his umpiring partner left the field. Enraged by O'Day's decision, the Giants filed a protest but were turned down by National League president Harry Pulliam.

This tie game meant all the difference to the two teams, who finished the regular season in a flat-footed deadlock. It came down to a tie-breaking game on October 8 to decide the pennant. The Giants lost 4–2, and even though Merkle didn't even play in that deciding game, his name became forever linked with the infamous "Merkle's Boner"—no matter that he went on to become an excellent defensive first baseman and a respectable hitter.

Owen's Passed Ball

October 1941. Thirty-three years after Merkle's Boner, a normally sure-handed catcher let down the Brooklyn Dodgers at the worst possible moment. With Brooklyn trailing the Yankees two games to one in the World Series and clinging to a 4–3 lead in the ninth inning of Game 4, All-Star catcher Mickey Owen failed to catch what should have been a game-ending third strike to Tommy Henrich, who swung and missed. As the ball glanced off Owen's glove and squirted away toward the Brooklyn dugout, Henrich raced to first, igniting a four-run rally for the Yankees that earned them a miraculous 7–4 victory. Now up three games to one and with momentum on their side, the Yankees beat Owen's Dodgers the next day to wrap up the World Series.

"It was all my fault," said Owen in a report filed the next day in *The New York Times*. "It wasn't a strike. It was a great breaking curve that I should have had. But I guess the ball hit the side of my glove."

Ironically, earlier in the season Owen had set the NL record for catchers with 476 consecutive errorless chances accepted, also setting a Dodger record with a season-high .995 fielding percentage. Despite these achievements, and his election to the All-Star team in each of the next three years, he would never live down his blunder of 1941. That single play, rather than Owen's defensive excellence over time, would remain firmly embedded in the memories of Brooklyn fans and in the annals of baseball.

Between Buckner's Legs

October 1986. Call it "The Curse of the Bambino," if you will. With the Red Sox leading Game 6 of the World Series by two runs, the New York Mets found themselves with no one on base and two out in the bottom of the tenth, on the verge of elimination. As Red Sox fans jubilantly began to prepare for postgame parties, the Mets suddenly strung together three consecutive singles, bringing them within a run and putting the tying run on third base.

Mookie Wilson stepped up to the plate, and Sox reliever Bob Stanley threw a wild pitch that eluded catcher Rich Gedman, allowing Kevin Mitchell to score and Ray Knight to advance to second. With the game tied, Wilson then chopped a bouncer down the first base line. As Boston fans watched helplessly, and Mets fans looked on with mounting joy, the ball skipped between Bill Buckner's legs and slid down the right-field line. It's debatable whether Buckner would have had a play on the speedy Wilson, but the error made no doubt about the outcome, allowing the winning run to score from second base and handing the Red Sox yet another defeat in their quest for a world title.

After the game, Red Sox manager John McNamara faced a barrage of questions regarding his decision not to replace the aging and hobbled Buckner with utilityman Dave Stapleton as a defensive caddy. It was a maneuver McNamara had used throughout the season, but one he decided to forgo because he wanted Buckner on the field to celebrate the world championship. Alas, it was Buckner's error that ensured there would be no Red Sox celebration. The Mets took Game 7 as well, overcoming a three-run deficit to win the game and the Series. And Buckner, who otherwise would have been recalled as a gritty and skilled .289 lifetime hitter, would forever be linked in infamy with a World Series collapse.

Dusty Rhodes: One-Year Wonder

Most of Dusty Rhodes's baseball career embodied mediocrity. Yet in 1954, he was the toast of the town—and a pitcher's worst nightmare.

✳   ✳   ✳   ✳

JAMES LAMAR RHODES of Mathews, Alabama, was a substitute outfielder. A career Giant (1952–59), he hit an underwhelming .253 during that time. His field play and throwing arm were comically bad. He stole only three bases. This devoted bourbon enthusiast often stayed out late to fully enjoy his intoxicating hobby. Disregarding 1954, Dusty's lifetime stats were even worse: .238, with only 240 career base hits. A handful of players have exceeded that *in one season.*

What Happened in '54?

In 1954 the United States test-fired its first H-bomb, and Dusty—well, Dusty went nuts. Maybe it was radiation, or maybe he was upset because Joe DiMaggio married Marilyn Monroe. Whatever, Rhodes hit .341 with 15 homers and put together a Ruthian .695 slugging average. When Giants manager Leo Durocher looked down the bench for a pinch hitter, most of the guys would look away. Dusty would be loosening up with a bat, saying: "Ah'm your man, Skip."

In the World Series, it got ridiculous. Dusty hit .667 with seven RBI. He won Game 1 in extra innings with a pinch homer. He tied Game 2 with a pinch hit, stayed in, and hit another homer. In Game 3, Dusty singled in two runs with the bases loaded and had six at-bats, four hits, and two homers. The Giants swept Cleveland, and Dusty manned the broom. He won the Babe Ruth Award for best Series performance.

In 1955 Rhodes hit a sweet .305 in 187 plate appearances, but by '56 he was regular Dusty again, hitting an anemic .217 in 244 at-bats.

8 Memorable Ad Campaigns

Some commercial messages last only for the 30 seconds that they exist in real time, while others linger with us for decades. Here are some amusing ads that have stood the test of time.

✳ ✳ ✳ ✳

1. **Coca-Cola: "The pause that refreshes" (1929):** With the advent of the Great Depression, corporate America worried that sales would suffer. Not so with Coca-Cola, whose ads depicted carefree people and an idealized view of American life when real life was rather dreary. During the first year of the campaign, sales actually doubled! The economy may have been depressed, but "the pause that refreshes" appears to have been just what Americans needed to lift their spirits.

2. **Clairol: "Does she . . . or doesn't she?" (1956):** ". . . Only her hairdresser knows for sure." When there's only one female employee in the copywriting department, you give her a shot at the product geared toward women. Shirley Polykoff, who coined the phrase that jump-started the home hair-coloring industry, felt that a woman had the right to change her hair color without everybody knowing about it. The campaign lasted for 15 years, and Clairol's sales increased by 413 percent in the first six years!

3. **Volkswagen: "Think Small" (1959):** In 1959, art director Helmut Krone and copywriter Julian Koenig came up with this "less is more" message geared toward car buyers. Like the VW Beetle, the ads were simple and uncluttered, featuring photos of the car against a plain background. Can you sell a car with a headline that reads "Lemon"? Sure! In the ad, Volkswagen was pointing out that the car in the photo didn't make it off the assembly line because one of the many inspectors found a blemish. "We pluck the lemons; you get the plums," was the slogan.

4. **McDonald's: "You deserve a break today" (1971):** In 1970, Needham, Harper & Steers successfully pitched an upbeat, catchy melody to McDonald's, but they struggled with the lyrics. Noticing that the word break continuously surfaced in focus groups, copywriter Keith Reinhard finally wrote the perfect lyrics for the jingle. Within the next few years, global sales jumped from $587 million to $1.9 billion. The song was named the top jingle of the 20th century by Advertising Age.

5. **Miller Lite Beer: "Tastes great, less filling" (1974):** This campaign peppered with ex-jocks contained more than 200 commercials, and its lively debate entertained sports fans for nearly two decades. Is Miller Lite good because of the taste or because you can drink a ton of it and still have room for nachos? During the first five years of the campaign, sales of Miller Lite took off from just under 7 million barrels a year to more than 31 million barrels, breaking the all-time record for beer makers. A guy's gotta be full after that!

6. **Federal Express: "Fast Talker" (1982):** These memorable ads are breathtaking... literally, you might gasp for air when watching the TV spots. When writer Patrick Kelly and art director Mike Tesch discovered John Moscitta, Jr., who could speak more than 500 words a minute, they knew

he would be perfect for ads for the overnight delivery service. When director Joe Sedelmaier put his quirky spin on the concept, the spots were discussed around watercoolers across the country.

7. **Apple Computer: "1984" (1984):** This is the TV spot that made the Super Bowl about more than just football. Based on George Orwell's book *1984*, the commercial pitted the new Macintosh computer against the totalitarian control of Big Brother and the Thought Police (represented by other computer companies). Depicting an apocalyptic view of the future, the ad opened with a zombielike crowd fixated on a huge screen, then an Amazon woman entered and hurled a hammer into the screen, shattering it. The ad's creators, Lee Clow and Steve Hayden, won every advertising award that year for this venerable commercial.

8. **Nike: "Just Do It" (1988):** When ad exec Dan Wieden met with a group of Nike employees to talk about a new ad campaign, he told them, "You Nike guys . . . you just do it." The result was one of the most effective taglines in advertising history. During the first ten years of this award-winning campaign, Nike's percent of the sport shoe market shot up from 18 to 43 percent.

Reasons to Lose the Remote

9 Famous TV Flops

Everyone loved Lucy, and most even loved Raymond, but much of TV heaven is littered with the carcasses of shows that looked great on the drawing board but flopped miserably on the small screen. Check out this list of some memorable flops.

✳ ✳ ✳ ✳

1. **Supertrain:** If you can find romance on *The Love Boat*, why not on a train? The show *Supertrain* was filled with reasons

why not, derailing after airing on NBC from February to May 1979. Actors such as Tony Danza, Vicki Lawrence, and Joyce DeWitt hopped onboard the *Supertrain* to cavort in an Olympic-size swimming pool, gym, and discotheque while traveling more than 200 miles per hour. The original million-dollar, large-scale model electric train set with cameras attached crashed during its first demonstration, but nobody at the network saw this as a bad sign. The show suffered from poor reviews and low ratings, and the high production costs combined with the U.S. boycott of the 1980 Summer Olympics (which cost NBC millions in ad revenue), nearly bankrupted the network.

2. **Pink Lady and Jeff:** *Pink Lady and Jeff* aired for six weeks in 1980 and made network executives see red. The show combined musical numbers by a Japanese female singing duo called Pink Lady and sketch comedy starring comedian Jeff Altman. The show was produced by Sid and Marty Krofft, famous for creating the landmark children's series *H. R. Pufnstuf* and *The Donny and Marie Show*, and special guests included Sid Caeser, Sherman Hemsley, Blondie, and Jim Varney. The girls knew very little English and had to learn their song lyrics and lines phonetically, one reason why critics said *sayonara*.

3. **The Chevy Chase Show:** Chevy Chase, one of the original cast members of *Saturday Night Live*, was unable to use his humorous pratfalls to save *The Chevy Chase Show*, a weeknight talk show that was canceled in 1993 after only five weeks and is often referred to as "The Edsel of Television." Chase later appeared in a commercial for Doritos, in which he made a humorous reference to the show.

4. **Cop Rock:** *Cop Rock* might have done better if it was called *Rock Around the Cop*, but the combination musical/police drama went down the donut hole in 1990 after only 11 episodes. Even with a theme song by Randy Newman

and scripts written by Steven Bochco (creator of *Hill Street Blues*), *Cop Rock* still bombed due to scenes such as a jury singing a gospel song "He's Guilty." Bochco later redeemed himself with *NYPD Blue*.

5. **You're in the Picture:** Jackie Gleason was famous for saying "How sweet it is," but a game show he hosted called *You're in the Picture* wasn't so sweet at all. The first and only episode aired live on January 20, 1961, and featured celebrity contestants sticking their heads into a scene painted on plywood, and then trying to guess what the scene was by asking Gleason questions. After the disaster aired, Gleason convinced CBS to let him go on the next week and apologize to viewers under the title *The Jackie Gleason Show*. He did, and *The Jackie Gleason Show* aired for eight more weeks as a talk show before the network pulled the plug for good.

6. **Me and the Chimp:** Working with animals on television is always a risk, something *That Girl* costar Ted Bessell found out when he shared top billing with a chimpanzee. From January to May 1972, *Me and the Chimp* was produced by Tom Miller and Garry Marshall, who later went on to create *Happy Days* and *Laverne & Shirley*. The show centered around a family who found a chimp wandering around the neighborhood and decided to keep it hidden from their neighbors. Bessell was able to change the original working title from *The Chimp and I*, so at least he was the top banana.

7. **Turn-On:** On February 5, 1969, *Turn-On*, became the first show to get canceled before the premier episode had finished airing. Created by Ed Friendly and George Schlatter, producers of *Rowan & Martin's Laugh-In*, this show utilized a barrage of "hi-tech" media such as computer graphics, animation, signs flashing sexual innuendos, and electronically distorted, synthesized music. Guests included Tim Conway, who later did a long run on *The Carol Burnett*

Show, but *Turn-On* was turned off by most everyone who tuned in.

8. **Who's Your Daddy?:** The popular '90s slang phrase Who's your daddy? eventually appeared in everything from movies to a country music song by Toby Keith. That didn't help a 2005 reality show on Fox called *Who's Your Daddy?*, which was canceled after one episode. The show took a woman who had been adopted as an infant and placed her in a room with eight men, one of whom was her biological father. If she chose the correct man as her father, they would win a big cash prize; if she chose the wrong man, the money would go to him instead. The show was blasted by adoption rights organizations, so Fox decided not to broadcast the other five episodes that had been produced.

9. **My Mother the Car:** *My Mother the Car*, typically named the worst TV show of all time, aired on NBC from 1965 to 1966. It starred Jerry Van Dyke as the owner of a 1928 Porter convertible possessed by his deceased mother (Ann Sothern), whose voice came out of the car radio. Although written by Allan Burns and Chris Hayward, who had success with *The Munsters*, the show was panned by critics. Still, *My Mother the Car* managed to survive a year, but in the end, a country that loved a talking horse just wasn't ready for a talking car.

The Short-Lived 1942 German Invasion of America

Why did the least effective sabotage operation in history fail so very miserably?

✳   ✳   ✳   ✳

IN JUNE 1942, two Nazi submarines delivered eight saboteurs to America's coast—four to Long Island and four to Florida. Their mission: implement a series of industrial bombings and spread fear in the heart of the enemy. The men, trained agents of the Nazi intelligence unit known as the *Abwehr*, were chosen for their impeccable Nazi credentials, knowledge of American culture, and fluent English. The teams were trained to use explosives, given approximately $50,000 for expenses and bribes, and supplied with a list of contacts written in invisible ink on handkerchiefs.

Within two weeks of landing, however, all eight members of Operation Pastorius were in FBI custody and waiting to stand trial for their lives.

Flawed From the Start

The captain of submarine U-202, Kptlt. Lindner, was decidedly unhappy with his mission. He was to deliver four saboteurs to the New York coast and then make his way south to prey on enemy shipping. Lindner suspected that the saboteurs lacked true Nazi fervor and dedication to their mission. He was nervous that, if captured, they would reveal essential details about the U-boats. If Lindner had known how much information the saboteurs' leader, George Dasch, would eventually relay to the Americans, he would certainly have shot him on sight.

As it was, Kptlt. Lindner successfully got the men ashore, after which U-202 became moored on a sandbar. With daylight only a few hours away, Lindner could not afford to await the tide. He ordered a series of furious, noisy maneuvers, which—after several attempts—succeeded in freeing the submarine.

On the beach, Dasch and the members of his team encountered a young Coast Guard seaman named John Cullen who soon became suspicious. Rather than kill the guardsman, Dasch offered a bribe, which Cullen, outnumbered, pretended to accept. When Cullen returned with other seamen, they were in time to see the conning tower of U-202 slip beneath the waves; soon thereafter they unearthed explosives and uniforms hastily buried by the Germans.

On the Montauk Highway

The Montauk Highway runs east toward Montauk and west to the Amagansett Railroad Station with trains to New York City. Shaken by their encounter with the guardsmen, the Germans began to walk east, away from their immediate goal. The rising sun soon corrected their direction, however, and as the secret agents miserably retraced their steps alongside the highway, numerous cars—including a truck full of Coast Guard seamen—passed them. Against the odds, however, the Germans reached the rail station and—from there—the anonymous safety of the city.

How to Prove You're a Nazi

The saboteurs separated into two pairs and ensconced themselves in downtown New York City hotels. With the authorities alerted to their presence, the men grew increasingly nervous while Dasch did nothing beyond purchasing new clothes for nearly a week. After speaking at length about his intentions with fellow saboteur Ernest Peter Burger, Dasch called the FBI office in New York and stated that he would have information for J. Edgar Hoover in two days. He then traveled by rail to Washington, D.C., where he checked into a hotel and phoned the FBI. Using the pseudonym Franz Daniel Pastorius, Dasch demanded to speak with J. Edgar Hoover regarding important information about German agents.

Whatever hopes for a sensational, thankful, or decisive response Dasch might have held prior to phoning the FBI, however, rapidly dissipated as the G-man took a message and subsequently dismissed him as a crank caller. Dasch then went to the bureau in person and was sent from office to office with his fantastic story of submarines, explosives, and German agents extant in both New York and Florida.

Finally, after he dropped $84,000 in cash on an agent's desk, the FBI took Dasch seriously and interrogated him for nearly 13 hours. During the course of the interrogation, Dasch outlined everything from the probable whereabouts of the other agents to the diving depth of the submarines that had carried them to America.

Why Did Dasch Turn Traitor?

George Dasch was 39 years old at the time of Operation Pastorius; he felt that the world had passed him over for too long. First, as a poor German immigrant to the United States in the 1920s, he detested the dreary, unimportant work available to him. And the Nazis were unable to provide him with the recognition and glory that he considered his due.

During the course of his confession to the FBI, Dasch claimed that he had never intended to carry out his destructive mission; rather, he had meant to turn himself in from the beginning. Whether Dasch really expected a parade in his honor or was merely hedging his confession in hopes of lenient treatment is uncertain. What is known is that Dasch and Burger's death sentences were commuted to lengthy prison terms while the other six would-be saboteurs died in the electric chair.

After the war Dasch was deported to Germany, where he was viewed as a traitor and a coward. A subsequent book by Dasch about his experiences failed to bolster his reputation. George Dasch died in 1992.

Toy Story

So, we know the elves make toys—but where do the toys go from there? For almost 150 years, FAO Schwarz has been the first name in fun.

✳ ✳ ✳ ✳

No NAME IS as synonymous with toys as FAO Schwarz, and the story of the company is a true American success story. But did you know that while this paragon of playtime may be a New York institution, it actually got its start in Baltimore?

The four Schwarz brothers left Germany for America in the mid-1800s. They settled in Baltimore, where they worked for Theodore Schwerdtmann, owner of a retail store for imported goods. Henry and younger brother Frederick August Otto (the "F.A.O." in FAO Schwarz) imported toys from other countries, including Germany, France, and Switzerland, for Schwerdtmann & Co, which became Schwerdtmann & Schwarz in 1871.

In 1870, Frederick left to open another branch, the Schwarz Toy Bazaar, in New York. Henry took over Schwerdtmann & Schwarz in 1872, and brothers Gustave and Richard ran their own toy stores in Philadelphia and Boston.

The brothers pooled their purchasing power to bring a wide variety of European toys and trinkets to American stores. At the time, stores that sold only toys were all but nonexistent. Most Americans gave their children handmade toys rather than storebought playthings. There was no Toys "R" Us; instead, toys cropped up on a shelf or two at local general stores. Baltimore, however, was another story. A disproportionately large population of German immigrants lived in this shipping center. As the Schwarz clan tapped directly into that market, demand spread.

Frederick would often request specific changes from European manufacturers, making many of the toys on FAO's shelves Schwarz exclusives. This practice became a tradition, as evidenced by the unique and lavish displays in the stores, particularly the giant keyboard made famous by Tom Hanks in the 1988 movie *Big*.

The venerable American toy icon experienced financial woes at the turn of the 21st century and changed ownership several times, but its flagship New York store continues to be a must-see attraction for tourists and toy enthusiasts alike.

Battle for the Sky

When auto magnate Walter Chrysler erected his stylish art deco skyscraper in 1928, he closely guarded its intended height, hoping to outdo others with equally lofty intentions. Thus began New York's skyscraper wars.

✳   ✳   ✳   ✳

THE PROSPERITY OF the 1920s encouraged a major trend among developers: Lacking horizontal space in which to grow their empires, New York builders looked to the sky. Here, in this untapped landscape of altitude, skyscrapers could offer not only vast amounts of commercial space, but breathtaking views to boot. A select few aspired for the top prize: World's Tallest Building. Only one building at a time could hold the coveted title, of course, but anybody who undertook that sort of costly construction might create enough excitement and publicity to offset—for everybody—the increased costs of gunning for the top. For the ultimate winner, success would cement his name into the public psyche. Big money and overstuffed egos were in collusion, and the results would be fabulous.

High Hopes

The auto baron Walter Chrysler decided to enter the skyscraper sweepstakes in 1928. Chrysler hinted that his namesake structure on Lexington Avenue would be a building of monumental proportions but declined to divulge its intended height. Walter was noted for being coy in public, and his caginess here suggested that he was indeed shooting for the world mark.

A former General Motors vice president, John Jakob Raskob, was an equally ambitious sort. On 34th Street in 1929, he began construction of a tower soon to be called the Empire State Building. When he hired the architectural firm of Shreve, Lamb & Harmon, Raskob asked, "How high can you make it so it won't fall down?"

Tit for Tat

As buildings grew progressively taller, developers grew more concerned. "We thought we would be the tallest at 80 stories," declared Hamilton Weber, the rental manager for the Empire State Building. "Then the Chrysler went higher, so we lifted the Empire State to 85 stories, but only four feet taller than the Chrysler."

Four feet was the slimmest of margins. Raskob wondered if Chrysler and his boys were planning some sort of trick. They could easily conceal a rod in the building's spire and then raise it at the last moment to claim the title (which they in fact did at a later date). In Raskob's view, the Empire State Building needed a revamped plan that would guarantee its preeminence over all other skyscrapers.

It Needs a Hat!

While looking at a scale model of the Empire State, particularly at its flat, featureless roof, Raskob found his answer. "It needs a hat!" he shouted. But this would be no ordinary bonnet. This addition would be a functional mooring mast built to accommodate airships—a form of transport then coming into vogue. The building's designers took Raskob's forward-thinking suggestion and ran with it. They couldn't know it at the time, but their new plan would not only secure for them the title of world's tallest building, it would positively trounce Chrysler's 'scraper in the process.

A Champ Emerges

On May 27, 1930, the Chrysler Building opened for business. At some 77 stories and 1,046 feet tall, it became the WTB, beating the former champion, 40 Wall Street (72 stories, 927 feet) by a considerable margin. However, the Chrysler Building's reign was short-lived. On May 1, 1931, the Empire State Building swung open its doors. At 1,250 feet and 102 stories, it made Walter Chrysler's effort appear almost puny in comparison.

Although Walter Chrysler's building didn't hold the world title for very long, it would be a mighty tall mistake to write the structure off. With art deco styling so exquisite it routinely wins design awards, the Chrysler Building is widely viewed as a marvel of architectural style. Not the world's tallest, but surely among the most beautiful!

Broadway's Biggest Losers

Broadway is known for producing some of the world's largest shows ever seen on stage. Still, they can't all be Cats. *Here are some of the biggest tankers in Broadway history.*

✳   ✳   ✳   ✳

PROBABLY THE WORST play on Broadway, the stinker that all subsequent bombs have been compared to, was Arthur Bicknell's *The Moose Murders*. The script included one character who tried to have sex with his mother; meanwhile another character, dressed in a moose costume, was kicked in the groin by a quadriplegic. *New York Times* theater critic Frank Rich called it "the worst play I've ever seen on a Broadway stage." It had one performance at the Eugene O'Neill Theatre on February 22, 1983, before it was closed down.

Quick Closers

Another early closer was the 1966 stage version of the movie classic *Breakfast at Tiffany's*. Although it had big-name star Mary Tyler Moore playing Holly Golightly, the musical, nearly four hours long, was constantly being revised. *Breakfast* had its first preview on December 12, but producer David Merrick shut it down four nights later, saying the show's closing was preferable "rather than subject the drama critics and the public to an excruciatingly boring evening."

Another movie adaptation to bomb big on Broadway was a 1988 musical version of Stephen King's horror novel, *Carrie*, which closed after a measly five performances. Actress Barbara

Cook was actually nearly decapitated by a set prop, and lead actress Linzi Hateley's body microphone stopped working after the show's climactic blood-soaked scene. The $7 million show was the most expensive quick-to-close flop in Broadway history.

An older stinker on Broadway was *Portofino*, a confusing musical that combined an auto-racing storyline with witches, priests, and the devil. Opening on February 21, 1958, it seemed destined to bomb. It closed after only three shows. Famed theater critic Walter Kerr wrote, "I will not say that *Portofino* was the worst musical ever produced, because I've only been seeing musicals since 1919."

The High-flying Jacob Brodbeck

Jacob Brodbeck isn't very well known outside of the Lone Star State, but to many Texans he is the father of American aviation.

✳   ✳   ✳   ✳

WHEN IT COMES to American aviation history, folks from Fredericksburg and Gillespie County consider Orville and Wilbur Wright's accomplishment at Kitty Hawk in 1903 —lauded as the first successful piloted flight of a powered, heavier-than-air aircraft—to be no big deal. They boast that their local Jacob Brodbeck achieved that feat some 38 years before the Wright Brothers even got off the ground.

A Born Inventor

Born in Württemberg, Germany, in 1821, Brodbeck had an innate propensity for invention. According to some accounts, he tried inventing a self-winding clock; others claim he fashioned a watch that didn't need winding for months and was insulted when the kaiser of Württemberg offered him the cash equivalent of one cow for it.

In 1847, Brodbeck packed up his timepieces and belongings and made his way to Fredericksburg. Once settled on the Texas frontier, Brodbeck took teaching positions in various Gillespie County schools, married, and fathered 12 children. Yet he still somehow found time for inventing: He purportedly designed an ice-making machine and lessened Mrs. Brodbeck's domestic load by building her a windmill-powered washing machine.

Brodbeck embarked on a project in the 1860s that literally took his inventiveness to new heights. He envisioned what he called an "airship," a self-propelled flying machine that could carry a passenger and, potentially, replace the wagon and stagecoach— not a bad idea considering the Fredericksburg–San Antonio stagecoach was frequently robbed. It may have seemed like a pie-in-the-sky notion, but in 1863 he built a small prototype model sporting a rudder, wings, and a propeller powered by a coiled spring (similar to a clock spring) that wowed people at local fairs. Determined to make his airship idea fly, Brodbeck secured financial backing from some San Antonio businessmen and set about building the real thing.

Flying High in Luckenbach

By September 1865, Brodbeck's full-size airship was ready to take flight. The larger machine mirrored Brodbeck's earlier model, but it also contained a fuselage for the "aeronaut" (to use Brodbeck's term) and a boat propeller in case of an unexpected wet landing. On September 25, Brodbeck brought his airship to a field outside Luckenbach for its maiden voyage. Accompanying Brodbeck were his nervous investors, a handful of local newspaper reporters, and some curious onlookers.

Brodbeck climbed aboard the machine, engaged the spring-powered propeller, and in seconds, the airship was off the ground. Witnesses reported that Brodbeck piloted his airship for approximately 100 feet at a height of about 12 feet. For a few fleeting moments, Brodbeck's dream was a reality.

But everything literally came crashing down for Brodbeck when he was unable to rewind the spring coil, which caused the propeller to stall. The airship crash-landed into a chicken coop.

Unfortunately for Brodbeck, he had no photographic equipment in place to capture his airship in flight for posterity, and the press scribes deemed the debacle a nonstory. Worse, Brodbeck's financial backers bailed on him, leaving him without the cash needed to assemble another airship.

The Aftermath

What happened after is a matter of debate. Some say a despondent Brodbeck destroyed the wreckage of his airship and all his drawings. Others contend that he took his drawings to the 1900 St. Louis World's Fair seeking investors to bankroll the building of another airship—only to have the drawings stolen. No drawings, photos, or written accounts remain to verify Brodbeck's aeronautic achievement—only the faded word of long-dead eyewitnesses.

Up in Flames: The "Fireproof" Crystal Palace

How New York's attempt to emulate a London architectural triumph ended in financial and physical ruin.

✳ ✳ ✳ ✳

IN LONDON IN 1851, the first ever World's Fair was held. Opened by Queen Victoria and officially titled the Great Exhibition of the Works of Industry of All Continents, it was more commonly referred to as the Great Exhibition or the Crystal Palace Exhibition because of the vast, architecturally daring glass and cast-iron structure in which the expo was held. Two years later, New York City followed suit, staging the Exhibition of the Industry of All Nations inside its own Crystal Palace, a building whose glass and iron structure rendered it fireproof—or so its designers thought.

International Cachet, Domestic Glory

Located on 42nd Street between Fifth and Sixth avenues, on the Reservoir Square site that is now known as Bryant Park, the Palace was designed by Danish architect Georg Carstensen (who had helped develop Copenhagen's famed Tivoli Gardens) and his German compatriot, Charles Gildemeister. New York wanted to prove it could hold its own among the greatest cities on earth, and indeed, following the fair's grand opening in July 1853, Gotham enjoyed one of its first major tourist booms as more than a million people took in the artwork, consumer goods, and industrial products of no fewer than 4,000 exhibitors.

From house paint to fine paintings, farm tools to precision steam engines, the wares were ostensibly displayed to showcase the global fruits of the Industrial Revolution. However, like its London predecessor, the NYC exhibition clearly promoted domestic product and ingenuity above anything else. More than 15,000 panes of glass and 1,800 tons of iron were used to construct the giant cross-shaped structure, whose central 100-foot-diameter dome towered 123 feet above the city. If that sounds a little like London's centerpiece structure, well, imitation is the sincerest form of flattery. Unfortunately, what the New York fair *couldn't* duplicate was the first one's huge profits.

May 1, 1853, was scheduled to be the public opening of the New York Crystal Palace, but major construction setbacks delayed the launch for more than two months. Finally, on July 14, U.S. President Franklin Pierce unveiled the highly anticipated "Temple of National Industry." After opening festivities in which poets sang psalms and philosophers cited industry as the source of humanity's greatest accomplishments, relatively modest numbers of people shelled out $10 for season tickets to the exhibition, while others paid the single-day admissions of 50 cents for adults and 25 cents for the kiddies.

The Embarrassment of Destruction

Several hotels were built to accommodate the visitors, yet after the initial burst of enthusiasm, there wasn't sufficient continuing public interest to avert a financial disaster. By March 1854, the expo's financiers were $100,000 in debt, and their attempt to correct this by recruiting the leadership of circus huckster P. T. Barnum was clearly a desperate move. Barnum may have been a successful businessman, but his carny expertise hardly lent itself to the requirements of a prestigious industrial exhibition. By the time the fair closed on November 1, 1854, the deficit had risen to around $300,000.

Thereafter, the huge glass cathedral was leased out as a concert venue and a convention center. But that came to an end when, just after 5:00 P.M. on October 5, 1858, during the 30th Annual Fair of the American Institute, fire broke out in a room storing wood patterns that had been used in the building's construction. Forget all of the iron and glass: Courtesy of high winds and ineffective extinguishers, the dome collapsed within 15 minutes, and just five minutes later the entire Crystal Palace was in ruins. To ensure there were no major injuries, New York firefighters evacuated about 2,000 people, but about half a million dollars of merchandise and machinery were destroyed—along with the last vestiges of a sparkling "fireproof" structure that had been intended to elevate a nation's pride.

Toxic Times Beach

Nestled in the flood plains of the Meramec River just outside St. Louis is the tiny town of Times Beach, Missouri. In 1972, it became the site of one of the nation's worst chemical disasters when it was discovered that the oil sprayed onto the town's dirt roads to solve a dust problem was actually Agent Orange. How could this ever happen?

✳   ✳   ✳   ✳

A Deadly Solution

IN THE EARLY 1970s, the small 480-acre town of Times Beach and its approximately 1,200 residents hit on a cost-effective solution to the town's growing dust problem: Instead of paving the roads, which was too expensive for the lower-middle-class community to afford, why not have the roads sprayed with oil? This was hardly considered a crazy idea; many dirt-road towns followed the same practice, since oil was deemed much more effective than water.

Professional waste-hauler Russell Bliss was hired to do the deed and sprayed the roads with oil at regular intervals from 1972 to 1976, at a cost of six cents per gallon. Former residents remember local children following Bliss's truck as he drove through town, playing and sliding in the thick oil slick it left behind. But for some reason, the streets turned purple after Bliss drove through; birds dropped dead in ditches; puppies and kittens were stillborn. No one suspected Bliss was dredging "The Beach" with poison.

Bliss-fully Ignorant

What the town didn't know was that Bliss was mixing the oil with waste he'd been subcontracted to haul for a company downstate, the Northeastern Pharmaceutical and Chemical Company (NEPACCO).

During the Vietnam War, NEPACCO manufactured the highly toxic Agent Orange; the waste clay and water Bliss removed from the plant contained levels of dioxin 2,000 times higher than the dioxin content in Agent Orange. Bliss, who later professed ignorance of the dioxin-laced oil, used his deadly blend not only on the town of Times Beach but on several local horse stables as well.

In 1971, after a routine stable spray left 62 horses dead, stable owners became suspicious of Bliss, who claimed his spray was simply old engine oil. Nevertheless, the owners began tracking Bliss's actions, and after other stables reported similar problems, the Centers for Disease Control and Prevention (CDC) launched an investigation. In late 1979, a NEPACCO employee admitted to the company's use of dioxin—a poison so toxic that it is considered the deadliest chemical made by humankind.

Back to the Beach

Amazingly, the citizens of Times Beach remained in the dark about dioxin until some three years later when, on November 10, 1982, a local reporter called city hall with news that the town may have been among the sites contaminated by Russell Bliss. The Environmental Protection Agency (EPA) called shortly after to verify the news, and on December 4, official testing confirmed the town's dioxin contamination level was 33,000 times more toxic than what the EPA deemed safe.

Days later came the death knell for tiny Times Beach: The Meramec River crested at 43 feet, flooding the town and spreading dioxin-contaminated soil even further throughout the community and its surrounding areas. On December 23, the town's officials issued a horrifying holiday message: If you're here, leave; if you're gone, don't come back.

By 1985, not only had the entire area been evacuated (with the exception of an elderly couple who refused to leave), but the governor had issued an executive order dissolving the town. The site was officially quarantined. Security checkpoints reminiscent of international border controls were set up along the perimeter to keep visitors and former residents from trespassing.

Route 66 State Park

Following its evacuation, the area once known as Times Beach sat empty for more than a decade—a modern-day ghost town—before the federal government began its clean-up efforts in March 1996. By June 1997, more than 265,000 tons of contaminated soil had been removed from the area and destroyed (using an incinerator made by Syntex, the parent company of NEPACCO).

In October 1999, the state of Missouri opened Route 66 State Park on the grounds of what was once Times Beach. Now verified as clean and toxin-free, the site features hiking trails, picnic tables, and a multitude of flora and fauna. The only original building still standing is the park's visitor center: formerly the Times Beach Steiny's Inn, formerly the headquarters of the EPA's clean-up efforts, and today, a testament to the area's checkered past.

Other Contaminated U.S. Communities

The Love Canal: In the late 1800s, William T. Love planned to build a model community at this site near Niagara Falls. By 1920, the canal had been abandoned due to a lack of funding, and it became a dumping site for the Niagara Falls township. In the 1940s, Hooker Chemical was permitted to dump 21,000 tons of waste in the abandoned canal; a decade later, a school was constructed on top of it and a housing development built nearby.

Though no one suspected contamination at the time, in the late 1970s, health issues began surfacing among residents, who were ultimately relocated and paid $129 million in retribution by Hooker.

Picher, Oklahoma: The same zinc and lead mines that put Picher on the map are wiping it out. Following the mine closures in the 1970s, officials discovered that contaminated mine waste was spread across 25,000 acres and poisoning residents. Still, many people refused to leave until 2007, when federal buyouts made it worth their while.

Centralia, Pennsylvania: When workers set a routine fire to burn trash in this tiny mining town in 1962, they unwittingly ignited an exposed vein of highly flammable anthracite (hard) coal. Though firefighters quickly extinguished flames on the surface, the fire continued to rage below the earth, rapidly spreading beneath the town and releasing harmful carbon monoxide into homes. After 20 years and $7 million spent (unsuccessfully) fighting the fire, the state government decided to call it quits and demolish the town, though as of 2010, less than a dozen people remain. The fire continues to burn today.

Millennium Park

This once-controversial undertaking is now one of the Windy City's preeminent attractions.

* * * *

CHICAGO'S LAKEFRONT IS its greatest asset. But for decades, miles of the shore were dominated by industrial infrastructure. Train tracks, which had been built a few hundred yards offshore during the 19th century, separated the people of Chicago from the body of water that made their city one of the fastest growing in history. Its downtown area was a mess of steel and concrete divorced from the natural beauty and serenity that surrounded it. The eyesores drove Chicago's wealthiest residents into the northern and western suburbs, where they had access to the lake or to large swaths of greenery.

The grandeur of Grant Park, the city's turn-of-the-century Beaux Arts solution to its malaise, was a wonder for the city. It utilized the neat patches of grass and complex geometric gardens for concerts, festivals, and everyday leisure. But the northwest tip of the park still left a gape of commuter trains, parking spaces, and abandoned railcars—all owned and maintained by the Illinois Central Railroad company—that sullied an otherwise idyllic lakeside setting. That all changed in 1997, when the city won rights to the space above the tracks. Use of the space was debated for some time before plans were drawn to build a massive parking structure. In addition, the parking structure would be covered by about 25 acres of recreational public space.

The details were vague, and plans for the park quickly fell behind schedule. The city sought the expertise of superstar architect Frank Gehry, who had recently won several prestigious awards and international recognition for a series of magnificent buildings in locales as varied as Bilbao, Spain, and Cleveland, Ohio. Gehry's reluctance to sign on to the plan created a major roadblock in construction of the parking garage and the park itself, which Mayor Richard M. Daley hoped would be the city's newest artistic playground. What had originally been a $150 million plan had ballooned to more than $200 million—and that was just the beginning.

Finally, exasperated by the city's mismanagement of the site and the funds and its inability to attract Gehry to the project, the Pritzker family came to the rescue. They ponied up $15 million for what would become the Jay Pritzker Pavilion, home to Frank Gehry's glimmering steel band shell, topped off by enormous frills of stainless steel.

Complete with a Bike Station Worth Millions

Ameritech and Chicago-based Banc One each donated $5 million, and William Daley, former secretary of commerce and the Midwest chair of J.P. Morgan-Chase (and, naturally, the brother of Mayor Richard Daley) arranged for the bank to underwrite the project, allowing for expansions in the city's original plans. The federal government offered an additional $3.1 million in grant money for a bike station under the park. That might sound a little steep for a bike station, but this area—which is complete with showers and a café—was built to encourage motorists to bike downtown instead of drive, and it has been wildly successful.

Soon, the city's large and lofty philanthropic community began giving money to the project, requesting with each donation another large piece of public art, a garden, or a monument commemorating the gift.

The results include London-based artist Anish Kapoor's interactive steel sculpture *Cloud Gate*—affectionately dubbed "The Bean" by its legion of fans—which reflects the city's skyline in a panoramic arch; Spanish artist Jaume Plensa's Crown Fountain, two towers of glass bricks with the projected faces of Chicagoans behind a streaming wall of water; and the Lurie Garden, which (at five acres) was the largest rooftop garden in the world at the time of its construction.

When all was said and done, Millennium Park's price tag was about $475 million, but more than half of that was provided through grants and private donations. The city's bill was, in the end, a little large for its britches, but we're willing to bet that will slip your mind as you watch dozens of kids from all over the city splash with delight in Crown Fountain on a hot Chicago summer day.

Baseball's Darkest Hour

Baseball's Golden Age was preceded by its darkest hour: the 1919 World Series–fixing scandal.

✳   ✳   ✳   ✳

THE CHICAGO HERALD *and* Examiner described him as "a little urchin," the young lad who emerged from the crowd outside a Chicago courthouse on that September day in 1920 and was said to have grabbed Joe Jackson by the coat sleeve. The newspaper's report of the exchange went like this:

"It ain't true, is it?" the lad said.

"Yes, kid, I'm afraid it is," Jackson replied.

"Well, I'd never have thought it," the boy exclaimed.

Nowhere did the newspaper report that the boy demanded, "Say it ain't so, Joe," although this version of the story was passed down through the generations. A few years before his 1951 death, Jackson told *Sport Magazine* that the story was made up by a sportswriter. He said the only words exchanged on the way out of the courthouse that day were between him and a law enforcement officer.

What *is* so is this: Members of the 1919 Chicago White Sox committed baseball's cardinal sin, deliberately losing the World Series to the Cincinnati Reds for pay. It was a scandal that would go down in sports history.

Ripe for a Fix

Two years after their 1917 world championship, the White Sox took the American League pennant. The White Sox were favored to defeat Cincinnati in the World Series—heavily favored, in some gambling circles. By all accounts, Sox infielder Chick Gandil made contact with gamblers and indicated that the Series could be thrown. He immediately involved 29-game-winner Eddie Cicotte, and others followed: Jackson, pitcher Claude Williams, infielders Buck Weaver and "Swede" Risberg, outfielder Oscar "Happy" Felsch, and utility man Fred McMullin. Some of the players would play lead parts in the fixing of games. Others, notably Weaver and some say Jackson, knew about the plan but were not active participants.

When the Series began, the players were promised a total of $100,000 to throw the games. By the time the Reds won the Series in eight games, the payout was considerably less, and whispers about what had taken place began swelling to a roar. Sportswriters speculated about a possible fix even before Cincinnati wrapped up the Series, but nobody wanted to believe it could be true.

Conspiracy to Defraud the Public

The 1920 season began with rumors about gambling in other big-league dugouts. In September a grand jury convened to examine instances of gambling in the game, and the jury soon looked at the 1919 World Series. Eight White Sox players were called to testify, and several admitted knowledge of the fix. All eight were indicted for conspiracy to defraud the public and injure "the business of Charles Comiskey and the American League." Although the group was acquitted due to lack of evidence, the damage had been done.

Bring in the Judge

The Black Sox were not as fortunate on the scales of baseball justice, as Judge Kenesaw Mountain Landis, baseball's first commissioner, suspended all eight players for life. It was a crushing blow for Chicago, and for Weaver and Jackson in particular. While Gandil had received $35,000 and Cicotte $10,000 for the fix, Weaver received nothing. Actually, it was proven that he had *turned down* an invitation to participate in the scam. And Jackson, considered one of the greatest outfielders and hitters in the history of the game, hit .375 with six RBI in the 1919 Series while playing errorless defense.

Many still clamor for Shoeless Joe to be enshrined in the Hall of Fame, arguing that his numbers support the claim that he did nothing to contribute to the fixing of the 1919 World Series. However, the $5,000 he accepted from the gamblers sealed his fate as a tragic figure in baseball's most infamous 20th-century scandal.

Say it ain't so, Joe.

Too bad it is.

Not Quite Hotcakes: Product Disasters

It's true that you can't win 'em all, and when you're in the business of making new things, you can pretty much count on a spectacular flop now and then. Here's a sampling of some of the biggest.

✳　✳　✳　✳

New Coke When Coca-Cola CEO Roberto Goizueta introduced a new Coke formula in a 1985 press conference, he proclaimed it, "the boldest single marketing move in the history of the consumer goods business" and the "surest move ever made." The company concocted the new, sweeter formula to compete with Pepsi, and after conducting 200,000 taste tests and spending a whopping $4 million on research and development, executives were convinced they had a hit. But they never gauged how strongly people would react to original Coke being pulled from the shelves. When the new formula debuted, angry customers jammed Coca-Cola's lines with more than 1,000 calls per day, and the press opened up with both barrels. Within three months, the company was selling "Coca-Cola Classic" alongside the new version, and within a year, it decided to scrap New Coke entirely.

Smokeless Cigarettes In the 1980s, R.J. Reynolds spent $325 million to launch Premier, a new cigarette without the smoke and ash that nonsmokers hate. The biggest problem seemed obvious: Nonsmokers don't buy cigarettes. On top of that, the smokeless cigarettes tasted bad, smelled bad, and cost 25 percent more than regular cigarettes. R.J. Reynolds pulled the product from the market quickly but apparently didn't learn its lesson. In the 1990s, R.J. Reynolds dropped $125 million to develop the smokeless Eclipse cigarettes. Nobody liked those either—especially after they learned the filters contained glass fibers. The idea went up in smoke.

Earring Magic Ken In 1993, Mattel released what they intended to be a cooler, more modern boyfriend for Barbie. But the new Ken—sporting an earring, necklace, mesh shirt, lavender vest, and blonde highlights—suggested something very different to most people. The doll actually sold very well (due in large part to adult collectors), but it was pulled from the shelves in less than a year because of parents and church groups.

Windows Vista When Microsoft's new operating system launched in 2006—years behind schedule and missing promised features—it was so sluggish, glitchy, and hard to use that PC manufacturers established programs to "downgrade" new PC owners to the previous system, Windows XP. After spending billions to develop what was supposed to be a computing revolution, Microsoft soon found itself soothing customers with promises of a new system, Windows 7.

Gerber Singles In a 1974 push to expand beyond the diaper demographic, Gerber introduced baby-food-style dishes intended for childless adults. Packaged in the same iconic jars as the original baby food, the "Singles" line certainly didn't appeal to real swinging singles.

The Edsel Ho-hum cars are nothing unusual, but the gap between hype and results put the 1958 Edsel in a class by itself. In an effort to compete with General Motors, Ford launched a midpriced division, alongside the budget Ford and the high-end Mercury/Lincoln lines. They spent an unprecedented $400 million in research and development before building a single car. But then they tossed an initial sleek design and sacrificed engineering quality to shrink production costs. They also ignored a year of naming research and opted for "Edsel," the name of Henry Ford's son, even though market research subjects associated it with "weasel." To make the car stand out, they outfitted it with a bizarre grille that one reviewer described as "an Oldsmobile sucking a lemon." In the marketing blitz leading up to the 1957 debut, Ford boasted, "There has never been a car like the Edsel." The company predicted it would sell more than 200,000 cars in the first year—around 5 percent of the U.S. market at the time. In reality, they only sold 64,000 the first year, 44,891 the second, and 2,846 the third before finally halting production.

Blowing a "Razz"-berry

Since 1981, the Golden Raspberry Awards, or Razzies, have been presented annually in Hollywood to "honor" the year's worst achievements in film.

✳   ✳   ✳   ✳

THE RAZZIES ARE voted upon by the Golden Raspberry Award Foundation, which, unlike the Academy of Motion Picture Arts and Sciences, is open to members of the public. A Razzie Award consists of a plastic raspberry painted gold atop a reel of Super 8 film. Razzies are presented in categories such as Worst Picture, Worst Director, Worst Actor, Worst Actress,

Worst Screenplay, and Worst Screen Couple. When Ben Affleck was presented with the Worst Actor Razzie on *Larry King Live* in 2003 for his performances in *Gigli, Daredevil,* and *Paycheck,* he accidentally broke the award, which is valued at a whopping $4.97. Razzies founder John Wilson recovered it, sold it on eBay, and raised enough money to pay for the theater rental for the following year's ceremony.

"I'd Like to Thank the Academy..."

Although many superstars have won Razzie awards, only a few have actually accepted the award in person. Halle Berry collected her Worst Actress Razzie at the 2004 ceremony for her performance in *Catwoman* and mocked the Oscar acceptance speech she gave when she won for *Monster's Ball* (2001). The audience greeted her description of *Catwoman* as a "god-awful movie" with laughter and enthusiastic applause.

Director Paul Verhoeven attended the awards ceremony to accept the Worst Picture and Worst Director Razzies for his box-office dud *Showgirls* (1995). Screenwriter Brian Helgeland became only the fourth person to voluntarily accept his Golden Raspberry Award and the first person to win both a Razzie and an Oscar in the same year. His Worst Screenplay Razzie for the Kevin Costner flop *The Postman* (1997) countered his Academy Award for Best Adapted Screenplay for *L.A. Confidential* (1997). Rumor has it that Helgeland likes to display both awards side-by-side on his mantle.

The Razzies' Biggest Winners ... or Losers

* Two movies have won seven Razzie Awards: *Showgirls* (1995) and *Battlefield Earth* (2000). But *I Know Who Killed Me* (2007) set a new Razzie record by winning eight of the not-so-coveted awards.

* *Gigli* (2003) was the first and, so far, the only movie to win Razzies in each of the top five categories: Worst Picture, Worst Director, Worst Actor, Worst Actress, and Worst Screenplay.

* Sylvester Stallone has been the recipient of the most Razzie Awards, with 30 nominations and 10 wins, including Worst Actor of the Decade for his performances in *Rhinestone* (1984), *Rambo: First Blood Part II* (1985), *Rocky IV* (1985), *Cobra* (1986), *Over the Top* (1987), *Rambo III* (1988), *Lock-Up* (1989), and *Tango & Cash* (1989).

* Madonna leads the way for female Razzie winners with five wins plus a Worst Actress of the Century award.

* In 2004, Ben Stiller was nominated as Worst Actor for a record five different movies: *Along Came Polly*, *Dodgeball*, *Starsky & Hutch*, *Envy*, and *Anchorman*, but Ben Affleck won for *Surviving Christmas* and *Jersey Girl*.

* Winning three Razzies for *Norbit* (2007), Eddie Murphy became the first person to win a Golden Raspberry Award for both male and female performances in the same film.

* The only non-Hollywood people to win Razzies are President George W. Bush, Defense Secretary Donald Rumsfeld, and Secretary of State Condoleezza Rice, who all appeared in Michael Moore's 2004 documentary *Fahrenheit 9/11*.

* Actors have won both Razzies and Oscars during their careers (although not for the same performance) include: Marlon Brando, Charlton Heston, Faye Dunaway, Laurence Olivier, Roberto Benigni, Halle Berry, Liza Minnelli, and Nicole Kidman.

* Tom Cruise and Katie Holmes were the Golden Raspberry Award winners in a one-off category for their performance in 2005 as the Most Tiresome Tabloid Target. Not surprisingly, neither actor attended the ceremony to collect the award.

A Ticket to Ride

For William Rand, the railroad boom proved to be the ticket to a publishing empire.

✳   ✳   ✳   ✳

IT MAY BE hard to believe that Rand McNally, a company known for its highway maps, actually got its start before the automobile. This publishing giant dates its inception to 1856—a time when the burgeoning rail industry was hailed as the future of the United States. Bostonian William Rand knew opportunity when he saw it; he packed his bags and headed to Chicago, an area destined to become a railroad hub due to its prime location on the shores of Lake Michigan. Rand set up a small printing shop and got to work producing rail tickets.

Two years later, Rand hired Irish immigrant Andrew McNally, an experienced printer. By 1868, the men had become partners, establishing Rand McNally & Company and assuming control over the *Chicago Tribune*'s printing shop. Business increased as the pair began printing railway timetables along with the tickets.

Grace Under Fire

In 1871, disaster struck Chicago as the Great Fire swept the downtown area. With flames racing toward the plant, Rand and McNally had the foresight to bury two printing presses in the sand along Lake Michigan. A mere three days later, the men had the presses up and running in a newly rented shop. This little nugget of company lore remains a source of pride more than a century later.

Mapping Out the Future

By 1872, Rand McNally's future success was on the map— quite literally. Using an innovative new printing technology that relied on wax engraving, Rand McNally & Company included their very first map in a railroad guide. The wax engraving process allowed the company to mass-produce maps in a cost-effective fashion. By 1880, Rand McNally employed 250 workers and had become the largest producer of maps in the United States. Rand McNally's reputation as a premier mapmaker allowed the company to branch out into the educational publishing market with globes, atlases, and yearly geography textbooks that included pictures, diagrams, and maps.

Navigating Success

Rand retired at the turn of the century, and McNally died of pneumonia in 1904. McNally's descendants continued to run the firm successfully. Not surprisingly, Henry Ford's mass-produced automobiles proved to be a boon to the mapmaking business. In 1907, Rand McNally began producing its popular *Photo Auto Guides*, which added arrow overlays to maps to help automobile owners find their way around—perhaps marking the last time in history that American men would actually seek out directions when driving. Renowned aviator Charles Lindbergh boosted sales further when he revealed that he used Rand McNally railroad maps to navigate.

In the 1940s, the company published the work of Thor Heyerdahl, a maverick anthropologist and geographer who believed that the Polynesian people descended from ancient South Americans who had sailed to the distant South Pacific islands. The scientific community largely rejected Heyerdahl's theories, but when Rand McNally published *Kon-Tiki: Across the Pacific by Raft*, the book sold more than a million copies in its first few years. It is still in print today.

Over the years, maps and atlases have remained at the center of the company's business, but the firm has kept pace with the times by offering trip-planning services online. Although the McNally family sold their interest in the company in the 1990s, the firm is still based in the Chicago area and remains one of the world's most respected cartography firms.

The *Titanic* of New York

Although the PS General Slocum *was smaller than the RMS* Titanic *and acquired less notoriety after its tragedy, its demise brought with it a substantial loss of life. Yet, quite unlike the fate of the doomed White Star liner, the Slocum disaster occurred scant yards from shore in full view of horrified onlookers.*

✳   ✳   ✳   ✳

The Best Laid Plans

I T WAS SUPPOSED to be a day of fun. The PS *General Slocum*, a 235-foot side-wheel passenger ship owned by New York's Knickerbocker Steamship Company, had been chartered for June 15, 1904, by St. Mark's Evangelical Lutheran Church to take parishioners up the East River to a church picnic. Onboard were over 1,300 people anxious to flee the hot, noisy, metropolis. The outing had become familiar. The largely German congregation had enjoyed this cruise for 17 consecutive years and knew what to expect. As in the past, the ship would cruise north up the turbulent river and then track east across the vast blue expanse of Long Island Sound. When the vessel made landfall, revelers would find themselves at bucolic Locust Grove, on Eatons Neck, Long Island. But this year would be different. Tragically different.

Disaster in the Making

Many believe that the *General Slocum* was doomed from the outset. During its trouble-plagued life, the craft had run aground no fewer than three times and had suffered three serious collisions with other ships. At least these mishaps might be explained away by bad luck. Not so easy to defend was the frightful shape that the *Slocum* was in. It's as if the vessel's owners were tempting catastrophe. How else to explain rotted life preservers so brittle that they crumbled when handled, and fire hoses so seriously decayed that they'd burst if put to task? Ship safety demanded a regular infusion of capital. From the look of things, this was a commitment that the Knickerbocker Steamship Company wasn't willing to make.

Fanning the Flames

Just half an hour into the journey, trouble arose when a 12-year-old boy alerted Captain Van Schaick to an onboard fire. Unfortunately, the captain dismissed the boy's words as a prank. It would be ten full minutes before Van Schaick would learn the truth. The *Slocum* had indeed caught fire and by now was almost consumed by it. Even as panicked passengers tried to flee the flames by flinging themselves into the treacherous East River, floors began to collapse upon those unfortunate souls riding below deck. A full-scale disaster was underway.

Inexplicably, Van Schaick chose to proceed at full speed upriver rather than beach the craft along the riverbank. The captain would later claim that he was trying to keep the fire from spreading to riverside oil tanks and flammable buildings. Whatever Van Schaick's motivation, the decision literally fanned the flames into an even deadlier firestorm. When the vessel eventually beached at North Brother Island, tremendous carnage had occurred. Of the more than 1,300 people on board, an estimated 1,021 had burned or drowned. On the other hand, the vast majority of crew members—including the seriously injured Van Schaick—survived. This outcome invited condemnation later from people seeking answers to the whys and wherefores.

Retribution

After a major tragedy plays out, the blame game begins. In Captain Van Schaick, his crew, and the steamship company, the public had the perfect villains. Had the accused not created a ridiculously unsafe condition by ignoring safety equipment? Had regular fire drills routinely been skipped?

Above all, why had the captain not grounded his boat alongside the riverbank? Such a move would certainly have enabled more to escape.

In the end, Van Schaick was the only one tried in court. He was convicted of criminal negligence and misconduct and was sentenced to ten years at New York's Sing Sing Prison. Today, a marker in Tompkins Square Park serves as the only memorial to the *Slocum* tragedy, which is surpassed in number of deaths in the city's history only by $^9/_{11}$.

Inventive Women

If you think men have the market cornered on inventions, think again. It turns out that the fairer sex is responsible for some of history's most notable breakthroughs.

✳ ✳ ✳ ✳

WOMEN CAME UP with ideas and specifications for such useful items as life rafts (Maria Beasley), circular saws (Tabitha Babbitt), medical syringes (Letitia Geer), and underwater lamps and telescopes (Sarah Mather). Giuliana Tesoro was a prolific inventor in the textile industry; flame-resistant fibers and permanent-press properties are among her many contributions. The Tesoro Corporation holds more than 125 of her textile-related patents.

Not surprisingly, some well-known inventions by women are associated with the home. In the late 1950s, Ruth Handler drew inspiration from watching her daughter and her daughter's friends play with paper dolls. After noticing that the girls used the dolls to act out future events rather than those in the present, Handler set out to create a grown-up, three-dimensional doll. She even endowed it with breasts (though their proportions were later criticized for being unrealistic). Handler named her creation after her daughter, and the Barbie doll was introduced in 1959. Handler, incidentally, was one of the founders of the toy giant Mattel.

Of course, not all female inventors have been interested in cookies and dolls. Consider Mary Anderson. While taking a trip from Alabama to New York City just after the turn of the twentieth century, she noticed that when it rained, drivers had to open their car windows to see. Anderson invented a swinging-arm device with a rubber blade that the driver operated by using a lever. In 1903, she received a patent for what became known as the windshield wiper; by 1916, it was standard on most vehicles.

Movie actress Hedy Lamarr's invention was a matter of national security. Lamarr, born Hedwig Eva Maria Kiesler in Austria, emigrated to the United States in the 1930s. In addition to leading the glamorous life of a film star, she became a pioneer in the field of wireless communication.

Lamarr and composer George Anthiel developed a secret communications system to help the Allies in World War II—their method of manipulating radio frequencies was used to create unbreakable codes. The invention proved invaluable again two decades later when it was used aboard naval vessels during the Cuban Missile Crisis.

The "spread spectrum" technology that Lamarr helped to pioneer became the key component in the creation of cellular phones, fax machines, and other wireless devices. How's that for inventive?

Chapter 10

Love and Marriage

Proposals: The Preposterous

Lovers who want to pop the question in a memorable way might be inspired—or deterred—by the stories of the following people who definitely achieved memorability.

※ ※ ※ ※

Ready for Prime Time

IN 2006, RAND Fishkin decided to propose to his girlfriend via a TV ad on Super Bowl Sunday... until he found out it was going to set him back $2.5 million. Fishkin spread the word online, which garnered attention from several media outlets, but he could only raise $85,000. However, CBS wouldn't lower their price, so for just $3,000, Rand purchased a local ad that ran during his girlfriend's favorite show. She saw the commercial, said yes, and the rest of the money was donated to charity.

Baby, Light My Fire

In 2005, Todd Grannis of Grants Pass, Oregon, lit himself on fire, jumped into a swimming pool, and then swam over to his girlfriend, Malissa, to ask for her hand in marriage. This stunt, which nobody should ever try at home, was overseen by a stuntman and was executed while paramedics and a safety crew stood by. Grannis was shown how to wrap his body in protective garments before igniting for a few seconds. After recovering from the horror she must have felt when she saw her boyfriend go up in flames, Malissa said yes.

From Crush to Crash

In 2006, Adam Sutton had it all planned out. He would take his girlfriend, Erika Brussee, up in a chartered plane and ask her to look out the window, high above Rome, Georgia, where family members would be holding a large sign with his proposal written on it. But instead, she saw flames just before the plane crashed onto the runway. No one was seriously injured, and Brussee did say yes, but the ring was lost in the rubble.

22 Romantic Kissing Spots in America

What makes a place romantic enough to inspire a long, passionate kiss? The answer differs for all couples, but one universal answer seems to apply: Being together in beauty— whether in a natural setting or a creation of the human imagination—can certainly help affections flow freely.

✳ ✳ ✳ ✳

1. **Verde Hot Springs, Arizona:** Hot passions won't cool off at these secluded hot springs. Wintertime water temperatures reach 96 degreesF and soar higher in summer. Soak in pools fit for two, or in seclusion underneath cliff overhangs.

2. **Mendocino Headlands State Park, California:** If the town of Mendocino wasn't tantalizing enough for romance, there's the adjacent state park where kissing spots are as common as tidal pools. Explore gentle pathways leading along rugged coastline to secluded beaches, hidden grottoes, and sea arches. On foggy days, a cool mist caresses cheeks and lips, so snuggle up to stay warm.

3. **San Juan Skyway (U.S. 550 between Durango and Ridgway), Colorado:** Reach the height of romance on this high and mighty scenic loop in south central Colorado. The 14 summits along the route—all above 14,000 feet—lead

lovers toward the sky and to unsurpassed vistas. Even at lower elevations, there's no romantic letdown. The old mining towns of Durango, Telluride, and Silverton—all mother lodes of romantic ambience—highlight this 236-mile stretch of highway.

4. **Amelia Island, Florida:** A sun-kissed beach certainly qualifies as a smooching spot, but if lovers want more drama, Amelia Island delivers. More than just sand and surf, the island increases the pucker-up potential with delights of the Deep South: gnarled oak trees dripping with Spanish moss, footbridges crisscrossing windswept dunes, and wide, unspoiled Atlantic beaches. Study the birds and the bees while kayaking through gentle tidal creeks where egrets and herons await.

5. **Na Pali Coast State Park, Hawaii:** Heaven and Earth merge at this exquisite state park, located on the untamed northern side of Kauai. Journeying by foot (the only way to go) into the verdant rainforests and deep valleys flanked by mile-high cliffs is like stepping into untouched Hawaii. There's nothing here but you and nature. Whisper "Aloha" to each other at one of the secret crescent beaches that dot the shoreline, many perfect for a little au naturel action.

6. **Chicago's Navy Pier Ferris Wheel, Illinois:** Take to the sky to smooch! Nighttime is prime time to whirl around, snuggled together on a swinging seat, and view Chicago's fabulous skyline from this 150-foot-tall Ferris wheel.

7. **Cumberland Falls, Kentucky:** Bring a flashlight, hold hands, and venture deep into the woods to cast your eyes upon a romantically rare and unforgettable moonbow. A moonbow is a lunar rainbow that occurs at night, and Cumberland Falls (dubbed the "Niagara of the South") serves up this optical phenomenon on clear, moon-bathed nights. There's no pot o' gold at the bow's end, but the romantic reward of a moonlit kiss should prove satisfying.

8. **Haakwood State Forest Campground, Michigan:** Howl at the moon and snuggle under the stars for a bit of rugged romance in this remote part of the state. For a taste of civilization, hop into the car and drive along Lake Michigan's coastline to watch the sun's last show of the day.

9. **Ruins of Windsor, Mississippi:** Hauntingly romantic and oh-so-southern, the largest antebellum mansion in Mississippi still captivates lovers despite its ruined status. Twenty-three massive Corinthian columns are all that remain of this Civil War survivor. (A careless smoker caused the mansion's demise in 1890.) Stroll the lush grounds together and imagine days "gone with the wind"... and fire.

10. **Meadville Ghost Town, Nebraska:** No spooks out here, just simple solitude, a slice of history, and a charming general store. Meadville isn't exactly easy to reach, but therein lies its quiet allure. Once you've made it, explore the blacksmith shop, farmhouse, and the 1890 cabin used by newlyweds in the days before honeymoon suites. At the renovated general store—the only business for miles— warm up by the wood-burning stove, sip wine, and share an old-fashioned smooch.

11. **Valley of Fire, Nevada:** Spark the romantic kindling in this tiny, fiery desert state park, located an hour from Las Vegas. Hide in the narrow arroyos, cuddle underneath overhanging rock formations, or spread out on the slickrock with only lizards to keep you company. There are numerous hiking trails, many with peekaboo views of Lake Mead.

12. **Pitcher Mountain Trail, New Hampshire:** Grab a small jug of New Hampshire's famous cider in nearby Stoddard, then stroll past blueberry fields and grazing Scottish Highland cattle to reach the summit of Mount Pitcher. The bald, flat mountaintop boasts the "softest rock in New Hampshire" for picnics and offers head-twirling views of

the Presidential Range, the Berkshires, and Vermont foothills. The 15-minute hike is easily accessible, and encountering another couple is considered a crowd.

13. **Cape May, New Jersey:** When it comes to wooing your beloved, Cape May delivers all that's needed. During the day, stroll together through the area's numerous gardens and wildlife sanctuaries or beachcomb for Cape May's famous "diamonds"—pieces of quartz polished by the waves. Savor the romance with a horse-drawn carriage ride through the gaslit streets of the old Victorian town.

14. **White Sands National Monument Moonlight Walk, New Mexico:** Moonlight has never before exerted such an attraction for lovers. When the moon's out in full force, these gypsum sand formations—the largest in the world—glow. Stroll hand-in-hand under the brilliant New Mexico night sky and steal a kiss under the approving eye of the man in the moon.

15. **Lake Metigoshe, North Dakota:** Straddling the U.S.-Canadian border, Lake Metigoshe is as far north as you'll get in the state . . . making it the prime place to watch the northern lights dance or the Milky Way sparkle while bundled together in a blanket. There are no crowds to interfere with romance and no bright city lights to hinder stargazing.

16. **The Richland Carousel, Ohio:** Love makes the world go 'round, so keep on spinning by kissing aboard one of the carousel's ornate animals. This indoor merry-go-round keeps hearts and hands toasty in the winter, and, when things heat up in the summer, an airy breeze cools lovers as they twirl into the sunset.

17. **McConnell's Mill Bridge in McConnell's Mill State Park, Pennsylvania:** Back in horse-and-buggy days, a young fella could steal plenty of kisses as he and his sweetie rode underneath a long covered bridge, hence the nickname

"kissing bridges." Pennsylvania boasts 213 such bridges, and a favorite is McConnell's Mill Bridge spanning scenic Slippery Rock Creek. At 96 feet long, there are plenty of kisses to be had while slowly traveling through.

18. **Providence Athenaeum, Rhode Island:** Amidst the library stacks, there's romance and history...but not just in the books. Edgar Allan Poe spent hours hidden away in this 1838-era building reading poems to his love, Sarah Whitman. Choose your favorite love poem and tuck back into the stacks together for some riveting recitation of passionate passages.

19. **Landsford Canal State Park, South Carolina:** It's not Venice, and canoes aren't gondolas, but you can glide along with the same romantic notions at this charming state park. Canoe the Catawba River canals or simply stroll along the riverside trails. Whichever mode of transport suits your style, the surroundings won't cease to amaze. Stone bridges, canal locks, and an old mill add a touch of history, while the rare spider lilies that bloom along the rocky shoals give a sense of the exotic.

20. **McDonald Observatory, Texas:** Like everything else in Texas, the night sky is big...and up in these parts it's darker than cowboy coffee—choice conditions for stargazing and kissing. At this remote observatory, starry-eyed lovers intent on romance can look toward the heavens for some unexpected celestial surprises but also find earthly delights. Relish romantic moments far from civilization (the nearest major town is 160 miles away), and be sure to wish upon a lone star.

21. **Barboursville Vineyards, Virginia:** Raise a toast to the state motto—"Virginia is for Lovers"—at this vineyard and winery nestled in the foothills of the Blue Ridge Mountains. As if sipping wine at a lovely vineyard wasn't enough to captivate your romantic attention, there are also

enchanting ruins to explore. The remains of an early 19th-century mansion designed by Thomas Jefferson are tucked away in the boxwoods.

22. **American Camp, San Juan Island, Washington:** Duck out of sight into secluded, sheltered coves or hide together in the tall grass. No one will see you, except for perhaps one of the rabbits. American Camp at the windswept southern end of San Juan Island doesn't let up on spectacular scenery or hidden spots. Find your own little beach and savor views of the Olympic Peninsula and Cascade Mountains. Between kisses, watch for orcas breaching in Puget Sound.

Wedding Announcements

These married names say more than the sum of their parts.

✳ ✳ ✳ ✳

MANY FACTORS ARE taken into consideration as couples decide whether to keep, blend, or hyphenate their surnames: preservation of a family name, political beliefs, feminist values, professional identities, and more.

But no matter how well intended, some name combinations are not a match made in heaven. Having one of the following odd-ball combos could doom you to a lifetime of constantly having to spell, explain, and put up with "Are you serious?" looks from colleagues, neighbors—and even your own family.

✳ Badde-Mann

✳ Beebe-Makar

✳ Berger-King

✳ Best-Freund

✳ Betten-Kind

✳ Bichen-Carr

✳ Bird-Hunter

✳ Bogg-Downe

✳ Brake-Fast

✳ Brick-Laer

✳ Bumm-Diehl

✳ Bumm-Rapp

* Crabb-Appel
* Dills-Pickle
* Doll-Fase
* Ferris-Wheeler
* Flower-Garton
* Fuller-Bottom
* Gott-Milk
* Hotze-Duff
* Lacy-Bumm
* Lyon-Heartt
* Mann-Slaughter
* Near-Farr
* Pancake-Stack
* Papa-Baer
* Poore-Mies
* Poore-Yu
* Rose-Bloom
* Schlapp-Bottom
* Stock-Potts
* Storey-Ours
* Uder-Panak
* Wonder-Barr
* Wynnen-Hand

* Darling-Valentine
* Dollor-Bett
* Dudley-Downer
* Fisher-Mann
* Flower-Mill
* Gold-Fisch
* Hare-Kutter
* Hunt-Peck
* Lemon-Dropp
* Macon-Bacon
* Mash-Schupp
* Nutt-Endouin
* Pan-Frye
* Picken-Finger

18 Hopelessly Devoted Couples

Behind every good man is a great woman. Can you match up the following couples who stayed together till death (or the end of TV syndication) did them part?

✴   ✴   ✴   ✴

1. Robin Hood	a. Betty Bloomer
2. Clark Kent	b. Cleopatra
3. Kermit	c. Dale Evans
4. Romeo	d. Elizabeth Barrett
5. Marc Antony	e. Gracie Allen
6. JFK	f. Harriett Hilliard
7. Ricky Ricardo	g. Jacqueline Bouvier
8. Prince Albert	h. Juliet
9. Robert Browning	i. June Carter
10. Gerald Ford	j. Lauren Bacall
11. Fred Flintstone	k. Lois Lane
12. Ronald Reagan	l. Lucy McGillicuddy
13. Johnny Cash	m. Maid Marian
14. Ozzie Nelson	n. Miss Piggy
15. John Lennon	o. Nancy Davis
16. Humphrey Bogart	p. Queen Victoria
17. Roy Rogers	q. Wilma Slaghoople
18. George Burns	r. Yoko Ono

1. m; 2. k; 3. n; 4. h; 5. b; 6. g; 7. l; 8. p; 9. d; 10. a; 11. q; 12. o; 13. i; 14. f; 15. r; 16. j; 17. c; 18. e

Cakes through the Ages

We'll give you a slice of wedding cake history...

✳ ✳ ✳ ✳

When in Rome

NEXT TIME YOU enjoy a slice from a six-tiered mocha wedding cake with raspberry-almond icing, give a quick thankyou to the ancient Romans who started the tradition. Granted, their "wedding cake" was more of a barley loaf broken over the wife's head for luck. When the Romans invaded England in A.D. 43, they brought along this tradition, effectively laying the foundation for wedding cakes to come.

Pie in the Sky

In medieval England, guests stacked spiced buns in front of the bride for luck; if she and the groom could reach over them to kiss, it foretold a prosperous (and fertile) future.

The 17th century saw the rise of the "bride's pie"—an elaborately decorated pastry filled with a concoction of lamb testicles, oysters, cow innards, and spices. Other variations included the more palatable "matrimony pie" filled with dried fruit, and the "bride's cake," made of currants sandwiched between short bread and baked over a fire.

With the availability of sugar and home ovens in the 18th century, more contemporary-looking cakes began to emerge. But refined sugar was still pricey—a bride who had a cake with white icing clearly came from money. For everyone else, a simple plum cake or brandied fruitcake, which had a longer shelf life, was the wedding cake du jour.

The brandied fruitcake followed the pilgrims to Plymouth Rock and remained a custom in America until 1840, when Queen Victoria and Prince Albert changed the face of wedding cakes on both sides of the Atlantic.

Tiers of a Crown

Covered in white icing, hence known as "royal icing," Vicky and Al's multi-tiered masterpiece set the precedent for generations of towering cakes. No matter that bakers hadn't yet figured out how to stack cakes—they just made the bottom layer actual cake, while the rest was just layers of icing.

Prince Leopold's 1882 wedding cake was the first to feature stacked cakes, a look achieved by allowing the icing in between each layer to harden. It wasn't until the 20th century that bakers employed the modern practice of using wooden pillars to support each tier. With refined sugar now a staple, the tiered cake became a wedding must-have for most of the 20th century.

Fast Facts: Wedding Cakes

* On average, wedding cakes will run you anywhere from $3-$12 a slice.

* For that smooth, flawless frosting look, you'll want fondant, which is a thick, chewy form of sculptable frosting. It's a must if you want edible flowers, bows, etc., but watch out—that fondant will increase the price of your cake considerably.

* Queen Victoria and Prince Albert's wedding cake was nine feet around, weighed in at 300 pounds, was 14 inches high, and was actually served at the wedding breakfast.

* Originally, the wedding "cake" was just grains of wheat that were thrown on the happy couple as a symbol of fertility and prosperity.

* In 2004, chefs at the Mohegan Sun Hotel and Casino in Uncasville, Connecticut, baked a 15,032-pound wedding cake—it holds the record for largest wedding cake ever. (Nearly 5,000 pounds of the total weight was just frosting!)

* In the Middle Ages, couples would kiss over a pile of scones and bread—the taller the pile, the more luck they would have. But a French chef visiting London in the 16th century decided this tradition was in need of his help; he created an iced, multi-layered cake, instead, and the trend caught on.

* Careful of hidden costs: Most tiered wedding cakes must be delivered and assembled on site by the bakery—trust them, they're professionals—and delivery charges can be $50 to $100 or more, depending on travel logistics and cake size. (Some bakeries charge a cake-cutting fee, too.)

* Wedding cake toppers can be found on the cheap, but those who go all out can purchase Swarovski crystal cake toppers that can cost several hundred dollars or more.

Weddings the Wiccan Way

A Wiccan wedding, while not the norm, could be to your liking.

✳ ✳ ✳ ✳

WEDDINGS ARE STEEPED in time-honored tradition—and yet there are few other events in life with so many opportunities for self-expression. For some brides and grooms, this self-expression goes deeper than matching the color of the bridesmaids' dresses to the flowers. These couples personalize their ceremony by adopting a theme that expresses their spiritual beliefs and values. In this case, a Wiccan wedding.

Set the Scene Naturally

So how exactly does one throw a Wiccan or pagan wedding? Let's start with the basics: Nature is highly revered in the Wiccan and pagan religions, so ceremonies are often held outside, and pagan couples usually decorate the ritual area with an assortment and abundance of flowers.

The altar should be arranged with two white candles, flower-scented incense, and a willow wand. (The willow tree, which frequently appears in folklore and mythology, is considered the tree of enchantment. It is sacred to poets and significant in the life cycles of birth and death. It takes its place on the altar as a sacred object just as a cross might be displayed at a Christian wedding.) Additionally, cakes and wine may be displayed on the altar to be shared at some point during the ritual.

The witnesses are usually arranged in a circle, either sitting or standing, depending on how long the ceremony will last. The priest or priestess may want to call attention to the symbolism of the circle as an object without beginning or end.

Some couples wear traditional, formal wedding garb (a long white dress and veil for the bride; tuxedo or suit for the groom), and other couples dress in Celtic attire. Fortunately, there are no rigorous rules governing dress code for a pagan or Wiccan wedding, so couples may dress as their tastes , finances, and climate allows.

The Ties that Bind

The priest or priestess invokes the beings of air, fire, water, and earth and directs the couple to remember the qualities their union should possess. (Scripts for a Wiccan service are easily found on various Web sites.) The couple may light a unity candle, as is done in traditional weddings, or incorporate other elements of non-pagan weddings if they choose.

Finally, the bride and groom cross arms and join hands, creating the infinity symbol. The clergyperson loosely wraps the couple's hands with a cord or ribbon, and they state their vows. Most of us are familiar with the symbolism of wedding rings, but in a pagan or Wiccan ceremony, a rope or cord is the primary symbol of unity. In the ceremony known as *handfasting*, the ritual of tying the bride's and groom's hands together, is the culminating act—on par with the exchanging of wedding rings. Handfasting can occur either as a marriage ceremony or as betrothal. Either way, this is where the phrases "tying the knot" and "the ties that bind" come from, as the bride and groom literally have their hands fastened together, signifying their formal contract to be husband and wife.

Centuries ago, handfasting was customary in Great Britain— especially in rural areas where weeks or months could pass before a clergyman happened to travel through your village. So, eager couples bypassed the need for clergy by clasping hands, publicly declaring themselves married, and consummating their bond. It was the ancient equivalent of today's common-law marriages.

In modern Wiccan ceremonies, the cord is knotted, the union is blessed, and the couple is publicly presented to their family and friends. You will still need to obtain a marriage license for the ceremony to be considered legally binding. But some couples consider the public performance of the ceremonial act to be sufficient. Legalities aside, the pagan/Wiccan handfasting ceremony can be a beautiful and memorable way to literally and metaphorically tie the knot!

A Walk Down the Aisle

This ancient ritual still has a modern (but different) meaning.

✳ ✳ ✳ ✳

Getting Paid to Give Her Away

How many heads of cattle do you think you're worth? How about chickens? What about acres of land? Fortunately, American women don't have to speculate about their personal value in terms of commodities, but there are many cultures where that is still the case when it comes to wedding planning. Marriages were once based on social and economic pragmatism rather than love or compatibility, and for centuries, a groom's family was expected to pay a "bride's price" before a wedding could take place.

In this scenario, the groom's family was essentially reimbursing the bride's family for her lost labor. Their daughter would no longer be available to work and help support the family, and they required compensation for this. On the wedding day, the father of the bride would present his daughter to the groom and give her away, verbally acknowledging their compensatory agreement had been fulfilled and that her family of origin had no further claim to her.

From a contemporary point of view, it's hard to believe there was ever a time when a woman had so few rights and privileges that she didn't have the choice of whom to marry. Of course, the age-old tradition of "giving away" the bride is still popular—although no longer as a conveyance of property from father to husband.

Making It Modern

While some progressive-thinking brides feel a father escorting his daughter down the aisle is a remnant of a patriarchal system that failed to recognize women as the equals of men, it doesn't have to be interpreted literally (or historically). Some brides may chafe at the "giving away" ritual as an artifact of arranged marriages, but modern brides can put their own spin on the old tradition.

Christian brides, for example, sometimes prefer to interpret the ritual as an expression of the Bible verse that describes how a man and woman will leave their families and "become one." The subtext in this case is that the bride and groom are giving up their old support systems—and their identities with their original families—in exchange for new ones.

Usually, the way this plays out is that the father of the bride walks his daughter down the aisle of the church or ceremony site. Once the bride and her father have arrived at the front of the room, he may lift up her veil and give her a kiss or hug. At this time, the father may take the groom's hand and place it with the bride's hand or simply step back, allowing the bride and groom to stand as a couple. For a modern twist, some brides have their mother accompany them down the aisle as well.

"Who Gives this Woman to Be Married?"

Nowadays, it's not uncommon to hear a father respond to the above, "'Her mother and I do" or "We do." He may even reply, "She gives herself freely, with her family's blessing." Or, the parents may reply in unison. Some couples have taken the evolution further by having the question posed to both the bride's parents and the groom's, for a more egalitarian touch.

Although the origins of some traditional wedding practices may seem archaic and out of touch, remember: They can be adapted to fit your modern sensibilities and, most importantly, help define your new life as a couple. Having the father and/or mother "give the bride away" has come to mean something few brides would turn away from: That the people who raised her embrace her future husband and approve of the marriage. Just a little tinkering with the language, and any self-respecting bride can confidently start her wedding off with a traditional expression of her parents' support—and be ensured a tear-jerker moment!

Something Old: Saving the Top Tier

Most people have a few mysterious, unidentifiable things in their freezer. And if it belongs to a newlywed couple, you can be pretty sure that one of those tinfoil lumps is wedding cake.

✳   ✳   ✳   ✳

Saving the top tier of the wedding cake is a tradition that traces its roots to Europe in the late 19th century. People used to make significant cakes not only for weddings but for christenings, too. It was hoped, even assumed, that a couple would hold a christening at least nine months after their wedding, so the two ceremonies were often linked—as were the cakes. Couples thought it would be nice to save some of their wedding cake to serve at their first christening, coming full circle on the whole "commitment" thing.

This trend resulted in the cakes themselves changing a bit; tiered wedding cakes became logical. The bottom tier was for the party, the middle tier was for giving away to guests, and the top tier was to save for later. It helped that wedding cakes back then were often brandy-soaked, fruitcake-like affairs that lent themselves to preserving for long periods of time.

Times Change, Traditions Remain (for Better or Worse)

Over the past 100 years or so, the length of time between the wedding day and the christening or baptizing of a couple's first child has gradually gotten longer, so the two events have become less connected. People still save the top tier, but the reason for doing so has shifted. Nowadays, most couples want to save cake to enjoy on their one-year anniversary, simply as a reminder of their special day.

The question of whether or not this actually makes sense has been under debate over the past few years, however. It's a nice idea, but in reality, modern wedding cakes won't last in a freezer much longer than three months. Today's wedding cakes are made with buttercream, lots of eggs and sugar, chocolates, fruit fillings, and nuts—ingredients that simply don't freeze well in the long-term. It's not good news for the couple that wants to save their cake…but sometimes a frozen block of goo is a frozen block of goo—even if it has sentimental value.

But I Love Stale, Waxy Cake!

If you still want to save your top tier (or just a slice) of your wedding cake, no one is going to stop you. You probably paid dearly for it, the trend is still popular, and it *is* cake, after all. If you do attempt it, however, there are important steps to take.

Well before your reception, find a plastic container big enough to fit the top tier with an airtight lid. Make sure your caterer or reception hall manager has this container and your instructions ready. As soon as the cake is cut, the top tier or slice should be put into the container, then put into a fridge as soon as possible—time is of the essence. Ideally, not much time would pass between that stage and the freezing stage, which involves wrapping the container itself in tinfoil and hoping for the best.

Have Your Cake and Eat It Too

A memorable one-year wedding anniversary isn't going to hinge on whether or not you get to savor the exact cake you ate one year earlier. But if having that flavor is important to you, there are other ways you can create it.

Most bakers save recipes or use the same ones again and again, so ask your baker if he or she can create a fresh, mini- version of your wedding cake on your anniversary. (It is guaranteed to taste better than last year's.) You could also try baking your own version or, perhaps most fun of all, discovering a new dessert or kind of cake that becomes your special yearly anniversary tradition.

Once Wasn't Enough

These famous serial spouses married their way into infamy.

❊   ❊   ❊   ❊

WHEN FAMOUS COUPLES wed, their stories are as apt to end in infamy as they are with "happily ever after." Unless they give marriage another go-round, that is. These celebrity paramours managed to marry the same person twice—with a divorce in between.

But why would a celeb marry an ex-spouse again? It may depend on the reasons they divorced in the first place. Becoming older and "wiser" may have revealed new insight into problems that once plagued them as a couple. From this new, more sophisticated perspective, they value the good parts of the relationship and can make a commitment to managing conflict in a more healthful way. Or it could just be the amazing makeup sex.

Richard Burton and Elizabeth Taylor

This couple tops the list of twice-married celebs. Movie-star-turned-fragrance-maven Elizabeth Taylor got married eight times, twice to Richard Burton. Sixteen months after their first divorce, they tied the knot again. That marriage was about as short-lived as the divorce, lasting less than a year.

Don Johnson and Melanie Griffith

Melanie Griffith and Don Johnson said Las Vegas "I do's" when she was only 18 years old. The two divorced, and Melanie moved on to marry Steven Bauer. When drug and alcohol addiction overwhelmed her career, she and Bauer divorced, and Melanie turned to Don for support. They reconciled, wed again, and—you guessed it—divorced again.

Marshall Mathers and Kim Scott

Troubled shock-rapper Marshall Mathers (whose stage name is Eminem) married high school sweetheart Kim Scott after an on-again/off-again relationship that spanned a decade. The marriage came to an end after Scott attempted suicide and then sued her husband for depicting her violent death in one of his songs. As if that wasn't enough drama, they remarried five years later—but divorced within a year.

Travis Barker and Shanna Moakler

Former Blink-182 drummer Travis Barker and beauty queen Shanna Moakler turned their volatile relationship into a reality television show on *Meet the Barkers*. The two filed for divorce in 2006 (it was finalized in 2008), but when Travis was injured in a plane crash, Shanna ran to his bedside. In subsequent interviews, Shanna revealed the fiery crash reignited their affections: "We would like to renew our vows and have another wedding. When you almost lose a loved one, it makes you appreciate things you took for granted." To date, however, official nuptials have yet to take place.

Steven Crane and Lana Turner

Apparently, the postman isn't the only one who rings twice! Seven-times-wed actress Lana Turner wed second husband Steven Crane twice. Why? Their first marriage was annulled in a shocking paperwork snafu. Turns out, Crane's divorce from an earlier wife wasn't the real deal.

Robert Wagner and Natalie Wood

Academy Award–winning actress Natalie Wood rose to fame as a teen, starring in plays and movies such as *Miracle on 34th Street*, *West Side Story*, and *Rebel Without a Cause*. Apparently, she found *Love with the Proper Stranger* twice in husband Robert Wagner. Although Wood—like many other Hollywood starlets—has multiple marriages to her credit, her last marriage didn't end in divorce but rather at the time of her accidental drowning at age 43.

Italian Wedding Customs

Many of the wedding customs we observe in the United States trace their roots to Italy. Perhaps you can incorporate some of these buone ideas into your own wedding plans...

❋ ❋ ❋ ❋

Doing as the Romans Did

FROM AQUEDUCTS TO art, we still "do as the Romans do" in many ways, including the way we celebrate marriage. Pre-wedding banquets, gifts for the bride and groom, and the ring as a symbol of union are all Roman customs that have continued to this day. Most weddings were held in June, since they were forbidden during Advent or Lent, and August was so hot and sticky it was considered unlucky. Nuts and wheat were thrown over the newlyweds after the ceremony as a symbol for fertility, and everyone ate until they were stuffed.

Most Roman weddings were arranged by the parents, however, and a dowry was paid by the bride's father to the groom. A pig was sacrificed before the meal, and a parade from the church to the bride's new house ended in the bride smearing the doorposts with oil and fat.

After that, she took to the bed, since ancient Romans were pretty clear that marriage was there for procreation.

Italian Weddings Today

Of course, Italian wedding customs have evolved over the centuries. And since there are so many distinct regions of Italy, wedding protocol varies depending on where you are; for example, Southern Italian weddings are generally bigger, showier events than the intimate weddings to the North. But the following are a few customs that you'll still find alive and well in many parts of Italy:

* On either side of the door of the church, a small olive tree is placed for good luck during the ceremony.

* No purple! Italians believe purple brings bad luck.

* Italian brides used to have a trousseau, or hope chest, full of linens and silk nightgowns passed down through the women in the family. Though it's less common to have a hope chest today, middle-class families will often give their daughter all the linen belonging to her mother or her grandmother on her big day.

* It's still popular to dance the "Tarantella," a lively group dance.

* "*Viva gli sposi!*" or "Long live the couple!" is shouted throughout the day and is usually followed by a toast.

* Guests at an Italian wedding get a small gift, called a bomboniere. The bomboniere are placed in a basket, and the bride walks around the tables, greeting well-wishers and giving out the gifts before the cutting of the cake.

* The bride and groom rarely have a bridal party; instead, they choose a witness.

You Are Going to Talk About the Food, Right?

Maybe one of the biggest advantages of getting married Italian style is that you get to enjoy the food. Italian cuisine is known worldwide for being extraordinary—and always plentiful.

Appetizers, breads, pastas, soups, meat dishes, salads, fruits, and desserts will be in abundance at an Italian wedding. It's not unheard of to enjoy 12 or more courses during the reception. Coffee, espresso, sweet liqueurs for the women and harder stuff for the men, and, of course, wine flows freely and everyone is encouraged to eat, drink, and make merry in the name of the happy couple. Plates of fried dough, twisted into bow-tie shapes and covered with powdered sugar, are often served for extra luck.

Many people have enjoyed Italian wedding cake, a decadent white cake filled with coconut and topped with cream cheese frosting. This cake is so good, it's actually on the menu at some restaurants—one more example of just how influential the Italian wedding has become.

Bachelor Parties and Bridal Showers

Pre-wedding rituals for men and women…

✳   ✳   ✳   ✳

Stag Night

THE FIRST BACHELOR parties date back to fifth-century Sparta, when soldiers would gorge themselves on food and drink the night before one of them got married. Instead of gifts, the men took up a collection and, at the end of the night, presented a bag of money to the groom—so he could still afford to party with his buddies after his wife took control of the household finances. (Strip clubs weren't part of these celebrations, but that's probably just because they weren't really around in ancient times.)

Bachelorette, or "hen," parties didn't come into fashion until the late 1960s and '70s, when liberated women decided they deserved to party just as hard as the guys.

Shower Power

More traditional for brides-to-be is the shower, which many say can be traced to the Dutch. Hundreds of years ago in Holland, a maiden fell in love with a poor miller, but her father refused to allow the marriage—because clearly the broke-as-a-joke miller couldn't provide a "properly set up" home. Rallying to her defense, the bride's friends "showered" her with household items to help her get settled—and ultimately marry the miller.

England may be another point of origin for the bridal shower. A friend of the bride felt she couldn't afford a nice-enough gift to convey the magnitude of her happiness for the engaged couple. So she convinced the bride's other friends to pool their resources and shower the bride with several smaller gifts. A version of the story suggests the English girl had heard about the Dutch bride and took her cue from that.

The Common and the Covenant

There is more than one way to be married!

✳ ✳ ✳ ✳

Skipping the Ceremony-Thingy

CAN YOU BE married without the marriage license or the wedding? In about a dozen states in the United States, yes. While grounds vary from state to state, common law marriage typically declares couples legally wed if they live together, file joint tax returns, and willfully regard themselves as husband and wife in all traditional respects.

Not Just Playing House: The Rules

A common law marriage abides by the same rules as traditional marriage. And common law couples must follow the same legal divorce procedures—including potentially being on the hook for alimony. The upside? Along with establishing a higher level of commitment to the relationship, they may receive spousal privileges such as inheritance rights; tax and employer-benefit advantages; and in the event of a life-or-death situation, visitation and decision-making powers.

The Covenant Contract

While some perceive common law marriage as a shortcut to matrimony, covenant marriage lies at the other end of the spectrum. Fed up with trivialized weddings and quickie divorces? Well, covenant marriage advocates a truer interpretation of "'til death do us part." What constitutes a marriage as "covenant"? The couple is required to undergo premarital counseling to ascertain compatibility and clarify the gravity of the covenant agreement. The martial pact is super-highly binding. Once a covenant marriage is entered into, it's for the long haul. Only a very few allowances will dissolve the marriage.

The Blame Game

No way out? Well, unlike traditional marriage, covenant marriage does not permit a no-fault divorce. Meaning: Start the finger pointing, because someone's gotta be unequivocally to blame. Divorce can be obtained—after first seeking mandatory counseling. But there must be proven "blame," with adultery, abandonment, abuse, or a felony criminal conviction as primary acceptable reasons.

A Polarizing Practice

The movement has found minimal but steadfast support. For most covenant crusaders, entering into a near-iron-clad union demonstrates a well-intentioned show of devotion. However, the practice has also provoked some vocal detractors. According to dissenters, covenant marriage puts the "institutionalization" in the institution of marriage. Since acts of adultery and certain types of abuse may be difficult to prove in court, covenant critics fear that individuals (mostly women) will be trapped in a potentially harmful situation.

Covenant Marriage: A Love Story

Perhaps the most famous poster couple for covenant marriage is former Arkansas governor and 2008 presidential hopeful

Mike Huckabee and his wife Janet. Eighteen years old and unable to afford a proper ring at the time for his high school sweetheart, Mike proposed to Janet with a soda can pull-tab. After a year of marriage, the couple was devastated when Janet was diagnosed with cancer of the spine. Doctors grimly reported that if she lived, she would likely be permanently wheelchair-bound. Well, Janet recovered her ability to walk, but she was told she likely would never bear children. Three children later, Mike and Janet renewed their lifelong commitment by upgrading to a covenant marriage on Valentine's Day 2005.

Not Winning any Popularity Contests

Only a few states legally recognize and enforce the terms of covenant marriage. In 1997, the state of Louisiana blazed the trail and enacted the first covenant marriage law. And Arkansas and Arizona also hopped on board. Yet, in those three states combined, less than 5 percent of married couples go the covenant route.

Fast Facts: Weddings

* It's common for couples in India and China to cut down on costs by displaying a fake wedding cake. Made of cardboard and wax, it's just for show, not for dessert, though the uppermost tier is sometimes the real thing.

* A honeymoon will run you about $4,500, depending on the trip.

* Every wedding dress needs alterations; the average bride will schedule between two and three fittings before her big day.

* These days, many engaged couples choose a bakery or specialty wedding cake store for their cake, but most supermarkets make wedding cakes, too. Supermarket cakes account for more than $280 million of wedding cake sales.

* Gamophobia is the fear of marriage.

* On average, an engagement ring runs around $4,411. Couples spend approximately $2,067 for his-and-hers wedding bands.

* Not so long ago, wedding cakes were predominately white cake with white frosting. These days, chocolate devil's food cakes are more popular, and fruit fillings such as pear, blood orange, coconut, and lime frequently top a bakery's most-wanted list.

* Accessories such as shoes and undergarments can cost about one-third of the price of the dress itself.

* Roughly 46 percent of brides purchase their gowns on sale.

* Don't want to do things the traditional way? Cupcake tiers have become increasingly popular as alternatives to the wedding cake. Other couples serve towers of truffles, slices of tiramisu, or even "cakes" made by stacking doughnuts.

Long Road to Love

Paving the way for the acceptance of interracial marriage hasn't always been easy...

✳   ✳   ✳   ✳

Love for the Lonely

UNTIL 1662, INTERRACIAL marriage was legal in every British colony in North America. It's not hard to imagine why: The white women of England and Western Europe were very wary of the long, dangerous journey to the Colonies and even more frightened of what they might find once they arrived, yet the white male settlers were lonely and needed mates. Many were more than happy to take Native American brides or to satisfy their lusts with African American slave mistresses. Who was going to stop them? Colonial men were all in the same boat, so to speak, and political and religious leaders feared anarchy if natural desires were not satisfied.

The Law Intervenes

As the decades went on and more Caucasian women arrived on the American shore, however, laws began to change. Colonial leaders no longer saw any "excuse" for white men to carry on with women of other races. In 1662, lawmakers in Virginia doubled the fine for fornication between white men and black women. In 1664, interracial marriage was banned completely in Maryland. And by 1750, every southern colony, along with Massachusetts and Pennsylvania, had outlawed the practice—though those who were already married when laws were passed were rarely hunted down and forced to separate. When interracial marriages were nullified, most of the white men involved in them simply chose to keep on living with their partners, whether their relationships were recognized by law or not.

Though the word "miscegenation" is rarely used anymore, from 1863 on, it was a term used to describe marriage, cohabitation, or sex between members of different races. Originally coined during the Civil War in an attempt to vilify the Abolitionist movement and scare the public about the results of outlawing slavery, the word "miscegenation" was widely known, but often, it was not the actual legal term used to prosecute those who broke such laws. Instead, the parties would be charged with the more generic sounding "felony adultery" or "felony fornication." Thus, local authorities could prosecute people for engaging in interracial sex and/or marriage without raising too many questions outside their own communities.

Federal anti-miscegenation amendments were proposed in the U.S. Congress in 1871, 1912, and 1928, but no nationwide law against interracial marriage was ever passed.

A Loving Change

Religious institutions began to speak out about the issue in the mid-20th century. The Presbyterian Church, the Unitarian Universalist Association, and the Roman Catholic Church all expressed disgust at anti-miscegenation laws and support for interracial couples who wanted to marry, and these weighty opinions seemed to finally turn the tide. In the 1950s, anti-miscegenation laws finally began to be struck down. Arizona, California, Colorado, Idaho, Indiana, Maryland, Montana, Nebraska, Nevada, North Dakota, Oregon, South Dakota,

Utah, and Wyoming all legalized interracial marriage within just a little over a decade.

Many other states clung tenaciously to their anti-miscegenation laws, however, and it took a federal ruling to legalize interracial marriage everywhere in America. Richard Perry Loving, a white man, and his wife Mildred Loving, a black woman, filed suit against the state of Virginia for denying their marriage that had taken place in the District of Columbia and for prosecuting them under Virginia's anti-miscegenation law. In 1967, after the Supreme Court's decision in the Lovings' favor in the case of *Loving v. Virginia*, interracial couples were suddenly free to marry not only in Virginia but in Alabama, Arkansas, Delaware, Florida, Georgia, Kentucky, Louisiana, Mississippi, Missouri, North Carolina, Oklahoma, South Carolina, Tennessee, Texas, and West Virginia. The battle for love and justice that had lasted hundreds of years was finally over.

On the "Threshold" of Tradition

Why does the groom carry the bride over the threshold? It's all in the good luck that follows.

✳ ✳ ✳ ✳

Avoiding Evil

THE CENTURIES-OLD ORIGINS of this practice range from the mystical to just plain bizarre. In ancient times, it was thought that the spirits of the dead could attach themselves to the living—and brides were particularly at risk.

To make matters worse, these spirits congregated near doorways, so when a bride walked across the threshold, they entered through her feet. These bodiless interlopers were believed to doom newly minted couples to a tragic end. The spirits wreaked havoc on the bride, causing everything from physical ailments to mental illness. To prevent this kind of relationship carnage, grooms played it safe by carrying their brides over thresholds. It stands to reason: If a bride's feet never touched the threshold, then she could never be possessed by the wayward spirits.

In the Roman Empire, grooms carried brides over thresholds for luck. If a bride tripped while stepping across the threshold into her new home, bad luck rained down on the marriage and abode. Carrying the bride through the doorway was a way to aovid this danger.

Lifting a bride over the threshold also eliminated fodder for the rumor mill. If a bride rushed across the threshold of her own volition, she may have seemed too enthusiastic to offer her virginity. By carrying her across the threshold, a groom could avoid scandal and his betrothed could appear suitably reluctant and demure.

Or Avoiding Escape

Perhaps the most disturbing origin of this now-symbolic gesture is the role it played in medieval times, when brides were often kidnapped. Carrying a bride across the threshold prevented her from escaping of her own volition.

Marriage by Proxy

What is a proxy marriage? Do both parties have to be in the same country or on the same continent? Can anyone do it, or is it just for those serving in the military?

✳ ✳ ✳ ✳

He/She Does

THE REASON THERE are so many questions about proxy marriage is because the laws vary so widely from country to country, and here in the United States, from state to state.

In the United States, only five states allow marriage by proxy: California, Colorado, Kansas, Montana, and Texas. In a proxy marriage, either the bride or groom is not physically present for the ceremony, and someone stands in for that missing person based upon a power of attorney.

They Do

A double proxy marriage is one in which two representatives stand in for both parties. Double proxy marriages are much harder to obtain and are only legal in Montana. Even there, laws vary from county to county, and in many Montana counties, at least one party must physically be there to pick up the marriage license. In the United States, proxy marriages are most often obtained by those serving in the military and are exceedingly rare amongst the general populace. In California, proxy marriages are available only to members of the military currently on active duty.

Historically speaking, probably the most famous proxy marriage was that of Napoleon Bonaparte to Archduchess Marie Louise in 1810. But proxy marriages still make headlines today: Cosmonaut Yuri Malenchenko was orbiting the earth in a space station on August 10, 2003, when he married Ekaterina Dmitriev, who looked radiant in a long, white gown at NASA's Johnson Space Center in Houston, Texas. A close pal stood in for Yuri as his agent, and the couple blew kisses to each other via video link.

The Much-Married Tommy Manville

Thomas Franklyn Manville Jr.—flamboyant Manhattan socialite and heir to the Johns-Manville asbestos fortune—earned minor celebrity and a place in Guinness World Records for being the American man married the most times in the 20th century.

✳   ✳   ✳   ✳

MANVILLE APPEARED TO revel in his reputation and frequently made self-deprecating comments that made for memorable sound bites...

"I propose to anybody... Sort of an introduction."

During his lifetime (1894–1967), Manville racked up 13 marriages to 11 different women. Why the hankering to get hitched? Well, part of his marriage compulsion may have been motivated by financial gain. You see, when Tommy's wealthy father died, his father's will set up a trust for Tommy—but he was only entitled to withdraw from the interest. However, the will reportedly stipulated that Tommy would receive a million dollars from the principal when he married. The loophole? It didn't specify that only the first marriage was eligible for the big payout!

"I've only had lunch with her once or twice, [but]... I think this could be one of the richest experiences of my life."

The above statement was made while Manville was still married to his eighth wife. He was referring to a brunette nightclub singer named Ruth Webb. Ruth managed to avoid becoming wife number nine, but perhaps Manville regretted that he went another route...

"I'm done with blondes."

Manville's love of women and reciting marital vows was only matched by his passion for fast cars. In fact, as a parting favor, Manville typically gifted each wife with an automobile on their way out. Other than that, Manville barely had to tap into his $20 million bank account while freeing himself from his first eight marriages.

But wifey number nine, blond bombshell Anita Frances Roddy-Eden, caused quite a headache. When they wed in 1952, the dancer was 30 years Manville's junior. And she didn't age much in the 12 days they were married. She hauled the eccentric playboy to court and took the stand with accusations of "extreme mental cruelty." Among her claims: Manville drank excessively, and when she questioned his morning gin consumption, he threatened to kill her with a gun.

Plus, he allegedly hung photos of his previous wives around the house and constantly talked about his exes. She even said that while they were still married, he tried proposing to her twin sister, Juanita Patino, the ex-wife of a Bolivian tin tycoon. A bit of a sassy character herself, Roddy-Eden Manville remarked that if they were unable to come to terms with a satisfactory settlement, then "I am still his wife, and I am going to be the widow Manville!"

"She cried, and the judge wiped her tears with my checkbook."

Ultimately, Roddy-Eden Manville walked away with $260,000—a sizable sum at the time and significantly more than any of her predecessors received. She went on to pen and publish a biography entitled *The Many Wives and Lives of Tommy Manville.*

"When I meet a beautiful girl, the first thing I say is will you marry me? The second thing I say is how do you do?"

Over the years, Manville's notoriety made its mark on popular culture. Anita's book inspired a campy musical by Jackie Curtis called *Lucky Wonderful: 13 Musicals About Tommy Manville.* Manville is also referenced in Irving Berlin's song "What Chance Have I With Love." Furthermore, it is widely believed that Manville was the basis for Gary Cooper's serial marrying character in the 1938 movie *Bluebeard's Eighth Wife.*

Meant for Each Other

The Chinese have an enduring history of special wedding superstitions and practices.

✳   ✳   ✳   ✳

About Last Night

IN ANCIENT CHINA, some of the most popular wedding rituals took place the night before the big day. The "installation of the bridal bed" was a big to-do for the groom. As implied, a newly purchased bed was installed. The bed was scattered with lotus seeds, dates, pomegranates, and peanuts, and children were invited to scramble for items on the bed as an omen of offspring to come.

Slumber Party

For her part, the bride spent the night with her girlfriends in a secluded part of the house, called the "cock loft." True story, and no, it's not a loft full of male chickens. There she could vent about her troubles and would probably receive tips to prepare for marriage.

At Western sleepover parties, fixing each other's hair is a mainstay, and the ancient Chinese had their own version. Both bride and groom would separately perform a four-part combing ritual. The first comb-through marked "from beginning 'til the end." The second combing represented "harmony from now 'til old age." The third signified "sons and grandsons." The fourth would bring "good wealth and a long lasting marriage."

Here Comes the Groom

To claim his beloved, the groom would lead a parade to the bride's home. Firecrackers and drums both announced his upcoming arrival and warded away evil spirits. The bride's attendants would not surrender the bride until they were appeased with packets of money from the groom's party.

Flinging Flowers

Overzealous luck-seekers are distracted by flowers tossed in self-defense.

✳ ✳ ✳ ✳

It's Tradition

NUPTIAL LORE ASSERTS that the unwed woman who catches the bouquet will be the next to marry, but the origins of this practice are a bit more sinister. Intrigued? Let's head to medieval Europe for some (albeit disturbing) answers.

Distracting the Desperate

In the early 14th century, brides didn't keep their wedding gowns for posterity; instead, after the wedding, the dress was torn to shreds—with the bride still wearing it. Single women chased the bride, yanking the dress to shreds because the bits of fabric were good luck to the oh-so-desperate-to-wed. As the bride attempted to escape with her new husband, she threw the wedding bouquet to distract mad-with-envy throngs.

A century or two later, brides wanted to keep attendees' paws off their increasingly couture creations, so gown-tearing fell out of fashion. Still, tossing the bouquet remained a winsome tradition. Why? Flowers are a symbol of fertility.

Better Safe than Sorry

Today, the modern bouquet-throwing tradition sometimes has disastrous effects. In July 2009, a couple in Italy actually caused an aircraft to fall out of the sky during the process. It seems the bouquet became tangled in the ultra-light's tail rotor.

It's no wonder some brides opt to skip the bouquet toss—and the risk of a stampede. Instead, they award a small, token bouquet to each bridesmaid or pass a singular flower from the bouquet to each single woman at the reception.

But where's the sport in that?

Bouquet Breakdown

The color and scent of flowers create a festive look, along with memories that will last a lifetime.

✳ ✳ ✳ ✳

Ancient Times

✳ Ancient Greeks are credited with introducing the idea of wedding flowers around the 5th century B.C. Flowers and plants, such as ivy, were used to create a crown for the bride to wear, which represented a gift of nature. The ivy stood for everlasting and unbreakable love—and had the bonus of warding off evil spirits.

✳ Evil spirits being a concern in early times, brides of ancient Rome also carried herbs under their veils to ward them off, as well as to express fidelity and fertility.

✳ Bridesmaids of old were given the task of creating these floral arrangements for the bride as a token of thanks. But it might be the bridesmaids who deserved the appreciation. Instead of flowers, they carried bouquets of strong smelling herbs, such as garlic and rosemary, to ward off evil spirits.

17th Century

✳ The language of flowers is credited to the people of Turkey back in the 1600s. Couples used certain types and colors of flowers to send messages. It was only natural to continue that symbolism on the wedding day by mixing certain flowers in the bouquet.

Victorian Times

✳ Symbolism went a step further by the early 1800s, when lovers sent one flower to convey a message. Unfortunately, otherwise beautiful flowers got a bad rap by being assigned a negative message—which meant there was no place for them in the bridal bouquet!

* The marriage of Queen Victoria to Prince Albert marked the replacement of herbs with fresh flowers. However, dill, known as the herb of lust, was still often tucked into floral arrangements and consumed by the bride and groom.

Late 19th Century
* A small circular bouquet called a posy was all the rage in the late 1800s. It was followed by a variation known as a biedermeier, which originated in Switzerland. This was a tightly formed bouquet that was carefully arranged in concentric circles of colored flowers. One ring would be made up of one type of flower, and the next ring, another. Orange and lemon peels were often included for their pleasing fragrance.

1900s
* Arm sheafs were favorites of brides around the turn of the century. Popularized by actress Sarah Bernhardt, these bouquets looked just like the sheaf of flowers presented to the actress after an outstanding performance. Instead of being held in front of the bride, this natural-looking arrangement would be cradled in her arms, or draped over a single arm with the stems showing.

* Composite-flower bouquets were an ingenious creation by florists. Unable to obtain fresh flowers from around the world the way we do today, florists created their own "roses" by using petals of the gladioli. Known as galleria, they were sometimes used as part of a bridal bouquet but were more often worn separately as a corsage or adornment on the bridal hat.

1910s
* So began the start of a long-running trend: the shower bouquet. If you can't picture what it looked like, consider that another name for it is a cascading bouquet. Think of it as the hanging plant of bouquets, with flowers and vines trailing down.

1920–30s:

* The cascading bouquet was very popular for the next two decades, reaching its peak by the late 1930s. In an effort to make a few changes to what brides already knew and liked, the bouquet became larger and more exaggerated. Some were so large that they nearly concealed the bride. These bouquets were decorated with ribbons, which were incorporated right into the floral design. Long streamers tied with "lover's knots" flowed from the bouquet. These small knots ran the length of the ribbon, and small buds and foliage were inserted. When brides threw the bouquet, the lucky girl who caught it untied one of these knots and made a wish that was supposed to come true. For a more rustic look, some brides added large turkey feathers that were tucked around the edges.

1940s:

* As the war effort spread across the country, cascading bouquets were suddenly too showy. Most brides gave up the bouquet altogether in favor of a simple corsage pinned to her suit or dress.

1980–90s:

* The shower bouquet made a bit of a comeback in the '80s as people tried to emulate Princess Diana and her cascading bouquet. Variations of this style continued into the '90s and peaked with the teardrop bouquet, which featured an elegant overflow of flowers forming a teardrop shape over the bride's clasped hands.

2000s:

* One modern tradition has the bride giving a single flower to her mother as she walks down the aisle and another flower to her new mother-in-law on her way back out.

* The idea of dogs bearing flowers on their collar or leash has become popular among canine-loving couples that include their pets in the ceremony.

✳ The start of a new millennium marked a trend toward anything and everything in terms of wedding flowers. Some brides choose to carry traditional bouquets; others carry original creations with unexpected elements.

The Continuous Circle of Love

We think of engagement and wedding rings as symbols of eternal love. The use of rings dates back thousands of years, but their meaning and makeup has changed over time.

✳   ✳   ✳   ✳

Ancient Egypt: About 4,800 years ago, the first recorded exchange of wedding rings took place in ancient Egypt. When a groom placed a ring on his bride's finger, it demonstrated his confidence in her ability to take care of their home.

2nd Century B.C.: Brides in ancient Rome were given a gold ring, but there was a catch—they were only allowed to wear it in public since it was too valuable to wear while doing household chores. These brides also had a second ring made of iron to wear around the house.

860 B.C.: Christians started to exchange rings in wedding ceremonies. The bands were usually very ornate, engraved with doves, lyres, and two linked hands. The Church felt these rings were "heathenish," however, and discouraged their use.

13th Century: Wedding and engagement rings became noticeably simpler—more a symbol of a couple's union than a piece of jewelry. The symbol was deemed so important that if a groom couldn't afford to buy a ring, he rented one for the ceremony.

16th Century: It had long been common practice to wear a wedding ring on the third finger of the left hand, but this tradition was formalized in The Book of Common Prayer, written by the son of King Henry VIII.

17th Century: Silver became the metal of choice in England and France for the popular poesy (or posy) rings of the time. The wedding ring was inscribed with a poesy, or love poem, either inside or out.

19th Century: Plain gold bands were very common in the 1800s. Other rings of this time period were set with pearls or small diamonds, and some even used turquoise to symbolize the forget-me-not flower.

Early 1900s: Delicate designs were the rage in the Edwardian era. Rings were made of platinum—or gold set with silver or platinum—to better show off the center diamond.

1910s: Old-mine and old-European cut diamonds were the most popular gemstone. The high crown of this cut sparkled beautifully in the candlelight.

1920s: Art deco was the trend for these "modern" brides, and rings took on the look of the times. Geometric designs and colored stones ruled the day.

1930s: Wedding bands were narrow, in keeping with the economics of the Depression era, but the widespread choice of 18kt or 14kt gold for the rings illustrated how important they were to a new bride or groom.

1940s: Platinum was needed for the war effort, so brides substituted silver for their wedding bands. Jewelry hoarding was not uncommon.

1950s: Before 1940, only about 15 percent of grooms wore wedding bands. By the Korean War, that number was 70 percent.

1960s: Platinum, silver, and white gold took a backseat to yellow gold. This popular metal was usually set with diamonds for a simple ring that really sparkled.

1970s: Free love was the order of the day, and a classic ring like your mother had just wouldn't do. Nugget and antique finishes became very popular because of their more rustic, natural look. They may have been expensive, but they didn't look it.

1980s: Artisan rings lost their popularity, and brides turned to cathedral or dome mountings for their rings. The diamond was often set up high on a band that was a quarter to three-eighths of an inch wide, with smaller baguettes on the side.

1990s: The '90s brought a renewed interest in white gold—often with yellow gold accents.

2000s: Whether it's the generation or the economy, today's brides are returning to a simpler look. Diamond solitaires (usually .5 to 1 carat) are the most popular engagement ring style. Today's brides like the look of a silver ring and are usually choosing white gold as the metal. Sterling can tarnish, and the cost of platinum is out of reach for many newly engaged couples.

* In a custom of the 17th century, the bride passed pieces of wedding cake through her ring. She then gave a piece to the unmarried girls who slept with it under their pillows, hoping to dream of their future husbands. The practice ended when brides decided it might be bad luck to remove their rings so soon after the wedding.
* In a wedding ceremony, the ring bearer carries the wedding rings from the entrance of the church to the bride, groom, and ceremony officiant. Typically, the ring bearer is a nephew or young brother (or a niece or a young sister) of the bride or groom but can also be any relative or child of a relative or friend.

Old Weddings' Tale

Did you know it's bad luck to spot a lizard on the way to your wedding ceremony? Find out why superstitions are still a powerful part of wedding lore.

※　　※　　※　　※

WEDDINGS ARE NOTHING if not surrounded by superstition. Whether it's on the way to the wedding, during the ceremony, or after the fact, any number of omens or actions can bring bad luck.

Saturday Superstition

Although now a universally popular day for ceremonies, there was a time when Saturday weddings were scandalous. Why? Several superstitions imply a Saturday marriage means an early death for the bride or groom.

Saturday isn't the only risky calendar date. The early church prohibited couples to marry during certain religious seasons, such as Lent. Ignore the antiquated ruling—even today—and it's believed bad luck will befall you. Hence, the popular saying in Great Britain, "Marry in Lent, live to repent."

Ancient Romans refused to marry in May, which was the month when sacrifices were made to the dead. Later, Great Britain's Queen Victoria even refused to allow her children to wed in May.

Black Cat, Good Luck

It's long been purported that a cat—black or any other hue—can bring good luck to a marriage. If a cat sneezes in the home of the bride on the eve (or some sources say on the actual day) of her wedding, a blanket of good luck will cover her wedding day. First, find your cat...

And, to be on the safe side, a bride should always personally feed the household cat before leaving for the church on her wedding day. The act is believed to bring lasting happiness to her married life.

Don't have a cat? Request one on your gift registry. At one time in England, it was believed that a bride who received a black cat on her wedding day would have the best of luck.

Of course, wedding superstitions don't always involve animals of the feline persuasion. It's unlucky if a pig crosses the path of a bride on her wedding day, and if she spots a lizard on the way to her wedding, she might as well go back home.

Save the Soul with Rice

As long as people have been getting married, they've been avoiding supernatural spirits and their ethereal intents. In fact, to prevent trouble with the spirit world, guests began throwing rice when newly betrothed couples departed. The idea was that the tiny grains would assuage the injured feelings of spirits who really didn't like to see mortals happy.

Rice also played an important role for the groom. It was used as a charm to keep the groom's soul in his body. Turns out the souls of grooms had a penchant for running away from impending marital responsibilities.

In recent years, however, tossing this grain fell out of favor—largely because of an oft-repeated myth that the uncooked rice would be eaten by birds that would then explode as the rice expanded in their tiny bellies. According to the USA Rice Federation, however, uncooked rice is a harmless food for birds. Still, an increasing number of couples opt to have guests toss birdseed, release butterflies, or blow bubbles. There's no word on whether tiny bubbles cause bad luck.

Considered by the Ming dynasty to be the color of good luck, a traditional Chinese bride dons a red dress, red shoes, and a red silk veil. She may change clothing one or more times throughout the day.

Chase Away the Evil Spirits

While most weddings are full of good cheer, Norwegian weddings go a little further. The wedding couple takes steps to chase away evil spirits on this special day. Not a bad way to begin.

✳   ✳   ✳   ✳

Norsk Nuptials

NORWEGIAN FOOD IS known for its lack of color and taste— everything is white. But the country itself is beautiful, and each region brings a tradition of colorful clothing and designs that make a Norwegian wedding one to remember.

The More the Merrier

Weddings in Norway are usually much smaller than weddings in the United States. Guests are primarily close family and friends. Norwegian weddings also include a procession to the church. In the old days, a fiddle player led the way, followed by the bride and groom, then her parents, the bridesmaids, the flower girl and ring bearer, and finally the guests.

Wedding off Evil

In a traditional Norwegian wedding, the groom—and his groomsmen—wear a *bunad,* which is a woolen suit of short pants worn with stockings and a white silk shirt, a vest, and a topcoat. Colorful designs specific to the groom's birthplace (or ancestry) embellish the plain material and make it unique.

The bride's look is a more elegant one: a white or silver gown. Instead of a veil, she wears a silver or gold crown with silk ribbons. But most importantly, small spoon-shape bangles hang over the crown, and they make a musical sound when the bride moves her head from side to side. It's the sound created by these melodious bangles that chases away the evil spirits. What a responsibility!

The bridesmaid gowns are purposefully chosen to be very similar to the bride's wedding dress but in a different color. This is another way to trick the evil spirits—so they are unable to identify the wedding couple.

Let Them Eat Cake

Music is an integral part of the Norwegian ceremony. "Come To The Wedding" is one traditional song played at most Norwegian weddings. The bride and bridesmaids typically dance at the actual wedding ceremony—also to chase away the evil spirits.

But the reception is still a big part of the day. Besides the food and music, it is a time for toasts—from just about everybody involved. A traditional wedding cake, called a *kransekake,* is often served, but many times other cakes accompany it as well. The kransekake is a white-tiered cake made of almond paste in the shape of rings that decrease in size as they approach the top. One bride's traditional Norwegian wedding served a chocolate sour cream cake, flanked by two kransekake. Each was decorated by placing a small bouquet of flowers in the top and tiny Norwegian flags in the rings. The couple saved the top ring to cut on their first anniversary and found it to be tastier than most frozen cakes.

Guests often bring additional cakes for the cake table, too. And these extra cakes are a good idea, because after a night of dining and dancing, a traditional Norwegian wedding should be capped off with *nattmat*, or night food: hot dogs, soup, and sandwiches, followed by more cake.

Jumping the Broom

For hundreds of years, African American slaves had no power or control over their own lives—yet they continued to marry, bringing their own tradition to a well-known ceremony.

✳ ✳ ✳ ✳

A Bittersweet Tradition

AS SLAVES, THEY could be sold away from their spouses, parents, children, and friends at a moment's notice, and once sold, they almost never saw those loved ones again. Yet despite knowing this awful reality, slaves continued to fall in love and marry, hoping against hope that one day they would have the legal right to possess their own bodies and call themselves families.

Of course, the marriages of slaves had no standing in the white world and were either ignored or debased by slave owners. To most slave owners, all that mattered was that their slaves were having children and creating more human property—whether they called it "marriage" or not was irrelevant. But many slaves had adopted the Christian religion of their masters, and the marriage ceremony meant a great deal to them, even if it meant nothing legally. Other slaves usually performed slave weddings, though once in a while a white minister would agree to preside.

Though the customs that grew out of slave weddings varied from place to place in the southern United States, one was almost universal: jumping the broom. After the vows were taken, a broom would be placed on the ground before the couple, and the two would jump over it—into the land of matrimony.

This act may not have meant anything to people in the "outside world," but it meant something to the couple's immediate circle, as well as to the entire slave community: These two people were now married. Everyone else, hands off.

The roots of the tradition of jumping the broom go all the way back to Africa, where brooms were a potent symbol of domestic life. In Ghana, brooms were waved over the heads of the newlyweds at the feast following the wedding ceremony. In other parts of Africa, on the day after her wedding, the young bride would be expected to participate in a ritual in which she and her female in-laws swept out her new home. This signified her willingness to adapt to her new family and cooperate with them in communal work. Like many other African customs and symbols, the broom ritual followed slaves to America and evolved over hundreds of years.

Bringing Back the Broom

In the mid-20th century, many whites had never heard of jumping the broom, and even some African Americans were unaware of it. But Alex Haley's 1976 book, *Roots: The Saga of an American Family*, changed all that. In one of the most famous scenes in the reality-based novel, Haley's ancestor, the slave Kunta Kinte (or "Toby"), is married to Bell, the cook on his master's estate. After taking their vows, Kunta and Bell jump the broom.

When a blockbuster miniseries based on the book was aired in 1977, 130 million viewers watched actors John Amos and Madge Sinclair recreate this moment.

Roots was not the only thing in the 1970s to stir memories of slave traditions, however. Black leaders, civil rights groups, and black churches were encouraging African Americans to learn their history and take pride in their customs, even those—perhaps *especially* those—that grew out of great pain and suffering. Black couples began to reincorporate jumping the broom into their weddings, and now it is an almost expected part of the African American matrimonial experience. When discouraged at a church ceremony—for example, a Catholic wedding mass—it can easily be moved to the reception, but it's a tradition many African American brides and grooms insist on honoring in remembrance of those who had nothing else.

Japanese Wedding Traditions

While a modern Japanese bride won't likely find a fan at her doorstop to begin the marital journey, plenty of century-old habits remain.

✳   ✳   ✳   ✳

IN OLDEN-DAYS JAPAN, the process of matching a young man to a well-suited lady was a formal interview called the *Mi-Ai*. The gentleman caller would visit his prospective bride's home and submit to some mutual judging. If he was satisfied with what he saw and learned, the suitor would leave behind a token of his intentions: a Japanese fan.

Lady in White

Along with a white kimono, a traditional Japanese bride paints her skin pale white from head to toe. She may also wear a white hood that serves as a veil to hide her face or an elaborate ornamental hat. In either case, the headgear is said to cover her "horns," or imperfections, such as jealousy or selfishness.

Bottoms Up

While alcohol is often a key component of Western wedding receptions, it's actually incorporated into the traditional Shinto Japanese wedding ceremony. The bride's and groom's families face each other, and nine sips of sweet sake are taken. After drinking, the couple is considered unified and may be officially introduced to each other's respective families.

Wife Garb Swap

After the ceremony, the bride will change into a different kimono and may later change at least one more time, often into more modern or Western-influenced attire. Symbolically, this demonstrates that she is prepared to return to her daily life.

A Long-Ago Wedding Remembered

Though there are many medieval pageants, parades, and "faires" all around the world, one of the biggest and best reenactments of the Middle Ages is in Landshut, Bavaria (Germany), and celebrates a wedding that happened long, long ago.

✳ ✳ ✳ ✳

To Marry Means to Ally

THE LANDSHUT WEDDING is held every four years in remembrance of the wedding of George (Georg) of Bavaria to Princess Hedwig (Jadwiga) of Poland, which took place way back in 1475.

In 1474, the Ottoman Turks threatened the borders of Bavaria and Poland. And the leaders of these two countries knew they must appear to be strong allies against any possible invasion. What better way to show their combined strength than to marry the offspring of the two royal families? The marriage was negotiated in Cracow before the bride and groom ever met, but that was no big deal back in those days; royal children knew it was their duty to marry for political and religious reasons, not for love. Most "regular" people didn't even marry for love at that time, so the elaborate prenuptial arrangements wouldn't have struck anyone as strange or cold. That was just the way it was.

Hedwig and George Get Hitched

Hedwig Jagiellonica was the eldest daughter of King Casimir IV Jagellion and his wife, the Archduchess Elisabeth of Austria. In a portrait painted in her youth, she appears quite pretty, with dark eyes; a long, straight nose; and a rather small, prim mouth. Her groom, who was also known as George the Rich, was the son of Louis IX the Rich and his wife, Amalia of Saxony. It took Hedwig two months to travel from her home in Poland to Landshut, but once she got there, she certainly couldn't complain that they didn't "put on the dog" for her. Numerous members of the royal family, the aristocracy, and the Catholic hierarchy feted her, plus, Salzburg's Archbishop Bernhard von Rohr agreed to perform the wedding.

Hedwig and George were married in St. Martin's Church in Landshut. Construction of the church had begun in 1380, and it would not be finished until 1500, but enough of it was standing so that the wedding could be held. After the ceremony, the couple led a parade through the Old Town to the Town Hall as 10,000 spectators cheered them on. And it's a good thing Louis IX was "the Rich," because all those people had to be fed and supplied with alcoholic beverages. It's estimated that they gobbled up 40,000 chickens, 320 bullocks, 1,500 sheep, 1,300 lambs, and 500 calves. The amount of beer and wine consumed is not known, but one can assume that it was enormous.

Landshuter Hochzeit

In 1902, a group of Landshut citizens formed a society called *Die Förderer* (The Sponsors) and proposed to reenact the famous wedding of Hedwig and George every four years. The first bridal procession took place one year later, and the pageant has grown larger and more extravagant with every production.

Over a century later, more than 2,000 participants (out of a population of 60,000) don medieval costumes to re-create the spectacle, and thousands more attend just to enjoy the show. The pageant goes on for three weeks, usually in late June and early July. Reenactors portray "life in the quarters"; joust as knights on horseback; play the music of 1475 on historically correct instruments; and dance as their ancestors once did, masquerading in colorful masks and regaling the crowds with juggling and jokes as jesters and fools.

It is considered a great honor to be one of the official actors in the Landshut Wedding, as the costumes are very expensive and maintained with the greatest care. One must have been born in Landshut to participate; however, all the citizens of Landshut and all the tourists who come to Landshut to see the pageant are encouraged to get into the spirit. The men of the town even grow their facial hair out for months before the pageant begins!

Fast Facts: Wedding Superstitions

* Tying tin cans to the bride and groom's car will frighten away evil spirits.

* Victorian bridal couples were said to have very good luck if they married on the groom's birthday.

* Rain is the bride's old boyfriends crying over her.

* After toasting, it is good luck for the bride and groom to smash their glasses. That ensures the glasses will never be used for a better reason.

* It is bad luck for the bride to make her own dress.

* Bridesmaids dress similar to the bride to confuse the evil spirits.

* In Mexico, it is bad luck for the bride to wear pearls. It signifies the tears she will cry in her marriage.

* Don't let the groom see the bride in her wedding dress before the ceremony!

* If it rains and everything still goes smoothly, that means the couple was able to work under pressure to overcome obstacles and will continue to do so throughout their marriage.

* A penny in the bride's shoes will bring wealth in her marriage.

* It is good luck to encounter a frog on the way to the church. Just don't kiss it!

* Rain on the wedding day means the couple will be blessed with good fortune and fertility.

* If the new mother-in-law throws a shoe over the bride's head as she leaves the church, the two of them will be friends forever. (If she throws the shoe at the bride's head, well...)

Bad Brides

These ladies may have gone a little over the top on their wedding days. And we don't mean with the decorations...

* * * *

Married Mugshot

IN MARCH OF 2009, newlyweds Jade and Billy Puckett left their wedding reception, only to be caught in a "March Madness" DUI sting that was being conducted by deputies in Harris County, Texas. When Billy was charged with driving under the influence, Jade became belligerent and was charged with public intoxication. But it didn't end there! Jade claimed she was not allowed to change clothing and was humiliated when an unidentified male in the courtroom took photos of her in her wedding dress—photos that wound up on the Internet. She filed a formal complaint with the Harris County Precinct 8 Constable's office just days after her arrest.

Bridezilla Indeed!

Mark Allerton and Teresa Brown were friends for 16 years before they got hitched in a 2007 fairy-tale wedding at a castle in Aberdeen, Scotland. The castle is used in the popular British soap opera *Monarch of the Glen*, but the fight Mark and Teresa got into after the ceremony was even more dramatic than the show. According to police, Teresa attacked Mark with one of her stiletto heels, leaving him with a bleeding puncture wound on his head. Teresa spent two days in jail, but Mark stood by her, saying they had no plans to split. The bride claimed her freak-out was caused by a reaction to the antidepressant she was taking. Note: Brides and grooms might want to adjust those meds before the wedding.

Breaking up the Band

Elmo Fernadez and his wife Fabiana had been married in a civil ceremony long before, but in 2008, they decided to renew their vows in a religious ceremony in Port Chester, New York. Everything was going swimmingly until the reception, when the band explained that they could only play music when the DJ was not playing. Fabiana didn't care for that excuse and went on a rampage, knocking over a set of $600 conga drums and destroying other equipment valued at $350. Girlfriend just wanted her money's worth! The cops hauled in Fabiana, her husband, and her daughter that night.

Celebrity Wedding Ruckus

In 2007, groom Carlos Barron and bride Tara Hensley were arrested on their wedding night after partying at a Huntington, South Carolina, nightclub called Envy. Police said they had no choice but to arrest the couple and three other members of the wedding party after they received a report of shots fired, and the crowd refused to disperse. But when it was revealed that one of the arrestees was Cincinnati Bengals running back Quincy Wilson, the boys in blue had a little more 'splainin' to do.

Two Birds with One Threat

Diane Carnes did something not-too-bright on the day before her March 2008 wedding. It seems Diane thought it would be convenient to schedule her wedding at the Scotts Bluff County, Nebraska, courthouse while she was already there taking care of a pesky suspended license violation problem. Her license had been revoked after a DUI, but she got caught driving again. At her trial, Diane threatened one of the jurors, but no matter—she scheduled her wedding for the next day and went on home. The thing is, threatening a juror is a little bit illegal, so when Diane showed up the next day for her wedding, she was arrested. What a way to start a new, married life!

Quiz

Show what you know about weird, obscure, or fun wedding facts with this wedding trivia quiz.

✳ ✳ ✳ ✳

1. In the Czech Republic, a prospective bride's future in-laws might place this in plain view to test her skill before granting their blessing:

    a. Bed
    b. Broom
    c. Baby

2. In Nigerian culture, where does the bride-to-be go with her female relatives to learn how to be a wife?

    a. Etiquette class
    b. Brothel
    c. Fattening room

3. According to the Scottish tradition of Creeling, what must the groom carry across the village on his back until his bride is satisfied with his strength?

    a. His bride
    b. Bagpipes
    c. Basket of stones

4. What does the French wedding custom of *coupe de marriage* mean?

   a. The couple toasts themselves with a two-handled cup
   b. The groom's family bestows a new car upon the happy couple
   c. Eloping

5. What celebrity wedding ceremony reportedly included the vows, "And when she's older, do you keep her still?" "I do."

   a. Tom Cruise and Katie Holmes
   b. Ashton Kutcher and Demi Moore
   c. Donald Trump and Melania Knauss

6. What might French relatives bang outside of the newlywed couple's room?

   a. Drums
   b. Pots and pans
   c. Cowbells

Answers: 1. b; 2. c; 3. c; 4. a; 5. a; 6. b

Chapter 11

Screen, Stage, and Song

Behind the TV Shows of Our Time

❋ Before he became a hugely famous movie star, Jim Carrey played a cartoonist on the 1984 flop sitcom *The Duck Factory.*

❋ The Chia Pet company once made a mohawked Mr. T Chia model.

❋ When Mary Tyler Moore named her production company MTM, she decided to spoof MGM's production slate of a lion roaring by using a tiny kitten meowing in her own production slate.

❋ Chuck Woolery, best known as the host of such game shows as *Wheel of Fortune* and *Love Connection,* once belonged to a psychedelic rock group named Avant Garde. The band had a minor hit with a song called "Naturally Stoned."

❋ Art Carney is best known for his role as dopey Ed Norton on The Honeymooners, but he went on to win an Academy Award in 1974 for his role in the film *Harry and Tonto.*

❋ One of the silliest attempts to capitalize on the 1970s women's movement was a very short-lived sitcom called *The Feminist and the Fuzz.* No, it wasn't about whether to shave one's armpits or not—it was just about a cop and a "women's libber."

* As an example of how prevalent the smoking habit once was, the 1971 TV movie *Cold Turkey* was about a town in which every adult citizen agrees to give up smoking at the same time.

* *Ferris Bueller,* an unsuccessful sitcom based on the movie *Ferris Bueller's Day Off,* costarred a very young Jennifer Aniston.

* When NBC aired the series finale of *Seinfeld* in 1998, the TV Land cable channel didn't even try to compete. Instead, they broadcast a sign that read, "WE'RE TV FANS; WE'RE WATCHING SEINFELD."

* Football legend Joe Namath once wore Beauty Mist pantyhose in a commercial to show that Beauty Mist could "make any legs look like a million dollars." He quickly reassured viewers of his heterosexuality by adding with a wink, "… especially your legs."

* Before he was the voice of Mister Ed, actor Allan "Rocky" Lane starred in a number of B-movie westerns.

Solo Mission

Thanks to paper cups and a doting husband, Dora Hall achieved her dreams of stardom.

✳ ✳ ✳ ✳

Promotional Materials

DON'T KNOW WHO Dora Hall is? Don't fret—you're not alone. Hall was an obscure performer from the 1960s who was once called "the undisputed queen of vanity entertainment." She dreamed of making a career as a singer and actor but had very little performing experience—and well, she also came up a bit short in the talent department. Nevertheless, her utterly supportive husband, Leo Hulseman, was determined to make her show biz dreams come true.

Leo was founder of the Illinois-based Solo Cup Company, which made products such as disposable cups, bowls, and plates. Throughout the '60s, Leo paid for Dora to make a variety of record releases—featuring everything from country songs and show tunes to rock classics such as Elvis Presley's "I'm All Shook Up"—all of which were recorded on Solo subsidiary labels or affiliates, such as Calamo, Cozy, and Dot. Dora's albums were given away for free with Solo cups and plates as a "special promotion."

Dora Hits the Big Time

Leo then founded a TV production company in California called Premore Inc. Because Dora dreamed of being much more than a recording artist, Leo financed several elaborate TV specials (just one cost $400,000!), all of which were filmed at Premore. These quirky specials, such as *Rose on Broadway* and *Once Upon a Tour*, aired in the '70s and '80s, and they featured a now-elderly Dora as she sang and danced her way through various lighthearted story lines. She collaborated with the likes of Donald O'Connor, Rich Little, Ben Blue, Scatman Crothers, and Frank Sinatra Jr. What Dora lacked in sheer talent, she made up for in pizzazz and sparkly pantsuits.

Hall passed away in 1988, the grandmother of 16. Not much has been written about her career; thus, much about her remains a mystery. Even so, some people look back with fondness on her endearingly earnest performances.

The Late, Great Buddy Holly

One of the first rock 'n' rollers, Buddy Holly shone brightly but for only a very short time.

✳ ✳ ✳ ✳

NAMED AFTER A Texas Ranger who was a Confederate colonel during the Civil War, home of Texas Tech University, and center of the largest contiguous cotton growing region in the world, Lubbock is a pure West Texan city on the South Plains. The city will always be known as the hometown of Buddy Holly—a local boy who became a rock 'n' roll legend and whose life was tragically cut short. Charles Hardin Holley was born in Lubbock on September 7, 1936. The fourth child of Lawrence and Ella Holley, he was nicknamed Buddy by his mother. Although he only lived to age 22, Buddy Holly was one of the most influential musicians of early rock 'n' roll, and many of his songs have become American classics.

Early Promise

The Holleys were a musical family, and as a boy, Buddy learned to sing and play several instruments. By the time he entered seventh grade in 1949, he could hold his own on the guitar, the banjo, and the mandolin. At J. T. Hutchinson Junior High School, he began playing together with another seventh grader, Bob Montgomery. They were inspired by the country music they heard on radio shows such as *The Grand Ole Opry* and *Louisiana Hayride* and started several bands while still in junior high. In high school, Buddy and Bob had their own music show on Lubbock's KDAV radio station, and they started listening to black rhythm and blues musicians and a young new star named Elvis Presley.

Presley barnstormed through Lubbock in early 1955, and after seeing him perform, Holly decided that music was his life's ambition. Buddy and Bob opened for Presley when he returned to Lubbock in October 1955. Later that month, the duo performed with Bill Haley and His Comets at another local concert. A Nashville talent agent was in the audience, and shortly afterward, Buddy Holly signed a contract with Decca Records. The record company misspelled his last name as "Holly," which became his stage name.

The Hits Start Coming

Holly left Lubbock for Nashville and later New York, forming a band he named The Crickets. Sales of their early recordings were disappointing, but in May 1957, Buddy Holly and The Crickets released a single, "That'll Be the Day," which topped charts in the United States and Great Britain. In December of that year, the band performed their first hit and another, "Peggy Sue," on *The Ed Sullivan Show*.

Holly's music was sophisticated for early rock 'n' roll, and he was a masterful lead and rhythm guitarist and lyricist. He was one of the first rock stars to write, produce, and perform his own songs, and The Crickets set the template for the standard rock 'n' roll band: two guitars, bass, and drums.

International Influence

In March 1958, the band began a 25-day tour of England, an event that many rock historians consider a turning point in popular music. Holly was wildly popular in Britain, and his performances directly inspired musicians who would lead the "British Invasion" of the United States a few years later. Paul McCartney recalls watching The Crickets perform live on London television. Keith Richards, who would become lead guitarist for The Rolling Stones, attended one of the concerts. Even Holly's fashion choices—black horn-rimmed glasses and Ivy League three-button jackets—would influence early English rock.

During the last year of his life, Holly recorded and toured constantly. He returned to Lubbock in August 1958 to marry Maria Elena Santiago, a receptionist at a New York music company, who he had met two months earlier—he proposed on their first date.

Under the pressures of the road, Buddy Holly and The Crickets parted ways after a final tour in the fall of 1958.

An Unexpected End

In January 1959, Holly, with a new band behind him, started a three-week group tour across the Midwest with other young stars on the bill, including Dion and the Belmonts, Ritchie

Valens, and J. P. "The Big Bopper" Richardson. The weather was frigid, and the tour buses had continuous problems—one of Holly's band mates had to be hospitalized for frostbite. On February 2, they performed in Clear Lake, Iowa, a last-minute addition to the schedule. Eager to avoid another long bus trip in the cold weather, Holly chartered a private airplane to fly him to the tour's next date. The plane crashed soon after take-off, killing Holly, Richardson, Valens, and pilot Roger Peterson.

Holly's funeral was held on February 7, 1959, at the Tabernacle Baptist Church in Lubbock, and he was buried at the City of Lubbock Cemetery in the eastern part of the city. His headstone uses the correct spelling of his last name, Holley, and features a carving of his Fender Stratocaster guitar.

In Memory Of...

Holly remains Lubbock's most famous native son. Hutchinson Junior High School and Lubbock High School have several tributes to the late musician on their campuses. A life-size statue of Holly playing his Fender guitar is the centerpiece of Lubbock's West Texas "Walk of Fame," an outdoor tribute to the region's artists and musicians.

In 1997, the city of Lubbock purchased a renovated train station downtown and started the Buddy Holly Center, a museum dedicated to Holly's life and music, as well as more general Texas art and music. The center houses an extensive collection of Buddy Holly memorabilia, exhibits on other West Texas musicians, and a fine art gallery. Displays include Holly's Fender Stratocaster, songbooks, photographs, fan mail, posters, stage clothing, and a hand-tooled guitar strap he made as a teenager. Personal items from Holly's boyhood in Lubbock include a pair of his glasses, a wooden slingshot, his report cards, and his collection of 45 rpm records.

The Holley family home in Lubbock is a private residence and is not open for tours.

38 Celebrity Siblings

1. Ben and Casey Affleck

2. Kevin and Matt Dillon

3. Sean and Mackenzie Astin

4. Jim and John Belushi

5. River and Joaquin Phoenix

6. Sean and Neil Connery

7. Don and Jim Ameche

8. James Arness and Peter Graves

9. Groucho, Harpo, Chico, Zeppo, and Gummo Marx

10. Ron and Clint Howard

11. Beau and Jeff Bridges

12. Charlie Sheen and Emilio Estevez

13. Moe, Curly, and Shemp Howard (The Three Stooges)

14. Dennis and Randy Quaid

15. Fred and Ben Savage

16. Dean and Guy Stockwell

17. Dick and Jerry Van Dyke

18. Donnie and Mark Wahlberg

19. Keenan Ivory, Damon, Marlon, and Shawn Wayans

20. Pier Angeli and Marisa Pavan

21. David, Rosanna, Patricia, and Alexis Arquette

22. Hilary and Haylie Duff

23. Zsa-Zsa, Eva, and Magda Gabor

24. Joan Fontaine and Olivia de Havilland

25. Margaux and Mariel Hemingway

26. Phylicia Rashad and Debbie Allen

27. Meg and Jennifer Tilly

28. Justine and Jason Bateman

29. Jane and Peter Fonda

30. Jake and Maggie Gyllenhaal

31. Warren Beatty and Shirley MacLaine

32. John and Joan Cusack

33. Michael and Virginia Madsen

34. Julia and Eric Roberts

35. Alec, Daniel, Billy, and Stephen Baldwin

36. Ashley and Wynonna Judd

37. Jessica and Ashlee Simpson

38. Nick and Aaron Carter

Roles of a Rebel

This Indiana boy lived only 24 years, but his legend as an American icon continues to thrive. He began his showbiz career in a Pepsi commercial, standing around a jukebox with a group of teens singing "Pepsi-Cola hits the spot." Within a decade, Dean had two Oscar nominations. Sadly, both were posthumous.

✳ ✳ ✳ ✳

IN 1955, DEAN bought a Porsche Spyder, bragging that it could reach speeds of 150 miles per hour. Upon hearing this, actor Alec Guinness told him not to set foot inside the car because he would be dead before the week was out. Six days later, Dean's body was pulled from the twisted wreckage of his new car on a stretch of California highway. Dean's career was cut short, but his legacy lives on in the movies he left behind.

1. **Fixed Bayonets** (1951): James Dean's first movie role was far from "cushy." This Korean War film was the first to depict the violence of combat. Director Samuel Fuller was given free reign to portray the grisly "kill or be killed" premise of the film, and he took it! Actors and camera crews were pushed to their physical limits, including lead actors Richard Basehart, Gene Evans, and Michael O'Shea. Twenty-year-old Dean was uncredited in the film and had only one line, which was cut in the final production.

2. **Sailor Beware** (1952): Dean's next film was a nice departure from Korean combat. With Dean Martin and Jerry Lewis at the helm, production must have been more pleasant. This Paramount film took only five weeks to film, and even though it technically deals with the military, the plot centers around a good-natured bet between sailors that involves kissing girls. Dean went uncredited again, playing a guy in the locker room, but at least his line wasn't cut.

3. **Has Anybody Seen My Gal?** (1952): Rock Hudson carried this film about a wealthy older man trying to decide if the family of his former love is worthy of inheriting his estate. James Dean remained one of many guys with a bit part. Specifically, he's on a bar stool at a soda fountain without any lines. He's credited as "youth at soda fountain." .

4. **East of Eden** (1955): Dean's first major film role gave him top billing along with Julie Harris, Raymond Massey, and Burl Ives. Dean played Cal Trask, who competes with his brother for their father's love. This was Dean's only major film released while he was alive. The role landed him an Oscar nomination for Best Actor, although it sadly came posthumously. However, Ernest Borgnine won for his role in *Marty*.

5. *Rebel Without a Cause* (1955): This is the film for which James Dean is best remembered. It came out just a month after his tragic death, and costarred teens Natalie Wood and Sal Mineo. Dean played the new kid in town, Jim Stark, who finds trouble when searching to replace the love that is lacking in his family life. A daring commentary on tough teenage existence, this movie pitted boys against each other in knife fights that used real switchblades. The actors wore chest protectors under their shirts, but Dean still ended up with a cut on his ear.

6. *Giant* (1956): Rock Hudson worked one last time with James Dean, and this time legendary star Elizabeth Taylor rounded out the top billing. Dean played Jett Rink, a ranch hand who became a Texas oil tycoon. The actor finished shooting his scenes just days before he died, but a few voice-over lines still needed to be recorded, so actor Nick Adams stepped to the microphone to read the part of Jett Rink. Dean received a second posthumous Oscar nomination for Best Actor for this role. Rock Hudson was also nominated, but the award went to Yul Brynner for his role in *The King and I*.

Hollywood's Self-Censorship Machine

Today's moviegoers are accustomed to using the letter-ratings system to decide if a film is suitable viewing for themselves or their children. Thus, the decision to view films with violent or sexual content currently rests on the shoulders of the moviegoers themselves. The Motion Picture Association of American (MPAA) began the letter-ratings system in 1968. Prior to that, Hollywood was governed by a different method of censorship, which was known as the Motion Picture Production Code, or the Hays Code.

✳ ✳ ✳ ✳

What Is the Production Code?

THE PRODUCTION CODE was a lengthy set of guidelines used to control the content of Hollywood movies from 1930 to 1968, though it was only strictly enforced from 1934 to the mid-1950s. Censorship via the Code occurred during the production of a movie, so by the time it was completed, it had already been through the approval process and therefore was suitable for all ages. In this system, it was the film industry that was responsible for what patrons saw on the big screen. Like the letter-ratings system, the Code is an example of self-regulation; it is not administered by the government as are censorship systems in some other countries.

Nude Hippos No Longer Allowed!

The Production Code was not just a list of forbidden acts; it was a complex system of guidelines that controlled how American institutions, values, and ideals should be depicted in Hollywood storytelling. The Code was authored by Father Daniel A. Lord, a Catholic priest and professor of drama, and Martin Quigley, a Catholic layperson who published trade magazines for the film industry. They imbued the Code with a moral agenda, which is clear from its three general principles: "No film should lower the moral standards of those who see it; the correct standards of life should be presented; and, the law should not be ridiculed, nor should sympathy be created for its violation."

The Code forbade certain behaviors, such as profanity, sexual perversion (including prostitution), white slavery, miscegenation, and nudity or partial nudity. Even animated characters were not exempt: Betty Boop was completely altered and desexualized after the advent of the Code, and Walt Disney was forced to add tutus to the dancing hippos in *Fantasia* (1940), which were originally "nude."

However, the bulk of the Code amounted to guidelines on how to deal with facets of American ideology. For example, religion was never to be condemned or criticized; democracy and the trial-by-jury judicial system could not be attacked or depicted as unfair; and outlaws and other lawbreakers could not be treated with sympathy. Gangster films such as *The Public Enemy* (1931), *Little Caesar* (1931), and *Scarface* (1932) thrived during the early 1930s, but after the strict enforcement of the Code, it became difficult to feature a criminal in a leading role for fear of treating him too sympathetically.

Separate Beds

In retrospect, the Code's most talked-about guidelines are those regarding marriage. Marriage and family were sanctified as the most righteous of social institutions and therefore should be the goal of all good female characters. Often, leading ladies in films expressed the opinion that they would gladly give up their career or goals if the right man came along, whether it was part of the plot or not. This was to appease the Code, which suggested that both career women and girls with low morals be "punished" within the story lines of films because those lifestyles did not illustrate the sanctity of marriage. Additional Code rules on marriage and sex stated that sexual relations should not be depicted in a way that suggested sex was typical behavior. The Code's administrators interpreted this to mean that even married couples in the movies had to sleep in separate beds, as in the Spencer Tracy and Katharine Hepburn classic *State of the Union* (1948).

The film industry adopted the Code after the advent of sync-sound movies in 1927, when religious groups, social groups, and children's advocacy organizations pressured Hollywood to clean up its act, or they would lobby the government to do it for them. Movie studios were already battling individual state censorship boards, who often edited out offending scenes or altered inappropriate intertitles (title cards between the scenes of silent movies) without asking the studios' permission. Because each state had its own set of guidelines, a film print making the rounds of distribution could conceivably be edited in one state, but there was no way to ensure that the footage was restored before the print was shipped to the next state. Therefore, the studios decided to adopt the Code in 1930 on a voluntary basis. As might be expected, the studios did not always adhere to the Code, so in 1934, it became mandatory. After that, no Hollywood movie could be distributed or exhibited without a seal of approval from the Code office, which was included in a film's opening credits.

Moral Compensation

Contrary to popular belief, the Code did not ban immoral behavior, crime, or even sexual situations because those behaviors are the essence of drama. Instead, it guided the depiction of those behaviors, and the Production Code Administration (PCA) worked with studios and filmmakers to ensure that the Code was followed without compromising artistic integrity. The PCA reviewed each project at script stage, at first cut, and then at final cut, so that filmmakers could address problems during the production process. The PCA strongly advocated the idea of "compensating moral values." That is, if a film featured a corrupt politician, then an honest politician needed to be included to show that democracy was a valid institution even if there was the occasional bad apple.

If a studio felt strongly about a requested change, they could appeal it. One of the most famous appeals was on behalf of *Gone with the Wind* because of the famous line, "Frankly my dear, I don't give a damn." The line was originally cut by the PCA but was reinstated after producer David O. Selznik protested, arguing that it had been made famous by the book.

The Code on Trial

During the 1950s, a series of Supreme Court decisions questioned the constitutionality of the Code, weakening its hold over Hollywood. At the same time, filmmakers such as Otto Preminger began to openly violate the Code with films such as *The Moon Is Blue* (1953) and *The Man with the Golden Arm*

(1955) until it was forgotten completely by the early 1960s. Though still on the books, filmmakers paid little attention to the Code as they continued to escalate depictions of sex and violence. Finally, in 1968, the Code was discarded in favor of the letter-ratings system still used today.

19 Popular TV Shows of the 1960s

1. Candid Camera

2. The Andy Griffith Show

3. Bonanza

4. The Red Skelton Show

5. Gunsmoke

6. The Lucy Show

7. Gomer Pyle U.S.M.C.

8. The Beverly Hillbillies

9. The Dick Van Dyke Show

10. Gilligan's Island

11. My Three Sons

12. Lassie

13. The Munsters

14. Bewitched

15. Green Acres

16. Get Smart

17. Batman

18. The Twilight Zone

19. I Dream of Jeannie

Acting Up in School

Where else but Manhattan will you find a high school that has inspired a television series, an off-Broadway show, and two movies? "The Fame high school" is everything you saw in the movies—and more.

✳ ✳ ✳ ✳

THEY COME TO La Guardia High School from all over the city, from all kinds of homes, with dreams of becoming pop stars, ballet dancers, opera divas, painters, and instrumentalists. After they leave this unique public school four years later, many of them become stars.

A Fine Pedigree

Jennifer Aniston, Adrien Brody, Bela Fleck, Ben Vereen, Steven Bochco, NPR's Susan Stamberg, Eartha Kitt, Isaac Mizrahi, Wesley Snipes, and Al Pacino are just a few of the scores of big names you'll find on the La Guardia alumni rolls. And there's more talent waiting in the wings.

Safe to say, no high school on earth has produced more notable performers than Fiorello H. La Guardia High School of Music & Art and Performing Arts, located on Amsterdam Avenue across the street from Lincoln Center.

First, there's the name, a nod to one of NYC's greatest mayors, Fiorello La Guardia. La!, as its students call it, was originally two public schools, the High School of Performing Arts in the theater district, which taught 600 students, and a smaller, 300-student sister school, High School of Music & Art in upper Manhattan. Both schools were highly respected and graduated stellar talents over the years, but they both struggled financially, leading to the merger in 1961.

The new institution was named for the iconic La Guardia in 1969, in honor of his founding of Music & Art. In 1984 the new school moved to its current, well-equipped home, which comes complete with a 1,150-seat concert hall, a 450-seat theater, and a small "black box" theater, plus dance and musical studios, a recording studio, and an art gallery—all of this in addition to the usual classrooms and labs.

La Guardia is one of nine specialized high schools in the city and the first high school in the country to offer a free, publicly funded professional education in the arts.

Grueling

La Guardia continues the grand tradition of Performing Arts and Music & Art, with a complete college prep academic curriculum, supplemented with three or four hours of daily work in a student's particular discipline. Do you doubt that many high school kids really want to work as hard as all that? In 2008, more than 9,000 students applied for a place in La Guardia's freshman class. Only 664 were accepted.

The application process is daunting, especially considering that all the applicants are young kids in eighth and ninth grade. The requirements are stiff. Students' academic records and artistic achievements are considered; visual artists must present a 10- to 20-piece portfolio of their work, then participate in a drawing class in which they sketch a live model, create a still life from memory, and draw on an assigned subject. Dancers take part in ballet and modern dance classes, and if called back, take more classes and do a solo performance. Musicians perform a solo piece and then must pass tests that gauge rhythm, tonal memory, and sight-reading. Students interested in the backstage world may audition for the technical theater program.

A Complete Education

Get through all of that and you're in—in for some serious sweat, that is. There are no snap courses at La Guardia. The academic curriculum is the same as that followed by students in high schools around the city and includes a heavy schedule of social studies, English, math, foreign languages, science, and physical ed.

The instruction is superb. The full-time dance instructors have performed with the country's most prestigious dance companies. Master classes for musicians are likely to be taught by members of the New York Philharmonic or the City Opera.

Many of the 2,700 students take honors and advanced-placement classes, and the school boasts a graduation rate of 97 percent.

Even with all this going on, La Guardia students enjoy a full array of extracurricular activities and clubs to fill their spare time (as hard as it is to believe they have any), from yearbook, Key Club, and the literary magazine to the anime club, knitting for charity, Embracing the Inner Child, and the Enigmatology and Film Club. Many students participate in a full calendar of theater, opera, and concerts. Especially gifted incoming ninth-graders may be chosen to participate in the DaVinci Scholars, a four-year enrichment program for math and science wizards. And if you think French horn players don't like sports, listen up. La Guardia students compete very successfully in the city-wide public school league. The school offers 10 boys' sports and 13 sports for girls, as well as sports for all, such as bowling and fencing.

Student life? Well, famous people stop by from time to time to chat, and during Spirit Week the cafeteria has an open mic. But this isn't the movies, so there's no dancing on the tables, and everyone sweats the theatrical and musical production auditions. Just as they do everywhere, seniors get measured for caps and gowns.

Just an Ordinary High School?

A glance at the student handbook leaves the impression that La Guardia is like any other American high school. Students are reminded that they are not to bring cell phones to school or loiter in front of the building after class. Bring a note from home after an illness. Get a bathroom pass. But then you come across the section that instructs kids on appropriate audience etiquette and another on blackout days, when students are excused from classes for rehearsals.

The annual picture of the La! senior class is shot at Bethesda Fountain in the middle of Central Park, and graduation exercises take place in Avery Fisher Hall at Lincoln Center. The school provides a unique education that lets kids take full advantage of all that New York has to offer. It's an education, and then some!

Beatlemania New York Style!

In August 1965, the Beatles took New York by storm—and ushered in the British Invasion.

✳   ✳   ✳   ✳

THE BEATLES OWE New York City a huge debt for their popularity in the United States. *The Ed Sullivan Show*, one of the first American television shows to feature the Fab Four, helped introduce them to a music-hungry public early in 1964. But it was their concert at Shea Stadium on August 15, 1965, that sealed the deal.

It was a musical event unlike any other. The Beatles arrived in the United States on August 13 and the next day recorded a live segment for *The Ed Sullivan Show*. The concert at Shea Stadium, home of the New York Mets, was the first leg of their U.S. tour. The opening acts that day were the King Curtis Band, Cannibal and the Headhunters, Brenda Holloway, the Young Rascals, and Sounds Incorporated.

Getting the Beatles to Shea Stadium proved to be a logistical nightmare. Because of extraordinarily heavy traffic leading to the ballpark, the band was transported by limo to the Manhattan East River Heliport, where they boarded a helicopter that took them to the roof of the World's Fair building in Queens. There, the boys were loaded into the back of an armored Wells Fargo van for the trip to the stadium. When it was their turn to play, they raced through a tunnel to the stage, which had been erected at second base.

Play Louder, Mates, I Can't Hear You

Unfortunately, the crowd of 55,600 hysterically screaming fans produced such a din that the four musicians literally could not hear themselves play. This proved especially difficult for Ringo, whose drums were supposed to set the beat for each song. But positioned behind the others, he couldn't see or hear what the rest of the band was doing. Immediately after their 12-song set, the boys fled to the armored van for a quick escape.

The concert was filmed for a somewhat truncated documentary record of the event, *The Beatles at Shea Stadium*, which premiered on the BBC in England on March 1, 1966.

Tin Pan Alley

A place that was once synonymous with songwriting is long gone, yet the popular music it produced will last forever.

✳   ✳   ✳   ✳

I F YOU'RE A student of classic popular music, you'll hear these in your head as soon as you read the titles: "In the Good Old Summertime," "Give My Regards to Broadway," "Shine on Harvest Moon," "By the Light of the Silvery Moon," "Let Me Call You Sweetheart." And try these: "Alexander's Ragtime Band," "Swanee," "Baby Face," "Ain't She Sweet," "Happy Days Are Here Again," "Take Me Out to the Ball Game," "God Bless America." These and many, many more hit songs of the late 19th and early 20th centuries sprang from the West 28th Street district in lower Manhattan between Fifth and Sixth avenues, which was once known as Tin Pan Alley.

Why *Tin Pan Alley?* Well, legend has it that newspaper writer Monroe Rosenfeld coined the name after hearing the dissonant sound of multiple composers simultaneously pounding pianos in music publishers' offices that were located practically on top of each other. Others attribute the name to Roy McCardell's May 1903 article in *The World*, titled "A Visit to Tin Pan Alley, Where the Popular Songs Come From."

Beauty and Business

Although the "tin pan" racket may have given some neighbors plenty of headaches, the music itself often provided a lot more pleasure, since it was created by such legends as Irving Berlin, Hoagy Carmichael, George M. Cohan, Scott Joplin, Jerome Kern, Cole Porter, and Fats Waller, as well as the songwriting teams of George and Ira Gershwin; Al Dubin and Harry Warren; Buddy DeSylva, Lew Brown, and Ray Henderson; Gus Kahn and Walter Donaldson; Bert Kalmar and Harry Ruby; and Arthur Freed and Nacio Herb Brown.

Until the latter part of the 19th century, major publishers of American music were scattered throughout the country, with particular concentrations in New York, Chicago, Boston, Philadelphia, St. Louis, Cincinnati, Baltimore, Cleveland, Detroit, and New Orleans. However, when a post-Civil War boom in the purchase of pianos resulted in a massive increase in demand for sheet music of songs to play on them, the industry began to assemble in the city that was already the main center for the performing arts: New York. There, at 51 West 28th Street, M. Witmark & Sons initially led the way by providing new music for free to established performers as a means of plugging its song catalog. Soon others followed suit, including the Robbins Music Corporation, the Remick Music Company, the E. B. Marks Music Company, and Shapiro, Bernstein & Company, as well as the firms headed by Irving Berlin and fellow composer Harry Von Tilzer.

Writing to Order

During these early years, composers and lyricists of proven ability usually signed exclusive contracts with a particular company and then wrote to order, producing songs to suit current trends. These were often created for Broadway and vaudeville, escapist entertainment required upbeat numbers with catchy melodies. The music publishers were happy to oblige, especially in the wake of Charles K. Harris's 1892 waltz song, "After the Ball," which sold more than two million copies of sheet music during that year alone. This was big business, and pop songs of both commercial and—in many cases—long-lasting appeal were churned out to satisfy the public's appetite for romantic ballads, novelty songs, and dance tunes, as well as ragtime, jazz, and blues.

By 1907, most of the major publishers had relocated from West 28th Street to the West 30s and beyond, yet the Tin Pan Alley moniker prevailed until sheet music sales declined in line with the ascent of radio and the record player during the early 1930s. Thereafter, the Tin Pan Alley style and business model became anachronisms, and the scene was long gone by the time rock 'n' roll rose to prominence a quarter-century later.

The Best of Broadway!

The Great White Way boasts a million lights—and nearly as many memorable shows and performances. Here's a look at the ten longest-running shows in Broadway history.

✳ ✳ ✳ ✳

ON BROADWAY, SUCCESS is measured in many ways, such as rave reviews and boffo box-office. And then there's the length of time a show can attract an appreciative audience. These are Broadway's top ten longest-running shows, with a tally of their single-run performances.

1. *The Phantom of the Opera* (9,000+ performances). Andrew Lloyd Webber's musical version of the Gaston Leroux classic is the longest-running and most financially successful production in Broadway history, and shows no signs of slowing down. It crossed the 9,000 barrier in September 2009. Touring productions have brought the show to every major city, and the play was even adapted as a motion picture. On Broadway, they don't get any bigger.

2. *Cats* (7,485). Another Andrew Lloyd Webber musical hit, *Cats*—based on *Old Possum's Book of Practical Cats* by T. S. Eliot—ended its run in 2000 after 18 continuous years on Broadway, making it one of the most popular productions ever. If you missed it, don't worry—a road production will almost certainly make it to your town eventually.

3. *Les Misérables* (6,680). Based on the novel by Victor Hugo, this wildly successful production closed in 2003, only to reopen three years later to satisfy demand from audiences who missed it the first time around.

4. *A Chorus Line* (6,137). A Broadway production about, naturally enough, the chorus line of a Broadway production, *A Chorus Line* is one of the most acclaimed shows in Broadway history. In its first year it won nine Tony Awards, in addition to the 1976 Pulitzer Prize for Drama. Like *Les Misérables*, it closed its doors only to reopen in 2006 as a very successful revival.

5. *Oh! Calcutta!* (5,959 as a revival). *Oh! Calcutta!* got its start Off Broadway because of its then-startling presentation of full frontal nudity. The staid Great White Way wasn't ready for that when audiences first saw *Oh! Calcutta!* in 1969. However, in 1976 the play reopened on Broadway and played continuously for the next 13 years.

6. *Chicago* (5,500+ as a revival). First produced in 1926 as a play, *Chicago* hit Broadway in 1975 as a musical, closed, then reappeared in revival in 1996. In 2002, a movie version of the play, starring Renée Zellweger and Catherine Zeta-Jones, helped generate even more interest, resulting in a production that still has legs. It tallied its 5,500th performance in February 2010.

7. *Beauty and the Beast* (5,461). Based on the 1991 Disney animated hit, this musical production was a surprise hit on Broadway, where it ran for an impressive 13 years. And like most Broadway successes, touring companies still bring it to appreciative audiences.

8. *The Lion King* (5,200+). Another musical based on an elaborate Disney cartoon feature, *The Lion King* hit Broadway in 1997 to instant acclaim and a rabid desire for tickets. A favorite of young and old alike, it won a Tony Award for Best Musical. It achieved 5,200 performances in May 2010.

9. *Rent* (5,124). When it premiered on Broadway in April 1996, *Rent* created huge buzz over its story of a group of poor, young artists who struggle with life in the shadow of AIDS. *Rent* received immediate critical acclaim and went on to win four Tony Awards, including Best Musical, as well as the 1996 Pulitzer Prize for Drama.

10. *Miss Saigon* (4,092). An updated version of Puccini's *Madame Butterfly* set against the Vietnam War, *Miss Saigon* took Broadway by storm when it premiered in April 1991 following a successful run in England. Audiences were wowed by the musical's extravagant sets, and many in the original cast impressed critics. Indeed, *Miss Saigon* won Tonys for Best Actor in a Musical, Best Actress in a Musical, and Best Featured Actor in a Musical.

Bragging Rights

Lincoln Center for the Performing Arts, located on Columbus Avenue between 62nd and 66th streets in Manhattan, is the largest performing arts center in the nation—and one of the most prestigious.

✳   ✳   ✳   ✳

STRETCHING OVER 16 ACRES, it is made up of 12 resident institutions that encompass pretty much all of the popular arts. Some of the most famous include the Julliard School (which has produced more artistically talented individuals than you can shake a baton at), the Metropolitan Opera, the New York Philharmonic, the New York City Ballet, and the Lincoln Center Theater.

President Dwight Eisenhower broke ground for the center on May 14, 1959, and predicted that it would become "a mighty influence for peace and understanding throughout the world." The center's first building, Philharmonic Hall—now known as Avery Fisher Hall—opened three years later. Total construction cost: $185 million.

A variety of auditoriums and halls, both expansive and intimate, host Lincoln Center's varied programs. The largest is the 3,900-seat Metropolitan Opera House, home stage of the Metropolitan Opera. Avery Fisher Hall, home stage of the New York Philharmonic, is the center's second largest facility with 2,738 seats. Smaller venues include the 268-seat Walter Reade Theater, which hosts screenings by the Film Society of Lincoln Center, and the 299-seat Mitzi E. Newhouse Theater, which show-cases off-Broadway productions and other shows.

When New Yorkers are in the mood for top-notch entertainment, Lincoln Center for the Performing Arts is always at the top of their list. It presents more than 400 unique events each year, including American Songbook, Great Performers, the Mostly Mozart Festival, Midsummer Night Swing, and the Emmy Award-winning Live from Lincoln Center. So do yourself a favor and drop by the next time you're in town—your inner critic will love it.

Memorable Movie Weddings

People dream of finding "movie love." But having a movie wedding may not be the best idea—they never seem to go smoothly.

❋   ❋   ❋   ❋

The Graduate

Mrs. Robinson: "Elaine, it's too late."

Elaine: "Not for me."

The most memorable scene in this movie is sans wedding: the iconic shot through Mrs. Robinson's (Anne Bancroft) stocking-covered leg as Benjamin Braddock (Dustin Hoffman) hedges, "Mrs. Robinson, you're trying to seduce me." Mrs. Robinson may have had her way with our confused new grad, but it's her daughter, Elaine, who becomes the true object of Ben's affection. At the end of the day—or literally, the end of the film—it's a climatic wedding scene that elicits major emotion. Depending on the viewer, the scene is either touching or hilarious (intentional or otherwise). It's the mother of all "speak now or forever hold your peace" scenes.

Highlight: Furious that Elaine is set to marry another, Ben tries to stop it, despite obstacles. First, his car runs out of gas. So a persistent Ben runs the rest of the way. Sweaty and disheveled, he bangs on the church glass screaming, "ELAINE!" And after showing off some self-defense moves and charging an aisle of people, he wields a giant cross to deter the upset throng, and he and Elaine make a run for it. Ben flags down a bus, and their escape is complete.

Father of the Bride

George Banks: "I used to think a wedding was a simple affair. Boy and girl meet, they fall in love, he buys a ring, she buys a dress, they say 'I do.' I was wrong. That's getting married. A wedding is an entirely different proposition."

You've heard that the joy is in the journey, not the destination. When it comes to wedding movies, the drama and comedy are aplenty on the road to the altar, rather than at the event itself. The *Father of the Bride* remake follows the expensive, wonderful, expensive, romantic, expensive wedding planning process through all of its joys and frustrations. Good thing parents-of-the-bride George and Nina Banks (Steve Martin and Diane Keaton) have wedding planner extraordinaire Franck Eggelhoffer (Martin Short) and his loyal executive assistant Howard Weinstein (B. D. Wong), to navigate them through the countless decisions. Chic seafood or cheaper chicken? Can son Matt invite his friend, Cameron, if Cameron promises not to eat?

Highlight: George's supermarket meltdown that lands him in jail.

My Big Fat Greek Wedding

Maria Portokalos: "Toula, on my wedding night, my mother, she said to me, 'Greek women, we may be lambs in the kitchen, but we are tigers in the bedroom.'"

Toula Portokalos: "Eww. Please let that be the end of your speech."

From *Miss Congeniality* to *She's All That*, makeover movies are a Hollywood mainstay. Toula (Nia Vardalos, who also penned the screenplay, based on her stand-up show) is crushing hardcore on Ian (John Corbett). To everyone's surprise, he finds her shy, clumsy shtick adorable! Only in the movies, right? Ian willingly jumps through mega hoops to win over her large, loud family. And hey, Joey Fatone from N'Sync plays one of her cousins. Sadly, aforementioned hoop jumping does not include trimming Ian's mullet. Maybe Toula should have tried spraying Windex on it in his sleep.

Highlight: Watching Ian's super-straight parents interact with the rowdy Greeks. *Opa!*

Four Weddings and a Funeral

Carrie: "Having a good night?"

Charles: "Yes. It's right up there with my father's funeral for sheer entertainment value."

Serial monogamist Charles (Hugh Grant) attends a few weddings—and one funeral, obviously—with his mates, including flatmate Scarlett (Charlotte Coleman), gregarious Gareth (Simon Callow), straight-laced Matthew (John Hannah), bumbling Tom (James Fleet), and cynical Fiona (Kristin Scott Thomas). He meets and becomes infatuated with an American, Carrie (Andie MacDowell). Unfortunately, Carrie is already promised to Hamish, a Scottish bloke with quite possibly the worst teeth in all of Great Britain. Yet the charm of Charles's blinking and stammering prevails, and he and Carrie end up together.

Highlight: Of the four weddings, the most memorable is the first, with Mr. Bean as a new priest who botches the ceremony.

Betsy's Wedding

Stevie Dee: "I could be whatever you need. I could do anything for the woman I love. I believe in saying what you feel. You are the blood in my veins; I would walk through fire for you. I will always be available; I belong to you."

This flick cracks the list if only for the opportunity to see *The Breakfast Club*'s Clare and Allison reunited post high school. This time around, Molly Ringwald plays Betsy, a woman with the same dreadful fashion sense as her *Pretty in Pink* character. Ally Sheedy plays cop older sister Connie, who embarks on a romance with shady mobster Stevie Dee (Anthony LaPaglia). Sharing the screen are the talents of patriarch Alan Alda and the late, great Madeline Kahn.

Highlight: Any scene with LaPaglia

The Godfather: Carlo (Gianni Russo) and Connie (Talia Shire)

Old School: Frank "the Tank" (Will Farrell) and Marissa (Perrey Reeves)

Wedding Crashers: Um, pick one.

Honeymoon in Vegas: Jack (Nicholas Cage, in Flying Elvis impersonator gear) and Betsy (Sarah Jessica Parker, in showgirl costume)

My Best Friend's Wedding: Michael (Dermot Mulroney) and Kimmy (Cameron Diaz)

Steel Magnolias: Jackson (Dylan McDermott, not to be confused with Dermot Mulroney) and Shelby (Julia Roberts)

Behind the Films of Our Time

* The cover of the novel *Twilight* shows a close-up of what appears to be Edward's hands holding an apple. The filmmakers wanted to duplicate that for the movie version, so Bella drops an apple, and Edward picks it up and gently holds it in his hands, offering it to her. According to the director, the scene took 13 takes to get right.

* Fifty-one-year-old Gary Cooper wore very little, if any, make-up in the 1952 movie *High Noon*, to better show the worry lines on his face.

* Four Academy Award-winning movie titles contain animal names, but the movies aren't about those animals. They are *One Flew Over the Cuckoo's Nest* (1975); *The Deer Hunter* (1978); *Dances With Wolves* (1990); and *The Silence of the Lambs* (1991).

* The first movie directed by a woman to gross over $100 million in the United States was *Big*, directed by Penny Marshall in 1988.

* John Travolta's white disco suit in 1977's *Saturday Night Fever* later sold for $145,000.

* The 1996 horror movie *Scream* was the unlikely setting for a romance between costars Courtney Cox and David Arquette. They did two sequels to the movie, got married in 1999, and had a daughter together before divorcing in 2013.

* *The Dark Knight* is the first Batman film that didn't have the name "Batman" in the title.

* For the women who think Sean Connery was the sexiest spy: You might be surprised to learn that Connery wore a toupee in all of his James Bond movies, even the 1962 hit, *Dr. No.*

* Finding a backer in 1981 for *A Nightmare on Elm Street* was a nightmare. The show's original investor backed out days before filming, and two weeks in, the producers had run out of money. Line producer John Burrows used his credit card to float the show until new backers were found.

* Brooke Shields was taller than her costar Christopher Atkins in *The Blue Lagoon,* so the director frequently had her walking and standing in a trench so that she would appear shorter.

Crossing Ed Sullivan

Throughout the 1950s and '60s, a spot on The Ed Sullivan Show *could be a career-maker—but if you angered the host, watch out. Here are some famous folks who dared cross the mighty Ed Sullivan.*

* * * *

Bo Diddley Beat

I N NOVEMBER 1955, rock 'n' roller Bo Diddley was set to perform the up-tempo song "Bo Diddley" on the show. Sullivan, however, didn't like it. He told Diddley instead to play

"Sixteen Tons" by Tennessee Ernie Ford. Though the performer begrudgingly agreed, he instead roared into "Bo Diddley." The result was a riotous number that inspired a wave of future musicians from the Rolling Stones to Bruce Springsteen—and a lifetime ban of Diddley from the show.

Incurring Sullivan's Wrath

In the early 1960s, Jackie Mason was a rising young comedian who had already logged numerous appearances on *The Ed Sullivan Show*. In October 1964, Mason was doing his bit on the show, when Sullivan began gesturing frantically to Mason to wind up his routine. Sullivan held up two fingers (for two minutes) and then one.

"They're giving me the finger," Mason reportedly said. "Well, I've got some fingers for you—and you." He began making his own exaggerated finger motions. Did he flip off Sullivan? Maybe yes, maybe no. (Mason denies it.) But a furious Sullivan was certain he had, and he began a campaign to destroy Mason's career. Mason filed suit against Sullivan. Eventually the two reconciled.

For their 1967 performance, the Rolling Stones were told to change their lyrics from "Let's spend the night together" to "Let's spend some time together." Singer Mick Jagger did as he was told, but he theatrically rolled his eyes while singing the censored version.

After being specifically told not to sing the lyric "Girl we couldn't get much higher" (and then doing so anyway), the Doors were officially banned from the show. And Elvis Presley wasn't totally banned from the show—only certain parts of him. Sullivan didn't allow the singer's gyrating hips to be shown.

Box Office Disasters

We admire the best, but sometimes we can't look away from the worst.

✳   ✳   ✳   ✳

Cutthroat Island

Some movies are so dismal, they bankrupt an entire company. Such was the case with the Geena Davis pirate movie *Cutthroat Island*. With a budget of $115 million, this 1995 movie made only $10 million at the U.S. box office. In the process, it bankrupted production company Carolco Pictures. In fact, *Guinness World Records* ranks *Cutthroat Island* as the biggest money loser of all time.

Howard the Duck

There was a time when comic book superheroes didn't guarantee big grosses. *Howard the Duck*, the 1986 movie based on a wisecracking, cigar-smoking duck created by Marvel Comics, offers proof. The movie had a budget of $38 million but only made $16 million at the domestic box office.

Bad reviews sunk this film, and many critics still place it on their lists of all-time worst movies. Executive producer George Lucas made some questionable choices, including spending $2 million on a duck suit that looked like something from a bad Godzilla movie.

Speed Racer

Speed Racer was supposed to be one of the breakout hits of the 2008 summer movie season. Instead the film, directed by the Wachowski brothers of *Matrix* movie fame, ranked as the biggest loser of that summer.

Speed Racer cost $120 million to make but earned only $44 million at the box office. While the film is considered a technological marvel, its bright colors and endless onslaught of computer-generated effects gave audiences headaches. After bad word of mouth, the crowds stayed away. It took just 60 days to shoot *Speed Racer*. They may rank as the costliest 60 days in Warner Bros. history.

The Secret Side of Elvis

Being the King of Rock 'n' Roll is not all it's cracked up to be.

✳   ✳   ✳   ✳

SPARKLING WHITE JUMPSUIT, shiny black pompadour, soulful eyes, and shimmying hips—that's the mythic image of Elvis Presley everyone knows and loves. But although he was a revolutionary recording artist and the King of Rock 'n' Roll, Elvis was also made of darker stuff. From his obsession with guns to his bizarre behavior regarding his mother's corpse and a long fascination with occult teachings, Elvis had a secret side that his publicists preferred to keep under blue suede wraps.

I Remember Mama

Born on January 8, 1935, in Tupelo, Mississippi, to Vernon and Gladys Presley, Elvis Aaron came into the world along with a stillborn twin brother, Jesse Garon. It was an early tragedy that haunted Elvis for most of his life. The family was poor—a situation made worse when Vernon was sent to prison for forging a check. At age three, Elvis was suddenly the man of the house.

After Vernon's release in 1948, the family moved to Memphis, Tennessee. Even as his recording career began to take off in the mid-'50s, Elvis and his mother remained incredibly close and devoted to one another. She lived with him at his Graceland estate until her death in 1958.

To say Elvis did not take his mother's death well would be an understatement, and his grief morphed into often bizarre behavior. Family and friends worriedly noted that he seemed obsessed with his mother's corpse.

Later, he talked at length to friends about the technical details of the embalming process. When Gladys's glass-topped coffin was brought to lie in state at the Graceland mansion, Elvis threw himself on the corpse. Elvis also threw himself on her coffin as it was being lowered into the ground. Recording artist Barbara Pittman said he was screaming and had to be restrained. Afterward, he carried his mother's nightgown everywhere for more than a week.

Don't Be Cruel

When Elvis began dating 14-year-old Priscilla Beaulieu in 1959, he showed another strange side—the control freak. He asked her to dye her hair the same jet black as his own; the couple looked so similar that people thought they were twins. He chose her wardrobe and once became upset over an imperfect polish job on one of her toenails. He also required her to carry a concealed handgun.

Of course, Elvis sometimes carried as many as five guns himself, and was in the habit of shooting objects that irked him. A television with poor reception? *Blam!* Shattered console televisions were constantly dragged out of the Jungle Room at Graceland. Elvis once even shot his Ferrari after it stalled on the road.

Got My Mojo Workin'

Elvis continued to feel haunted by the loss of his brother and mother, and he grew desperate for some sort of spiritual answer. For a time, he sought solace in the beliefs of a hair stylist named Larry Geller. Elvis confessed to Geller that as a young child, he often heard a voice and wondered if it was his dead brother. Geller, something of a New Age mystic, introduced Elvis to metaphysical books and to his own philosophy that—as redundant as it sounds—the purpose of life was to find one's purpose in life. Presley staff member Alan Fortas said Elvis referred to Geller as his guru and to himself as "the divine messenger."

Elvis began carrying a numerology book with him that he consulted to help him decide which gifts to bestow on any given individual. His metaphysical journey ended after he tripped and hit his head in 1967, after which he was "deprogrammed" by his manager Colonel Tom Parker.

In the end, Elvis apparently had enough, and his collection of metaphysical books wound up in flames in a burn pit on the grounds of Graceland. But when Elvis was found dead in his bathroom on August 16, 1977, he was wearing the symbols of three religions: an Egyptian ankh, a Jewish Star of David, and a Christian crucifix.

Behind the Music of Our Time

* Harry Belafonte was the first black male singer to top the British music charts.

* The Bellamy Brothers' country hit, "If I Said You Had a Beautiful Body (Would You Hold It Against Me)" was based on a quip from comedian Groucho Marx.

* Marvin Gaye's hit single, "I Heard It Through the Grapevine," is a cover—Smokey Robinson and the Miracles recorded it first.

* In the late '70s, many unlikely rock groups caved into pressure from their record companies and recorded a disco song—even hippie icons The Grateful Dead. Their dance track "Shakedown Street" was recorded for an album of the same name that went gold in 1978.

* The best-selling pop duo in history is Hall & Oates, whose hits include "Rich Girl," "Kiss on My List," and "Private Eyes."

* Nick Lowe's 1979 hit "Cruel to Be Kind" coincidentally peaked at No. 12 on four music charts around the world—the United States, the United Kingdom, Canada, and Australia. Think of the odds!

* In 1997, Hanson's debut single, "MMMBop," went to the top of the charts in both the United States and Britain in the same week.

* One of the biggest rock groups ever to come out of Europe is The Scorpions, who have sold more than 100 million albums worldwide.

* When asked about Nirvana's influences after the release of *Nevermind*, Kurt Cobain said, "We sound like The Knack and The Bay City Rollers being molested by Black Flag and Black Sabbath."

* Screamin' Jay Hawkins made a major music blunder when he decided to follow up his million-selling hit "I Put a Spell on You" with a song called "Constipation Blues." Many radio stations refused the track simply because of its title.

* The name of the band Everything but the Girl, who had a big hit with "Missing" in 1995, came from the sign outside a furniture store in Hull, England: "For your bedroom needs, we sell everything but the girl."

7 Outrageous Hollywood Publicity Stunts

The movie industry isn't exactly shy about self-promotion. After all, the Academy Awards began in 1928 simply to generate press coverage for the movies and stars of the day. Here are some of the wildest feats in the long history of movie publicity.

✳ ✳ ✳ ✳

1. **Gone With the Wind (1939):** The search for the actress to play Scarlett O'Hara in the screen version of Margaret Mitchell's novel created much hoopla as the casting director traveled the country holding open auditions. After three years of interviews and auditions with stars such as Katherine Hepburn, Paulette Goddard, and Lana Turner,

the role went to Vivien Leigh, who had appeared in a few films, but remained largely unknown outside of Great Britain. Frankly, the public didn't seem to give a damn, and *Gone With the Wind* became the highest grossing film in movie history (adjusted for inflation). Its original release and seven rereleases over the years have raked in nearly $2.7 billion in today's figures.

2. **Down Missouri Way (1946):** This musical features an agriculture professor who secures a movie role for her trained mule, Shirley. To promote the film, a studio publicity man led Shirley, with an ad for the movie on her back, down Fifth Avenue in New York City, and into the restaurant overlooking Rockefeller Plaza's ice rink. Managers naturally refused to seat the animal. The press showed up to record the event, so it accomplished the publicist's mission…but it didn't appear to do much for the movie, which was not a box office smash.

3. **Teacher's Pet (1958):** Clark Gable and Doris Day star in this comedy about a newspaper editor. For publicity purposes, Paramount filmed 50 Hollywood newsmen sitting at desks and gave a few of them lines in the film. What better way to get reporters to focus on your movie than to put them in it? The buzz may have worked; the *New York Times* placed *Teacher's Pet* in its top ten of 1958, and the movie received two Oscar nominations.

4. **Mr. Sardonicus (1961):** Colombia Pictures executives told director William Castle to film an alternate, happy ending for this dark movie. Castle turned the episode into a publicity opportunity, giving audience members thumbs-up and thumbs-down cards to "vote" for the main character's fate. Castle apparently understood human nature well—there are no accounts of audiences wanting a happy ending.

5. The Blair Witch Project (1999): Producers intimated that this thriller's documentary style was authentic and implied that the footage making up the entire movie had been discovered after three student filmmakers searching for the so-called "Blair Witch" disappeared in the woods of rural Maryland. They even listed the film's lead actors (the supposed filmmakers) as "missing, presumed dead" on the Internet Movie Database before the movie's release. The stunt seemed to work: The movie made the *Guinness Book of World Records* for the highest box-office-proceeds-to-budget ratio in film history. It cost only around $35,000 to make but pulled in more than $140 million in the United States and more than $248 million worldwide.

6. Office Space (1999): The corporate "cube farm" is the target of both this cult classic—which follows coworkers who rebel against their less-than-rewarding work environment—as well as its publicity stunt. For a week, the studio had a man sit inside a Plexiglas work cubicle on top of an office building overlooking Times Square. Everyone from Howard Stern to nearby office workers expressed sympathy. The publicity helped promote the film, which ranked number 65 on Bravo's 2006 list of the 100 funniest movies of all time.

7. Borat (2006): As the title character, British actor Sacha Baron Cohen played Borat, a misspeaking journalist from Kazakhstan. In 2006, Secret Service officers prevented Cohen (dressed as Borat) from entering the White House where he hoped to invite "Premier George Walter Bush" to a screening of the film. His antics even prompted the Kazakh government to remind audiences that the obnoxious character does not properly represent the country's values. Whether due to Cohen's shenanigans, generally positive reviews, or word-of-mouth, the film made more than $248 million worldwide.

Frankly Freakish: The Crazed Genius of Frank Zappa

This Mother of Invention lived his rock 'n' roll life to the fullest.

✳ ✳ ✳ ✳

Chemical Kid

FRANK ZAPPA WAS born feet-first with his umbilical cord snagged around his neck on December 21, 1940. Such a wild beginning belied his music career based on unrelenting contrariness.

The fertile seeds of Zappa's creativity and rebellious nature were sown in his unusual childhood. He was the oldest of four children born to an Italian mother and a Greek-Arab, Italian-born father. Growing up, Zappa suffered many ailments that may have been related to his father Francis's job as a chemist for the defense industry in Baltimore. Safety standards were rather lax at the time, and Francis often came home swathed in bandages where he had allowed dangerous substances to be tested on his body for bonus pay.

The family also once lived close to a mustard gas facility, and Francis kept a large sack of the insecticide DDT, a potent carcinogen, in the hall closet because he believed that it was harmless enough for a person to eat.

Shuffled from school to school, Zappa never quite fit in. The tall, sickly boy was also tormented by sinus problems, which were probably only exacerbated when radium pellets were shoved up his nostrils as a supposed cutting-edge treatment.

Left to his own devices, Zappa began playing guitar as a teenager, an instrument he mastered in an amazingly short time. His influences were wildly varied: Soul, jazz, doo-wop, and avant-garde composers such as Igor Stravinsky and Varèse all played a part in his musical coming-of-age.

Jailhouse Shock

After high school, Zappa fell in with a succession of small local bands until he eventually bought his own recording studio in Cucamonga, California. By the mid-'60s, Zappa was in a band called the Mothers (short for a vulgar phrase); with this band he threw himself into creating music that exposed what he considered the world's hypocrisy. The group changed its name to the Mothers of Invention after their nervous record company insisted on a more benign moniker. The group's first album, *Freak Out!* blew up the 1966 charts.

Home, Home on the Strange

Married twice but well-known for dalliances with other women, Zappa had a chaotic personal life. In early 1968, he and his second wife, Gail, moved into a Los Angeles log cabin-style mansion built by cowboy movie legend Tom Mix. The rambling estate soon attracted a growing gaggle of musicians, staff, and hangers-on. The couple felt it was too crowded, so they bought a second home in Laurel Canyon and redecorated it Zappa-style: The reception area was done entirely in purple, a mural of fire-breathing dragons enlivened the living room, and in the basement lurked a ten-foot-long plastic shark.

And then there's the matter of their children. Apparently the Zappas didn't own a traditional baby name book, as their four children are named Moon Unit, Dweezil, Ahmet, and Diva Muffin.

Legend Low-Down

Although Zappa maintained a no-holds-barred attitude toward subject matter for his music and films, not all popular beliefs about Zappa's depravity are true. Unlike most rock stars of the day, Zappa seldom used drugs. Probably the most persistent (and disgusting) Zappa myth is that he once ate human excrement on stage. The rumor spread rapidly among his groupies; after concerts, girls would wait in line to present him with their own carefully collected stool samples. (Uh, thanks.)

Zappa died of prostate cancer in 1993 at age 52, with an astonishing 64 albums under his belt. And his legacy lives on in a variety of ways. Many of Zappa's orchestral compositions are still played by classical music ensembles. Also, a gene and several species of invertebrates, such as the *Pachygnatha zappa* spider, have been named after him. And outer space aficionados can look to the starry heavens and know that somewhere in the night sky flies an asteroid that will forever be known as Zappafrank.

Behind the Films of Our Time

* Linda Fiorentino played the female lead in *Men in Black*, after winning the role—and $1,200—in a poker game against director Barry Sonnenfeld.

* Would the Rodgers and Hammerstein musical *Oklahoma!* have been as popular with its original name, *Away We Go?*

* In *Forrest Gump*, the background music that's playing while Forrest is in the bathroom at the Kennedy White House is the theme from *Camelot*, in reference to the name often used to describe President John F. Kennedy's life and administration.

* The characters' names in *WALL-E* have real meaning: WALL-E stands for "Waste Allocation Load Lifter Earth-class," and EVE stands for "Extraterrestrial Vegetation Evaluator."

* Phillip Alford, who played Jem Finch in the 1962 classic *To Kill A Mockingbird*, didn't really want to try out for the part, but his mom told him he could miss a half-day of school if he went to auditions.

* When Brad Pitt chipped a tooth filming *Fight Club*, he waited until the movie was completed before getting it capped, thinking the chipped tooth would better fit the part.

* Watch out for the fruit! When you see an orange in the *Godfather* movies, it means someone is about to die, or at least have a close call.

* Although Mega City in *The Matrix* is not real, the street references are of real streets in Chicago, hometown of the writers, the Wachowski Brothers.

* The 1994 film *The Shawshank Redemption* was only a minor hit at the box office, but was one of the best moneymaking videos of all time. It was voted the number-one Must See Movie of All Time by Capital FM in London and took top spot in the IMDb Top 250 movies as voted by viewers.

* The props department built a door that could be easily broken for the set of *The Shining*. Unfortunately, Jack Nicholson, who once had worked as a volunteer fire marshal, didn't know his own strength. The door broke much too easily and one that held up a little longer had to be constructed.

D'oh! I Know That Voice!

Since its TV premiere in 1989, The Simpsons *has become a genuine cultural phenomenon. Being invited to appear (well, vocally, anyway) in an episode is a high honor. Here are some celebrities who have stepped up to the mic.*

✳ ✳ ✳ ✳

Going Incognito

NOT EVERY CELEB wants their name on the credits. Take "John Jay Smith," for example. He voiced the character of Leon Kompowsky, a burly white guy institutionalized because he thought he was singer Michael Jackson, right down to the high-pitched voice and dance moves. But John Jay Smith was actually a pseudonym for the real Michael Jackson, a longtime *Simpsons* fan. Interestingly, the character's singing was done by Jackson impersonator Kipp Lemon.

Jackson wasn't the first big name to appear on the show incognito. Oscar-winning actor Dustin Hoffman, listed as "Sam Etic" in the credits, voiced Mr. Bergstrom, a sympathetic substitute teacher who inspires Lisa Simpson.

More Stars Than Homerpalooza

Most of the Fab Four have appeared on *The Simpsons* (minus John Lennon, of course). Paul McCartney and his late wife, Linda, were in a memorable episode called "Lisa the Vegetarian." A song plays during the closing credits that, when played backward, is really a lentil soup recipe read by Paul. Other celebrities who have appeared on the show include:

* Meryl Streep

* James Earl Jones

* The Ramones

* Elizabeth Taylor

* Johnny Cash

* Buzz Aldrin

* Hugh Hefner

* Stephen Hawking

* Stephen King

* Gore Vidal

* Tom Wolfe

* Roger Clemens

* Ken Griffey Jr.

* Johnny Carson

* Mick Jagger

* Aerosmith

The Red Special

Queen guitarist Brian May was a legend, and so was his guitar, dubbed the Red Special. Even more impressive, May and his father built the entire guitar by hand using mostly household items.

✳   ✳   ✳   ✳

SOME OF THE most influential songs to come out of the 1970s belong to the bombastic rock band Queen. Part of the band's unique sound was certainly the incredible vocal prowess of late singer Freddie Mercury. But just as unique were the sounds coming out of guitarist Brian May's guitar.

May's family was rather poor. So when young May decided he wanted an electric guitar, he and his father, Harold, an electronics whiz, decided to build one. The pair began construction around 1963; it took more than two years to build the guitar. When it was completed, everyone marveled at the unique sounds May was able to coax out of the red guitar, often using a sixpence coin rather than a guitar pick. Here's what went into the making of legend.

Mantle from a 100-year-old fireplace: When one of his neighbors was getting ready to throw out his old mantle, May took it to use for the guitar's neck, hand-carving the entire piece.

Mother-of-pearl buttons: Once the neck was carved, May turned his attention to the fretboard. For this he raided his mother's sewing kit for mother-of-pearl buttons.

Oak table: The Mays needed something for the guitar's body. An old oak table was perfect, since the oak would be strong enough to support any pressure May used on the neck of the guitar.

Bicycle saddlebag holder and a knitting needle: Every guitarist knows you can't have a good guitar without a tremolo bar. So May took part of a metal saddlebag holder and bent it, creating the bar.

He then used the plastic tip from one of his mother's knitting needles to cap the bar off.

A knife and some motorcycle springs: May and his father took an old, hardened steel knife-edge and bent it into a v-shape. They then took two valve springs from a motorcycle and connected them to the knife-edge to complete the tremolo system.

Behind the Films of Our Time

* Dogs rule. Terry the dog got $125 a week to play Toto in *The Wizard of Oz.* Meanwhile, the folks who played the Munchkins only received $50 a week.

* Director Steven Spielberg planned to use M&Ms as the candy that attracted the alien in the movie *E.T.*, but he couldn't get the rights from the company. Reese's Pieces went on to film fame as the replacement.

* Not only did Gary Cooper turn down the offer to play Rhett Butler in *Gone with the Wind*, but he was also very vocal in his feeling that the movie would be a flop. "I'm just glad it'll be Clark Gable who's falling on his face," he said, "not Gary Cooper." Of course, the movie went on to win the Oscar for Best Picture in 1939—and a Best Actor nomination for Gable, who played Rhett.

* Sarah Michelle Gellar and Freddie Prinze Jr. met on the 1997 set of *I Know What You Did Last Summer.* They were engaged by 2001, got married, had a child, and are still going strong.

* The phrase "Let's get out of here" may give you that déjà vu feeling. It's the line that has been used most often in films.

* Shiloh Jolie-Pitt, daughter of Brad Pitt and Angelina Jolie, appeared with her dad in *The Curious Case of Benjamin Button* as Benjamin and Daisy's daughter. She was 10 months old at the time.

* It may look gross in the movie, but the pile of human waste that Jamal jumps into in *Slumdog Millionaire* is actually made of peanut butter and chocolate.

* Would the horror movie *Halloween* been such a hit if it had been called by its original title, *The Babysitter Murders?*

* Heath Ledger posthumously won 32 Best Supporting Actor awards for his role as The Joker in *The Dark Knight*, including an Oscar, a Golden Globe, and a Critic's Choice Award.

* In *The Green Mile*, the prison guards are seen wearing uniforms, but guards didn't typically wear uniforms in 1935, when the movie was set.

Weird Science!

Don't trust motion pictures to get their science straight.

✳ ✳ ✳ ✳

If Indy Was a Weightlifter

AT THE BEGINNING of *Raiders of the Lost Ark* (1981), Indiana Jones snatches an ancient gold idol off its pedestal by substituting a small bag of sand that he believes to be of equal weight. Then, with the idol tucked safely in one arm, our intrepid archeologist hightails it out of the booby-trapped temple.

It's a thrilling scene, but it had real scientists tearing out their hair, because the science was all wrong. Gold is twice as heavy as lead, so assuming that the idol was made entirely of the precious metal, it would weigh at least 60 pounds—too much for a man to carry in one hand.

Raiders of the Lost Ark is just one example of bad movie science. In fact, many movies—particularly sci-fi films and thrillers with stories based in science—get more science wrong than right. According to physicists, one of the most common errors in sci-fi movies is a scene of a rocket whooshing through space, or something loudly blowing up in space. As anyone who has taken even a basic science class knows, sound needs air to travel, and space is a vacuum. No air, no sound. So much for a big bang.

Not Fast Enough

The Keanu Reeves-Sandra Bullock action thriller *Speed* (1994) drew a laugh from scientists by ignoring one of the most basic laws of physics: gravity. If you've seen the movie, you'll remember the scene in which the bus must leap a level gap in a freeway bridge. There's no ramp to propel the bus over the abyss—it just flies over the gap at a speed of 70 miles per hour. In real life, gravity would cause the bus to plummet to the ground, regardless of how fast it was going.

Not-So-Superman

Superman (1978), starring Christopher Reeve, was a fun flick full of flawed science (and we're not talking about how, exactly, Superman is able to fly). In one scene, Superman saves Lois Lane after she falls from a tall building by flying up and snatching her in midair. It looks cool, but in reality Lois would be hurt or even killed because she falls into Superman's arms with the same force as if she had hit the ground. (You can test this concept by tossing a water balloon with a friend at greater and greater distances. The farther the distance, the more difficult it is to catch the balloon without breaking it.)

In another scene, Superman is able to travel back in time by reversing the Earth's rotation. Even ignoring the fact that time has nothing to do with a planet's rotation, the scene fails because Superman flies in the opposite direction from where he needs to go to make such a thing happen.

More So-Called Science

The Core (2003) is so rife with scientific inaccuracies as to be laughable. The movie is about a group of scientists who must burrow to the center of the Earth in order to save the planet. About 700 miles down, the group stops to stretch their legs.

Oddly, the gravity is normal there, which doesn't make sense because a large percentage of the Earth's mass (which is key to gravity) is now above them. In other words, gravity toward the center of the Earth would be much less than on its surface.

Sadly, the science in *Armageddon* (1998) is even worse. One of its most egregious errors is the falling rain on the asteroid that Bruce Willis and his team are sent to destroy. A celestial body must have an atmosphere to produce rain, and asteroids have no atmosphere, and therefore no rain.

Physics-Friendly Movies

Not all movies are rife with bad science. In fact, some actually get it right. One of the best examples is Stanley Kubrick's opus *2001: A Space Odyssey* (1968), which demonstrates the use of centrifugal force to generate artificial gravity, and craft flying silently through airless space. Equally laudable is *Apollo 13* (1995), which strives to adhere as closely as possible to the true story upon which it was based.

Real or Hollywood?

The Texas cowboy in Hollywood and TV westerns is one of the most enduring characters in popular culture. The fact that many of the fine actors who played these roles were born far from Texas is a credit to their skills. See if you can pick out and put a check mark beside the names of the real Texans by birth from this list of famous Hollywood Western actors.

1. _____ Chill Wills

2. _____ James Arness

3. _____ Gene Autry

4. _____ William Boyd (Hopalong Cassidy)

5. _____ Roy Rogers

6. _____ Dale Evans

7. ____ Gabby Hayes

8. ____ John Wayne

9. ____ Clint Eastwood

10. ____ Richard Boone

11. ____ Glenn Ford

12. ____ Gary Cooper

13. ____ Dennis Weaver

14. ____ Audie Murphy

15. ____ Alan Ladd

16. ____ Tom Mix

17. ____ Tex Ritter

18. ____ Slim Pickens

19. ____ Randolph Scott

20. ____ Will Rogers

21. ____ Richard Widmark

1. Yes—Seagoville, Texas; 2. No—Minneapolis, Minnesota; 3. Yes—Tioga, Texas; 4. No—Hendrysburg, Ohio; 5. No—Cincinnati, Ohio; 6. Yes—Uvalde, Texas; 7. No—Wellsville, New York; 8. No—Winterset, Iowa; 9. No—San Francisco, California; 10. No—Los Angeles, California; 11. No—Ste.-Christine, Quebec; 12. No—Helena, Montana; 13. No—Joplin, Missouri; 14. Yes—near Kingston, Texas; 15. No—Hot Springs, Arkansas; 16. No—Mix Run, Pennsylvania; 17. Yes—Murvaul, Texas; 18. No—Kingsburg, California; 19. No—Orange County, Virginia; 20. No—Oologah, Oklahoma; 21. No—Sunrise Township, Minnesota

From Chicago to Hollywood

Some of Hollywood's brightest stars, past and present, have roots in Chicago and its environs. Here are 20+ Chicagoans, including some famous siblings, who have dazzled Tinseltown with their talent.

✳ ✳ ✳ ✳

✳ **Jim and John Belushi** (Wheaton)

✳ **Jack Benny** (Waukegan)

✳ **Joan and John Cusack** (Evanston)

✳ **Dennis Farina** (Chicago)

✳ **Harrison Ford** (Park Ridge)

✳ **Charlton Heston** (Evanston)

✳ **Bonnie Hunt** (Chicago)

✳ **Jennifer Hudson** (Chicago)

✳ **Bernie Mac** (Chicago)

✳ **Michael and Virginia Madsen** (Chicago)

✳ **Jenny McCarthy** (Chicago)

✳ **Mr. T** (Chicago)

✳ **Bill Murray** (Wilmette)

✳ **Bob Newhart** (Oak Park)

✳ **Gary Sinise** (Highland Park)

✳ **Vince Vaughn** (Lake Forest)

✳ **George Wendt** (Chicago)

✳ **Jeremy Piven** (Evanston)

It Wasn't Always a Wonderful Life

For many, watching It's a Wonderful Life *(1946) is as much a part of the Christmas season as listening to carols and exchanging gifts. Spend the holiday without George and Mary Bailey, Clarence Oddbody, and Zuzu's rose petals? Why, you might as well not bother putting up a tree! But when this beloved holiday classic was initially released, it proved an uncharacteristic flop at the box office.*

✳   ✳   ✳   ✳

DURING THE 1930S, director Frank Capra could seemingly do no wrong. Starting with the classic screwball comedy *It Happened One Night* in 1934, he created a series of wildly successful films that won acclaim from critics and devotion from audiences while vaulting the fledgling Columbia Pictures into the ranks of Hollywood's top studios. In hits such as *Mr. Deeds Goes to Town* (1936), *You Can't Take It with You* (1938), and *Mr. Smith Goes to Washington* (1939), Capra spun tales of idealistic individuals who defended the moral high ground and protected our social institutions against greed and corruption. Though the themes of his films were viewed by some as simplistic, they resonated with audiences who saw in them the same struggles they faced during the long years of the Great Depression.

But in 1946, when Capra released the story of George Bailey, a common man who sees himself as a failure but comes to understand the value of his life through a bit of divine intervention, it marked the start of a long slide in popularity for the famous director. Moviegoers rejected the film at the box office, and it lost money despite being nominated for five Oscars. Some hold that the audiences who embraced the filmmaker's uplifting messages in the previous decade had become jaded and weary after the horrors of World War II and found no use for what they now saw as Capra's naive encouragement.

Others contend that George Bailey's discovery of what might have been is depicted as a nightmare of loss and bitterness that survivors of war and hard times didn't want to be reminded of. Whatever the reason for its failure, it wasn't until the 1970s, when *It's a Wonderful Life* became a staple of holiday television programming, that Americans finally embraced Capra's heart-warming Christmas flick.

From the Playing Field to the Silver Screen

Athletes and actors both showcase their abilities on the highest stage, often receive impressive compensation for their efforts, and bask in the adulation of an adoring public. Here are a few athletes who transferred their talents to the silver screen. In some cases, their acting talents equaled or surpassed their athletic accomplishments.

✳ ✳ ✳ ✳

Jim Brown (1935–)

ONE OF THE greatest running backs to ever lug the loaf, Brown was named first team All-Pro in eight of the nine seasons he played with the Cleveland Browns from 1957 to 1965. Brown brought the same intensity and determined professionalism to Hollywood, appearing in more than 30 films including The *Dirty Dozen* (1967), *The Running Man* (1987), and *Mars Attacks* (1996).

Chuck Connors (1921–1992)

A center for the Boston Celtics (1946) and an outfielder with the Brooklyn Dodgers (1949) and Chicago Cubs (1951), Connors shifted his focus from sports to the silver screen. From 1958 to 1963, Connors was better known as the star of TV's *The Rifleman*. He was also a well-respected movie actor who appeared in acclaimed films such as *Pat and Mike* (1952), *Old Yeller* (1957), *The Big Country* (1958), and *Flipper* (1963).

Sonja Henie (1910–1969)

The winner of three Olympic gold medals in figure skating, Sonja Henie translated her success on the ice into a dignified film career that made her a major box-office attraction. Signed by renowned Hollywood studio head Darryl Zanuck to a long-term contract in 1936, Henie appeared in films including *One in a Million* (1936), *Sun Valley Serenade* (1941), and *The Countess of Monte Cristo* (1948).

Chuck Norris (1939–)

A professional karate champion who held the middleweight world title from 1968 to 1974, Norris brought his martial arts skills to Hollywood and opened a school frequented by stars. This opened the door to a film career. In the 1980s, he starred in a string of successful films including *Missing in Action* (1984), *Code of Silence* (1985), *Firewalker* (1986), and *The Delta Force* (1986). He also played the title character in the TV series *Walker: Texas Ranger*, which ran from 1993 to 2001.

Paul Robeson (1898–1976)

Prior to carrying films such as *Show Boat* (1936) and *Song of Freedom* (1936) with his sonorous, booming baritone, Paul Robeson studied law at Columbia University and played for the Milwaukee Badgers, one of the founding franchises of the NFL. A member of the College Football Hall of Fame, Robeson also appeared in films such as *Jericho* (1937), *King Solomon's Mines* (1937), and *The Proud Valley* (1940).

Woody Strode (1914–1995)

One of the first African Americans to play in the NFL when he suited up with the Los Angeles Rams in 1946, Strode found even greater fame as an actor, earning a Golden Globe award nomination for *Spartacus* (1960). A favorite of legendary director John Ford, Strode appeared in four of Ford's films, including *Two Rode Together* (1961) and *The Man Who Shot Liberty Valance* (1962), but he gave the performance of his career in the great director's *Sergeant Rutledge* (1960).

O. J. Simpson (1947–)

He's now notorious for activities not related to sports or cinema, but it's hard to ignore the impact Simpson had on his two chosen pursuits. A Hall of Fame running back with the Buffalo Bills and San Francisco 49ers from 1969 to 1979, Simpson brought his acting skills to the silver screen in films such as *The Cassandra Crossing* (1976), *Capricorn One* (1978), and *The Naked Gun* series, in which he exhibited a flair for comedy.

Carl Weathers (1948–)

Before trading body blows with Sylvester Stallone in the *Rocky* film franchise, Weathers played professional football with the NFL's Oakland Raiders (1970) and the CFL's British Columbia Lions (1971–1973). Weathers, who also has a flair for comedy, has shared the screen with Adam Sandler in *Happy Gilmore* (1996) and *Little Nicky* (2000).

Johnny Weissmuller (1904–1984)

The winner of five Olympic gold medals in swimming, Weissmuller set 51 world records and retired from his amateur swimming career undefeated. He was able to translate his success in the pool into a stellar Hollywood career, appearing in more than 30 films including 12 *Tarzan* flicks and another dozen entries in the *Jungle Jim* franchise.

First City of Comedy

A group of U of C students staged a theatrical revolution.

✳   ✳   ✳   ✳

WHO COMES TO mind when you try to think of the funniest people you've ever seen? Stephen Colbert of *The Colbert Report*? Tina Fey of *30 Rock*? Steve Carell of *The Office*? Bill Murray or John Belushi of *Saturday Night Live*?

All these comedic actors have something in common: They honed their skills in Chicago. Forget hog butchering, deep-dish pizza, and architecture. The City of the Big Shoulders' real gift to the world is comedy. From Mike Nichols directing *The Graduate* to Tina Fey taking time out from *30 Rock* to transform herself into Sarah Palin, a long parade of Chicago-trained actors, writers, and directors have kept America in stitches.

Games Lead to Brilliance

How did a working-class midwestern city become a major source of showbiz talent? It started in the 1950s at the University of Chicago, where the lack of a drama department did not stop students from forming their own theater group. One of those students was Chicagoan Paul Sills, who had learned improvisational theater games from his mother, Viola Spolin, and taught them to his fellow actors as a way to develop their skills. In improv, actors build a sense of trust and timing among themselves by performing scenes created on the spot— out of their own imaginations—rather than from scripts.

Inspired by their improv work, Sills and a group of actors established their own cabaret-style comedy theater group, the Compass Players, and made improv a part of the show. Audiences were encouraged to suggest types of characters and settings, and the actors would use that information to create comedy sketches that focused on political and social humor. Buoyed by their success, Sills and other Compass members opened their own club on North Wells Street in 1959 and called it the Second City. The troupe gained notoriety as a proving ground, propelling Alan Arkin, Joan Rivers, David Steinberg, Robert Klein, and others to national fame.

By the 1970s, Second City's workshops were as renowned as its shows, and young actors from around the country made the pilgrimage to Chicago to learn comic improv, hoping for a shot at the big time. The shows themselves had evolved into polished, rehearsed revues, though the material continued to be developed through improv. Second City went from notable to legendary in the late 1970s after alums Belushi, Murray, Gilda Radner, and Dan Aykroyd helped establish *Saturday Night Live*.

A Comic Boom

In the 1980s, with its hot reputation and an influx of eager young performers, Chicago saw an explosion of improv-based comedy shows and workshops, each offering its own spin on the form. At ImprovOlympic (later called iO), Second City veteran Del Close taught a technique he called "the Harold," a long-form style of improv that created complex performances that were more like short plays than comedy skits. Annoyance Theatre, established by Mick Napier, a respected director at Second City, succeeded in pushing improv into darker, more experimental areas. Annoyance's *The Real Live Brady Bunch* was a breakout hit that was remounted successfully in New York and triggered a nationwide revival of interest in the popular 1970s sitcom, while *Co-ed Prison Sluts* ran for an amazing 11 years—a record in Chicago musical-theater history.

As the growth of cable TV offered more room for comedy programming in the 1990s and 2000s, Chicago continued to funnel talent to the coasts. Andy Dick, Rachel Dratch, Jeff Garlin, Sean Hayes, Mike Myers, Bob Odenkirk, Amy Poehler, Andy Richter, Amy Sedaris, and others maintained the city's 50-year tradition of breeding comic innovation.

Left Behind on the Cutting Room Floor

Filmmakers face tough calls while editing films, and sometimes, deleting a scene can completely change the final product. Would these flicks still have been box-office gold if the following scenes had been left in?

✳ ✳ ✳ ✳

The Wizard of Oz (1939)

TALK ABOUT A different path for the yellow brick road: The original treatment of *The Wizard of Oz* included a massively expensive musical scene called "The Jitterbug." The scene—which took five weeks to shoot and cost producers a whopping $80,000—had Dorothy, the Scarecrow, the Tin Man, and the Cowardly Lion being attacked by a group of jitterbugs as they enter the Haunted Forest. What is a jitterbug, you ask? It's commonly described by film buffs as a "furry pink and blue mosquitolike rascal" that buzzes around people, giving them the jitters.

Despite the work that went into the elaborate scene and accompanying song, MGM decided it made the movie too long. Legend has it that studio execs were also concerned that viewers would associate the scene with the then-popular dance of the same name, which could ruin the idea that Oz was a fantasy world and would one day make the movie seem dated.

King Kong (1933)

These days, it's hard to imagine that the 1933 classic *King Kong* was ever too scary to sit through. For audiences back then, however, the giant gorilla was a frightful sight—so much so that producers had to slice a scene out of the movie just to make it more tolerable.

The original *King Kong* included a scene in which Kong shook a log bridge, sending several sailors falling into a ravine below, where giant spiders were waiting to eat them alive. Yikes! During the initial preview, the scene supposedly caused people to scream and even get up and leave the theater. According to producer Merian C. Cooper, it "stopped the picture cold," so the human-eating spiders were removed from the scene.

Dr. No (1962)

James Bond's initial introduction to the world wasn't as the character's creators originally intended. *Dr. No*, the first installment in the James Bond franchise, saw several chops before hitting the big screen, including one major change to the movie's climax. The original version showed Honey Ryder, the first Bond girl, being attacked by giant crabs just before 007 swoops in to rescue her. The consensus, though, was that the crabs weren't creepy enough. Apparently, their crawling was a bit too slow to be truly scary, so the crustaceans got the ax.

Other modifications were made to tone down the violence in *Dr. No.* One scene, for example, was meant to have Bond shooting the villain six times, but the British Board of Film Classification thought that was a bit excessive, so it asked producers to pare it down to two gunshots instead.

Big (1988)

This blockbuster starring Tom Hanks got a big change before its debut. In the movie, Hanks plays a 12-year-old boy who magically transforms into an adult after making a wish on a carnival machine. But the final product featured a drastically different ending from what test audiences first saw.

Hanks's character, Josh, falls in love with a woman when he is living the life of an adult male. The version we know ends with Josh deciding to leave her behind when he wishes to become a child again. The woman, it appears, accepts this fate and moves on with her life.

But it's been rumored that the first version of the film didn't end there. A supposed subsequent scene showed Josh, back as a child and back in school, meeting a new girl in his class. And, you guessed it, that new girl is his former adult flame, who had gone to the carnival machine and wished to become a child herself so the two could stay together. However, that ending has never shown up on DVD releases and may have been wishful thinking on the part of fans who wanted a fairy-tale ending.

Titanic (1997)

The historical epic that broke box-office records and won 11 Academy Awards almost missed out on its dramatic ending. The movie ends with the elderly Rose—played by Gloria Stuart—throwing her "Heart of the Ocean" diamond necklace over the side of the research ship and into the ocean. Simple and beautiful, right? It almost wasn't.

Titanic originally went on for another nine minutes during which crew members approached Rose, thinking she was going to jump over the edge and end her life. They tried to talk her out of committing suicide, and then, when they realized she was just throwing the necklace overboard, they tried to convince her to keep it. Not quite as poetic, is it?

Steven Spielberg's Tall Tale

There's an oft-repeated myth that celebrated director Steven Spielberg got his big break in the movie industry by sneaking onto the Universal Studios lot, taking over a vacant office, and pretending to be an established filmmaker. The story has evolved and gained momentum over the years due in large part to Spielberg's own frequent embellishments.

✳   ✳   ✳   ✳

SPIELBERG'S FIRST VERSION of the story has the 21-year-old future director bluffing his way past the guards at Universal in 1969, dressed in a cheap suit and carrying a briefcase. Once inside the gates, he coolly took over a vacant office for two and a half months before allegedly being chased off the lot by none other than "The Master of Suspense" himself, Alfred Hitchcock. A second take on the tale pushes the action back to 1965, with a 17-year-old Spielberg touring the studio on a tram. According to this version of the story, the young auteur-to-be simply snuck away from the tour group during a bathroom break and found an empty office. Thereafter, he took the tour every day, got off the tram, and appropriated the office, even slapping his name on the door.

As colorful as these stories are, and as much as countless film school graduates wish they were true, the real story of how Spielberg broke into the industry is far more mundane. When Steven was 16, his father arranged for him to visit the studio and spend a day with his friend Chuck Silvers, who was an assistant to the editorial supervisor. The following year, Silvers secured Spielberg a summer job on the lot as an unpaid clerical assistant working for a woman named Julie Raymond. He ran errands for her for two summers while working on his own scripts. As Raymond later told Spielberg's biographer: "He made up a lot of stories about finding an empty editing office and moving into it. That's a bunch of *@$#!" It seems that when it comes to telling compelling stories, Spielberg doesn't limit himself to his scripts.

How to Get a Star on the Hollywood Walk of Fame

They say you'll know you've made it in Hollywood when they give you your very own star on the Hollywood Walk of Fame, which is located along Hollywood Boulevard. But just how do all those celebs go about getting their very own star? Well, read on, because you might be surprised at just how easy it is to get one.

Q: Who can apply for a star?

A: Anyone who makes/made their living in one of five categories: Live Theater/Performance, Motion Pictures, Radio, Recording, and Television.

Q: How does one begin the application process?

A: Complete and mail in a nomination form by the end of May to be eligible for a star in June of the following year. The form must be accompanied by a bio and a photo of the nominee, their qualifications, and a list of their contributions to the community. In addition, applicants must be sponsored by agents, fan clubs, producers, or local businesses, who provide a letter of agreement.

Q: What criteria must a star applicant meet?

A: For someone to be considered for a star, the applicant must have been involved with the entertainment industry for more than five years and/or have made contributions to the community. Applicants must also agree to attend a dedication ceremony if they are accepted. The Walk of Fame has been criticized for withdrawing an honor if a star refuses to appear in person.

Q: Who decides who gets a star?

A: Each year, the Walk of Fame Committee, which is part of the Hollywood Chamber of Commerce, is responsible for choosing from the submitted applications to select a new group of entertainers to receive stars on the Hollywood Walk of Fame. Once the Committee has made its selections, they still must be approved by the Hollywood Chamber of Commerce's Board of Directors and the City of Los Angeles' Board of Public Works Department.

Q: How many people are awarded a star each year?

A: The committee annually nominates up to 20 people to receive a star.

Q: How many people apply for a star each year?

A: On average, the Committee receives 300 applications per year.

Q: Do you have to be alive to get a star?

A: No. Every year, one star is awarded posthumously. However, friends and family must wait five years after the entertainer's death before submitting an application. The Committee has been criticized for its failure to honor many industry pioneers because they lack a presence among the public and there are no family members to pony up the fee.

Q: Do people get to choose where their star goes?

A: No, the stars are placed in areas as they are awarded. Stars are also faced in alternating opposite directions so that people walking either way on the sidewalk can read them.

Q: How much does each star cost?

A: Each recipient must pay $25,000 to the Walk of Fame Trust upon receiving his or her star.

Q: How do people find out if they've been awarded a star?

A: Each June, the Committee announces who will receive a star the following year.

Q: What are the stars made of?

A: The stars are made of coral terrazzo with brass accents.

Q: How can I get directions to a specific star after it's in place?

A: The Hollywood Chamber of Commerce hosts an online search engine that notes the location of current stars.

Q: Can I attend the presentation ceremony when the stars are unveiled?

A: Yes, the ceremony is open to the general public.

Q: What if an applicant doesn't get picked?

A: Applicants are permitted to reapply as many times as they like.

The Making of *King Kong*

Very few movies have had the kind of cultural impact enjoyed by King Kong (1933). Its iconic imagery is familiar to almost everyone, and it remains a critical favorite more than 75 years after its premiere. In fact, the American Film Institute included King Kong on its list of the Ten Best Fantasy Films of all time.

✳   ✳   ✳   ✳

A King Is Born

WHEN KING KONG premiered in March 1933, audiences were awestruck by the work of talented special effects technicians who brought the film's giant dinosaurs to life and gave the massive gorilla Kong a personality that moviegoers could relate to.

The driving force behind *King Kong* was Merian C. Cooper, who came up with the concept of a primitive gorilla trapped in the concrete jungle of New York City. For his film, Cooper had planned on using real gorillas and lizards—that is until he met Willis O'Brien, a stop-motion animator who was using the process to create lifelike dinosaurs for a movie called *Creation*.

When the expensive production of *Creation* was canceled, O'Brien approached Cooper about using stop-motion animation in his gorilla movie. Cooper brought the idea to David O. Selznick, the vice president in charge of production at RKO Pictures, who shared Cooper's enthusiasm for the project. He authorized a special effects test reel, which convinced the brass at RKO that *King Kong* could be just the thing to pull the studio out of debt.

Produced from a script by James Ashmore Creelman and Ruth Rose, *King Kong* was a groundbreaking movie for its time. O'Brien and his crew vastly improved the stop-motion animation process, giving Kong facial expressions and convincing reactions to the action around him. As a result, both Kong and the film's dinosaurs look amazingly lifelike.

A Miniature Marvel

Though King Kong appears to be as much as 50 feet tall in the movie, the real Kong measured just 18 inches. Marcel Delgado crafted the model as an articulated metal skeleton and covered this armature with foam rubber, latex, and rabbit fur. For close-ups and scenes in which Kong holds Fay Wray, full-size arm, hand, and head models were made. A full-size leg was created for scenes in which Kong steps on natives as he rampages through the island village. (Contrary to claims made years later, the original King Kong was never portrayed by a man in a gorilla suit.)

The movie also required the creation of various articulated dinosaurs and other creatures, all of which, like Kong, were brought to life by stop-motion animation.

Many of the movie's key scenes required the use of rear-screen projection, which allowed actors Fay Wray and Bruce Cabot to appear seamlessly in scenes with, and react to, Kong and the other terrifying denizens of Skull Island. RKO shared a special Academy Award with Fox Film Corp. and Warner Bros. for developing a more reliable rear-screen projection system during the production of *King Kong*.

Hollywood's First Scream Queen

Fay Wray was already an established actress when she appeared in *King Kong*. She spends much of the movie screaming as Kong carries her through the jungle and protects her from various dangers—though all of her screams were recorded after filming was completed.

Most of *King Kong* was filmed in or around the RKO studio and back lot in Culver City, California. The huge wall and gate that protects the natives of Skull Island from Kong was reportedly first used in Cecil B. DeMille's 1927 production *The King of Kings*. The producers of *King Kong* also economized by using jungle sets from *The Most Dangerous Game*, which was being filmed at RKO at the same time as *King Kong*. Some of the same mattes, such as the giant log across the ravine, can be clearly identified in both films.

King Kong cost around $670,000 to make and was a tremendous success. It grossed more than $1.7 million during its initial release and had a role in saving RKO from financial ruin. A sequel, *The Son of Kong*, was immediately put into production and released in December 1933. However, its smaller budget and rushed production schedule were evident, and it didn't fare nearly as well as the original.

Questionable Kongs

The giant gorilla character Kong did not appear in the movies again until 1962, when Japan's Toho Studios pitted him against Godzilla in a movie that annoyed fans of the original, even though Kong took the prize for toe-to-toe combat. An updated version of *King Kong* starring Jessica Lange was produced in 1976 by Dino DeLaurentiis, who decided to go with legendary makeup artist Rick Baker in a gorilla suit for the portrayal of Kong, instead of using stop-motion animation. Even though the remake earned an Oscar for special effects, fans of the original were outraged and the movie was vilified by critics. In 2005, Peter Jackson, an avowed *King Kong* fan, released his own affectionate remake of the original, relying on state-of-the-art computer effects to bring Kong, the horrifying creatures of Skull Island, and 1930s-era New York City to the big screen. Despite a host of enthusiastic critical raves, ticket sales for this 187-minute take on *Kong* were mediocre at best (it cost $207 million to produce but collected just $218 million in America), making it a major disappointment at U.S. box offices. The picture did far better business abroad.

In addition to its two official remakes and related sequels, *King Kong* has spawned scores of "big monkey" movies over the decades, including the 1949 classic *Mighty Joe Young*, with effects by Willis O'Brien and his protégé, Ray Harryhausen. King Kong has also appeared in television commercials and in print advertising, comic books, and elsewhere.

Beauty may have killed the beast in the movie, but the big gorilla's status as a groundbreaking cinematic icon will live forever.

* Merian C. Cooper's original idea for *King Kong* was inspired in part by the story of how Komodo dragons—first brought to New York's Bronx Zoo in 1926 by adventurer W. Douglas Burden—died quickly in captivity. Cooper envisioned a battle between a live, captured African gorilla and a Komodo dragon for his film project,.

The Dummy Did It

Many of Hollywood's most oddball flicks seem to feature ventriloquists and their wooden sidekicks. It's a subgenre of filmmaking that contains more movies than you might think. Here are some of the best:

❋ ❋ ❋ ❋

The Unholy Three (1925)

IN THIS SILENT thriller, Lon Chaney plays a sideshow ventriloquist named Echo who teams up with a strong man and a dwarf to rob people by selling them talking parrots. Of course, the parrots talk only when Echo, in disguise as an old lady, is around to make them talk via ventriloquism. When customers complain that their birds won't speak, Echo and his diminutive colleague, who is disguised as a toddler, drop by their homes, which they case for future robberies. A silent movie about ventriloquism might seem odd, but Chaney, whose makeup mastery is one of the highlights of the movie, manages to make it work.

The Great Gabbo (1929)

In this early talkie, German director-turned-actor Erich von Stroheim portrays The Great Gabbo, a ventriloquist who slowly goes insane and starts to channel his innermost desires through his dummy, Otto. Trivia buffs will be interested to learn that this obscure little film was actually referenced in an episode of *The Simpsons*.

The Unholy Three (1930)

This remake of the 1925 silent film of the same name was Lon Chaney's first—and last—talkie (he died a couple of months after its release). The story is essentially the same as the original, with Chaney again playing sideshow ventriloquist/master criminal Echo, who joins forces with some of his carny colleagues for a series of Park Avenue heists. Harry Earles reprises his role as Tweedledee, the dwarf with crime in his heart.

Charlie McCarthy, Detective (1939)

Edgar Bergen and his dummy, Charlie McCarthy, were one of the most popular radio and motion picture ventriloquist acts of the 1930s and '40s. In this flick, the duo investigate the mysterious death of a newspaper editor with ties to the mob. Bergen and Charlie appeared in numerous movies over the years, including *You Can't Cheat an Honest Man* (1939) starring W. C. Fields.

Dead of Night (1945)

This critically acclaimed British film is actually an anthology of supernatural horror vignettes. Its concluding segment is about a ventriloquist, played by Michael Redgrave, who is driven insane when his dummy appears to come to life.

Devil Doll (1964)

Also from England, this horror flick concerns a ventriloquist/hypnotist named The Great Vorelli, who enlists his very animated dummy, Hugo, to help him get rid of his clingy mistress, Magda.

Magic (1978)

Long before he terrified audiences as Hannibal Lecter in *The Silence of the Lambs* (1991), Anthony Hopkins made audiences squirm as an unbalanced ventriloquist named Corky, who is psychologically tormented by his dummy, Fats. Richard Attenborough directed and William Goldman wrote the screenplay based on his best-selling novel of the same title.

Pin (1988)

This psychological thriller features a life-size medical mannequin instead of a traditional ventriloquist's dummy, but it frightens just the same. Terry O'Quinn plays Dr. Linden, a father who finds that he can teach his children about the body most effectively through the dummy, which he calls Pin, short for Pinocchio. When Dr. Linden dies, his disturbed son, Leon (David Hewlett), adopts Pin as part of the family with horrifying consequences.

Dummy (2002)

Academy Award-winner Adrien Brody stars as Steven, a man who has great difficulty expressing himself until he takes up ventriloquism. By speaking through his dummy, Steven learns to overcome his crippling social phobias and discovers that he finally has the fortitude to pursue the girl of his dreams. Illeana Douglas and Milla Jovovich costar.

Dead Silence (2007)

James Wan and Leigh Whannell, the duo behind the popular *Saw* horror franchise, teamed up to make this entertaining flick about a small town haunted by a group of dolls owned by a ventriloquist named Mary Shaw. Shaw had been murdered years earlier by townsfolk who believed she was responsible for the death of a young boy. Though the dolls were buried with Mary, they start appearing before the individuals responsible for her death, foreshadowing their own grisly doom.

Oscar: The Scoop on the Statue

The gold-plated statue that symbolizes silver screen success has had a rich and varied history, so much so that it deserves its own Tinseltown tribute. Here are a few tasty tidbits that honor Hollywood's holy grail.

✳   ✳   ✳   ✳

✳ The silver screen status symbol was first dubbed "Oscar" in 1934 when Margaret Herrick, the Academy's librarian, remarked that the statue bore a striking resemblance to her uncle, Oscar Pierce. The gilded prize officially became known as Oscar in 1939.

✳ From 1942 until 1944, Uncle Oscar was plastered—quite literally. Because of a shortage of metal during World War II, the icon was molded from mortar instead of being gilded with gold. Later, the recipients were allowed to exchange their awards for gold-plated ones.

* The first Academy Award winner who refused to accept an Oscar was writer Dudley Nichols, who turned down his statue for the 1935 film *The Informer* because the Writers Guild was on strike at the time.

* Three-time Academy Award recipient Jack Nicholson reportedly uses one of his screen sculptures as a hat stand.

* In 2000, 55 Oscar statues were stolen from a loading dock by a pair of pilfering employees. Fifty-two of the busts were found by a man rummaging through a downtown garbage bin. In a twist only Hollywood could have scripted, the step-brother of the hero who found the missing merchandise was charged in the theft. Later in 2000, another statue turned up in the possession of lawyer Stephen Yagman. The 54th missing Oscar was discovered in 2003 when law enforcement agents raided a home in a drug bust. One of the legendary statues remains at-large.

* The saga of the stolen statue has also plagued actors William Hurt and Whoopi Goldberg. Hurt's prize was ripped off in 2005 while he was relocating. Whoopi's was clipped when she sent it back to the Academy to be cleaned. Goldberg's gilded guy was discovered in a downtown trash bin in 2002. Hurt's prize is still on the loose.

Slasher Films

It's easy for most of us to rattle off the iconic killers who rule the cinematic landscape of slasher films—Freddy, Jason, Michael Myers, Leatherface. But their reigns of terror were actually made possible by another, more obscure movie maniac.

* * * *

W E ALL KNOW the basic scenario that inevitably plays out in the standard slasher film: An unstoppable killer stalks a group of teens or young adults in a remote setting, using various sharp or pointy objects to dispatch them in workmanlike fashion until one would-be victim manages to do him in (until the next sequel, anyway). From the late 1970s through the 1980s, Hollywood made enormous profits by churning out dozens of these teen screamers. The films never used big-name actors and rarely deviated from the formula. All it seemed to take to draw in audiences was a killer who brought a modicum of creativity to his work and amassed a respectable body count.

As disturbing and provocative as these films were, they had a tendency to offer a surprisingly conventional moral subtext. The killers usually suffered some cruel injustice in their formative years, and their murder sprees were often motivated by a quest for justice, as misdirected and twisted as it might seem.

More importantly, the victims commonly engaged in some kind of socially unacceptable behavior—promiscuity, drug use, the betrayal of a friend—right before meeting their gruesome fates. The lone survivor, often a female (known as "the last girl" in horror terminology), would always be guiltless of any such transgressions.

Michael Myers Breaks Through

Although some early examples of the genre by independent filmmakers—such as Tobe Hooper's *The Texas Chain Saw Massacre* (1974) and Bob Clark's *Black Christmas* (1974)—became well known in the early 1970s, film historians generally cite *Halloween* (1978) as the first mainstream slasher film. Directed by a young John Carpenter, *Halloween* featured capable actors—including Jamie Lee Curtis in her big-screen debut—and focused more on suspense than on the killings.

The film was widely hailed as a modern horror masterpiece and is still remembered for its disturbing opening scene, in which the camera offers the killer's perspective as he commits his first murder. As a result, the viewer sees things through the eyes of a psychopathic killer. Critics at the time thought the technique was too disturbing because it forced audience members to identify with a psychopath who equates sex with violence. However, its success led to an onslaught of low-budget knockoffs, most notably the *Friday the 13th* series.

The popularity of these films eventually waned, though the late 1990s saw a resurgence of the genre with the *Scream* franchise, which freshened up the genre by featuring recognizable stars and having the characters make references to classic slasher films. More recently, series such as *Hostel* and *Saw* found a niche by delving into new levels of cruelty and violence, though they don't follow the traditional slasher premise.

These movies established a new subgenre sometimes referred to as gornography, or torture porn. These cousins to the slasher movie feature villains who don't just kill their victims but torture them in remarkably horrific and protracted ways.

Fuad Who?

Ironically, the explicit gore that seems to be so innovative in these recent torture films actually harkens back to cinema's true original slasher—Fuad Ramses.

Never heard of him? You're not alone. But *Blood Feast*, the 1963 film that featured him, made movie history by graphically depicting dismembered corpses and bloody entrails for the first time. Fuad, you see, was bent on performing a cannibalistic ritual that would resurrect an ancient Egyptian goddess.

Right before the viewers' eyes, he kills a succession of young women and savagely harvests their body parts—chopping off limbs, gouging out brains, even tearing out a tongue with his bare hands. Produced on a budget of $25,000 by sexploitation pioneers Herschell Gordon Lewis and Dave Friedman, the poorly made film raked in $4 million and paved the way for all the slasher and gore films that would follow.

Films Based on Fact When, In Fact, Those Facts Were Fiction

Directors and writers frequently take creative license when adapting a real-life story or historical event for the big screen. The filmmakers are after a universal truth, not a literal one, so audiences tend to allow for a few distorted or left-out facts. But when the facts that form the foundation of the film are false, perhaps that creative license should be revoked. Below are some examples of films that were seemingly based on real events but altered some major facts.

✳ ✳ ✳ ✳

Birdman of Alcatraz (1962)

GOING BY THE title alone, one might assume that convict Robert Stroud (played by Burt Lancaster in the film) earned his famous nickname by raising and breeding canaries inside the walls of Alcatraz. However, prison records show that all of Stroud's aviary activity actually took place at Leavenworth Federal Penitentiary in Kansas when he was imprisoned there from 1912 to 1942. When Stroud was transferred to Alcatraz, he was not permitted to continue his work with birds.

The Texas Chain Saw Massacre (1974)

The opening sequence of the film purports that the story about to be shown on-screen is based on real events that happened on August 18, 1973. However, the actual movie wrapped filming on August 14, 1973, four days before the supposed events even occurred. The movie was actually based loosely on the murders committed by Wisconsin serial killer Ed Gein between 1947 and 1957.

Midnight Express (1978)

In this flick, American Billy Hayes gains his freedom from a Turkish prison by impaling the head guard on a clothes rack, stealing his keys and uniform, and escaping. In real life, the head guard that tortured and threatened Hayes during his stay in prison was actually killed in a café outside the prison by another former inmate.

The Untouchables (1987)

In a key plot point of the movie, Al Capone crony Frank Nitti kills two members of Treasury agent Eliot Ness's team before being killed himself when Ness pushes him off the courthouse roof during Capone's trial. In reality, Nitti never killed any Treasury agents and didn't meet his demise by being tossed from a roof. In fact, there is no evidence to suggest that any of Ness's men died. Nitti was imprisoned with Capone in 1931 and committed suicide in 1943.

Braveheart (1995)

In Mel Gibson's Academy Award-winning film, the decisive battle between the followers of Scottish resistance leader William Wallace and the English forces led by John de Warenne is fought on a wide, open plain. But history tells us that the bloody barrage that saw the Scottish troops decisively defeat the English actually took place on and near Stirling Bridge where it crosses the River Forth.

Remember the Titans (2000)

In this motivational tale, Gerry Bertier, the defensive leader of the T. C. Williams high school football team, is paralyzed in a car accident before the championship game, and his injury inspires the team to persevere and eventually win the state championship. Bertier really was severely injured in an automobile accident, but the injury didn't occur until after the season ended. He actually played in the championship game and helped the team win the Virginia state title.

A Beautiful Mind (2001)

In Ron Howard's stirring film, mathematician John Nash (played by Russell Crowe) gives a moving acceptance speech after winning the Nobel Prize in Economics. Truth be told, Nash actually received the Nobel Memorial Prize for

Economics, which was not one of the prizes originally established by Alfred Nobel in 1895. Instead, it is named in honor of him and is endowed by a bank. Nobel prizes are only awarded for Chemistry, Physiology or Medicine, Literature, and Peace—and Nash did not speak at the ceremony.

21 (2008)

In this film, an MIT professor named Mickey Rosa teaches a group of predominantly white students to count cards at casino blackjack tables and use the technique to win millions. However, while the basic facts are accurate, the students who were involved in the cheating scheme were not white; they were Asian American, and there was no professor. Three university graduates formed the team and helped teach them the methods they used.

Actors, Actresses, and Directors

Anagrams are new words or phrases made by rearranging the letters of the original word or phrase. Check out the new phrases made by rearranging the letters of the names of these Hollywood stars.

❇ ❇ ❇ ❇

Gillian Anderson	Darling alien son
Christian Bale	Bat lair niches
Drew Barrymore	Merry wardrobe
Kim Basinger	Brisk enigma
Pierce Brosnan	Carbine person
Nicolas Cage	Laconic sage
George Clooney	Ego, cool, energy
Sean Connery	On any screen
Russell Crowe	Swell courser

Willem Dafoe	Media fellow
Robert De Niro	Inert brooder
Leonardo DiCaprio	A periodical donor
Ralph Fiennes	Fine shrapnel
Ashton Kutcher	Hot hunk recast
Leonard Nimoy	My alien donor
Natalie Portman	Planet animator
Martin Scorsese	Stress or cinema
William Shatner	Win? Hell, I'm a star!
Sylvester Stallone	Tell Sly: Veteran S.O.S.
Oliver Stone	No overt lies
Meryl Streep	Slyer temper
Donald Sutherland	Haunted landlords

For Some, Acting Just Isn't Enough

Movie stars are talented people. Sometimes that talent transcends the silver screen and transmits over the airwaves too. Here are some songs by a few stars who tried their luck in the music biz as well.

✳   ✳   ✳   ✳

"Tammy" by Debbie Reynolds

THIS *SINGING IN the Rain* (1952) costar had the best-selling single by a female artist in 1957, thanks to this ditty from *Tammy and the Bachelor.*

"Purple People Eater" by Sheb Wooley

Wooley, who appeared in *High Noon* (1952), *Giant* (1956), and *Hoosiers* (1986), had a No. 1 hit in 1958 with this oddball ode to a man-munching monster.

"Ballad of Thunder Road" by Robert Mitchum

This tune, cowritten and sung by Mitchum, was intended to be the theme song to the movie *Thunder Road* (1958). But when Mitchum decided that there was no place for it in the film, he released it as a single in conjunction with the movie. However, it is never actually heard in the film.

"Old Rivers" by Walter Brennan

The winner of three Academy Awards, this quivering and gravelly voiced actor hit the Top Five with this ballad in 1962.

"Johnny Angel" by Shelley Fabares

In 1962, while portraying Mary Stone on *The Donna Reed Show*, Fabares recorded this hit tune aimed at teen girls. She went on to appear in three Elvis Presley films and later costarred on the popular sitcom *Coach*.

"MacArthur Park" by Richard Harris

As an actor, Richard Harris was nominated for an Academy Award for his roles in *This Sporting Life* (1963) and *The Field* (1990). He also scored a No. 1 hit with this seven-and-a-half-minute pop tune in 1968.

"Wanderin' Star" by Lee Marvin

This song, from the movie *Paint Your Wagon*, was recorded by actor Lee Marvin and became a No. 1 hit in England in 1970.

"Basketball Jones" by Cheech and Chong

Hemp-hewn hipsters added musical parody to their comedic repertoire with this bouncy canticle in 1973, which reached No. 15 on *Billboard*'s Top 100 charts.

"Let Her In" by John Travolta

The former Sweathog and future *Saturday Night Fever* fave hit the Top Ten with this piece of fluff in 1976.

"King Tut" by Steve Martin

The banjo-strumming wild and crazy guy cashed in on the King Tut craze with this tune that hit the Top 20 in 1978.

"Rocket Man" by William Shatner

The star of the original *Star Trek* TV series sang this Elton John classic at the 1978 Sci-Fi Awards, where it was caught on tape for posterity.

"Party All the Time" by Eddie Murphy

This Rick James-penned tune hit the charts in 1985 and was once voted the eighth-worst song of all-time by *Blender* magazine.

"Heartbeat" by Don Johnson

In 1986, the future star of *Harley Davidson and the Marlboro Man* (1991) and *Guilty as Sin* (1993) rode his *Miami Vice* popularity to No. 5 on charts with this guitar-laden tune.

"She's Like the Wind" by Patrick Swayze

The star of *Dirty Dancing* (1987) and *Ghost* (1990) had a Top Ten hit with this ballad that he cowrote and sang for the *Dirty Dancing* soundtrack.

"Looking for Freedom" by David Hasselhoff

The timing of this 1989 song made it a hit in Eastern Europe. Pop music lovers in that part of the world embraced the Hasselhoff tune as an anthem just as the fall of communism began.

"Acid Tongue" by Jenny Lewis

Teen idol and star of more than a dozen movies in the 1990s, the cofounder of indie rockers Rilo Kiley released this gem in 2008.

"Anywhere I Lay My Head" by Scarlett Johansson

The *Lost in Translation* (2003) star released an album of Tom Waits tunes to mixed reviews in 2008.

Sing and Shout!

Cleveland beat out many others to host the Rock and Roll Hall of Fame and Museum.

✳ ✳ ✳ ✳

ROCK 'N' ROLL is a uniquely American musical art form, so it's only natural that the hall of fame and museum created to celebrate it would be located in the rockin' Midwest metropolis of Cleveland.However, it wasn't always intended that way. During the facility's early planning stages, those in charge envisioned the Hall of Fame being housed in a New York City brownstone. Luckily, Cleveland officials managed to change their minds.

The Committee for Cleveland

The Rock and Roll Hall of Fame and Museum was the brainchild of Atlantic Records founder and chairman Ahmet Ertegun, who, in 1983, approached other industry honchos with the idea of an organization that would "recognize the people who have created this music which has become the most popular music of our time." A nonprofit organization, which would later become the Rock and Roll Hall of Fame Foundation, was established, and a special committee was appointed to develop the criteria for nomination.

In October 1985, representatives of Cleveland and the State of Ohio approached the foundation with the idea of a creating a major museum in the Buckeye State. Other cities soon threw their hats into the ring, including New York, Philadelphia, New Orleans, San Francisco, and Memphis. Each had much to offer, but the foundation ultimately threw its support behind the city of Cleveland.

International Appeal

Internationally renowned architect I. M. Pei was selected to design the hall of fame and museum, despite his admission that he "didn't know a thing about rock and roll." (The foundation gave him a crash course by taking him to musical meccas such as Memphis and New York.) Groundbreaking took place on June 7, 1993, and the museum opened with a ribbon-cutting ceremony on September 1, 1995. The VIPs in attendance included Cleveland Mayor Michael White, Ohio Governor George Voinovich, *Rolling Stone* publisher Jann Wenner, Little Richard, and Yoko Ono.

Performers are eligible for nomination into the museum 25 years after the release of their first recording. In addition to artists, the museum also honors "non-performers" such as producers, songwriters, inventors, and "early influences" of the musical genre as we know it today. The first inductees into the hall included Chuck Berry, James Brown, Ray Charles, Sam Cooke, Fats Domino, The Everly Brothers, Buddy Holly, Jerry Lee Lewis, Elvis Presley, and Little Richard. Bluesman Robert Johnson, country singer Jimmie Rodgers, and boogie-woogie player and composer Jimmy Yancey were honored as early influences.

More than Memorabilia

A remarkable array of permanent exhibits makes up the hall of fame and museum, paying tribute to everything from the performers to the cities that helped define specific trends. Exhibits focus on specific artists as well as music of the 1950s, a recreation of Sun Studios where Elvis Presley first recorded, rhythm and blues, and Ohio's own musical heritage. Each year, the museum also unveils a major temporary exhibit. In years past, this has included an examination of the psychedelic era of the 1960s, the life and career of Elvis Presley, and a look at rock 'n' roll fashion.

Of greatest interest to most visitors is the hall of fame and museum's astounding collection of rock 'n' roll memorabilia, which includes everything from clothing and instruments, to vintage concert posters and the pieces of scratch paper upon which were scribbled the lyrics of some of rock 'n' roll's best-known songs. Music can be heard in a lot of venues around the world, but when it comes to rock 'n' roll, there's simply no place like Cleveland.

The Wilhelm Scream

In the early days of the film industry, it was hard to find a good scream. Before the invention of sound bites, directors who required a blood-curdling shriek from actors often got rather paltry-sounding yelps. That is, at least until Private Wilhelm entered the scene.

✳ ✳ ✳ ✳

That Hurts!

IN THE 1951 WAR classic *Distant Drums*, a soldier is dragged under water by an alligator as he wades through a treacherous Florida swamp. After the filming was completed, sound engineers recorded a series of screams that were added during post-production.

Two years later, in *The Charge at Feather River*, a soldier named Private Wilhelm (played by Ralph Brooke) takes an arrow in the leg. Similar to modern sound engineering processes, the *Distant Drums* scream was resurrected from a vault and added to Wilhelm's impalement scene.

The Real "Wilhelm"

What became known as the Wilhelm Scream is actually thought to be the handiwork of a popular television and screen actor named Sheb Wooley. He and other actors from *Distant Drums* were asked to contribute various sound bites to the film.

Wooley later went on to play in classics such as *High Noon* with Gary Cooper, Clint Eastwood's *The Outlaw Josey Wales*, and the hit television series *Rawhide*. But it was Wooley's contribution to radio, the hit song "Purple People Eater," that overshadowed his success as the originator of the Wilhelm Scream.

Over the years, the Wilhelm Scream has enjoyed something of a cult following. One of the scream's biggest fans was Ben Burtt, the sound-effects creator for the original *Star Wars* in 1977. While perusing the sound archives of Warner Bros. Studios (who owned the rights to the Wilhelm Scream), he came across the scream and decided to use it in his film. He became so fond of it that it became his signature sound bite in other productions including the *Indiana Jones* series. More than 50 years later, moviegoers can still hear Private Wilhelm.

Misheard Lyrics

We've all misheard our share of lyrics. Some mistakes might even make the song better...or at least stranger.

✳   ✳   ✳   ✳

Pink Floyd, "Another Brick in the Wall, Part 2"
Correct: "No dark sarcasm in the classroom"
Wrong: "The ducks are hazards in the classroom"

Moody Blues, "Nights in White Satin"
Correct: "Nights in white satin"
Wrong: "Knights speaking Latin"

Ohio Players, "Love Rollercoaster"
Correct: "Rollercoaster of love"
Wrong: "Hold that bus sir, for love"

Bonnie Raitt, "Something to Talk About"
Correct: "Let's give them something to talk about"
Wrong: "Let's go get something at Taco Bell"

Bay City Rollers, "Saturday Night"
Correct: "S-A-T-U-R-D-A-Y night"
Wrong: "I say: 'Eat a rock! Eat a rock! Right!'"

The Go-Gos, "Our Lips Are Sealed"
Correct: "Our lips are sealed"
Wrong: "I licked a seal"

John Lennon, "Give Peace A Chance"
Correct: "All we are saying, is give peace a chance"
Wrong: "Yes we are sailing / Give Jesus Pants"

Red Hot Chili Peppers, "Can't Stop"
Correct: "Can't stop the spirits when they need you"
Wrong: "Can't stop the ferrets when they need food"

Skid Row, "18 And Life"
Correct: "18 and life you got it, 18 and life ya know"
Wrong: "18 and a licensed driver, 18 on the Maginot"

Bachman-Turner Overdrive, "Takin' Care Of Business"
Correct: "Takin' care of business"
Wrong: "Baking carrot biscuits"

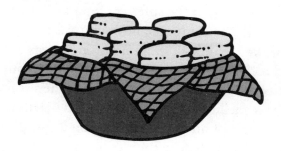

Chapter 12

True Crime and Murderous Mayhem

Fumbling Felons, Part I

Smile!

In October 2007, a man decided to steal a camera from a store in Connecticut. His technique might have been perfect except for the surveillance camera that caught him on tape. The criminal seems to have remembered to keep his face well-hidden from that camera. Clever! The surveillance camera, however, caught the would-be thief taking a picture of himself with another display model, which he put down and left behind in the store, just before walking out with a different $400 camera in hand. Brilliant!

Don't Call Us...

A man in St. Charles, Missouri, stole a computer and printer from a driver's license facility in October 2007. The printer could be used to produce fake driver's licenses or other identification, but only with the software found on the PC. That's thinking ahead! The computer, however, was inoperable without a special key to unlock it. Summoning all his cunning, the thief called tech support two days later asking to buy the software for the make and model of the printer he'd stolen from the driver's license facility. He ingeniously used his middle name, but he provided a phone number he'd previously given to the FBI in an unrelated identity theft case.

A Quick U-Turn

A man accused of drug possession successfully eluded police after being chased from Ontario, Oregon, into the neighboring state of Idaho. Shortly after crossing the state line, however, the criminal decided to turn around and go back to Oregon. He quickly made his way to the parking lot of a Wal-Mart, where he surrendered to the authorities. He reportedly told the arresting state trooper that he had done this because he didn't want to go to jail in Idaho.

Drunk Dialing

In April 2007, a man in Germany stole a cell phone and made a clean getaway. Police decided to call the stolen phone, figuring it was worth a shot to see if they could get any information. The thief answered. The officer on the other end told him, "You've won a crate of beer," but they needed the thief's location to drop it off. He happily gave his full address. Police believe the man was drunk.

Reruns Are Always Annoying

In July 2006, a convenience store supervisor in Edinburgh, Scotland, conspired with a friend to rob his store of more than three thousand dollars and to beat him up for good measure. Their plan seemed foolproof. Police arrived at the store to find the safe open and the supervisor bleeding from repeated blows to the head and body. Upon further investigation, however, the security camera footage showed the supervisor opening the door on his day off and walking in with his friend. The 20-year-olds, known to gamble together, admitted to staging the whole thing.

Don't Drink and Mow

A Martinsburg, West Virginia, man was accused of drunk driving on his riding lawn mower in October 2007—a mile from his home. After an officer—still in his police car—asked the man to pull over, the man "sped" away on his mower. The officer then jumped out of his car, chased the mower on foot, and caught up to it after a short jog. The officer allegedly found a case of beer strapped to the front of the riding mower. When the driver refused a field sobriety test, the authorities held him on $7,500 bond.

Man of a Thousand Faces

A disguised man robbed a bank in Manchester, New Hampshire, in July 2007. That may not be so unusual, but unfortunately for him, the man had disguised himself as a tree. He walked into the bank with leaves and branches duct-taped to his face and body and demanded money. Despite his face being somewhat obscured, someone recognized the robber after seeing footage released from a bank security camera. An anonymous tip led police straight to the man later that night.

Always Know Your Customer

On September 19, 2007, in Charleston, West Virginia, a 19-year-old sent a text message to his friend asking if he "wanted to buy some reefer." The teen received a text message back saying simply "yes," and a meeting was arranged. What the young man didn't know was that his friend had changed his cell phone number and that the number to which he sent the text belonged to a state trooper. Oops. The teenager was charged with delivery of a controlled substance and possession with intent to deliver marijuana.

8 Outrageous Lawsuits

One of the benefits of living in a democratic country with a well-established judicial system is the opportunity to use the courts to achieve justice and set wrongs right. But there is a drawback—some folks go to court about things that make most of us shake our heads. Take a look at these odd cases and judge for yourself.

✳   ✳   ✳   ✳

1. **All Toys Are Not Equal:** Jodee Berry, a Hooter's waitress in Florida, won the restaurant's sales contest and thought

she'd just won the new Toyota that her bosses said the champion would get. The prize was actually a toy Yoda, not a Toyota, so she left her job and sued the franchisee for breach of contract and fraudulent misrepresentation. The force was with Berry—the out-of-court settlement in May 2002 allowed her to pick out any Toyota car she wanted.

2. **Fingered as a Scam:** In March 2005, Ann Ayala filed a claim against a Wendy's franchise owner, asserting that she had found a fingertip in a bowl of chili. But authorities found no evidence of missing fingers at the accused restaurant. Suspicion turned on Ayala, who dropped the suit when reporters discovered that she had previously accused several other companies of wrongdoing.

3. **No Good Deed Goes Unpunished:** In July 2004, two teenage girls in Colorado baked cookies and delivered them to their neighbors. But the door-knocking apparently scared Wanita Young, who had an anxiety attack, went to the hospital, and sued the girls' families. A local judge awarded Young almost $900 for medical expenses but denied her half-baked demand for nearly $3,000 in itemized expenses, including lost wages and new motion-sensor lights for her porch.

4. **Bubbles Aren't Always Fun:** Early on the morning of July 7, 2001, a prankster dumped detergent into a public park fountain in Duluth, Minnesota, creating a mountain of bubbles. A few hours later, passerby Kathy Kelly fell down and suffered several injuries. She sued the city because it had not cleaned up the suds (on Saturday morning) or posted warnings to citizens urging them not to walk through the slippery wall of bubbles. A jury in March 2004 found the city 70 percent responsible for Kelly's injuries—leaving her with only 30 percent of the blame—and thus awarded her $125,000.

5. **School Responsible for Bad Break-Up:** In February 2004, a New York court ordered a school district to pay a former student $375,000 when his two-year affair with a school secretary ended. The young basketball star claimed that the break-up brought "emotional and psychological trauma," ruining any prospects for a professional hard-court career. The jury determined that the school was culpable for failing to supervise the secretary properly. It also ordered the secretary to pay the student another $375,000—even though she had not been named in the lawsuit.

6. **Trespass at the Owner's Risk:** Let's say you're illegally sneaking onto a railroad's property so you can get a view from the top of a boxcar—and then an electrical wire above the car electrocutes you. What do you do? Obviously, you sue the railroad! In October 2006, a jury awarded more than $24 million to two young men who were severely burned while atop a parked railroad car in Lancaster, Pennsylvania, in 2002. The jury said that, although they were trespassing, the 17-year-old boys bore no responsibility. Instead the blame fell entirely on Amtrak and Norfolk Southern for failing to post signs warning of the danger from the electrified wires that power locomotives. For medical costs, pain and suffering, and "loss of life pleasures," one boy received $17.3 million and the other $6.8 million.

7. **Sue the Pants Off Them:** In 2005, in one of the most outrageous lawsuits of recent times, Roy Pearson, a Washington, D.C. judge, sued a small mom-and-pop dry cleaner for $54 million for misplacing his pants. The shop's owners, Jin and Soo Chung, returned the pants a week later, but Pearson refused them, saying they were not his $800 trousers but a cheap imitation. He also sued the Chungs and their son $1,500 each, per day for more than a year, claiming that the store's signs, which read "Satisfaction Guaranteed" and "Same Day Service," were fraudulent. In 2007, a judge ruled in favor of the Chungs and ordered

Pearson to pay the couple's court costs, and possibly their attorney fees as well.

8. **Spilling the (Coffee) Beans:** This list can only end with the most notorious of lawsuits: Stella Liebeck, of Albuquerque, sued McDonald's in 1992 after spilling a cup of the restaurant's coffee, which burned her lap severely and hospitalized her for a week. Two years later, a jury awarded her $160,000 in direct damages and $2.7 million in punitive damages, which a court later reduced to $480,000. Both parties appealed, and they eventually settled out of court for an undisclosed amount—surely enough for her to buy McDonald's coffee for the rest of her life. Liebeck inspired the creation of the Stella Awards, which highlight particularly "wild, outrageous, or ridiculous lawsuits."

John Wesley Hardin—the Old West's Deadliest Gun?

Some credit this Texan with as many as 50 kills. Some call him a misunderstood Southern folk hero. What most obscures the facts about John Wesley Hardin is Hardin himself. He wrote a self-serving autobiography late in life, taking responsibility for many killings and painting himself as a sort of avenging angel against wrong. Some of his statements have been corroborated; others can't be.

✳   ✳   ✳   ✳

✳ Hardin was born a minister's son in Bonham, Texas, in 1853. His parents named him for Methodism's founder, John Wesley.

✳ John was 12 when the Civil War ended, and postwar Texas bred desperadoes and made them into folk heroes: The average white Texan of the day looked most leniently upon anyone who showed hostility to the Yankee occupiers.

* As a child, he was outdoorsy even by rural Western standards. John was an adventuresome young man, hunting and exploring with guns and dogs at an early age. This would later stand him in good stead when he spent several years with large numbers of people from Kansas, Indian Territory, or Texas chasing him around the bush and all the way to the Florida panhandle.

* Hardin killed his first man when he was 15. After volleys of bragging, he and a crony wrestled with a local freedman named Mage Holshousen, a mature fellow with a brawny reputation. Two teens against a big strong guy wasn't as uneven as it sounds. Hardin murdered Holshousen the next day with a .44, point blank. The spree was on.

* Though a white jury at the time probably wouldn't have convicted John, he still went on the lam. At 16, he had a brief stint teaching school while the heat died down.

* Hardin claims to have done some killing—two white soldiers, one African American soldier—in his early adult life while working as a cowboy for relatives. During this time, he also mastered the fine arts of spitting chew, gambling, and drinking—habits that would work against him for the rest of his life.

* Hardin's killings, alleged and claimed, followed a pattern: A situation would arise involving gambling and drinking, and someone would say the wrong thing. Given the opportunity to escalate things or calm them down, Hardin would do the former. All evidence says he was the epitome of pistol wizardry, a brilliant quick-draw artist and dead shot. Likewise, no one doubts his homicidal temper. He had allegedly killed 12 men by the time he was 17.

* How did Hardin get away with so many murders? Chalk it up to the times. There was little legal infrastructure in the West during his youth, but there was a lot of vigilante

justice. If you kept moving, you could probably duck the consequences. He also had an uncanny ability to make friends with law enforcement; it seems he could be a likeable guy when he wasn't drunk and losing at cards. He could also be a dangerous man to pursue—sneaky and willing to lay in wait rather than run.

* The cattle business led Hardin through Indian Territory (now Oklahoma), with more alleged killings along the way, and up to Abilene, Kansas. Abilene was a wild cattle trailhead, and J. B. "Wild Bill" Hickok was its marshal. A town full of rowdy, drunken gamblers? John Wesley Hardin? This would not end well.

* The story goes that Hickok at one point tried to confront and disarm Hardin, and that Hardin proffered the pistols, then did the "border roll" (reversing the firearms in his hands to point them, loaded and ready, at Marshal Hickok). It's possible. Reliable accounts say that Hardin was a master of this trick, which was mostly a way for kids to shoot themselves by mistake while trying to impress their friends. We can only be sure that Hickok never disarmed Hardin, because John later shot someone and hurried out of Abilene.

* By the time Hardin got back to his home state, he'd supposedly ended 23 lives, and he was 18 years old.

* Hardin married and had children. His descendants naturally still take an interest in their kinsman. That's more than can be said for Hardin, who mostly neglected his entire family. That he was usually hiding out from the law isn't a great excuse; the law might have stopped bothering him had he stopped putting holes in people.

* Back in Texas, Hardin finally killed enough people to interest the law in hunting him down. He fled across the South to Florida with a big price on his head, using the name John Swain. Lawmen subdued him in a passenger rail car at

Pensacola and hauled him back home to stand trial for murder. He was convicted of second-degree murder in 1877, and the jury sentenced him to 25 years of hard labor.

✳ Texas governor James Hogg released Hardin several years early. Why? Hardin's wife and the mother of his children had died while he was imprisoned, and he had kept his nose clean during the later part of his sentence. Hardin had done 17 years, and at the age of 42, he was now free to become a peaceable attorney and author.

✳ Unfortunately, he was also free to resume his habits of drinking and gambling. This led to more confrontations, more killings, and a rapid downward spiral. A constable finally shot John Wesley Hardin dead in 1895 without warning as he played dice in the Acme Saloon in El Paso.

✳ According to legend, the constable who killed Hardin, John Selman, did so over an unpaid debt. Apparently, Hardin had actually hired Selman to kill another man, allegedly the husband of a woman with whom Hardin was having an affair. Although Selman carried out his end of the bargain, Hardin neglected to pay him for the job. As a result, Selman tracked Hardin to the saloon and ended his life as well.

✳ Hardin's death tally could be as low as 20 or could have exceeded 50. Although he went out of his way in his autobiography to claim kills and paint himself as the ultimate bad guy, there may perhaps have been murders he didn't bother to mention. Was John Wesley Hardin comfortable with or perhaps even addicted to killing? On that charge, the record is fairly clear.

The Giant Straw Goat of Gävle

Every year at Christmas, the Southern Merchants of Gävle, Sweden, erect a straw goat. Nearly every year, vandalism gets their goat.

✳   ✳   ✳   ✳

Y OU'D THINK IT would be the final straw: On December 22, 2009, in Gävle, Sweden, just three days before Christmas, an unknown culprit snuck up to the 43-foot-tall straw goat in the town square and set fire to the big ol' billy. The tradition of building a Swedish Yule goat began in 1966, and the tradition of vandalizing it started shortly thereafter. In fact, this was the 24th torching of the famous Gävle goat. Some years the goat goes up in flames mere hours after it's erected. Other goats have been smashed, run over by cars, and had their legs removed. Thus far, only ten of the goats have survived past Christmas. Still, the town continues the tradition. If the goat is destroyed before St. Lucia Day (December 13), it is often rebuilt.

Advertising man Stig Gavlén came up with the idea of building the goat to attract people to Gävle businesses. The Southern Merchants, a local association, provided financing for the first goat— which was built by the local fire department—on December 1, 1966, and it went up in flames at midnight on New Year's Eve. Successive goats were also vandalized, to the point that the Southern Merchants stopped building them for 15 years, and the task fell to the Natural Science Club of the School of Vasa. Their goats, too, often succumbed to flames. Today, there are two Gävle goats—one by the Southern Merchants and one by the Natural Science Club.

In 2001, a tourist from Ohio, was apprehended and spent 18 days in jail for setting fire to the goat, but often the culprits are never caught. There have been Webcams on the goat, but vandals have tampered with those as well. It's safe to say that at this point, the Gävle goat is an endangered species!

Growing Up Capone

He's the racket guy everyone's heard of, and most people associate him with Chicago. But Al Capone was in fact a native Brooklynite.

✳ ✳ ✳ ✳

ALPHONSE GABRIEL CAPONE entered the world January 17, 1899, in Brooklyn. Papa Capone came from a town just south of Naples, while Mama hailed from a smaller town farther south, near Salerno. Alphonse was the fourth child (and fourth son) for Gabriele and Teresina Capone; three more boys and two girls (one survived infancy) would follow. Gabriele was a barber, while Teresina made dresses. They initially lived near the Navy Yard and then moved to Park Slope.

Fourteen-year-old Alphonse was a promising student, but he was naturally foul tempered. One day, after his sixth-grade teacher hit him, he swiftly retaliated against her with a punch. Not surprisingly, such behavior was frowned upon. The principal whaled the daylights out of Alphonse, who had had enough and quit school.

Street Education

Because Alphonse was drawn to the action, he began hanging out near the John Torrio Association. Torrio's Five Points Gang had begun in Manhattan's notorious neighborhood of that name and ex-panded into Brooklyn. Now, Torrio was a prominent local racketeer and pimp, and he'd occasionally hire Alphonse to carry out errands.

Torrio came to trust Alphonse immensely over time, and he and Frankie Yale, another notorious Brooklyn thug and loan shark, mentored young Alphonse in crime. Another early Brooklyn associate was Salvatore Lucania, who, after a slight name change, became world famous as "Lucky" Luciano.

In 1918 Alphonse got his girlfriend pregnant. They married and moved to Chicago, where Torrio advised his protégé that fortunes were to be made—and thus ended both the youth and the New York days of Al Capone. His subsequent rise—and fall—in the Chicago underworld was brutal and startling and, well, that's another story!

Fumbling Felons, Part II

Give Her a Break

Ohio police pulled over 42-year-old Nancy M. Lang's van after they noticed her driving erratically. They suspected that she might be driving under the influence, so they submitted her to the usual sobriety tests. Lang couldn't stand on one leg or walk in a straight line when asked, but she voluntarily performed several jumping jacks and a cartwheel to show she could still drive. Lang was charged with a DUI, driving with an expired registration, and driving with a suspended license. Her excuse? According to police reports, she offered, "Please, give me a break. I'm drunk."

Burglary and Ethics

Two burglars in North Yorkshire, England, committed a crime when they stole a laptop computer owned by 24-year-old Richard Coverdale. All went well until the pair took a look at the computer. They were surprised to see videos and pictures of child abuse and pornography disturbing enough that they decided to turn it over to the police. Coverdale confessed to several counts of sexual offenses and was sentenced to 3¹/₂ years in jail. The original perpetrators got a little leniency for their belated honesty: They both got one year of community service.

It's Not a Field Trip

An undercover policeman in Toronto, Canada, was a little surprised when a suspected drug dealer met him for an arranged drug deal—with his five children in tow. That's right: The guy brought along his two teenagers, a 10 year old, an 11 year old, and a toddler while he sold cocaine. After buying the drugs, the detective followed the man back to his car where he found additional cocaine and two knives. The dad was arrested and charged with selling cocaine, possession with the intent to sell, and possession of a weapon. The Children's Aid Society took the kids into protective custody. Apparently, this was not an appropriate way to participate in Bring Your Kids to Work Day.

When You're Hungry, You're Hungry

In Appleton, Wisconsin, a burglar reportedly entered an unlocked apartment but didn't steal any of the "valuables" within. No, this thief had a particular goal in mind and took six eggs, a container of beef ravioli, a pizza, a can of peaches, and a Hot Pocket (chicken-and-broccoli variety). The October 2007 crime apparently occurred sometime between 8:30 A.M. and 12:30 P.M.—prime snacking hours!

Taking the Credit

In Britain, two 18-year-olds were arrested for vandalizing a children's campsite. They apparently broke into the facility late one night, smashed plates and dishes, and discharged fire extinguishers. One of the boys decided to write his name in black permanent marker on the wall, boasting that he "was here!" The two wrote the name of their gang, as well. Police simply entered the vandal's name into the computer system for all the information they needed. The boys were quickly arrested. As punishment, they were fined and ordered to perform community service.

The Lap of Luxury

In an attempt to help pay for her and her boyfriend's drug-dealing debts, a woman in Providence, Rhode Island, rented a limo and attempted to rob a bank. The woman hired the driver to take her to the airport, but she asked him to stop at a bank's drive-through lane, where she got out of the limo and handed a teller a note. The note demanded money and claimed that there were two bombs inside the bank. In response, the teller hit the panic button. The would-be bank robber immediately got back in the car without any money, and the limo driver pulled off, unaware of what had occurred. Police eventually arrested the woman and charged her with attempted bank robbery.

It Works in the Movies

In Silver Springs Shores, Florida, a man was charged with commercial burglary, possessing tools for burglary, and felony criminal mischief. The enterprising criminal had a plan to break into a drugstore by removing an air-conditioning cover and gaining access to the air vent. He was going to crawl through it to get into the store, but instead he got stuck until the store opened the next day—ten hours later! In his defense, the man claimed he "heard a cat" and was trying to "chase" it.

Odd Ordinances

✳ North Carolina law forbids the use of elephants to plow cotton fields.

✳ Possessing a lottery ticket in North Carolina is illegal, resulting in up to $2,000 in fines. You'd need to have a winning ticket to pay it off.

✳ Shooting a Native American on horseback in North Dakota is legal only if you are in a covered wagon.

✳ Women may not wear patent leather shoes in public in Ohio.

✳ In Bexley, Ohio, it is illegal to install and use a slot machine in an outhouse.

✳ You'd better grocery shop on Saturday in Columbus, Ohio, because it is against the law to sell corn flakes on Sunday.

✳ Oklahoma law prohibits anyone from taking a bite from another person's hamburger.

✳ In Wynona, Oklahoma, birdbaths are off-limits to mules.

* You may not read a comic book while driving a car in Oklahoma.

* Oregon fish have discriminating palates—you may not use canned corn as bait.

* Sorry, but there's no juggling without a license in Hood River, Oregon.

* Pennsylvania law puts unusual restrictions on appliances— you may not sleep on top of a refrigerator outdoors.

* "Swept under the rug" is more than just a saying in Pennsylvania. Housewives are actually banned from hiding dirt and dust under a rug in a residence.

* It's only the best for convicts in Wisconsin, where butter substitutes are prohibited in state prisons.

* Store windows in La Crosse, Wisconsin, may not display a naked mannequin.

Bloody Angle: The Most Violent Place in New York?

If you're looking for some NYC history but don't feel like hitting a museum, take a trip over to Chinatown and check out Bloody Angle. This infamous area at the bend in Doyers Street was the site of untold bloodshed for years.

* * * *

LOWER MANHATTAN TODAY is quite the place to be. The East Village is full of restaurants and boutiques; SoHo offers high-end shopping and crowds of tourists; the Lower East Side is hipster central, and, of course, the crocodiles that inhabit Wall Street keep that area bustling. But not so long ago, the southern end of the island was rife with gangs, prostitution rings, corruption, and general debauchery.

Chinatown, a neighborhood that became "official" (and ghet-toized) around 1882 with ratification of the Chinese Exclusion Act, was particularly active in terms of violence and chaos. Secret societies called "tongs" were formed to protect and support Chinese American residents, but before long the groups were simply gangs that spent their time dealing in criminal activity—and they weren't afraid to use violence against anyone who didn't like it. Many different tong gangs existed, and they didn't all get along. Unrest grew, and by the end of the 19th century and beginning of the 20th, the Tong Wars were on. Few participants made it through alive.

Doyers Street: A Bad Part of Town

Running more or less north and south between Pell Street and the Bowery, Doyers Street is just one block long. Halfway down the block, Doyers turns sharply—hence the "angle" part of Bloody Angle's name. This turn provided a great spot for ambush, and the battling gangs knew it. In 1909, the bloodiest tong war in Chinatown history began when a gang that called themselves the Hip Sings killed an On Leong comedian for being disrespectful. The ensuing war was ruthless, and its locus was the bend in Doyers Street. From then on, the spot would be known as the Bloody Angle.

Herbert Asbury, whose book *The Gangs of New York* was later made into a hit movie by Martin Scorsese, wrote, "The police believe, and can prove it as far as such proof is possible, that more men have been murdered at the Bloody Angle than at any other place of like area in the world." The tongs were vicious and showed no mercy: If you got in their way, you were a goner.

Adding to the danger of the area was a warren of underground tunnels. Connecting buildings and adjacent streets, the tunnels were frequented by gang members who used them to facilitate their dastardly deeds. An assassin would ambush and kill a victim and then disappear down into the tunnels. Several minutes later the killer would emerge, far from the scene of the crime.

Plenty of places near Bloody Angle offered killers opportunities to calm their nerves with a drink—and nail down an alibi. Gang hangouts included The Dump, The Plague, The Hell Hole, and McGuirck's Suicide Hall.

New Violence, and a Cleanup

Eventually, the Tong Wars quieted down, at least for protracted periods of time. By 1930, it was mostly safe to take Doyers if you were passing through Chinatown. But then in the late 1980s, crack cocaine gripped New York, and as a result, gangs grew once again, this time with astonishing wealth and savage violence. Bloody Angle returned to being the most dangerous block in the city as the Chinese Flying Dragon gang launched a turf war against the Vietnamese Born to Kill (or BTK) gang.

Successful anticrime crusades by mayors Giuliani and Bloomberg in the 1990s and 2000s cleaned up much of New York, including Chinatown. Today, Bloody Angle is more likely to be called "Hair Alley" because of the multitude of salons and barbershops located there. The local post office is there, too, nestled among restaurants and shops.

As for the hidden tunnels, most have either been closed up or repurposed by locals. A tunnel once used by criminals to escape capture in the 1900s is now a belowground shopping arcade— and don't worry, it's safe to shop there.

Sleep with the Fishes

Whether you're a fan of gangster movies or not, you've undoubtedly heard the phrase "sleep with the fishes." It may come as no surprise to find that the concept started with real, grisly events in New York City's East River.

* * * *

THE EAST RIVER is a tidal strait spanned by eight bridges and thirteen tunnels separating Long Island from Manhattan Island and the Bronx on the mainland. The lower portion, which flows between Manhattan and Brooklyn, was once one of the busiest shipping channels in the world. Although the East River is known for being filthy, experts claim it's not as polluted as it once was.

At one time, when New York City had more than its share of organized crime, it wasn't uncommon for gangsters—both the Mob and the Westies, an Irish gang from Hell's Kitchen—to murder their enemies and dump the bodies into the East River. This could be done in a few ways, none of which were for the faint of heart. Sometimes bodies were dismembered and chopped into pieces so they couldn't be identified if, and when, they washed ashore. (Intimidating the departed's survivors with bloody appendages was also effective, apparently.) Other times, entire bodies were disposed of in the water.

Legend has it that some gangs gave their victims—alive or dead—"cement shoes," literally encasing their feet in concrete so they sank to the bottom of the river and stayed there. We refer to it as a legend, however, because it doesn't appear to be true. There's no evidence of any gangster turning anyone into a human sidewalk (although they weren't against sometimes using cement or heavy rocks as an anchor).

Bodies occasionally still turn up in the East River as a result of murder or suicide, mostly in the warmer months from April to August. As the waters warm up after the winter, corpses decompose faster and produce gases that bring the bodies floating to the surface.

Pirates!

As long as cargo has been carried across the sea, there have been pirates who have tried to plunder the goods, or "booty." Learn more about what it meant to be a pirate in the good ol' days of privateering.

✳   ✳   ✳   ✳

The Genuine Arrr-ticle

MOST CONSIDER THE golden age of piracy to be from the 16th to 18th centuries. Pirates at this time could be found primarily sailing their ships around the Caribbean Sea, off the coasts of Arabia and North Africa, and in the South China Sea. These were major sea trade routes at the time, and the huge cargo ships there routinely transported everything from gold and silver to ivory, spices, and slaves. Anything of worth was desirable to the pirate, who could either use what he stole or sell it at a profit wherever his ship landed next.

Worth the Risk?

Being a pirate was a big gamble. Piracy was illegal, and punishment often meant torture and death by hanging. Basically, if you were caught pirating, you were toast.

But if you could remain free, privateering was a better occupation than many available on land. You could say that pirates were equal opportunity employers: blacks, West Indians, Arabs, and everyone in between were welcome to "go on the account," in other words, to sign up to work a pirate ship. Discrimination was almost nonexistent: If you could sail, steal, and keep a secret, you were in. Many black men enlisted, since their only other option was often forced slavery in Europe and in America. Criminals on the lam, as well as people who opposed their government, found asylum on a pirate ship (which numbered around 100 men, depending on the size of the vessel). Piracy was a refuge for many, but remember, if they were caught, they faced death.

Another Day at the Office

There were many jobs onboard the ship. There was the role of the captain, who acted as the commander of his onboard army. Captains, while indisputably in charge, were just as vulnerable as the rest of their men when it came to justice. If one pirate ship attacked another, the captain of the victorious fleet would ask the captured crew if their captain was a fair man. If he was, he lived. If not, he'd likely be thrown overboard. Famous pirate captains include "Black Sam" Bellamy and Blackbeard.

For others, most of their time privateering was spent like that of any mariner. The daily grind of mending the ship's ropes and sails, repairing rowboats, and swabbing the decks kept the sailors busy between attacks. Life onboard was much more lenient than that of, say, the British Royal Navy, but there was still a lot of work to be done, and each man was expected to pull his own weight.

There were specialty jobs, too. A surgeon (or someone with at least a little medical experience) was usually kept onboard, as well as a quartermaster, who dealt with counting money and keeping the peace. Other positions aboard a pirate ship included the cook, master gunner (in charge of ammunition), and boatswain (head of the cables, anchors, and such).

A Pirate's Life for Me

Food was scarce on the ship, though pirates tended to eat better than most other sailors. Dolphin and tuna meat was supplemented with yams, plantains, and other exotic fruits. Life onboard was crowded, dirty, and smelly, but the pirates kept their sense of humor. They were known to put on plays, play cards and dice, sing songs, and dance all day long, reveling in the freedom they enjoyed. There were even some crews that held mock trials, entertaining themselves with hypothetical scenarios of being caught and put on trial.

But what about all that booty? The notion of buried treasure has been debunked, unfortunately—when pirates had money, they spent it. When on land, the crew of a pirate ship could be found carousing in pubs and indulging in wine, women, and song until it was time to board the ship and sail in search of more treasure.

Fumbling Felons, Part III

Crime Really Stinks

Some people steal money or jewelry or even electronics. A few criminals have even stolen pedigree dogs. But a skunk? That's what a Sarasota, Florida, couple took from the Animal Crackers Pet Store in 2009. It's bad enough that the pair stole the $400 baby animal, but the real kicker is that the man tried to return the skunk the next day. Suspicious employees called the police, who charged the man with grand theft and the woman with accessory to the crime.

Don't Hold the Ketchup

In 2009, a Surprise, Arizona, woman surprised a Kentucky Fried Chicken employee, resulting in her own arrest. Monique Aguet was upset when she didn't get condiments with her order at the KFC drive-through, so she took matters into her own hands. She walked into the store boiling mad and confronted an employee who asked the irate woman to leave. The employee even followed her out to the parking lot. Aguet may not have gotten the food her way, but she did get her way in the fight: She started her car and backed up over the startled employee. Aguet was arrested on suspicion of assault with a deadly weapon and disorderly conduct.

Kitty Porn

A Jensen Beach, Florida, man accused of downloading more than 1,000 pictures of child pornography has an unusual claim—he says his cat did it. Keith R. Griffin said that when he left his computer after downloading some music, the cat leaped onto the computer keyboard. Griffin returned to his computer with unusual images on the screen. Oddly enough, officers on the scene didn't buy his story. He was arrested with bail set at $250,000.

Thirsty Thief

Store employees caught a man stealing two bottles of liquor at a store in Boynton Beach, Florida. The workers called the police, and when officers arrived on the scene, the thief was guzzling alcohol out of one of the bottles. His explanation? He said if he had to go to jail anyway, he might as well drink.

Three Times Is No Charm

In December 2005, an unmasked man in Frisco, Texas, attempted to break into three different ATM machines at three different locations with an ax! The machines are apparently built to withstand such an attack. Meanwhile, security cameras at each of the locations captured the incidents on tape. Television news quickly broadcast the footage, and the man, who saw how easily he'd be recognized, turned himself in shortly afterward. His bond was set for $20,000—for each ATM he tried to rob.

There's Nothing Like a Good Disguise

In Ashland, Kentucky, a man tried to rob a liquor store with his face completely wrapped in gray duct tape. Claiming to have a knife, the man threatened to harm the clerk if she didn't give him the money out of the cash register. The clerk complied, but as the robber tried to leave, the store manager pulled out a wooden club and chased him into the parking lot. Several employees joined in and tackled the robber. During a later interview, the suspect—who's since been indicted—claimed that he wasn't the robber, that he had no memory of entering the store, and that he couldn't remember police removing the duct tape.

Driving Through Adversity

A 40-year-old man with no arms and one leg received five years in prison in New Port Richey, Florida, for felony driving. The man once held a valid license, but it had been suspended several times in the previous 20 years. He had previously spent three years in prison for other offenses, such as habitually driving without a license and kicking a state trooper. (Details on how he kicked a state trooper were not forthcoming.)

Going to the Dogs

A woman and two men attempted to steal copper wiring and pipes from an abandoned nursing home in Gainesville, Georgia, in July 2007. The trio apparently ignored signs declaring that the property was owned by the Gainesville police department. And it wasn't just police property—it was a K-9 training facility (also clearly marked). Police dog handlers arrived and discovered the thieves, who dropped their tools and took off running. Naturally, the handlers released the entire K-9 unit to go after them. One thief ended up with a superficial dog bite on the buttocks. All were caught and charged with burglary.

More Odd Ordinances

* In Nevada, camels are not to be driven on the highway.

* In Elko, Nevada, the law states that everyone must wear a mask while on the street. That must make it easy for bank robbers.

* It is against the law to lie down on a sidewalk in Reno, Nevada.

* Picking seaweed from the beach is not considered legal in New Hampshire.

* Farmers, do you know where your cows are? Any cattle crossing New Hampshire state roads must be wearing a device that collects their feces.

* In New Hampshire, you cannot pay off your gambling debts by selling the clothes you are wearing.

* It's illegal for a man in New Jersey to knit during the fishing season.

- In Cresskill, New Jersey, cats must wear not one but *three* bells so that birds are forewarned of their whereabouts.

- There's no steak tartare in Ocean City, New Jersey—the selling of raw hamburger is prohibited.

- In Newark, New Jersey, it's against the law to sell ice cream after 6 P.M.—unless the customer has a note from his or her doctor.

- It is illegal to hunt in Mountain View Cemetery in Deming, New Mexico.

- New Yorkers can be fined $25 for flirting.

- Here's one that makes sense: The penalty for jumping off a building in New York is death.

- In New York, it's illegal to throw a ball at someone's head for fun. Spoilsports.

- It's perfectly legal to take home roadkill for dinner in West Virginia.

Masks Only a Robber Could Love

Do bank robbers actually wear Richard Nixon masks? Or is that just something we see in the movies? You might be surprised.

✳ ✳ ✳ ✳

Laughing on the Inside

HOLLYWOOD GAVE US *Quick Change* in 1990, in which Bill Murray dresses as a clown to rob a bank. In 2008's *Batman* movie *The Dark Knight*, the Joker and his gang dress in clown masks to rob a bank of their own.

In real life, a gang of six thieves, some of whom dressed in clown costumes, robbed a jewelry store in the Mexican city of Guadalajara in July 2009. They got away with at least 1.2 million pesos worth—about $900,000 USD—of stolen goods. Police, though, might get the last laugh: In October, prosecutors filed robbery charges against two alleged members of the gang.

I'm Not a Crook. Well . . .

Patrick Swayze and company robbed a bank while wearing the masks of former presidents in *Point Break* (1991). One of the robbers wore a Richard Nixon mask, while the others wore masks of Jimmy Carter, Lyndon Johnson, and Ronald Reagan.

In October 2009, a robber wearing his own Richard Nixon mask held up a Dunn County, Wisconsin, bank at gunpoint. No word on whether he declared "I am not a crook," before he fled the scene.

He's Not Really Going Skiing

Countless bank robbers in movies and television shows have worn ski masks. In January 2009, a robber in Stow, Ohio, followed suit. Obviously having been taught the value of good manners, Feliks Goldshtein waited in line at the National City Bank branch behind several other customers. When he finally reached a teller, though, his good manners disappeared. He refused to take off his mask when asked and instead pointed a gun at the teller. The police caught Goldshtein after only a short chase.

9 of the Grisliest Crimes of the 20th Century

Our TV screens are saturated with crime. Every night we witness more bizarre slayings and mayhem than the night before. Makes you wonder how far-fetched those scriptwriters will get. After all, real people don't commit those types of crimes, right? Wrong. In fact, the annals of history are crammed with crimes even more gruesome than anything seen on television. Here are some of the 20th century's wildest crimes.

✳   ✳   ✳   ✳

1. **Ed Kemper:** Ed Kemper had a genius IQ, but his appetite for murder took over at age 15 when he shot his grandparents because he wanted to see what it felt like. Nine years later, he'd done his time for that crime, and during 1972 and 1973, Kemper hit the California highways, picking up pretty students and killing them before taking the corpses back to his apartment, having sex with them, then dissecting them. He killed six women in that manner and then took an ax to his own mother, decapitating and raping her, then using her body as a dartboard. Still not satisfied, he killed one of his mother's friends as well.

   Upset that his crimes didn't garner the media attention he thought they warranted, Kemper confessed to police. He gleefully went into detail about his penchant for necrophilia and decapitation. He asked to be executed, but because capital punishment was suspended at the time, he got life imprisonment and remains incarcerated in California.

2. **Andrei Chikatilo:** Andrei Chikatilo was Russia's most notorious serial killer. The Rostov Ripper, as he came to be called, began his rampage in 1978 in the city of Shakhty, where he started abducting teenagers and subjecting them to unspeakable torture before raping and murdering them, and, often, cannibalizing their bodies. Authorities gave the crimes little attention, but as the body count grew, police were forced to face the facts—Russia had a serial killer.

   Chikatilo was actually brought in for questioning when the police found a rope and butcher knife in his bag during a routine search, but he was released and allowed to continue his killing spree. In the end, he got careless and was arrested near the scene of his latest murder. Under interrogation, he confessed to 56 murders. During the trial, he was kept in a cage in the middle of the court, playing up the image of the deranged lunatic. It didn't help his cause, though. He was found guilty and executed on February 14, 1994.

3. **Cameron Hooker:** With the assistance of his wife, Janice, in May 1977 Cameron Hooker snatched a 20-year-old woman who was hitchhiking to a friend's house in northern California. He locked her in a wooden box that was kept under the bed he shared with Janice, who was well aware of what lay beneath. During the next seven years, Hooker repeatedly tortured, beaten, and sexually assaulted the young woman. Eventually, she was allowed out of the box to do household chores, but she was forced to wear a slave collar. As time went by, Hooker allowed his prisoner more and more freedom, even letting her get a part-time job. Janice's conscience finally got the best of her, and she helped the young woman escape. After seven years of hell, the prisoner simply got on a bus and left. Hooker was convicted and sentenced to 104 years in a box of his own.

4. **Andras Pandy:** Andras Pandy was a Belgian pastor who had eight children by two different wives. Between 1986 and 1989, his former wives and four of the children disappeared. Pandy tried to appease investigators by faking papers to show that they were living in Hungary. He even coerced other children into impersonating the missing ones. Then, under intense questioning, Pandy's daughter Agnes broke down. She told authorities that she had been held by her father as a teenage sex slave and then was forced to join him in killing her family members, including her mother, brothers, stepmother, and stepsister. The bodies were chopped up, dissolved in drain cleaner, and flushed down the drain. Pandy was sentenced to life in prison, while Agnes received 21 years as an accomplice. To this day he still claims that all of the missing family members are alive and well in Hungary.

5. **Harold Shipman:** The most prolific serial killer in modern history was British doctor Harold Shipman, who murdered up to 400 of his patients between 1970 and 1998. Shipman was a respected member of the community, but in March

1998, a colleague became alarmed at the high death rate among his patients. She went to the local coroner, who in turn went to the police. They investigated, but found nothing out of the ordinary. But when a woman named Kathleen Grundy died a few months later, it was revealed that she had cut her daughter Angela out of her will and, instead, bequeathed £386,000 to Shipman. Suspicious, Angela went to the police, who began another investigation. Kathleen Grundy's body was exhumed and examined, and traces of diamorphine (heroin) were found in her system. Shipman was arrested and charged with murder. When police examined his patient files more closely, they realized that Shipman was overdosing patients with diamorphine, then forging their medical records to state that they were in poor health.

Shipman was found guilty and sentenced to 15 consecutive life sentences, but he hung himself in his cell in 2004.

6. **Fred and Rose West:** In the early 1970s, a pattern developed in which young women were lured to the home of Fred and Rose West in Gloucester, England, subjected to sexual depravities, and then ritually slaughtered in the soundproof basement. The bodies were dismembered and disposed of under the cellar floor. As the number of victims increased, the garden became a secondary burial plot. This became the final resting place of their own daughter, 16-year-old Heather, who was butchered in June 1983.

Police became increasingly concerned about the whereabouts of Heather. One day they decided to take the family joke that she was "buried under the patio" seriously. When they began excavating the property in June 1994, the number of body parts uncovered shocked the world. With overwhelming evidence stacked against him, Fred West committed suicide while in custody in 1995. Rose received life imprisonment.

7. **John Wayne Gacy:** In the mid-1960s, John Wayne Gacy was, by all outward appearances, a happily married Chicago-area businessman who doted on his two young children. But when Gacy was convicted of sodomy in 1968, he got ten years in jail, and his wife divorced him.

Eighteen months later, Gacy was out on parole. He started a construction company, and in his spare time, he volunteered as a clown to entertain sick children. He also began picking up homeless male prostitutes. After taking them home, Gacy would beat, rape, and slaughter his victims before depositing the bodies in the crawl space underneath his house.

In 1978, an investigation into the disappearance of 15-year-old Robert Piest led police to Gacy, following reports that the two had been seen together on the night the boy disappeared. Suspicions were heightened when detectives uncovered Gacy's sodomy conviction, and a warrant was issued to search his home. Detectives found a piece of jewelry belonging to a boy who had disappeared a year before. They returned to the house with excavating equipment and they made a gruesome discovery.

Gacy tried to escape the death penalty with a tale of multiple personalities, but it didn't impress the jury. It took them only two hours to convict him of 33 murders. On May 10, 1994, he was put to death by lethal injection.

8. **Ed Gein:** Ed Gein was the son of an overbearing mother who taught him that sex was sinful. When she died in 1945, he was a 39-year-old bachelor living alone in a rundown farmhouse in Plainfield, Wisconsin. After his mother's death, he developed a morbid fascination with the medical atrocities performed by the Nazis during World War II. This fascination led him to dig up female corpses from cemeteries, take them home, and perform his own experiments on them, such as removing the skin from the

body and draping it over a tailor's dummy. He was also fascinated with female genitalia, which he would fondle and, on occasion, stuff into women's panties and wear around the house.

He soon tired of decomposing corpses and set out in search of fresher bodies. Most of his victims were women around his mother's age. He went a step too far, however, when he abducted the mother of local sheriff's deputy Frank Worden. Learning that his missing mother had been seen with Gein on the day of her disappearance, Worden went to the Gein house to question the recluse. What he found there belied belief. Human heads sat as prize trophies in the living room along with a belt made from human nipples and a chair completely upholstered in human skin. But for Worden, the worst sight was in the woodshed. Strung up by the feet was the headless body of his mother. Her front had been slit open and her heart was found on a plate in the dining room.

Gein confessed but couldn't recall how many people he'd killed. He told detectives that he liked to dress up in the carved out torsos of his victims and pretend to be his mother. He spent ten years in an insane asylum before he was judged fit to stand trial. He was found guilty, but criminally insane, and died of heart failure in 1984, at age 77.

9. **Jeffrey Dahmer:** Jeffrey Dahmer looked like an all-American boy, but as a child, he performed autopsies on small animals, including neighborhood dogs. At age 18, he graduated to humans, picking up a 19-year-old boy and taking him home to drink beer. Dahmer attacked him with a barbell, dismembered his body, and buried it in the backyard. More abductions and murders followed, and Dahmer also began to eat his victims.

In 1989, Dahmer was sentenced to eight years in jail for child molestation but only served ten months. After his release, he immediately resumed the slaughter. In May 1991, Dahmer picked up a 14-year-old boy, gave him money to pose for suggestive photos, and then plied him with alcohol and sleeping pills. While the boy slept, Dahmer went to the store. Waking up alone, the boy fled but ran straight into Dahmer. When they were approached by police, Dahmer convinced the officers that the two were lovers. Upon returning to the apartment, Dahmer slaughtered the boy and then had sex with his corpse.

Two months later this scenario was virtually reenacted when a 31-year-old man escaped from the apartment. With handcuffs dangling from one arm, he approached a nearby police officer. This time the officer decided to check out the apartment. What the officer and his partner saw horrified them. Dismembered bodies, skulls, and internal organs littered the place, and a skeleton hung in the shower. When they opened the refrigerator, they were confronted with a human head. Three more heads were wrapped up in the freezer, and a pan on the stove contained human brains.

During the ensuing trial, another gruesome fact emerged— Dahmer had drilled holes into the skulls of some of his victims and poured in acid in an attempt to keep them alive as zombielike sex slaves. He was given 15 life terms, but in November 1994, he was beaten to death in prison.

Outlandish Laws

* Close the blinds! In Singapore, walking around in your house while nude is against the law—it's considered pornographic.

* Carrying a concealed weapon in Seattle is illegal if it's more than six feet long. Spears don't tuck into coats very well.

* Be kind to bivalves: In Maryland, it's illegal to mistreat oysters.

* In Arizona, it is illegal to refuse a person a glass of water. Aimed primarily at businesses, this law is meant to cut down on dehydration deaths among homeless people.

* A Virginia law states that bribery or corrupt practices are forbidden—unless you are a political candidate.

* Be careful how you break your eggs in England. Anyone caught breaking a boiled egg on the pointed end can be thrown in the "village stocks" for a day. This ordinance was put in place by King Edward VI and has yet to be overturned.

* Have a duel planned in Paraguay? If you're not a legal blood donor, you could be arrested.

* In Ohio, it is against the law to get a fish drunk.

* Cursing in French may sound elegant, but it's illegal in Montreal. Swearing in English is okay, though.

* Dressing in a hurry has its hazards in Thailand, where it's illegal to leave your house unless you're wearing underwear.

* In Israel it's illegal to pick your nose on the Sabbath.

* British law mandates that if you are driving a car, you must be in the front seat.

* A law in North Carolina forbids the use of an elephant to plow cotton fields.

* According to South Korean law, traffic officers must report all bribes they receive from motorists.

* In Providence, Rhode Island, you can buy toothpaste and mouthwash on a Sunday, but you can't buy a toothbrush.

* Members of the British Parliament are not allowed to enter the House of Commons in full armor. They can't die in Parliament, either.

* Massachusetts takes its clam chowder seriously—people there are legally forbidden to put tomatoes in it.

* Farmers in France, be aware—you may not name your pig Napoleon.

* In Italy, a woman wearing a skirt is considered feminine. A man in a skirt can be arrested.

* Atlanta does not allow anyone to tie a giraffe to a telephone pole. Perhaps they're worried the pole might get jealous?

* You may not use a feather duster to tickle a girl under the chin in Portland, Maine.

* The head of any dead whale found on British shores automatically becomes the property of the king. The queen gets the tail.

* Alabama strictly forbids wearing a fake moustache in church if it could cause laughter.

* Be careful to check the clock—it's illegal to flush a toilet after 10 P.M. in Switzerland.

* Bad for business: In Sweden, prostitution is legal. Hiring the services of a prostitute, however, is not.

* California law strictly forbids hunting animals from a moving vehicle—unless your target is a whale.

* Alaska does not allow waking a sleeping bear just to take its photograph. You can hunt it, though.

* Ladies, pay attention to your wardrobe choices when in Arizona. Certain cities still have laws that make it illegal for a woman to wear pants.

* Hawaii prohibits placing coins in one's ear.

* All males in England who are older than 14 must spend at least two hours per week practicing firing a longbow.

Cold and Clammy

Gangster "Crazy" Joe Gallo went about his underworld business with style and panache. If there was limelight to be sampled, chances are Gallo would be standing directly beneath it. Unfortunately for the crime boss, such flamboyance would trigger his early demise.

✳ ✳ ✳ ✳

Wise Guy of Note

IN SOME WAYS, Joe Gallo was a gangster ahead of his time. He certainly viewed himself that way. Here was a dutiful, workaday mobster who, for all of his limitations, saw opportunity in areas of criminal activity where others saw only strife. Before long, Gallo pioneered alliances with non-Mafia gangs that proved profitable all around. These unlikely but shrewd couplings of rival groups were masterful strokes.

But there was another side to Gallo that wasn't nearly as good for business: his public side. Much like Benjamin "Bugsy" Siegel before him, Gallo had a sense of flair, a taste for the good life, and plenty of celebrity friends.

Gallo and his boys were well- known for their keen sense of style. The wise guys looked like they had come straight from central casting in their black suits, narrow black ties, and darker-than-pitch sunglasses. Tabloids often ran covers of the boys done up in such "gangster chic." The public seemed to love it. The mob, not so much.

Gallo simply couldn't resist being the center of attention. And he liked to talk. In an enterprise that conducts its business well beneath the radar, this was *not* the preferred path.

Wild Child

Born on April 7, 1929, in the tough Red Hook section of Brooklyn, Gallo quickly rose from street criminal to key enforcer in the Profaci Crime Family. With help from brothers

Albert and Larry—as well as mobsters Frank Illiano, Nicholas Bianco, and Vic Amuso—no tactic seemed too ruthless or too bloody. In 1957, after allegedly rubbing out gangster Albert Anastasia in a barber chair at New York's Park Sheraton Hotel, Gallo (perhaps not unreasonably) asked mob boss Joseph Profaci for a bigger slice of the pie. The don's refusal sparked a turf war between the Gallo gang and the Profacis. The bloody feud continued into the 1960s, ultimately working to the favor of the Profacis.

Can't Win for Trying

After Joe Profaci died of cancer in 1962, power was transferred to his underboss, Joseph Magliocco, then later to Joseph Colombo. Due to Gallo's inability to achieve the exalted seat—as well as his ten-year incarceration for extortion—the mobster's leadership skills were placed in question. It wasn't that the Gallo boys didn't try. They had even gone so far as kidnapping Magliocco (during the Profaci-Gallo wars) in hopes that a human bargaining chip would bring them better profits. It didn't. In the long run nothing seemed to work out for the gang. The huge cash tributes that Profaci demanded of the Gallos prior to the kidnapping were suspended—but only for a brief period. After Magliocco was returned, the fees were reinstated. In the bloody dream of big-time money, Gallo and his crew had been effectively squeezed out of the action.

The Gang That Couldn't Shoot Straight

The gang's big ideas and general ineptitude caught the eye of *New York Post* columnist Jimmy Breslin, who lampooned them in his bestselling 1969 novel, *The Gang That Couldn't Shoot Straight.* A movie would follow with the buffoonish lead role (loosely based on Gallo's life) given to actor Jerry Orbach.

Things got interesting after the movie's release when Gallo, fresh out of prison, approached Orbach to set history straight. Oddly, the two men took to each other and became friends. Orbach was astonished by Gallo's grasp of art and literature and introduced him to his circle of friends. Soon, Gallo was hobnobbing with Hollywood figures and members of the literary set. Everybody, it seemed, wanted to meet this real-life *Mafioso* with the cultural dexterity to quote from such figures as Camus and Sartre. After rotting for ten long years behind bars and suffering countless indignities as Profaci's underpaid soldier, could Gallo's star finally be on the rise?

Stars in His Eyes

Although suspected in the recent assassination of boss Joe Colombo, Gallo announced that he was "turning legit" in 1972. The purportedly reformed mobster planned to write a book about his life and perhaps even try his hand at acting. This might explain why Gallo found himself in the company of Jerry Orbach, comedian David Steinberg, and columnist Earl Wilson at New York's Copacabana one night before his 43rd birthday. It may also explain why the mob no longer wanted Gallo around. In the eyes of syndicate members, they didn't come much riskier than a starstruck, publicity-mad mobster who invited the scrutiny of federal agents bent on destroying La Cosa Nostra. In fact, the only thing that might trump such an actionable offense would be a gangster who had taken the oath of omertà, only to go straight and announce plans to write a tell-all book.

Bad Clams

During the wee hours of April 7, 1972, the unlikely group disbanded. Gallo, his bodyguard Pete Diapoulas, and four women made their way to Umberto's Clam House on Mulberry Street. While mobsters regarded this popular Little Italy location as Mafia holy ground, a hit was nevertheless in the making. As Gallo and his bodyguard pondered menu choices with their backs to the door, one or two gunmen barged in. Hearing the danger, Gallo and Diapoulas instinctively rose and made a run for it. Despite their maneuvers, both men were hit. Diapoulas took a bullet to his hip (he would later recover) and Gallo caught no fewer than five slugs. The mortally wounded mobster wobbled out the front door, making it as far as his Cadillac before collapsing in a lifeless heap. While it wasn't quite the Hollywood ending that the mobster had hoped for, it was a Hollywood ending of sorts. The death of "Crazy" Joe Gallo had been every bit as flamboyant as his existence. To live in the limelight, to die in the limelight—maybe it was all somehow equal.

Fumbling Felons, Part IV

Click It and Ticket

If you're going to break the law by purse snatching, speeding, and leading the police on a high-speed chase, you may as well go all the way and break one more law by not wearing a seat belt. At least that's how Lawrence Neal of Detroit must have felt after his adventure. He committed the first three crimes, but it was the car seat belt that proved his undoing. During the chase, Neal tried to ditch the car on a front lawn and flee on foot, but got his foot tangled in the seat belt. He was dragged a few hundred feet and broke his leg in the process. Police caught up with him and brought him in on several charges.

Shoplifting Seagull Chooses Chips

Here's one thief that's actually popular with the locals. His name is Sam—Sam the seagull. No one knows how he got started on his life of crime, but he has been seen (and video-taped) walking into RS McColl Newsagents in Aberdeen, Scotland, and snatching a bag of Doritos with his beak. There's no breaking and entering; the bird simply strolls into the store while the door is open. Maybe it's the proximity of that brand of "crisps," or perhaps it's the look of the bag, but Sam steals the same type of chips each time. He's a savvy little thief, waiting until the coast is clear to make the grab. Then he walks right out and shares his loot with his bird buddies. People are so amazed and entertained by the fowl convict that they have begun to pay the 55 pence for his treat.

Where Do You Find Emma Christ in the Bible?

Emma Kim-Tashis Harrison sometimes goes by her married name: Emma Christ. Or rather, Mrs. Jesus Christ, the name she recently used when attempting to buy a $70,000 car in Jacksonville, Florida. Apparently when you write a check that large, the car dealership feels obligated to run an inquiry on it right away. And surprise, the check and the names on it were bad. The sheriff was called in and charged her with three felonies, including organized fraud. Harrison said her husband, Jesus Christ, would be stopping by the next week to sign papers and pick up the car.

Keep Your Pants On

A police officer in Spokane, Washington, took her van to the dealership for servicing. Later that day, a witness reported a naked man driving by repeatedly and pleasuring himself in a van. Turns out it was the officer's van. After the witness provided the plate number, police found the van back at the dealership—where the naked driver worked. He had apparently gone on a 16-mile test-drive! The man was charged and jailed for taking a motor vehicle without permission as well as for lewd conduct.

A Successful Robber Must Be Taken Seriously

A man in Inwood, West Virginia, attempted to rob a store with a gun-shape cigarette lighter. He disguised himself by wearing a pair of blue women's panties over his face. The store clerk, not surprisingly, thought it was a joke and refused to give up any money. Realizing that his plan was falling apart, the man hopped into a Jeep and fled into the night. Within a matter of minutes, the police stopped a vehicle matching the description given by the clerk. After searching the driver and the area, they found the pistol-shaped lighter and recovered the blue underwear nearby. Unlike the clerk, the police didn't treat the matter as a joke.

In the Driver's Seat

Apparently suffering from a powerful craving, a six-year-old boy in Colorado attempted to drive to Applebee's. He grabbed his grandmother's keys and placed his booster seat in the driver's seat. Although he managed to start the car, he couldn't get it out of reverse. The child backed up about 47 feet, crossing the street and hitting the curb. The car continued rolling an additional 29 feet before taking out a transformer and communications box. Fortunately, no one was injured. But it's still a mystery to investigators how the boy reached the gas pedal.

The Immovable ATM

In Milwaukee, three men tried to steal an ATM from a gas station. They smashed their SUV through the mostly glass wall where the ATM stood and then yanked on the machine. Discovering that it was bolted to the floor, they decided to wrap a rope around the ATM and tie it to the truck's bumper. But although the driver gunned the accelerator, the ATM refused to budge. They soon gave up completely. The sturdy and thief-proof ATM, although badly scratched, still stands where it always did, and it still works.

Criminals Behaving Nicely?

The following mixture of life's flotsam proves far and away that, like books, people can't always be judged by their covers.

✳   ✳   ✳   ✳

John Dillinger

Seen as a modern-day Robin Hood by many cash-strapped, Depression-era citizens, bank robber Dillinger took what he wanted when he wanted it. The public, angry at banks and the government for doing little to help them, cheered for the antihero's escape, but they weren't looking at the full picture. Dillinger and his gang were responsible for at least ten murders. And unlike Robin Hood, Dillinger didn't share his ill-gotten booty with those in need. Nevertheless, his charm carried him along until one fateful day when he agreed to meet the now-infamous "Lady in Red" (Ana Cumpanas) at Chicago's Biograph Theater. Unbeknownst to the gangster, Miss Cumpanas had sold him out to federal agents who had come to apprehend him. In the end, the popular gangster was cut down by a hail of bullets—a fitting end for a not-so-nice criminal.

John Gotti

It's amazing what a quick smile and a few block parties can do for one's popularity. Labeled the "Teflon Don" for his uncanny knack at evading prosecution, the Gambino family crime boss was beloved by his Queens, New York, neighbors. Each year, the cheerful don would stage an elaborate Fourth of July celebration, free of charge, solely for their benefit. When the Teflon finally wore off in 1992 and Gotti was convicted on murder and racketeering charges, no one defended him more passionately than his neighbors. But their faith was misplaced. In 2009, informant Charles Carneglia testified that Gotti had neighbor John Favara "dissolved in a barrel of acid" after the man accidentally killed Gotti's 12-year-old son in a car accident. So much for Gotti's good neighbor policy.

Theodore "Ted" Bundy

If a polite, good-looking law student on crutches asked for your assistance lifting heavy objects into his car, would you help him? For those obliging young women smitten by Bundy's boyish charm, such kindness equated to a death sentence. Bundy would be tried and convicted for the murder of Kimberly Leach, just one of more than 30 women he'd eventually admit to killing. Even Dade County Circuit Court Judge Edward D. Cowart appeared impressed by Bundy as he sentenced him to death. "You're a bright young man. You'd have made a good lawyer, and I would have loved to have you practice in front of me," said the judge in a fatherly tone. "But you went another way, partner." On January 24, 1989, 2,000 searing volts of electricity ensured that Bundy's "charm" could seduce no more.

John Wayne Gacy

Serial killer Gacy often donned a clown outfit to amuse children at local hospitals. He was seen as a pillar of society, working closely with the Jaycees and other groups for community improvement. But Gacy had a dark side that could repel even the most hardened criminals. His modus operandi was to drug, torture, and rape young men before killing and burying them under his house. Gacy died at the Stateville Correctional Center in Illinois on May 10, 1994, when a lethal injection shut his circus down permanently.

Charles Manson

As revolting as he now seems, there's no denying that Charles Manson once had a magnetic personality. Much like Svengali, the charismatic man had a knack for placing people under his spell. After this was accomplished, the rest was elementary. Such a talent could be used for good or evil purposes. Manson ran with the latter. In 1969, a group of faithful followers performed unthinkable acts on Manson's direct orders. The Tate/LaBianca murders rocked America for their unusual viciousness and revealed Manson as a deranged puppet master, bent on the death and destruction of humankind. Manson has spent the past four decades behind bars and by most accounts has lost all of his charm. A classic case of too little, too late.

Brazen Armored Car Heists

From Butch Cassidy to John Dillinger, bank robbers have captured the imagination of the American public. Here are some of the most brazen heists of armored cars in American history.

✳   ✳   ✳   ✳

The Great Vault Robbery, Jacksonville, Florida: $22 million

In March 1997, 33-year-old Philip Johnson, who made $7 an hour as a driver for armored-car company Loomis Fargo, took off with one of the cars he was supposed to be guarding.

Johnson pulled off the caper by waiting until the end of the night, when the armored cars returned to the Loomis Fargo vaults. Johnson tied up the two vault employees, loaded an armored car with about $22 million in cash, and took off.

He remained on the lam for more than four months, despite a half-million-dollar reward for his arrest. He was finally arrested crossing into the United States from Mexico in August 1997.

The majority of the money—which had been stashed in a rental storage unit in rural North Carolina—was recovered shortly afterward.

Dunbar Armored, Los Angeles, California: $18.9 million

Though not technically an armored-car robbery, the 1997 heist of $18.9 million dollars from the Dunbar Armored vaults in Los Angeles, is noteworthy for its meticulous planning and the fact that it is considered the largest armed cash robbery in American history.

The mastermind behind the theft was Dunbar Armored employee Allen Pace III, who used his knowledge of the vault's security system, along with his company keys, to gain access to the loot. Pace and his gang were eventually brought down when one of his cohorts, Eugene Hill, paid for something with a stack of bills banded in a Dunbar wrapper. That, plus a shard of taillight that had been the only piece of evidence left at the scene, was enough for investigators to crack the case. Despite the arrest of Pace and several coconspirators, nearly $10 million of the haul still remains unaccounted for.

Armored Motor Service of America, Rochester, New York: $10.8 million

In June 1990, a driver for the Armored Motor Service of America (AMSA) and his female partner stopped for breakfast at a convenience store near Rochester. While the female guard went into the store, a band of armed thieves attacked the driver, waited for the female guard to return, then ordered them to drive the truck to an unnamed location, where the thieves transferred the money to a waiting van, tied up the two guards, and escaped with the money. The total haul of $10.8 million ranked as one the largest heists in history. The robbery was also noteworthy for the fact that it remained unsolved for more than a decade. In 2002, though, the driver of the robbed AMSA truck, Albert Ranieri, admitted to masterminding the scheme.

Express Teller Services, Columbia, South Carolina: $9.8 million

In 2007, two young men overpowered an Express Teller Services armored car driver when he and his partners stopped to fuel up. They drove the car to a remote area, where two accomplices waited with another vehicle to transfer the cash. The theft of $9.8 million was one of the biggest in American history, but it wasn't particularly well executed. First, the thieves didn't bring a large enough vehicle or enough bags to take the nearly $20 million that was in the truck. Next, the bandits savagely beat one of the guards, while leaving the other one—who was later arrested as the mastermind—untouched. But the gang really did themselves in by going on a weeklong spending spree involving strippers, tattoos, and Mother's Day gifts. Not surprisingly, just about the entire gang was arrested less than a week later.

Even More Odd Ordinances

* In Chico, California, you'll be fined $500 if you set off a nuclear device within city limits.

* If you have the itch to rip those tags off your pillows and mattresses (that clearly say "Do Not Remove"), Colorado is the place for you. It's legal there to do so.

* It's illegal to offer to loan your neighbor your vacuum cleaner in Denver.

* Here's a law that might be easier said than done: In Sterling, Colorado, cats that run free must be fitted with a taillight.

* For a good evening view in Devon, Connecticut, you'd better walk west—it's illegal to walk backward after sunset.

* Moms might rejoice at this law: Silly string is prohibited in Southington, Connecticut.

* It's against the law to whisper in church in Rehoboth Beach, Delaware.

* Laws in Delaware prohibit you from flying over a body of water unless you are carrying ample supplies of food and drink.

* In case you wondered: It's not legal to sell your children in Florida.

* Floridians must have very clean clothes—it's illegal to shower naked there.

* If you don't want to end up in jail, don't have sex with a porcupine in Florida.

* In Georgia, watch your tongue around dead people. It's unlawful to swear in front of a dead body in a funeral home or coroner's office.

* Happy Hour is not quite as happy in Athens-Clarke County, Georgia. Selling two beers for the price of one is outlawed.

* Keep the speed down when biking in Connecticut. You aren't allowed to exceed 65 mph.

Bye-Bye Brewskis

As the largest 100-percent Canadian-owned brewery, Moosehead is one of the country's most beloved brand. In fact, a few Canadians have taken the opportunity to steal large quantities of the brew.

✳ ✳ ✳ ✳

Wanted: Beer and Bear

IN AUGUST 2004, a truck driver named Wade Haines was transporting 54,000 cans of Moosehead beer to Mexico, when suddenly the delivery went missing. Police found Haines's empty rig idling in a parking lot on the outskirts of Fredericton, New Brunswick. Soon afterward about 8,000 cans were found in a makeshift trailer that had overturned off the road in a wooded region near Woodstock, New Brunswick. But what happened to the rest of the brew?

The local population, the police, and the national media embarked on a frenzied search for the missing beer. Thousands of cans were recovered from the surrounding area, including in the woods and by a cemetery. In October, police discovered a marijuana farm that had 200 of the stolen cans, six of which showed clear signs of having been bitten by a bear. Neither the bear nor the farmers, however, could be located for questioning.

In another daring move, in September 2007, thieves used stolen tractors to heist two trailers holding 70,000 cans and 44,000 bottles of Moosehead, adding up to a loss of more than $200,000. Never fear, beer drinkers: Ontario was restocked with Moosehead a week later, a testament to the brewery's dedication to its fans.

Not Just for Canucks

In March 2008, Americans in Daytona Beach, Florida, apparently were willing to steal Moosehead as well. But unlike their Candian counterparts, the American thieves failed to steal actual beer; instead, the thieves made off with the company's 30-foot-tall inflatable bottle of Moosehead Light. To show it could take a joke, or perhaps to compensate the thieves for the blow-up bottle's lack of liquid, Moosehead offered a year's supply of beer for the return of the $5,000 display.

That's a Crime Too

* Kissing a woman while she's asleep is a crime in Logan County, Colorado.

* Men with mustaches are not allowed to kiss women in Eureka, Nevada.

* Any man who comes face-to-face with a cow has to remove his hat in Fruithill, Kentucky.

* Flirting in public is against the law in Little Rock, Arkansas.

* Michigan law states that a woman's hair is technically owned by her husband.

* It's illegal for kids under the age of seven to attend college in Winston-Salem, North Carolina (sorry, Doogie).

* Talking on the phone without a parent on the line is a crime in Blue Earth, Minnesota.

* You can't buy a lollipop without a doctor's note while church services are in session if you live in Kalispell, Montana.

* It's illegal to eat chicken with a fork in Gainesville, Georgia.

* You could go to jail for making an ugly face at a dog in the state of Oklahoma.

* A frog—yes, a frog—can be arrested for keeping a person awake with its "ribbit" noises in Memphis, Tennessee.

* Eating nuts on a city bus in Charleston, South Carolina, could cost you a $500 fine or even 60 days in jail.

Death from on High

When a troubled man exacted revenge from a lofty perch, a stunned nation watched in horror and disbelief. What could cause a man to kill indiscriminately? Why hadn't anyone seen it coming? Could such a thing happen again? Decades later the mystery continues.

✳ ✳ ✳ ✳

I N AN AMERICA strained by an escalating war in Vietnam, the 1966 headline still managed to shock the senses. The "Texas Tower Sniper" had killed his mother and wife before snuffing out the lives of 13 innocents on the University of Texas (UT) campus at Austin. At least the Vietnam conflict offered up motives. Like most wars, battle lines had been drawn, and a steady buildup of threats and tensions had preceded the violence. But here, no such declarations were issued. Bullets came blazing out of the sky for no apparent reason. After the victims breathed their last and the nightmare drew to a close, a stunned populace was left with one burning question: Why?

Undercurrents

Charles Whitman appeared to have enjoyed many of life's advantages. Hailing from a prominent family in Lake Worth, Florida, the future was Whitman's. But friction with his abusive father found Whitman seeking escape. After a brutal incident in which he returned home from a party drunk only to be beaten, and nearly drowned in a swimming pool, by his father, the 18-year-old Whitman enlisted in the Marines. He served for five years, distinguishing himself with a Sharpshooters Badge. After that he attended college at UT. During that period, he also married his girlfriend, Kathy Leissner.

Whitman's life plan appeared to be straightforward. After obtaining a scholarship, he would seek an engineering degree, hoping to follow it up with acceptance at officer's candidate school. But things didn't go as planned.

Opportunity Lost

After leaving the military, Whitman worked toward a variety of goals in and out of school. Unfortunately, the ex-Marine was fraught with failure, and his frustrations multiplied. In the spring of 1966, Whitman sought the help of UT psychiatrist Dr. Maurice Dean Heatly. In a moment of ominous foretelling, Whitman remarked that he fantasized "going up on the [campus] tower with a deer rifle and shooting people." The doctor, having heard similar threats in the past, was mostly unimpressed. Since Whitman hadn't previously exhibited violent behavior, Heatly took his statement as nothing more than an idle threat.

Surprise Assault

During the wee hours of August 1, 1966, Whitman's demons finally won out, and his killing spree began. For reasons still uncertain, the murderer kicked off his blood quest by first stabbing his mother in her apartment and his wife while she slept. Both died from the injuries.

Whitman then made his way to the UT campus and ascended the soon-to-be infamous tower. At his side he had enough provisions, weapons, and ammo to hole up indefinitely. Just before noon, he lifted a high-powered rifle and began shooting. He picked off victims one by one from the observation deck of the 307-foot-tall tower. Whitman's sharpshooting prowess (he once scored 215 points out of a possible 250 in target practice) added to the danger. When people finally realized what was happening, quite a few had already been cut down.

Lives Cut Short

As the attacks progressed, Austin police hatched a plan. Officers Ramiro Martinez and Houston McCoy snuck into the tower, surprising Whitman. Both sides exchanged fire. The 96-minute attack ended with two fatal shots to Whitman's head, compliments of McCoy's 12-gauge shotgun. The horror was over. In its ultimate wake lay 16 dead and 31 wounded. An autopsy performed on Whitman revealed a brain tumor that may have caused him to snap.

The authorities later found a note at his home. Its matter-of-fact tone is chilling to this day: "I imagine it appears that I brutaly [sic] kill [sic] both of my loved ones. I was only trying to do a quick thorough job. If my life insurance policy is valid ... please pay off all my debts ... Donate the rest anonymously to a mental health foundation. Maybe research can prevent further tragedies of this type."

The Sutton-Taylor Feud

When disputes fester, they can turn deadly. Such was the case with Texas's version of the Hatfields and McCoys. When the smoke cleared, and this long-standing feud died out, dozens lay dead in its wake.

✳   ✳   ✳   ✳

TEXAS'S FIGHT BETWEEN the Suttons and the Taylors claimed an estimated 30 to 50 people. In one of the state's longest and deadliest disputes, William E. Sutton and Creed Taylor did their hateful best to mow each other down. Eventually, family and friends joined each combatant in their unquenchable quest for revenge. For such loyalty, many paid the ultimate price.

So, What Do We Know?

Hatred between the families may have begun as early as the 1840s, when Sutton and Taylor lived in Georgia. By the 1860s, both families had relocated to Texas's DeWitt County, bringing their loathing with them.

In March 1868, a pivotal event occurred when accused horse thieves Charles Taylor and James Sharp were shot to death. This was followed by the Christmas Eve murders of Buck Taylor and Dick Chisholm. William Sutton was believed to be involved in both episodes. With the gauntlet thrown down, there was no turning back. The Taylors staged deadly ambushes, claiming a number of Sutton's soldiers. In 1872, Pitkin Taylor was shot and wounded, and he died six months later. His family swore revenge and enlisted kinsman and notorious outlaw John Wesley Hardin. Soon, Hardin and Jim Taylor disposed of Jack Helm, an agent of Sutton.

Settled?

This deadly tit-for-tat continued until the late 1870s, when Texas Rangers arrested eight men from the Sutton camp for killing Dr. Phillip Brassel and his son. By this time, the feud was so widespread and fragmented that no one was sure who fought for what or for whom. With witnesses understandably scared to testify against either side, the legal case fell apart. But the feud appeared to be over. With a whimper instead of a bang, the Sutton-Taylor feud had finally come to an end.

Fumbling Felons, Part V

Just Change the Oil

Not knowing anything about cars proved to be the downfall of a woman from San Antonio, Texas. After hiding 18 bags of marijuana under her hood, she went in for an oil change. The mechanic discovered the stash and called police who promptly arrested the woman on drug charges. She said she didn't realize they'd have to open the hood in order to change her oil.

Don't Move!

In Detroit, Michigan, two would-be robbers charged in to a store, waving guns in the air. One of them shouted, "Nobody move!" Just then the second robber made a sudden movement, surprising his buddy—who shot him.

Paying with Pot

When a customer at a McDonald's restaurant in Vero Beach, Florida, realized he didn't have enough cash to pay for his order, he offered to trade the clerk some marijuana for the food. The cashier declined the offer and called the police instead, describing the car in question. Police stopped the vehicle soon after and found—surprise, surprise—a baggie of weed. Now he'll be eating his Big Mac in the Big House.

Don't Ask and Certainly Don't Tell

On trial for a convenience store robbery in Oklahoma City, Dennis Newton fired his attorney and decided to represent himself in court. The alleged robber actually was handling the defense pretty well until the store manager took the stand. She identified him as the robber, and Newton blew up, shouting, "You're lying! I should have blown your head off!" Realizing his gaffe, he quickly added, "If I'd been the one who was there." But it was too late—the jury found him guilty within 20 minutes and recommended 30 years in jail.

Call It Multitasking

Apparently no one told Efe Osenwegie of Ontario, Canada, that he should keep his eyes on the road. When he was pulled over for speeding on Highway 401, police discovered he was watching a porn movie on a portable DVD player in the front seat. Osenwegie was charged with speeding and operating a motor vehicle with a television visible to the driver.

If Only He Could Have Stayed Awake

After a Campbelltown, Australia, man allegedly stole a car, he drove it to a local car wash. Maybe he wanted to wash off any evidence, or perhaps he was hiding out. Heck, maybe the guy just needed a nap. After an hour passed with him sleeping inside the stolen vehicle, the attendant called the police. The sleepy fella was charged with car theft and illegal use of a motor vehicle.

Where Are Those Keys?

When a Texas man robbed a pharmacy of hydrocodone and Xanax, he left his car running for a faster getaway. There was just one problem: He discovered that he had locked the keys inside the car. To add insult to injury (or vice versa in this case), when the man tried to flee the scene on foot, the police, who thought he was armed, shot him in the shoulder. Now he's really going to need those painkillers.

It Doesn't Pay to Lie

Sandy Hamilton of Lincoln, Nebraska, presumably left his house with no criminal intent whatsoever but managed to wander into trouble along the way. The 19-year-old was arrested after he was spotted walking around an area park with no clothes on. When the police stopped him, Hamilton claimed that a man had tried to rob him at gunpoint; when he said he had no money, the robber took his clothes instead. Police eventually concluded that Hamilton took off the clothes because he was hot. Unfortunately, after walking around naked for a while, he forgot where he left his clothes and concocted the story about the robbery. As a result of the lie, Hamilton was charged not only with indecent exposure, but also with suspicion of making a false statement to police.

Look Before You Leap

Jermaine Washington was so focused on his goal—robbing someone in New York City's Riverside Park—that he didn't even register what his victims looked like. If he'd taken a closer look, he would have realized that they were two of New York's finest, in uniform, no less. Washington pulled a fake gun; the officers pulled real guns, and Washington was promptly taken into custody.

Bluebeard in the Flesh

"All of the women for Johann go crazy!"

✳   ✳   ✳   ✳

IN 1905, WHEN the police finally caught up with Johann Hoch, he had already proposed to what would have been his 45th wife. His habit was to meet a lonely middle-aged woman, propose, marry her, and take her money in the space of about a week. Depending on Johann's mood, about a third of the women were murdered; the others were simply abandoned. Hoch's method of murder was slipping his new bride some arsenic, which was a perfect crime in those days. Arsenic was used in embalming fluid, so the minute an undertaker came into the house, convicting someone of arsenic poisoning was impossible.

The press was fascinated—how could an ugly man who spoke like a comedian with a German accent convince so many women to marry him? Why, his last Chicago wife (his 44th overall) had agreed to marry him while her sister (wife #43) was lying dead on her bed! *The Herald American*, which could be counted on to print the wildest rumors in town, claimed that Hoch used hypnosis on the women and that he had learned all he knew about murdering from the infamous H. H. Holmes.

Hoch's power over women made it seem as though he *must* have had access to some sort of magic spell. As his trial continued, wife #44, the woman who had first reported him to authorities, came to his cell daily to bring him money and beg him to forgive her. He received numerous letters containing marriage proposals while in prison. Any marriage would have been a short one—Johann was hanged in 1906.

Legend has it that as Hoch was about to be hanged, he said to the guards, "I don't look like a monster now, do I?" After the deed was done, one of the guards quietly replied, "Well, not anymore."

The Butcher Was a Wienie

So, the mugger is dead, your wife is dead, but you made it out unscathed? Something doesn't quite add up...

✳   ✳   ✳   ✳

IN 1920, BUTCHER Carl Wanderer, a veteran of the First World War, approached a drifter in a bar and offered him the princely sum of $10 to pretend to rob him. Wanderer explained that he was in the doghouse with his wife, but that if he punched a mugger in front of her, he'd look like a hero. The drifter agreed to the deal.

The next day, as Wanderer and his wife (who was due to deliver the couple's first child the following month) returned home from the movies, the drifter attacked them in the entryway of their apartment building. Wanderer pulled out a gun, shot the drifter to death, then turned and shot his wife to death too. Wanderer told police that his wife had tragically been killed during the ruckus.

For a couple of days, Wanderer was hailed as a hero. But the police—and, more importantly, the newspaper reporters—had an uneasy feeling about Wanderer's story. They were especially suspicious of the fact that he and the drifter had exactly the same model of pistol.

Reporters soon discovered that Wanderer had a girlfriend—a 16-year-old who worked across the street from Wanderer's butcher shop. Within weeks, Wanderer's story had fallen apart, and he broke down and confessed to the murders.

Initially put on trial only for the murder of his wife, Wanderer was sentenced to 25 years in prison. The newspapers were outraged that he hadn't been sentenced to hang and published the names and addresses of the jurors so that people could harass them. Eventually, Wanderer was rushed back into court to stand trial for the death of the drifter. This time, he was sentenced to death.

At his hanging, he entertained the reporters by singing a popular song of the day, "Old Pal Why Don't You Answer Me," just before his execution. One reporter said, "He shoulda been a song plugger." Another, however, said, "He should have been hanged just for his voice!" All were thankful Wanderer would sing no more.

The Whitechapel Club

Where the only light came from the skulls that lined the walls...

✳ ✳ ✳ ✳

IN THE LATE 19th century, in Chicago, the area bounded by Wells on the west, La Salle on the east, Washington on the north, and Madison on the south was known as Newsboy Alley. The back room of a club on Calhoun Place housed the strangest of all Chicago's press clubs: the Whitechapel Club.

Named for the neighborhood that had been terrorized by Jack the Ripper, the club was decorated with crime-scene photos. The members surrounded themselves with such images to show that they were gritty newspapermen who had seen it all; nothing could faze them. While the club had an aura of mystery, it was regularly featured in *The New York Times*. Rumors of strange rites held in the dark headquarters circulated throughout the city.

The Truth: They Liked to Drink

In reality, the only spirits that were actually raised here were held up in a glass. Indeed, while the program at the club on any given evening might feature readings of essays and poems by the club members (some of which could probably have been categorized as "crimes" on their own), the majority of the meetings seem to have been occupied with the same thing that went on at most private clubs: drinking. But at least the Whitechapel members knew how to mix a little drama in with their cocktails: The agenda for the evening would be written out on a rolled-up curtain that would be unrolled to reveal one event at a time. The first event of the night was generally "we drink," and the second was generally "we drink again."

Just as all crime sprees must come to a close, the club ended its five-year run in 1902. The building that housed the club was demolished, and the La Salle Hotel was built in its place. The hotel included a bar known as the Whitechapel Club until the hotel itself fell victim to the wrecking ball in the mid-1970s.

William Desmond Taylor

The murder of actor/director William Desmond Taylor was like something out of an Agatha Christie novel, complete with a handsome, debonair victim and multiple suspects, each with a motive. But unlike Christie's novels, in which the murderer was always unmasked, Taylor's death remains unsolved nearly 100 years later.

❋   ❋   ❋   ❋

O N THE EVENING of February 1, 1922, Taylor was shot in the back by an unknown assailant; his body was discovered the next morning by a servant, Henry Peavey. News of Taylor's demise spread quickly, and several individuals, including officials from Paramount Studios, where Taylor was employed, raced to the dead man's home to clear it of anything incriminating, such as illegal liquor, evidence of drug use, illicit correspondence, and signs of sexual indiscretion. However, no one called the police until later in the morning.

Numerous Suspects

Soon an eclectic array of potential suspects came to light, including Taylor's criminally inclined former butler, Edward F. Sands, who had gone missing before the murder; popular movie comedienne Mabel Normand, whom Taylor had entertained the evening of his death; actress Mary Miles Minter, who had a passionate crush on the handsome director who was 28 years her senior; and Charlotte Shelby, Minter's mother, who often wielded a gun in order to protect her daughter's tarnished honor.

Taylor's murder was the last thing Hollywood needed at the time, coming as it did on the heels of rape allegations against popular film comedian Fatty Arbuckle. Scandals brought undue attention on Hollywood, and the Arbuckle story had taken its toll. Officials at Paramount tried to keep a lid on the Taylor story, but the tabloid press had a field day. A variety of personal foibles were made public in the weeks that followed, and both Normand and Minter saw their careers come to a screeching halt as a result. Taylor's own indiscretions were also revealed, such as the fact that he kept a special souvenir, usually lingerie, from every woman he bedded.

Little Evidence

Police interviewed many of Taylor's friends and colleagues, including all potential suspects. However, there was no evidence to incriminate anyone specifically, and no one was formally charged.

Investigators and amateur sleuths pursued the case for years. Sands was long a prime suspect, based on his criminal past and his estrangement from the victim. But it was later revealed that on the day of the murder, Sands had signed in for work at a lumberyard in Oakland, California—some 400 miles away—and thus could not have committed the crime. Coming in second was Shelby, whose temper and threats were legendary. Shelby's own acting career had fizzled out early, and all of her hopes for stardom were pinned on her daughter. She threatened many men who tried to woo Mary.

In the mid-1990s, another possible suspect surfaced—a long-forgotten silent-film actress named Margaret Gibson. According to Bruce Long, author of *William Desmond Taylor: A Dossier*, Gibson confessed to a friend on her deathbed in 1964 that years before she had killed a man named William Desmond Taylor. However, the woman to whom Gibson cleared her conscience didn't know who Taylor was and thought nothing more about it.

The Mystery Continues

Could Margaret Gibson (aka Pat Lewis) be Taylor's murderer? She had acted with Taylor in Hollywood in the early 1910s, and she may even have been one of his many sexual conquests. She also had a criminal past, including charges of blackmail, drug use, and prostitution, so it's entirely conceivable that she was a member of a group trying to extort money from the director, a popular theory among investigators. But according to an earlier book, *A Cast of Killers* by Sidney D. Kirkpatrick, veteran Hollywood director King Vidor had investigated the murder as material for a film script and through his research believed Shelby was the murderer. But out of respect for Minter, he never did anything about it.

Ultimately, however, we may never know for certain who killed William Desmond Taylor, or why. The case has long grown cold, and anyone with specific knowledge of the murder is likely dead. Unlike a Hollywood thriller, in which the killer is revealed at the end, Taylor's death is a macabre puzzle that likely will never be solved.

Who Founded the Mafia?

This is like asking, "Who founded England?" or "Who founded capitalism?" The Mafia is more of a phenomenon than an organization—it's a movement that rose from a complicated interaction of multiple factors, including history, economics, geography, and politics.

✳   ✳   ✳   ✳

BY ALL ACCOUNTS, the Mafia came to prominence in Sicily during the mid-nineteenth century. Given Sicily's history, this makes sense—the island has repeatedly been invaded and occupied, and has generally been mired in poverty for thousands of years. By the mid-nineteenth century, Italy was in total chaos due to the abolition of feudalism and the lack of a central government or a semblance of a legitimate legal system.

As sociologists will confirm, people who live in areas that fall victim to such upheaval tend to rely on various forms of self-government. In Sicily, this took the form of what has become known as the Mafia. The fellowship, which originated in the rural areas of the Mediterranean island, is based on a complicated system of respect, violence, distrust of government, and the code of *omertà*—a word that is synonymous with the group's code of silence and refers to an unspoken agreement to never cooperate with authorities, under penalty of death. Just as there is no one person who founded the Mafia, there is no one person who runs it. The term "Mafia" refers to any group of organized criminals that follows the traditional Sicilian system of bosses, *capos* ("chiefs"), and soldiers. These groups are referred to as "families."

Although the Mafia evolved in Sicily during the nineteenth century, most Americans equate it to the crime families that dominated the headlines in Chicago and New York for much of the twentieth century. The American Mafia developed as a result of the huge wave of Sicilian immigrants that arrived in the United States in the late nineteenth and early twentieth centuries. These newcomers brought with them the Mafia structure and the code of *omertà*.

These Sicilian immigrants often clustered together in poor urban areas, such as Park Slope in Brooklyn and the south side of Chicago. There, far from the eyes of authorities, disputes were handled by locals. By the 1920s, crime families had sprung up all over the United States and gang wars were prevalent. In the 1930s, Lucky Luciano—who is sometimes called the father of the American Mafia—organized "The Commission," a faux-judiciary system that oversaw the activities of the Mafia in the United States.

Though Mafia families have been involved in murder, kidnapping, extortion, racketeering, gambling, prostitution, drug dealing, weapons dealing, and other crimes over the years, the phenomenon still maintains the romantic appeal that it had when gangsters like Al Capone captivated the nation. Part of it, of course, is the result of the enormous success of the *Godfather* films, but it is also due, one presumes, to the allure of the principles that the Mafia supposedly was founded upon: self-reliance, loyalty, and *omertà*.

So there you have it: a summary of the founding of the Mafia. Of course, we could tell you more, but then we'd have to . . . well, you know.

Fumbling Felons, Part VI

Bear Facts

For someone to shift the blame for their criminal behavior is one thing, but it always works best if the other person or thing happens to be alive. Police are sort of quick to catch on otherwise.

A police officer in Florida saw this firsthand when he stopped a van that was driving erratically. As he approached the van, he saw the driver was now sitting in the passenger seat. When the cop asked for the man's license and registration, the man indignantly informed him, "I wasn't driving. The guy in the back was." When the officer looked in the back of the van, all he saw was a huge stuffed teddy bear. However, since the teddy refused to bear all, the man was taken into custody.

The Eyes Have It

Two teenage thieves in Liverpool, England, had been quite successful at their previous scheme: driving around, then suddenly stopping at a random parked car. One would break into the auto while the other drove around the block. By the time he came back, his buddy would be waiting for him with the car radio, CD player, and whatever else they wanted. After successfully fencing the goods, the two hoods would be back on the street, looking for another victim.

The case was a difficult one for police to solve, particularly because of the random nature of the crimes. All the cops could do was increase their patrols of the area. One night two cops were slowly cruising down the street when their squad car's back door opened. In hopped a youth holding a car radio. "Hit it!" he yelled.

Obediently, the cops did; they raced the squad car around the block, and they handcuffed the unwitting thief. Quickly returning to the scene of the crime, the officers caught the hoodlum's accomplice as well. When they inquired why the boy with the radio had jumped into their vehicle, they discovered that he was nearsighted and had forgotten his glasses that evening. He had simply picked out a car that he thought was his friend's and hopped in.

It Pays to Follow the Styles

A 54-year-old man in San Francisco robbed several banks just seven days after being released from prison—for bank robbery. In February 2007, the man's probation officer took a photo of him on the day he was released. Still wearing the 1980s-style clothes and Members Only jacket in which he strode away from prison—but adding a new hairnet—the man proceeded to rob a bank. Authorities weren't able to positively identify the robber's face from the surveillance photos, but they were able to clearly distinguish his Members Only jacket, his hairnet, and the 1980s-era clothes he wore. He wasn't wasting any time, however, and robbed two more banks before police caught him. The images from the later robberies were widely distributed to police agencies—the bank robber's probation officer instantly recognized him and immediately contacted authorities with the man's name and address. The bank robber was apprehended later that night. He was identified due to the fact that he was still wearing the same clothes.

Choose Your Location Carefully

Perhaps he thought the lot was still vacant, or maybe he believed that no one would think to look for marijuana in such a place. Regardless of his reasoning, a 17-year-old male was arrested for growing nine marijuana plants in a wooded area of Ocala, Florida. Unfortunately for the teen, that wooded area belonged to the deputy chief of police. Neighbors noticed the teen acting suspiciously and asked why he was on the chief's property. He replied that he'd come from a skate park, but they didn't buy it. One neighbor went to where the teen had been spotted and found the illegal crop. The deputy chief was immediately notified.

Safety Goggles Wouldn't Have Helped

Two 19-year-olds were treated for minor burns and arrested after shoplifting gunpowder and PVC pipe from a Wal-Mart in Bayou Black, Louisiana, in July 2007. The youths had successfully gotten away from the store, but they didn't follow all the safety precautions that they should have. One of them subsequently set off the black powder when he flicked cigarette ashes near the open bottle. Following up on reports of a bang, police arrived to investigate. They found damage from an explosion in the kitchen and dining room. The duo was charged with shoplifting and possessing or making a bomb.

Ohio's Greatest Unsolved Mystery

From 1935 until 1938, a brutal madman roamed the Flats of Cleveland. The killer—known as the Mad Butcher of Kingsbury Run—is believed to have murdered 12 men and women. Despite a massive manhunt, the murderer was never apprehended.

✳   ✳   ✳   ✳

IN 1935, THE Depression had hit Cleveland hard, leaving large numbers of people homeless. Shantytowns sprang up on the eastern side of the city in Kingsbury Run—a popular place for transients—near the Erie and Nickel Plate railroads.

It is unclear who the Butcher's first victim was. Recent research suggests it may have been an unidentified woman found floating in Lake Erie—in pieces—on September 5, 1934; she would be known as Jane Doe I but dubbed by some as the "Lady of the Lake." The first official victim was found in the Jackass Hill area of Kingsbury Run on September 23, 1935. The unidentified body, labeled John Doe, had been dead for almost a month. A mere 30 feet away from the body was another victim, Edward Andrassy. Unlike John Doe, Andrassy had only been dead for days, indicating that the spot was a dumping ground. Police began staking out the area.

After a few months passed without another body, police thought the worst was over. Then on January 26, 1936, the partial remains of a new victim, a woman, were found in downtown Cleveland. On February 7, more remains were found at a separate location, and the deceased was identified as Florence Genevieve Polillo. Despite similarities among the three murders, authorities had yet to connect them—serial killers were highly uncommon at the time.

Tattoo Man, Eliot Ness, and More Victims

On June 5, two young boys passing through Kingsbury Run discovered a severed head. The rest of the body was found near the Nickel Plate railroad police station. Despite six distinctive tattoos on the man's body (thus the nickname "Tattoo Man"), he was never identified and became John Doe II.

At this point, Cleveland's newly appointed director of public safety, Eliot Ness, was officially briefed on the case. While Ness and his men hunted down leads, the headless body of another unidentified male was found west of Cleveland on July 22, 1936. It appeared that the man, John Doe III, had been murdered several months earlier. On September 10, the headless body of a sixth victim, John Doe IV, was found in the Kingsbury Run area.

Ness officially started spearheading the investigation. Determined to bring the killer to justice, Ness's staff fanned out across the city, even going undercover in the Kingsbury Run area. As 1936 drew to a close, no suspects had been named nor new victims discovered. City residents believed that Ness's team had run the killer off. But future events would prove that the killer was back . . . with a vengeance.

The Body Count Climbs

A woman's mutilated torso washed up on the beach at 156th Street on February 23, 1937. The rest would wash ashore two months later. (Strangely, the body washed up in the same location as the "Lady of the Lake" had three years earlier.)

On June 6, 1937, teenager Russell Lauyer found the decomposed body of a woman inside of a burlap sack under the Lorain-Carnegie Bridge in Cleveland. With the body was a newspaper from June of the previous year, suggesting a timeline for the murder. An investigation indicated the body might belong to one Rose Wallace; this was never confirmed, and the victim is sometimes referred to as Jane Doe II. Pieces of another man's body (the ninth victim) began washing ashore on July 6, just below Kingsbury Run. Cleveland newspapers were having a field day with the case that the "great" Eliot Ness couldn't solve. This fueled Ness, and he promised justice.

Burning of Kingsbury Run

The next nine months were quiet, and the public began to relax. When a woman's severed leg was found in the Cuyahoga River on April 8, 1938, however, people debated its connection to the Butcher. But the rest of Jane Doe III was soon found inside two burlap sacks floating in the river (*sans* head, of course).

On August 16, 1938, the last two confirmed victims of the Butcher were found together at the East 9th Street Lakeshore Dump. Jane Doe IV had apparently been dead for four to six months prior to discovery, while John Doe VI may have been dead for almost nine months.

Something snapped inside Eliot Ness. On the night of August 18, Ness and dozens of police officials raided the shantytowns in the Flats, ending up in Kingsbury Run. Along the way, they interrogated or arrested anyone they came across, and Ness ordered the shanties burned to the ground. There would be no more confirmed victims of the Mad Butcher of Kingsbury Run.

Who Was the Mad Butcher?

There were two prime suspects in the case, though no one was ever charged. The first was Dr. Francis Sweeney, a surgeon with the knowledge many believed necessary to mutilate the victims the way the killer did. (He was also a cousin of Congressman Martin L. Sweeney, a known political opponent of Ness.)

In August 1938, Dr. Sweeney was interrogated by Ness, two other men, and the inventor of the polygraph machine, Dr. Royal Grossman. By all accounts, Sweeney failed the polygraph test (several times), and Ness believed he had his man, but he was released due to lack of evidence. Two days after the interrogation, on August 25, 1938, Sweeney checked himself into the Sandusky Veterans Hospital. He remained institutionalized at various facilities until his death in 1965. Because Sweeney voluntarily checked himself in, he could have left whenever he desired.

The other suspect was Frank Dolezal, who was arrested by private investigators on July 5, 1939, as a suspect in the murder of Florence Polillo, with whom he had lived for a time. While in custody, Dolezal confessed to killing Polillo, although some believe the confession was forced. Either way, Dolezal died under mysterious circumstances while incarcerated at the Cuyahoga County Jail before he could be charged.

As for Eliot Ness, some believe his inability to bring the Butcher to trial weighed on him for the rest of his life. Ness went to his grave without getting a conviction. To this day, the case remains open.

The Butcher and the Thief

Meet the two charming fellows who inspired the children's rhyme: "Burke's the Butcher, Hare's the Thief, Knox the boy that buys the beef."

✳ ✳ ✳ ✳

The Cadaver Crunch

IN THE 1820s, Edinburgh, Scotland, was suffering from a "cadaver crunch." Considering the city was regarded as a center of medical education, the lack of bodies for students to dissect in anatomy classes posed a problem. At the time, the only legal source of corpses for dissection in Britain was executed criminals. Interestingly, at the same time that enrollment in medical schools was rising (as well as the need for cadavers), the number of executions was decreasing. This was due to the repeal of the so-called "Bloody Code," which by 1815 listed more than 200 capital offenses.

The growing need for corpses created a grisly new occupation. "Resurrection Men" dug up the newly buried dead and sold the bodies to medical schools. William Burke and William Hare decided to cut out the middleman: Over the course of a year, they murdered at least 15 people in order to sell their bodies.

A Grisly Business

The pair fell into the cadaver supply business on November 29, 1827. At the time, Hare was running a cheap boarding house in an Edinburgh slum. Burke was his tenant and drinking buddy. When one of Hare's tenants died still owing four pounds, Hare and Burke stole the tenant's corpse from his coffin and sold it to recover the back rent. Dr. Robert Knox, who taught anatomy to 500 students at Edinburgh Medical College, paid more than seven pounds for the body.

Encouraged by the profit, Burke and Hare looked for other bodies to sell to Knox. Their first victim was another tenant at the boarding house, who fell ill a few days later. Burke and Hare "comforted" the sick man with whiskey until he passed out, and then smothered him. The result was a body that looked like it had died of drunkenness, and had no marks of foul play.

Over the course of the next year, Burke and Hare lured more victims into the lodging house. They sold the bodies to Knox, who not only accepted them without question, but increased the pair's payment to ten pounds because of the "freshness" of the bodies they provided.

Their initial targets were strangers to Edinburgh, but Burke and Hare soon began to take more risks, murdering local prostitutes and "Daft Jamie," a well-known neighborhood character. People began to talk about the disappearances, and Knox's students began to recognize the bodies brought to them for dissection.

The End of Burke and Hare

Burke and Hare's mercenary killings ended on October 31, 1828, when Burke lured an old Irish woman named Mary Docherty to the house. James and Ann Gray, who were also boarders at the time, met Docherty there. Docherty was invited to spend the night, and arrangements were made for the Grays to board elsewhere. The next morning, the Grays returned and found the old woman's body under the bed. Although they were offered a bribe of ten pounds a week to keep quiet, the Grays ran for the police.

Hare testified against Burke in exchange for immunity. He was released in February 1829 and disappeared from the historical record, though popular legend claims he ended his life a blind beggar on the streets of London. Burke was tried for murder, found guilty, and hung. Although there was no evidence that Knox had any knowledge of the murders, angry crowds appeared at his lectures and tore his effigy to shreds. He eventually moved to London.

Fittingly, Burke's corpse was turned over to the Edinburgh Medical College for "useful dissection." A bit more oddly, skin from his body was used to bind a small book.

The murders led to the passage of the Anatomy Act of 1832, which provided new legal sources for medical cadavers and eliminated the profit motive that drove Burke and Hare to opportunistic murder.

Fumbling Felons, Part VII

Now It Can Be Told

In 2003, a jewelry heist occurred at a department store in Temecula, California. Two armed men and a getaway driver all got away—until the driver got in touch with his inner muse. In 2005, Colton Simpson published a memoir, *Inside the Crips: Life Inside L.A.'s Most Notorious Gang*. Touting its author as the mastermind, Colton's book described details uncannily similar to the actual jewelry heist. Colton discussed waiting outside while two others robbed the store and the fact that he scouted out the jewelry section two days prior. As a result of California's "Three Strikes You're Out" law, Colton received 126 years in prison for his literary spirit!

Do You Have Change for a Bill?

Since 1969, the largest U.S. bill in circulation is the $100 bill. Despite this fact, on October 6, 2007, a man walked into a Pittsburgh supermarket and attempted to pay for his purchase with a one-million-dollar bill! When the cashier refused to accept it and the store manager confiscated the bill, the customer flew into a rage. He was subsequently held in the county jail.

Sorry, Wrong Number

A man in Escatawpa, Mississippi, intended to call the local TV station after watching a news story. Angry, he apparently wanted to complain about not receiving a FEMA trailer after Hurricane Katrina. Meaning to dial 411 for the station's number, the man accidentally dialed 911. Panicking, he hung up on the dispatcher. The dispatcher, concerned, requested police to check if anyone needed assistance. When police arrived at the address from where the phone call was made, no one answered the door. Thinking the residents might be in trouble, police broke in and found the 56-year-old caller and four others in a full methamphetamine lab.

Next Time, Carry a Flashlight

A burglar broke into a German sports club around 3: 00 A.M. Needing to see what he was about to steal, he turned on the first light switch he could find. That turned on the floodlights and sprinkler system for the football field outside. The grounds-keeper for the sports club could see the light from his nearby home and immediately contacted the police. The man was quickly arrested.

Keep It to Yourself

A 60-year-old man in Duisburg, Germany, decided to appeal his court conviction for streaking at a girls' soccer match. Perhaps believing it might help his case, the man stripped off all his clothes in the courtroom when the jury adjourned for deliberation. Needless to say, it did not, and new charges were immediately filed.

The Internet Knows Everything

Two burglars broke into an indoor amusement center in Colorado Springs, Colorado. Police suspect that they had inside help, as the felons had keys, pass codes, and combinations. What they didn't have, however, was information about the safes—which took them more than 75 minutes to open. Security footage showed them fumbling with the dials. In an attempt to obscure the lens of a security camera, the bungling duo sprayed it with WD-40 lubricant, which cleaned the lens instead. Eventually, one of the burglars left the room. Police later checked a computer in a nearby office and found that the thief had performed Google searches for "how to open a safe" and "how to crack a safe." It must have helped. The two easily opened the safes after that, escaping with cash, a laptop computer, and a PlayStation, totaling more than $12,000.

Don't Display Your Own Evidence

An Italian university student was arrested in 2007 for marijuana charges after dropping his cell phone. Apparently, the student had taken a picture of himself in front of a marijuana plant and then inexplicably used that picture as a screen saver on his phone. That wasn't so bad, until he lost the phone. A retiree found it and turned it over to the police. Upon seeing the picture, police called the student in, where he promptly broke down and confessed to everything, including the location of his crop. He was immediately arrested.

Take Your Name Tag with You

In June 2007, a man who was admitted to a Newark, New Jersey, hospital was arrested for vandalizing the hospital's helicopter. He apparently left the emergency room and walked onto the helipad. Perhaps searching for drugs, the man entered the helicopter and ransacked it. Damages were estimated around $55,000. The vandal, however, left behind his grocery store name tag in the helicopter. Police swiftly arrested him.

Another Set of Odd Ordinances

* It is illegal to drive while sleeping in Tennessee.

* In Danville, Pennsylvania, all fire hydrants must be inspected one hour before a fire.

* It is illegal to throw pickle juice on a trolley in Rhode Island.

* It's not legal to wear transparent clothes in Providence, Rhode Island. Spoilsports.

* A Spartanburg, South Carolina, law forbids people from eating watermelon in the Magnolia Street Cemetery.

* Snowball throwers can expect a $50 fine in Provo, Utah.

* No runaway grooms: If a man promises to marry a woman in South Carolina, he is bound by law to do so.

* You cannot fire a missile without a permit in South Carolina.

* It is against the law to lie down and go to sleep in a cheese factory in South Dakota.

* Movies that depict police officers as being beaten or treated badly are banned in South Dakota.

* It is not legal to use a lasso to catch a fish in Tennessee. Though good luck trying.

* In Memphis restaurants, no pie may be taken home or given to fellow diners.

* Shooting a buffalo is prohibited from the second story of a hotel in Texas.

* Criminals in Texas must give their victims written or verbal notice 24 hours in advance, explaining what crime is about to be committed.

* You may not dust any public place with a feather duster in Clarendon, Texas.

Berkowitz's Reign of Terror

For one year, a murderous madman who called himself the Son of Sam held New York City hostage. Terrified residents stopped going outside, and some women even changed their appearance for fear of provoking the mysterious serial slayer. At its height, the police effort to catch the killer involved more than 200 determined detectives.

✳ ✳ ✳ ✳

BETWEEN JULY 1976 AND July 1977, New Yorkers couldn't pick up a newspaper or turn on the television without hearing about the notorious serial killer who referred to himself in cryptic letters only as the Son of Sam. He struck seemingly at random, primarily attacking young women, and by the time he was finally captured on August 10, 1977, six people were dead and seven gravely wounded.

The Son of Sam turned out to be a troubled loner named David Berkowitz, who told investigators upon his capture that demons in the form of howling dogs had instructed him to kill.

The Seeds Are Planted

Berkowitz had led a distressed life almost from the beginning. Abandoned as a baby, he was adopted by Nathan and Pearl Berkowitz, a middle-class couple who gave him a loving home. But Berkowitz grew up feeling scorned and unwanted because he was adopted. He made few friends, was viewed by neighbors as a bully, and did poorly in school.

When Pearl Berkowitz died of breast cancer in 1967, her son fell into a deep depression, and his emotional problems steadily worsened. His father remarried in 1971, and the animosity Berkowitz expressed toward his new stepmother eventually caused the newlywed couple to flee to Florida. Berkowitz, just 18, found himself alone in New York.

On Christmas Eve 1975, Berkowitz's internal rage reached the boiling point, and he stalked the streets with a knife, looking for someone to kill. He later told police that he stabbed two women that night, though police could locate only one, a 15-year-old girl named Michelle Forman who survived multiple stab wounds.

Berkowitz fled the Bronx and moved into a two-family home in Yonkers, where his mental state continued to decline. Barking dogs kept him awake at night, and Berkowitz eventually perceived their howls as demonic commands to kill. He moved out of the house and into a nearby apartment, where he became convinced that his neighbor's black Labrador retriever was also possessed. After shooting the dog, Berkowitz came to believe that its owner, a man named Sam Carr, also harbored demons.

The Shootings

The voices in his head eventually encouraged Berkowitz to once again seek victims on the street. On July 29, 1976, he shot Jody Valenti and Donna Lauria as they sat chatting in a car outside of Lauria's apartment. Lauria died instantly from a shot to the throat; Valenti survived.

In the months that followed, Berkowitz continued his nocturnal attacks, using a distinctive .44 Bulldog revolver to dispatch his victims.

October 23, 1976: Carl Denaro and Rosemary Keenan were shot while sitting in a parked car. Denaro was struck in the head, but both survived.

November 26, 1976: Donna DeMasi and Joanne Lomino were attacked by Berkowitz as they walked home from a late movie. DeMasi survived with minor injuries; Lomino was left paralyzed.

January 30, 1977: Christine Freund and her fiancé, John Diel, were shot as they sat in a parked car. Freund was killed, Diel survived.

March 8, 1977: College student Virginia Voskerichian was shot and killed while walking home from class.

April 17, 1977: Valentina Suriani and her boyfriend, Alexander Esau, were shot and killed. Police found a note signed "Son of Sam."

June 26, 1977: Judy Placido and Sal Lupu were shot in their car after a night of dancing at a local disco. Both survived.

July 31, 1977: Bobby Violante and Stacy Moskowitz were both shot while sitting in a parked car. Moskowitz was killed, and Violante lost the vision in one eye and partial vision in the other.

Sam Speaks Up

At the scene of the Suriani-Esau shootings in April, police found a rambling, handwritten letter from Berkowitz in which he referred to himself as "Son of Sam." In the note, Berkowitz revealed that he felt like an outsider and was programmed to kill. He told police that to stop his murderous rampage, they'd have to shoot him dead. Forensic psychiatrists used the letter to develop a psychological profile of "Son of Sam" and concluded that he likely suffered from paranoid schizophrenia and thought himself a victim of demonic possession.

As the daily papers splashed gruesome details of each new killing across their front pages, New Yorkers began to panic. Women with dark hair cut their locks short or bought blond wigs because the killer seemed to have a penchant for brunettes. Many New Yorkers simply refused to go outside after it grew dark.

A ticket for parking too close to a fire hydrant finally led to David Berkowitz's capture. Two days after the Violante/Moskowitz shootings, a woman named Cacilia Davis, who lived near the murder scene, called police to report seeing a strange man, later identified as Berkowitz, loitering in the neighborhood for several hours before snatching a parking ticket off the windshield of his car and driving away.

New York police detectives, working with the Yonkers police, decided to pay a visit to Berkowitz. They examined his car, parked outside his apartment, and spotted a rifle on the back seat. A search of the vehicle also revealed a duffel bag containing ammunition, maps of the crime scenes, and a letter to a member of the police task force charged with finding the Son of Sam.

Arrest and Aftermath

Berkowitz was arrested later that evening as he started his car. He immediately confessed to being the Son of Sam, telling the arresting officers, "You got me. What took you so long?"

In court, David Berkowitz admitted to six murders and received six life sentences, though he later recanted his testimony and claimed to have pulled the trigger in only two of the killings. The others, he said, had been committed by members of a Satanic cult to which he belonged. Despite his claims, no one else was ever charged in association with the Son of Sam killings.

Murder, Inc.

A gun; an ice pick; a rope; these were some of the favorite tools of Albert Anastasia, notorious mob assassin. When he wasn't pulling the trigger himself, this head of Murder, Inc.—the enforcement arm of New York's Five Families Mafia—was giving the orders to kill, beat, extort, and rob on the mob-controlled waterfronts of Brooklyn and Manhattan.

✳   ✳   ✳   ✳

BORN IN ITALY in 1902 as Umberto Anastasio, Anastasia worked as a deck hand before jumping ship in New York, where he built a power base in the longshoremen's union. Murder was his tool to consolidate power. Arrested several times in the 1920s, his trials were often dismissed when witnesses would go missing. It wasn't long before he attracted the attention of mob "brain" Lucky Luciano and subsequently helped whack Joe "the Boss" Masseria in 1931, an act that opened the way for Luciano to achieve national prominence within the organization.

Luciano put Anastasia, Bugsy Siegel, and Meyer Lanksy in charge of what became known as Murder, Inc., the lethal button men of the Brooklyn Mafia. With his quick temper and brutal disposition, Anastasia earned the nickname "Lord High Executioner."

A psychopathic assassin named Abe "Kid Twist" Reles was a key man of Murder, Inc., but turned prosecution witness when he was arrested in 1940. Reles fingered Anastasia, only to "fall" from his hotel room while under protective custody.

A History of Violence

Anastasia climbed the next rung in the mob ladder by ordering the violent 1951 deaths of the Mangano brothers and ultimately taking over the Mangano family. Eventually, however, he alienated two powerful rivals, Vito Genovese and Meyer Lansky. On October 25, 1957, as Albert Anastasia dozed in a barber's chair at New York's Park Sheraton Hotel, he was riddled by two masked gunmen (possibly Larry and Joe Gallo), who acted on orders from Genovese. Anastasia had evaded justice for decades, but he couldn't escape the violence he himself cultivated in organized crime.

Mafia Buster!

Joseph Petrosino was one of the first New York cops to take on the Mafia. He was clever, fearless—and effective.

✳ ✳ ✳ ✳

THE NAME JOSEPH Petrosino means nothing to most New Yorkers—unless they're police officers, who regard the guy as a legend. In the first decade of the 20th century, Petrosino established himself as one of the toughest, most effective detectives in NYPD history. His beat was Little Italy, and he spent much of his career going toe-to-toe with the Mafia. It was a war that ultimately cost him his life.

Takin' Names

Petrosino was brought into the department by Captain Alexander Williams, who had watched Petrosino tangle with local thugs on the city streets. Petrosino didn't meet the police height requirement, but in addition to being tough as nails, he spoke fluent Italian and was familiar with the local culture. Williams quickly realized that Petrosino could be an invaluable asset to the force.

The NYPD put Petrosino to work as a sergeant in 1883. He wasted no time making his presence known within the city's Italian community. Strong and fearless, Petrosino became a brawler when necessary, but he also knew the value of quiet detective work. (Dedication and fearlessness eventually elevated him to the rank of lieutenant.) To gather intelligence, for instance, Petrosino routinely disguised himself as a tunnel "sandhog" laborer, a blind street beggar, and other urban denizens who can slip around unnoticed.

Petrosino solved plenty of crimes during his career, but it was his labor to eliminate the vicious gangs preying on Italian immigrants that made him famous. Italian gangsters started setting up shop in the city around 1900, bringing murder, theft, and extortion with them. Petrosino made it his mission to end their reign of terror.

Unspeakable Violence

Foremost among Petrosino's gangland foes was Vito Cascio Ferro, whom some consider one of the inspirations for Mario Puzo's *The Godfather*. Ferro arrived in New York from Sicily in 1901, already a mob boss to be feared and respected. Petrosino made no secret of his desire to implicate Ferro in the gruesome murder in which a body had been dismembered and stuffed in a barrel. As Petrosino closed in, Ferro fled to Sicily, vowing that he would get his revenge.

Meanwhile, Petrosino continued to battle the various gangs plaguing Little Italy. Kidnapping and murder were on the rise, as was the use of bombs. (In one terrifying incident, Petrosino managed to extinguish a bomb's fuse with his *fingers* just seconds before the bomb was set to explode.) Determined to stay ahead of the criminals, Petrosino established the nation's first bomb squad, teaching himself and his crew how to dismantle the deadly devices.

In 1908, Vito Ferro again attempted to reach into New York, this time through an intermediary—a murderous Sicilian named Raffaele Palizzolo. At first, clueless city officials embraced Palizzolo, who claimed to want to eliminate the Black Hand, as the Mafia was also called. But Petrosino was skeptical and tailed Palizzolo everywhere. This forced Palizzolo to return to Sicily, much to Ferro's anger.

All the News That's Fit to Blab

Petrosino's boss, Police Commissioner Theodore Bingham, was eager to eliminate New York's Mafia menace once and for all. Early in 1909 he sent Petrosino on a clandestine trip to Italy to meet with law enforcement officials there and gather intelligence. Because the underworld had put a price on his head, Petrosino made the trip disguised as a Jewish merchant named Simone Velletri. Unfortunately, his mission didn't remain a secret for long: While Petrosino was still in transit, the *New York Herald* ran a story that he was on his way to Italy specifically to gather information on Italian gangsters. The source? Bingham, who had stupidly confided in a reporter.

By the time Petrosino arrived in Italy, news of his mission had spread throughout the local underworld. Ferro ordered a hit. On March 12, 1909, two gunmen cut down Petrosino.

The detective's funeral was one of the largest in New York history. Thousands of police officers and citizens lined the streets as the procession traveled through the city to Calvary Cemetery in Long Island. The journey took five and a half hours—a fitting journey for a good man who lived and died for the rule of law.

One Last Set: Odd Ordinances

* The town of Rumford, Maine, has made it illegal to bite your landlord under any circumstances.

* Slurping soup is against the law in New Jersey.

* Mixing cornmeal with wheat flour is frowned upon in Maryland.

* Barbers aren't allowed to eat onions in Waterloo, Nebraska, between 7 A.M. and 7 P.M.

* No one can go to a theater within four hours of eating garlic in Gary, Indiana.

* Wearing a hat in a theater could cost you in Wyoming, but only if it happens to block anyone else's view of the show.

* It's illegal to offer someone a glass of water without a permit in Walden, New York.

* Peeling an orange in a hotel room in California is a crime.

* Bristow, Oklahoma, mandates that all restaurants serve customers one peanut per every glass of water.

* Serving wine in a teacup is against the law in Topeka, Kansas.

* Restaurant owners can't offer margarine in Vermont unless they have a public notice posted.

* Eating in a restaurant that is on fire is a crime in Chicago.

* It's illegal for a girl to ask a guy out on the phone in Dyersburg, Tennessee.

* In Whitesville, Delaware, women aren't allowed to propose to men.

* Portland, Maine, has outlawed any tickling of girls under the chin with a feather duster.

* Kissing without first wiping your lips is not allowed in Riverside, California. You also have to use carbonated rose water for the lip cleansings.

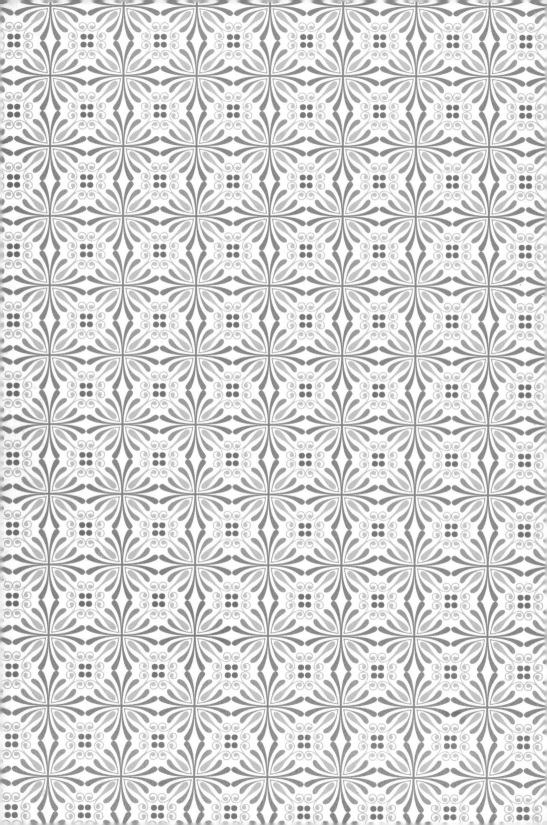